RIGHTS AND REMEDIES UNDER FEDERAL GRANTS

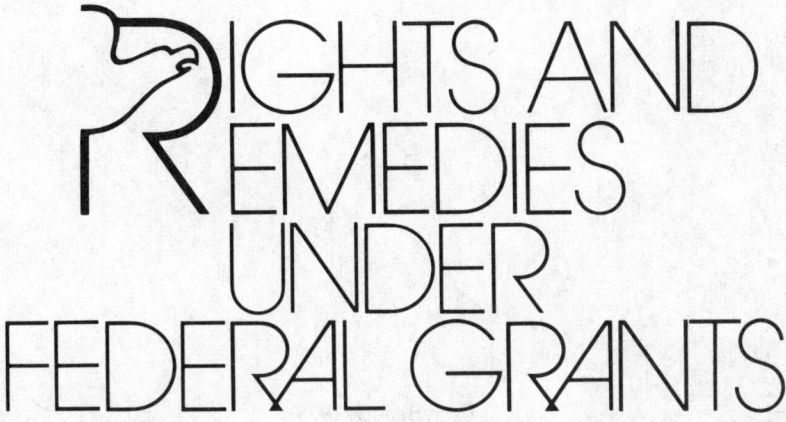

Rights and Remedies Under Federal Grants

Richard B. Cappalli
Professor of Law
Temple University School of Law

The Bureau of National Affairs, Inc., Washington, D.C.

Copyright © 1979
The Bureau of National Affairs, Inc.

Library of Congress Cataloging in Publication Data

Cappalli, Richard B.
  Rights and remedies under Federal grants.

  Includes index.
  1. Grants-in-aid—United States. 2. Subsidies—United States.
I. Title.
KF6733.C33   343'.73'074   79-12004
ISBN 0-87179-304-0

International Standard Book Number: 0-87179-304-0
Printed in the United States of America

To my wife Paula,
for her loveliness,
charm, and constant
support

Acknowledgments

Temple University School of Law has, to a large extent, underwritten this book, providing research assistance, secretarial support, and, most importantly, time. I am particularly indebted to our Dean, Peter J. Liacouras, for his magical way of making resources appear and for his personal encouragement.

Several students have joined me in this venture. Dante Antonio Cancelli and Richard Serafini labored through a long, hot summer working on the tedious compilations necessary to bring order to this massive and complex field. Nancy Shickler worked with me the following summer, and I am grateful for her always dependable work. Thanks, also, to George Krueger who worked on a paper under my supervision which enabled me to incorporate into the text analogies to the Contract Disputes Act of 1978. Don Rogers, though forewarned, cheerfully undertook the final review of citations and the compilation of the tables. His quick but precise work was invaluable. A special note of thanks is due Cheryl Young who forsook livelier job opportunities to work with me.

Finally, I would like to acknowledge the many hours of patient and careful labor of Keith Wall, who typed the many drafts. Without his accuracy I would have soon abandoned the work.

Contents

Acknowledgments vii
List of Abbreviations xiii
1. Introduction: The Emerging Law of Federal Grants 1
2. The Theory and Structure of Grants 28
    Constitutional Bases 28
    Purposes of Federal Grants 34
    Types of Grants 38
    Federal Grant Requirements 45
3. Agency Enforcement of Grant Conditions 53
    Legal Bases 53
    Monitoring Compliance 63
        Standard Practices 65
        Special Monitoring 66
        Subgrantee Compliance 71
    Methods of Enforcement 79
        Grant Principles and Remedial Options 80
        Voluntary Compliance Efforts 93
        Fiscal Sanctions 95
        Specific Performance 103
4. Expanding Bases of Judicial Intervention 108
    Standing 108
        The Old Theories 110
        New Standing Principles 111
        Grants-in-Aid and Protected Interests 117
        Core Interests 118
        Fringe Interests 126
        Special Interests 132
        Surviving Limitations 137

x / *Rights and Remedies Under Federal Grants*

        Federal Court Subject Matter Jurisdiction   146
            Federal Question Jurisdiction   147
            Civil Rights Jurisdiction   150
            Mandamus Jurisdiction   153
            U.S. Court of Claims   155
        The Demise of Government Legalese   155
        Reviewability   157

5. Legal and Practical Limits on the Judicial Role   162
        Remaining Barriers   162
            Primary Jurisdiction   163
            Scope of Review   165
        Adequacy of the Judicial Forum   168

6. The Federal Grant: A Unique Legal Creation   172

7. Due Process and Federal Grants   180
        Basic Principles   180
        Grantee Due Process: Threshold Considerations   185
        The Property Question   188
            Seekers of Formula Grants   193
            Seekers of Discretionary Grants   201
            Holders of Federal Grants   207
        The Liberty Question   211
        The Range of Deprivations   219

8. The Right of States to Fair Process   225

9. Grantee Hearing Rights: Withholding of Entitlements   244
        Congressional Practice   244
        Administrative Practice   265

10. Terminations of Competitive Grants   272
        Statutory Rights   272
        Regulations   280

11. Grant Suspensions   285

12. Rights of Applicants for Federal Funds   289
        Formula Funding Decisions   289
        Discretionary Initial Grant Awards   296
        Refunding Proposals   300

13. Subgrantees   307

14. Two Special Cases   314
        Nondiscrimination   314
            Racial Discrimination   316
            Discrimination Based on Handicap   324

                Sex Discrimination   325
                Age Discrimination   327
            Fellowships   329
15. Guideposts for Reform   331
            A Grantee Bill of Procedural Rights   332
                Notice and Opportunity To Be Heard   333
                The "Timing" Issue   336
                Sanctions   339
                Denials of Grant Applications   344
            The Grant Disputes Board   345
                Jurisdiction and Structure   350
                Procedures   353
            Justifications   356
16. No Man's Land   359

Table of Books, Articles, Reports, and Other
    Secondary Sources   365
Table of Statutes Cited   371
Table of Citations to the Code of Federal Regulations   381
Table of Cases   385
Index   393

List of Abbreviations

AFDC—Aid to Families With Dependent Children
AFGE—American Federation of Government Employees
AFSCME—American Federation of State, County, and Municipal Employees
APA—Administrative Procedure Act

CAMP—Comprehensive Area Manpower Plan
CETA—Comprehensive Employment and Training Act
CORE—Congress on Racial Equality

EDA—Economic Development Administration
EPA—Environmental Protection Agency
ETA—Employment and Training Administration

FMHA—Farmers Home Administration
FNS—Food and Nutrition Service

HEP—Health Education Project
HEW—Department of Health, Education and Welfare
HUD—Department of Housing and Urban Development

LEA—local educational agency
LEAA—Law Enforcement Assistance Administration
LSC—Legal Services Corporation

NAACP—National Association for the Advancement of Colored People
NIE—National Institute of Education
NIH—National Institute of Health

OCR—Office of Civil Rights
OE—Office of Education
OHD—Office of Human Development
OMB—Office of Management and Budget
OSHA—Occupational Safety and Health Act

PHS—Public Health Service

SBA—Small Business Administration
SEA—state educational agency
SLO—state liaison official

UMTA—Urban Mass Transportation Administration

1

Introduction: The Emerging Law of Federal Grants

"This spectacular expansion of both the size and scope of grant programs has engendered surprisingly little case law on the administration of federal grants. However, there is no doubt that an ever increasing number of cases in this area will be presented, especially to [the United States Court of Appeals for the District of Columbia] with its unique jurisdiction over many grant-dispensing agencies. . . . [T]here currently is a need for a fuller body of law concerning this slumbering giant. . . ." *

The rights and responsibilities of federal grantors and grantees are rapidly becoming a major area of litigation in the federal courts. In the late 1960s the national Legal Services Program greatly increased the availability of free attorneys for the poor in civil cases. This produced an explosion of cases testing the legality of various state practices under the major grant-in-aid programs, most notably welfare, medical assistance, and public housing. *King* v. *Smith*,[1] decided by the U.S. Supreme Court in 1968, was the first U.S. court decision to invalidate a state regulation as inconsistent with federal requirements under the Aid to Families With Dependent Children Program.[2] In hindsight this is an

---

* *Southern Mut. Help Ass'n* v. *Califano*, 574 F.2d 518, 522 (D.C. Cir. 1977) (footnote omitted).
[1] 392 U.S. 309 (1968).
[2] Berney *et al., Legal Problems of the Poor: Cases and Materials* 614 (1975).

2 / *Rights and Remedies Under Federal Grants*

amazing fact considering that this federal-state program had been operating for more than three decades with a vast expenditure of public resources over this period. While the lawyers may have been slow out of the gate, one could not criticize their stride once moving. Indeed, the Supreme Court viewed "with concern" the "escalating involvement of federal courts in [the] highly complicated area of welfare benefits," but the Court could find no congressional intention to "deprive federal courts of their traditional jurisdiction to hear and decide federal questions in this field." [3]

These controversies have been initiated on behalf of the individual beneficiaries of federally assisted social programs. The suits typically seek to expand eligibility, to increase the scope of services and the level of benefits, and to protect the dignity and humanity of the people dependent on public services. Both federal and state agencies are usually sued: the former for not enforcing federal standards; the latter for allegedly violating them. Belt-tightening at the state and local government level ordinarily takes the form of cutbacks in the reach, scope, and quality of public services financed in part by federal grants. Those harmed by such economy measures seek out free legal services (or vice versa), and suit is initiated on the ground that federal constitutional, statutory, or regulatory standards prohibit the practice. Similarly, fiscal austerity and taxpayer revolt may translate into increased demands on program beneficiaries—greater accountability, self-help, public exposure, and the like. Program actions of this nature are also grist for the judicial mill. Given the hard economic times of the 1970s, it's not surprising to report that this category of litigation has not abated.

Suits have also been brought in considerable numbers by private parties claiming injury from federally supported projects. Some of the earliest cases involving grants-in-aid, for instance, were generated by the impact of the urban renewal program on private business and individuals.[4] Businessmen have never enjoyed the idea of competition supported by federal tax dollars and are quick to sue when it happens. While the average American might

[3] *Rosado* v. *Wyman*, 397 U.S. 397, 422 (1970).
[4] See *Allied-City Wide, Inc.* v. *Cole*, 230 F.2d 827 (D.C. Cir. 1956); *Gart* v. *Cole*, 263 F.2d 244 (2d Cir.), *cert. denied*, 359 U.S. 978 (1959); *Harrison-Halsted Community Group, Inc.* v. *Housing & Home Fin. Agency*, 310 F.2d 99 (7th Cir. 1962); *Pittsburgh Hotels Ass'n, Inc.* v. *Urban Redev. Auth.*, 309 F.2d 186 (3d Cir. 1962), *cert. denied*, 372 U.S. 916 (1963); *Berry* v. *Housing & Home Fin. Agency*, 340 F.2d 939 (2d Cir. 1965).

vaguely support social programs, the location of a low-income housing project next door will quickly trigger a visit to a lawyer's office. Federal programs, particularly those involving physical development, deeply affect those on and near the path of progress. So it is not unexpected that federal grants for urban renewal, roads, housing, waste disposal, and sewage treatment will bring forth complaints of hardship from these projects' neighbors.

A third group, never timid about suit, is composed of those who do business with grantees. A significant portion of the billions in federal grant dollars winds up in the coffers of businesses that trade with grantees in products and services. A fair right to do business is typically what is sought. For example, one of the earliest lawsuits involving a federal grant was brought under the health facilities construction program (Hill-Burton) by a low-bidding construction company which was not awarded the building contract.[5]

None of the above is unusual. An accepted part of the American way of life is vindication of rights through the courts. Those harmed by government action sue, and as the sphere of government action widens the volume of disputes increases.

What *is* unusual is the explosion of cases in a fourth category —disputes between the agencies dispensing federal grants and those public and private institutions receiving or seeking them.

Not too long ago only a handful of federal court cases involving grantor-grantee disputes could be found, though a variety of grant programs had been operational since the turn of the century.[6] In 1923, the Commonwealth of Massachusetts challenged in the highest court the power of the United States to establish a program of grants to the states for child and maternal health.[7] In 1947, the Supreme Court dealt with the power of the Federal Government to penalize a state grantee which had violated its commitment under the grant not to play politics with federal dollars.[8]

Over these early years the lower federal courts also fielded an occasional grantor-grantee dispute. The state of Indiana tested in

---

[5] *Clement Martin, Inc.* v. *Dick Corp.*, 97 F. Supp. 961 (W.D. Pa. 1951) (suit dismissed for lack of cause of action under federal competitive bidding requirements).
[6] See generally Advisory Commission on Intergovernmental Relations, *The Intergovernmental Grant System: An Assessment and Proposed Policies: Categorical Grants: Their Role and Design* 15–47 (1978) [hereinafter cited as *Categorical Grants*].
[7] *Frothingham* v. *Mellon*, 262 U.S. 447 (1923).
[8] *Oklahoma* v. *U.S. Civil Serv. Comm'n*, 330 U.S. 127 (1947). See also *Ohio* v. *U.S. Civil Serv. Comm'n*, 65 F. Supp. 776 (S.D. Ohio 1976).

4 / *Rights and Remedies Under Federal Grants*

court a cutoff of welfare funds for the aged.⁹ This action by the Federal Security Administration was provoked by a state law which permitted public inspection of welfare roles in contravention of a federal confidentiality statute. In another case, a rare agency finding that a state plan did not conform to federal standards led to an unsuccessful court challenge.¹⁰ A third suit was successfully brought by the United States to recover a $1,976 grant overpayment to a school district.¹¹ In a series of school cases, the U.S. Department of Justice sought, with mixed results, to implement desegregation by way of specific performance of grant requirements.¹² Finally, these early years reveal only two reported cases in which suit was filed by a disappointed seeker of a federal grant. In one case, the action was dismissed on a preliminary motion,¹³ and in the other the grantor's decision was affirmed as within its discretion.¹⁴

In contrast, this decade has witnessed a sharp and steady increase in the number of instances in which grantees have challenged federal agency action in court. The tone was set, perhaps, by the "impoundment" cases of 1973. In that year the Nixon Administration froze appropriated funds under several programs in order to combat inflation by reducing the rate of federal spending. This led to dozens of court cases in which states, local governments, and community groups successfully challenged the legality of this executive action.¹⁵ We may speculate that the

---

⁹ *Indiana ex rel. Indiana State Bd. of Pub. Welfare* v. *Ewing*, 99 F. Supp. 734 (D. D.C. 1951), *vacated as moot*, 195 F.2d 556 (D.C. Cir. 1952).

¹⁰ *Arizona* v. *Hobby*, 221 F.2d 498 (D.C. Cir. 1954) (sovereign immunity bars suit).

¹¹ *United States* v. *Independent School Dist. No. 1*, 209 F.2d 578 (10th Cir. 1954). Hopefully, the United States was interested in its principles more than its pocketbook. Grantors today beg grantees to find ways to spend such amounts rather than going through the book work of returning the funds.

¹² Compare *United States* v. *County School Bd.*, 221 F. Supp. 93 (E.D. Va. 1963) (right to seek specific performance); and *United States* v. *Sumter County School Dist. No. 2*, 232 F. Supp. 945 (E.D. S.C. 1964) (same); with *United States* v. *Madison County Bd. of Educ.*, 326 F.2d 237 (5th Cir.), *cert. denied*, 379 U.S. 929 (1964) (statutory remedy of withholding funds is exclusive); and *United States* v. *Bossier Parish School Bd.*, 220 F. Supp. 243 (W.D. La. 1963), *aff'd per curiam*, 336 F.2d 197 (5th Cir. 1964), *cert. denied*, 379 U.S. 1000 (1965) (grantee did not agree to immediate integration of schools).

¹³ *Paducah Junior College* v. *Secretary of Health, Educ. & Welfare*, 255 F. Supp. 147 (W.D. Ky. 1966) (plaintiff lacked standing).

¹⁴ *School City* v. *Derthick*, 273 F.2d 319 (7th Cir. 1959).

¹⁵ See, e.g., *Train* v. *City of New York*, 420 U.S. 35 (1975); *State Highway Comm'n* v. *Volpe*, 479 F.2d 1099 (8th Cir. 1973); *Louisiana* v. *Weinberger*, 369 F. Supp. 856 (E.D. La. 1973); *Illinois ex rel. Bakalis* v. *Weinberger*, 368 F. Supp. 721 (N.D. Ill. 1973); *Pennsylvania* v. *Weinberger*, 367 F. Supp. 1378 (D. D.C. 1973); *Community Action Programs Executive Directors Ass'n* v. *Ash*, 365 F. Supp. 1355 (D. N.J. 1973); *National Council of Community Mental Health Centers, Inc.* v. *Weinberger*, 361

Introduction / 5

victories in the impoundment cases taught grantees that the courts could be used to hold the Federal Government to account in its grant activities. A wide variety of adverse federal agency actions were subsequently tested. These included: grant terminations;[15a] denial of reimbursement for grantee expenditures;[16] refusals to refund grantees at the end of a project period;[17] determinations that a plan submitted for federal approval did not meet applicable standards or that a grantee violated mandatory conditions placed on the grant;[18] suspension of a grant for suspected violation of federal standards;[19] imposition of a fiscal penalty on a grantee;[20] underfunding of a grantee;[21] denial of a grant;[22] imposition of federal grant conditions claimed to be unconstitutional or viola-

---

F. Supp. 897 (D. D.C. 1973); *Oklahoma v. Weinberger*, 360 F. Supp. 724 (W.D. Okla. 1973); *Local 2677, AFGE v. Phillips*, 358 F. Supp. 60 (D. D.C. 1973).

[15a] *Southern Mut. Help Ass'n v. Califano*, 574 F.2d 518 (D.C. Cir. 1977).

[16] *California ex rel. Dep't of Transp. v. United States* (II), 561 F.2d 731 (9th Cir. 1977); *California ex rel. Dep't of Transp. v. United States*, 547 F.2d 1388 (9th Cir.), *cert. denied*, 434 U.S. 857 (1977); *County of Alameda v. Weinberger*, 520 F.2d 344 (9th Cir. 1975); *California By and Through the Dep't of Transp. v. United States*, 551 F.2d 843 (Ct. Cl.), *cert. denied*, 434 U.S. 857 (1977); *Texas v. United States*, 537 F.2d 466 (Ct. Cl. 1976); *Arizona v. United States*, 494 F.2d 1285 (Ct. Cl. 1974); *State Dep't of Pub. Welfare v. Weinberger*, 388 F. Supp. 1304 (W.D. Tex. 1975), *modified sub nom., State Dep't of Pub. Welfare v. Califano*, 556 F.2d 326 (5th Cir. 1977), *cert. denied*, 99 S. Ct. 78 (1978); *Florida v. Mathews* (II), 422 F. Supp. 1231 (D. D.C. 1976).

[17] *National Consumer Info. Center v. Gallegos*, 549 F.2d 822 (D.C. Cir. 1977); *Economic Opportunity Comm'n v. Weinberger*, 524 F.2d 393 (2d Cir. 1975); *Spokane County Legal Servs., Inc. v. Legal Servs. Corp.*, 433 F. Supp. 278 (E.D. Wash. 1977).

[18] *Mayor of Baltimore v. Mathews*, 562 F.2d 914 (4th Cir. 1977), *vacated then aff'd*, 571 F.2d 1273, *cert. denied*, 99 S. Ct. 184 (1978); *Nebraska Dep't of Rds. v. Tiemann*, 510 F.2d 446 (8th Cir. 1975). Compare *Hospital Ass'n of New York State, Inc. v. Toia*, 438 F. Supp. 866 (S.D. N.Y. 1977) (subgrantees sue grantor and grantee alleging nonconformity of state plan).

[19] *United States v. Virginia*, 569 F.2d 1300 (4th Cir. 1978); *Community Progress, Inc. v. Martinez*, 420 F. Supp. 204 (D. Conn. 1976); *Red School House, Inc. v. Office of Economic Opportunity*, 386 F. Supp. 1177 (D. Minn. 1974).

[20] *Maryland v. Mathews*, 415 F. Supp. 1206 (D. D.C. 1976); *Vermont v. Brinegar*, 379 F. Supp. 606 (D. Vt. 1974).

[21] *City of Los Angeles v. Adams*, 556 F.2d 40 (D.C. Cir. 1977).

[22] *Township of Benton v. County of Berrien*, 570 F.2d 114 (6th Cir. 1978); *Jacksonville Port Auth. v. Adams*, 556 F.2d 52 (D.C. Cir. 1977); *Advocates for the Arts v. Thomson*, 532 F.2d 792 (1st Cir.), *cert. denied*, 429 U.S. 894 (1976); *Board of Educ. v. Dep't of Health, Educ. & Welfare*, 532 F.2d 1070 (6th Cir. 1976); *School Comm. v. Anrig*, 520 F.2d 577 (1st Cir. 1975); *Apter v. Richardson*, 510 F.2d 351 (7th Cir. 1975); *Township of River Vale v. Harris*, 444 F. Supp. 90 (D. D.C. 1978); *City of Macon v. Marshall*, 439 F. Supp. 1209 (M.D. Ga. 1977); *City of Beaver Falls v. Economic Dev. Admin.*, 439 F. Supp. 851 (W.D. Pa. 1977); *Clark v. Richardson*, 431 F. Supp. 105 (D. N.J. 1977); *City of Grand Rapids v. Richardson*, 429 F. Supp. 1087 (W.D. Mich. 1977); *City of Benton Harbor v. Richardson*, 429 F. Supp. 1096 (W.D. Mich. 1977); *Lewis v. Richardson*, 428 F. Supp. 1164 (D. Mass. 1977); *Mid-America Regional Council v. Mathews*, 416 F. Supp. 896 (W.D. Mo. 1976); *Grassetti v. Weinberger*, 408 F. Supp. 142 (N.D. Cal. 1976); *Michigan Head Start Directors Ass'n v. Butz*, 397 F. Supp. 1124 (W.D. Mich. 1975); *Northeast Community Organ., Inc. v. Weinberger*, 378 F. Supp. 1287 (D. Md. 1974).

6 / *Rights and Remedies Under Federal Grants*

tive of statutory law;[23] withholding of required grantor approval;[24] undue delay in awarding grants;[25] imposition of erroneous matching rates;[26] and approval of allegedly illegal grant regulations.[26a] Not only the case volume is up but the stakes are incredibly high. In what must be the largest out-of-court settlement in the history of the law, Congress recently settled a series of lawsuits between 19 states and HEW for $543,000,000![27]

It would be a mistake, however, to assume a faddish aftermath of the impoundment cases which will soon pass. Even before these cases were filed and won, disgruntled grantees had begun to march to court in steadily increasing numbers.[28] What we really see is a substantial number of overt grantor-grantee controversies beginning toward the end of the 1960s, bulging in 1973, steadily growing through this decade, and showing no signs of abatement.

---

[23] *North Carolina ex rel. Morrow v. Califano*, 445 F. Supp. 532 (E.D. N. Car.), *aff'd mem.*, 435 U.S. 962 (1978); *Florida v. Matthews* (I), 526 F.2d 319 (5th Cir. 1976); *Romeo Community Schools v. U.S. Dep't of Health, Educ. & Welfare*, 438 F. Supp. 1021 (E.D. Mich. 1977); *City of New York v. Diamond*, 379 F. Supp. 503 (S.D. N.Y. 1974).

[24] *Maryland-Nat'l Capital Park & Planning Comm'n v. Lynn*, 514 F.2d 829 (D.C. Cir. 1975).

[25] *National Ass'n of Regional Councils v. Costle*, 564 F.2d 583 (D.C. Cir. 1977); *County of Los Angeles v. Coleman*, 423 F. Supp. 496 (D. D.C. 1976), *aff'd per curiam sub nom., County of Los Angeles v. Adams*, 574 F.2d 608 (D.C. Cir. 1978).

[26] *Ibid.*

[26a] *Florida v. Weinberger*, 492 F.2d 488 (5th Cir. 1974).

[27] The cases involved $2.5 billion in reimbursement claims under the welfare program. The compromise was achieved by legislative action. See Pub. L. 95-291, June 12, 1978, 42 U.S.C. §1397a note. Although the legal validity of the state claims was never proved, the compromise resolved "a long-standing and difficult issue between the Federal Government and the States" and "awesome" litigation prospects. See H.R. Rep. No. 1114, pt. I, 95th Cong., 2d Sess. 5, 7 (1978).

[28] See *Port Auth. v. United States*, 432 F.2d 455 (Ct. Cl. 1970) (reimbursement); *Commission on Aging v. Finch*, 430 F.2d 667 (5th Cir. 1970) (reallocation of formula funds to another jurisdiction); *Mil-Ka-Ko Research & Dev. Corp. v. Office of Economic Opportunity*, 352 F. Supp. 169 (D. D.C. 1972), *aff'd mem.*, 497 F.2d 684 (D.C. Cir. 1974) (denial of refunding); *Monmouth Legal Servs. Organ. v. Carlucci*, 330 F. Supp. 985 (D. N.J. 1971) (same); *Arizona State Dep't of Pub. Welfare v. Dep't of Health, Educ. & Welfare*, 449 F.2d 456 (9th Cir. 1971), *cert. denied*, 405 U.S. 919 (1972) (nonconformity); *Connecticut State Dep't of Pub. Welfare v. Dep't of Health, Educ. & Welfare*, 448 F.2d 209 (2d Cir. 1971) (same); *Gardner v. Alabama*, 385 F.2d 804 (5th Cir. 1967), *cert. denied*, 389 U.S. 1046 (1968) (same); *Board of Pub. Instruction v. Finch*, 414 F.2d 1068 (5th Cir. 1969) (noncompliance); *Marable v. Alabama Mental Health Bd.*, 297 F. Supp. 291 (M.D. Ala. 1969) (same); *Lee v. Macon County Bd. of Educ.*, 270 F. Supp. 859 (M.D. Ala. 1967) (same); *Rubinstein v. Mayor of Baltimore*, 295 F. Supp. 108 (D. Md. 1969) (termination of grant); *In re School Board*, 475 F.2d 1117 (5th Cir. 1973) (voiding of grant for misrepresentation in application); *School Bd. v. Richardson*, 332 F. Supp. 1263 (N.D. Fla. 1971) (claimed underfunding of plaintiff); *East Oakland-Fruitvale Planning Council v. Rumsfeld*, 471 F.2d 524 (9th Cir. 1972) (denial of grant); *Wu v. National Endowment for Humanities*, 460 F.2d 1030 (5th Cir.), *cert. denied*, 410 U.S. 926 (1972) (same); *Kletschka v. Driver*, 411 F.2d 436 (2d Cir. 1969) (same); *South Dakota v. Volpe*, 353 F. Supp. 335 (D. S.D. 1973) (fiscal penalty for noncompliance).

Introduction / 7

We must also note that here we are counting only the reported decisions. That typically represents only a small percentage of the controversies. The bulk are settled before or during suit, or are judicially decided without a reported opinion.

What underlies this phenomenon? Part of the explanation is technical. Doctrinal change during this period produced considerably easier access to the federal courts. These jurisdictional considerations will be examined later in this book. Here we shall endeavor to understand the root causes of friction, the antagonisms which block conciliation.

One of the root causes must surely be that the federal grant has become highly demanding in terms of the procedural and substantive conditions which encapsulate the offer of financial aid. In the next chapter we shall describe most of these conditions. Their growth in number and complexity has made the federal grant-in-aid an instrument of governance fraught with pitfalls. Recent reports characterize these grant requirements in sweeping terms:

- "[A] web of entangling regulations has bureaucratized the system of federal grants-in-aid." [29]

- "The complexity and volume of paperwork involved in the project grant process was by far the most frequently identified problem by both city and county officials. . . . This problem probably approximates what many people would identify as 'red tape.'" [30]

- "Analyses of existing generally applicable policy requirements have revealed four interrelated problems of major significance to state and local grantees. . . . (1) [T]he lack of federal awareness of the costs that national policy conditions impose on grantees; (2) the inadequacy of present federal grant allocations and other funds to meet both the basic objectives of grants-in-aid and the additional goals established by national policy conditions as presently formulated; (3) the insensitivity of national policy conditions to the diverse needs, resources, and capacities of the state and local government grantees; and (4) the ineffective interagency coordination of national policy conditions and the consequent inconsistencies among agency regulations issued pursuant to each condition." [31]

- "This long list of national policy objectives attached to grant programs continues to grow year by year. . . . [T]his adds up to a

[29] *Categorical Grants, supra* note 6, at 276 (resolution of U.S. Conference of Mayors).
[30] *Id.* at 279.
[31] *Id.* at 237.

8 / *Rights and Remedies Under Federal Grants*

three-way tug-of-war. The specific program objectives enacted by Congress (the reason for the grant program) compete with a large number of generally applicable national policy objectives (to which the government is also committed) and with a series of administrative simplification efforts needed to make the programs workable within reasonable cost and time limitations. Upon encountering this complex situation, grant recipients have good reason to wonder whether or not they can comply with all of these requirements and objectives and still benefit from the program." [32]

• "This growth of categorical aid to universities and colleges has brought with it the expected controls born of the need for stewardship in the use of these Federal monies. Many institutions are critically dependent on this Federal support. As wave after wave of regulations, surveys, and compliance activities have hit, they have until recently endured with suffering and silence, while resources made scarce by shrinking dollars have been diverted to administrative and accountability functions." [33]

In short, those who receive federal grants currently face a burden of complying with federal standards which has never been stiffer. Evidence also exists that the Federal Government is stepping up its efforts to police compliance with the terms of financial aid agreements.[34] One example is provided by HEW. That agency is allocating 1,102 professional employees to the single task of enforcing the nondiscrimination duties of HEW grantees.[35]

The number of players in the grantsmanship game has also skyrocketed in the past few years. We have roughly tabulated the number of institutions and agencies in the United States directly receiving federal financing: [36]

State government agencies	1,800
Minor cities, counties, and other general government	38,000
Agencies of major cities and counties	5,200
Elementary and secondary school districts	16,000
Special governmental districts	23,000
Regional bodies	1,800
Colleges and university units	10,000
Hospitals	6,000
Community action agencies	900
Legal services organizations	320
Research and development organizations	1,500
Community nonprofit organizations	8,000
	112,520

Introduction / 9

This impressive grantee total results, of course, from the massive number of aid programs enacted by Congress in the past 14 years.

In this book we include within the concept of a grant-in-aid cash assistance to governments and private institutions conditioned upon compliance with federal requirements. We have followed the classification scheme of the *Catalog of Federal Domestic Assistance,* published by the Office of Management and Budget, which defines grants as either "formula"—"[a]llocations of money to states or their subdivision in accordance with distribution formula prescribed by law or administrative regulation, for activities of a continuing nature not confined to a specific project"—or "project" —"[t]he funding, for fixed or known periods, of specific projects or the delivery of specific services or products without liability for damages for failure to perform. . . ."[37] Excluded from consideration in this study are other forms of federal assistance such as: procurement contracts; benefits to individuals; loans; loan insurance and guarantees; insurance; sale, exchange, or donation of property and goods; use of federal property, facilities, and equipment; provision of specialized services; advisory services and counseling; dissemination of information; training conducted directly by federal agencies; investigation of complaints; and federal employment.

We have surveyed the statutes and regulations underlying approximately 90 percent of the grant programs—by our count[38] 700 programs administered by 24 federal departments and agencies. Sheer volume has precluded the study of all.

Particularly worthy of mention in this explosive growth of programs of the U.S. government are those which have carried federal aid to the thousands of local governmental units which run America. General revenue sharing is the most well known of these and, despite its popular name, it is a "grant" of federal aid taken from general appropriations and conditioned upon compliance with federal standards.[39] Of lesser fame but of equal economic

---

[32] *Id.* at 233–34.
[33] Commission on Federal Paperwork, *Education* 91 (1977) (Report of the Interagency Task Force on Higher Education Burden Reduction).
[34] See Chapter 3, notes 58–117, *infra,* and accompanying text.
[35] 43 Fed. Reg. 7050 (1978).
[36] The underlying calculations are on file with the author at Temple University School of Law.
[37] Office of Management and Budget, *Catalog of Federal Domestic Assistance* xix (1978 update).
[38] Some of the difficulties involved in counting grant programs are explored in *Categorical Grants, supra* note 6, at 124–27.
[39] State and Local Fiscal Assistance Act of 1972, 31 U.S.C. §§1221–1265.

importance are the "temporary" antirecession grants.[40] Then there are the three major aid programs enacted on "block grant" [41] principles which direct federal dollars to states and general purpose local governments to fight crime, unemployment, and blight.[42] In combination, these programs mean that it is the very rare town or county in this country which is not receiving some federal aid. That, in turn, means that thousands of local officials are facing compliance problems and issues for the first time.

Adding to the boiling brew is the simple fact that vast amounts of badly needed dollars are at stake. Grant controversies are not likely candidates for small claims court. On the contrary, millions of dollars are frequently at stake—dollars which fiscally strapped governments and nonprofits cannot afford to lose for alleged infractions of federal rules. The quantities almost defy imagination, even in these days of the cheap dollar. The Federal Government is now spending, each year, 85 billion dollars under these grant programs.[43] That does not include, as previously stated, payments to individuals from the trust funds like Social Security. And the grant total is actually a few billion dollars higher because the budget definition of grants excludes research and demonstration grants to universities and other nonprofits.[44]

As a share of the total federal budget, grants-in-aid have increased from 5.3 percent in 1950, to 7.6 percent in 1960, to 12.2 percent in 1970, and to an estimated 17.4 percent in fiscal year 1979.[45] In terms of gross outlays, the following table summarizes the historical growth pattern of federal grant outlays during the twentieth century: [46]

[40] Title II, Public Works Employment Act of 1976, 42 U.S.C. §§6721–6736; Local Public Works Capital Development and Investment Act of 1976, 42 U.S.C. §§6701–6710.

[41] "[T]he block grant . . . may be defined as a grant that is given chiefly to general purpose governmental units in accordance with a statutory formula for use, largely at the recipient's discretion, in a variety of activities within a broad functional area." *Categorical Grants, supra* note 6, at 6.

[42] Omnibus Crime Control and Safe Streets Act of 1968, 42 U.S.C. §§3701–3796c; Comprehensive Employment and Training Act of 1973 (CETA), 29 U.S.C. §§801–999; Housing and Community Development Act of 1974, 42 U.S.C. §§5301–5317.

[43] Office of Management and Budget, "Special Analysis H, Federal Aid to State and Local Governments," in *Special Analyses, Budget of the United States Government, 1979* at 175 (Jan. 1978) (estimate for fiscal year 1979) [hereinafter cited as *Special Analysis H*].

[44] *Id.* at 185.

[45] *Id.* at 184, Table H-5.

[46] See *id.* at 175; R.H. Leach, *American Federalism* 167–68 (1970); Advisory Commission on Intergovernmental Relations, *Fiscal Balance in the American Federal System* 140–45, Table 22 (Oct. 1967) [hereinafter cited as *Fiscal Balance*]; M. Grodzins, *The American System* 49–50, Table 2; 61, Table 5 (1966).

1915: $5,500,000
1937: $296,000,000
1947: $1,100,000,000
1962: $7,400,000,000
1968: $17,300,000,000
1970: $25,000,000,000
1977: $68,400,000,000
1979: $85,000,000,000 (est.)

The total dollars dedicated to federal grant-in-aid programs also include the local matching share required under most grant programs. The Office of Management and Budget estimates this, on the whole, as an additional 25 percent.[47] Thus, total dollars invested in federal grants-in-aid reach around $106 billion annually, excluding university research grants.

As one might guess from the raw data on federal grant outlays, such assistance has become an increasingly important factor in state and local government finance. As a percentage of total state and local revenues federal aid has increased from 10.4 percent in 1950 to an estimated 27.5 percent in fiscal 1978.[48]

Many dollars, multiple programs, new players, complex and demanding conditions—the picture is emerging but is still incomplete. While the above vastly multiplies the number of encounters, it does not necessarily engender conflict. Indeed, a system of rapid and peaceful decision making could theoretically stifle potential disputes.

That was the ideal and model. In 1937 Professor Corwin, the great constitutionalist, coined the phrase "cooperative federalism"[49] to describe the emerging forms of national-state cooperation exemplified by the grant-in-aid. The phrase was adopted during the presidency of Lyndon B. Johnson and the years of the Great Society to describe and justify the massive entry of the Federal Government, by means of grant programs, into areas previously left to states, local government, and private charity. Thus popularized, the catch phrase was picked up by the Supreme Court in *King* v. *Smith*[50] and has regularly been used by the

[47] *Special Analysis H, supra* note 43, at 187.
[48] *Id.* at 184, Table H-5.
[49] Corwin, "National-State Cooperation—Its Present Possibilities," 8 Am. Law School Rev. 687, 704 (1937).
[50] 392 U.S. 309, 316 (1968).

Court to describe the essential nature of a grant-in-aid.[51] Although the Justices have failed to fill the phrase "cooperative federalism" with explicit content, it seems to be a shorthand way of emphasizing not only the voluntary basis of local participation but also the concept that considerable autonomy remains vested in grantees to deal with the shape, content, and administration of the aided programs despite mandated federal standards.[52]

Although the rubric for grant programs was changed during the Nixon presidency to the "new federalism," the focus on federal-state-local cooperation was not reduced. In fact, the new direction was toward the easing of potential tensions through structural reform. The "block grant" symbolized this effort to reduce federal controls over the use of grant funds and to strengthen the role of state and local governments.[53]

That ideal may, in an earlier day, have been actualized in the field. Older studies of the grant-in-aid system emphasized the smooth, professional relationships between federal grant administrators and their state agency counterparts.

> "Before the 1960s, the typical grant-in-aid programs were not used to resolve problems of national concern but were established to help state or local governments accomplish their respective objectives—'to help them get farmers out of the mud'. . . . In general, federal agencies saw their role as one of technical assistance rather than of control: they offered advice and worked with the states to improve programs initiated by the states, and they did not substitute their policy judgments for those of state and local agencies. . . . Federal review and control of grant distribution in earlier decades was designed to accomplish the objectives of efficiency and economy in order to safeguard the federal treasury, and was not generally intended to affect the substance of grant programs."[54]

Though the small and relatively simple grant system has not existed for almost two decades, the model of frictionless grantor-

---

[51] *Dandridge* v. *Williams*, 397 U.S. 471, 478 (1970); *New York State Dep't of Social Servs.* v. *Dublino*, 413 U.S. 405, 413 (1973); *Batterton* v. *Francis*, 432 U.S. 416, 420 (1977).

[52] See *King* v. *Smith*, 392 U.S. 309, 318 (1968); *New York State Dep't of Social Servs.* v. *Dublino*, 413 U.S. 405, 413 (1973); *Wheeler* v. *Barrera*, 417 U.S. 402, 416 (1974); *United States* v. *Orleans*, 425 U.S. 807, 818 (1976); *Batterton* v. *Francis*, 432 U.S. 416, 431–32 (1977).

[53] See, e.g., R.H. Leach, *American Federalism* 16–17 (1970).

[54] A.S. Harbert, *Federal Grants-in-Aid: Maximizing Benefits to the States* 4 (1976) (citations omitted). See also M. Derthick, *The Influence of Federal Grants: Public Assistance in Massachusetts* 196–216 (1970); M. Grodzins, *The American System* 60–70 (1966).

grantee relations lives on. It has now, however, become a fantasy. The new grant system, the one created in 1964 and thereafter,[55] is characterized by domineering federal agencies and strong-handed federal authority.

To be sure, the grantor-grantee relationship established by statutes and regulations readily lends itself to the unilateral exertion of power by the fund-giver. A reading of any grant-in-aid statute and its accompanying regulation will support that conclusion. We find a set of obligations, often great in number and complexity, imposed on the grantee as a prerequisite to the transfer of federal funds. The policing agent is the federal department or agency delegated administrative authority by the grant statute. Under this structure a stream of authoritative assertions by one side, the grantor, is naturally to be expected.

This book is not a critical study of those conditions. We do not even pretend to study more than a small part of them. The task would be monumental—substantive program conditions exist by the thousands. We accept the conditional federal grant-in-aid as a given, leaving to others the task of suggesting better ways of dispensing federal aid.[56] And in speaking of absolutist tendencies, we do not have in mind the federal agency faithfully discharging its statutory responsibilities, but rather the grantor issuing ultimatums to grantees from a background of ambiguous rules and facts. That, to our knowledge, has been the practice.

Admittedly our evidence is impressionistic and not based on empirical study. Indeed, we are tempted to simply bootstrap back to the swell of federal court cases as evidence of federal arbitrariness. That, however, may simply be evidence of grantee overreaching and not federal domination. Though our data are scant on this point, our opinion is strongly held. Ultimately we leave it to our readers to reject or confirm our characterization of federal agency attitudes and actions.

Support for our belief that federal grantor officials strong-arm grantees is drawn primarily from the author's 12 years in the field,

---

[55] See M. Reagan, *The New Federalism* 55 (1972) (80% of grant programs enacted after 1960); Cappalli, "Federal Financing in the Commonwealth of Puerto Rico," 38 U. P. R. L. Rev. 1, 16–17 (1970); Tomlinson & Mashaw, "The Enforcement of Federal Standards in Grant-in-Aid Programs: Suggestions for Beneficiary Involvement," 58 U. Va. L. Rev. 600 (1972) [hereinafter cited as Tomlinson]. See generally *Categorical Grants, supra* note 6, at 15–47.

[56] See, e.g., W.W. Heller, *New Dimensions of Political Economy* (1966) (seminal work advocating revenue sharing); M. Reagan, *The New Federalism* 89–141 (1972) (advocates block grants over revenue sharing). See generally *Fiscal Balance, supra* note 46.

14 / *Rights and Remedies Under Federal Grants*

three of which were spent as a governor's aid in charge of $1.5 billion worth of federal programs. There is no lack, however, of corroborating sources. Arbitrary federal grantor actions have been documented in numerous federal cases, and have often provoked unusually strident criticism from the bench.[57] While political scientists have stressed the cooperative nature of federal assistance and the numerous restraints on arbitrary action, there is some recognition of the antistate and antilocal bias of federal grantor officials.[58] In a brilliant article published in the *Harvard Law Review,* the Professors Cahn document and thoroughly analyze the subject of arbitrary federal grantor action, characterizing the federal grant system as a "no man's land of official anarchy." [59] Other lawyers have observed much of the same.[60]

In speaking of domineering federal agencies we also have in mind the grantor agency which utilizes its control over discretionary grant funds to "convince" grantees to follow agency policies. Those who unquestioningly accept the "recommendations" of district, regional, or central federal officials can expect warm treatment in their petitions for discretionary grants. Those who challenge either the legality or wisdom of federal policy or practice can expect the contrary. A marvelous example is provided by a fairly recent case.[61] The U.S. Department of Housing and Urban Development sent a circular to local housing authorities which "urged" them to set rent schedules which would promote greater numbers of wealthier tenants in public housing. A U.S. court of appeals found the practice to be violative of the statute under which the project was funded. In defense of its action, HUD

---

[57] E.g., *Human Resources Management, Inc.* v. *Weaver,* 442 F. Supp. 241 (D. D.C. 1978); *Cole* v. *Lynn,* 389 F. Supp. 99 (D. D.C. 1975); *Grumman Ecosystems Corp.* v. *Gainesville-Alachua County Regional Elec., Water & Sewer Facilities Bd.,* 402 F. Supp. 582 (N.D. Fla. 1975); *School Bd.* v. *Dep't of Health, Educ. & Welfare,* 390 F. Supp. 13 (S.D. Fla. 1974), *rev'd on other grounds,* 525 F.2d 900 (5th Cir. 1976); *Red School House, Inc.* v. *Office of Economic Opportunity,* 386 F. Supp. 1177, 1186–87 (D. Minn. 1974); *Monmouth Legal Servs. Organ.* v. *Carlucci,* 330 F. Supp. 985 (D. N.J. 1971). See also *County of Alameda* v. *Weinberger,* 520 F.2d 344 (9th Cir. 1975); *Maryland* v. *Mathews,* 415 F. Supp. 1206 (D. D.C. 1976); *State Dep't of Pub. Welfare* v. *Weinberger,* 388 F. Supp. 1304 (W.D. Tex. 1975), *modified sub nom., State Dep't of Pub. Welfare* v. *Califano,* 556 F.2d 326 (5th Cir. 1977), *cert. denied,* 99 S. Ct. 78 (1978).

[58] R.H. Leach, *American Federalism* 17–18 (1970).

[59] Cahn & Cahn, "The New Sovereign Immunity," 81 Harv. L. Rev. 929, 930 (1968).

[60] See, e.g., Tomlinson, *supra* note 55, at 618–19; Wallick & Montalto, "Symbiosis or Domination: Rights and Remedies Under Grant-Type Assistance Programs," 46 Geo. Wash. L. Rev. 159, 160 (1978).

[61] *Fletcher* v. *Housing Auth.,* 491 F.2d 793 (6th Cir.), *vacated and remanded for reconsideration,* 419 U.S. 812 (1974), *aff'd on reconsideration,* 525 F.2d 532 (1975).

argued that its circular was a mere suggestion. The Sixth Circuit replied:

> "For us to accept this argument . . . would be to blind ourselves to the realities of cooperative federalism in this case. The record is clear that the sole reason for [the Housing Authority of Louisville's] implementation of HUD Circular No. 7465.12 was the desire to conform to HUD's wishes. HUD's desires . . . took the form of a demand through HUD's control over HAL's federal funding." [62]

This book is primarily an effort to bring a semblance of order to the "anarchy" found by the Cahn's. To a great extent the text is merely expository, an attempt to analyze and rationally order the "law" of federal grants. While there are those who have suggested that such a work be undertaken,[63] we know of no predecessor. Because of the newness of the field and the lack of prior comprehensive legal study, we have minutely documented our assertions by massive citation to grant statutes, regulations, and cases. Our "law"—the broader, more comprehensive principles—is drawn out of this positive law. We will shortly sketch the magnitude of that effort. Here, we humbly hope for understanding if our readers spot an occasional mistake and hold in their hands, from time to time, a regulation which conflicts with our statement.

Yet we do not pretend to be value- or theory-free. This work is polemical and tendentious, though hopefully not pretentious. We do have a guiding premise—a thread which weaves throughout and which ties the knot at the end. The premise is simply that grantor policing of federal conditions need not and should not be a unilateral affair. The argument will be advanced that in many instances the Constitution requires that grantees be given realistic opportunities to demonstrate that their actions are consistent with federal law.

Chapters 4 and 5 discuss in considerable detail the access which grantees have to the federal courts. But that is not our focus. On the level of debate we stress notice and hearing opportunities at the administrative level. The ability of a grantee to seek redress in the courts may be a factor in determining the type of process which an administrative agency must afford,[64] but does not relieve

---

[62] *Id.* at 799.
[63] E.g., Mason, "Current Trends in Federal Grant Law—Fiscal Year 1976," 35 Fed. B.J. 163, 164–65 (1976).
[64] E.g., *Mathews* v. *Eldridge*, 424 U.S. 319, 349 (1976).

16 / *Rights and Remedies Under Federal Grants*

the executive branch from its obligation not to deprive a person of "life, liberty, or property, without due process of law." [65] For various reasons, the availability of judicial review is, alone, insufficient to comport with the fundamental procedural fairness demanded by Due Process in the context of adverse administrative decisions. First, the costs, delays, and hazards of litigation may make that type of hearing an insufficient opportunity for redress.[66] Second, when administrative action works a substantial deprivation, the government must afford notice and an opportunity to be heard *prior to* a final decision on the matter.[67] This prior opportunity can only be within the administrative process since judicial review would be available only after final agency action. Third, and most importantly, the commands of Due Process extend to all branches of government.

To our legal arguments will be added policy considerations which we think demonstrate that, apart from constitutional mandates, federal cooperative programs can achieve greater success if grantees are afforded a meaningful role in elucidating the scope, meaning, and applicability of federal grant requirements. In our discussion, we shall explore the nature of the basic "right" which flows to the grantee as a result of its commitments—the right to the grant funds.

We will also consider the case, if any, of those who *seek* federal assistance, a separate but related topic. Here too it has been our experience that federal grantor agencies have been insensitive to considerations of procedural fairness. While the constitutional and practical Due Process factors are fundamentally different between seekers and holders of federal aid, the issue of procedural equity is posited in both cases.

This book, therefore, will carry us directly into one sector of the blossoming field of federal grant law: the adverse actions which federal agencies may take against recipients or potential recipients of federal grants and the legal opportunities of the latter to influence those injurious decisions. Two broad areas are subsumed, with multiple variations in each: first, the imposition of sanctions against grantees for violation of the terms of the grant; second, denials of funding to applicants for federal assistance.

[65] U.S. Const. amend. V.
[66] See, e.g., *Memphis Light, Gas & Water Div.* v. *Craft*, 436 U.S. 1, 20–21 (1978); *Escalera* v. *New York City Housing Auth.*, 425 F.2d 853, 864 (2d Cir.), *cert. denied*, 400 U.S. 853 (1970).
[67] E.g., *Goldberg* v. *Kelly*, 397 U.S. 254 (1970).

Introduction / 17

Before moving on to the law, however, we should posit one more basic inquiry. Even if the dollars, programs, players, and conditions have greatly expanded, and even if one might fairly label the federal grantor agencies as autocratic, none of that guarantees a fight. It takes two to do battle.

Indeed, the number of reported grantor-grantee controversies while growing is still strikingly small given the magnitude of the grant-in-aid business. It is doubtful that any individual in the Federal Government even knows how many grant agreements are in effect at any one time, though we may crudely guess that at least 300 thousand such agreements are consummated or extended each year between the Federal Government and recipient states, local governments, schools, hospitals, community groups, and research organizations. Many of these grants are subsequently parceled out by states and other primary recipients to numerous subgrantees, raising the total of grants and grantees even higher. The number of separate conditions attached to each grant will vary from program to program but about 30 is the average.[68] Even these rough calculations provide some demonstration that thousands of compliance questions are potentially eruptible every moment of every day. Adding to that the many disappointments suffered each year by seekers of federal grants, we see even more clearly the fertility of the field for disputes.

Thus, here we will flip the coin over and guess why so relatively few grantor-grantee disputes have, up to now, made their way into the courts or the press.

Heading the list of probable factors is the tremendous leverage which grantors exercise over grantees. That power has two separable elements: psychological and practical. The recipient of grant funds does not sense the attributes of ownership. Rather, possession of the grant is considered gratuitous, fortuitous, fragile. For many years, arbitrary government action was shielded by the idea that government benefits, including grants-in-aid, were mere "gratuities" or "privileges" which could be withheld or recalled on a bureaucratic whim.[69] Two decades ago, a noted scholar challenged the absence of a legal regimen: "The new expectations progressively brought into existence by the welfare state must be thought of not as privileges to be dispensed unequally or by

---

[68] See Chapter 2, notes 90-136, *infra*, and accompanying text.
[69] See, e.g., *Smith* v. *Board of Comm'rs*, 259 F. Supp. 423 (D. D.C. 1966). See generally K.C. Davis, *Administrative Law Text* §§7.12-.14 (3d ed. 1972).

arbitrary fiat of government officials but as substantial rights in the assertion of which the claimant is entitled to an effective remedy, a fair procedure, and a reasoned decision."[70] The call for recipient protection was subsequently picked up and persistently elaborated by a young professor at Yale Law School,[71] and, eventually, the Supreme Court exorcised the "right-privilege" distinction as a basis for denying equality or procedural fairness in the distribution of government benefits.[72] And grants-in-aid, once awarded, are shielded by the same principles of entitlement.[73]

We shall demonstrate that the holder of a federal grant has considerable security of tenure in the grant and, in some cases, even applicants for federal funds have rights to their receipt. Yet until the existence of those entitlements is understood and, more importantly, believed, the psychological impotence of grantees will produce passive obedience to the dictates of federal officials.

The second aspect of federal agency leverage is the reality that grantor officials are in a position to visit considerable harm upon a "noncooperating" grantee. An institution dependent on federal assistance, be it a state agency, local unit of government, or nonprofit corporation, must seriously consider the side effects of a compliance battle with the United States. Though it may win on the particular issue, the resulting strain on the relationship could produce a bloody aftermath. Its requests for discretionary funds, once warmly received, may now be found lacking in merit or not quite as promising as other proposals. Its grant reports may be studied for deficiencies with unusual zeal. On-site inspections may become uncommonly frequent. Given the complexity of grant requirements, as well as their frequent ambiguity, something can usually be found lacking in the operations of even the most conscientious and capable grantee.

---

[70] H.W. Jones, "The Rule of Law and the Welfare State," 58 Colum. L. Rev. 143, 155 (1958).

[71] See Reich, "The New Property," 73 Yale L.J. 733 (1964); Reich, "Individual Rights and Social Welfare: The Emerging Legal Issues," 74 Yale L.J. 1245 (1965); Reich, "Social Welfare in the Public-Private State," 114 U. Pa. L. Rev. 487 (1966). See also Van Alstyne, "The Demise of the Right-Privilege Distinction in Constitutional Law," 81 Harv. L. Rev. 1439 (1968).

[72] E.g., *Shapiro* v. *Thompson*, 394 U.S. 618, 627, n. 6 (1969); *Goldberg* v. *Kelly*, 397 U.S. 254, 262, n. 8 (1970); *Graham* v. *Richardson*, 403 U.S. 365, 374 (1971). Compare *Richardson* v. *Belcher*, 404 U.S. 78, 80–81 (1971) (despite the characterization of public benefits as "property," Congress retains the power to make substantive changes in entitlements).

[73] See, e.g., *Texas* v. *United States*, 537 F.2d 466 (Ct. Cl. 1976). But see *School Bd.* v. *Richardson*, 332 F. Supp. 1263, 1268 (N.D. Fla. 1971) ("The funds in question here constitute a gratuity provided by Congress. . . .").

Introduction / 19

Another reason grantees have not been contentious is undoubtedly the supposed mastery which federal agencies have over the rules governing grants. As the creators of most of that vast body of intricate and interrelated commands, they are presumed to speak from a position of knowledgeability.

To analyze properly this factor we must briefly discuss the nature of federal grant law. We can refer to such "law" if we mean no more than the total body of rules which governs the dispensation of grant funds. In these terms, this would be a composite of the following elements:

(1) *Grant-in-Aid Statutes*—Our research included examination of 66 separate grant statutes ranging from a few to several hundred pages in length. It is, of course, not only the statutes but also their legislative histories which must be examined.

(2) *Appropriations Acts*—Grant-in-aid statutes contain "authorization" sections which permit funding of the programs established in the act through the appropriations process. Such sections establish the programs' life span by specifying the fiscal years for which appropriations are authorized. In most cases the authorization clause establishes the upper limit of appropriations, but increasingly Congress is permitting the appropriation of "such sums as may be necessary," thus referring all fiscal decisions to the appropriations process. Appropriations are, of course, necessary to bring a grant program to life.

Appropriations bills are theoretically limited to the funding of programs whose substance is shaped by separate legislation. Under congressional procedures the insertion of substantive provisions in appropriations bills is improper.[74] This principle, however, is frequently violated,[75] and the "courts are bound to follow Congress's last word on the matter even in an appropriations law."[76]

(3) *Program Regulations*—The practice is for the agencies to implement each grant program by means of a separate

[74] *City of Los Angeles* v. *Adams*, 556 F.2d 40, 48–49 (D.C. Cir. 1977); *Local 2677, AFGE* v. *Phillips*, 358 F. Supp. 60, 74–75, n. 15 (D. D.C. 1973).
[75] E.g., *Beal* v. *Doe*, 432 U.S. 438, 447, n. 14 (1977) (limit on use of Medicaid funds in appropriations act); *City of Hialeah* v. *U.S. Housing Auth.*, 340 F. Supp. 885 (S.D. Fla. 1971) (appropriations legislation authorized localities to reject low-income housing projects).
[76] *City of Los Angeles* v. *Adams*, 556 F.2d 40, 49 (D.C. Cir. 1977).

regulation. During the course of our research approximately 400 grant regulations were studied.

(4) *"Cross-Cutting" Statutes*—Congress has occasionally passed a grant statute applicable to all or most programs and aimed at standardizing covered practices. Examples include the Intergovernmental Cooperation Act of 1968,[77] the Joint Funding Simplification Act of 1974,[78] the National Environmental Policy Act of 1969,[79] the Uniform Relocation Assistance and Real Property Acquisitions Policies Act of 1970,[80] Title VI of the Civil Rights Act of 1964,[81] and the Federal Grant and Cooperative Agreement Act of 1977.[82] Each of these statutes is implemented by a series of administrative regulations.

(5) *Central Management Rules*—Coordinating federal agencies, primarily the Office of Management and Budget, have attempted to coordinate, standardize, and simplify the grant practices of the dozens of federal agencies and bureaus operating programs.[83]

(6) *Departmental Administrative Regulations*—In addition to regulations implementing specific programs, federal agencies have promulgated standards which cover the gamut of programs under their authority.[84]

(7) *Informal Guidelines*—Grantor agencies have traditionally utilized a wide variety of informal methods of conveying instructions, rules, suggestions, information, and other mes-

---

[77] 42 U.S.C. §§4201–4244.
[78] 42 U.S.C. §§4251–4261.
[79] 42 U.S.C. §§4321–4367.
[80] 42 U.S.C. §§4601–4655.
[81] 42 U.S.C. §§2000d–2000d-4.
[82] Pub. L. 95-224, Feb. 3, 1978, 41 U.S.C. §§501–509.

[83] See, e.g., OMB Cir. No. A-102, "Uniform Administrative Requirements for Grants-in-Aid to State and Local Governments," 42 Fed. Reg. 45827 (1977) [hereinafter cited as OMB Cir. A-102]; OMB Cir. No. A-110, "Grants and Agreements With Institutions of Higher Education, Hospitals and Other Nonprofit Organizations," 41 Fed. Reg. 32015 (1976) [hereinafter cited as OMB Cir. A-110]; OMB Cir. No. A-95, "Evaluation, Review, and Coordination of Federal and Federally Assisted Programs and Projects," 41 Fed. Reg. 2052 (1976).

[84] See, e.g., 45 C.F.R. pt. 74, 43 Fed. Reg. 34076 (1978) (HEW principles for administration of grants); 45 C.F.R. pt. 100a (OE principles for administration of direct project grants); 45 C.F.R. pt. 100b (OE principles for administration of state formula grants). When reissuing HEW's basic administrative regulation with amendments, the Acting Secretary announced the department's intention to follow up with "conforming changes" to grant program regulations and manuals and, "[w]herever feasible," to do so by "simply eliminating language on topics covered" by 45 C.F.R. pt. 74. See 43 Fed. Reg. 34077 (1978). This type of initiative is much needed, even though the sheer volume of program regulations and manuals guarantees an extremely slow revision process and, thus, many months of duplication and conflict.

sages to grantees. These include manuals, handbooks, pamphlets, directives, instructions, circulars, and memoranda. Because the operating principles of federal grant agencies are primarily and authoritatively contained in the *Code of Federal Regulations* and the *Federal Register,* these have been our primary reference sources for administrative grant law. We have also refrained from extensive utilization of informal agency guidelines because of their ambiguous legal stature.[85]

(8) *Grant Agreements*—One might suppose that the actual terms of federal grant agreements would be an important source of grant law. The opposite is true. Because grant agreements faithfully track the conditions imposed by statute and regulations, they infrequently provide a fresh source of federal grant law. The major exception is where additional conditions are imposed on a grantee through special clauses in the grant agreement.[86] And, of course, certain terms like grant amount, project period, and budget are unique to each grant.

(9) *Court Decisions*—Increasingly the courts have been called upon to interpret grant statutes and regulations. This book utilizes the leading decisions, but does not pretend to cite all relevant cases.[87]

Thus, there is a "law of federal grants" if we mean no more than a vast chain of sovereign commands. Yet this vast outpour of norms governing grantor and grantee conduct bears few of the hallmarks of mature legal systems. Congress has approved a massive number of grant statutes, caring little about the quality of its draftsmanship [88] and less about the need to consolidate the opera-

---

[85] See *California ex rel. Dep't of Transp.* v. *United States,* 547 F.2d 1388, 1389–90 (9th Cir.), *cert. denied,* 434 U.S. 824 (1977); *United States* v. *Jefferson County Bd. of Educ.,* 372 F.2d 836, 857–58 (5th Cir. 1966), *cert. denied,* 389 U.S. 840 (1967); Chapter 3, note 38, *infra.* We must clarify, however, that agency procedures not published in the *Federal Register* are binding upon those with "actual and timely notice" of their terms. See §3(a)(1) Administrative Procedure Act, 5 U.S.C. §552(a)(1); *Human Resources Management, Inc.* v. *Weaver,* 442 F. Supp. 241 (D. D.C. 1978).

[86] See Chapter 3, notes 34–36, *infra,* and accompanying text.

[87] Another source of grant law is the opinions of administrative bodies authorized to adjudicate grant controversies. Decisions of HEW's Grant Appeals Board are summarized in 45 C.F.R. pt. 16. The decisions in other administrative grant-in-aid hearings are not published.

[88] A call was made in 1968 for more precision in grant statutes so that "deviation is clearly recognizable and more nearly objectively determinable." Cahn & Cahn, "The New Sovereign Immunity," 81 Harv. L. Rev. 929, 944 (1968). Our study of grant statutes shows little improvement.

tional principles common to each such enactment.[89] The executive branch has triply compounded the problem by spewing forth incredible masses of prolix and tortuous regulations.[90] To some extent, it has tried to bring the beast under control through central directives, but these are as lacking in clarity and coverage as the grant-in-aid statutes and their implementing program regulations.

The occasional foray of the courts into the domain has produced astonishment at the morass encountered: "as complex a legislative mosaic as could be conceived by man"; [91] like "King Minos's labyrinth in ancient Crete." [92] Narrow decisions are typical. In the unfamiliar terrain of grant programs, the courts have generally been hesitant to engage in discussion of legal principles beyond the specific issues raised in the case.

Scholars have generally lacked the fortitude, experience, patience, or resources to look beyond specific programs.[93] While some

[89] The only example of a statute which attempts to consolidate operational principles of a group of grant-in-aid programs is the General Education Provisions Act, 20 U.S.C. §§1221–1234e.

[90] The Cahn's have characterized federal grant regulations as "[t]ypically silent at critical junctures, unreadable, and unmanageable." Cahn & Cahn, "The New Sovereign Immunity," 81 Harv. L. Rev. 929, 949 (1968). By executive order President Carter has adopted the following policy:

"Regulations shall be as simple and clear as possible. They shall achieve legislative goals effectively and efficiently. They shall not impose unnecessary burdens on the economy, on individuals, on public or private organizations, or on State and local governments."

§1 Exec. Order 12044, 43 Fed. Reg. 12661 (Mar. 3, 1978). The order covers grant-in-aid regulations. *Id.* at §6(a), 43 Fed. Reg. at 12664. The factors motivating the new policy were summarized in a prologue to the proposed executive order:

"Too often, regulations are written in technical or legalistic terms which are not understood by those who must comply with them. They are sometimes issued without sufficient understanding of their consequences by agency officials and without adequate review and comment from other Federal agencies, state and local governments, and the general public. The purpose of the Executive Order would be to increase public and governmental participation in the development of regulations, to permit effective oversight of regulations by agency managers and to improve agency analysis and awareness of the consequences of their regulations." 42 Fed. Reg. 59740, 59741 (1977) (proposed executive order—"Improving Government Regulations").

Under the rubric "Operation Common Sense," the Secretary of HEW has launched a project to review and revise 6,000 pages of HEW grant regulations and to improve HEW's processes for developing regulations. See 42 Fed. Reg. 59555 (1977). Secretary Califano announced proudly that the project has removed more than 300 obsolete pages from the *Code of Federal Regulations*, see 43 Fed. Reg. 23122 (1978), while revealing that the financial assistance arms of HEW were developing 215 new *sets* of regulations! See *id.* at 23123–42.

[91] *City of New York* v. *Richardson*, 473 F.2d 923, 926 (2d Cir.), *cert. denied*, 412 U.S. 950 (1973) (Aid to Families With Dependent Children).

[92] *City of Hartford* v. *Towns of Glastonbury*, 561 F.2d 1032, 1052 (2d Cir. 1977), *cert. denied*, 434 U.S. 1034 (1978) (community development program).

[93] See Mason, "Current Trends in Federal Grant Law—Fiscal Year 1976," 35 Fed. Bar J. 163, 165 (1976). Even scholars of administrative law make only passing reference to the field of grants-in-aid. See, e.g., Verkuil, "The Emerging Concept of Administrative Procedure," 78 Colum. L. Rev. 258, 300–301 (1978).

economists and political scientists have done overviews of the grant-in-aid system, legal scholars have, with few exceptions, focused only on legal issues arising in specific grant programs, or an occasional theme such as impoundment which has caught their fancy. One writer speculates that lawyers "consider public grants as being beyond the reach of legal demands" because they have been "[l]ulled perhaps by the resemblance to private gifts. . . ." [94]

Even private law publishers have ignored the field to a large extent. Law digests, encyclopedias, and other research tools do not group the case law arising from grants-in-aid under that category, but rather scatter the cases throughout traditional organizational concepts such as "Administrative Law and Procedure," "United States," "Colleges and Universities," "Hospitals," "Municipal Corporations," "State," and the like. This makes such sources unusable in researching grant issues which cut across program lines. There are numerous loose-leaf services in the field. These highlight current developments. But they focus on specific programs and do not provide a substantive and analytical framework for the masses of data they collect.

Despite the lack of consolidation, guides, and interpretive analysis, one might still move comfortably amidst the thicket if the purpose and reach of each rule, and its relation to others, could be ascertained with some ease and certainty. But the federal machinery which has spewed out this vast body of dictates has seemingly concerned itself little with the quality (in this sense) of its rule making. Ambiguity, gaps, and contradictions are rampant.

One can readily understand, therefore, the unease felt by a grantee facing a compliance directive of a federal agency. Such order, usually based on some federal official's interpretation of a section of a regulation or program manual drafted by another federal official (unknown and unavailable) in interpretation of a higher command drafted by another (also anonymous and long gone), may be dead wrong. Yet, lacking the tools and training to challenge such interpretation, and conscious of the need to maintain cordial grantor relations, the grantee is likely to abide by the federal decision.

Another factor is that until recently procedural mechanisms did not exist which a grantee could utilize to challenge federal directives. The appeal system of the Department of Health, Education and Welfare, for example, was created only four years

---

[94] Willcox, "The Function and Nature of Grants," 22 Ad. L. Rev. 125 (1970).

ago.[95] Even today, numerous grantor agencies offer no routes under which formal grantee challenges to adverse federal decisions can be brought. Excluding statutorily mandated procedures, we have been unable to locate hearing standards and procedures for administrative challenges to adverse grantor decisions for many federal departments which dispense grants and/or their operating divisions.[96] The prevailing practice appears to be that a federal agency will afford formal administrative hearing opportunities only when Congress has so mandated.[97] Some agencies will afford grantees an informal opportunity to be heard, such as through a written response to charges or an informal meeting.[98] But it appears that few agencies have voluntarily established formal appeal procedures after the grantor has made certain adverse final decisions.[99] Judicial review of such decisions is increasingly possible [100] but is subject to severe restrictions.[101]

To speak of grantee "rights" in the absence of effective procedures for their vindication is, of course, to speak of gossamer and puffs of smoke.

[95] See 40 Fed. Reg. 33936 (1975).
[96] Department of Agriculture; Department of Commerce; Department of the Interior; Department of Justice; Department of Labor; Federal Highway Administration; Urban Mass Transportation Administration; Federal Aviation Administration; Appalachian Regional Development Commission; and National Foundation on the Arts and Humanities.
[97] See, e.g., §401(h) Federal Civil Defense Act of 1950, 50 U.S.C. app. §2253(h), implemented at 32 C.F.R. pt. 1803 (Department of Defense, civil defense grants); §111 Housing and Community Development Act of 1974, 42 U.S.C. §5311, implemented at 24 C.F.R. §570.913 (HUD, community development grants); §§509, 510 Omnibus Crime Control and Safe Streets Act of 1968, 42 U.S.C. §§3757–3758, implemented at 28 C.F.R. pt. 18 (LEAA, crime control grants); §§104, 106 Comprehensive and Employment Training Act of 1973, 29 U.S.C. §§814, 816, implemented at 29 C.F.R. §§98.16, 98.40–98.46 (ETA, employment and training grants); §507 Intergovernmental Personnel Act of 1970, 42 U.S.C. §4767, implemented at 5 C.F.R. §900.204 (Civil Service Commission, intergovernmental personnel grants); §604 Community Services Act of 1974, 42 U.S.C. §2944, implemented at 45 C.F.R. §§1050.115-1–1050.115-121, 1067.2 (Community Services Administration, community action grants); §412 Domestic Volunteer Services Act of 1973, 42 U.S.C. §5052, implemented at 45 C.F.R. pt. 1206 (ACTION, domestic volunteer services grants); §§1006(b)(1), 1006(b)(2), 1011 Community Services Act of 1974, 42 U.S.C. §§2996e(b)(1), 2996e(b)(2), 2996j, implemented at 45 C.F.R. pts. 1606 [43 Fed. Reg. 32769 (1978)], 1618, 1623 [43 Fed. Reg. 21883 (1978)] (Legal Services Corporation, legal services grants); §212 Public Works Employment Act of 1976, 42 U.S.C. §6732, implemented at 31 C.F.R. §52.90 (Office of Revenue Sharing, antirecession grants); §123(b) State and Local Fiscal Assistance Act of 1972, 31 U.S.C. §1243(b), implemented at 31 C.F.R. §§51.200–51.225 (Office of Revenue Sharing, general revenue sharing).
[98] See Chapter 7, note 88, *infra*, and accompanying text.
[99] See 45 C.F.R. pt. 16 (HEW); 40 C.F.R. pt. 30, subpts. H, J (EPA); 7 C.F.R. pt. 1900, subpt. B, 43 Fed. Reg. 52461 (1978) (Farmers Home Administration). The Department of Housing and Urban Development has extended to grantees its procedures for the suspension and debarment of contractors. See 24 C.F.R. pt. 24.
[100] See Chapter 4.
[101] See Chapter 5.

Introduction / 25

The equitable treatment of thousands of grantees discharging public responsibilities is a sufficiently important goal to justify a close examination of the process currently afforded. If this effort results in a fairer shake for individual grantees, it is worthwhile. Broader goals, however, may also be served by reforms which realign the balance of power between federal agencies and their grantee clients.

Some political theorists have asserted in recent years that American federalism is no longer accurately described as two separate systems of government, federal and state, distinct and autonomous in their separate spheres. Rather, federal, state, and local governments are actively involved in virtually all functions of government, and federal-state cooperation, not separation, is characteristic.[102] The new federalism model has been principally produced by the federal grant-in-aid which has deeply enmeshed the U.S. government in many fields once thought the exclusive province of the states. If one believes that state and local governments still have an important and independent role in American society, one must necessarily be disturbed by the spectre of their meek obedience to grant-giving central authorities. One may admit the need and constitutional propriety of attaching conditions to the dispensation of federal grants without conceding unilateral and arbitrary power to federal agencies in the interpretation of those conditions and their application to specific cases. If some balance of power is to remain between the states and the United States, governmental grantees must be given realistic opportunities to challenge the reach and impact of federal grant requirements. The concept of "cooperative federalism" is meaningless if the terms of such "cooperation" are dictated by one side. Because states and their subdivisions are the recipients of most federal grant money,[103] the creation and strengthening of grantee Due Process rights will serve federalism, even the new model, well.

Due Process may be additionally justified for all sides in terms of programmatic goals. The categorical federal grant, with its multitude of strings, has been severely attacked as a misguided

---

[102] M. Grodzins, *The American System* 60 *et seq.* (1966); R.H. Leach, *American Federalism* 14–15 (1970); Reagan, *The New Federalism* 3–12 (1972); "Developments in the Law—Section 1983 and Federalism," 90 Harv. L. Rev. 1133, 1184 (1977).

[103] See generally Department of the Treasury, *Federal Aid to States: Fiscal Year 1977* (undated). Excluding revenue sharing and block grants, which would raise the percentage even higher, the Advisory Commission on Intergovernmental Relations estimates that 75% of the total grant funds go to state and local governments. *Categorical Grants, supra* note 6, at 91.

and inefficient way to attack social problems which pervade communities throughout the country. Many now see that knowledge and appreciation of local conditions reside, not surprisingly, at home and not in a distant Capitol. The continued existence of hundreds of highly conditioned, prepackaged grant-in-aid programs bears witness that central planners continue to hold sway. Yet even the most fervent centralists would admit that the grant can function most effectively when moulded to the specific needs and conditions of the community in which it operates, and that the recipients are best able to achieve that functional redesign. Federal administrators, however, tend to interpret and apply grant conditions literally and unsympathetically. Local variations and improvisations, even if fully defensible in terms of program goals, are viewed askance. The text of most grant conditions is sufficiently loose to permit sensible results in the varying situations to which they are applied. Therefore, adequate hearing opportunities could, through the ventilation of compliance issues in the full context of the operational impact of federal conditions, inject flexibility where possible and desirable.

This book begins with a sketch of the purposes and constitutional foundations of federal grant programs, their basic structure, and a brief discussion of the kinds of requirements which are imposed on recipients of federal funds. We then move into an analysis of the compliance powers of federal grantors. Our discussion of the remedies and sanctions available to grantors may be of particular assistance in the development of the law because of the rampant confusion and uncertainty. The role of the federal judiciary in policing grantor and grantee actions is then considered. We beg forgiveness from our nonlawyer readers for the highly technical nature of this discussion. Some areas of the law defy simplification.

In Chapter 6 we finally reach the point where most writers would have started: What is a federal grant? We feel that such a discussion needs the knowledge and analysis provided by the first five chapters. Most of our readers will not be troubled by lack of preliminary definitions because of prior familiarity with the field.

Our Due Process analysis will begin with the Constitution, examining the extent to which grantees can call upon first principles when faced with injurious federal action. This is followed by a detailed discussion of the hearing opportunities presently

Introduction / 27

accorded recipients of federal funds under congressional enactments and administrative regulations. Hopefully our readers will have the patience to plow through what will seem like endless detail. To the extent possible, piles of statutes and regulations have been summarized and culled for what is either the most relevant or representative of current practices. After this section, we will consider two special Due Process questions: noncompliance with civil rights obligations, and the rights of individuals who are recipients of federal training grants. The former is given separate consideration because it has received an unusual degree of attention from Congress and grantor agencies; the latter is set apart because federal grants to individuals present some considerations not found in institutional funding.

In our concluding chapters we lay the groundwork for future reform efforts. Even recognizing that the congressional agenda is tight with weighty matters, we feel that our proposal for a Grantee Bill of Procedural Rights is sufficiently important and needed to receive active consideration. On the other hand, our proposal for a Grant Disputes Board, while sensible, may be a distant dream. On the broadest level, we hope that our research and analysis can bring some rationality to an unnecessarily sprawling network of rules.

2
The Theory and Structure of Grants

Constitutional Bases

Through the grant-in-aid Congress has massively injected itself into domains traditionally occupied by states, local governments, and private institutions—probably to a greater degree than through its regulatory activities. The intrusion is effected in two ways. First, the use to which grant funds may be dedicated is closely defined in the grant statute and regulations, which has led to the descriptive label "categorical" grant. When combined with the usual requirement that the grantee contribute a specified share of total program costs ("matching"), the categorical grant not only federally defines the activities of local institutions but also shifts their resources to them. At present, approximately 37 percent of the total fiscal resources available to state and local governments is being dedicated to congressionally shaped programs and projects.[1] The second method of federal intervention is the series of requirements, other than restrictions on fund uses, which are typically attached to the grant. To qualify for financial support a grant applicant must commit itself to comply with a host of specifications such as personnel, civil rights, citizen participation, fiscal management, and organizational standards.[2]

---

[1] See Chapter 1, notes 47–48, *supra*, and accompanying text. Federal grants compose 27.5% of total state and local revenue to which grantees add an additional 9.2% as matching funds.
[2] See generally notes 90–136, *infra*, and accompanying text.

Despite the obvious impact of the federal grant in shifting governmental power to the national level, the constitutional validity of the categorical-conditional grant is firmly entrenched. Supreme Court decisions have established that Congress may utilize the General Welfare Clause [3] to establish and fund grant-in-aid programs independently of its enumerated powers. Further, conditions on the receipt and use of federal funds which might otherwise be an impermissible infringement of state and local sovereignty are valid because of the voluntary acceptance of such stipulations by grantees.

One leg of the constitutional base upon which hundreds of grant programs have been erected was first established in *United States* v. *Butler* [4] in 1936. While accepting the traditional view that the Federal Government has only such powers as have been expressly conferred by the Constitution and those reasonably to be implied from the granted powers, the Court in that case espoused the Hamiltonian position that the power to lay and collect taxes for the general welfare is a grant of authority additional to the enumerated powers. Only two restrictions exist on the power: Congress must effectuate the general welfare by means of tax revenues—i.e., through its spending power; and the appropriations must be dedicated to purposes of nationwide and not just local benefit.[5] Although this 1936 decision struck down the federal legislation under review as too local in nature to comport with the reserved rights of states under the Tenth Amendment, subsequent Supreme Court decisions have unanimously accepted *Butler*'s reading of the General Welfare Clause.[6] Further, only one year after the *Butler* decision Justice Cardozo significantly expanded that power by affording Congress great latitude in determining whether the nation's welfare will be served by the uses to which its appropriations are dedicated. He stated:

> "Nor is the concept of the general welfare static. Needs that were narrow or parochial a century ago may be inter-woven in our day with the well-being of the Nation. What is critical or urgent changes with the times. . . . When money is spent to promote the general welfare, the concept of welfare or the opposite is shaped

---

[3] U.S. Const. art. I, §8, cl. 1.
[4] 297 U.S. 1 (1936).
[5] *Id.* at 64–67.
[6] See *Steward Mach. Co.* v. *Davis*, 301 U.S. 548, 586 (1937); *Helvering* v. *Davis*, 301 U.S. 619, 640 (1937); *Ivanhoe Irrigation Dist.* v. *McCracken*, 357 U.S. 275, 294 (1958); *Rosado* v. *Wyman*, 397 U.S. 397, 423 (1970).

by Congress, not the states. So the concept be not arbitrary, the locality must yield." [7]

Butler affirmed the power of Congress to use the General Welfare Clause to promote the general well-being of the country in the context of legislation which provided federal payments directly to farmers. The authority of Congress to provide assistance by way of grants to states and localities was not involved. The compatibility of federal stipulations with state sovereignty was not, therefore, directly in issue and was not addressed. That question, however, had already been presented to the Supreme Court 13 years before *Butler*. In *Frothingham* v. *Mellon* [8] the state of Massachusetts launched a broadside constitutional attack on the power of Congress to invade local prerogatives by way of grants to states. Although the Court found the challenge to be a nonjusticiable political question and purported not to reach the merits of the constitutional claim, its dicta strongly suggested a solution:

> "Probably it would be sufficient to point out that the powers of the state are not invaded, since the statute imposes no obligation but simply extends an option which the state is free to accept or reject. . . . Nor does the statute require the states to do or yield anything. If Congress enacted it with the ulterior purpose of tempting them to yield, that purpose may be effectively frustrated by the simple expedient of not yielding." [9]

The second leg validating the constitutionality of federal grants-in-aid—the voluntary surrender of state prerogatives through the acceptance of federal aid and its accompanying conditions—was thus born in Supreme Court dicta in 1923.

A natural line of attack on this waiver theory is to question its compatibility with reality. Under political and economic pressure, what state can realistically resist federal largesse? That attack was confronted directly and repulsed in *Steward Machine Company* v. *Davis*.[10] In his typically colorful style Justice Cardozo refused to examine a state's motives in exercising the participatory option. He stated:

---

[7] *Helvering* v. *Davis*, 301 U.S. 619, 640–41, 645 (1937). See also *Buckley* v. *Valeo*, 424 U.S. 1, 90 (1976).
[8] 262 U.S. 447 (1923).
[9] *Id.* at 480, 482.
[10] 301 U.S. 548 (1937).

"[T]o hold that motive or temptation is equivalent to coercion is to plunge the law into endless difficulties. The outcome of such a doctrine is the acceptance of a philosophical determinism by which choice becomes impossible. Till now the law has been guided by a robust common sense which assumes the freedom of the will as a working hypothesis in the solution of its problems." [11]

Stressing that the state was free at any time to withdraw its participation,[12] the Court found that the "essence of [its] statehood is maintained without impairment." [13]

Following *Steward Machine,* the Supreme Court has repeatedly affirmed that conditional federal grants do not invade state sovereignty as long as participation is optional [14] and the grantee is free to withdraw.[15] Thus, even if Congress lacked the power to impose a standard of conduct directly on state and local institutions, it can do so indirectly by way of conditions attached to federal grants-in-aid. The most explicit holding on this point is *Oklahoma v. United States Civil Service Commission.*[16] While the Court admitted that Congress could not directly regulate the local political activities of state officials, it upheld such restrictions as permissible conditions on federal grants, noting that Oklahoma had in fact adopted the option of not complying with the condition and paying the fiscal penalty.[17]

Many cases have accepted the power of Congress to condition its grants without inquiring into the impact of the condition on state sovereignty, presumably on the assumption that the voluntary acceptance of the condition normally makes such an inquiry

---

[11] *Id.* at 590. The argument had found more ready acceptance in *United States* v. *Butler,* 297 U.S. 1 (1936), in which Justice Roberts found that a farmer's choice of accepting or rejecting federal payments was "illusory." *Id.* at 71.

[12] *Steward Mach. Co.* v. *Davis,* 301 U.S. 548, 592–93, 595–96 (1937).

[13] *Id.* at 597.

[14] Stress on the voluntary nature of grantee participation is found in *Oklahoma v. U.S. Civil Serv. Comm'n,* 330 U.S. 127, 143–44 (1947); *Rosado v. Wyman,* 397 U.S. 397, 408 (1970); *id.* at 427 (Douglas, J., concurring); *Lau v. Nichols,* 414 U.S. 563, 568–69 (1974); *Batterton v. Francis,* 432 U.S. 416, 420, 431–32 (1977); *Quern v. Mandley,* 436 U.S. 725, 734 (1978).

[15] See *Rosado* v. *Wyman,* 397 U.S. 397, 421 (1970); *Wheeler* v. *Barrera,* 417 U.S. 402, 425–26 (1975).

[16] 330 U.S. 127 (1947).

[17] *Id.* at 143–44. See also *Arizona State Dep't of Pub. Welfare* v. *Dep't of Health, Educ. & Welfare,* 449 F.2d 456, 473–74, n. 25 (9th Cir. 1971), *cert. denied,* 405 U.S. 919 (1972); *School Bd.* v. *Richardson,* 332 F. Supp. 1263, 1267 (N.D. Fla. 1971).

irrelevant.[18] However, a 1976 Supreme Court decision, *National League of Cities* v. *Usery*,[19] may have cracked open the door for federalism-based challenges to grant conditions.

In *Usery* the Supreme Court held that federalism and the Tenth Amendment constitute an affirmative limitation on congressional action under the Commerce Clause and struck down the extension of federal wage and hour standards to state and local employees. The Court found that the activities regulated by Congress were attributes of state sovereignty, that the functions were essential to the separate and independent existence of the states, and that on balance the national interest did not justify the intrusion.

Although the Court expressly indicated that it was reserving opinion on exercises of congressional power via grants-in-aid,[20] some have been unable to resist the temptation to speculate whether federalism and the Tenth Amendment limit the power of Congress to impose conditions on grants. More than one writer, in fact, advocates that each federal grant-in-aid condition should be subjected to an *Usery*-type analysis.[21] What is suggested would be, in essence, the creation of general revenue sharing by judicial action! While a student author labors hard to demonstrate that the voluntary nature of state participation in grants-in-aid is unreal,[22] this overlooks the basic facts that the Supreme Court has rejected inquiry into state motivation in accepting grants-in-aid and has repeatedly emphasized the voluntary basis of grants. Thus, the fundamental distinction between mandating and offering

---

[18] See, e.g., *Ivanhoe Irrigation Dist.* v. *McCracken*, 357 U.S. 275, 295 (1958); *King* v. *Smith*, 392 U.S. 309, 333, n. 34 (1968); *Lau* v. *Nichols*, 414 U.S. 563, 569 (1974); *Nebraska Dep't of Pub. Rds.* v. *Tiemann*, 510 F.2d 446, 448 (8th Cir. 1975); *Connecticut State Dep't of Pub. Welfare* v. *Dep't of Health, Educ. & Welfare*, 448 F.2d 209, 215 (2d Cir. 1971); *Ohio* v. *U.S. Civil Serv. Comm'n*, 65 F. Supp. 776 (S.D. Ohio 1946). But see *Vermont* v. *Brinegar*, 379 F. Supp. 606 (D. Vt. 1974) (conditions on federal highway grant tested by impact on state sovereignty and degree of coercion). Compare *County of Los Angeles* v. *Coleman*, 423 F. Supp. 496, 502, n. 27 (D. D.C. 1976), aff'd per curiam sub nom., *County of Los Angeles* v. *Adams*, 574 F.2d 608 (D.C. Cir. 1978) (federalism objection belongs to state not county).

[19] 426 U.S. 833 (1976).

[20] *Id.* at 852, n. 17.

[21] See Dam, "The American Fiscal Constitution," 44 U. Chi. L. Rev. 271, 293 (1977); Comment, "Toward New Safeguards on Conditional Spending: Implications of *National League of Cities* v. *Usery*," 26 Am. U. L. Rev. 726 (1977); Note, "Municipal Bankruptcy, the Tenth Amendment, and the New Federalism," 89 Harv. L. Rev. 1871, 1884 (1976).

[22] Comment, "Toward New Safeguards on Conditional Spending: Implications of *National League of Cities* v. *Usery*," 26 Am. U. L. Rev. 726, 738–46 (1977).

federal requirements is likely to preclude use of *Usery* in the grants field. That point was made emphatically in a recent decision of the United States Court of Appeals for the District of Columbia:

> "We add . . . that the Tenth Amendment contention, even assuming the County has standing to press it, is equally unpersuasive. In no way does the administrative scheme diminish the states' sovereign responsibilities. If a state is empowered by its constitution and laws to order local jurisdictions not to participate in the planning and programming process—and hence to forgo the opportunity to seek federal funding—nothing in the challenged rules prohibits it from doing so. Consequently, any impact on the states from observance of the regulations is but a necessary concomitant of Congress' evident desire to assure that the federal funds be spent wisely." [22a]

Although a condition not reasonably related to the purposes of the grant might be challengeable,[23] if the rational relation can be shown the condition will be upheld. The Court will not be inclined to tamper with an institution that has been described as a "major social invention" which has created modern cooperative federalism and which has kept state government alive despite political and financial bankruptcy.[24]

The issue was posed to the U.S. Supreme Court in a 1978 challenge brought by North Carolina to a grant condition in the National Planning and Resources Development Act.[25] The Court summarily affirmed a three-judge decision rejecting the constitutional contention.[26] The lack of an opinion, however, leaves us guessing whether all conditions on federal grants are free from *Usery* analysis or whether this particular requirement—that a state

---

[22a] *County of Los Angeles v. Adams*, 574 F.2d 608, 609 (D.C. Cir. 1978).

[23] See *United States v. Butler*, 297 U.S. 1, 85–86 (1936) (Stone, J., dissenting); Comment, "Federal Conditional Spending Power: A Search for Limits," 70 Nw. U. L. Rev. 293 (1975); Note, "Emerging Concepts of Federalism: Limitations on the Spending Power and National Health Planning," 34 Wash. & Lee L. Rev. 1133, 1143–44 (1977).

[24] Reagan, *The New Federalism* 82–83 (1972).

[25] Title XV, Public Health Service Act, 42 U.S.C. §§300k–300n-5.

[26] *North Carolina ex rel. Morrow v. Califano*, 445 F. Supp. 532 (E.D. No. Car.), aff'd mem., 435 U.S. 962 (1978).

34 / *Rights and Remedies Under Federal Grants*

certify the need for public or private health facilities construction—was not a sufficiently serious encroachment on state sovereignty.[27]

Purposes of Federal Grants

The "classic" objectives of fiscal aid have been defined as general support, stimulation, equalization, and demonstration.[28] We shall discuss these purposes in that order.

The bulk of federal grant dollars goes to support the efforts of state and local governments to provide public services. The Advisory Commission on Intergovernmental Relations has described the motivations underlying such assistance as follows:

> "The evolution of the categorical grant-in-aid system indicates that it has grown as a consequence of Congressional determination (1) that the achievement of certain specific national objectives requires additional public expenditures, (2) that these expenditures should be made through State and local governments rather than directly by the National Government, and (3) that State and local governments lack the resources or motivation to make them on their own." [29]

Once the concept of the proper governmental role in America became fixed on the side of active involvement in the resolution of social problems,[30] the preemptive taxing power of the national government probably made inevitable massive federal entry into the domestic assistance field. State and local revenues could not keep pace with the ever-increasing demand of the citizenry for services. Lobby groups focused their attention on Washington, quickly learning that once Congress was persuaded to enact a

---

[27] One should anticipate inhospitable treatment of the *Usery* argument in the lower federal courts. See, e.g., *Natural Resources Defense Council, Inc.* v. *Costle*, 564 F.2d 573, 579–80 (D.C. Cir. 1977); *Stiner* v. *Califano*, 438 F. Supp. 796, 799–800 (W.D. Okla. 1977). Before the North Carolina case was summarily affirmed, lower courts even rejected a federalism argument focusing on the imposition of labor standards through grant conditions. See *City of Macon* v. *Marshall*, 439 F. Supp. 1209 (M.D. Ga. 1977) (preservation of collective bargaining employee rights as condition of federal mass transit aid); *Local 519, Amalgamated Transit Union* v. *LaCrosse Municipal Transit Util.*, 445 F. Supp. 798 (W.D. Wis. 1978) (same).

[28] *Fiscal Balance, supra*, Chapter 1, note 46, at 5. See generally S.J. Mushkin & J.F. Cotton, *Sharing Federal Funds for State and Local Needs: Grants-in-Aid and PPB Systems* (1969); A. Harbert, *Federal Grants-in-Aid: Maximizing Benefits to the States* (1976); Reagan, *The New Federalism* 66–77 (1972).

[29] *Fiscal Balance, supra*, Chapter 1, note 46, at 149.

[30] See generally Woodward, "Reality and Social Reform: The Transition From Laissez-Faire to the Welfare State," 72 Yale L. J. 286 (1962).

grant program, the lure of federal matching funds would prove irresistible to states and localities.

What was not so clear was that the form of federal aid should be fiscal assistance to lower levels of government rather than direct national provision of benefits and services. We have seen that the General Welfare Clause offers Congress the option of either providing public services on its own or supporting the efforts of other units of government and private institutions. Eight hundred separate grant programs show, of course, that in the great majority of cases Congress has chosen the latter alternative. The popularity of the grant-in-aid is readily understandable. First, in many areas it seemed senseless to create parallel federal machinery when a structure of state, local, and private institutions already existed to provide the same or comparable services. Second, aid in the form of grants to state and local governments guaranteed widespread political support for federal intervention, while direct federal development was more likely to foster local jealousy and hostility. Third, the matching grant could be effectively utilized as a prod to increased state and local financial participation, pulling local governmental revenues into areas deemed of national priority. Fourth, the grant-in-aid offered a unique opportunity to improve the administration of state and local governments once the conditioning of a federal grant was found constitutionally acceptable. Finally, the grant-in-aid avoided, or at least muted, hard political questions of federal-state relations. The old conceptions of federalism—the constitutional division of authority and functions between national and state governments—could be honored in theory, while as a practical matter congressionally determined categories of assistance orchestrated governmental priorities and grant conditions implemented national policies.

Whatever the motivation, the important point for our purposes is that in the grant-in-aid Congress chooses as the beneficiary of its largesse other institutions, governmental and private, which are the direct service providers.[31] One notes some confusion in judicial opinions about the primary beneficiaries of grants-in-aid.[32]

[31] Congress frequently makes this point explicitly in its statement of purposes in grant-in-aid legislation. See, e.g., §100 Omnibus Crime Control and Safe Streets Act of 1968, 42 U.S.C. §3701.

[32] Compare, e.g., *City of Grand Rapids* v. *Richardson*, 429 F. Supp. 1087, 1093 (W.D. Mich. 1977) (local public works grants; primary beneficiary is unemployed worker); and *City of Beaver Falls* v. *Economic Dev. Admin.*, 439 F. Supp. 851, 854 (W.D. Pa. 1977) (same); with *Clark* v. *Richardson*, 431 F. Supp. 105, 116 (D. N.J. 1977) (local public works grants; local governments have protectable rights). See also *Southern Mut. Help Ass'n* v. *Califano*, 574 F.2d 518, 528–34 (D.C. Cir. 1977) (Wilkey, J., dissenting).

The simple point is often lost that the grant "aids" other institutions which, in turn, aid individuals. In the background of grant statutes one will, of course, always find congressional discussion of the needs of individuals to which federal expenditures should be directed. That discussion is essential to the determination of national expenditure priorities. But once the grant vehicle is chosen the individual becomes the secondary or indirect beneficiary of federal bounty.

The point is more than academic. The focus of rights and responsibilities under a federal grant may hinge on proper conceptions such as these. To the extent that one misconceives the ultimate recipient of federally assisted benefits and services as the primary object of federal concern, the nature and extent of grantee rights become dubious. The example most relevant for our purposes is the Due Process question. When the Federal Government takes unfavorable action on a grant, to whom is process owed? Conceiving the grantee as a mere conduit of federal dollars aimed primarily at the grantee's clients improperly shifts our concern for procedural equity away from the grantee with potentially mischievous consequences.[33]

We have made passing reference to the "stimulative" effect of federal grants, a second objective of fiscal aid. The idea is to induce state and local governments to inject their funds into new types of services or expand their financial support for existing programs. The inducement is the availability of federal grants; the stimulator of increased local financial participation is the requirement that new federal dollars be matched in some predetermined ratio by local revenues. The great majority of federal grants-in-aid requires such matching, and often blends the double motives of stimulation and general support.[34] It appears that Congress has judged, in many programs, that state and local revenues are insufficient to provide the desired level of services, but not so bankrupt that additional dollars cannot be squeezed out of these levels of government by way of matching requirements. Congress has usually been right. The states have left few matchable dollars in the federal till.

A third objective, equalization, will be described in detail later in the text. What is equalized to some extent is the financial

---

[33] See, e.g., Chapter 8, *infra*, at pp. 230–33.
[34] See *Fiscal Balance, supra*, Chapter 1, note 46, at 5 (objectives of fiscal aid "not clearly differentiated" under present system).

capability of states in different sectors of the country. States with fewer taxable resources are provided proportionately higher shares of federal aid, or even singled out for special grant programs.[35]

The three goals of support, stimulation, and equalization particularly characterize the heavily funded formula grant programs which we shall discuss in the next section. Another set of grant programs has a different thrust, the promotion of knowledge, information, and technology. These are the federal research, demonstration, or research and demonstration grants. Here the federal aim is primarily to learn. The chief beneficiary of such efforts is the Federal Government itself. The goal is not to assist other social institutions in the discharge of their locally defined functions but rather to utilize their capabilities to accomplish federal purposes. These programs are quite akin to the buying of goods and services through contracts and, in fact, the contract and grant are often used interchangeably.[36] As might be expected, the shape of such assistance is moulded by the difference in goals. Federal definition of anticipated products of the sponsored projects tends to be tighter, discretion in the selection of grantees is vested in the grantor, and the federal contribution to project costs is higher.

In addition to the primary objectives of federal grants described above, the Federal Government has utilized grant conditions to improve standards in the aided programs. The grant has also been a convenient vehicle for the achievement of national policies which transcend the particular grant, such as civil rights and environmental protection. Finally, the grant has been a powerful force in the improvement of the administration of state and local governments. Typical grant conditions have included merit standards for personnel policies, program planning and budgeting criteria, modern systems for fiscal accounting and re-

[35] See Appalachian Regional Development Act of 1965, 40 U.S.C. app. §§1–405; Title V, Public Works and Economic Development Act of 1965, 42 U.S.C. §§3181–3196.

[36] Unsolicited contractual agreements are listed in the Office of Management and Budget, *Catalog of Federal Domestic Assistance* (1978 update), as project grants, see *id.* at xix, although the form of agreement will differ if the contractual vehicle is chosen. The Federal Grant and Cooperative Agreement Act of 1977, Pub. L. 95-224, Feb. 3, 1978, 41 U.S.C. §§501–509, forces agencies to categorize their assistance by purpose, but does not preclude the use of both grants and contracts in implementing a particular program.

While either instrument may be used, the resolution of disputes arising under them differs dramatically since controversies involving procurement contracts are governed by the mature disputes machinery culminating in the Contract Disputes Act of 1978, Pub. L. 95-563, Nov. 1, 1978, 41 U.S.C. §§601–613.

38 / *Rights and Remedies Under Federal Grants*

porting, disentanglement of politics and programs, and greater citizen input in program development and implementation.

Types of Grants

Congress has created such a bewildering array of federal domestic assistance programs that generalizations are hazardous. Out of the mass of detail, however, emerge three classes of grant, distinct in purpose and structure.[37]

One broad grouping subsumes those programs which support ongoing activities of other public entities, principally state and local governments. Indeed, the label grant "in-aid" arises from these programs which provide supplementary federal financing to institutions already engaged in the provision of traditional public services. Programs of this type include assistance to states and local governments for: feeding[38] and education[39] of public school children; health services[40] and hospitals;[41] libraries;[42] law enforcement;[43] public welfare;[44] housing and community development;[45] vocational training;[46] public employment;[47] highway[48] and air-

---

[37] See generally *Categorical Grants, supra,* Chapter 1, note 6.

[38] See National School Lunch Act of 1946, 42 U.S.C. §§1751–1769a; Child Nutrition Act of 1966, 42 U.S.C. §§1771–1788.

[39] See, e.g., Act of Sept. 30, 1950, Pub. L. 81-874, 20 U.S.C. §§236–246; Act of Sept. 23, 1950, Pub. L. 81-815, 20 U.S.C. §§631–647; Elementary and Secondary Education Act of 1965, 20 U.S.C. §§2701–3386, as rewritten by §101 Education Amendments of 1978, Pub. L. 95-561, Nov. 1, 1978; Education of the Handicapped Act, 20 U.S.C. §§1401–1461; Emergency School Aid Act, 20 U.S.C. §§1601–1619; Special Projects Act, 20 U.S.C. §§1851–1853, 1861–1867.

[40] See, e.g., Title III-B, Public Health Service Act, 42 U.S.C. §§243–247c (comprehensive health services); Title X, Public Health Service Act, 42 U.S.C. §§300–300a–8 (family planning); Title V, Social Security Act, 42 U.S.C. §§701–716 (crippled children and maternal and child health care services); Title XIX, Social Security Act, 42 U.S.C. §§1396–1396k (Medicaid).

[41] See Title XVI, Public Health Service Act, 42 U.S.C. §§300o–300t.

[42] See Library Services and Construction Act of 1956, 20 U.S.C. §§351–364.

[43] See Omnibus Crime Control and Safe Streets Act of 1968, 42 U.S.C. §§3701–3796(c); Juvenile Justice and Delinquency Prevention Act, 42 U.S.C. §§5601–5751.

[44] See, e.g., Title IV-A, Social Security Act, 42 U.S.C. §§601–611 (AFDC); Title IV-B, Social Security Act, 42 U.S.C. §§620–626 (child welfare services); Title XX-A, Social Security Act, 42 U.S.C. §§1397–1397f (social services).

[45] See, e.g., Housing and Community Development Act of 1974, 42 U.S.C. §§5301–5318.

[46] See, e.g., Rehabilitation Act of 1973, 29 U.S.C. §§701–796i; Vocational Education Act of 1963, 20 U.S.C. §§2301–2461; Titles II, pts. A–C, III, IV, VIII, Comprehensive Employment and Training Act of 1973, 29 U.S.C. §§841–852, 871–886, 891–945, 991–999.

[47] See, e.g., Titles II-D, VI, Comprehensive Employment and Training Act of 1973, 29 U.S.C. §§853–859, 961–970.

[48] See Federal-Aid Highway Act of 1973, 23 U.S.C. §§101–407.

port [49] construction; outdoor recreation facilities; [50] and sewage systems and treatment plants.[51]

Despite the variety of fields, the statutes establishing such programs share several common characteristics. First, federal funding is expected to be provided in predictable amounts year after year. In most programs of this type Congress technically retains financial control through yearly authorizations and appropriations,[52] but the possibility of a cutoff or drastic reduction of funds is remote. The needs to which such aid is directed are important and persistent, producing consistent political support and heavy funding.[53] Second, program appropriations are divided among the states by means of a statutory formula. The allocation system employs weighted statistical factors considered relevant to the measurement of the dimension, in each jurisdiction, of the particular social problem addressed by the grant program. The need of each state is translated into dollar amounts of federal aid by slotting the state's relevant demographic, social, and economic data into the statutory formula and comparing them to the total need. The money share of each state, therefore, will roughly correspond to its share of the problem. The use of a mandatory formula for the allocation of funds among the states results in the common practice of labeling this category as "formula" grants.[54]

---

[49] See Airport and Airway Redevelopment Act of 1970, 49 U.S.C. §§1701–1743.
[50] See Land and Water Conservation Fund Act of 1965, 16 U.S.C. §§460L–460L(22).
[51] See Federal Water Pollution Control Act, 33 U.S.C. §§1251–1376.
[52] See Chapter 1, *supra,* at p. 19. The major exception is the program in which appropriations are "open-ended." Congress commits itself to appropriate whatever funds are necessary to provide the federal share of state-determined program costs. See, e.g., §§401, 403, Social Security Act, 42 U.S.C. §§601, 603 (Aid to Families With Dependent Children).

A good discussion of the different varieties of congressional budget authority can be found in *National Ass'n of Regional Councils* v. *Costle,* 564 F.2d 583, 586–87 (D.C. Cir. 1977).

[53] Although some 20% of the federal grant programs utilize a formula in the distribution of monies, these programs account for about 70% of the total grant outlays. See Cappalli, *Federal Aid to Puerto Rico* Tables A & B (1970).

[54] Setting forth one of the more simple allocation formulas might serve to clarify the brief description in the text. Title V, Older Americans Act of 1965, 42 U.S.C. §§3056–3056f, establishes a grant program for projects which provide community service employment opportunities for low-income elderly. The statute divides funds among the states and the District of Columbia as follows:

"(3) The Secretary [of Labor] shall allot for projects within each State the remainder of the sums appropriated for any fiscal year . . . so that each State will receive an amount which bears the same ratio to such remainder as the product of the number of persons aged fifty-five or over in the State and the allotment percentage of such State bears to the sum of the corresponding product for all States, except that (A) no State shall be allotted less than one-half of 1 per centum of the remainder of

40 / *Rights and Remedies Under Federal Grants*

A third characteristic of such programs is that each state initially qualifies for its formula grant through the submission of a document ordinarily described in the statutes as a "state plan." [55] This is the vehicle by which the state commits itself to abide by the conditions which Congress attaches to the funds. As program revisions add or amend such requirements, the state must submit

---

the sums appropriated for the fiscal year for which the determination is made, or $100,000, whichever is greater, . . .

"(4) For the purpose of this subsection—

"(A) The allotment percentage of each State shall be 100 per centum less that percentage which bears the same ratio to 50 per centum as the per capita income of such State bears to the per capita income of the United States, except that (i) the allotment percentage shall in no case be more than 75 per centum or less than $33\frac{1}{3}$ per centum . . .

"(B) the number of persons aged fifty-five or over in any State and in all States, and the per capita income in any State and in all States, shall be determined by the Secretary on the basis of the most satisfactory data available to him. . . ." §506(a), *id.*, 42 U.S.C. §3056d(a).

The formula translates each state's need for this type of grant into a dollar share of the appropriation by utilizing comparative statistics on the number of elderly and the incidence of poverty among this group. The latter is measured roughly, using state per capita income levels. The greater a state's share of the total national population of poor elderly, the greater its share of program funds, and vice versa.

§506(a) has other features typical of grant-in-aid distribution formulas. First, the distribution based on comparative needs is limited by floors and ceilings. Each state is guaranteed $100,000, or more if the available appropriation exceeds $20 million. Funds are, therefore, shifted out of the need distribution into the guaranteed allotment of high-income, low-elderly-population states. Also, the influence of the per capita income factor is tempered by the high and low boundaries of 75% and $33\frac{1}{3}$%. Second, the Secretary is authorized to utilize a specified percentage of the total program appropriation for discretionary grants. See §506(a)(1), *id.*, 42 U.S.C. §3056d(a)(1). This explains the reference to the "remainder" in the first sentence of the quoted section. Third, the administering agency is given discretion to select the sources of data. This is uncommon. In most formulas one finds a requirement that the data be provided by the Department of Commerce or other specific source. See, e.g., §2002(a)(2)(A), Social Security Act, 42 U.S.C. §1397a(a)(2)(A) (state grants for social services distributed by respective state populations; Department of Commerce supplies data). Fourth, the use of the respective state per capita incomes as a distribution factor is typical. It not only serves to gauge the size of the beneficiary population in each state but also measures the taxing capacity of each state and, hence, its ability to fund a particular program from its own revenues.

We have excised from the quoted section the special rules for distributing funds among Puerto Rico and the territories. For a detailed review of such provisions, see Cappalli, "Federal Financing in the Commonwealth of Puerto Rico," 38 U. P. R. L. Rev. 1, 43–92 (1970).

Congress will occasionally direct the administering federal agency to develop the specific details of the allocation formula. §302(a) Comprehensive Alcohol Abuse and Alcoholism Prevention, Treatment and Rehabilitation Act of 1970, 42 U.S.C. §4572(a), for example, directs the Secretary of HEW to establish by regulation "a methodology to assess and determine the incidence and prevalence of alcohol abuse within the States." The allocation formula is set forth in 42 C.F.R. §54a.102, 42 Fed. Reg. 60398 (1977).

[55] See, e.g., §613 Education of the Handicapped Act, 20 U.S.C. §1413; 45 C.F.R. §121a.110–.151, 42 Fed. Reg. 42480–84 (1977) (required contents of state plan). The word "plan" is a misnomer. The document does not specify long- and short-term goals and the staged processes for achieving them. Rather, it contains a series of assurances and descriptions concerning compliance with federal grant requirements.

appropriate modifications to its approved plan.[56] A fourth feature common to formula programs is that once a state has submitted suitable assurances it is entitled to its allotment of funds. The statute will normally instruct the administrator to approve all plans and modifications thereof which contain the requisite assurances,[57] and there is usually an additional mandate to "make payments."[58] The federal administering agency has authority to disapprove a state plan which does not conform to federal standards,[59] but once approved has no further discretion to retain the state's allocation.[60] A fifth feature of formula grants is the requirement that each state dedicate sufficient local revenues to the program to satisfy the statutory "matching" ratio. Two different matching systems are utilized. In numerous programs the ratio of federal and state shares of total program costs is the same for all grantees.[61] The second system is to vary the federal share in inverse proportion to the recipient's financial capacity, usually measured by the area's per capita income.[62] Federal aid would not have the desired effect of increasing the total financial resources devoted to meeting the particular need if state and local governments were permitted to supplant local budgets with newly arrived federal dollars. Where federal allocations are sufficient to cover all local revenues at the statutory matching ratio, each local dollar withdrawn will cost an additional federal dollar if the match is fifty-fifty and more if the federal share of program expenditures is higher. Such "two for one" pressure ordinarily suffices to maintain local efforts [63]

---

[56] See, e.g., *National Welfare Rights Organ.* v. *Finch*, 429 F.2d 725 (D.C. Cir. 1970) (nonconformity hearings on failure of Nevada and Connecticut to modify welfare plans).
[57] See, e.g., §613(c) Education of the Handicapped Act, 20 U.S.C. §1413(c).
[58] See, e.g., §620, *id.*, 20 U.S.C. §1420.
[59] See, e.g., §613(c) Education of the Handicapped Act, 20 U.S.C. §1413(c).
[60] See, e.g., *Kennedy* v. *Mathews*, 413 F. Supp. 1240 (D. D.C. 1976) (impoundment of formula grants for nutrition projects for elderly illegal).
[61] See, e.g., §304(d)(1)(A) Older Americans Act of 1965, 42 U.S.C. §3024(d)(1)(A) (state administrative expenses: 75 percent federal; 25 percent state). For program expenses the state determines the matching ratios for its subgrantees, with a 90 percent federal percentage ceiling for fiscal years 1979 and 1980 and an 85 percent ceiling for fiscal year 1981. §304(d)(1)(B) *id.*, 42 U.S.C. §3024(d)(1)(B).
[62] See, e.g., §423 Social Security Act, 42 U.S.C. §623.
[63] If the grant statute does not impose a local share requirement, in most cases it will directly prohibit the recipient from substituting federal for local dollars. A typical nonsupplantation provision reads as follows:

"[S]uch plan must—. . . provide reasonable assurance that Federal funds made available under this part for any period will be so used to supplement and increase (but not supplant) the level of the State, local, and other non-Federal funds that would in the absence of such Federal funds be made available for the programs described in this part, and will in no event replace such State, local, and other non-Federal funds;" §223(a)(19) Juvenile Justice Delinquency and Prevention Act of 1974, 42 U.S.C. §5633(a)(19).

42 / Rights and Remedies Under Federal Grants

and, in any event, avoids supplantation. The matching requirement may even have the effect of attracting additional local dollars into a program. When congressional appropriations outstrip a program's local financing, available federal dollars may be lost for lack of sufficient matching funds. States have been generally reluctant to let such dollars return to Washington and will often revamp their budgets to avoid such losses.[64] Finally, the matching ratio will ordinarily remain constant over the life of a formula program, or the federal share may even be increased if state and local governments are financially strained.[65] Unlike other types of grant programs, the underlying theory is not to move the Federal Government gradually out of the program's financing. Rather, because the need for federal aid is produced by the heavy costs of the public services being sponsored and the insufficiency of state and local revenues to finance them, financial involvement of the United States will persist as long as these precipitating social and economic factors continue.

In a second category of federal grants the United States promotes new initiatives to understand, ameliorate, or solve social problems of national scope. This category includes a multitude of research and demonstration efforts.[66] Several factors distinguish this type of "project" grant from the formula program. Aid is not simply a supplement to the traditional, ongoing activities of other political institutions, but instead is aimed at creating new knowl-

[64] *Fiscal Balance, supra,* Chapter 1, note 46, at 202–03.

[65] See, e.g., Thomas & Luken, "Balancing Incentives and Conditions in the Evolution of a Federal Program: A Perspective on Construction Grants for Waste Water Treatment Plants," 4 Publius 43 (1974) (over 16-year period federal share increased from 30% to 75%). See generally *Categorical Grants, supra,* Chapter 1, note 6, at 114–15. Despite broad support for reducing matching requirements in federal grant programs, see, e.g., *Fiscal Balance, supra,* Chapter 1, note 46, *passim,* the Office of Management and Budget reported:

"Most general purpose and broad-based grants significantly reduce or eliminate the requirement that recipients match Federal funds with their own. Despite the increase in these grants, matching requirements for all grants have not changed significantly. In 1972, State and local governments were estimated to provide approximately $1 of matching funds for $3 of Federal aid, and this ratio is virtually unchanged for 1977. The decrease in matching requirements for general-purpose and broad-based aid has been offset by the significant growth in programs such as Medicaid, which requires substantial matching aid." *Special Analysis H, supra,* Chapter 1, note 43, at 187.

[66] See generally *Fiscal Balance, supra,* Chapter 1, note 46, at 153–55. Whether a program or project is or is not a demonstration may, at times, be difficult to discern. See, e.g., *National Council of Community Mental Health Centers, Inc.* v. *Weinberger,* 361 F. Supp. 897, 901–902 (D. D.C. 1973); *California Welfare Rights Organ.* v. *Richardson,* 348 F. Supp. 491, 498 (N.D. Cal. 1972). Various federal grant programs originated in experiments and, after proving their worth, were enacted on a more permanent basis. See, e.g., *Batterton* v. *Francis,* 432 U.S. 416, 419 (1977) (Aid to Families With Dependent Children—Unemployed Parent).

edge and methodology in areas where state and local governments have assumed no or minimal responsibility. The conditions attached to formula grants may modify state and local programs, sometimes substantially,[67] but the primary ingredients of such programs are locally determined. In the research and demonstration grants, in comparison, the United States carefully shapes the goals and uses of grant funds. Grant statutes establishing research and demonstration efforts are ordinarily phrased broadly. It is the executive branch, through implementing regulations, that defines with considerable precision the parameters of grantee activities. A second distinguishing characteristic is that the federal effort is anticipated to be transitory. Once research or demonstration goals are achieved or found unobtainable, federal financial involvement ceases. Thus, federal research and demonstration efforts come and go with great frequency. A third way in which such grants differ from the formula type is that their aim is not to solve or deal with a social problem wherever it exists throughout the country, but instead to lay the foundation for such an effort through better understanding of a problem's nature and dimensions, and development of methods of attacking it. Grant funds, therefore, need not be spread from state to state. Similarly, the choice of grantee is not preordained. No institution can claim presumptive rights to such funds as the exclusive or principal agency in a jurisdiction authorized to engage in the particular activity being financed. Also, the goal of such grants—the creation of new knowledge—compels careful consideration of the prior experience, capabilities, and other credentials of prospective grantees.

These distinguishing characteristics result in a grant-in-aid structure considerably different from the formula type. Eligibility for such grants is defined broadly, ranging from state agencies to individuals. A typical eligibility section reads as follows:

> "The administrator . . . shall . . . render financial and other assistance to appropriate public (whether Federal, State, interstate, or local) authorities, agencies, and institutions, private agencies and institutions, and individuals in the conduct of and to promote the coordination of research, investigations, experiments, training, demonstrations, surveys, public education programs and studies relating to —. . . ."[68]

[67] See, e.g., §402(a) Social Security Act, 42 U.S.C. §602(a)(29 requirements for receipt of federal welfare aid); §1902(a) Social Security Act, 42 U.S.C. §1396a(a) (39 standards for federal Medicaid assistance).
[68] §8001(a) Solid Waste Disposal Act, 42 U.S.C. §6981(a).

44 / Rights and Remedies Under Federal Grants

The grantor is delegated broad discretion both in selecting grantees and determining funding levels.[69] Project periods are sharply defined, with no express or implied commitment to additional funding when budgeted amounts are exhausted.[70] While some local contribution to project expenses is usually required, the essentially national focus of the effort is reflected in a high federal contribution to project costs. If fixed by statute, the federal share of a research or demonstration statute will range from 75 to 100 percent; in many cases the administering agency is authorized to negotiate the matching rate.[71] Finally, requests for grants are made through applications which meticulously elaborate the project goals, design, budget, and personnel, as well as the prior experiences, resources, and capabilities of the applicant.[72]

In a third category of federal grant the congressional aim is to improve the delivery of existing services through increased financing, yet the formula grant system is not feasible. A social problem may not be sufficiently uniform throughout the country to permit a formula distribution of appropriated funds. Instead, need for federal financial assistance can best be determined by consideration of individual cases on the basis of the specific information supplied in grant applications. That individualized treatment is achieved by delegating discretion in the funding process, exercised on the basis of such information, to the program's administrator. Although statutes establishing such programs do not preordain the distribution of funds throughout the country, in many cases the administering agency is exhorted to spread the funds "equitably" among the states and between urban and rural areas.[73] It may also be that within any state a number of public and private institutions are providing, or are capable of providing, such services, and that a discriminating selection of grantees will best promote the effective use of federal funds. In some cases Congress may be unhappy with the structure and performance of established institutions and may create, through grants, new orga-

---

[69] See Chapter 7, notes 72–73, *infra*, and accompanying text.

[70] See generally Chapter 12, notes 53–57, *infra*, and accompanying text.

[71] Compare, e.g., §8006(b)(2) Solid Waste Disposal Act, 42 U.S.C. §6986(b)(2) (75% federal); with §8004(c), *id.*, 42 U.S.C. §6984(c) (maximum practicable local share).

[72] See, e.g., OMB Cir. A-102, *supra*, Chapter 1, note 83, at Attachment M, "Standard Forms for Applying for Federal Assistance" (state and local governments); OMB Cir. A-110, *supra*, Chapter 1, note 83, at Attachment M, "Standard Forms for Applying for Federal Assistance" (nonprofits).

[73] See, e.g., §405(h) Special Projects Act, 20 U.S.C. §1864(h) (community education programs).

nizations to deliver services.[74] Thus, although the type of activity being supported by the United States is characteristic of the formula program, Congress adopts the grant structure used for research and demonstration.[75] Alternatively, Congress may require the administering agency to provide a grant to all eligible applicants, but give the administrator discretion to determine the size of each.[76]

While the three types of federal grants-in-aid described above are readily distinguishable, and constitute the bulk of grant programs, a fair number of programs do not neatly fit into these categories. In some programs, funds are allocated among the states by formula yet on a discretionary basis the grantor determines which projects to fund and at what levels.[77] In others, Congress has chosen the discretionary grant structure when the type of activity being sponsored would seem to lend itself readily to a formula approach.[78] Programs may also shift from one category to another. For instance, having proven its worth a demonstration program may be moved into the formula category of mandated grants.[79]

Federal Grant Requirements

From the beginning, federal grants contained various conditions on their receipt and use. For example, land grants to the states for the support of agricultural colleges established under the Act of July 2, 1862, 12 Stat. 503, required state legislatures to assent to the following conditions: Any monies from the endowment funds or interest on such which might be "lost" had to be

---

[74] The premier examples are community action agencies, see §§211–213 Community Services Act of 1974, 42 U.S.C. §§2791, 2795, 2796, and health systems agencies, see §§1512, 1513 Public Health Service Act, 42 U.S.C. §§300"l"-1, 300"l"-2.

[75] See, e.g., Title VII, Elementary and Secondary Education Act, 20 U.S.C. §§3221–3261, as rewritten by §101 Education Amendments of 1978, Pub. L. 95-561, Nov. 1, 1978 (bilingual education).

[76] See, e.g., §17 Child Nutrition Act of 1966, 42 U.S.C. §1786 (special supplemental food program).

[77] See, e.g., Title V, Older Americans Act of 1965, 42 U.S.C. §§3056–3056f (community service employment for senior citizens).

[78] For example, the competitive grants awarded under Title I of the Public Works and Economic Development Act of 1965, 42 U.S.C. §§3131–3137, could easily be distributed by statutory formula. Cf. §108(a)(3) Local Public Works Capital Development and Investment Act of 1976, 42 U.S.C. §6707(a)(3), as amended by §105 Pub. L. 95-28, May 13, 1977.

[79] Compare, e.g., §17 Child Nutrition Act of 1966, 42 U.S.C. §1786, with H.R. Rep. No. 92-1387, 92d Cong., 2d Sess., in *1972 U.S. Code Cong. & Admin. News* 3395, 3397–98 (explaining the "pilot" nature of the special supplemental food program).

replaced by the state; the interest earned on the endowment fund had to be used only for agricultural colleges; the funds could not be used for physical facilities; the funds had to be returned if a state failed to establish at least one such college within five years; and each state had to submit annual progress reports.[80] *Cornell University* v. *Fiske* [81] reveals a fascinating early instance of a state's successful evasion of a federal condition. States receiving land script in place of land could not locate and sell the donated public land. Having difficulty in selling the script, New York utilized an elaborate "strawman" scheme.

Even revenue-sharing grants are conditioned upon compliance with federal standards such as reports on use of funds, public hearings on proposed uses, nondiscrimination, and fiscal accountability requirements.[82]

We can safely say, therefore, that each federal grant of whatever type will always be accompanied by a host of federal requirements. The focus in this section is on standard grant conditions imposed by statutes and regulations, though we recognize the power of federal grantor agencies to impose special conditions on grantees if such conditions are consistent with the grant statute.[83] These conditions are not an unconstitutional invasion of state authority, even though Congress could not impose them in the absence of the grant.[84] The theory is that a grantee can always avoid their imposition by refusing to accept federal funds.[85] Such federal requirements must, however, pass constitutional muster under the Bill of Rights.[86]

Because most right, responsibility, and remedy issues will arise in the context of an alleged violation of a grant requirement, we are obliged to at least describe them. We will offer just a thumbnail sketch, enough to provide a feel for the nature and variety of compliance questions which may arise during the course of a grant.

First, however, a brief word on the nature of federal standards found in grant statutes. A basic characteristic of such standards is

---

[80] See *Cornell Univ.* v. *Fiske*, 136 U.S. 152, 179–80 (1890).

[81] 136 U.S. 152 (1890).

[82] See §§121–123 State and Local Fiscal Assistance Act of 1972, 31 U.S.C. §§1241–1243.

[83] See, e.g., Chapter 3, notes 34–36, *infra*, and accompanying text; Tomlinson, *supra*, Chapter 1, note 55, at 604–605.

[84] See *Oklahoma* v. *U.S. Civil Serv. Comm'n*, 330 U.S. 127 (1947).

[85] *Id.* at 144.

[86] See, e.g., *Shapiro* v. *Thompson*, 394 U.S. 618, 641 (1969) ("Congress may not authorize the States to violate the Equal Protection Clause").

that they focus on structures and processes rather than the results which grant systems are aimed at producing. The focus is on "inputs" rather than "outputs." [87] The difficulties of measuring the success of benefit programs and in monitoring compliance with result-oriented standards explain the indirect approach.[88] We should note that Due Process rights for grantees are even more imperative on questions involving compliance with output standards since the "success" of particular programs will invariably involve imprecise measuring devices and the application of a plethora of specific program "facts" to the output standards. Similarly, Congress may utilize "incentive" payments to achieve compliance with federal goals.[89] Such incentives, geared to program results, are also meat for the adjudicative grinder.

Every grantee will face a set of housekeeping rules—provisions of an administrative nature aimed at insuring that grant funds are guarded, spent, and accounted for in a businesslike manner. Federal standards are established for: financial management systems;[90] regular reports of financial transactions and status;[91] monitoring and reporting of program performance;[92]

---

[87] See Tomlinson, *supra*, Chapter 1, note 55, at 607.

[88] *Ibid*. We should point out an increasing tendency on the part of Congress to try to measure program results and to reward or penalize accordingly. For example, in the recently rewritten program for educationally deprived children, state agencies are required to develop standards for measuring the effectiveness of local education projects and are authorized to deny grant applications on the basis of proved ineffectiveness. See §§164, 167 Elementary and Secondary Education Act of 1965, 20 U.S.C. §§2811, 2814, as rewritten by §101 Education Amendments of 1978, Pub. L. 95-561, Nov. 1, 1978. The House Education and Labor Committee stated:

"With respect to quality programming, the Committee wishes to clarify its intent in requiring that State educational agencies review and take into consideration pertinent evaluations prior to approval of an application. The Committee intends that State educational agencies determine whether the project described in the application reflects the results of evaluations of that project, i.e., State educational agencies should not routinely approve applications for project designs which previous evaluations have demonstrated are of little value in raising the achievement level of participants."

H.R. Rep. No. 95-1137, 95th Cong., 2d Sess. 45 (1978). See also §104 Comprehensive Employment and Training Act of 1973, 29 U.S.C. §814 (approval of prime sponsor plans based, in part, on "past performance" and having a plan adequately designed "to carry out an effective and well-administered program").

[89] See, e.g., §402 Social Security Amendments of 1977, Pub. L. 95-216, Dec. 20, 1977 (incentive payments to states for achieving low error rates in AFDC determinations).

[90] See, e.g., OMB Cir. A-102, *supra*, Chapter 1, note 83, at Attachment G; OMB Cir. A-110, *supra*, Chapter 1, note 83, at Attachment F.

[91] See, e.g., OMB Cir. A-102, *supra*, Chapter 1, note 83, at Attachment H; OMB Cir. A-110, *supra*, Chapter 1, note 83, at Attachment G.

[92] See, e.g., OMB Cir. A-102, *supra*, Chapter 1, note 83, at Attachment I; OMB Cir. A-110, *supra*, Chapter 1, note 83, at Attachment H; 42 Fed. Reg. 43842 (1977) (Community Services Administration).

48 / *Rights and Remedies Under Federal Grants*

retention of project records and access for federal examiners; [93] bonding and insurance required of companies contracting with the grantee; [94] ownership and disposition of income produced by the grant; [95] acquisition, identification, preservation, and disposition of real and personal property acquired with grant funds; [96] competitive procurement of property and services; [97] and allowable expenditures under the grant.[98] Procedures are also established to cover grantee requests to modify the approved budget.[99]

A second set of grant requirements will emanate from the particular grant statute establishing the program under which funds are awarded. We shall refer to these hereafter as "programmatic" conditions. Although such conditions will differ from program to program, several appear with great frequency. The "matching" requirement, we have seen, is common to both formula and competitive grants.[100] While this requisite of providing a certain share of total program costs will be statutorily established, legislative provisions do not attempt to determine what types of grantee contributions may properly count toward the local match, or how such contributions are to be proved. Administrative regulations of general applicability fill this hiatus.[101] In a number of programs Congress may not only require a local contribution but also forbid the grantee from lowering the fiscal support it provided for the activity before receiving federal funds.[102] This stipulation is commonly called "nonsupplantation" or "maintenance-of-effort." Unlike the matching conditions under which the grantee loses

---

[93] See, e.g., OMB Cir. A-102, *supra,* Chapter 1, note 83, at Attachment C; OMB Cir. A-110, *supra,* Chapter 1, note 83, at Attachment C.
[94] See, e.g., OMB Cir. A-102, *supra,* Chapter 1, note 83, at Attachment B; OMB Cir. A-110, *supra,* Chapter 1, note 83, at Attachment B.
[95] See, e.g., OMB Cir. A-102, *supra,* Chapter 1, note 83, at Attachment E; OMB Cir. A-110, *supra,* Chapter 1, note 83, at Attachment D.
[96] See, e.g., OMB Cir. A-102, *supra,* Chapter 1, note 83, at Attachment N; OMB Cir. A-110, *supra,* Chapter 1, note 83, at Attachment N.
[97] See, e.g., OMB Cir. A-102, *supra,* Chapter 1, note 83, at Attachment O; OMB Cir. A-110, *supra,* Chapter 1, note 83, at Attachment O.
[98] See, e.g., OMB Cir. No. A-87, 39 Fed. Reg. 27133 (1974) (cost principles applicable to grants and contracts with state and local governments); 42 Fed. Reg. 21391 (1977) (proposed OMB circular; cost principles for grants and contracts with nonprofits).
[99] See, e.g., OMB Cir. A-102, *supra,* Chapter 1, note 83, at Attachment K; OMB Cir. A-110, *supra,* Chapter 1, note 83, at Attachment J.
[100] See notes 61–65, 71, *supra,* and accompanying text.
[101] See, e.g., OMB Cir. A-102, *supra,* Chapter 1, note 83, at Attachment F; OMB Cir. A-110, *supra,* Chapter 1, note 83, at Attachment E.
[102] See, e.g., §2003(b) Social Security Act, 42 U.S.C. §1397b(b) (grants to states for social services). This requirement is in addition to a required state "match" of 10% for family planning expenditures and 25% for other social services. See §2002(a)(1), *id.,* 42 U.S.C. §1397a(a)(1).

The Theory and Structure of Grants / 49

only the federal funds it fails to match, the maintenance-of-effort requirement will ordinarily have to be satisfied to receive any part of the particular grant.[103] An alternative technique aimed at prodding grantee contributions to the total program effort is to require neither a "match" nor a maintenance-of-effort, but instead include the grantee's local contribution effort as a factor in the formula which determines the size of the grant allotment.[104] Another common programmatic condition is that of citizen participation.[105] The goal is to involve those individuals who will be directly affected by the grant activity in its planning and execution. The forms of citizen participation will vary from program to program, but four models are found with frequency: the public hearing; [106]

---

[103] See, e.g., §2003(c)(1) Social Security Act, 42 U.S.C. §1397b(c)(1); *Shepheard* v. *Godwin*, 280 F. Supp. 869 (E.D. Va. 1968).

[104] See, e.g., §111(a)(2) Elementary and Secondary Education Act of 1965, 20 U.S.C. §2711(a)(2), as rewritten by §101 Education Amendments of 1978, Pub. L. 95-561, Nov. 1, 1978 (payments to local education agencies for education of disadvantaged children).

[105] The issue of grantee compliance with federal requirements for beneficiary and citizen involvement in program planning and execution has generated a considerable amount of litigation. See, e.g., *Texas Acorn* v. *Texas Area 5 Health Systems Agency, Inc.*, 559 F.2d 1019 (5th Cir. 1977); *Martinez* v. *Mathews*, 544 F.2d 1233 (5th Cir. 1976); *School Comm.* v. *Anrig*, 520 F.2d 577 (1st Cir. 1975); *Lopez* v. *Luginbill*, 483 F.2d 486 (10th Cir. 1973), *cert. denied*, 415 U.S. 927 (1974); *Chacon* v. *Hodgson*, 465 F.2d 307 (7th Cir. 1972); *Davis* v. *Shultz*, 453 F.2d 497 (3d Cir. 1971); *Arizona State Dep't of Pub. Welfare* v. *Dep't of Health, Educ. & Welfare*, 449 F.2d 456 (9th Cir. 1971), *cert. denied*, 405 U.S. 919 (1972); *North City Area-Wide Council, Inc.* v. *Romney*, 428 F.2d 754 (3d Cir. 1970), *cert. denied*, 406 U.S. 963 (1972); *Community Progress, Inc.* v. *Martinez*, 420 F. Supp. 204 (D. Conn. 1976); *NAACP, Santa Rosa-Sonoma City Branch* v. *Hills*, 412 F. Supp. 102 (N.D. Cal. 1976); *Ulster County Community Action Comm., Inc.* v. *Koenig*, 402 F. Supp. 986 (S.D. N.Y. 1975); *Comprehensive Group Health Servs. Bd. of Directors* v. *Temple Univ.*, 363 F. Supp. 1069 (E.D. Pa. 1973); *New York City Coalition for Community Health* v. *Lindsay*, 362 F. Supp. 434 (S.D. N.Y. 1973); *Lower East Side Neighborhood Health Council-South, Inc.* v. *Richardson*, 346 F. Supp. 386 (S.D. N.Y. 1972); *Feliciano* v. *Romney*, 336 F. Supp. 1340 (S.D. N.Y. 1971); *Lower Kensington Civic Ass'n* v. *Watson*, 330 F. Supp. 1257 (E.D. Pa. 1971); *North Phila. Community Bd.* v. *Temple Univ.*, 330 F. Supp. 1107 (E.D. Pa. 1971); *North City Area-Wide Council, Inc.* v. *Romney*, 329 F. Supp. 1124 (E.D. Pa. 1971) (on remand), *cert. denied*, 406 U.S. 963 (1972); *Coalition for United Community Action* v. *Romney*, 316 F. Supp. 742 (N.D. Ill. 1970); *Owens* v. *School Comm.*, 204 F. Supp. 1327 (D. Mass. 1969); *Benson* v. *City of Minneapolis*, 286 F. Supp. 614 (D. Minn. 1968). See generally A.A. Altshuler, *Community Control: The Black Demand for Participation in Large American Cities* (1970); *Citizen Participation: Effecting Community Change* (E.S. Cahn & B.A. Passett, eds. 1971); H.W. Hallman, *Neighborhood Control of Public Programs: Case Studies of Community Corporations and Neighborhood Boards* (1970); R.M. Kramer, *Participation of the Poor: Comparative Community Case Studies in the War on Poverty* (1969); D.P. Moynihan, *Maximum Feasible Misunderstanding: Community Action in the War on Poverty* (1969); Burke, "The Threat to Citizen Participation in Model Cities," 56 Cornell L. Rev. 751 (1971); Kirp, "Community Control, Public Policy, and the Limits of Law," 68 Mich. L. Rev. 1355 (1970); Rein & Miller, "Citizen Participation and Poverty," 1 Conn. L. Rev. 221 (1968); Note, "Participation of the Poor: Section 202(a)(3) Organizations Under the Economic Opportunity Act of 1964," 75 Yale L. J. 599 (1966).

[106] See, e.g., 23 U.S.C. §128 (federal aid for highway construction).

the advisory committee; [107] citizen involvement on grantee policy-making boards; [108] and employment in the grant program of individuals from the populations being served.[109] A fourth programmatic requirement which frequently appears controls the type of organizational structure which must be established as a prerequisite to the receipt of funds. Congress will at times mandate the creation of specially organized bodies [110] or force modifications in existing agencies and organizations [111] as a condition on the receipt of funds. The "single state agency" requirement,[112] under which only one agency is permitted to administer a grant, is a common example of the theme of mandated organizational structures. Another standard condition is that grantees perform regular self-evaluations.[113] Increasingly the task of analyzing program performance is being transferred to grantees with the Federal Government reviewing such assessments, rather than placing primary evaluation obligations on the grantor agency.[114]

In grant programs which finance the provision of funds and services to individuals, Congress will concern itself, often in meticulous detail, with the targeting of its funds, the services which may and must be provided, the processing of individual cases, and the possible discriminations and partialities of state and local governments. Thus, service programs typically include federal standards for determining eligibility for benefits, both individual [115] and geographic.[116] Mandated procedures for the process-

---

[107] See, e.g., §306(a)(6)(G) Older Americans Act of 1965, 42 U.S.C. §3026(a)(6)(G).
[108] See, e.g., §211 Community Services Act of 1974, 42 U.S.C. §2791.
[109] See, e.g., §307(a)(11) Older Americans Act of 1965, 42 U.S.C. §3027(a)(11); §606 Education of the Handicapped Act, 20 U.S.C. §1405.
[110] See, e.g., statutes cited note 74, *supra*.
[111] See, e.g., §1202 Higher Education Act of 1965, 20 U.S.C. §1142a (state postsecondary education commissions).
[112] See, e.g., §402(a)(3) Social Security Act, 42 U.S.C. §602(a)(3). §204 Intergovernmental Cooperation Act of 1968, 42 U.S.C. §4214, authorizes the head of the grantor agency to waive such requirement upon a showing that an alternative structure will be more efficient and effective.
[113] See, e.g., §613(a)(11) Education of the Handicapped Act, 20 U.S.C. §1413(a)(11).
[114] See, e.g., 40 C.F.R. §35.744, 42 Fed. Reg. 56056 (1977) (self-evaluation of solid waste programs); 45 C.F.R. §§1050.80-1–1050.80-3 (Community Service Administration; procedures for local evaluations).
[115] See, e.g., §§602(1), 612(2)(B), 612(2)(C) Education of the Handicapped Act, 20 U.S.C. §§1401(1), 1412(2)(B), 1412(2)(C). See also *Maryland* v. *Mathews*, 415 F. Supp. 1206, 1209–11 (D. D.C. 1976) (detailed description of multiple factors involved in welfare eligibility determinations).
[116] For the major federal grant programs it is typically provided that program benefits be available throughout the grantee's jurisdiction. See, e.g., §402(a)(1) Social Security Act, 42 U.S.C. §602(a)(1) (Aid to Families With Dependent Children "shall be in effect in all political subdivisions of the State").

The Theory and Structure of Grants / 51

ing of individual applications for benefits are common,[117] as well as procedures for handling the grievances of disappointed applicants or terminated recipients.[118] Prohibitions on the dispensation of aid in a political or discriminatory manner will usually be found in the grant statute.[119] Requirements are also legislated to control the types of services which may be supported with federal aid,[120] and often to mandate the provision of services considered essential to program success.[121]

Another stratum of grant conditions derives from national policies which cover all activities of the Federal Government, including its grant-giving function ("cross-cutting" conditions). A prime example of national policy requirements is civil rights provisions which protect all persons in the United States from discrimination on the grounds of race, color, or national origin in any program supported by federal aid,[122] including construction contracts made by recipients of federal funds.[123] Similar protection is afforded the handicapped,[124] females,[125] drug and alcohol addicts,[126] and the aged.[127] Additional national policies covering grant programs include: special procurement treatment for minor-

---

[117] See, e.g., §§402(a)(4), 402(a)(10) Social Security Act, 42 U.S.C. §§602(a)(4), 602(a)(10).

[118] See, e.g., §402(a)(4) Social Security Act, 42 U.S.C. §602(a)(4) ("fair hearing" for denial or delay in welfare application approval); §615 Education of the Handicapped Act, 20 U.S.C. §1415 ("impartial due process hearing" for grievances concerning handicapped educational services). In the wake of *Goldberg* v. *Kelly*, 397 U.S. 254 (1970), there has been a spate of grant agency regulations affording program beneficiaries Due Process rights even when the grant statute does not impose such requirement. See, e.g., 7 C.F.R. §246.24, 42 Fed. Reg. 43223–24 (1977) (special supplemental food program).

[119] See, e.g., §131 Comprehensive Employment and Training Act of 1973, 29 U.S.C. §833 (prohibits political activities); §132, *id.*, 29 U.S.C. §834 (nondiscrimination).

[120] See, e.g., §103 Rehabilitation Act of 1973, 29 U.S.C. §723.

[121] See, e.g., §402(a) Social Security Act, 42 U.S.C. §602(a) (*passim*).

[122] See, e.g., Title VI, Civil Rights Act of 1964, 42 U.S.C. §§2000d–2000d-4.

[123] See, e.g., Exec. Order No. 11246, 30 Fed. Reg. 12319 (1965).

[124] §504 Rehabilitation Act of 1973, 29 U.S.C. §794.

[125] A general prohibition against discrimination on the basis of sex, applicable to all federally assisted programs, has not yet been enacted; rather, this federal standard has been implemented on a piecemeal basis. See, e.g., Title IX, Education Amendments of 1972, 20 U.S.C. §§1681–1686 (covers all federally assisted education programs); §704 Public Health Service Act, 42 U.S.C. §292d (covers federally assisted health education); §855 Public Health Service Act, 42 U.S.C. §298b-2 (covers nurse training grants); §110 Local Public Works Capital Development and Investment Act of 1976, 42 U.S.C. §6709 (covers grants for projects authorized by Act).

[126] See §407 Drug Abuse Office and Treatment Act of 1972, 21 U.S.C. §1174 (prohibits discrimination against drug abusers in admission and treatment by federally supported hospitals); §321 Comprehensive Alcohol Abuse and Alcoholism Prevention, Treatment and Rehabilitation Act of 1970, 42 U.S.C. §4581 (same; alcohol abusers and alcoholics).

[127] See Age Discrimination Act of 1975, 42 U.S.C. §§6101–6107.

52 / *Rights and Remedies Under Federal Grants*

ity businesses; [128] the promotion of personnel systems based on merit; [129] environmental protection; [130] equitable treatment of persons or businesses displaced by federal grant activities; [131] uniform procedures for the acquisition of real property with federal funds; [132] protection of the confidentiality of personal information about individuals collected in performance of a federal grant; [133] payment of competitive wages; [134] nondisplacement of workers; [135] and protection of private businesses from federally financed competitors.[136]

---

[128] See, e.g., §106(f)(2) Local Public Works Capital Development and Investment Act of 1976, 42 U.S.C. §6705(f)(2), as added by §103 Pub. L. 95-28, May 13, 1977.
[129] See 5 C.F.R. pt. 900, subpt. F, "Standards for a Merit System of Personnel Administration," 44 Fed. Reg. 10238 (1979).
[130] See National Environmental Policy Act of 1969, 42 U.S.C. §§4321–4347.
[131] See Uniform Relocation Assistance and Real Property Acquisitions Policies Act of 1970, 42 U.S.C. §§4601–4655.
[132] *Ibid.*
[133] See, e.g., §1106 Social Security Act, 42 U.S.C. §1306 (confidentiality of information collected by federal agencies in administration of Social Security Act).
[134] See, e.g., §125 Comprehensive Employment and Training Act of 1973, 29 U.S.C. §827.
[135] See, e.g., §122(c)(1), *id.*, 29 U.S.C. §824(c)(1).
[136] See, e.g., §723(a)(4) Community Services Act of 1974, 42 U.S.C. §2983b(a)(4) §702 Public Works and Economic Development Act of 1965, 42 U.S.C. §3212.

3

Agency Enforcement of Grant Conditions

Legal Bases

On a superficial level the grant-in-aid project appears similar to a normal contractual undertaking.[1] Mutual and dependent sets of valuable promises run between the grantor and the grantee. Like a contract for the sale of goods or services, the grantor commits itself to pay in certain amounts and at certain times for a package of acts and products to be delivered by the grantee.

The analogy, however, is false. While there are areas of overlap, federal grant law differs fundamentally from that of federal procurement.[2] We shall postpone until Chapter 6 a full discussion of the distinctions. Here we will begin with some of the primary considerations.

Contract law in America evolves from the fundamental premise that the commitments on each side, whether written or oral, are known from a study of their contents. Should irreconcilable unhappiness about the other side's performance occur, the

---

[1] For a typical grant-in-aid agreement, see 43 Fed. Reg. 5491-94 (1978) (Farmers Home Administration; rural development planning grant agreement).

[2] See Mason, "Current Trends in Federal Grant Law—Fiscal Year 1976," 35 Fed. B. J. 163, 164–68 (1976). A parallel set of hearing rights is provided for the ventilation of federal procurement grievances. See generally Contract Disputes Act of 1978, Pub. L. 95-563, Nov. 1, 1978, 41 U.S.C. §§601–613; 44 Fed. Reg. 12519 (1979) (interim final rule; uniform rules of procedure for boards of contract appeals.)

parties march to court with documents and witnesses for judicial interpretation of what was mutually promised and whether those promises were fulfilled. While the parameters and contents of those promises may occasionally be controlled by legislative and judicial prescriptions, the parties to agreements are permitted to design and enjoy (or suffer) their own beds. Enforcement of contracts, then, is primarily a matter of divining the meaning of the words the parties chose to express their intentions, insuring that such commitments are consistent with public policy, finding the facts, and comparing the evidence to what was agreed.

In comparison, the grant agreement and award is but a small cloth of a larger bundle. First, the statute authorizing and defining the scope and terms of the particular grant-in-aid program under which the award was made must be consulted for a primary understanding of the rights and responsibilities of grantor and grantee. Most grant agreements executed by the United States contain standard phraseology obliging the grantee to abide by the Act under which the funds are authorized and awarded.[3] One typically cautious federal draftsman, for example, wrote the following term into a federal-state highway agreement:

> "The State, through its Highway Department, having complied, or hereby agreeing to comply, with the terms and conditions set forth in (1) Title 23, U.S. Code, Highways, (2) the Regulations issued pursuant thereto, and (3) the policies and procedures promulgated by the Federal Highway Administrator and the Director of Public Roads. . . ."[4]

But whether or not such a clause is inserted and whether or not the grantee has ever read it, the Act still controls.[5] As the constitutional document enabling, organizing, defining, and controlling the award of funds via grant instruments, it governs all expenditures made pursuant to its authorizations. The Supremacy Clause guarantees also that the grant-in-aid statute shall be preemptively authoritative.[6] While a violation of the Supremacy Clause does not automatically invalidate conflicting state law, regulations, and

---

[3] See, e.g., *Johnson v. Redevelopment Agency*, 317 F.2d 872, 874 (9th Cir. 1963); *Texas v. United States*, 537 F.2d 466, 470 (Ct. Cl. 1976); *Corum v. Beth Israel Medical Center*, 359 F. Supp. 909, 912, n. 3 (S.D. N.Y. 1973); *English v. Town of Huntington*, 335 F. Supp. 1369, 1371–72 (E.D. N.Y. 1970).

[4] See *Barnhart v. Brinegar*, 362 F. Supp. 464, 473 (W.D. Mo. 1973).

[5] See, e.g., *Maryland Nat'l Capital Park & Planning Comm'n v. Lynn*, 514 F.2d 829 (D.C. Cir. 1975).

[6] U.S. Const. art. VI, cl. 2. See, e.g., *Carleson v. Remillard*, 406 U.S. 598, 601 (1972); *Rosado v. Wyman*, 397 U.S. 397, 422–23 (1970).

practices, the grantee must choose whether to accept and honor the federal condition (if possible) or to maintain its local policy and forfeit federal assistance.[7] Since the agency entrusted with the administration of the law must abide by its terms, implementing rules, regulations, guidelines, and forms of agreement cannot conflict with the statute;[8] nor could a grantee rely upon conflicting agency policy to justify any act or activity violative of the statutory commands. Neither formally nor informally is the agency permitted to waive grant terms and conditions imposed by the authorizing legislation,[9] unless the grant statute itself permits the waiver of specified conditions.[10]

Unlike contract law, the initial understanding of the details of the mutual commitments of grantor and grantee must, then, be sought in the words and intent of Congress. What the individual parties to the grant agreement meant and understood by the terms of their commitments might be quickly overridden, though this statement must be tempered by the deference which courts give to federal agency regulations, interpretations, and practices.[11] Enforcement of grant-in-aid conditions is, therefore, in the first instance a matter of turning to the statute and its legislative history to determine the intentions of Congress, if any, as to the matter in dispute.

Parenthetically, the primacy of the authorizing statute creates conditions under which administering agencies can effectively "mousetrap" grantees. Either formally, by regulation or guideline, or informally, by tacit agreement, the grantor agency permits the grantee to engage in a questionable practice. Since the grantor has both enforcement discretion [12] and a duty to interpret the authoriz-

[7] See notes 132–148, *infra*, and accompanying text.
[8] See, e.g., *Townsend v. Swank*, 404 U.S. 282, 286 (1971); *Graham v. Richardson*, 403 U.S. 365, 380–81, n. 11 (1971); *King v. Smith*, 392 U.S. 309, 333, n. 34 (1968); *Maryland v. Mathews*, 415 F. Supp. 1206 (D. D.C. 1976).
[9] See, e.g., *National Ass'n of Neighborhood Health Centers, Inc. v. Mathews*, 551 F.2d 321 (D.C. Cir. 1976); *City of Hartford v. Hills*, 408 F. Supp. 889, 901, n. 48 (D. Conn. 1976), *rev'd sub nom., City of Hartford v. Towns of Glastonbury*, 561 F.2d 1032 (2d Cir. 1977), *cert. denied*, 434 U.S. 1034 (1978).
[10] See, e.g., §1115 Social Security Act, 42 U.S.C. §1315 (waiver of statutory conditions authorized for experimental, pilot, or demonstration projects); *Aguayo v. Richardson*, 473 F.2d 1090 (2d Cir. 1973), *cert. denied*, 414 U.S. 1146 (1974); *California Welfare Rights Organ. v. Richardson*, 348 F. Supp. 491 (N.D. Cal. 1972). Compare *Coalition for United Community Action v. Romney*, 316 F. Supp. 742 (N.D. Ill. 1970) (temporary waiver of statutory relocation requirements within Secretary's discretion).
[11] See notes 17–18, *infra*, and accompanying text.
[12] See notes 118–120, *infra*, and accompanying text.

ing statute, it could justify its action on either count. The administrator might be bowing to political pressure, might be uncertain as to the legality of the practice, or might simply be ignoring it because of the press of other affairs. Yet the obligatory duty of the agency to enforce the statute empowers it to turn against the grantee on the particular practice at any time. *County of Alameda* v. *Weinberger*[13] provides a clear example. Following a General Accounting Office audit, the Department of Health, Education and Welfare reversed its two-year-old policy of reimbursing California at a 75 percent rate for certain welfare services. It applied a 50 percent rate and unilaterally recouped $11 million by deducting that amount from current quarterly grants. The Ninth Circuit affirmed the issuance of a preliminary injunction against HEW, finding that the county was likely to prevail on the merits. The court suggested, without deciding, that to the extent that HEW's approval of California's plan conflicted with its own guidelines, "it is entirely possible" for the approval to take precedence over the department's guidelines.[14] One cannot always count on sympathetic courts. The supremacy of the grant statute creates tremendous grantor leverage over grantees, as well as the potentiality for abuse of the enforcement power. It is doubtful whether judicial "estoppel" doctrines could be utilized to check such reversals of policy by granting agencies. A leading work in the procurement field expresses the principle in the following terms:

> "The basic rule is that an individual can only commit the Government to acts and relationships in accordance with the express powers granted to him by the agency. An individual who is not expressly authorized to enter into contracts cannot make a contract which is enforceable against the Government. An individual who is authorized to enter into contracts binding the Government cannot commit the Government to clauses which vary from those established by the regulations unless the regulations specifically permit such deviations. In a similar manner, one who is otherwise authorized to act for the Government cannot bind the Government by acting in a manner other than as predetermined by the regulations."[15]

Estoppel would effectively condone the continuance of statutory violations, something the courts would be reluctant to permit no

[13] 520 F.2d 344 (9th Cir. 1975).
[14] *Id.* at 351.
[15] R. Scurlock, *Government Contracts and Grants for Research: A Guide for Colleges and Universities* 15 (Nat'l Ass'n of College & Univ. Business Officers 1975).

matter how justifiable the grantee's reliance or how painful the new directives.[16]

The provisions of federal grant-in-aid statutes, like other laws, run the gamut from incredibly broad and vague to meticulously detailed and specific. As in other areas, Congress relies on the executive branch for the implementation of grant-in-aid programs, including the interpretation and instrumentation of the statutory scheme by way of agency regulations. When Congress delegates broad rule-making authority to an executive agency, as is typical in federal grant statutes,[17] regulations properly promulgated under such authority will be judicially upheld if "reasonably related" to the purposes of the legislation.[18] While Congress can control

---

[16] See, e.g., *United States* v. *Brady,* 385 F. Supp. 1347, 1351 (S.D. Fla. 1974) ("when the government seeks to enforce a public right or protect a public interest it is acting in its sovereign capacity and cannot be disabled by past actions of its officers or agents").

[17] See, e.g., §602 Community Services Act of 1974, 42 U.S.C. §2942:

"In addition to the authority conferred upon the Director [of the Community Services Administration] by other sections of this Act, the Director is authorized, in carrying out the functions of the Director under this Act, to . . . (n) establish such policies, standards, criteria and procedures, prescribe such rules and regulations . . . as the Director may deem necessary or appropriate to carry out the provisions of this Act";

§1102 Social Security Act, 42 U.S.C. §1302:

"The Secretary of the Treasury, the Secretary of Labor, and the Secretary of Health, Education and Welfare, respectively, shall make and publish such rules and regulations, not inconsistent with [the Social Security Act], as may be necessary to the efficient administration of the functions with which each is charged under this Act."

§431 General Education Provisions Act, 20 U.S.C. §1232, is a unique provision which controls, in considerable detail, the issuance of regulations by divisions of HEW which administer education grants. "Regulation" is broadly defined as "any rules, regulations, guidelines, interpretations, orders, or requirements of general applicability." Each substantive provision of a regulation must be followed by a citation to the legal authority on which it is based. Every regulation has to be proposed in the *Federal Register,* the public must be given 30 days to submit comments, and the Commissioner of Education is obliged to reconsider the regulation in light of such submissions. The 30-day requirement can be waived, however, if the Commissioner, the House Committee on Education and Labor, and the Senate Committee on Labor and Public Welfare all agree that the delay will cause "extreme hardship" for the program beneficiaries. Once the regulation is published in final form it cannot become effective for an additional 45 days, during which time Congress may rescind the regulation by adopting a concurrent resolution which finds the regulation inconsistent with the law it implements. §431 also mandates that the Commissioner of Education promulgate final regulations within 240 days of the enactment of new or amended educational programs.

Whether Congress can control the executive branch in this fashion has provoked a spate of commentary. For a few of the better pieces, see Bruff & Gellhorn, "Congressional Control of Administrative Regulation: A Study of Legislative Vetoes," 90 Harv. L. Rev. 1369 (1977); Watson, "Congress Steps Out: A Look at Congressional Control of the Executive," 63 Calif. L. Rev. 983 (1975); Comment, "Congressional Oversight of Administrative Discretion: Defining the Proper Role of the Legislative Veto," 26 Am. U. L. Rev. 1018 (1977).

[18] *Mourning* v. *Family Publications Serv., Inc.,* 411 U.S. 356, 359 (1973).

58 / *Rights and Remedies Under Federal Grants*

agency interpretative discretion by the degree of explicitness in its statutory language,[19] the norms found in grant statutes tend to be tremendously imprecise. This, in turn, places great authority in the administrator. Another way Congress may control agency discretion is through statements of intent and interpretation in committee reports. But for most of the standard clauses found in grant-in-aid legislation, including grantee hearing rights, the legislative history is typically barren. While domestic assistance programs generate reams of background materials, most of the discussion focuses on the need for the legislation, the substance of the legislation in terms of dollars and programs, special problems which may have arisen in past implementation, and the principal programmatic conditions. For "boilerplate" clauses the only mention is usually found in the "section-by-section analysis" in congressional committee reports, where the statutory language is repeated verbatim without further analysis.

All grant-in-aid statutes designate a specific department or agency of the executive branch to implement the program, and sometimes will even require the creation of a new office within a federal department to carry out the grant activity.[20] They also typically authorize, in general terms as just mentioned, the head of the agency to prescribe such regulations as may be necessary to carry out the assigned functions. In the great majority of cases the administering agencies have promulgated such regulations.[21] Thus, one is likely to find for each grant-in-aid program a separate set of program regulations implementing the authorizing statute.

It is standard doctrine in the federal courts that agency regulations which are authorized by statute and consistent with the legislation have the force of law.[22] Until properly amended, such regulations bind not only the grantee but also the grantor. As one court authoritatively stated:

---

[19] Recall the expression of this thought, beautiful despite the mixing of metaphors, by Mr. Justice Harlan in *Rosado* v. *Wyman*, 397 U.S. 397, 412 (1970):
"The background of §402(a)(23) reveals little except that we have before us a child born of the silent union of legislative compromise. Thus, Congress, as it frequently does, has voiced its wishes in muted strains and left it to the courts to discern the theme in the cacaphony of political understanding. Our chief resources in this undertaking are the words of the statute and those common sense assumptions that must be made in determining direction without a compass."

[20] See, e.g., §731 Elementary and Secondary Education Act of 1965, 20 U.S.C. §3241, as rewritten by §101 Education Amendments of 1978, Pub. L. 95-561, Nov. 1, 1978 (Office of Bilingual Education).

[21] See Chapter 1, *supra*, at pp. 19–20.

[22] See, e.g., *Batterton* v. *Francis*, 432 U.S. 416, 425, n. 9 (1977).

"There are intimations that Department of Agriculture officials have not read their agency regulations to mean what they appear plainly to say. . . . But these officials are not less bound than the rest of us to obey their own formal and authoritative rules."[23]

Therefore, a second stratum of rights and responsibilities is created by the promulgation of program regulations. These rules ordinarily contain both additional terms and conditions of the grant award and greater detail as to the meaning and methods of compliance with statutory conditions.

The requirement of complying with all applicable agency regulations is sometimes extended to the grantee by way of appropriate language in the grant award instrument,[24] and always, of course, in the introductory clauses of the regulations themselves. As in the case of the authorizing statute, the regulations would cover grantee activity regardless of formal extension of their authority in the grant agreement.

In addition to the grant-in-aid statute and its implementing regulations, a network of federal statutes aims at implementing important national policies throughout all financial assistance programs or certain categories of programs.[25] Examples of such crosscutting conditions include nondiscrimination requirements, mandated procedures for intergovernmental cooperation, processes to protect the environment, standards for relocating persons displaced by federally assisted activities, land acquisition policies, labor standards, and protection from the disclosure of confidential information. These, too, form part of the primary stratum of grantee commitments, as well as the packages of agency regulations which implement such national standards.

A third element of the legal foundation for enforcing grant-in-aid conditions is the set of assurances provided by the grantee.

---

[23] *Justice v. Board of Educ.*, 351 F. Supp. 1252, 1260, n. 20 (S.D. N.Y. 1972) (citations omitted). See also, e.g., *North City Area-Wide Council, Inc. v. Romney*, 428 F.2d 754 (3rd Cir. 1970), cert. denied, 406 U.S. 963 (1972) (HUD's actions violated its own citizen participation guidelines); *Crane v. Mathews*, 417 F. Supp. 532 (N.D. Ga. 1976) (HEW acted illegally by failing to apply its regulation on the protection of human subjects); *Grumman Ecosystems Corp. v. Gainsville-Alachua County Regional Elec., Water & Sewer Facilities Bd.*, 402 F. Supp. 582 (N.D. Fla. 1975) (EPA violated its procurement regulations); *Torres v. Butz*, 397 F. Supp. 1015 (N.D. Ill. 1975) (FNS violated its school lunch regulations).

Despite the rule, the Cahns report that agency violation of regulations is endemic. See Cahn & Cahn, "The New Sovereign Immunity," 81 Harv. L. Rev. 929, 949 (1968).

[24] See, e.g., 45 C.F.R. §121a.236, 42 Fed. Reg. 42487 (1977); note 4, *supra*, and accompanying text.

[25] See Chapter 2, notes 122–136, *supra*, and accompanying text.

60 / *Rights and Remedies Under Federal Grants*

If the program is one distributing funds by formula, a "State plan" will usually be required.[26] The word "plan" is normally a misnomer. For most programs the document is nothing more than a form preprinted in Washington which reiterates the grant conditions.[27] The state agency preparing the plan simply checks "yes" to each of the conditions and fills in any blanks. The process of signifying consent to federal terms for project grant applications is similar. In the application package, the prospective grantee finds several pages of boilerplate language parroting statutes and regulations.[28] By applying for funds the grantee consents to each of the terms. No negotiation of administrative, crosscutting, or programmatic standards occurs. The only exceptions are when Congress has explicitly authorized the administering agency to waive certain conditions,[29] or when the condition is imposed by regulation and the agency has decided to entertain waiver requests.[30] To insure flexibility in the application to specific cases of its own program rules, a grantor agency may provide generally that nonstatutory program standards can be waived. Regulations covering the Community Development Block Grant Program, if not required by statute, can be waived by the Secretary of HUD in cases of "undue hardship." [31] Some agencies have, however, opted to deny themselves such a waiver power.[32] This latter policy is aimed at promoting the fair and uniform application of rules to all applicants and grantees,[33] but the disadvantage is that it forces the agency to approve and promulgate any specific waiver with the same formality as its program regulations.

The federal grantor agency does possess some ability to tailor special provisions in the grant agreement in order to deal with particular problems.[34] The implementation power of the agency

[26] See Chapter 2, notes 55–56, *supra,* and accompanying text.
[27] See, e.g., 45 C.F.R. §§121a.110–.151, 42 Fed. Reg. 42480–84 (1977) (state plan for education of handicapped). The process is known as a "proclaimer system" under which the states "merely check off the existence of various provisions in their state plans on a standardized form." Tomlinson, *supra,* Chapter 1, note 55, at 623.
[28] See, e.g., OMB Cir. A-102, *supra,* Chapter 1, note 83, at Attachment M, part V (assurances).
[29] See notes 9–10, *supra,* and accompanying text.
[30] See, e.g., 45 C.F.R. §§1068.25-1–.25-2, 42 Fed. Reg. 53600 (1977) (Community Services Administration; waivers of local share requirement imposed by regulation).
[31] 24 C.F.R. §570.4, 43 Fed. Reg. 4382 (1978).
[32] E.g., 45 C.F.R. §100a.483 (1976) (Office of Education).
[33] See 43 Fed. Reg. 1768 (1978).
[34] See, e.g., *AFSCME, Greater Cleveland Dist. Council 78 v. City of Cleveland,* 484 F.2d 339 (6th Cir. 1973) (special hiring restrictions placed on only two of 900 emergency employment grants); *New York City Coalition for Community Health v. Lindsay,* 362 F. Supp. 434, 439, n. 2 (S.D. N.Y. 1973) (additional conditions imposed on New York City health planning grant).

Agency Enforcement of Grant Conditions / 61

is not limited to promulgating uniform regulations. It includes the authority to structure conditions applicable only to an individual grantee if the circumstances so warrant and if the special requirement is consistent with the authorizing statute. Public Health Service regulations, for example, frequently contain language like the following:

> "The Secretary may, with respect to any grant award, impose additional conditions prior to or at the time of any award when in his judgment such conditions are necessary to assure or protect advancement of the approved activity, the interest of the public health, or the conservation of grant funds." [35]

If the grantor has doubts about the financial stability or viability of an applicant, special payment, matching, or reporting conditions may be imposed.[36] The grantor may, similarly, be concerned about the management capability of an applicant. It may wish to require, as a condition of the grant, that the entity undertake specified organizational, personnel, and administrative reforms. If the applicant has been found to have violated one or more grant conditions in past project periods, the grantor agency may wish to draft special compliance requirements to avoid repetition of the conduct. Given the volume of grants that federal agencies must administer, however, special negotiation of grant terms and conditions is unusual. In most cases each grantee under the same federal program will face an identical set of responsibilities.

At this point, we might profitably pause to consider the complexity of grant compliance from the recipient's perspective. It is now juggling various documents in an effort to understand what it has promised to do: the authorizing statute; the legislative history of that act; other applicable federal statutes and their histories and regulations; program rules; agencywide regulations implementing standard grant-in-aid conditions; and the grant agreement. If so much were not at stake, it would be humorous to note that the Grants Administration Manual of the Office of Human Development commences with a primer on the hierarchical authority of different types of rules:

> "The policies and procedures included herein are subject to applicable Federal law and regulations and any changes made thereto adopted subsequent to its publication. In the event these

[35] 42 C.F.R. §57.13.
[36] See, e.g., 45 C.F.R. §1302.3-1 (Head Start).

62 / *Rights and Remedies Under Federal Grants*

policies and procedures conflict with applicable Federal laws, regulations and policies, the following order of precedence shall prevail:

"1. Federal Legislation
"2. Federal Regulations
"3. Terms and Conditions of Grant Award
"4. OHD Grants Administration Manual
"5. HEW Grants Administration Manual" [37]

Admittedly, much of what the grantee surveys is boring repetition: The statutory provision is repeated in the congressional committee report, the program regulation, the department regulation, and the grant agreement. But since each of these documents is drafted by different individuals, frustrating variances in language frequently appear and lead to confusion as to meaning and intent.

Now the grantor agency comes to the rescue with interpretive and descriptive matter and forms. It publishes and distributes to grantees thick volumes labeled "manuals" or "guidelines" or "handbooks" or "directives." By means of such documents the agency tries to put in understandable English what is meant by the various commands in the relevant statutes and regulations. Necessary specificity is added, implementing procedures are established, statutory directives are reduced to printed forms, illustrative examples are set forth for guidance, and so forth.

The enforceability of the directives in such manuals is often open to debate.[38] Their terms may bestow discretion upon the grantee or be couched as mandates. They are obviously subject to the higher commands of the statute and regulations, but if consistent with such they may generate additional, enforceable grantee obligations.

Thorpe v. *Housing Authority* [39] holds that when directives are contained in documents other than regulations, whether they are mandatory depends primarily on the intention of the issuing agency. This is to be determined both by the language utilized in the publication and direct evidence on intent from the agency itself. Thus, *Thorpe* held that HUD circulars were obligatory because HUD manuals indicated that rule changes made by means

---

[37] 42 Fed. Reg. 21047, 21049 (1977).
[38] See *United States* v. *Jefferson County Bd. of Educ.*, 372 F.2d 836, 857–58 (5th Cir. 1966), *cert. denied*, 389 U.S. 840 (1967).
[39] 393 U.S. 268 (1969).

Agency Enforcement of Grant Conditions / 63

of circulars were binding, the language of the circular itself was phrased in nondiscretionary terms, and HUD indicated by letter to the Court that it considered the circular binding.[40] The same principles would apply to determine the force of other types of agency issuances.[41] The absence of public participation in the rule-making process, however, may cost these informal agency issuances the judicial deference which they would otherwise be accorded.[42] Also, while a "matter relating to . . . loans, grants, benefits, or contracts" is exempted from the rule-making requirements of the Administrative Procedure Act,[43] several grantor agencies have declined the exemption.[44] In this situation, rules contained in manuals, circulars, handbooks, and the like are not binding if they are not promulgated according to the APA.[45]

The mosaic of federal grant law, then, is a multileveled series of dictates to grantees. Each of these commands may generate independent grantee obligations or may add meaning and depth to a hierarchically superior provision. In a compliance context, the grantor can dip into any level to justify its position.

Monitoring Compliance

Unlike the ordinary contractual situation in which the buyer of goods or services is indifferent to the methods employed by the provider in achieving the end product, the federal grantor is statutorily obliged to entangle itself to some extent in the operational activities of its clients. For instance, in the daily operations of the grantee, federal standards must be met as to employment practices, nondiscrimination, property procurement, record systems and maintenance, citizen participation, and numerous programmatic conditions. Federal involvement in determining grantee compliance with mandated performance standards, however, does

[40] See also *Brown v. Housing Auth.*, 471 F.2d 63 (7th Cir. 1972) (HUD circular binding); *Housing Auth. v. U.S. Housing Auth.*, 468 F.2d 1 (8th Cir. 1972), cert. denied, 410 U.S. 927 (1973) (same). Compare *Bromley-Heath Modernization Comm. v. Boston Housing Auth.*, 459 F.2d 1067 (1st Cir. 1972) (HUD circular couched in terms of exhortation not binding).

[41] See, e.g., *Afton Alps, Inc. v. United States*, 392 F. Supp. 543 (D. Minn. 1974) (EDA directive); *West Coast Constr. Co. v. Oceano Sanitary Dist.*, 311 F. Supp. 378 (N.D. Cal. 1970) (Fm. H.A. instruction).

[42] See *American Ass'n of Councils of Medical Staffs of Private Hosps., Inc. v. Mathews*, 421 F. Supp. 848, 854–55, n. 11 (E.D. La. 1976).

[43] §4(a)(2), 5 U.S.C. §553(a)(2).

[44] See, e.g., *Center for Auto Safety v. Tiemann*, 414 F. Supp. 215, 222, n. 6 (D. D.C. 1976).

[45] *City of New York v. Diamond*, 379 F. Supp. 503, 515–18 (S.D. N.Y. 1974).

not amount to daily supervision of grantee operations; hence, federal monitoring and enforcement of grant conditions do not convert the grantee into a federal agency or instrumentality either to impose liability on the United States for the torts of grantee employees [46] or to find "Federal action" for constitutional purposes.[47] Similarly, the mere receipt of federal funds by a private entity is insufficient to find "state action" under the Fourteenth Amendment.[48]

After February 3, 1979, federal agencies must utilize cooperative agreements and not grants if the principal purpose of the relationship is support or stimulation of the recipient and "substantial involvement" of the federal agency is contemplated.[49] The Office of Management and Budget has provided guidance to the agencies on the meaning of that vague phrase.[50]

Constant surveillance, however, is not the general practice—and with good reason. A unique feature of the grantor-grantee relationship is that both parties share the common goal of achieving congressionally defined ends. The antagonisms likely to be provoked by continuous probing into grantee affairs would undermine the cooperative nature of the activity. Should an adversarial posture result, the likelihood of effective and efficient achievement of project goals would be severely diminished. In judging how much monitoring it will carry out, a federal administrator must also consider the costs. Every dollar spent by the grantor in investigating, and by the grantee in proving, compliance is a dollar diverted from achieving program purposes. While the argument is always available, of course, that each federal condition contains a legitimate and important "purpose," that word is used here in the sense of the broader and ultimate program

---

[46] *United States* v. *Orleans*, 425 U.S. 807 (1976).
[47] *Hines* v. *Cenla Community Action Comm., Inc.*, 474 F.2d 1052 (5th Cir. 1973).
[48] E.g., *Ascherman* v. *Presbyterian Hosp. of Pac. Medical Center, Inc.*, 507 F.2d 1103, 1105 (9th Cir. 1974); *Aasum* v. *Good Samaritan Hosp.*, 395 F. Supp. 363 (D. Ore. 1975), aff'd, 542 F.2d 792 (9th Cir. 1976); *Cannon* v. *University of Chicago*, 406 F. Supp. 1257 (N.D. Ill.), aff'd, 559 F.2d 1063 (7th Cir. 1976), rev'd on other grounds, 96 S. Ct. 1946 (1979). But see *Don* v. *Okmulgee Memorial Hosp.*, 443 F.2d 234, 235 (10th Cir. 1971) (receipt of federal funds may be "significant"); *Stanturf* v. *Sipes*, 335 F.2d 224, 226 (8th Cir. 1964), cert. denied, 379 U.S. 977 (1965) (assumed for purposes of decision that receipt of federal funds is state action).
[49] §§6, 10(b) Federal Grant and Cooperative Agreement Act of 1977, Pub. L. 95-224, Feb. 3, 1978, 41 U.S.C. §§505, 509(b).
[50] 43 Fed. Reg. 36863 (1978).

goals.⁵¹ Moreover, constant oversight is largely impossible. Given the huge volume of grants and contracts through which the Federal Government carries out its programs, it would not be too far from the mark to say that half the federal budget would have to be dedicated to supervising the expenditure of the other half. The reality is that federal agency budgets permit only modest oversight activities,⁵² and lack of agency oversight means that federal conditions, even important ones such as maintenance of effort and limits on fund uses, may be so widely ignored as to be nonoperational in practice.⁵³

Standard Practices

At the beginning of a project period the grantee has committed itself to comply with the various terms and conditions of the grant by applying for federal funds either through submission of a plan or a project application. One of those conditions is the maintenance of program records ⁵⁴ and another is the submission, ordinarily on a quarterly basis, of fiscal and program reports.⁵⁵ It is primarily through such record and reporting systems that the grantor keeps tabs on recipient activities. Reports are scanned by federal technicians for completeness and compliance and, on a random basis, audits and on-site inspections of grantees are conducted.⁵⁶

Several features of the standard practice assure its minimum effectiveness in determining compliance. The system relies, almost exclusively in most cases, on good faith reporting by grantees. In providing information on its own activities, a recipient which is conscious of noncompliance is ordinarily able to prepare reports which on their face do not reveal any deficiency. Also, the required reports themselves do not comprehensively cover program conditions. Fiscal reports can reveal noncompliance on matching

---

51 See *California Welfare Rights Organ.* v. *Richardson,* 348 F. Supp. 491 (N.D. Cal. 1972), which includes the issue whether mandated requirements are part of a grant program's objectives.
52 See Tomlinson, *supra,* Chapter 1, note 55, at 623–25.
53 See, e.g., Advisory Commission on Intergovernmental Relations, *The Intergovernmental Grant System: An Assessment and Proposed Policies: Summary and Concluding Observations* 41–42, 66–67 (1978).
54 See Chapter 2, notes 90–93, *supra,* and accompanying text.
55 See Chapter 2, notes 91–92, *supra,* and accompanying text.
56 See, e.g., 45 C.F.R. §§1050.80-1-.80-3, Attachment A, 42 Fed. Reg. 43842 (1977) (Community Services Administration; rules and forms for monitoring and reporting program performance).

requirements and budget items, but little else. Programmatic reports are often nothing more than sketchy, self-serving statements about the grantee's progress in achieving its goals and commitments. In fact, most of the grant terms are not subject to any reporting. Deficiencies could be spotted by on-site program reviews, but most grantees are never audited or inspected because of limited federal agency oversight budgets.

In the big money programs, systematic review and audit are more common.[57] Inspections by federal employees will probe the operational realities of the grantee to validate adherence to preselected, or sometimes all, program conditions. Federal audit teams will examine the grantee's fiscal records to verify reported expenditures, determine cost allowability, and substantiate the local match.

Special Monitoring

In several recent enactments, congressional concern over past or potential noncompliance by grantees has prompted the insertion in the grant-in-aid statute of special monitoring directives and procedures. In some, the administering agency is directed to review on an "annual" or "periodic" basis the activities of each grantee to determine compliance.[58] One statute specifically requires the agency to make its own inspections and not to rely exclusively on grantee reports.[59] The most explicit congressional mandate of this nature is in the revised Vocational Education Act.[60] It requires the Commissioner of Education to make specific written findings concerning the compliance of each state plan with the Act's provisions, and further directs the Commissioner to refuse plan approval until "he is satisfied that adequate procedures are set forth to insure that the assurances . . . will be carried out." [61]

In most grant programs the administering agency has complete discretion on the handling of "tips" from third parties which point to possible grantee illegality. A steady stream of complaints

[57] See, e.g., 45 C.F.R. §§201.10–.13 (1977) (public assistance). But see Tomlinson, *supra*, Chapter 1, note 55, at 619–29 (inadequate compliance monitoring of Aid to Families With Dependent Children).
[58] See, e.g., §314(d)(3) Public Health Service Act, 42 U.S.C. §246(d)(3); §1612(c) Public Health Service Act, 42 U.S.C. §300p-2(c).
[59] §18(f) Occupational Safety and Health Act of 1971, 29 U.S.C. §667(f).
[60] Vocational Education Act of 1963, 20 U.S.C. §§2301–2461, as amended by Pub. L. 94-482, Oct. 12, 1976.
[61] §109(a)(1) Vocational Education Act of 1973, 20 U.S.C. §2309(a)(1).

and allegations flows into federal offices from dissatisfied recipients or applicants for grantee services, groups which lost out in the grant competition, opposing politicians or political groups, coalitions and organizations advocating beneficiary rights, discharged employees, and disgruntled taxpayers. In many programs, it would be an impossible burden for the administrator to run down each and every accusation.

Prior to its amendment in 1978, the Comprehensive Employment and Training Act departed from this tradition by requiring investigations when the Department of Labor received a "formal" allegation of noncompliance from an "affected" unit of local government which received funds through a prime sponsor.[62] Because most federal formula programs involve a pass-through of funds to other governmental units or nonprofit organizations,[63] the unusual CETA provision cannot be rationalized by reference to the program structure; however, the requirement is understandable when one takes into account the conflicts engendered by a program in which federal funds may flow through a state or local government controlled by one political party to smaller units controlled by another. CETA also mandated an investigation of an allegation received from "any other interested person" if it was "supported by substantial evidence." [64] Because the Department of Labor determined both the credentials of the complainant and what was "substantial," the provision was, in effect, hortatory.[65]

In the 1978 rewriting of CETA,[66] even stricter monitoring has been demanded by Congress. While "[o]n the whole" the Senate Human Resources Committee found that CETA was being operated "with integrity," it noted "abuses." [67] The committee specified various illegalities:

> "There have been instances of political patronage in the filling of CETA jobs. There have been abuses with respect to nepotism and conflicts of interest. There have been instances where private employment agencies have charged unemployed workers for referring them to a CETA job. There have been instances in which records

[62] §108(b)(2) Comprehensive Employment and Training Act of 1973, 29 U.S.C. §818(b)(2) (1976).
[63] See Chapter 9, note 20, *infra,* and accompanying text.
[64] §108(b)(2) Comprehensive Employment and Training Act of 1973, 29 U.S.C. §818(b)(2) (1976).
[65] See 29 C.F.R. §98.46.
[66] Comprehensive Employment and Training Act Amendments of 1978, Pub. L. 95-524, Oct. 27, 1978.
[67] S. Rep. No. 95-891, 95th Cong., 2d Sess. 42 (1978).

68 / *Rights and Remedies Under Federal Grants*

have been withheld from the Secretary's investigations, and in some cases destroyed. Embezzlement has occurred, as has the improper spending of CETA funds for personal entertainment and travel. In some cases grievances have been either ignored, or there has been interminable delay in their resolution. The penalizing of a participant or a staff person who has filed a grievance or cooperated in an investigation has also occurred. Some prime sponsors have not equitably served the significant segments of the population by age, race, sex, and national origin. Two of the greatest abuses have been the substitution of CETA workers for regular employees (thus defeating the purpose of the act to create additional jobs for the unemployed) and the use of CETA funds to bolster the pension funds of State and local governments (with no benefit going to the temporary CETA workers). . . ." [68]

These findings provoked the insertion of a tough complaints and sanctions section into the Act.[69] The provisions [70] dealing with Department of Labor monitoring now call for mandatory investigation of complaints of illegality from any "interested person or organization" and also for investigations whenever the Secretary has "reason to believe" that any grantee or subgrantee is violating CETA, the law's regulations, or the terms of its approved plan. In the latter case, the investigation can be triggered by an audit, a report, an on-site review, or "otherwise." The section further requires primary grantees to establish grievance procedures for the expeditious processing of complaints filed by "participants, subgrantees, contractors, and other interested persons." An individual or organization must seek a remedy through the grantee complaint system before resorting to the Department of Labor.

Title X of the Community Services Act,[71] which establishes the Legal Services Corporation, creates a remarkable and *sui generis* monitoring system. Besides directing the corporation to monitor and evaluate grantees to insure compliance with the Act and applicable rules, regulations, and guidelines,[72] Congress established an unparalleled watchdog mechanism. In each state is created an "Advisory Council" charged with notifying the corporation of any "apparent violation" of the federal law and regulations by a grantee.[73] The corporation has read the Act as requiring

[68] *Ibid.*
[69] §106 Comprehensive Employment and Training Act of 1973, 29 U.S.C. §816.
[70] §§106(a), (b) *id.*, 29 U.S.C. §§816(a), (b).
[71] 42 U.S.C. §§2996–2996k (also entitled "Legal Services Corporation Act").
[72] §1007(d) Community Services Act of 1974, 42 U.S.C. §2996f(d).
[73] §1004(f), *id.*, 42 U.S.C. §2996c(f).

the councils to forward to its Washington, D.C., headquarters all written allegations of grantee noncompliance, and also as imposing on the corporation the duty to investigate and resolve all such complaints.[74]

The program, originally funded under the Economic Opportunity Act, has stirred considerable controversy because of the law reform, political organizing, and street advocacy activities of poverty lawyers.[75] The compromise struck in the new law is to permit continuation of the program but to control carefully the activities of employees of both the corporation and its grantees. Unlike other grant-in-aid programs, the Legal Services Corporation Act bristles with prohibitions on employee conduct.[76] To effectuate such controls, special monitoring was devised.

The uniqueness of the legal services scheme is not in the use of a mechanism for the receipt and review of accusations but in the creation at the state level of a special watchdog body independent of both grantee and grantor. In various programs the Office of Education has followed the recommendations of the Administrative Conference of the United States [77] by directing state educational agencies to establish internal procedures for the receipt and investigation of complaints of noncompliance.[78] The state educational agency must accept and investigate promptly all written allegations from any individual or organization that the agency itself or a local educational agency has violated the grant-in-aid law or regulations. The complainant has to be given the opportunity of presenting evidence, the complaint procedures must be publicized, and the agency is obliged to report to the Office of Education the disposition of all such complaints. In at least one program, the grantee is required to appoint a complaints officer and publicize his name and address.[79]

Another strategy recently utilized to police compliance with

---

[74] 45 C.F.R. §§1603.5–.6.

[75] See, e.g., George, "Development of the Legal Services Corporation," 61 Cornell L. Rev. 681, 682–99 (1976).

[76] See, e.g., §1006(b)(5) Community Services Act of 1974, 42 U.S.C. §2996e(b)(5). See generally Note, "Depoliticising Legal Aid: A Constitutional Analysis of the Legal Services Corporation Act," 61 Cornell L. Rev. 734 (1976).

[77] See Recommendation 71-9, "Enforcement of Standards in Federal Grant-in-Aid Programs," 1 C.F.R. §305.71-9.

[78] See, e.g., 45 C.F.R. §116.6 (education of disadvantaged); 45 C.F.R. §118.19 (violation of private school participation requirement); 45 C.F.R. §134.102 (same). Congress adopted such a system recently in the Comprehensive Employment and Training Program. See §106(a) Comprehensive Employment and Training Act, 29 U.S.C. §816(a).

[79] See 45 C.F.R. §121a.602 (education of the handicapped).

grant conditions is to require special compliance reports from grantees. In the State Medical Facilities Construction Program, the authorizing statute directs the Secretary of HEW to prescribe by regulation the "manner" and "means" by which each entity receiving financial assistance shall be required to demonstrate compliance with its assurances.[80] Not content with that directive, Congress imposes on each recipient the nonwaivable obligation of regularly submitting data and information which "reasonably supports the entity's compliance with such assurances." [81]

Congress has generally not mandated the creation of special federal offices to determine compliance with grant-in-aid conditions. The responsibility falls on each federal office administering a grant program, along with other grantor functions. To promote internal efficiency, however, the major federal departments have created central audit offices which conduct fiscal reviews of the department's grantees.[82] Similarly, civil rights issues are centrally handled. Another exception is found in the Buckley Amendment which establishes standards concerning grantee use and correction of student educational records. That provision directs the Secretary of HEW to establish or designate an office and review board within HEW to investigate, process, review, and adjudicate violations and complaints of alleged infractions.[83] Except for the conduct of hearings, none of the Secretary's responsibilities under this

---

[80] §1602(6) Public Health Service Act, 42 U.S.C. §300o-1(6). The Medical Facilities Construction Program has spawned a significant number of cases involving compliance issues, particularly the question whether grantee hospitals have provided sufficient free medical services to indigents. See, e.g., *Stanturf* v. *Sipes*, 335 F.2d 224 (8th Cir. 1964), cert. denied, 379 U.S. 977 (1965); *Saine* v. *Hospital Auth.*, 502 F.2d 1033 (5th Cir. 1974); *Cook* v. *Oshner Foundation Hosp.*, 319 F. Supp. 603 (E.D. La. 1970); *Corum* v. *Beth Israel Medical Center*, 359 F. Supp. 909 (S.D. N.Y. 1973). See also *Clement Martin, Inc.* v. *Dick Corp.*, 97 F. Supp. 961 (W.D. Pa. 1961) (alleged noncompliance with bidding procedures); *Simkins* v. *Moses H. Cone Memorial Hosp.*, 323 F.2d 959 (4th Cir. 1963), cert. denied, 376 U.S. 938 (1965) (racial discrimination).

[81] §1602(6) Public Health Service Act, 42 U.S.C. §300o-1(6).

[82] See S. Rep. No. 95-1071, 95th Cong., 2d Sess. 7–8 (1978). In response to an "epidemic" of "fraud, abuse and waste in the operations of Federal departments and agencies and in federally-funded programs," see *id.* at 4, Congress established the Office of Inspector General in 14 executive departments and agencies. Inspector General Act of 1978, Pub. L. 95-452, Oct. 12, 1978. The legislation built upon a prior law which had established such an office in HEW. See Title II, Pub. L. 94-505, Oct. 15, 1976, 42 U.S.C. §§3521–3527. These laws mandate a central audit office in most of the major grant-giving departments, as follows: Agriculture, Commerce, HEW, HUD, Interior, Labor, Transportation, Community Services Administration, and the Environmental Protection Administration. The impact of such offices on grantee audits remains, of course, to be seen.

[83] §438 General Education Provisions Act, 20 U.S.C. §1232g. Enforcement regulations are found at 45 C.F.R. §§99.60–99.67.

law can be carried out in any of the regular offices of the Department.

Subgrantee Compliance

Programs involving a pass-through of funds to subgrantees pose special compliance problems. All federal conditions apply to both the main and the subsidiary recipient. This general rule stems from various drafting techniques. One is the simple expedient of attaching the condition to the federal dollar itself ("Assistance under this Act shall not be spent . . ."). A variant on this theme is to attach the condition to the "program" which means, under common usage, all activities at every level ("In this program . . ."; "In the administration of this program . . ."). Another method is to issue a command to the federal administrator which must be obeyed whether or not there is privity with the recipient ("The Secretary shall . . ."). A fourth way is to impose the obligation on all "recipients" of federal funds, making the act of receiving the assistance the factor which triggers the federal standard without regard to the recipient's position as grantee, subgrantee, or sub-subgrantee ("The recipient shall . . ."). A fifth technique, commonly found in pass-through programs, is to impose the standards through a series of guarantees from the principal recipient ("Such plan/application shall provide assurances that . . ."). In such cases it is less clear that the federal standards contained in the assurances reach down to subgrantees, but the issue is rarely reached because the grantee typically imposes the totality of federal standards in the subgrant agreement. An acquaintance of the author explained that in his position with a community action agency he was responsible for drafting subgrant agreements. Lacking guidance from the federal grantor, the official simply stapled together the dozens of pages of rules applicable to his agency, added a few of his own, and had the subgrantees sign.

Federal standards which originate with the administering agency may or may not apply to subgrantees. That is a question of policy choice. The power to issue implementing regulations is sufficiently broad to authorize the extension of program rules to subgrantees.[84] Not too long ago HEW dealt with the "important and difficult issue" [85] whether to impose its departmentwide grant administrative regulations, 45 C.F.R. Part 74, to subgrantees

---
[84] See notes 17–19, *supra*, and accompanying text.
[85] 43 Fed. Reg. 34076 (1978).

receiving their funds through state agencies and other primary grantees. The original position of HEW

> "intentionally did not require States and other grantees to administer subgrants strictly in accordance with the same standards that Federal agencies follow in administering grants. To do so, HEW felt, would be an unwarranted intrusion into the affairs of States and other grantees and could affect their ability to administer the subgrants effectively." [86]

The final regulation, however, reversed this position on the ground that "the interest of subgrantees lies in having the same rights and and protections as do grantees." [87] That comment is true, but only to a degree. The circulars [88] of the Office of Management and Budget which require grant-giving agencies like HEW to standardize their administrative practices in accordance with the central rules were motivated by the desire to simplify and unify agency practices across the field of federal grants.[89] To some extent, therefore, 45 C.F.R. Part 74 protects subgrantees by preventing the issuance of more rigorous administrative requirements by the operational division of HEW administering the particular grant program. The reality nonetheless remains that Part 74 is a long series of *federal rules*. The deception in HEW's explanatory comment is the assumption that all areas regulated by Part 74 would have been covered in its absence. That is far from clear. Federal program regulations are rarely as comprehensive as Part 74 and state practices are simply not known.

Though little is known about grantee management of subgrantees, there must be some degree of supervision. It is standard in grant law that if the subgrantee is out of compliance, the grantee is automatically in violation.[90] Thus, both the Federal

[86] *Ibid.*
[87] *Ibid.*
[88] See Chapter 1, note 83, *supra.*
[89] See Advisory Commission on Intergovernmental Relations, *The Intergovernmental Grant System: An Assessment and Proposed Policies: Improving Federal Grants Management* 93–143 (1977).
[90] See, e.g., 29 C.F.R. §97.165(a). This result is typically assured by requiring a general assurance from the grantee that the "program" will comply with all relevant federal standards. See, e.g., §435(b)(1) General Education Provisions Act, 20 U.S.C. §1232d(b)(1) (boilerplate assurance for all education "flow-through" formula grants): "An application . . . shall set forth assurances . . . that each program will be administered in accordance with all applicable statutes, regulations, program plans, and applications. . . ." The "program" being the totality of activities, the grantee's assurance is violated each time a subgrantee is found in violation. In practice, however, the grantor would either proceed directly against the subgrantee or against the grantee on the different ground of failing to discharge its enforcement responsibilities.

Government and its principal grantee are vitally concerned with subgrantee performance.

There is surprisingly little in the federal grant-in-aid statutes and regulations addressing the question of subgrantee supervision. In most programs it appears that the federal grantor has delegated to its grantee responsibility for the supervision of subgrantee activities. To protect itself, the grantee creates a system of reports and inspections parallel to the system imposed on it by the grantor.[91]

A beacon was recently shone into the vast and shadowy world of subgrantees. The National Institute of Education studied the practices of state educational agencies in supervising local school district expenditures of grants under the Elementary and Secondary Education Act. The Institute's findings, as summarized by the House Education and Labor Committee, were as follows:

> "The major responsibility for managing and monitoring Title I local school district programs is shouldered by the State educational agencies. NIE discovered, though, that many States are confused as to their exact responsibilities and authority in the area of . . . monitoring and enforcing compliance. NIE attributes this confusion to the ambiguity and degree of difficulty of the statute and to the inconsistency of Federal monitoring. . . .
>
> "As a consequence, NIE found that States have adopted widely different administrative policies and that some do not fulfill all of their responsibilities. Most seriously, NIE concluded, the failure of Title I's legal framework to provide clear guidance has in some cases led to State practices that may not be in compliance. For example, some State application forms request only limited information from local school districts and may result in these States approving programs that do not meet all requirements. A review of audit policies also disclosed that several State educational agencies do not conduct audits of compliance with every regulation, as required by law, but only audits of total expenditures." [92]

The legislative response to those findings was swift and stern. An elaborate set of monitoring and enforcement responsibilities for state educational agencies was inserted in the massive Title I program for educationally disadvantaged children. The primary purpose of these provisions is "to clarify administrative respon-

---

[91] See, e.g., *Natonabah* v. *Board of Educ.*, 355 F. Supp. 716, 729–32 (D. N.M. 1973).

[92] H. R. Rep. No. 95-1137, 95th Cong., 2d Sess. 41 (1978) (hereinafter cited as H. Rep. 1137).

sibility at each level." [93] Because they are likely to serve as the model for future grant statutes and amendments, it is worthwhile to examine this scheme in some detail.[94] To some extent this study will take us into areas, like sanctions and remediation, which are separately considered in the immediately following section of the text. This "preview" is justified, however, by the benefits derived from seeing the potentially revolutionary Title I system as a whole.

The program for enforcement of subgrantee responsibilities consists of three basic components: systems enabling an SEA to inform itself of subgrantee practices; explicit authority vested in the SEA to penalize and correct improprieties; and responsibility of the SEA to the Office of Education for carrying out the monitoring and enforcement.

Three techniques are employed for monitoring. Primary is the periodic audit for which each SEA "shall make provision." [95] The statute now establishes minimum federal standards for audit coverage. The audit not only must guarantee the integrity of financial transactions and reports but must also verify "compliance with applicable statutes, regulations, and terms and conditions of the grant or subgrant." [96] The SEA has discretion to determine the frequency of audit, but must consider the nature, size, and com-

---

[93] *Id.* at 3.

[94] It is interesting to compare the treatment of subgrantee compliance in another major grant statute completely rewritten by the 95th Congress, the Comprehensive Employment and Training Act of 1973. This program is carried out through almost 450 prime sponsors, see S. Rep. No. 95-891, 95th Cong., 2d Sess. 5–6 (1978), and an estimated 50,000 subgrantees. Commission on Federal Paperwork, *Employment and Training Programs* 44 (1977). While the "complaints and sanctions" section of the Act was considerably expanded last year, the focus is primarily on the Secretary of Labor's enforcement obligations and powers in the context of prime sponsor violations. See §106 Comprehensive Employment and Training Act of 1973, 29 U.S.C. §816, as rewritten by §2 Comprehensive Employment and Training Act Amendments of 1978, Pub. L. 95-524, Oct. 27, 1978. Prime sponsor enforcement of subgrantee obligations is a condition of federal funding and the statute authorizes the Secretary to take action against a grantee "that has not taken appropriate action against its subcontractors, subgrantees, and other recipients." See §106(d)(1) *id.*, 29 U.S.C. §816(d)(1). The Secretary may withhold the prime sponsor's funds, in whole or part, or may move directly against the subgrantee, or may order the grantee to take appropriate legal action against the subgrantee in violation.

[95] See §170 Elementary and Secondary Education Act of 1965, 20 U.S.C. §2817, as rewritten by §101 Education Amendments of 1978, Pub. L. 95-561, Nov. 1, 1978.

[96] This responds to the finding of the National Institute of Education that most SEAs were skipping compliance issues in their audits and including only financial matters. See H. Rep. 1137, note 92, *supra*, at 48. The House Education and Labor Committee expressed its belief that the Commissioner of Education should collaborate with HEW's Office of Inspector General and Office of General Counsel to establish compliance guidelines for nonfederal auditors; the committee also specified three federal standards of "fundamental" importance. See *id.* at 49.

plexity of each activity subject to scrutiny. The SEA is further responsible for "timely and appropriate" resolution of audit findings and recommendations, pursuant to "written procedures." A second method for discovering violations is through complaints from individuals and organizations.[97] Each SEA is mandated to establish a system for receiving and investigating complaints of violations of program rules.[98] The agency must establish time limits for the resolution of complaints and completion of investigations, not exceeding 60 days in the absence of "exceptional circumstances." The parties must be given an opportunity to present evidence and to question witnesses and other parties. The SEA must also liberally disseminate information concerning the availability of the complaints process. The third monitoring focus occurs during the process of SEA review of grant applications from local educational agencies.[99] In determining whether to approve such applications, the SEA must determine that each applicant is not and will not be in violation of grant conditions. To that end the SEA must study the results of audits, complaints, evaluations, and monitoring reports.

The second leg of the new Title I "law and order" thrust is the explicit investiture of enforcement powers in the SEA.[100] The grantee/subgrantor has several whips, but each must be preceded by reasonable notice and opportunity for a hearing [101] and the subgrantee is guaranteed the right to appeal SEA final sanction deci-

[97] §168 Elementary and Secondary Education Act of 1965, 20 U.S.C. §2815, as rewritten by §101 Education Amendments of 1978, Pub. L. 95-561, Nov. 1, 1978. Local education agencies must establish comparable complaints mechanisms. See §128 *id.*, 20 U.S.C. §2738. If the complaint is lodged at that level, the SEA has appellate jurisdiction from LEA final decisions. A parallel system is also mandated for the federal level. See §184 *id.*, 20 U.S.C. §2834. The House Education and Labor Committee described the three sections as a "comprehensive, interlocking complaint resolution system." H. Rep. 1137, note 92, *supra,* at 47.

[98] §168 Elementary and Secondary Education Act of 1965, 20 U.S.C. §2815, as rewritten by §101 Education Amendments of 1978, Pub. L. 95-561, Nov. 1, 1978.

[99] §164 Elementary and Secondary Education Act of 1965, 20 U.S.C. §2811, as rewritten by §101 Education Amendments of 1978, Pub. L. 95-561, Nov. 1, 1978.

[100] The legislative history makes clear that prior to the 1978 amendments the SEAs possessed "implied authority" to enforce Title I's requirements, see H. Rep. 1137, note 92, *supra,* at 47, and the amendments simply "clarify" and make explicit that authority. See *id.* at 3–58 *(passim).*

[101] §164(c) Elementary and Secondary Education Act of 1965, 20 U.S.C. §2811(c), as rewritten by §101 Education Amendments of 1978, Pub. L. 95-561, Nov. 1, 1978 (application disapproval; prior "reasonable notice and opportunity for a hearing"); §170(b) *id.*, 20 U.S.C. §2817(b) (audit "appeals process"); §169(a) *id.*, 20 U.S.C. §2816(a) (payment withholding; "reasonable notice and opportunity for a hearing . . . before an impartial decisionmaker").

76 / *Rights and Remedies Under Federal Grants*

sions to the Commissioner of Education.¹⁰² One device, discussed in the previous paragraph, is the disapproval of grant applications based on uncorrected past violations or an inadequate showing that future compliance will be achieved. This aspect of SEA supervision was considered of particular importance by the House Education and Labor Committee. It stated:

> "The Committee feels that application approval is perhaps the most important function performed by State educational agencies under Title I. It enables the State educational agency to determine whether an applicant agency has complied with applicable program requirements before the applicant agency implements the program or project described in the application. In addition, the review and approval process gives the State educational agency an opportunity to . . . place the applicant agency on notice as to practices which would be considered unacceptable under Title I. . . .
>
> "Furthermore, the effects of approving an application that does not meet all the applicable requirements can include costly audit exceptions and appeal to the Audit Hearing Board; a determination that illegal expenditures must be reimbursed; burdensome attempts to achieve compliance in mid-year; or even litigation by Title I parents and children seeking to insure that their rights are protected. A well designed application approval process can help applicant agencies avoid such compliance problems." ¹⁰³

Another sanction device is the recovery of federal funds which were found, at the end of the audit resolution process, to have been "misspent" or "misapplied." ¹⁰⁴ If the LEA fails to respond to an SEA's payment demand, the matter may be referred to the Office of Education for the prosecution of a collection action. Repayment must be from nonfederal sources or unrestricted federal receipts. The SEA is also empowered to invoke the usual sanction ¹⁰⁵ of payment withholding, in whole or part, "until it is satisfied that there is no longer any . . . failure to comply." ¹⁰⁶

We shall see that despite the authorization of severe sanctions for violation of grant conditions, the initial compliance thrust is

---

102 §169(d) *id.*, 20 U.S.C. §2816(d); §170(d) *id.*, 20 U.S.C. §2817(d); §425(a) General Education Provisions Act, 20 U.S.C. §1231b-2.

103 H. Rep. 1137, note 92, *supra,* at 42.

104 §§170(b), (c), (e) Elementary and Secondary Education Act of 1965, 20 U.S.C. §§2817(b), (c), (e), as rewritten by §101 Education Amendments of 1978, Pub. L. 95-561, Nov. 1, 1978.

105 See generally Chapter 9, *infra*.

106 §169 Elementary and Secondary Education Act of 1965, 20 U.S.C. §2816, as rewritten by §101 Education Amendments of 1978, Pub. L. 95-561, Nov. 1, 1978.

to seek, whenever possible, voluntary compliance.[107] The aim of grantor enforcement of federal standards is to obtain obedience to the rules without causing unnecessary harm to the program. This aim is also expressed at the subgrantee level in the form of "compliance agreements." [108] If a compliance agreement with the violator is feasible, the SEA is authorized to forsake or discontinue the withholding sanction. Such an agreement must specify the corrective action to be taken by the LEA, must cover all violations which provoked the withholding proceeding, and must specify its duration.[109]

An additional sanction, or better "quasi-sanction," available to the SEA is to shame the violator into compliance by means of public notice of the misdeed.[110] Indeed, such a public communication is required whenever the state imposes the withholding sanction. The SEA is required to advise the district advisory council of the action and also to take "such additional action as may be necessary to bring the State action to the attention of the public."

In federal programs the grantee typically does no more than "assure" the grantor that it will comply with the terms of the grant. It need offer no plan or program of compliance. This strategy has been rejected in the new Title I monitoring and enforcement program. In its application for state participation in Title I the SEA must give the normal assurance that it

> "will adopt and use proper methods of administering each applicable program, including— . . . monitoring of agencies, institutions, and organizations responsible for carrying out each program, and the enforcement of any obligations imposed on those agencies, institutions, and organizations under law. . . ." [111]

That, however, does not end the matter. For the Title I program the SEA must also submit to the Commissioner a plan for carrying

---

[107] See notes 169–180, *infra,* and accompanying text.

[108] §169(c) Elementary and Secondary Education Act Amendments of 1965, 20 U.S.C. §2816(c), as rewritten by §101 Education Amendments of 1978, Pub. L. 95-561, Nov. 1, 1978.

[109] The Education and Labor Committee made clear, in reporting this section, that when a subgrantee violates a compliance agreement, negotiation of another such agreement is impermissible, and that such agreements may not be used "to reduce or forgive any amount of funds which final State audit resolution determinations have determined were misspent or misapplied and must be repaid." H. Rep. 1137, note 92, *supra,* at 46.

[110] §169(b) Elementary and Secondary Education Act of 1965, 20 U.S.C. §2816(b), as rewritten by §101 Education Amendments of 1978, Pub. L. 95-561, Nov. 1, 1978.

[111] See §§162(b), 182(a) *id.,* 20 U.S.C. §§2802(b), 2832(b); §435(b)(1) General Education Provisions Act, 20 U.S.C. §1232(b)(1).

out these obligations with the detail required by Office of Education regulations.[112] This plan must contain: a program of regular site visits to LEA projects, with specification of the matters to be reviewed during such visits; procedures to cross-check and verify information supplied by subgrantees; procedures for regular audits and recovery of disallowed expenditures; and systems for handling and resolving complaints from individuals and organizations.

While the thrust of these amendments is to place the enforcement burden at the grantee/subgrantor level, the statute makes plain that the Federal Government reserves the power to move against subgrantees directly.[113]

The Education Amendments of 1978 [114] dealt in more generalized fashion with the monitoring and enforcement of subgrantee duties in other SEA-administered "flow-through" grant programs. In essence, a watered-down version of the Title I scheme, just reviewed, was extended to the numerous other formula grant education programs by means of a new Section 434 inserted in the General Education Provisions Act.[115]

The new provision clarifies the power of the administering state board or agency to enforce subgrantee duties through appropriate sanctions. These include the usual remedies of suspension of payments, withholding of payments pending compliance, and refusal to approve subgrant applications. In the latter two cases the sanction must be preceded by reasonable notice and opportunity to be heard "before an impartial hearing officer"; in the case of a preliminary suspension, the subgrantee must be given a prior "show cause" opportunity. Unlike Title I, a monitoring and enforcement plan of action is not required by the statute. Rather, the Commissioner of Education is authorized to require such plan in the federal programs of his choice. Similarly, the Commissioner is given discretion as to the contents of a state enforcement system, with the statute only suggesting periodic on-site visits, regular audits, and complaints systems. As in Title I, these specific responsibilities are backed up by a more generalized state assurance that it will adequately monitor and enforce federal program and administrative standards.[116]

---

[112] §171(a) Elementary and Secondary Education Act of 1965, 20 U.S.C. §2821(a), as rewritten by §101 Education Amendments of 1978, Pub. L. 95-561, Nov. 1, 1978.
[113] See §§185, 186 id., 20 U.S.C. §§2835, 2836.
[114] Pub. L. 95-561, Nov. 1, 1978.
[115] 20 U.S.C. §1232c.
[116] §435(b)(1) General Education Provisions Act, 20 U.S.C. §1232d(b)(1).

While the section does not mandate a strict compliance program, as in Title I, it creates that possibility for the balance of the Office of Education's formula programs by empowering the Commissioner to establish the Title I system by regulation. If the Commissioner were to take a hard-line approach, federal compliance issues would innundate America's educational systems. The new provision may not theoretically change "the law," but it could certainly have a profound impact on grant practices. For this reason, the following appraisal of the House Education and Labor Committee rings hollow:

> "Furthermore, nothing in these new provisions should be interpreted as radically changing the present relationship of the Federal government to the States or to local school districts. These amendments, rather, are meant merely to lay out responsibilities more clearly so that no confusion exists about each governmental level's respective duties.
>
> "It must always be remembered that education is primarily the responsibility of States. . . ." [117]

Methods of Enforcement

If a federal agency obtains information that one of its grantees is not following an applicable statute, regulation, instruction, or assurance, it will have several methods of remedying the violation. Naturally, for *de minimus* or unintentional violations not affecting program performance or effectiveness, a phone call is usually all that is required. The agency can also choose to ignore insubstantial violations which are more of form than substance, or which do not undermine program goals and important federal policies.

The latter alternative is available because the grantor has prosecutorial discretion. Noncompliance sections of grant statutes sometimes demand sanctions after a finding of substantial noncompliance ("shall") and sometimes simply authorize fiscal penalties ("may").[118] Although the majority of noncompliance sections speak in mandatory terms, the command is relevant only after a formal determination of violations following notice and an opportunity to be heard. Thus, the federal grantor has discretion

---

[117] H. Rep. 1137, note 92, *supra*, at 144.
[118] Compare, e.g., §314(g)(3) Public Health Service Act, 42 U.S.C. §246(g)(3), with §1611(b), *id.*, 42 U.S.C. §300p-1(b). See generally statutory sections cited in Chapter 9, note 2, *infra*.

to determine whether it will force a noncompliance hearing or will ignore or informally settle the matter. When, as in most cases, the statute is silent on the sanction question, no prosecutorial duty arises and normal administrative discretion applies. At the insistance of third parties, however, a court might force the federal agency to move against a noncomplying grantee.[119] The U.S. Court of Appeals for the District of Columbia has held that courts may review agency enforcement decisions for abuse of discretion.[120]

Should the decision be made that the violation is serious, or if Congress has withdrawn agency enforcement discretion,[121] the grantor must consider the options available for formal remedial action.

Grant Principles and Remedial Options

Before analyzing the specific remedial alternatives open to federal grantor agencies we must describe certain characteristics of a federal grant-in-aid which impact on enforcement possibilities. The federal grant is a unique institution in American law. Several lower federal courts have sloshed through this unfamiliar terrain with common law boots, treating the grant as just another form of contract species.[122] The following discussion may make for surer treading.

We have seen that the constitutional authority for grants-in-aid is provided by the General Welfare Clause.[123] Congress may utilize its tax revenues to provide for national social and economic needs. In so doing, it may opt for the direct, nationwide provision of benefits, as in the Social Security program, or for indirect federal involvement through grant assistance to other service-providing institutions. In analyzing the constitutional propriety of any particular grant program, it is ordinarily irrelevant whether

---

[119] See *Poirrier* v. *St. James Parish Police Jury*, 372 F. Supp. 1021 (E.D. La. 1974), aff'd per curiam, 531 F.2d 316 (5th Cir. 1976). But see *Arthur C. Logan Mem. Hosp.* v. *Toia*, 441 F. Supp. 26 (S.D. N.Y. 1977) (court cannot order grantor to hold a compliance hearing).

[120] *Adams* v. *Richardson*, 480 F.2d 1159, 1161–63 (D.C. Cir. 1973).

[121] See generally notes 58–83, *supra*, and accompanying text.

[122] See, e.g., *United States* v. *Independent School Dist. No. 1*, 209 F.2d 578 (10th Cir. 1954); *United States* v. *Frazer*, 297 F. Supp. 319, 322–23 (M.D. Ala. 1968); *United States* v. *Sumter County School Dist. No. 2*, 232 F. Supp. 945, 950 (E.D. S.C. 1964); *United States* v. *County School Bd.*, 221 F. Supp. 93, 103 (E.D. Va. 1963). The disease is particularly acute, not surprisingly, in the Court of Claims. See, e.g., *California By and Through the Dep't of Transp.* v. *United States*, 551 F.2d 843 (Ct. Cl.), cert. denied, 434 U.S. 857 (1977).

[123] See Chapter 2, notes 3–7, *supra*, and accompanying text.

the national government had the authority to do the job directly, under the General Welfare Clause or some other constitutional grant of power, because Congress has chosen to avoid difficult questions of federal-state relations by means of the cooperative grant device. Participation in the assistance program being voluntary, a state surrenders its authority over local affairs to the extent and degree it deems advisable. Should federal grant conditions be considered unduly intrusive, the state may decide not to participate when the program assistance is first offered, or may withdraw its participation if Congress subsequently adds offensive standards. One may rail against the concept of voluntary surrender as either unreal (economic and political pressures on the states give them no choice) or unnecessary (Congress could have commanded the same conditions), but it is firmly imbedded in law and practice.[124] It is a principle under which Congress has acted for decades, under which billions of dollars have been distributed, and under which a radical but highly commended [125] transformation of our federal system has occurred. It is also a principle which the Supreme Court has shown no inclination to abandon.[126]

In a recent case, the State of Illinois purported to withdraw from a federally assisted emergency welfare program after a federal court of appeals held that the state could not determine its own standards for individual eligibility.[127] The U.S. Supreme Court did not balk at the proposition. On the contrary, it stated:

> "As the Court of Appeals readily conceded, its holding in *Mandley I* that federal eligibility standards are mandatory upon States that adopt the optional [Emergency Assistance] program in no way obligates a State to continue that program. The federal definition of eligibility in §406(e), like the other provisions of Title IV of the Social Security Act, simply governs the dispensation of federal funds. . . . And while Congress may attach strings to its offer of federal funding, it does not require the States to accept any federal funds at all." [128]

[124] A recent study found "the emergence of a tiny but perceptible trend toward recipient (especially state) refusal to participate in certain programs. . . ." Advisory Commission on Intergovernmental Relations, *The Intergovernmental Grant System: An Assessment and Proposed Policies: Summary and Concluding Observations* 66 (1978).

[125] See, e.g., R.H. Leach, *American Federalism* 193 (1970); M. Grodzins, *The American System* 62–63 (1966); Reagan, *The New Federalism* 82–88 (1972).

[126] See Chapter 2, notes 14–15, *supra*, and accompanying text; cf. *Wyman v. James*, 400 U.S. 309 (1971) (by accepting welfare, beneficiary voluntarily accepted home visit condition).

[127] See *Quern v. Mandley*, 436 U.S. 725, 730–31 (1978).

[128] *Id.* at 734 (citations omitted).

From the constitutional norm of voluntary participation we can derive several important limitations on the power of the United States to enforce its grant standards.

First, federal grant conditions are applicable only to those institutions which have accepted and are utilizing the funds to which the conditions are tied.[129] It is the receipt of federal funds and the voluntary acceptance of the attached terms which springs their authority. A state, county, city, district, or private group is free to engage in the practices of its choice if it abstains from federal financing and does not violate any law outside of the grant program. Once it receives federal funds, however, the commands of the grant statute become applicable to the recipient and the Supremacy Clause makes impermissible any conflicting state or local law, regulation, or practice.[130]

Chief Justice Burger has stated the correct principle in these terms:

> "In dealing with these cases—and the other AFDC cases on the Court's docket—it seems appropriate to keep clearly in mind that Title IV of the Social Security Act governs the disposition of federal funds and that it does no more than that. True, Congress has used the 'power of the purse' to force the States to adhere to its wishes to a certain extent; but adherence to the provisions of Title IV is in no way mandatory upon the States under the Supremacy Clause. The appropriate inquiry in any case should be, simply, whether the State has indeed adhered to the provisions and is accordingly entitled to utilize federal funds in support of its program." [131]

Second, by ending its participation in the program the grantee can withdraw its consent to federal intrusion, affirm its local policy and authority, and moot the Supremacy Clause issue, assuming that the withdrawal itself does not violate other constitutional norms.[132] While expressions in some Supreme Court opinions seem

---

[129] *James* v. *Valtierra*, 402 U.S. 137, 140 (1971); *Rhodes* v. *City of Chicago*, 516 F.2d 1373, 1377 (7th Cir. 1975).

[130] See, e.g., *Townsend* v. *Swank*, 404 U.S. 282, 285 (1971).

[131] *Id.* at 292 (concurring opinion). See also *Florida* v. *Mathews* (I), 526 F.2d 319 (5th Cir. 1976); *City of Macon* v. *Marshall*, 439 F. Supp. 1209 (M.D. Ga. 1977).

[132] If the grantee has violated the constitutional rights of individuals as well as federal grant conditions, the equitable power of federal courts to remedy the harm done by constitutional violations is likely to be sufficiently broad to order continued utilization of federal funds by the offending grantee. See *Hills* v. *Gautreaux*, 425 U.S. 284 (1976). If the act of refusing continued receipt of federal funds is *itself* a violation of constitutional norms, such as equal protection, federal judicial power to interdict the withdrawal would appear to exist, although the

to suggest that state laws and regulations are invalid under the Supremacy Clause if they conflict with federal grant policy,[133] the premise unarticulated in those cases is that *the invalidity persists only to the extent that the grantee continues to receive federal funding.*

The 1974 *Wheeler* v. *Barrera*[134] decision clearly makes this important point. The Supreme Court affirmed lower court findings[135] that a Missouri school system's program for the education of the disadvantaged, financed under Title I of the Elementary and Secondary Education Act, violated the statutory condition that Title I services be provided in private schools on a basis comparable to what was being offered to public school children. The difficulty of complying with the requirement was considerable in view of Missouri constitutional and statutory law which prevented the education of private school children in public schools during regular class hours and also the assignment of public school teachers to give special classes in parochial schools. The tension between Missouri law and the federal comparability policy did not lead to the invalidation of the former. Rather, the Court presented the grantee with three options: first, use its educational imagination to devise programs which achieved comparability without violating state law; second, achieve parity by lessening its public school effort; or, third, withdraw from participation in the program, even though this option might be "undoubtedly least attractive for the educationally deprived children."[136]

The withdrawal alternative was not invented in *Wheeler*. It was consistent with prior decisions of the Court.[137] It was also consistent with the constitutional bases of grant-in-aid programs, even though grantee withdrawal would promote hardship to the individuals benefiting from the services. In the context of grants-in-aid for welfare assistance Justice Douglas explained:

---

issue has not, to our knowledge, been decided. See *Richmond Welfare Rights Organ.* v. *Snodgrass,* 525 F.2d 197, 206 (9th Cir. 1975) (dicta); *Justice* v. *Board of Educ.,* 351 F. Supp. 1252, 1264, n. 30 (S.D. N.Y. 1972) (dicta).

[133] See *Carleson* v. *Remillard,* 406 U.S. 598, 601 (1972); *Townsend* v. *Swank,* 404 U.S. 282, 285 (1971).

[134] 417 U.S. 402 (1974).

[135] See *Barrera* v. *Wheeler,* 475 F.2d 1388 (8th Cir. 1973), *aff'd,* 417 U.S. 402 (1974).

[136] *Wheeler* v. *Barrera,* 417 U.S. 402, 425 (1974).

[137] See, e.g., *Rosado* v. *Wyman,* 397 U.S. 397, 420–22 (1970); *Oklahoma* v. *U.S. Civil Serv. Comm'n,* 330 U.S. 127 (1947).

84 / *Rights and Remedies Under Federal Grants*

"State participation in federal welfare programs is not required. States may choose not to apply for federal assistance or may join in some, but not all, of the various programs, of which AFDC is only one. That a State may choose to refuse to comply with the federal requirements at the cost of losing federal funds is, of course, a risk that any welfare plaintiff takes. . . . As long as a State is receiving federal funds, however, it is under a legal requirement to comply with the federal conditions placed on the receipt of these funds; and individuals who are adversely affected by the failure of the State to comply with the federal requirements in distributing those federal funds are entitled to a judicial determination of such a claim." [138]

Third, a logical corollary of the above principles is that a court, upon finding a violation of federal grant conditions, should not enjoin the conflicting state law, regulation, or practice, but instead should prohibit the grantee from continuing to utilize federal funds until consistency with federal policy is achieved.[139] Similarly, if the federal administrator is before the court he can be ordered to cease providing assistance until compliance is achieved. An outright prohibition of the state policy which conflicts with federal grant conditions would improperly eliminate the withdrawal option and violate the voluntary nature of federal grant programs and, hence, raise the delicate federalism questions which Congress chose to avoid by means of the grant-in-aid mechanism.

The upshot of the above is that, absent special circumstances,[140] the only prospective remedy available to the United States for the violation of federal grant conditions is fiscal—the withdrawal of

[138] *Rosado* v. *Wyman*, 397 U.S. 397, 427 (1970) (concurring opinion). See also *Richmond Welfare Rights Organ.* v. *Snodgrass*, 525 F.2d 197, 205–206 (9th Cir. 1975) (footnote omitted):

"Defendant's June 18, 1973, election to terminate all participation in the National School Lunch Program was a decision political in nature. The individual defendants herein, not the courts, were elected and empowered to make precisely such decisions. If defendants ultimately and lawfully adopt what may be perceived as an inhumanly callous position, the matter is one for the correction by the voters of the district, not for us. . . . We recognize the danger inherent in the termination alternative and appreciate plaintiff's frustration when confronted with it, but we cannot deny its availability under the law to school districts not found in violation of constitutional rights."

[139] See, e.g., *Rosado* v. *Wyman*, 397 U.S. 397, 420–22 (1970).

[140] One special circumstance is when the grant has been received and spent, as in a construction project, and federal conditions continue to apply to the subsidized facility. Because the fiscal sanction is no longer viable, specific performance of the condition may be ordered. See notes 222–227, *infra*, and accompanying text.

federal funding.¹⁴¹ The court may enjoin the federal defendant from supplying further assistance to a noncomplying program ¹⁴² or enjoin the grantee from utilizing federal funds until conformity with grant standards is achieved,¹⁴³ but may not directly order compliance and continued use of federal funds.¹⁴⁴

A few examples drawn from the cases may help clarify this extraordinary limit on federal enforcement powers:

(1) A grant statute authorizes operational assistance to local public schools providing education to children of federal employees. A prerequisite of such assistance is that the amount of any state aid to such schools not be influenced by this federal aid. A state passes a law which deducts from state aid, dollar-for-dollar, any such federal payments received by local schools. Although every local school district thereby becomes ineligible for such federal aid and the program is totally frustrated, the state cannot be enjoined from implementing its law. Congress has not prohibited such a state law; rather, it has chosen to enforce the standard by conditioning the payment of federal funds on compliance. The state may validly opt to decline the federal funds by making ineligible entities and governmental units over which its jurisdiction extends.¹⁴⁵

(2) A grant statute requires that an agreement to cooperate be executed between the local government where the aided activity is to be developed and the grantee. A local government enters into such an agreement. Prior to the execution of the grant, the city experiences a change of political parties and wishes to revoke the agreement. In the absence of a contrary provision in the federal grant statute or regulation which establishes that the city's initial

---

[141] See, e.g., *Richmond Welfare Rights Organ.* v. *Snodgrass*, 525 F.2d 197, 205–206 (9th Cir. 1975); *Philadelphia Anti-poverty Action Comm.* v. *Rizzo*, 502 F.2d 306 (3rd Cir. 1974), *cert. denied*, 419 U.S. 1108 (1975). But see *Arizona State Dep't of Pub. Welfare* v. *Department of Health, Educ. & Welfare*, 449 F.2d 456, 464, n. 9 (9th Cir. 1971) (dicta); Cahn & Cahn, "The New Sovereign Immunity," 929, 967–68, n. 138 (1968) (suggesting intermediate sanctions).

[142] See, e.g., *Torres* v. *Butz*, 397 F. Supp. 1015 (N.D. Ill. 1975).

[143] See, e.g., *Shaw* v. *Governing Bd.*, 310 F. Supp. 1282 (E.D. Cal. 1970).

[144] See, e.g., *Lopez* v. *Luginbill*, 483 F.2d 486, 489 (10th Cir. 1973), *cert. denied*, 415 U.S. 927 (1974); *Arthur C. Logan Mem. Hosp.* v. *Toia*, 441 F. Supp. 26, 27 (S.D. N.Y. 1977).

[145] The facts are drawn from *Shepheard* v. *Godwin*, 280 F. Supp. 869 (E.D. Va. 1968), in which the court incorrectly enjoined the implementation of the state law. See also *Hergenreter* v. *Hayden*, 295 F. Supp. 251 (D. Kan. 1968). The correct analysis is set forth in *County of Los Angeles* v. *Adams*, 574 F.2d 608, 609 (D.C. Cir. 1978).

consent is continuous and irrevocable, the city should be able to withdraw as a matter of federal law.[146]

(3) The head of a grantee agency is removed by the mayor of a city. The action allegedly violates the conditions of the grant, although under local law the mayor has the power of dismissal. Even if the mayor's action violates the grant terms, the court may not order reinstatement of the employee. It can only force the grantee to forgo federal funding until it brings itself into compliance with the grant statute and regulations.[147]

(4) A state develops a highway project with the intention of obtaining federal financial assistance. To insure consistency with federal standards it obtains necessary clearances from the Federal Highway Administration, but has not yet received or expended federal funds. A court finds that the project violates national environmental standards. At this point the state can refuse federal participation and continue to develop the project free from the grant constraints.[148]

This constitutional limit on the enforcement power of the Federal Government in the context of federal grant standards is extraordinary because it means, essentially, that: (1) whenever the Federal Government questions the legality of a grantee's actions it runs the risk of total program frustration through grantee withdrawal; (2) whenever a fiscal sanction is imposed the individual program beneficiaries are the losers in the amount by which the program level is reduced. The paradox is, of course, that the grantor has ended up punishing the very persons it sought to aid through the federal standards and their enforcement. The sanction only works through the *threat*.

---

[146] The contrary decision in *Cuyahoga Metro. Housing Auth.* v. *Harmody*, 474 F.2d 1102 (6th Cir. 1973), is supported by neither reason nor authority.

[147] See *Philadelphia Anti-poverty Action Comm.* v. *Rizzo*, 502 F.2d 306 (3d Cir. 1974), *cert. denied*, 419 U.S. 1108 (1975).

[148] It is submitted that the contrary decision in *Named Individual Members of the San Antonio Conservation Soc'y* v. *Texas Highway Dep't*, 446 F.2d 1013 (5th Cir. 1971), *cert. denied*, 406 U.S. 933 (1972), is wrong. The majority reasoned that the project became "federal" once approval was sought and obtained from the United States, and hence had to conform to federal standards whether or not the grantee opted to utilize only state funds thereafter. This is inconsistent with the withdrawal principle established in *Rosado* v. *Wyman*, 397 U.S. 397 (1970), and *Wheeler* v. *Barrera*, 417 U.S. 402 (1974). The Fifth Circuit feared "the circumvention of an Act of Congress," *Named Individual Members of the San Antonio Conservation Soc'y* v. *Texas Highway Dep't*, *supra* at 1027, forgetting that the grant-in-aid conditions are relevant only when federal funds are utilized. The dissent correctly reasoned that because federal funds had not been utilized, the court lacked authority to enjoin the completion of the project as a purely state action. *Id.* at 1029.

Congress recently dealt with this conundrum in federal education grant programs. In the case in which an audit disallowance results in a recovery from the grantee, the Commissioner of Education can return 75 percent of those funds to the violator.[149] That "arrangement" is conditioned upon: correction of the violating practice; a planned use of the returned funds which would "achieve the purposes of the program"; and a planned use "for the benefit of the population that was affected by the failure to comply or by the misexpenditures that resulted in the audit exception." The provision, in effect, permits a 25 percent fiscal sanction in cases selected (without the guidance of statutory standards) by the Commissioner. It deals with the fiscal sanction paradox by creating its own puzzle. To the extent that the Commissioner invokes this new power there will be a corresponding disincentive to federal standard compliance. After all, the grantee's gamble has been reduced by 75 percent. It would seem, then, that discriminating use of this penalty-reduction provision is called for. Relatively innocent violations, "close call" infractions, and cases where the remedy can be closely tailored to a group particularly burdened by the grantee infraction would be likely candidates.[150]

The Education Amendments of 1978 [151] enacted a second strategy to deal with the problem of program frustration through fiscal penalties. In the Title I program for educationally deprived children the Federal Government is authorized to seek repayment of funds that have been "misspent" or "misapplied." [152] An identical power is given to state educational agencies in their supervisory role over local educational agencies.[153] In both cases the party subject to the adverse audit determination must repay from local financial resources. The House Education and Labor Committee spoke at length about the importance of this rule:

> "The Committee is concerned that some State policies for the recoupment of misspent funds under this title permit the State

[149] §456 General Education Provisions Act, 20 U.S.C. §1234e.
[150] "Small" claims are dealt with in the audit section. Disallowances not exceeding $50,000 can be compromised in whole or part by the Commissioner of Education. §452(f) General Education Provisions Act, 20 U.S.C. §1234a(f). The Commissioner need only determine that collection "would not be practical or in the public interest," and that the violation has been corrected and will not recur. The public must be notified of the intention to compromise and given an opportunity to submit views.
[151] Pub. L. 95-561, Nov. 1, 1978.
[152] §185(b) Elementary and Secondary Education Act of 1965, 20 U.S.C. §2835(b), as rewritten by §101 Education Amendments of 1978, Pub. L. 95-561, Nov. 1, 1978.
[153] §170(c) *id.*, 20 U.S.C. §2817(c).

88 / *Rights and Remedies Under Federal Grants*

> educational agency to subtract the amount of the misexpended funds from a local educational agency's allocation and do not require that such misexpenditures be repaid from non-Federal sources.
>
> "It is not the Committee's intent that the intended beneficiaries of the program, educationally deprived children, be penalized because a local educational agency may misspend funds under this title in one year and then have the misspent funds subtracted from its allocation in another year. If such a policy were permitted, the program's intended beneficiaries would be penalized twice for the misdeeds of a local educational agency. First, they would receive less Title I services in the year the funds were misspent. Second, they would receive less Title I services in the year the allocation was reduced by the amount of the misexpenditures, unless the misspent funds were repaid from non-Federal sources." [154]

Assuming the misuse of funds involved giving services to ineligible recipients or giving unauthorized services, the committee is quite correct in its fear. Recovery from local funds reduces the impact on individuals affected by the illegality, but it does not make them whole. Nothing in the law requires the recovered funds to be put back into the violator's program, so the initial, single loss remains.[155]

The need for such a provision is particularly clear in a program, like Title I, which is financed entirely by federal funds. It may also be a valuable addition to matching grant programs, though maintenance-of-effort provisions would have to be utilized to prevent a grantee from repaying the debt from the locally budgeted program share.[156]

Another unique feature of federal grants-in-aid which impacts on enforcement potential is that the recipient normally commits itself only to use its best efforts to achieve program goals. Most grant programs do not attempt to bind the grantee to any specific results. Instead, broad goals or aims are established and certain methods and processes thought conducive to the achievement of

---

[154] H. Rep. 1137, note 92, *supra,* at 47–48.

[155] The penalty-reduction provision, §456 General Education Provisions Act, 20 U.S.C. §1234e, applies but only when the "Commissioner has recovered funds." If the SEA collects from an LEA, the provision on its face cannot be invoked. Thus, the LEA would in all cases be advised to refuse repayment, forcing the SEA to turn the matter over to the Commissioner for collection. See §170(e) Elementary and Secondary Education Act of 1965, 20 U.S.C. §2817(e), as rewritten by §101 Education Amendments of 1978, Pub. L. 95-561, Nov. 1, 1978.

[156] Inexplicably, a comparable provision is not found in the General Education Provisions Act. See §452(e) *id.,* 20 U.S.C. §1234a(e).

those goals are mandated.[157] Under this structure the grantee is free from federal interference as long as it complies with the required processes. The end product may be a terrible disappointment to the federal administrator, and during the course of the project he may be aware that poor results are being attained, but absent a violation of grant conditions he lacks the authority to stop the program or project. The federal grantor may, of course, work with the grantee to try to improve performance, it may render unfavorable evaluations,[158] and it may try to find violations to justify the termination of federal funding,[159] but absent such violations it cannot terminate the grant or force modifications. Under these circumstances the only remedy available to the grantor is to deny refunding of the project when its term expires, and to make that possibility known in advance to the grantee as a prod to improvement. It may also take the unsuccessful performance into account in determining whether to fund other applications of the grantee for discretionary funds.[160] If, however, the program is financed by a formula grant and the grantee, despite its unsatisfactory achievements, is entitled to continuation funding, the threat of unfavorable action on future proposals is not viable. The only course available to the grantor is to modify future program requirements by proposing statutory amendments or to improve its regulations to correct the deficiencies. This, in fact, is what principally causes the constant congressional tinkering with grant-in-aid statutes.

In yet another fundamental way the federal grant is so unlike the traditional forms of agreement that the remedies which normally accompany a breach of contract cannot be confidently transposed to the grant agreement. We have seen the many types of conditions which are typically attached to federal grants and their multiple purposes. Unlike contract stipulations which describe in detail the product or service to be delivered, the grant stipulation focuses on certain procedures for project development and administration with the end product described only in broad terms. Also, many grant conditions are not even geared to the goals of the particular grant program, but serve independent national policies. Racial discrimination, for example, may occur within a

[157] See Chapter 2, notes 87–88, *supra*, and accompanying text.
[158] See, e.g., *Gaines v. Martinez*, 353 F. Supp. 780 (N.D. Tex. 1972).
[159] See *id.* at 792–93.
[160] See Chapter 7, notes 105–116, *infra*, and accompanying text.

highly effective project and may not have influenced the project's success, but is not permitted in view of separate national aims. The nature of many federal grant stipulations is such that their breach may not influence program results at all or may only slightly affect those results.

This attenuation between means and ends could produce unseemly and senseless results if the federal enforcement powers were to be indiscriminately applied despite a showing of successful program performance. In many cases proof of grantee illegality would not necessarily mean that federal funds were not being effectively utilized in terms of achieving program goals. A grantee, for instance, might have consistently violated federal merit requirements for personnel decisions, but during the period of noncompliance might also have conducted a highly successful program from the perspective of the end results sought by the grant statute. The same might hold true for purely administrative matters such as financial management systems, record keeping, and reporting. Another example would be a grantee technically in violation of federal citizen participation requirements. While not meeting federal standards, the grantee might have been permitting a meaningful citizen role and the variance between the federal standard and actual performance might have had little effect on program outputs. In instances such as these the fiscal sanction is an inadequate resolution of the problem. It would seem theoretically possible for the grantor to determine that all federal funds expended during the period of noncompliance were illegally spent and present a bill for that amount. Yet those reclaimed funds might well have been put to their intended use despite the procedural or administrative irregularity. Recoupment would seem to be a penalty totally disproportionate to the proved shortcoming. It would also frustrate the broader goals of the grant-in-aid program on behalf of lesser purposes. The means would effectively defeat the ends.

A similar problem arises with respect to prospective enforcement. The grantor might terminate or suspend funding for the period needed to achieve compliance. If correction can be quickly effected, the fund shutoff might not be overly harmful.[161] But if time is needed to remedy the illegality, the termination of federal funding might destroy the project.

[161] See, e.g., *Community Progress, Inc.* v. *Martinez*, 420 F. Supp. 204 (D. Conn. 1976).

The two remedial problems—proportionality between offense and sanction and condition enforcement leading to program frustration—also exist even when it can be demonstrated that the illegal action of the grantee has adversely affected the achievement of the goals of the grant-in-aid. The starkest example is when the grantee has diverted federal funds to impermissible uses. That is clearly the most serious breach a grantee can commit. Yet a considerable portion of the funds may have been properly utilized. Common sense would lead us to assume that the fiscal sanction will be limited to the amount of diverted funds. That, however, is far from certain. While grantor agencies could take the sensible approach, it appears that they could also seek to recoup all federal funds spent during the period the illegal diversion was occurring or shut off all future funding until the diverted amount is replaced by the grantee.[162] The same remedial problems also present themselves when the grantee fails to provide the amount of local share promised or fails to maintain its financial effort.[163]

Several cases in the lower federal courts have involved the types of remedial problems discussed above. Lacking guidance from grant statutes and regulations, the courts have generally adopted ad hoc pragmatic solutions.[164] The relocation plan in an urban renewal project which had utilized federal assistance was found to have violated federal law. The court enjoined the grantee from further displacements of residents of the project area until a complying plan was submitted. The judge rejected the imposition of broader sanctions, stating:

> "The court concludes, however, that it is not necessary for the protection of plaintiffs' interests to now indicate any invalidation of these payments [grants and loans already expended] or to immediately and unconditionally restrain future similar financing of the project—although that power is reserved by the court to the extent hereinafter set forth. To completely restrain federal financing at this point might in the long run injuriously affect

---

[162] See notes 187–214, *infra,* and accompanying text.
[163] See text, *infra,* at pp. 98–103 for further discussion of the problem.
[164] In addition to the cases discussed in the text, see *Bartels* v. *Biernot,* 427 F. Supp. 226 (E.D. Wis. 1977) (upon a showing of compelling need and good faith efforts to comply with the rights of the handicapped, federal urban mass transit funds would be released); *Texas* v. *United States By and Through the Community Servs. Admin.,* 426 F. Supp. 74 (W.D. Tex. 1976) (court refrains from voiding grant for grantor noncompliance with A-95 consultation requirement; grant enjoined for 60 days to give consultation opportunity).

the whole project and all concerned—including plaintiffs themselves." [165]

In another decision involving a past period of noncompliance, which could have led to an order requiring repayment of federal funds spent during that time, the court avoided the issue by accepting a stipulation of the lawyers that the plaintiff was not interested in such a remedy.[166] In the Chicago revenue-sharing controversy the plaintiff's request that Chicago be required to return $135 million in revenue-sharing funds spent during the period the city's police department was violating civil rights requirements was rejected by the court on the ground that the government had not sought this sanction and had "great discretion in such matters." [167] In a recent case the lower court balked at granting relief which would have threatened the economic viability of a low-rent housing project where the building was constructed and 90 percent occupied.[168]

While the federal courts are to be commended for their common sense approach to the sanction problem, it is ultimately unsatisfactory to permit the evolution of a federal common law of grant remedies. Stripped of the body of contract remedy doctrines, the courts would not be simply applying traditional law to typical cases. The remedial jurisprudence would have to be evolved from the whole cloth of federal grant theory, policy, purpose, and practice. Hard work might solve the problem of the unfamiliarity of the federal bench with this budding field of American law. But the question remains whether Congress and the executive branch should, by inaction, delegate this task to the courts. Determining the range of permissible sanctions for the violation of federal grant conditions would appear more appropriate for congressional than judicial resolution. The effects of sanctions on the functioning of the grant system could be serious. Remedial policy has as legitimate a claim to congressional attention as do grant responsibilities and rights. Should Congress fail to discharge this task, then grantor agencies should fill the breach through their regulatory

---

[165] *Western Addition Community Organ.* v. *Weaver,* 294 F. Supp. 433, 440 (N.D. Cal. 1968), *vacated sub nom., Western Addition Community Organ.* v. *Romney,* 320 F. Supp. 308 (N.D. Cal. 1969).
[166] *North City Area-Wide Council, Inc.* v. *Romney,* 428 F.2d 754, 758 (3d Cir. 1970), *cert. denied,* 406 U.S. 963 (1972).
[167] *United States* v. *City of Chicago,* 411 F. Supp. 218, 246 (N.D. Ill. 1976), *modified,* 549 F.2d 415 (7th Cir. 1977). The court did, however, impound Chicago's future shares of federal allocations until the city brought itself into compliance.
[168] *Stanback* v. *Harris,* 444 F. Supp. 1143, 1147 (D. D.C. 1978).

power. Its daily involvement in grant administration and familiarity with grant compliance issues should imbue the executive branch with sufficient knowledge and experience to evolve a coherent, sensible remedial policy.

More fundamentally, the absence of clear remedial standards works a basic injustice to grantees. Under the present situation a grantee knows only that any violation of any grant condition could produce draconian fiscal consequences. While some grantees are aware that federal agencies generally do not abuse their sanction powers and usually impose severe fiscal sanctions only as a last resort, the threat of stiff financial penalties shifts bargaining power so strongly to the grantor that on any compliance question the federal perspective is likely to prevail, regardless of the merits. Only the rare grantee willing to forgo needed federal funding will be able to withstand that pressure. An adequate grantee bill of rights must include not only a clear description of the limits of grantor remedial power but also fiscal sanctions proportionate to the seriousness of the derelictions.

Voluntary Compliance Efforts

It has been long and widely recognized that the fiscal sanction, the only effective tool generally available to a federal agency to effectuate compliance, by terminating or cutting into the grantee's program budget is paradoxically self-defeating. Quotes from two different sources are representative:

> "[T]he principal sanction presently available to Federal agencies for securing compliance is to cut off the flow of Federal funds. This sanction raises a serious problem because, unless its threatened imposition prompts compliance, it stops worthwhile programs and adversely affects the interests of the innocent private persons whom the Congress intended to benefit through the program of Federal financial assistance." [169]

> "At the outset, it seems appropriate to take note of the importance of this case. It is important because the real parties in interest are not parties to the controversy which gave rise to this litigation. The real parties in interest are the blind, the maimed and crippled, helpless old people, and innocent babies and children who

---

[169] Administrative Conference of the United States, Recommendation No. 71-9, "Enforcement of Standards in Federal Grant-in-Aid Programs," 1 C.F.R. §305.71-9.

are too immature even to realize that their fate is involved in these proceedings." [170]

The basic mission of both grantor and grantee is to carry out the goals of the grant-in-aid statute, whether that be the provision of goods or services to ultimate beneficiaries or the conduct of research, training, or demonstrations. Defunding perforce guarantees frustration of statutory purpose. To promote legality in the *methods* employed to carry out the purpose of the grant, the financial sanction strips the grantee of the *means* of so doing.

One is not surprised to find, therefore, that the primary method employed by the Federal Government to secure grantee compliance is informal pressure. In virtually all noncompliance situations the grantee is given the opportunity to correct the defective aspects of its program before any sanctions are imposed. Most compliance regulations stress negotiation of voluntary compliance as the first step,[171] and it also appears that in practice major cutoffs of federal funds are truly a last resort.[172]

A few examples may serve to clarify these general statements. The Social and Rehabilitation Service [173] regulations implementing the Aid to Families With Dependent Children Program state simply that if a review reveals "serious problems with respect to compliance with any Federal requirement, the State agency is required to correct its practice so that there will be no recurrence of the problem in the future." [174] The regulation further indicates that noncompliance hearings are "generally not called . . . until after reasonable effort to resolve the questions involved by conference and discussion with State officials," [175] and that notification of a hearing does not "foreclose further negotiations with State officials." [176]

---

[170] *Gardner* v. *Alabama*, 385 F.2d 804, 806 (5th Cir. 1967), *cert. denied*, 389 U.S. 1046 (1968) (termination of $100 million in federal welfare funds).

[171] E.g., 45 C.F.R. §1618.5(a), 41 Fed. Reg. 51608 (1976).

[172] See, e.g., *Rosado* v. *Wyman*, 397 U.S. 397, 426 (1970) (Douglas, J., concurring); *King* v. *Smith*, 392 U.S. 309, 326, n. 23 (1968); *Arizona State Dep't of Pub. Welfare* v. *Department of Health, Educ. & Welfare*, 449 F.2d 456, 461 (9th Cir. 1971), *cert. denied*, 405 U.S. 919 (1972); *Gardner* v. *Alabama*, 385 F.2d 804, 808 (5th Cir. 1967), *cert. denied*, 389 U.S. 1046 (1968).

[173] The Social and Rehabilitation Service has been abolished and its functions transferred to the Office of Human Development Services, the Health Care Financing Administration, and the Social Security Administration. 42 Fed. Reg. 13262 (1977). New regulations have been proposed at 43 Fed. Reg. 38319 (1978).

[174] 45 C.F.R. §201.13(b) (1977).

[175] 45 C.F.R. §201.6(c) (1977).

[176] *Ibid.*

Agency Enforcement of Grant Conditions / 95

The grants manual of HEW's Office of Human Development announces that, for any program administered by that office, the recipient will be notified in writing of the nature of any problem "serious enough to cause the granting office to consider termination." [177] Within 30 days, the grantee can respond by "describing the action or the plan designed to correct the deficiency." [178]

An interesting prologue to the enforcement regulations of the Legal Services Corporation provides insight into the reluctance of federal grantors to initiate fiscal sanctions against grantees. It states:

> "The Act specifically mentions only termination of financial support to recipients as a means of general enforcement, but such a severe remedy probably would be unwarranted in most instances. It was necessary therefore to provide other methods of enforcement. . . . To allow maximum latitude for informal resolution of violations, this Part does not specify what kind of remedial action, short of suspension or termination, should be taken when the Corporation finds a violation of the Act. It is anticipated that some initial violations may be due to uncertainty about the proper interpretation of the Act. In such instances, it should be sufficient to notify the recipient that its interpretation of the Act is erroneous. In other cases, the Corporation may instruct the recipient to remedy the matter according to its own procedures. It is expected that the Corporation will take formal action to remedy a violation only after other means have failed." [179]

The pursuit of informal methods of obtaining grantee compliance is a sensible approach adopted by federal agencies as a function of their administrative responsibilities. The practice has received congressional approbation in various statutes which impose conditions on the receipt of federal aid and forbid the imposition of sanctions until efforts to secure voluntary compliance have failed.[180]

Fiscal Sanctions

The ultimate sanction which the United States can visit upon an uncooperative recipient of federal funds is to terminate the

---
[177] 42 Fed. Reg. 21047, 21076 (1977).
[178] *Ibid.*
[179] 41 Fed. Reg. 51608 (1977).
[180] See, e.g., §106(i) Comprehensive Employment and Training Act, 29 U.S.C. §816(i); §602 Civil Rights Act of 1964, 42 U.S.C. §2000d-1. See also §§169(c), 186(c) Elementary and Secondary Education Act of 1965, 20 U.S.C. §§2816(c), 2836(c), as rewritten by §101 Education Amendments of 1978, Pub. L. 95-561, Nov. 1, 1978 ("compliance agreement"; at discretion of grantor).

grant in whole or part. "Termination" is ordinarily defined as the cancellation of federal assistance under a grant at any time prior to the scheduled date of completion.[181] This doom is usually preceded by a "suspension," which is defined as "an action by a Federal grantor agency which temporarily suspends Federal assistance under the grant pending corrective action by the grantee or pending a decision to terminate the grant by the grantor agency."[182] The grantee will be officially informed that it has materially failed to comply with terms of the grant, and that it must stop incurring obligations. During the suspension period the grantee will be allowed, in most cases, to take the action necessary to correct the notified deficiency.

If the program is a continuing one and the noncompliance issue comes to a head toward its anniversary date, the federal grantor can use its refunding power as leverage.[183] It can refuse to award assistance for the new project period or defer action on the grant application pending compliance.

Suspension, termination, and deferral can all have devastating effects on grantee operations. Faced with recalcitrance, however, the government may have little alternative but to impose such sanctions. Yet in a large, multifaceted program if the defect does not substantially vitiate the entire operation, the grantor has discretion to tailor the sanction to the offense. If the violation stems from a subgrantee's action, for example, it is theoretically possible to suspend or terminate the entire funding of the grantee.[184] Such overkill has little to recommend it, particularly when it would close down the operations of other, innocent subrecipients. In such a situation, the grantor has power to target its enforcement to the particular violator by cutting off only its flow of funds.[185] Similarly, when the grantee's violation taints a portion of the program which is separable from the rest, a partial sanction directed to that specific activity would be possible and desirable.

Upon learning of serious grantee derelictions, federal officials may be tempted to shut off the spigot immediately and completely. The temptation may be particularly great if it is anticipated that

[181] See, e.g., OMB Cir. A-102, *supra*, Chapter 1, note 83, at Attachment L, para. 2(c); OMB Cir. A-110, *supra*, Chapter 1, note 83, at Attachment L, para. 2(a).
[182] OMB Cir. A-102, *supra*, Chapter 1, note 83, at Attachment L, para. 2(d). See also OMB Cir. A-110, *supra*, Chapter 1, note 83, at Attachment L, para. 2(b).
[183] See Chapter 7, notes 76–79, and Chapter 12, notes 49–77, *infra*, and accompanying text.
[184] See, e.g., 29 C.F.R. §97.165(a).
[185] See Chapter 9, notes 25–26, *infra*, and accompanying text; Chapter 14, *infra*, at pp. 316–17, 325–27; Chapter 15, *infra*, at p. 342.

recoupment of illegal expenditures will be difficult and there is uncertainty as to when the violation began. If the action contemplated is a stoppage of advances for future expenses, nothing would appear to prevent such a step. When payments are on a reimburseable basis, however, equity may lie with the grantee which has incurred obligations on the reasonable expectation of reimbursement. In this case federal agencies are instructed not to withhold payments "for proper charges" incurred by recipients. The payment obligation of federal grantor agencies reads in full:

> "Unless otherwise required by law, grantor agencies shall not withhold payments for proper charges made by State and local governments at any time during the grant period unless (a) a grantee has failed to comply with the program objectives, grant award conditions, or Federal reporting requirements, or (b) the grantee is indebted to the United States and collection of the indebtedness will not impair accomplishment of the objectives of any grant program sponsored by the United States. Under such conditions, the grantor may, upon reasonable notice, inform the grantee that payments will not be made for obligations incurred after a specified date until the conditions are corrected or the indebtedness to the Federal government is liquidated." [186]

The payment obligation imposed by this regulation seems toothless because the grantor judges whether any charge has been "proper." If an illegality taints all expenditures and the date it began is unclear, the government can assume as early a date as it pleases and consider all subsequent fund obligations to be improper. Further, under the guideline the grantor agency has unilateral power to determine noncompliance, so notify the grantee, and withhold any further payments until corrective action has been taken. Thus, by the simple expedient of imposing a suspension the grantor seems empowered to withhold all payments, whether reimbursements or advances.

Many grantees receive federal funds under several different grant-in-aid programs, and in order to exert extra leverage a grantor may wish to shut off all such payments. Congress has, on occasion, authorized such an enforcement technique.[187] But absent

---

[186] OMB Cir. A-102, *supra*, Chapter 1, note 83, at Attachment J, para. 7. See also OMB Cir. A-110, *supra*, Chapter 1, note 83, at Attachment I, para. 7 (identical standards for grants to nongovernmental entities).

[187] See, e.g., §616(a) Education of the Handicapped Act, 20 U.S.C. §1416(a) (sanctions may be extended to any grant program authorizing aid for education of handicapped children).

98 / *Rights and Remedies Under Federal Grants*

explicit statutory authority this course of action is not permissible. The government would, in effect, be violating its payment obligations under one program for the purpose of discharging its enforcement obligations under another. Each grant program is authorized and established independently of others, with its own set of rights and duties. Thus, noncompliance must be judged on a program-by-program basis.

When a grant recipient is found to have violated its responsibilities, expenditures made by it during the period of noncompliance may be illegal. Its commitment is to spend federal funds only for the specified purposes and in the specified manner; infractions of those commitments might vitiate the use of part or even all of the federal funds. The United States, besides looking toward future compliance, might seek reimbursement for past illegal expenditures.

The extent and manner by which federal agencies may seek refunds for illegal grantee expenditures are unclear, the great majority of grant-in-aid statutes being silent on the question. Because traditional contract principles are inapropos to an understanding of grant rights and responsibilities,[188] one cannot simply assume that grantee breaches give rise to correlative grantor rights, such as the right to recapture improperly expended funds. The source of both liability and remedy must emanate explicitly or implicitly from the grant statutes, regulations duly enacted and consistent with the statute, or provisions in the grant agreement.[189] Although Congress has occasionally provided in express terms for the recovery of federal payments through deductions from subsequent payments or lawsuits,[190] the existence of such authorizations should not be taken as evidence that recovery is precluded in programs lacking them. It is equally probable that Congress was doing no more than making explicit an administrative enforcement right otherwise implicitly held.[191] The correct analysis is that the statutory duty of federal agencies to administer grants-in-aid is necessarily accompanied by the power to enforce grant conditions

---

[188] See generally Chapter 6, *infra*.
[189] See Chapter 9, notes 42–43, *infra*, and accompanying text.
[190] See notes 203–214, *infra*, and accompanying text; Chapter 9, note 42, *infra*, and accompanying text.
[191] See H. Rep. 1137, note 92, *supra*, at 47; cf. *Natural Resources Defense Council, Inc.* v. *Costle*, 564 F.2d 573, 580 (D.C. Cir. 1977) (dictum; federal conditions enforceable by withholding grant payments despite absence of statutory authority); Tomlinson, *supra*, Chapter 1, note 55, at 682 (specific enforcement of federal conditions).

through reasonable means. By regulation, therefore, the grantor can empower itself to recover federal payments illegally expended by the grantee, either by deductions from future payments, withdrawal of advanced funds, or lawsuits when the first two alternatives are not available. The typical audit disallowance, in fact, is a clear example of the exercise of this implicit authority. If the grantor, however, has failed to establish such a right of recapture through provisions in the grant agreement or duly promulgated regulations, it may well have forfeited its ability to impose the sanction in the absence of explicit statutory authority.[192] Because of such failure, no legal basis would exist for the sanction; it would also be unfair to grantees to subject them to unannounced and improvised detriments.

Office of Management and Budget rules authorize federal grantor agencies to recover from future payments the amount of any grantee "indebtedness" to the United States if the collection "will not impair the accomplishment of the objectives of any grant program sponsored by the United States."[193] This directive is fuzzy. Without a definition of what constitutes a debt, one must assume that the grantor can unilaterally conclude that the grantee is indebted based on noncompliance information, calculate the amount of the putative debt, and deduct. The government must further conclude that such deduction will not adversely affect the grantee's project. This is a strange caveat. Unless one is willing to assume that there is considerable "fat" in grant budgets, it is hardly possible to conceive of a budget deduction of any appreciable size which will not materially affect the achievement of the objectives of any federally supported program.

Federal agencies have traditionally considered themselves empowered to draw back from advances or withhold from future allocations any amounts of past illegal expenditures.[194] They have also considered themselves able to notify a grantee of the amount of past illegal expenditures and demand payment.[195] Though there has not been a precise formulation of policy or procedure on the matter, it appears that such grantor action does not authorize the grantee to reduce future program activities because of the budget

---

192 *School Bd.* v. *Department of Health, Educ. & Welfare,* 525 F.2d 900, 908–909 (5th Cir. 1976) (repayment sanction void for lack of express authority).
193 See note 186, *supra,* and accompanying text.
194 See, e.g., 45 C.F.R. §100a.53(b) (Office of Education).
195 See note 186, *supra,* and accompanying text.

deficit caused by the deduction.[196] In this manner a grantee lacking independent sources of revenue can effectively be forced to terminate a project if the grantor is unwilling to revise its scope.

Federal grantor agencies need, of course, the power to recover grant funds in a wide variety of situations. If a grantee has utilized substantial misrepresentations to obtain an award, the grantor must be able to recover all federal funds transferred to the grantee.[197] If inaccurate estimates of grant needs lead to overpayments, the Federal Government must have authority to reclaim the excess.[198] If a grant condition is violated and no effective remedy is available other than a lawsuit to recover federal contributions, the power to sue should exist.[199] It is, however, unacceptable either to define those powers in such broad and ambiguous terms that grantees have no real notice of their potential liability, as is typical of agency regulations, or to fail to define such powers at all, leading to uncertainty on both sides.[200]

In *Gardner v. Alabama*[201] the State of Alabama could not guarantee that subgrantee providers of welfare services would honor the nondiscrimination obligation. It feared a subsequent lawsuit against the state by HEW to recoup federal welfare payments on the ground that these subrecipients had violated the civil rights assurance. The court decided that such a lawsuit would not be brought, not because it was precluded by law or regulation but because the Secretary of HEW had so stipulated to the court.[202]

Some of the newer grant statutes specifically address the question of federal recovery of illegal expenditures. The coastal energy impact program established by Section 308 of the Coastal Zone Management Act, for example, focuses on state expenditures of federal funds for unauthorized purposes.[203] The Secretary of

---

[196] See, e.g., 29 C.F.R. §98.15(b).
[197] See *In re School Bd.*, 475 F.2d 1117 (5th Cir. 1973) (Office of Education voided grant and ordered repayment of all federal funds).
[198] See, e.g., *United States v. Independent School Dist. No. 1*, 209 F.2d 578 (10th Cir. 1954).
[199] See, e.g., *United States v. Brady*, 385 F. Supp. 1347 (S.D. Fla. 1974) (facility partly financed with federal funds transferred to private party before expiration of stipulated 20-year term).
[200] *School Bd. v. Department of Health, Educ. & Welfare*, 525 F.2d 900, 908–909 (5th Cir. 1976) (repayment sanction void for lack of express authority). See also *Poirrier v. St. James Parish Police Jury*, 372 F. Supp. 1021, 1026 (E.D. La. 1974), aff'd per curiam, 531 F.2d 316 (5th Cir. 1976) (court suggests that grantor seek a judicial determination of its powers to enforce a grant condition).
[201] 385 F.2d 804 (5th Cir. 1967), cert. denied, 389 U.S. 1046 (1968).
[202] *Id.* at 815.
[203] §308(b)(6) Coastal Zone Management Act, 16 U.S.C. §1456a(b)(6).

Commerce is directed to review "in a timely manner" state uses of grant dollars in order to determine compliance with the statute's description of eligible activities. If such outlays are unauthorized, the Federal Government is explicitly given a right of recovery. Further, coastal states must give advance assurances that they will be able to return to the United States any amounts illegally expended. The administering agency has by regulation established various methods of recovery, including: modification or termination of a state's Section 308 grant or other grants under the Act; the withholding of future financial assistance under any section of the Act; imposition of the same sanctions in any program administered by the Department of Commerce; and a lawsuit against the state for the recovery of illegally expended funds.[204]

While Section 308 establishes policies and procedures only for that specific grant program, it raises some interesting questions. From its very existence one may infer that in its absence the grantor agency would not have authority to recover illegal expenditures from a grantee. A better reading would be that Congress has made explicit that which would be implicitly authorized under the grantor agency's administrative power.[205]

Second, the focus on recovery of unauthorized expenditures leads to the strong implication that recovery may be sought only for this type of illegality. This would be a sensible policy. Grantee mistakes take many shapes and forms, and not all of these will impact to the same degree on program performance. The most serious deviation would normally be the diversion of federal funds to unauthorized purposes; this would inevitably cause frustration of statutory goals. Other illegalities may impair program effectiveness or violate uniform federal policies, but may not seriously frustrate achievement of the ends of the funded activity. As previously mentioned, the recovery response by the federal grantor will severely debilitate the grantee's ability to perform in the future and probably should be reserved exclusively for the case of unauthorized expenditures. Congress followed this tack in recent amendments to the Housing and Community Development Act. Where reviews and audits uncover illegalities in program operations, tainted funds will be recaptured or deducted from future

[204] 15 C.F.R. §931.97.
[205] See note 191, *supra,* and accompanying text.

grants only if the error was expenditure on illegal activities.[206] In the program for educationally deprived students, Congress had in mind the use of federal funds for ineligible students or services [207] when it imposed a repayment obligation for funds "misspent" or "misapplied." [208] Unfortunately, these words so lack precision that the repayment obligation ends up being coextensive with the audit responsibility which, in turn, has been expanded to cover all types of grantee improprieties.[209]

Third, the requirement of assurances of repayment is curious. It is doubtful whether a state agency or other entity which does not have independent revenue-raising power could provide a meaningful assurance. It certainly could not bind a state legislature to appropriate funds to cover federal recoveries. Nor could it commit a governor to shift funds from the budget of other agencies to cover the deficit. Nor could such an assurance enable a grantee to play with its own authorized budget in violation of state law. At best, the assurance can only mean that the state agency or governor will use its best efforts to cover any deficits by way of new state appropriations.

The new Medical Facilities Construction Program contemplates the situation of a finding of noncompliance which cannot be remedied by grantee corrective action. Typically that would be a past unauthorized expenditure. If that occurs, the Secretary of HEW is directed to withhold future federal grants to the state under the program "until the State concerned repays or arranges for the repayment of Federal funds" expended for noncomplying projects.[210]

The Comprehensive Employment and Training Act is a third statute which addresses the question of recovery of past illegal expenditures. Unfortunately, it shares the same vice of overbreadth and ambiguity that characterizes grant regulations. The Act authorizes the Secretary to withhold from entitlement allocations any amounts expended during past fiscal years in violation

---

[206] See §104(e) Community Development Act of 1977, Pub. L. 95-128, Oct. 12, 1977, amending §104(d) Housing and Community Development Act of 1974, 42 U.S.C. §5304(d); §119(h) id., 42 U.S.C. §5318(h), as added by §110(b) Community Development Act of 1977, Pub. L. 95-128, Oct. 12, 1977.

[207] See H. Rep. 1137, note 92, supra, at 49.

[208] §§170(c), 185(b) Elementary and Secondary Education Act of 1965, 20 U.S.C. §§2817(c), 2835(b), as rewritten by §101 Education Amendments of 1978, Pub. L. 95-561, Nov. 1, 1978.

[209] See §§170(a), 185(a) id., 20 U.S.C. §§2817(a), 2835(a) ("compliance with applicable statutes, regulations, and terms and conditions . . .").

[210] §1612(b) Public Health Service Act, 42 U.S.C. §300p-2(b).

of any of the numerous conditions imposed by the statute, program regulations, or any provision in the grant agreement.[211] As an alternative recovery technique, in cases of fraud or "abuse" the statute authorizes the Secretary of Labor to require the grantee to run the program as planned with its own funds, presumably until it has made up the diverted federal grant.[212] While fraud is a settled legal term, "abuse" is not, and the Act, while providing some examples,[213] does not define the term.

If a grantee has exhausted its federal funds and is not to be the recipient of future outlays, the government is stripped of the fiscal enforcement alternatives previously discussed. A lawsuit seems to be the only remedy for recovering illegal expenditures, assuming the grantee has reachable resources. One might expect this common situation to be explicitly covered by grant statutes and regulations, but surprisingly most do not. The few statutory precedents deal primarily with federal construction funds. Typically the grantee commits itself for a period of years to a specified use of the federally financed facility. Failing such use, the United States is authorized to sue to recover its outlays for the project.[214] Apart from the construction situation, most program regulations do not specify, explicitly or implicitly, the grantor's power to sue to recover the amount of federal funds illegally used from noncontinuing grantees. As we have previously argued, without either statutory or regulatory authority, such damage suits should be precluded.

Specific Performance

At the beginning of this section we demonstrated that under grant theory and Supreme Court decisions direct enforcement of grant conditions by way of mandamus or specific performance is impermissible. The grantee generally cannot be forced to continue to receive federal funds in view of its voluntary participation. The acceptable way to achieve compliance is to stop the flow of federal funds, shifting to the grantee the choice of complying or forfeiting support. Similarly, if a grant has been approved in viola-

---

[211] §106(g) Comprehensive Employment and Training Act of 1973, 29 U.S.C. §816(g).
[212] See text accompanying note 216, *infra*.
[213] §123(g) Comprehensive Employment and Training Act of 1973, 29 U.S.C. §825(g).
[214] See, e.g., §225 Community Mental Health Centers Act, 42 U.S.C. §2689m.

tion of federal standards but no federal funds have yet been transferred, the proper remedy is to enjoin the federal agency from granting or the recipient from receiving payments until the illegality has been removed.[215] It would be improper to require the prospective grantee to accept the grant under a complying program. Even when the grantee has illegally diverted federal funds, it may be constitutionally impermissible to force the grantee to run the program with its own funds until the misspent amounts are covered. A recent congressional precedent supports our theory in this and the previous cases.

In the 1978 revision of the Comprehensive Employment and Training Act, Congress added the following section:

> "The Secretary may withhold funds otherwise payable under this Act in order to recover any amounts expended in any fiscal year in violation of any provision of this Act, any regulation promulgated pursuant to this Act, or any term or condition of assistance under this Act. In the event of any such withholding which results from fraud or abuse, the Secretary may order the prime sponsor to conduct the program as specified in the applicable plan on the basis of funds other than funds under this Act and may enforce such order by appropriate civil action, unless the prime sponsor elects to terminate participation as a grantee under this Act." [216]

As is seen in the last clause in this provision, the grantee retains the voluntary quit option even in its most unappealing circumstances—when the grantee has defrauded the Federal Government or otherwise abused its right to participate in federal funding.

The Education Amendments of 1978 [217] seemingly deal with the specific performance issue by creating a new administrative remedial option for education grants denominated the "cease and desist order." [218] The technique is applicable only to state and local education agency grantees/subgrantees. It is explicitly phrased as an option to grant payment withholding and can be used in the same circumstances—whenever the Commissioner of Education has reason to believe that the recipient is not complying with any applicable requirement of law. The proceeding starts with the issuance by the Commissioner of a complaint stating the charges and containing a notice of hearing before the new Educa-

---

[215] See, e.g., *Lloyd* v. *Regional Transp. Auth.*, 548 F.2d 1277 (7th Cir. 1977).
[216] §106(g) Comprehensive Employment and Training Act of 1973, 29 U.S.C. §816(g).
[217] Pub. L. 95-561, Nov. 1, 1978.
[218] §454 General Education Provisions Act, 20 U.S.C. §1234c.

tion Appeal Board. The respondent then carries the burden of showing cause why a cease and desist order should not issue. If the board finds the existence of a violation, it issues a written report with findings of fact and an order "requiring the State or the local educational agency to cease and desist from the practice, policy, or procedure which resulted in such violation." This order may be enforced, presumably in cases of recalcitrance, by the withholding of grant funds or by referring the matter to the Attorney General "whose duty it shall be to cause appropriate proceeding to be brought for the enforcement of the order."

The technique looks and smells like injunctive relief which corrects the noncomplying practice or act while continuing the program. Yet the new section does not explicitly address the question whether the grantee/subgrantee can respond to such an order by closing down the federal program. Nothing in the section precludes that possibility. While this interpretation would drain the substance from the section, leaving little more than a fancy name for the normal withholding procedure, the technique is not really a different alternative lying between voluntary negotiations and payment stoppage. When the Commissioner opts for a cease and desist order, he does no more than choose not to suspend payments prior to the Due Process hearing. This is permissible without the authority of the new section.[219] In all other respects, the provision adds little to a normal withholding proceeding; only new words and more explicit procedures. Perhaps the section simply serves to clarify that the hearing board has the alternative of issuing a cease and desist order in place of the usual decision that grant payments should be stopped pending compliance.[220] Unfortunately, the legislative report does not clarify the above questions.[221]

Under certain conditions, however, specific performance may be an appropriate remedy. If the grant money has been received and spent, and if the grant requirement continues in force after the completion of the project, the fiscal withholding remedy is no longer available as an enforcement measure. The typical situation is when a facility has been constructed with federal support and conditions attached to the grant require specified uses of the facility after project completion. While a damage suit to recover the

---

[219] See §453 *id.*, 20 U.S.C. §1234b.
[220] Also, §454(e)(2) *id.*, 20 U.S.C. §1234c(e)(2), performs the important function of removing prosecutorial discretion from the Attorney General.
[221] See H. Rep. 1137, note 92, *supra*, at 143.

106 / *Rights and Remedies Under Federal Grants*

federal outlay may be possible,[222] it will ordinarily be an unsatisfactory solution. If the grantee has reachable local resources, the United States may be able to recoup its outlay. Yet the purposes of the original grant-in-aid will have been destroyed.[223] If the noncomplying grantee should be receiving federal support under other programs, it may be possible to effectuate recovery by deductions from these grants,[224] but this enforcement technique will necessarily divert these subsequent outlays from their authorized uses. And in both cases the ultimate beneficiaries suffer.[225]

Congress has occasionally dealt with this particular situation by explicitly authorizing an action for specific performance.[226] The absence of statutory authority, however, should not preclude the remedy. It is no violation of the principle of voluntary participation in grants-in-aid to enforce conditions which persist after the grant funds have been expended. Those conditions attached to the funds received and spent and their voluntary acceptance committed the grantee for the duration of the stipulations. This is distinguishable from the more common situation in which the grantee must be allowed to receive or reject *new* federal funds which carry with them new future obligations. While not analyzing the problem in these terms, a majority of the federal courts have accepted an action for specific performance under these circumstances.[227]

Specific performance of grant conditions may also be obtainable, on occasion, within the term of the project period. It would be natural to assume that at least during the period for which the

[222] See, e.g., §225 Community Mental Health Centers Act, 42 U.S.C. §2689m; *United States* v. *Madison County Bd. of Educ.*, 326 F.2d 237, 241 (5th Cir.), *cert. denied*, 379 U.S. 929 (1964).

[223] See, e.g., *Poirrier* v. *St. James Parish Police Jury*, 372 F. Supp. 1021, 1025 (E.D. La. 1974), *aff'd per curiam*, 531 F.2d 316 (5th Cir. 1976); *United States* v. *County School Bd.*, 221 F. Supp. 93, 102–103 (E.D. Va. 1963).

[224] See, e.g., 15 C.F.R. §931.97.

[225] See *Euresti* v. *Stenner*, 458 F.2d 1115, 1119 (10th Cir. 1972). That is the price which the principles of federalism often exact, see notes 169–170, *supra*, and accompanying text, but it should not be unnecessarily paid.

[226] See, e.g., §1612(c) Public Health Service Act, 42 U.S.C. §300p-2(c).

[227] See *Euresti* v. *Stenner*, 458 F.2d 1115 (10th Cir. 1972); *Bossier Parish School Bd.* v. *Lemon*, 370 F.2d 847 (5th Cir.), *cert. denied*, 388 U.S. 911 (1967); *United States* v. *Sumter County School Dist. No. 2*, 232 F. Supp. 945 (E.D. S.C. 1964); *United States* v. *County School Bd.*, 221 F. Supp. 93 (E.D. Va. 1963). But see *United States* v. *Madison County Bd. of Educ.*, 326 F.2d 237 (5th Cir.), *cert. denied*, 379 U.S. 929 (1964); *United States* v. *Bossier Parish School Bd.*, 336 F.2d 197 (5th Cir. 1964) (per curiam), *cert. denied*, 379 U.S. 1000 (1965). Compare *Poirrier* v. *St. James Parish Police Jury*, 372 F. Supp. 1021, 1026 (E.D. La. 1974), *aff'd per curiam*, 531 F.2d 316 (5th Cir. 1976) (United States has obligation to seek judicial determination of question whether condition specifically enforceable).

grantee has agreed to observe federal requirements the grantor may compel compliance. Yet there are two problems with specific performance during the term of the grant. One is the practical reality that project periods, tied to the yearly appropriations cycle, rarely extend beyond one year. That is too short a time to make the specific performance remedy viable. By the time the noncompliance situation becomes known and judicial enforcement of federal requirements obtained, the project period will have expired or be about to expire. Because the grantee cannot be forced to run the project beyond the agreed period, the specific performance remedy would be futile. The second problem is that grantees have traditionally had the legal ability to terminate the grant at will.[228] Most likely in pursuance of the concepts of "assistance" and "voluntariness" underlying the grant-in-aid, federal regulations have typically permitted the grantee to end the project at any time upon notification to the grantor. The grantee need only write to the grantor specifying the reasons for termination, the effective date, and, if a partial termination is desired, the portion to be terminated.[229] That power, of course, would undercut completely the remedy of specific performance. Current Office of Management and Budget grant administration rules, however, seem now to preclude at will terminations during the project period.[230] When inconsistent agency regulations are brought into line with these OMB directives, the specific performance remedy should be available during project periods and might be a helpful enforcement tool when violations are caught early in a grant term.

---

[228] See *Rubinstein v. Mayor of Baltimore*, 295 F. Supp. 108 (D. Md. 1969) (Public Health Service grant); Mason, "Current Trends in Federal Grant Law—Fiscal Year 1976," 35 Fed. B. J. 163, 167 (1976) ("The grant is assistance, therefore, the grantee may choose unilaterally to stop and merely gives up his right to further funding"); Willcox, "The Function and Nature of Grants," 22 Ad. L. Rev. 125, 129 (1970).

[229] See, e.g., 45 C.F.R. §100a.496(a)(2) (Office of Education); 45 C.F.R. §1424.10(a)(2) (National Institute of Education).

[230] See OMB Cir. A-102, *supra,* Chapter 1, note 83, at Attachment L, para. 5(b): "The grantor agency or grantee may terminate grants in whole, or in part, when both parties agree that the continuation of the project would not produce beneficial results commensurate with the further expenditure of funds. The two parties shall agree on the termination conditions. . . .";

OMB Cir. A-110, *supra,* Chapter 1, note 83, at Attachment L, para. 4(b)(same).

4
Expanding Bases of Judicial Intervention

Standing

Central to this decade's explosive judicial intervention in the field of grants-in-aid is the demise of that once staunch soldier guarding the courthouse doors: standing. The doctrine of standing is a multifaceted judicial creation aimed at shielding the courts from certain types of litigants, primarily those who seek judicial declarations of illegality in order to promote their principles rather than their pocketbooks or persons.[1] *Flast* v. *Cohen*[2] emphasized that standing focuses primarily "on the *party* seeking to get his complaint before a federal court" and only secondarily "on the *issues* he wishes to have adjudicated." Thus, the focus is on the credentials of the plaintiff who seeks to invoke the judicial power. Only those who have such a personal stake in the matter presented as to assure a hard fight on the merits carry such credentials. In a seminal case the Supreme Court required that the following test be met:

> "The party who invokes the power [of judicial review] must be able to show not only that the statute is invalid but that he has sustained or is immediately in danger of sustaining some direct injury as the result of its enforcement, and not merely that he suffers in some indefinite way in common with people generally." [3]

[1] See, generally, Nowak *et al.*, *Constitutional Law* 68–83 (1978); Tribe, *American Constitutional Law* 79–113 (1978).
[2] 392 U.S. 83, 99 (1968) (emphasis in original).
[3] *Frothingham* v. *Mellon*, 262 U.S. 447, 488 (1923).

Two basic policies underlie the standing requirement. One is that judicial power does not extend to the resolution of abstract questions.[4] Courts are open only to mediate real controversies affecting the tangible interests of affected individuals and entities. The second is that courts cannot function effectively without significant input from parties and their counselors. Such input is likely to come only from those who have "alleged such a personal stake in the outcome of the controversy as to assure that concrete adverseness which sharpens the presentation of issues."[5]

It is beyond our scope to do more than outline the standing doctrine and sketch its application in the field of grants-in-aid. We would be remiss, however, in not pointing out that we have encountered rampant conceptual uncertainty in lower federal court opinions. The standing question has been posited in almost half of the cases in which the plaintiff alleges violation of federal grant standards by the grantor, the grantee, or both. While we shall see that certain resolutions of the standing issues have crystallized in the cases, the paths of reasoning leading to those results have been marked by considerable confusion, often bordering on incoherence.[6] The courts have had much difficulty in distinguishing questions of subject matter jurisdiction, reviewability, the validity of claims for relief, and standing.[7] Doctrines evolved for the purposes of determining reviewability of federal agency action under Section 10 of the Administrative Procedure Act have been mechanically and incorrectly transposed to resolve the question whether a cause of action may be implied under a federal statute.[8]

---

[4] See *Schlesinger v. Reservists Comm. to Stop the War*, 418 U.S. 208, 223 (1974).
[5] *Baker v. Carr*, 369 U.S. 186, 204 (1962).
[6] See, e.g., *Aguayo v. Richardson*, 473 F.2d 1090 (2d Cir. 1973), cert. denied, 414 U.S. 1146 (1974); *Johnson v. Morton*, 456 F.2d 68 (5th Cir. 1972); *Pullman, Inc. v. Volpe*, 337 F. Supp. 432 (E.D. Pa. 1971); *New York City Coalition for Community Health v. Lindsay*, 362 F. Supp. 434, 438–39 (S.D. N.Y. 1973).
[7] See, e.g., *South Suburban Safeway Lines, Inc. v. City of Chicago*, 416 F.2d 535 (7th Cir. 1969); *Local 519, Amalgamated Transit Union v. LaCrosse Municipal Transit Util.*, 445 F. Supp. 798, 801, 811 (W.D. Wis. 1978); *School Crossing Guards Ass'n v. Beame*, 438 F. Supp. 1275, 1280 (S.D. N.Y. 1977); *Pullman, Inc. v. Volpe*, 337 F. Supp. 432 (E.D. Pa. 1971).
[8] Numerous courts have applied the "zone of interests" test created for judicial review of federal agency action, see notes 20–25, *infra*, and accompanying text, even though the defendant was not a federal agency. See, e.g., *Gibson & Perin Co. v. City of Cincinnati*, 480 F.2d 936 (6th Cir.), cert. denied, 414 U.S. 1068 (1973); *Window Sys., Inc. v. Manchester Mem. Hosp.*, 424 F. Supp. 331 (D. Conn. 1976); *Comprehensive Group Health Servs. Bd. of Directors v. Temple Univ.*, 363 F. Supp. 1069 (E.D. Pa. 1973); *Corum v. Beth Israel Medical Center*, 359 F. Supp. 909 (S.D. N.Y. 1973); *Mathews v. Massell*, 356 F. Supp. 291 (N.D. Ga. 1973); *West Coast Constr. Co. v. Oceano Sanitary Dist.*, 311 F. Supp. 378 (N.D. Cal. 1970).

Precedents involving federal regulatory legislation have been undiscerningly applied to issues under federal grant legislation.[9] Finally, the courts have been reluctant to resolve the complex standing issues, frequently reaching the merits without deciding whether the threshold standing test was met.[10]

The Old Theories

In the decade beginning in the middle 1950s, people and businesses began to seek redress in the courts for injuries suffered as a result of faulty planning and execution of federally aided urban renewal projects. The initial judicial response to such lawsuits was quick and clean: Persons not parties to a grant agreement did not have standing to challenge compliance with federal grant conditions.

These standing decisions were premised on the theory that grant-in-aid statutes "create merely public rights, enforceable only by the agency charged with their administration. . . ."[11] Support for this proposition was drawn from the structure of the grant statutes and implementing grant agreements. The commitments of grantees pursuant to statutory directives ran to the United States as consideration for the latter's provision of financial aid. The statutes typically gave enforcement power to the United States, and this was interpreted as excluding the possibility of judicial bestowal of remedial power in third parties, absent explicit congressional authorization. The grant, therefore, placed rights and responsibilities in grantor and grantee alone, and the doors of the judiciary were open to mediate disputes only between the two.

Cogent reasons of public policy were advanced to justify this result. The "public good" sought through federally financed projects would be frustrated by the delay and expense of litigation if every objecting outsider could sue.[12] The complexities of major grant-in-aid efforts such as urban renewal counseled against judicial intervention and in favor of leaving the multitude of administrative choices and decisions in the expert hands of the agencies

---

[9] See notes 34–35, *infra*, and accompanying text.
[10] See, e.g., *Knoxville Progressive Christian Coalition* v. *Testerman*, 404 F. Supp. 783 (E.D. Tenn. 1975); *Shaw-Henderson, Inc.* v. *Schneider*, 335 F. Supp. 1203 (W.D. Mich.), *aff'd per curiam*, 453 F.2d 748 (6th Cir. 1971); *Fletcher* v. *Romney*, 323 F. Supp. 189 (S.D. N.Y. 1971).
[11] *Berry* v. *Housing & Home Fin. Agency*, 340 F.2d 939, 940 (2d Cir. 1965).
[12] *Ibid.*

Expanding Bases of Judicial Intervention / 111

charged with implementation.[13] Denying injured third parties access to the federal courts was not seen as depriving them of any remedy. The federal grantor agency would act as their surrogate by monitoring grantee compliance with federal standards, accepting and investigating citizen complaints, and requiring public hearings on project plans.[14]

Even if an outsider's complaint was directed against prejudicial federal agency action, the courts would not intervene. The Administrative Procedure Act offered judicial review of federal agency action which "aggrieved" or "adversely affected" an individual.[15] These words were read, however, as including only those who could show a "legal" wrong.[16] Since the grant statutes created just public rights enforceable only by the grantor agency, and no private rights, it was not possible for an outsider to suffer legally recognizable harm under the statute from the action of grantor or grantee.

Under the fabric of the old standing theory a showing of perceptible, direct, measurable harm from presumably illegal grantor or grantee activity was insufficient to invoke federal court protection. Plaintiffs harmed by grant-sponsored business competition were denied relief, even in the face of statutory provisions aimed at avoiding such uses of federal funds.[17] Violations of relocation requirements geared toward protecting individuals and businesses uprooted by urban renewal could not be remedied at the behest even of displacees,[18] nor did other residents of urban renewal areas have standing to challenge the activities of the parties to the grant.[19]

New Standing Principles

In 1970 two Supreme Court decisions rewrote the law of standing in cases involving claims of right under federal statutes or the

---

[13] See *Johnson* v. *Redevelopment Agency*, 317 F.2d 872, 874 (9th Cir. 1963).
[14] *Ibid.*
[15] 5 U.S.C. §702.
[16] See, e.g., *Harrison-Halsted Community Group, Inc.* v. *Housing & Home Fin. Agency*, 310 F.2d 99, 104 (7th Cir. 1962); *Paducah Junior College* v. *Secretary of Health, Educ. & Welfare*, 255 F. Supp. 147, 150–51 (W.D. Ky. 1966).
[17] See *Berry* v. *Housing & Home Fin. Agency*, 340 F.2d 939 (2d Cir. 1965); *Pittsburgh Hotels Ass'n, Inc.* v. *Urban Redev. Auth.*, 309 F.2d 186 (3d Cir. 1962), cert. denied, 372 U.S. 916 (1963).
[18] See *Johnson* v. *Redevelopment Agency*, 317 F.2d 872 (9th Cir. 1963).
[19] See *Harrison-Halsted Community Group, Inc.* v. *Housing & Home Fin. Agency*, 310 F.2d 99 (7th Cir. 1962); *Green St. Ass'n* v. *Daley*, 373 F.2d 1 (7th Cir. 1967).

112 / *Rights and Remedies Under Federal Grants*

Constitution.[20] The "legal right" concept embodied in earlier precedents [21] was rejected. Standing determinations were henceforth to be based on a dual inquiry: first, whether the plaintiff's allegations in the complaint showed some injury in fact to the plaintiff caused by the defendant's actions which purportedly violated the law; [22] second, whether the interests sought to be protected by the plaintiff were "arguably within the zone of interests" to be protected or regulated by the statutory or constitutional guarantee claimed to have been violated by the defendant's action.[23]

The twin decisions effectively shattered standing as a barrier to the federal courts. Any colorable claim of injury in a complaint would suffice to meet the threshold test. Further, it need only be "arguable" that the law allegedly violated by the defendant swept plaintiff's interests within its protective shield. And later Supreme Court cases eroded any vitality remaining in the standing doctrine. It was soon held that the injury claimed by plaintiff need not be economic; aesthetic, conservational, recreational, spiritual, and other like interests were cognizable and could be protected.[24] Nor need the alleged injury meet any test of substantiality, an "identifiable trifle" being sufficient.[25]

The Supreme Court has also been liberal in promoting suits by associations, institutions, and governments on behalf of their members and constituents. The doctrine of "associational standing" requires only the satisfaction of three simple tests: first, that one or more members of the association would have standing in their own right; second, that the interests sought to be protected are within the organization's goals; third, that the claim presented and the relief sought, such as declaratory or injunctive relief, do not require the presence of individuals in the action.[26] Associations, towns, and other entities have frequently been bestowed associational standing in cases involving federal grants-in-aid.[27]

---

[20] *Association of Data Processing Serv. Organs.* v. *Camp*, 397 U.S. 150 (1970); *Barlow* v. *Collins*, 397 U.S. 159 (1970).
[21] See, e.g., *Tennessee Elec. Power Co.* v. *Tennessee Valley Auth.*, 306 U.S. 118, 137–39 (1939).
[22] *Association of Data Processing Serv. Organs.* v. *Camp*, 397 U.S. 150, 152 (1970).
[23] *Id.* at 153.
[24] See *Sierra Club* v. *Morton*, 405 U.S. 727, 734 (1972).
[25] *United States* v. *Students Challenging Regulatory Agency Procedures*, 412 U.S. 669, 689, n. 14 (1973).
[26] *Hunt* v. *Washington State Apple Advertising Comm'n*, 432 U.S. 333, 342–43 (1977).
[27] See, e.g., *Rental Housing Ass'n, Inc.* v. *Hills*, 548 F.2d 388 (1st Cir. 1977) (association of landlords); *National Ass'n of Neighborhood Mental Health Centers, Inc.* v. *Mathews*, 551 F.2d 321 (D.C. Cir. 1976) (nationwide organization of com-

The Court later injected some tightness into the standing doctrine, though its exact extent is unclear. In *Simon v. Eastern Kentucky Welfare Rights Organization*,[28] the Court stressed that the "case or controversy" requirement of Article III of the Constitution mandated that federal court plaintiffs show: first, a causal link between defendant's allegedly illegal act and their injury; and, second, that they would be likely to benefit from corrective judicial action. Both prerequisites are essential to a case or controversy in the constitutional sense and, hence, mandatory to the invocation of federal judicial power. While these causal links need only be "fairly" proved, "unadorned" and "pure" speculation will not suffice. The liberality of an earlier decision which permitted an "attenuated line of causation"[29] would not be permitted henceforth.

These Supreme Court standing decisions involved a careful reinterpretation of Section 10 of the Administrative Procedure Act which provides for judicial review of federal agency actions at the behest of persons "aggrieved" or "affected" thereby.[30] What standing tests to apply when Section 10 was not available as authority for judicial review remained an open question. In the grant field this issue was primarily posed in cases where the allegedly illegal acts were performed not by the federal grantor but by the grantee. Also, even in cases where federal agency complicity in the illegality might be shown, the plaintiff sometimes opted to sue the grantee alone. In both situations Section 10 is of no assistance because Federal Government action is not in dispute. It was and is possible to read the new standing liberality as being confined to judicial review under Section 10, on the reasonable assumption that the Court's decisions were merely a reinterpretation of congressional

---

munity mental health centers); *City of Milwaukee* v. *Saxbe*, 546 F.2d 693 (7th Cir. 1976) (city enforcing rights of citizens); *Township of Ridley* v. *Blanchette*, 421 F. Supp. 435 (E.D. Pa. 1976) (town representing residents); *NAACP-Santa Rosa-Sonoma City Branch* v. *Hills*, 412 F. Supp. 102 (N.D. Cal. 1976) (association representing minorities and low-income persons); *Knoxville Progressive Christian Coalition* v. *Testerman*, 404 F. Supp. 783 (E.D. Tenn. 1975) (*inter alia*, neighborhood committees); *Jones* v. *Tully*, 378 F. Supp. 286 (E.D. N.Y. 1974), aff'd per curiam, 510 F.2d 961 (2d Cir. 1975) (civic association composed of neighborhood residents); *Local 2677, AFGE* v. *Phillips*, 358 F. Supp. 60 (D. D.C. 1973) (union representing employees). Compare *Hardy* v. *Leonard*, 377 F. Supp. 831 (N.D. Cal. 1974) (no injury to members of organization shown; only an ideological interest).

[28] 426 U.S. 26 (1976). See also *Warth* v. *Seldin*, 422 U.S. 490 (1975).

[29] See *Simon* v. *Eastern Ky. Welfare Rights Organ.*, 426 U.S. 26, 45, n. 25 (1976), discussing *United States* v. *Students Challenging Regulatory Agency Procedures*, 412 U.S. 669 (1973). Cf. *Evans* v. *Lynn*, 537 F.2d 571 (2d Cir. 1975), cert. denied, 429 U.S. 1066 (1977) (injury to plaintiffs insufficiently shown).

[30] 5 U.S.C. §702.

policy under the Administrative Procedure Act. This would leave the old and tough standing doctrine intact in suits against grantees alone, or in determining the standing question as to the grantee when both the federal agency and the grant recipient are joined as defendants.

That, however, has not been the approach of the lower federal courts. From the cases emerge four distinct ways of looking at the problem.

The first is the simplest—either pretend the issue does not exist or miss it in good faith. The standing issue is distinct from the question whether the plaintiff has a valid claim for relief.[31] It precedes the question of the substantive validity of plaintiff's claim on the law and facts. A plaintiff sues a grantee in federal court. No review of federal agency action is sought, putting Administrative Procedure Act review out of the picture. The plaintiff is obliged both to show standing and to state a valid claim for relief (a "cause of action" in the old style), or suffer dismissal. Lacking diversity or a special basis of federal court jurisdiction, the cause of action must be based on federal law to invoke federal question jurisdiction. Standing doctrines do not provide the solution, for we are instructed by the Supreme Court that standing is a preliminary jurisdictional matter which focuses on the plaintiff and not on his claim. Yet numerous courts have simply applied the new standing tests and decisions and have, further, allowed plaintiffs to proceed without ever inquiring whether plaintiffs had a valid cause of action.[32]

In another group of decisions, the courts have recognized the distinction between standing and claims and have explored the substantive validity of plaintiff's cause of action. Because there is rarely an explicit right to sue vested in the plaintiff by the federal grant statute, the question is ordinarily whether a cause of action may be "implied" under the grant legislation and regulations.

---

[31] Professor Lee Albert has cogently challenged the idea that standing and a cause of action are, in many cases, separable, see Albert, "Standing to Challenge Administrative Action: An Inadequate Surrogate for Claim for Relief," 83 Yale L. J. 425 (1974), with, however, little effect on the courts.

[32] See note 8, *supra,* and accompanying text. When the plaintiff sues both the Federal Government and the grantee, the court must pursue two separate inquiries: first, whether plaintiff has standing to seek judicial review of federal agency action; second, whether a valid claim for relief has been stated against the nonfederal defendant. The Seventh Circuit has twice failed to discern the second of the two issues. See *South Suburban Safeway Lines, Inc.* v. *City of Chicago,* 416 F.2d 535 (7th Cir. 1969) (denying standing); *Bradford School Bus Transit, Inc.* v. *Chicago Transit Auth.,* 537 F.2d 943 (7th Cir. 1976), *cert. denied,* 429 U.S. 1066 (1977).

That, however, has ordinarily not been much of a problem. These courts have simply utilized different words to effectuate the liberalized standing concepts.[33] The "zone of interests" becomes the question whether the legal provision relied on by the plaintiff was "intended" to protect his interest. The fact that enforcement power was vested in the grantor agency has not deterred the courts from finding a supplementary private cause of action; the analog in the standing decisions is that explicit congressional authorization for judicial review of federal agency decisions at the behest of state agencies does not preclude judicial review at the request of third parties. The grant program's purposes are seen as being promoted by private actions against grantees in the same way that standing to seek judicial review serves as a deterrent to grantor and grantee illegality.

A third approach, similar to the above, has been to borrow the Supreme Court tests [34] for implying a private cause of action under federal regulatory legislation.[35] The principle of voluntary participation in grant-in-aid legislation fundamentally distinguishes this type of federal activity from mandated regulatory

[33] See, e.g., *Gomez* v. *Florida State Employment Serv.*, 417 F.2d 569 (5th Cir. 1969); *Euresti* v. *Stenner*, 458 F.2d 1115 (10th Cir. 1972); *Mando* v. *Beame*, 398 F. Supp. 569 (S.D. N.Y. 1975). See also *Saine* v. *Hospital Auth.*, 502 F.2d 1033 (5th Cir. 1974); *Organized Migrants in Community Action, Inc.* v. *James Archer Smith Hosp.*, 325 F. Supp. 268 (S.D. Fla. 1971). In the two circuits which have readily accepted the implied cause of action theory, some contrary strains can be found. See *Schreiber* v. *Lugar*, 518 F.2d 1099, 1104–1105, n. 16 (7th Cir. 1975) (dicta: implied private action may not be brought under general revenue-sharing program); *Lopez* v. *Luginbill*, 483 F.2d 486, 489 (10th Cir. 1973), cert. denied, 415 U.S. 927 (1974) (no private cause of action in members of parents' advisory council). We are aware of only one case where a court found standing to secure judicial review of federal action, but, on the same facts, refused to find an implied cause of action against the grantee-defendant. See *Poirrier* v. *St. James Parish Police Jury*, 372 F. Supp. 1021 (E.D. La. 1974), aff'd per curiam, 531 F.2d 316 (5th Cir. 1976). Ordinarily, when suit is jointly brought against the grantor for failure to enforce federal standards and against the grantee for violation of the same standards, once the court finds standing to sue the former it will quickly find an implied cause of action against the latter. See *New York City Coalition for Community Health* v. *Lindsay*, 362 F. Supp. 434 (S.D. N.Y. 1973); *M.M. Crockin Co.* v. *Portsmouth Redev. & Housing Auth.*, 437 F.2d 784 (4th Cir. 1971).

[34] See *Cort* v. *Ash*, 422 U.S. 66 (1975): The four tests are: (1) whether plaintiff is within the class for whose particular benefit the statute was enacted; (2) whether legislative intent supports or denies a private action; (3) whether private suits would further the purpose of the statute; (4) whether the claim is in an area traditionally dealt with by state law and more properly the concern of the states. *Id.* at 78.

[35] See *Cannon* v. *University of Chicago*, 99 S. Ct. 1946 (1979); *Regents of the Univ. of Cal.* v. *Bakke*, 438 U.S. 265, 386–87 (1978) (White, J.); id. at 420, n. 28 (Stevens, J.); *Lloyd* v. *Regional Transp. Auth.*, 548 F.2d 1277 (7th Cir. 1977); *M.B. Guran Co.* v. *City of Akron*, 546 F.2d 201 (6th Cir. 1976); *People's Housing Dev. Corp.* v. *City of Poughkeepsie*, 425 F. Supp. 482 (S.D. N.Y. 1976). But see *Local 519, Amalgamated Transit Union* v. *LaCrosse Municipal Transit Util.*, 445 F. Supp. 798, 811 (W.D. Wis. 1978) ("anomalous" to apply *Cort* test to grant program).

legislation and counsels against unthinking transferrence of doctrines between the two fields.

A fourth method of analysis has been even more troublesome. A few courts have found authority for private actions against grantees in the federal grant agreement,[36] and the Supreme Court seems to have tacitly concurred.[37] The theory is that individual beneficiaries of federal grant programs are third-party beneficiaries of federal grant agreements. As such, they may enforce the stipulations in such agreements against the grantee. This perspective really adds little new to the implied cause of action theory, and, in fact, misfocuses the relevant inquiries. Federal grant agreements are not the primary vehicles under which federal conditions are extended to grantees.[38] The basic grantee obligations are imposed by the grant statute and regulations. They may or may not be repeated in the grant agreement, but they continue in effect. The grant agreement will, of course, fix the details of the project, such as the amount awarded, the parties, the itemized budget, the project period, the methods of payment, the matching ratio (if negotiable), and sometimes a few special obligations. Yet if the grant agreement were totally silent on the question of federal conditions, those imposed by relevant grant statutes and regulations would still govern the grantee.[39]

The third-party beneficiary theory, therefore, dips into what is, as far as grantee obligations are concerned, probably the least relevant document in the package creating the structure of grantee rights and responsibilities. It is mischievous because it apparently presumes that the parties to the agreement have bargained, on behalf of third parties, for certain commitments. That presumption we know to be false. Congress and the administering agency

---

[36] See *Lloyd* v. *Regional Transp. Auth.*, 548 F.2d 1277 (7th Cir. 1977); *Bossier Parish School Bd.* v. *Lemon*, 370 F.2d 847 (5th Cir.), *cert. denied*, 388 U.S. 911 (1967); *Corum* v. *Beth Israel Medical Center*, 359 F. Supp. 909, 912–13, n. 3 (S.D. N.Y. 1973); *Cook* v. *Ochsner Foundation Hosp.*, 319 F. Supp. 603, 605 (E.D. La. 1970). But see *M.B. Guran Co.* v. *City of Akron*, 546 F.2d 201, 203, n. 2 (6th Cir. 1976) (plaintiff only an "incidental beneficiary" of grant agreement); *Boston Pub. Housing Tenants' Policy Council, Inc.* v. *Lynn*, 388 F. Supp. 493, 496 (D. Mass. 1974) (plaintiffs "mere incidental beneficiaries"); *Mattingly* v. *Elias*, 325 F. Supp. 1374, 1382 (E.D. Pa. 1971), *rev'd on other grounds*, 482 F.2d 526 (3d Cir. 1973) ("difficult" and "novel" assumption).

[37] See *Miree* v. *DeKalb County*, 433 U.S. 25 (1977), discussed *infra* at pp. 139–40. See also *Lau* v. *Nichols*, 414 U.S. 563, 571, n. 2 (1974) (Stewart, J., concurring).

[38] See Chapter 3, *supra*, at pp. 53–63.

[39] See *Thorpe* v. *Housing Auth.*, 393 U.S. 268, 279 (1969): "Although the Circular supplements the contract in the sense that it imposes upon the Authority an additional obligation not contained in the contract, that obligation is imposed under HUD's wholly independent rule-making power."

have unilaterally imposed such conditions. Thus, a proper analysis must always end up asking whether the purposes and policies of the particular grant program will be served by allowing private suits—an inquiry which requires an understanding of the total grant program and not merely some words in the grant agreement.

We suspect that, despite the differences in legal theory and words, all of the four approaches discussed above end up utilizing the same factors in the same type of case. Beneath the verbiage we have found the same considerations governing the questions of standing, implied causes of action, and third-party beneficiaries. Does it appear that the plaintiff is within the class of persons protected by the legal provision he asserts was violated? Is he injured and is that injury the type of damage the provision was intended to avoid? Since the lawmaker has typically given no clues as to whether it would approve of private suits (or contrary signals are to be ignored, such as the vesting of enforcement powers in the grantor), what might the lawmaker have done if it had considered the question? What impact would private enforcement have on the grant program? We have also found that the lower federal courts have treated private plaintiffs with the same liberality on the question of implied causes of action as the Supreme Court has treated the question of standing to challenge federal agency action.

Thus, in the case review that follows we shall not attempt further to distinguish between true standing cases and those which more properly involve questions as to the validity of claims for relief. At another time we will perhaps return to the subject.

Grants-in-Aid and Protected Interests

Combining the countless decisions made daily in the administration of over one hundred billion dollars under some eight hundred separate grant-in-aid programs with the new standing tests—some injury to an interest arguably protected by the grant statute or a provision therein—we quickly see the devastating potential for litigation. Millions of individuals are affected by such decisions, and of those a substantial number can arguably lay claim to statutory protection.

We have seen the multiple purposes served by grant statutes and the host of conditions attached to federal funds. The enactment of public welfare legislation involves the conciliation of numerous interests. What normally emerges is a statute stating congressional goals in the broadest of terms (promising something for everyone). With those goals in mind, the program is shaped and conditioned, but the complex of interests served by each of the statutory prescriptions rarely surfaces with any degree of precision. Congress simply does not draft its grant legislation with questions of standing or zones of interest in focus. It is not surprising, therefore, that the liberal standing doctrine and the ambiguity of the grant statutes have, in the hands of the courts, combined virtually to destroy standing as an operational concept in cases involving third-party claims of grant illegality.

In presenting the numerous standing decisions, we shall attempt to impose some order on the cases through the following technique. Imagine two concentric circles. The inner circle is composed of what may be considered the "core" interests—those groups of individuals and entities with primary claims of entitlement under grant programs. The band created by the outer circle contains other groups of people and institutions affected by the grant activity, but whose claim to rights and entitlements is more attenuated and problematic. These interests we will denominate as "fringe." Imagine now a rectangle bisecting both circles. Within this area are claimants to rights under the grant statute which are broader in scope than the particular grant activity. These are the beneficiaries of national policy objectives which cut across program lines and permeate Federal Government activity of whatever nature. These we shall label "special" interests.

Core Interests

The standing of a grantee to challenge federal actions adversely affecting the grant has been conceded without much debate. More than three decades ago the Supreme Court, operating under the conservative standing concepts then in force, permitted a state grantee to challenge in court a federal agency decision; the grantor had imposed a fiscal penalty on the grant for violation of a grant condition.[40] The Court held that the grant statute gave the state a "legal right" to the receipt of funds, and analogized the action of the Federal Government to "private wrongs."

Even if the fiscal action of the Federal Government is more generalized, as when appropriated grant funds are uniformly low-

---

[40] *Oklahoma v. U.S. Civil Serv. Comm'n*, 330 U.S. 127, 134–37 (1947).

ered or shut off under a program, all affected grantees have standing to challenge the legality of the funding disruption. In the series of cases triggered by the 1973 executive impoundments, all affected grantees were held to have standing to challenge the freeze.[41] And over a strong dissent by Judge Friendly, the Second Circuit took the sensible position that a grantee could challenge the legality of a defunding decision. The plaintiff, a community action agency, was more than a mere conduit of federal funds aimed at the disadvantaged. It played an active role in fostering community development and self-help, and was clearly within the scope of interest protected by the Economic Opportunity Act.[42] The United States has not bothered to argue that a grantee does not have standing to collect monies owed to it under a grant agreement,[43] though not long ago it did have the temerity to suggest that grant funds were gratuities which could be withheld at the pleasure of the government.[44]

The lower federal courts have found the standing doctrine more difficult to apply when the plaintiff has been a disappointed applicant for a federal grant rather than a recipient. In the *Hood River* case,[45] decided by the Ninth Circuit, a nonprofit corporation which provided manpower services lost out in the competitive funding of migrant farmworker projects under the Comprehensive Employment and Training Act. The corporation then sued the Department of Labor, claiming that the winning grant was illegal because the recipient was ineligible and its application did not meet the Act's standards. The court denied the losing applicant standing to raise this claim. It reasoned that "the CETA program is aimed at aiding migrant workers, not the organizations which receive the funds"; thus, the plaintiff was not within the zone of interests to be protected by the Act.[46] Lack of familiarity with the

---

[41] E.g., *Local 2816, AFGE* v. *Phillips*, 360 F. Supp. 1092, 1097 (N.D. Ill. 1973); *Community Action Programs Executive Directors Ass'n* v. *Ash*, 365 F. Supp. 1355, 1359 (D. N.J. 1973).

In denying the government's motion to dismiss based, *inter alia*, on a standing argument, Judge Gesell remarked: "It is time this litany was displaced by a modicum of common sense. . . . These cases should move to higher courts for prompt, definitive determination shorn of the confusing inconsequential defenses so typical of Government legalese these days." *National Council of Community Mental Health Centers, Inc.* v. *Weinberger*, 361 F. Supp. 897, 900–901 (D. D.C. 1973).

[42] *Economic Opportunity Comm'n* v. *Weinberger*, 524 F.2d 393, 403–404 (2d Cir. 1975).

[43] See cases cited in Chapter 1, note 16, *supra*.

[44] *Texas* v. *United States*, 537 F.2d 466, 473 (Ct. Cl. 1976).

[45] *Hood River County* v. *United States By & Through the Dep't of Labor*, 532 F.2d 1236 (9th Cir. 1976).

[46] *Id.* at 1238.

120 / *Rights and Remedies Under Federal Grants*

grant-in-aid system probably explains this flawed reasoning. We have shown how the grant is directed primarily at state and local institutions to help *them* assist individuals in need.[47] Because there was no claim that the plaintiff was not eligible for a grant under the Act, the statute itself created in the plaintiff organization an entitlement to fair consideration of its grant applications. Not only was the plaintiff within the zone of interests to be served by the Act, it was at the very core of the zone.

The Ninth Circuit also argued that plaintiff failed to show injury in fact.[48] This position may often have substance. If, for instance, a grant applicant is one of many losers, the voiding of a grant to another does not mean that the released funds will be transferred to the winning plaintiff. The plaintiff has created another opportunity for itself and, to some extent, has increased its possibilities of being funded. But the grant may be rewarded to the original grantee under corrected standards and procedures, or may be awarded to an applicant other than the plaintiff. Favorable judicial action, therefore, may easily result in no relief to the plaintiff in violation of the teachings of the *Simon* case.[49] Looking at it from the prelitigation perspective, plaintiff may also be hard put to demonstrate that if illegality had not occurred in the original grant competition, it would have been awarded the funds or, at least, would have had a considerably better chance at the award.[50] This might be what the Ninth Circuit had in mind.

Simon, however, does not require certainty on either point. The injury to the plaintiff—in our context, denial of a grant—need only be "fairly" traceable to defendant's act—the illegal award of a grant to another. Similarly, whether judicial relief would result in a benefit to plaintiff must only be "likely"—that the plaintiff would receive the grant funds released by the court action. What is important is that both matters can ordinarily be proved, assuming that plaintiff is not tossed out of court on a preliminary standing determination before it has a chance to

---

[47] See Chapter 2, *supra,* at pp. 34–36.
[48] *Hood River County* v. *United States By & Through the Dep't of Labor,* 532 F.2d 1236, 1239 (9th Cir. 1976).
[49] *Simon* v. *Eastern Ky. Welfare Rights Organ.,* 426 U.S. 26 (1976).
[50] Where funding is in the discretion of the grantor agency, the federal agency's pique at having been sued by a rejected applicant may forever bury the applicant's chances. Being illegitimate, however, that factor could not be used in measuring plaintiff's postlitigation possibilities.

utilize discovery.[51] Because grant applications are almost universally ranked on a point basis, it would be no difficult matter to show where the plaintiff's grant application stood in relation to the others. Once shown, the *Simon* tests could then be applied to many cases with some ease. For example, if only five awards were made out of 50 applications and plaintiff's ranked fiftieth, illegality in any of the five awards did not injure plaintiff, nor would judicial action benefit plaintiff.[52] On the other hand, if plaintiff's application was the sixth ranked, both of the *Simon* tests are met.[53] For cases somewhere in the middle, judicial guesses as to probabilities would have to be made. But even in the tough middle cases, testimony of federal administrators could be made available on the issue of the probability of injury and relief.

More difficult *Simon*-type problems occur when federal agency action has precluded eligible applicants from applying for funds. In discretionary grant programs if a lawsuit is necessary to start the grant application process, there will be no way to determine the likelihood of the plaintiff's actually getting a grant. Recall, however, that the injury in fact need not be economic. If we consider the injury in these cases to be to the statutory right to apply for funds (as established in eligibility clauses), we need not concern ourselves with the probability of plaintiff's getting a grant. The injury is not to the receipt of funds but to the *opportunity* to compete for grants.[54] The only standing requirements would be plaintiff's eligibility for funds and interest in applying. This analysis would apply in cases where the grant program has been shut

---

[51] But cf. *Missouri ex rel. Missouri-St. Louis Metro. Airport Auth. v. Coleman*, 427 F. Supp. 1252 (D. D.C.), vacated, 564 F.2d 600 (D.C. Cir. 1977) (discovery of mental processes of decision makers denied). Assuming no exceptional countervailing equities, the plaintiff should be given preliminary injunctive relief to avoid the expenditure or lapse of funds, both of which might moot plaintiff's case before reaching the merits. See *Jacksonville Port Auth. v. Adams*, 556 F.2d 52 (D.C. Cir. 1977). But see *City of Beaver Falls v. Economic Dev. Admin.*, 439 F. Supp. 851, 854 (W.D. Pa. 1977) ("unilateral expectation" of grant; denial of preliminary injunction will, therefore, not cause irreparable harm).

[52] But see *City of Benton Harbor v. Richardson*, 429 F. Supp. 1096 (W.D. Mich. 1977), in which a low-ranking applicant was permitted to inquire into the propriety of a grant to another. The court did not address the standing problem.

[53] The easiest case is a head-on-head competition with one winner and one loser. The loser clearly has standing to challenge the legality of the award. See *Mid-America Regional Council v. Mathews*, 416 F. Supp. 896 (W.D. Mo. 1976); *Missouri ex rel. The Missouri-St. Louis Metro. Airport Auth. v. Coleman*, 427 F. Supp. 1252 (D. D.C. 1976), vacated, 564 F.2d 600 (D.C. Cir. 1977) (by implication). In order to challenge the legality of an award to another, the plaintiff must show, of course, that it is an eligible recipient. See *Wyoming ex rel. Wyoming Agricultural College v. Irvine*, 206 U.S. 278, 284 (1907).

[54] Cf. *Regents of the Univ. of Cal. v. Bakke*, 438 U.S. 265, 280–81, n. 14 (1978) (Powell, J.).

down by impoundment.[55] It also is relevant where the agency has failed to implement the program by approving needed regulations or taking other steps,[56] has improperly allocated grant funds among categories,[57] has failed to implement statutory priorities for grantees,[58] or has excluded certain institutions from consideration for grants in violation of statutory standards.[59]

In formula programs, an "opportunity" analysis is not necessary because once the application process is started eligible applicants are almost sure to receive their entitlements. Economic injury, therefore, flows naturally from illegal disruptions of the funding process.

In cases involving disappointed applicants for federal grants, the plaintiff has clear standing to challenge any abnormality in the funding process directly related to its own proposal, as opposed to the indirect impact of illegal awards to others. In *Clark* v. *Richardson*,[60] for example, plaintiff was allowed to challenge a federal agency's interpretation of the allocation formula in the grant statute. The reading of the statute suggested by the plaintiff would have considerably increased the pot of funds for which plaintiff's category of applicants was competing. The court's reply to the routine standing argument raised by the defendant is instructive:

> "[T]he Act, by creating a legal right on the part of certain cities, counties, and municipalities to apply and obtain grants for their public works projects, created a right to relief in those injured by an invasion of that right. . . . As the legal entity for the people in a certain geographical area, Hudson County as well as its County Executive and Board have an interest that falls within the zone of interests protected by the Act. There is no doubt that the statute was intended to ameliorate the unemployment problems of Hudson County. While Hudson County is seeking to vindicate its own interests as a legal entity, its interest is, to some extent, congruent with the interests of its unemployed residents." [61]

---

[55] See, e.g., *Rocky Ford Housing Auth.* v. *U.S. Dep't of Agriculture*, 427 F. Supp. 118 (D. D.C. 1977); *Community Action Programs Executive Directors Ass'n* v. *Ash*, 365 F. Supp. 1355 (D. N.J. 1973).
[56] See, e.g., *Minnesota Chippewa Tribe* v. *Carlucci*, 358 F. Supp. 973 (D. D.C. 1973).
[57] See *National Ass'n of Neighborhood Health Centers, Inc.* v. *Mathews*, 551 F.2d 321 (D.C. Cir. 1976).
[58] *Ibid.*
[59] See *Michigan Head Start Directors Ass'n* v. *Butz*, 397 F. Supp. 1124 (W.D. Mich. 1975).
[60] 431 F. Supp. 105 (D. N.J. 1977). See also *City of Benton Harbor* v. *Richardson*, 429 F. Supp. 1096 (W.D. Mich. 1977).
[61] *Clark* v. *Richardson*, 431 F. Supp. 105, 114, 116 (D. N.J. 1977).

Similarly, an applicant has standing to challenge the data used to rank its losing proposal.⁶² The broader proposition which emerges from these specific complaints is that a losing applicant for federal funds, or a recipient of formula funds unhappy with the amount, has standing to challenge the legality of the standards and procedures utilized by the grantor agency in evaluating the plaintiff's proposal. In *Apter* v. *Richardson*,⁶³ although the health research grant application was filed by an institution, the employee who prepared the proposal and was to be the project director had standing to challenge the denial of the grant. The Seventh Circuit found that it was "arguable" that "the legislative purpose underlying the [Public Health Service] Act can be fulfilled only by protecting the interest of medical personnel and medical faculties in fair and objective distribution of government grants." ⁶⁴

The ultimate, individual beneficiaries of grant programs have had standing to challenge illegal practices of both grantors and grantees since at least 1970 when the Supreme Court swept to one side the standard argument that enforcement power in the grantor agency should be considered the exclusive remedy.⁶⁵ The Court was "most reluctant to assume Congress has closed the avenue of effective judicial review to those individuals most directly affected by the administration of its program." ⁶⁶ In addition to welfare recipients, the courts have granted standing to individual beneficiaries of numerous grant programs, including: disadvantaged school children benefiting from federal education grants;⁶⁷ minorities and low-income individuals served by the Community Action

---

⁶² See *City of Grand Rapids* v. *Richardson*, 429 F. Supp. 1087 (W.D. Mich. 1977); *Lewis* v. *Richardson*, 428 F. Supp. 1164 (D. Mass. 1977).
⁶³ 510 F.2d 351 (7th Cir. 1975).
⁶⁴ *Id.* at 355.
⁶⁵ See *Rosado* v. *Wyman*, 397 U.S. 397, 420 (1970) (welfare recipients). The Court read *King* v. *Smith*, 392 U.S. 309 (1968), as an implicit holding on point. See also *National Welfare Rights Organ.* v. *Finch*, 429 F.2d 725 (D.C. Cir. 1970).
⁶⁶ *Rosado* v. *Wyman*, 397 U.S. 397, 420 (1970).
⁶⁷ *Lau* v. *Nichols*, 414 U.S. 563 (1974) (by implication).
 The principles announced in the text are less than certain in view of the ambivalence of the Supreme Court in *Regents of the Univ. of Cal.* v. *Bakke*, 438 U.S. 265 (1978), about implying a private cause of action under federal grant standards, at least with respect to civil rights requirements. Although Justices Stewart, Burger, and Rehnquist and the Chief Justice reached the question and affirmed a private cause of action under Title VI, Civil Rights Act of 1964, 438 U.S. at 418-21, Justice White strongly opposed any remedy other than government-initiated noncompliance proceedings, 438 U.S. at 379-87, and Justices Powell, Brennan, Marshall, and Blackmun did not address the question because it had not been litigated below, 438 U.S. at 281-84, 328.

124 / *Rights and Remedies Under Federal Grants*

Program; [68] residents of the service area of a Hill-Burton hospital; [69] public service employees salaried under the Emergency Employment Act; [70] actual [71] and prospective [72] tenants of federally supported public housing; needy residents of a town receiving community development funds; [73] unemployed workers who would benefit from public works projects; [74] and users of federally financed highways.[75]

The problem of proving a causal nexus between defendant's act and plaintiff's injury, which we discussed in the context of applicants for federal grants, also affects individuals who are potential beneficiaries of grant programs. If the plaintiff is suing to get a grant project underway, the question arises whether the plaintiff would be likely to receive benefits if the suit were successful. The lower federal courts have taken a liberal, pragmatic approach to this issue. If the facts alleged show some possibility that plaintiff will reap benefits from the litigation, the courts have been content.[76] Their common sense approach has been vindicated by a recent Supreme Court decision which requires no greater demonstration.[77]

Some federal programs cut such a wide swath that it is impossible to identify any particular group of individuals as the primary beneficiaries. Included in this gender of federal program are transportation projects, community development, and urban renewal. Similarly, federally financed projects may serve a particular population, but may directly and immediately affect other groups. A good example is the site location issue so common in public housing construction. In dealing with standing issues in cases involving this type of program, the courts have tended to focus on the geo-

---

[68] *Community Action Programs Executive Directors Ass'n* v. *Ash*, 365 F. Supp. 1355 (D. N.J. 1973); *Local 2816, AFGE* v. *Phillips*, 360 F. Supp. 1092 (N.D. Ill. 1973); *Local 2677, AFGE* v. *Phillips*, 358 F. Supp. 60 (D. D.C. 1973).

[69] *Carman* v. *Richardson*, 357 F. Supp. 1148 (D. Vt. 1973); *Poirrier* v. *St. James Parish Police Jury*, 372 F. Supp. 1021 (E.D. La. 1974), *aff'd per curiam*, 531 F.2d 316 (5th Cir. 1976).

[70] *Mando* v. *Beame*, 398 F. Supp. 569 (S.D. N.Y. 1975).

[71] *Thompson* v. *Washington*, 497 F.2d 626 (D.C. Cir. 1973).

[72] *Rocky Ford Housing Auth.* v. *U.S. Dep't of Agriculture*, 427 F. Supp. 118 (D. D.C. 1977); *Silva* v. *East Providence Housing Auth.*, 390 F. Supp. 691 (D. R.I. 1975).

[73] *NAACP-Santa Rosa-Sonoma City Branch* v. *Hills*, 412 F. Supp. 102 (N.D. Cal. 1976).

[74] *Lewis* v. *Richardson*, 428 F. Supp. 1164 (D. Mass. 1977).

[75] *Center for Auto Safety* v. *Tiemann*, 414 F. Supp. 215 (D. D.C. 1976).

[76] See, e.g., *Rocky Ford Housing Auth.* v. *U.S. Dep't of Agriculture*, 427 F. Supp. 118, 123–24 (D. D.C. 1977); *NAACP-Santa Rosa-Sonoma City Branch* v. *Hills*, 412 F. Supp. 102, 106 (N.D. Cal. 1976).

[77] See *Village of Arlington Heights* v. *Metropolitan Housing Dev. Corp.*, 429 U.S. 252, 264 (1977).

graphical boundaries of the project in dispute. Individuals, businesses, and organizations actually or potentially affected and physically located in or near the project area have usually been conceded standing to challenge possibly illegal grantee or grantor actions. In short, the "zone of interests" seems to have been translated into physical terms. Plaintiffs with standing have included displaced residents,[78] dismembered businesses,[79] town residents and committees concerned with equal rights,[80] nearby property owners concerned about the impact of public housing on property values and the quality of life,[81] and multiple interests affected by the location of highways [82] and railroads.[83] In such cases, however, physical location within the project area does not provide standing to litigate any and all issues. In *Sansom Committee v. Lynn*,[84] for example, residents and users of a block slated for urban renewal could challenge compliance with citizen participation, public hearing, and environmental standards; they did not, however, have standing to show that the grantor and grantee failed to avoid land speculation, for on this issue the law offered them no special protection. With that caveat, the locational approach is sensible. While such major activities benefit the entire community, county, or state, they have particular capability for harm or good to those within or in close proximity to the project area. The statutory zone of interest has been brought into physical focus through actual selection of project sites. Courts, however, should avoid hair-splitting geographical decisions, such as denying standing to a

---

[78] See, e.g., *Norwalk CORE v. Norwalk Redev. Agency*, 395 F.2d 920 (2d Cir. 1968) (urban renewal); *Talbot v. Romney*, 321 F. Supp. 458 (S.D. N.Y. 1970) (same); *Barnes v. Tarrytown Urban Renewal Agency*, 338 F. Supp. 257 (S.D. N.Y. 1971) (same); *Western Addition Community Organ. v. Weaver*, 294 F. Supp. 433 (N.D. Cal. 1968), *vacated sub nom., Western Addition Community Organ. v. Romney*, 320 F. Supp. 308 (N.D. Cal. 1969) (same); *Powelton Civic Home Owners Ass'n v. Department of Housing & Urban Dev.*, 284 F. Supp. 809 (E.D. Pa. 1968) (same).

[79] See, e.g., *M.M. Crockin Co. v. Portsmouth Redev. & Housing Auth.*, 437 F.2d 784 (4th Cir. 1971).

[80] See, e.g., *Norwalk CORE v. Norwalk Redev. Agency*, 395 F.2d 920 (2d Cir. 1968); *English v. Town of Huntington*, 335 F. Supp. 1369 (E.D. N.Y. 1969); *Jones v. Tully*, 378 F. Supp. 286 (E.D. N.Y. 1974), *aff'd per curiam*, 510 F.2d 961 (2d Cir. 1975) (public housing site selection).

[81] See *Shannon v. U.S. Dep't of Housing & Urban Dev.*, 436 F.2d 809 (3d Cir. 1970).

[82] See *Road Review League v. Boyd*, 270 F. Supp. 650 (S.D. N.Y. 1967) (plaintiffs included a town, wildlife sanctuaries, a residents' civic association, property owners, and a nonprofit corporation concerned with highway locations).

[83] See *Township of Ridley v. Blanchette*, 421 F. Supp. 435 (E.D. Pa. 1976).

[84] 366 F. Supp. 1271 (E.D. Pa. 1973). See also *Gart v. Cole*, 263 F.2d 244 (2d Cir.), *cert. denied*, 359 U.S. 978 (1959), in which landowners and tenants in the vicinity of an urban renewal project had standing to assert a violation of hearing requirements, but could not assert violations of bidding procedures.

126 / *Rights and Remedies Under Federal Grants*

business located across the street from an urban renewal project.[85]

Congress may single out for special attention a particular group of individuals even though a broader population is served by the grant program. A good example is provided by the hospital construction program. Financing by the Federal Government benefits all individuals within the hospital's service area. Congress, however, also focused on the indigent population by requiring Hill-Burton grantees to commit themselves to provide a reasonable volume of free services to the poor.[86] This congressional focus readily enabled the courts to find standing for indigent plaintiffs complaining of violations of that requirement.[87]

Fringe Interests

On the periphery of grant programs one encounters numerous interest groups with a stake in the effective functioning of a program or project. Employees of federal grant-giving agencies draw their daily bread from grant activity, as do staffs of grantee organizations. Thousands of profit or nonprofit companies sell their goods and services to grantees; in fact, such private businesses are often a potent lobbying force on behalf of the establishment, continuation, and funding of grant programs. On the other hand, the grant project might directly compete with private sector businesses. The taxpayer, too, has a stake in the proper expenditure of his contributions. We shall review the standing decisions on each of these groups.

In two of the impoundment cases, employees of both the federal agency being sued and grantee organizations joined as plaintiffs.[88] In each decision the court conceded standing to both groups of employees. Those decisions seem mistaken. While such employees are certainly affected—they were losing their jobs—proof of injury alone is not sufficient under standing doctrine. The affected parties must demonstrate legislative concern for their welfare. Yet Con-

---

[85] See *Gibson & Perin Co.* v. *City of Cincinnati*, 480 F.2d 936 (6th Cir. 1973), *cert. denied*, 414 U.S. 1068 (1973).

[86] The requirement can currently be found at §1604(b)(1)(J), Public Health Service Act, 42 U.S.C. §300o-3(b)(1)(J).

[87] See *Saine* v. *Hospital Auth.*, 502 F.2d 1033 (5th Cir. 1974) (implied cause of action against grantee); *Euresti* v. *Stenner*, 458 F.2d 1115 (10th Cir. 1972) (same); *Corum* v. *Beth Israel Medical Center*, 359 F. Supp. 909 (S.D. N.Y. 1973) (same); *Organized Migrants in Community Action, Inc.* v. *James Archer Smith Hosp.*, 325 F. Supp. 268 (S.D. Fla. 1971) (same); *Cook* v. *Ochsner Foundation Hosp.*, 319 F. Supp. 603 (E.D. La. 1970) (same).

[88] See *Local 2816, AFGE* v. *Phillips*, 360 F. Supp. 1092 (N.D. Ill. 1973); *Local 2677, AFGE* v. *Phillips*, 358 F. Supp. 60 (D. D.C. 1973).

gress does not establish grant programs in order to create employment in federal grantor agencies or in grantee organizations.[89] Staffs are necessary, of course, to implement government programs, but that is a necessary means and not a primary or even secondary goal of the grant-in-aid. *Hines* v. *Cenla Community Action Committee, Inc.*[90] takes the correct position. Plaintiff, discharged as executive director of a community action agency, tried to base a federal court suit on the grant statute which funded her employer. The Fifth Circuit rejected the attempt, holding that poverty-stricken individuals and families were the intended beneficiaries of the Economic Opportunity Act and not employees of grantee organizations. Similarly, because rights are held by the grantee and not its staff, an employee was denied standing to challenge the grantee organization's decision to terminate the grant.[91]

Two exceptions to the above rules would be appropriate. Because federal grant law generally requires that recipients observe merit standards in dealing with personnel, employees clearly fall within the zone of interests protected by that particular law.[92] Second, federal law might place special responsibilities in particular officials. In *Johnson* v. *Morton*[93] a State Liaison Official, appointed pursuant to outdoor recreation program regulations, sued to stop a federal-state project allegedly outside of state plan priorities. Federal law invested the SLO with authority to recommend projects to the grantor agency and to withdraw projects previously submitted, both powers serving the purpose of assuring that federal funds were channeled only into high-priority state projects. The court erroneously denied standing, being unable to find sufficient injury. It overlooked the fact that federal funds were being diverted to improper uses—an obvious injury—and that the SLO had special responsibilities to insure compliance with the statutorily required state priority plan.

A logical corollary of the proposition that grant programs do not serve the interests of individual grant officials and employees is that businesses hired by grantees cannot claim to fall under the

---

[89] The exception is when Congress directs that members of the beneficiary population be hired as employees of grantee organizations. See Chapter 2, note 109, *supra*, and accompanying text. These employees, as members of the group benefited by the program, would have standing.
[90] 474 F.2d 1052 (5th Cir. 1973).
[91] See *Rubinstein* v. *Mayor of Baltimore*, 295 F. Supp. 108 (D. Md. 1969).
[92] See *Norton* v. *Blaylock*, 285 F. Supp. 659 (W.D. Ark. 1968), *aff'd*, 409 F.2d 772 (8th Cir. 1969) (by implication).
[93] 456 F.2d 68 (5th Cir. 1972).

protective umbrella of a grant statute. This is the holding of a federal district court decision.[94] As part of its community development program, a city hired plaintiff organization to plan and develop a housing rehabilitation program. The city cancelled the contract and plaintiff sued, claiming violation of the nondiscrimination provision of the Housing and Community Development Act.[95] The court dismissed the action. While recognizing that organizations like plaintiff provide valuable services in implementing grant legislation, the court did not consider them "principal" beneficiaries. It declared:

> "To hold otherwise would bring within [the nondiscrimination provision's] ambit all manner of persons and organizations, such as landowners, concessionaires, and others, who may stand to gain or lose from urban housing development, but who are simply not the intended beneficiaries of the Act." [96]

On the other hand, a lower federal court permitted a contractor of the grantee to sue on the basis that the grantee was illegally expending grant funds.[97] The grantee was using federal funds to pay for its defense of a contract action brought by the plaintiff in the state courts. The court was impressed with the argument that the illegal diversion of funds would leave the grantee with less funds to satisfy its obligations to the plaintiff contractor, and failed to recognize that grant programs do not exist to serve the interests of such contractors.

Losing bidders for contracts with grantee organizations have frequently brought federal actions on the basis that the grantee failed to comply with federal standards for competitive bidding. Suit has been brought against the grantee in an attempt to void the winning bid and have the contract awarded to plaintiff,[98] or against the Federal Government seeking a cutoff of federal funds for violation of federal conditions,[99] or against both.[100] With just

---

[94] *People's Housing Dev. Corp.* v. *City of Poughkeepsie*, 425 F. Supp. 482 (S.D. N.Y. 1976).
[95] §109 Housing and Community Development Act of 1974, 42 U.S.C. §5309.
[96] *People's Housing Dev. Corp.* v. *City of Poughkeepsie*, 425 F. Supp. 482, 491 (S.D. N.Y. 1976).
[97] *West Coast Constr. Co.* v. *Oceano Sanitary Dist.*, 311 F. Supp. 378 (N.D. Cal. 1970).
[98] See *M.B. Guran Co., Inc.* v. *City of Akron*, 546 F.2d 201 (6th Cir. 1976); *Window Sys., Inc.* v. *Manchester Mem. Hosp.*, 424 F. Supp. 331 (D. Conn. 1976).
[99] See *Pullman, Inc.* v. *Volpe*, 337 F. Supp. 432 (E.D. Pa. 1971); *Shaw-Henderson, Inc.* v. *Schneider*, 335 F. Supp. 1203 (W.D. Mich. 1971).
[100] See *Clement Martin, Inc.* v. *Dick Corp.*, 97 F. Supp. 961 (W.D. Pa. 1951).

one exception,[101] these suits have foundered on the standing doctrine. Federal regulations imposing competitive bidding standards and procedures have been consistently read as protecting the public and the Federal Government, and not unsuccessful bidders.

Federal aid may, on occasion, be used to sponsor activities which compete directly with private businesses. When the potential for such conflict exists, Congress will ordinarily require that a determination be made prior to the grant that private businesses will not be adversely affected by the federally financed activity.[102] These protective clauses can be viewed from two different perspectives. The natural impulse is to assume that their purpose is to protect private businesses from "unfair" (i.e., government-sponsored) competition. Another perspective, however, focuses on the undemonstrated need for federal financing when the private sector is adequately servicing the public interest. From this viewpoint, the clauses protect not the private sector but rather the public interest in optimum use of public funds.

These different readings have led, not surprisingly, to a sharp division in the cases when private businesses have sued grantors and grantees. The earlier cases regularly denied standing, while the later decisions have permitted such plaintiffs to sue.

A series of early Supreme Court decisions established the proposition that when a company does not have a state law right to be free from competition, the threat of financial loss as a result of competition does not give standing to challenge the validity of a federal loan or grant which made the competition feasible.[103] These precedents were used in two urban renewal cases in which hotel owners complained of federally financed competition.[104] It is important to note that standing was denied in both cases even though the Housing Act required that a competent and independent analysis be made of the community's need for transient housing before urban renewal funds could be used for hotels and motels, and plaintiffs alleged that such study was lacking. A 1968

---

[101] See *Grumman Ecosystems Corp.* v. *Gainesville-Alachua County Regional Elec., Water & Sewer Facilities Bd.*, 402 F. Supp. 582 (N.D. Fla. 1975). On the standing question *Grumman* is distinguishable because the Environmental Protection Agency violated its own appeals procedures and also those of the Comptroller-General.

[102] See Chapter 2, note 136, *supra*, and accompanying text.

[103] See *Alabama Power Co.* v. *Ickes*, 302 U.S. 464 (1938); *Duke Power Co.* v. *Greenwood*, 302 U.S. 485 (1938); *Tennessee Elec. Power Co.* v. *T.V.A.*, 306 U.S. 118 (1939).

[104] See *Berry* v. *Housing & Home Fin. Agency*, 340 F.2d 939 (2d Cir. 1965); *Pittsburgh Hotels Ass'n* v. *Urban Redev. Auth.*, 309 F.2d 186 (3d Cir. 1962) (alternative holding).

Supreme Court decision did permit a private utility to challenge the Tennessee Valley Authority's expansion of its service into an area served by plaintiff.[105] The Court found that the particular statutory provision invoked reflected a legislative purpose to protect a competitive interest. But even following this 1968 decision, lower federal courts continued to deny standing to hurt businesses [106] and professions,[107] even when grants were carefully regulated to avoid duplication of services.

The latest cases, however, have been strongly influenced by *Data Processing* [108] and have readily found competitors to be within the zone of interests of protective clauses.[109] Even in the absence of a specific noncompetition clause, the First Circuit held that private landlords suffering from the loss of tenants to federal housing had standing to challenge the legality of the federal aid.[110] Section 8 of the Housing Act of 1937 [111] was read as placing first priority on the use of existing housing stock; thus, landlords should be protected from unnecessary new construction.

The last "fringe" group we shall consider is composed of those who foot the bill—federal and local taxpayers. The tough federal rules denying standing to contributors to the U.S. treasury have not slackened. In 1923, the *Frothingham* [112] decision found the interest of a federal taxpayer too "minute and indeterminable" and too "remote, fluctuating and uncertain" for purposes of the injury predicate of a constitutional case and controversy. *Flast* v. *Cohen* [113] in 1968 showed some tolerance of federal taxpayer suits challenging spending programs, but required a showing of specific constitutional limits on the spending power. *Flast* is a narrow exception which appears to be limited to church-state challenges

---

[105] See *Hardin* v. *Kentucky Util. Co.*, 390 U.S. 1 (1968).
[106] See *South Suburban Safeway Lines, Inc.* v. *City of Chicago*, 416 F.2d 535 (7th Cir. 1969).
[107] See *Troutman* v. *Shriver*, 417 F.2d 171 (5th Cir. 1969), *cert. denied*, 397 U.S. 923 (1970).
[108] *Association of Data Processing Serv. Organs.* v. *Camp*, 397 U.S. 150 (1970).
[109] See *Bradford School Bus Transit, Inc.* v. *Chicago Transit Auth.*, 537 F.2d 943 (7th Cir. 1976), *cert. denied*, 429 U.S. 1066 (1977); *Corrugated Container Corp.* v. *Community Servs. Admin.*, 429 F. Supp. 142 (W.D. Va. 1977); *Afton Alps, Inc.* v. *United States*, 392 F. Supp. 543 (D. Minn. 1974). Compare *Clinton Community Hosp. Corp.* v. *Southern Md. Medical Center*, 374 F. Supp. 450 (D. Md. 1974), *aff'd*, 510 F.2d 1037 (4th Cir.), *cert. denied*, 422 U.S. 1048 (1975) (corporation suffering competitive injury cannot advance environmental concerns).
[110] *Rental Housing Ass'n* v. *Hills*, 548 F.2d 388 (1st Cir. 1977).
[111] 42 U.S.C. §1437f.
[112] *Frothingham* v. *Mellon*, 262 U.S. 447 (1923).
[113] 392 U.S. 83 (1968).

to federal grant programs.[114] The lower federal courts have not been inclined to depart from these high court rulings; federal taxpayer standing has been regularly denied in third-party challenges to the legality of grant programs.[115]

Frothingham expressly left intact the rule that municipal taxpayers do have a sufficiently direct and determinable stake in the expenditure of municipal funds to have standing to challenge their use.[116] It is possible to develop an argument, based on municipal taxpayer standing, which would permit taxpayer challenges to the use of federal funds received by state and local governments. One could trace the effect which illegal expenditures of federal receipts would have on state or municipal tax liability. The simplest construct would be that: (1) illegal uses of federal funds by state and local governments could lead to forfeiture of those funds; (2) such illegal expenditures must be reimbursed from state and local budgets; (3) the deficit would have to be levied on state and local taxpayers; (4) therefore, the plaintiff has a sufficient stake as a state or local taxpayer to stop the illegality before the adverse consequences occur or get worse. Considering the facts that more than one quarter of state and local budgets is composed of federal receipts and that local tax rates are, indeed, dependent on actual and estimated receipts of federal funds, the argument is far from tenuous.[117] The problem, of course, is that it proves too much. By switching hats from federal to local taxpayer, the plaintiff has effectively sidestepped the federal taxpayer standing rule *in virtually all cases*. The fiscal sanction is always available to the Federal Government to enforce compliance with federal conditions, and such sanctions would always be felt to some extent by state and local taxpayers. Similarly, it might be argued that once federal grants are awarded to state and local governments they become the property of the grantees and, therefore, the relevant standing rule is that of the municipal and not the federal taxpayer.

Both arguments are squelched by the additional requirement under federal standing doctrine that plaintiff demonstrate that he is within the zone of interests protected or regulated by the

---

[114] See Nowak *et al.*, *Constitutional Law* 71–72 (1978).
[115] See, e.g., *South Suburban Safeway Lines, Inc.* v. *City of Chicago*, 416 F.2d 535 (7th Cir. 1969); *Troutman* v. *Shriver*, 417 F.2d 171 (5th Cir. 1969); *cert. denied*, 397 U.S. 923 (1970); *Clement Martin, Inc.* v. *Dick Corp.*, 97 F. Supp. 961 (W.D. Pa. 1951).
[116] *Frothingham* v. *Mellon*, 262 U.S. 447, 486 (1923).
[117] The argument was rejected in *Knoxville Progressive Christian Coalition* v. *Testerman*, 404 F. Supp. 783, 788 (E.D. Tenn. 1975), as "too tenuous" and accepted, without discussion, in *Shepheard* v. *Godwin*, 280 F. Supp. 869, 873 (E.D. Va. 1968).

relevant statutory or constitutional provision.[118] Yet one type of federal grant—general revenue sharing—is precisely aimed at providing fiscal relief to state and local taxpayers. Illegal expenditures of revenue-sharing funds not only could increase an individual's state and local tax liability but would thereby frustrate the very purpose of the federal program. Thus, in this situation it would appear that municipal taxpayer standing should suffice to permit taxpayer suits challenging the legality of revenue sharing implementation by state and local governments.[119]

Special Interests

In a prior section we described various standard federal grant conditions deriving from national policies which cut across the categorical lines of grant-in-aid programs.[120] These grant conditions are frequently imposed on all grant-in-aid programs by appropriate language in the statute which fixes the policy and standards. A particular standard may not be imposed in across-the-board fashion, but may appear in so many grant statutes that one can sense a uniform national policy emerging on an *ad hoc* basis.

The rights and responsibilities fixed by such standards are less directly related to the achievement of a particular grant objective than programmatic and administrative grant conditions. They serve interests to some extent independent of the thrust of the grant activity. For example, a crash hospital construction program could meet its primary goal of providing health services very effectively without accounting for its impact on the physical environment. Yet such federally sponsored projects must meet federal environmental standards because of an overriding national policy to protect the environment. We could, of course, define the object of our crash program as "building needed hospitals without harming the environment," but that obfuscates rather than helps analysis. The "zone of interests" standing test forces us to keep our differing zones separate.

[118] But see *Shepheard* v. *Godwin*, 280 F. Supp. 869 (E.D. Va. 1968). Taxpayers were allowed to enforce the nonsupplantation requirement of a federal education program, even though the purpose of the provision was not aimed at protecting taxpayers. The court failed to discuss the standing problem.

[119] In *Schreiber* v. *Lugar*, 518 F.2d 1099 (7th Cir. 1975), the court did not decide the standing question because it dismissed a citizen suit challenging the use of revenue-sharing funds on the ground of subject matter jurisdiction. It did, however, indicate doubts whether a citizen could allege a cause of action. *Id.* at 1104–1105, n. 16. *Mathews* v. *Massell*, 356 F. Supp. 291 (N.D. Ga. 1973), conceded standing.

[120] See Chapter 2, notes 122–136, *supra*, and accompanying text.

This section will consider the standing decisions on several of such "special" interests. We must keep in mind that because the plaintiffs asserting such interests are neither "core" nor "fringe" individuals within the framework of the particular grant program does not preclude standing under the ambit of the national policy being asserted. Similarly, the injury suffered may be only indirectly related to the expenditure of grant dollars.

The hundreds of federal grant programs superimposed on an even greater body of state and local programs have caused severe planning and coordination problems. Consultation has been the primary technique employed by the Federal Government to deal with the coordination crisis. The Intergovernmental Cooperation Act of 1968, for example, requires that:

> "All viewpoints—national, regional, State, and local—shall, to the extent possible, be fully considered and taken into account in planning Federal or federally assisted development programs and projects. State and local government objectives, together with the objectives of regional organizations shall be considered and evaluated...." [121]

This section has been implemented by a notification and clearinghouse system ("A-95") established by the Office of Management and Budget.[122] In essence, the A-95 system requires that applicants for grants under a great number of federal programs [123] provide designated state, local, and regional planning organizations with the details of their grant proposals. The federal grantor must give the notified organizations an opportunity to comment on the consistency of the proposals with state, regional, and local plans. In addition to A-95, numerous grant statutes have imposed consultation requirements to insure that the funded program or project is not contrary to state and local policies, plans, and programs.[124]

Such consultation standards promote the effectiveness of the particular grant program to which they attach. Grant activities which collide with state and local policies, plans, and programs are not likely to have easy sledding. Yet they go beyond that goal. Consultation insures that state and local officials know where

---

[121] §401(b) Intergovernmental Cooperation Act of 1968, 42 U.S.C. §4231(b).
[122] See 41 Fed. Reg. 2052–65 (1976). See generally Office of Management and Budget, *A-95: What It Is. How It Works* (1976).
[123] The programs subjected to A-95 are listed in Appendix I, Office of Management and Budget, *Catalog of Federal Domestic Assistance* (1978 update).
[124] See, e.g., §242 Community Services Act of 1974, 42 U.S.C. §2834 (gubernatorial veto power over community action grants).

134 / *Rights and Remedies Under Federal Grants*

federal dollars are headed, which better enables them to channel local resources intelligently. Similarly, it alerts federal officials to areas where state and local resources will be dedicated, thus making federal program development more rational. Consultation is also an essential element of the "cooperative" grant-in-aid. A system based on the voluntary cession of authority to the Federal Government is not likely to prosper if grant programs are launched without any participation of state and local officials. The right to be consulted assists in promoting the spirit of friendly partnership which, in turn, is basic to the success of all grants-in-aid.

If the consultation requirement is violated in a particular grant program, the above considerations strongly support standing in those officials vested by federal law with the right to be notified. Their interests are, indeed, the very interests to be protected. Such officials may, but need not, show any physical or measurable injury caused by the lack of consultation, such as the inconsistency of the federally sponsored project with a state or local plan. Violation of the cooperation requirement injures the intangible but important interest of coordination. A requirement that injury to local plans and projects be demonstrated would, effectively, make consultation rights unenforceable in many cases. The notification requirement could be ignored by the federal grantor or grantee in any case in which conflict was unlikely, and a later federal court standing decision would vindicate that guess.

The Fifth Circuit has taken a contrary position. In *Troutman* v. *Shriver* [125] a bar association sued the Office of Economic Opportunity for allegedly establishing a legal services program without complying with the statutory requirement that state and local bar associations be consulted beforehand.[126] The court dismissed for lack of standing, stating that "where, as here, the purpose of the statutory provision is simply to benefit the public at large by easing the task of administration of the statute, no right, nor legal standing, is conferred." [127] The court was also influenced by the fact that bar associations had only the authority to make suggestions and not a veto power. That myopic view of the goals of consultation is wrong, as previously explained. It also transports the notification obligation into the moral realm, for if those who

---

[125] 417 F.2d 171 (5th Cir. 1969).
[126] The present consultation requirement is found at §1007(f) Community Services Act of 1974, 42 U.S.C. §2996f.
[127] *Troutman* v. *Shriver*, 417 F.2d 171, 176 (5th Cir. 1969), *cert. denied*, 397 U.S. 923 (1970).

hold the consultation right can't enforce it, who can? Fortunately, a recent Ninth Circuit decision takes a view contrary to *Troutman* and holds that state and local agencies entitled to A-95 notification have standing to enforce the consultation requirement, although by the time the question was decided the grant had been given and expended, thus mooting the A-95 issue.[128]

Citizen participation requirements have been inserted into numerous grant programs which have a direct and important impact on community life.[129] These requirements present standing issues similar to those we discussed in the preceding paragraphs. Citizen participation in the planning and administration of grant programs is usually justified as a program effectiveness tool. The input of those who will be directly affected by the program is seen as an important informational source, leading to more relevant, better designed, and more readily accepted programs. Yet the citizen participation component of federal grants also serves the independent and broader purpose of participation—the abstract good of letting people who will be affected voice their feelings. It would, in some cases, be possible to demonstrate that citizen participation has hindered rather than helped a particular program.[130] But injury can still be shown if such participation, statutorily required, is eliminated or curtailed. The injury would be, of course, to the intangible but important right to be heard.

Numerous cases have been brought challenging grantee compliance with citizen participation requirements, and the standing issues have been fully explored. If an action is brought during the development stage of a grant program on the ground that citizens have not been involved in its planning, as required by federal law, any potential program beneficiary would be a proper plaintiff. Residents of a planned model cities area sued to enjoin federal funding of the project on the ground that the city-grantee had failed to honor the requirement of widespread citizen participation. The court easily found standing, stating:

> "The only effective means which plaintiffs have to assure citizen participation is to challenge the efficacy of the plan which, as they allege, excluded them. They are within the zone of interests protected by the Model Cities Act, and as residents of the area are

---

[128] *Hood River County* v. *United States By and Through the Dep't of Labor*, 532 F.2d 1236 (9th Cir. 1976).
[129] See Chapter 2, notes 105–109, *supra*, and accompanying text.
[130] See *Gaines* v. *Martinez*, 353 F. Supp. 780 (N.D. Tex. 1972).

within the class of persons which the statutory provision was designed to protect." [131]

The court recognized the stake of each area resident in having a voice in the program, either individually or through representatives, and rejected the argument that economic injury or specific individual rights be shown. If the grantee has established a citizen board or council, and the claim is that insufficient participation is being conceded, the board may sue in its own right or as an associational representative of community interests.[132] Presumably, any member of a citizen council would have standing to challenge the grantee's compliance with federal participation standards. Each would be an official spokesman for the public right to participation, whether or not the spokesman represents the interests of the program's beneficiary population. Thus, a wealthy businessman on a poverty program's advisory council would act as the surrogate of the business community's right to be heard, assuming, of course, that federal standards established such sectorial representation. The grantee cannot choke off citizen participation suits by disbanding previously recognized boards and councils. The courts have considered that disenfranchised boards continue to have a sufficient stake and continue to be within the zone of interests protected by citizen participation requirements.[133]

Standing to sue, or an implied cause of action, has easily been found when the plaintiff claims injury from violation of nondiscrimination requirements. Sex discrimination forbidden to recipients of federal educational funds subjects grantee schools, both public and private, to private actions implied under the nondiscrimination grant standard.[133a] Handicapped individuals can sue recipients of federal grants on a cause of action implied under Section 504 of the Rehabilitation Act of 1973 [134] which prohibits discrimination against the handicapped in all federal grant pro-

---

[131] *Coalition for United Community Action* v. *Romney,* 316 F. Supp. 742, 748 (N.D. Ill. 1970).

[132] See *Comprehensive Group Health Servs. Bd. of Directors* v. *Temple Univ.,* 363 F. Supp. 1069, 1092–93 (E.D. Pa. 1973); *North City Area-Wide Council, Inc.* v. *Romney,* 428 F.2d 754, 757 (3d Cir. 1970), *cert. denied,* 406 U.S. 963 (1972) (standing assumed without discussion). But see *Lopez* v. *Luginbill,* 483 F.2d 486 (10th Cir. 1973), *cert. denied,* 415 U.S. 927 (1974) (refusing to find implied cause of action in members of parents' advisory council).

[133] See *New York City Coalition for Community Health* v. *Lindsay,* 362 F. Supp. 434 (S.D. N.Y. 1973); *Lower East Side Neighborhood Health Council-South, Inc.* v. *Richardson,* 346 F. Supp. 386 (S.D. N.Y. 1972).

[133a] *Cannon* v. *University of Chicago,* 99 S. Ct. 1946 (1979).

[134] 29 U.S.C. §794.

grams.¹³⁵ Those suffering racial or ethnic discrimination have, under Title VI of the Civil Rights Act,¹³⁶ standing to seek review of federal agency action violative of these special rights ¹³⁷ and an implied cause of action against nonfederal violators.¹³⁸ Similarly, if a grant activity runs counter to the protective scheme of the National Environmental Policy Act,¹³⁹ any affected individual or organization can sue to enforce the Act's conditions.¹⁴⁰

Surviving Limitations

While the federal courthouse doors are now open to a great variety of complainants in cases involving grants-in-aid, the plaintiff seeking *damages* for violation of a grant condition may not be favorably received.

The idea that upon a showing of some injury a person within the zone of interests of a grant statute or a provision therein may sue the grantee for damages for violation of a grant standard has frightening implications for the system of grants-in-aid. A few examples will clarify the potential reach and impact of damage actions implied under grant statutes. In *Lau* v. *Nichols* ¹⁴¹ the Supreme Court found that the San Francisco school system had violated a duty, which attached to its receipt of federal educational grants, to provide equal learning opportunities to more than 3,000 Chinese students who did not speak English. An implied damage action would mean that each of these students could claim compensation from the city for the damages suffered because of years

---

¹³⁵ See, e.g., *Lloyd* v. *Regional Transp. Auth.*, 548 F.2d 1277 (7th Cir. 1977).
¹³⁶ 42 U.S.C. §§2000d to d-5.
¹³⁷ See, e.g., *Jones* v. *Tully*, 378 F. Supp. 286 (E.D. N.Y. 1974), *aff'd per curiam*, 510 F.2d 961 (2d Cir. 1975).
¹³⁸ See *Lau* v. *Nichols*, 414 U.S. 563 (1974) (by implication); *Bossier Parish School Bd.* v. *Lemon*, 370 F.2d 847 (5th Cir.), *cert. denied*, 388 U.S. 911 (1967). The statement in the text is probably correct, but less than sure in view of the severe split in the Supreme Court as to whether Title VI of the Civil Rights Act, 42 U.S.C. §§2000d to d-5, was intended by Congress to create a private cause of action. See *Cannon* v. *University of Chicago*, 99 S. Ct. 1946 (1979). At the present time a specific decision and Court majority is still lacking on this important issue.
¹³⁹ 42 U.S.C. §§4321–4347.
¹⁴⁰ See, e.g., *Sansom Comm.* v. *Lynn*, 366 F. Supp. 1271 (E.D. Pa. 1973) (residents and users of a block slated for urban renewal); *Township of Ridley* v. *Blanchette*, 421 F. Supp. 435 (E.D. Pa. 1976) (town).
¹⁴¹ 414 U.S. 563 (1974). The other examples in the text are drawn, *seriatim*, from the facts of the following cases: *Lloyd* v. *Regional Transp. Auth.*, 548 F.2d 1277 (7th Cir. 1977); *Saine* v. *Hospital Auth.*, 502 F.2d 1033 (5th Cir. 1974); *Barnes* v. *Tarrytown Urban Renewal Agency*, 338 F. Supp. 257 (S.D. N.Y. 1971); *Center for Auto Safety* v. *Tiemann*, 414 F. Supp. 215 (D. D.C. 1976); *Miree* v. *DeKalb County*, 433 U.S. 25 (1977); *Black* v. *Beame*, 550 F.2d 815 (2d Cir. 1977).

138 / *Rights and Remedies Under Federal Grants*

of incomprehensible teaching. A handicapped individual is injured because public transportation, which has received partial federal support, does not meet the affirmative federal obligations to provide equal treatment for the handicapped. An implied damage action would permit the recovery of damages from the grantee. A hospital which had received construction support under the Hill-Burton program violates its obligation to provide a reasonable volume of free services to indigents. A poor person denied medical treatment can sue for the resulting injuries following a denial of care. Inadequate compliance with federal relocation standards may lead to damage suits by individuals relocated in inadequate housing. A motorist is injured on a highway which does not meet federal construction or safety standards. Though tort law would not provide a remedy on the particular facts, a cause of action implied under federal standards leads to recovery for damages suffered. A plane crashes as a result of an airport condition which would not have existed if federal grant standards had been met. Each passenger has an implied cause of action under the grant-in-aid regulation. A welfare family disintegrates allegedly because of the state welfare agency's insufficient compliance with its obligation, under federal standards, to provide social and rehabilitation services. Damages are sought under an implied cause of action.

The essential problem is that traditional tort and contract standards would be replaced by a set of norms developed primarily by federal grantor agencies to further the goals of grant programs without consideration of the scope of potential grantee liability in individual damage actions. Apart from the federal standard, the grantee conduct might violate traditional duties. It is only when the plaintiff can find no relief under these traditional standards of liability that he needs to turn to federal grant conditions to save his action. While those conditions may have been erected to offer the plaintiff some degree of protection, their scope and detail might have differed substantially if their draftsmen knew they would be the predicates for damage actions.

The spectre is even more frightening when one considers that federal aid and, hence, federal standards now reach "nearly every area of state and local [government] activity . . . ," [142] that

---

[142] Advisory Commission on Intergovernmental Relations, *The Intergovernmental Grant System: An Assessment and Proposed Policies: Summary and Concluding Observations* 5 (1978).

"the conditions now attached to practically all federal assistance are infinitely more complex, more controversial (with more judicial decision making), more pervasive (in terms of the number of jurisdictions affected), and more penetrating (in terms of the focus of some on the internal operations of whole governmental jurisdictions) than their largely program-oriented predecessors of the mid-60's," [143]

and that

"the dynamics that shaped [this system] have been largely piecemeal, partial (in a program sense), heavily pluralistic (in terms of inputs and outputs), and perennial." [144]

Implied actions for damages would make the federal grant considerably less attractive to grantees and could considerably undermine the grant-in-aid system. With broad potential liability lurking at every corner, and facing the task of faithfully complying with hundreds of pages of ambiguous and often incomprehensible federal requirements, state and local institutions might sensibly opt out of the system. A good faith misstep along the way could expose the grant recipient to extensive financial liability, a weighty factor in evaluating the value of the federal grant. Should this scenario develop, federal grantor agencies would hesitate to write overly demanding standards into grant programs, thus leading eventually to a drop in the overall protection afforded grant program beneficiaries under the present system.

We can only sketch the nature of the problem here and further point out that it is more than academic. The Fifth Circuit has, unfortunately without much analysis, permitted a damage action to be implied under federal grant regulations.[145] The Second and Seventh Circuits recently rejected the proposition.[146] The Supreme Court, while not addressing the problem squarely, has given negative signals on the matter. In *Miree* v. *DeKalb County* [147] a plane crashed at a county airport which had received federal

[143] *Id.* at 66.
[144] *Id.* at 71.
[145] See *Gomez* v. *Florida State Employment Serv.*, 417 F.2d 569 (5th Cir. 1969); *Saine* v. *Hospital Auth.*, 502 F.2d 1033 (5th Cir. 1974).
[146] See *Black* v. *Beame*, 550 F.2d 815 (2d Cir. 1977); *Cannon* v. *University of Chicago*, 406 F. Supp. 1257 (N.D. Ill. 1976), *aff'd*, 559 F.2d 1063 (7th Cir. 1976), *rev'd on other grounds*, 99 S. Ct. 1946 (1979). In *Cannon*, while reversing the lower courts' denial of a private implied cause of action under a grant condition prohibiting sex discrimination, the Court did not address the issue of permissible relief.
[147] 433 U.S. 25 (1977).

support. Plaintiffs brought a diversity action in federal district court claiming, *inter alia,* to be third-party beneficiaries of the grant agreements. One of the grant conditions required that the use of land near the runway be compatible with airport operations. Defendant had permitted a garbage dump which attracted large birds. These, allegedly, caused the accident. The Court limited its inquiry to whether state or federal law governed the question of duties to third parties arising from the grant agreements, holding that state law should be applied. We have observed that the third-party beneficiary theory is no more than different verbiage for an implied cause of action.[148] Thus, the Supreme Court relegated to each state the power to determine whether violations by its grantees of conditions on federal grants shall lead to damage liability to third parties. Because plaintiffs did not assert federal question jurisdiction below, the Court purported to leave open the question whether an implied cause of action existed under the federal airport law and regulation. However, in dicta it stated: "The fact that this asserted basis of liability is so obviously an afterthought may be some indication of its merit. . . ."[149] The language could easily be read as disapproval, leading to the exceedingly strange result that state, but not federal, courts may create damage actions based on federal standards against recipients of federal grants.

It is surprising that lawyers have not pushed the point with more frequency in the lower courts. Most actions challenging violations of federal grant standards have sought declaratory and injunctive relief, but we can rest assured that damage suits in increasing numbers are in the offing.

A practical, though somewhat illogical, solution would be to permit the implied cause of action but only for prospective relief. Indeed, this result may be mandated by the Eleventh Amendment [150] in federal court suits seeking to impose monetary liability on states.[151] This would lead to active enforcement of federal grant conditions without running the risks previously mentioned. The illogic occurs only because the law is not accustomed to creating causes of action limited to certain types of relief. Yet the implied

[148] See text, *supra,* at pp. 116–17.
[149] *Miree* v. *DeKalb County,* 433 U.S. 25, 33–34 (1977).
[150] U.S. Const. amend. XI.
[151] *Edelman* v. *Jordan,* 415 U.S. 651 (1974). The Amendment's immunity, however, protects only state grantees, see *id.* at 667, n. 12, and does not apply at all to state court actions.

cause of action under a federal grant statute is, at bottom, a fictional process of finding nonexistent congressional intent to support the real basis of decision—the judicial judgment that a statute's goals can be better achieved by permitting private suits. Therefore, if the statutory scheme can be best implemented by actions limited to declaratory and injunctive relief, that path should be open.

Congress may, of course, explicitly create private claims for relief based on violations of federal conditions. The grantee cannot claim unfair surprise in view of the explicit statutory warning that poor administration may lead to citizen suits for damages, injunctive relief, or other relief authorized by Congress. It may be that such private litigation will discourage participation in the grant program by state and local institutions, but Congress can calculate that possibility in its political judgment. The legislature can also finance the program generously enough to tempt the grantee to take the bitter with the sweet.

There may be, indeed a recent example of such legislative action. Within a new and tough section on complaints and sanctions Congress added the following language to the Comprehensive Employment and Training Act of 1973:

> "The existence of remedies under this section shall not preclude any person, who alleges that an action of a prime sponsor or of any other recipient violates any of the provisions of the Act, from instituting a civil action or pursuing any other remedies authorized under Federal, State, or local law." [151a]

While an initial reading of the section (and, indeed, its very insertion within the statute) leads one to the impression that Congress has created private claims for relief under CETA by this language, closer examination reveals considerable ambiguity. Congress has not said that individuals can base a cause of action on CETA language and violations. It has said that the existence of sanctions in the hands of grantors and grantees (vis-à-vis subgrantees) should not be read as precluding suits by individuals. Such civil actions and "other remedies" must, however, be authorized by law. One aim of the section must be to assure that an action or activity by a CETA recipient which violates not only CETA grant conditions but also other federal and state statutes,

---

[151a] §106(l) Comprehensive Employment and Training Act of 1973, 29 U.S.C. §816(l).

such as criminal laws, can be punished and remedied by more than fiscal sanctions under the grant program. At that point, however, clarity stops. What about remedies for individuals created by the judiciary (precedents are, after all, "law") by implication from CETA language? At best, the statutory language may mean that the existence of remedies in the hands of government parties should not, by itself, preclude a court from implying private rights of action under particular CETA provisions in otherwise appropriate circumstances. It may simply be another troubling instance of congressional buck-passing. Congress is telling the courts that its intent is neutral on the implication question. The courts are to go through their four-factor analysis or other reasoning process, but they cannot presume a congressional intent to deny private claims from the existence of public enforcement mechanisms. At worst, Congress had no meaning as to implication of remedies under CETA by the judiciary and was unaware of the possible impact of its language.

The only truly clear thing is the confusion, sadly unexplicated by legislative history.[151b] Confused and confusing judicial standards have led to muddled legislative responses. Trapped in the quagmire is the potential or current grant recipient, unclear as to its potential risks and exposure in CETA participation.

A second area in which standing may prove to be a substantial barrier is the suit in which one jurisdiction sues a neighboring jurisdiction based on the latter's allegedly illegal use of grant funds. Before discussing the leading case on point, a brief discussion of the interjurisdictional goals and effects of grants-in-aid is necessary.

The economists often stress the need for federal grants to counteract the debilitating effect which "spillover" has on public programs.[152] Put in the simplest terms possible, spillover refers to the benefits which one jurisdiction receives from the social programs of another without participating in the financing of the effort. A state, for example, invests heavily in job training. A bordering state does nothing to improve the employability of its residents, but attracts industry by maintaining low tax rates. Employees trained in the neighboring state then move toward the

---

[151b] See S. Rep. No. 95-891, 95th Cong., 2d Sess. 16, 81 (1978); H.R. Conf. Rep. No. 95-1765, 95th Cong., 2d Sess. 125 (1978).
[152] See generally S.J. Mushkin & J.F. Cotton, *Sharing Federal Funds for State and Local Needs: Grants-in-Aid and PPB Systems (1969)*.

jobs. The "freeloader" state has thus accrued cost-free benefits from the efforts of its neighbor. Because of such spillover, jurisdictions are supposedly reluctant to finance certain types of programs in which the phenomenon is likely to occur, leading to an overall insufficient public financing in the particular area. The grant-in-aid is seen as offering a solution by moving the financial burden to a larger jurisdiction over whose borders little or no benefits will spill. Federal aid responds to interstate, regional, and local spillovers, the latter two where state aid has proved insufficient.

The standing problem arises when one jurisdiction violates the rules to the detriment of another. Assume that few states, counties, and cities are willing to invest their tax dollars in low-income housing for fear that poor families from outside will be attracted by the opportunity to secure decent dwellings.[153] The financial disincentive is counteracted by generous aid from the Federal Government. One jurisdiction takes the federal bounty and illegally diverts it to suburban swimming pools. Can the neighboring jurisdiction complain in court that this illegality has deprived it of the spillover benefits (reduction in its poverty population) accruing from federal financial support? That will depend, of course, on our reading of the purposes of the particular federal aid. It will ordinarily be a dubious and difficult proposition to demonstrate that a federal grant to X is aimed at providing help to Y. It is one thing to demonstrate that X would not have engaged in the activity without federal support because of possible spillover effects and quite another to carry that proposition to the further conclusion that the goal of the federal aid was to *promote* spillover. In most programs the conclusion cannot be drawn. Federal aid to X is just that—assistance to a jurisdiction to help it provide services to its own residents, not those of Y and Z.

City of Hartford v. *Towns of Glastonbury*[154] may be the exceptional case. In that controversy the Second Circuit, which takes the standing doctrine quite seriously,[155] had to wrestle with the prototype situation described above. The City of Hartford and its low-income residents were disturbed by the uses which

---

[153] The Constitution prohibits states and localities from restricting outsiders' access to such benefits by means such as residency requirements. See, e.g., *Shapiro* v. *Thompson*, 394 U.S. 618 (1969) (welfare benefits).
[154] 561 F.2d 1032 (2d Cir. 1976), *cert. denied*, 434 U.S. 1034 (1978).
[155] Perhaps *too* seriously. See, e.g., *Evans* v. *Lynn*, 537 F.2d 571 (2d Cir. 1975), *cert. denied*, 429 U.S. 1066 (1977); *Aguayo* v. *Richardson*, 473 F.2d 1090 (2d Cir. 1973), *cert. denied*, 414 U.S. 1146 (1978).

adjoining suburban towns were planning for their federal community development funds. Few of the dollars were going to be dedicated to low-income housing, thus denying Hartford residents the opportunity to move to greener valleys and denying Hartford the benefits of a smaller poverty population. They sued the towns and the Department of Housing and Urban Development, the grantor, charging that the defendants violated the statutory requirement that grant applications contain housing assistance plans which included estimates of the poverty population expected to reside in the applicant's jurisdiction during the next three years. HUD waived this last requirement because of the difficulty of making such estimates. Although the alleged illegality did not directly involve the defendants' use of grant funds, it was connected. If HUD had required the towns to support their housing plans with complete information, the data might have revealed insufficient quantities of low-income housing. The towns would have had to address and deal with such deficit in their housing assistance plans in order to receive community development funds.[156] In this manner, the lower income residents of Hartford might have gotten their greener valleys and the city itself would have benefited by losing some of its high-cost population of indigents. The exceptional nature of the case was that the housing and community development program has precisely this as one of its goals —ameliorating the decay problem of urban centers through the spatial decentralization of low-income housing.[157]

The district court found that plaintiffs had standing to assert the claim, that HUD's waiver violated the Act, and that the grantor should be enjoined from distributing grant funds to the towns until the legal deficiencies in the applications were corrected.[158] A panel of the Second Circuit affirmed.[159] Rehearing *en banc* was then ordered to reconsider the jurisdictional issue, considered of "exceptional importance," whether the municipality and its residents had standing to challenge a grant to a separate

---

[156] See *City of Hartford v. Towns of Glastonbury*, 561 F.2d 1032, 1035, n. 6 (2d Cir. 1976), *cert. denied*, 434 U.S. 1034 (1978).

[157] See *id.* at 1038–40, 1050, 1055–57.

[158] *City of Hartford v. Hills*, 408 F. Supp. 889 (D. Conn.), *rev'd sub nom., City of Hartford v. Towns of Glastonbury*, 561 F.2d 1032 (2d Cir. 1976), *cert. denied*, 434 U.S. 1034 (1978).

[159] *City of Hartford v. Towns of Glastonbury*, 561 F.2d 1032, 1033–48 (2d Cir. 1976), *cert. denied*, 434 U.S. 1034 (1978).

municipality.¹⁶⁰ A badly divided court finally dismissed the case for lack of standing.¹⁶¹

Glastonbury may be heralded as a major standing case, but at bottom the split decision centered on a factual dispute. The winning plurality discounted the issue of significance—whether the plaintiffs had a "legitimate, judicially cognizable interest in the benefits that should accrue to them under the Act" ¹⁶²—and then proceeded to decide that plaintiffs had failed to meet their burden under *Simon* ¹⁶³ and *Warth* ¹⁶⁴ of demonstrating that the illegal action caused injury to the plaintiffs and that judicial relief would remedy that injury. The court found it insufficiently probable that a correct estimate of housing needs would have resulted in the building of more low-income housing by the defendant towns. Also, because these defendants had already received their full allotments of housing grants, it was not likely that judicial action on the grant application would result in any benefit to plaintiffs. The dissenters differed on both counts, finding that correct housing need estimates might have affected the location and types of low-income housing and that the three-year housing plan would have an impact on future allocations of federal housing grants. Thus, *Glastonbury* turned on different images in the crystal ball.

In searching for positive benefits accruing to the plaintiffs from judicial relief, the district court, the original panel affirmance, and the *en banc* dissenters pointed to the fact that a judicial declaration of illegality in the grant applications might lead to the defendants' forfeiture of community development funds which, in turn, could benefit the City of Hartford through the assignment to it of reallocated funds. We would be remiss in not identifying the fundamental flaw in this analysis.¹⁶⁵ We have discussed this type of argument in the context of a losing applicant for a *competitive* grant successfully seeking to disqualify a winning applicant.¹⁶⁶ This, too, results in the release of grant funds which might benefit the plaintiff. In this context, plaintiff's claim of right is to have all grant applications judged under the same standards and

---

160 *Id.* at 1049.
161 *Id.* at 1049–59.
162 *Id.* at 1050.
163 *Simon v. Eastern Ky. Welfare Rights Organ.*, 426 U.S. 26 (1976).
164 *Warth v. Seldin*, 422 U.S. 490 (1975).
165 The plurality did not challenge the propriety of the argument. It simply found that it was improbable that the defendants would forfeit their allocations. *City of Hartford v. Towns of Glastonbury*, 561 F.2d 1032, 1051 (2d Cir. 1976), *cert. denied*, 434 U.S. 1034 (1978)..
166 See text, *supra*, at pp. 119–23.

procedures. Illegal deviation from such norms in favor of the winning applicant harms plaintiff not because of the grantee's use of the funds but because the plaintiff has lost its right to compete for all available grant monies. Damage is to that lost opportunity and judicial redress corresponds to the injury, the diverted funds being restored to the pot. The *Glastonbury* situation is fundamentally different. The City of Hartford was never entitled to compete for Glastonbury's formula allotment. Any benefits achieved through a reallocation of funds would be purely a windfall, with no correspondence to the illegality asserted by the plaintiffs. The logical flaw is the failure to see the disjunctive in the causal tests: injury to the plaintiffs caused by defendants' illegal act (denying spillover benefits) *and* relief to the plaintiffs unrelated to the injury (reallocated funds for building housing in Hartford, not Glastonbury). While the Supreme Court recently rejected the argument that standing required a direct relationship between the plaintiff's injury and the right being asserted,[167] it affirmed the need for a logical nexus between the injury alleged and the judicial remedy:

> "We . . . cannot accept the contention that, outside the context of taxpayers' suits, a litigant must demonstrate anything more than injury in fact and a substantial likelihood that *the judicial relief requested will prevent or redress the claimed injury* to satisfy the 'case and controversy' requirement of Art. III." [168]

Besides being illogical, the theory is dangerous. All formula programs provide for the reallocation of funds forfeited by eligible applicants.[169] To accept the theory advanced in *Glastonbury* is to open the doors to suits seeking to build up the reallocation pot by proving deficiencies in the proposals and programs of other jurisdictions.

Federal Court Subject Matter Jurisdiction

Subject matter jurisdiction refers to the power of courts to hear certain types or categories of cases. Lower federal courts have only the subject matter jurisdiction granted them by Congress.

---

[167] See *Duke Power Co. v. Carolina Environmental Study Group, Inc.*, 438 U.S. 59, 78–79 (1978).
[168] *Id.* at 79 (emphasis added) (footnote omitted).
[169] See Chapter 7, *infra*, at pp. 199–201.

Expanding Bases of Judicial Intervention / 147

Thus, a plaintiff in a grant controversy brought in a federal forum must allege in his pleadings [170] an appropriate statutory basis authorizing the court to hear his type of case, and, if challenged, must demonstrate some substance to his allegations.

This section shall quickly review the standard bases of federal court jurisdiction in cases involving grants-in-aid. We shall discuss the four vital sources of authority for federal court jurisdiction which have been successfully invoked in grant controversies, leaving for historians those statutes which have fallen by the wayside.[171] This primer on jurisdiction shows that in the great majority of grant-in-aid controversies the federal courts have been vested with adjudicatory power. This is true whether the dispute is between grantor and grantee, between a third party and the Federal Government, or between a third party and the grant recipient. We shall also demonstrate that here, as in the area of standing, recent developments have expanded the bases for judicial intervention in grant disputes.

Federal Question Jurisdiction

Section 1331 of the Judicial Code reads, in relevant part, as follows:

> "The district courts shall have original jurisdiction of all civil actions wherein the matter in controversy exceeds the sum or value of $10,000, exclusive of interest and costs, and arises under the Constitution, laws, or treaties of the United States, except that no such sum or value shall be required in any such action brought against the United States, any agency thereof, or any officer or employee thereof in his official capacity." [172]

---

[170] See Federal Rules of Civil Procedure 8(a).

[171] In *Califano* v. *Sanders*, 430 U.S. 99 (1977), the Supreme Court definitively answered the question (in the negative) whether §10 Administrative Procedure Act, 5 U.S.C. §705, provided an independent source of federal court subject matter jurisdiction in cases involving judicial review of federal agency action. Another statute which does not provide subject matter jurisdiction, though ritually incanted in plaintiffs' pleadings, is the Declaratory Judgment Act, 28 U.S.C. §2201. See, e.g., *Almenares* v. *Wyman*, 453 F.2d 1075, 1082, n. 9 (2d Cir. 1971), *cert. denied*, 405 U.S. 944 (1972). 28 U.S.C. §1337, which provides district court jurisdiction in cases involving Acts of Congress regulating commerce, will ordinarily be inapplicable to grant programs because they are based on the General Welfare Clause and not the Commerce Clause. Thus, a suit based on the Social Security Act cannot use 28 U.S.C. §1337 as a basis for jurisdiction. See *Aguayo* v. *Richardson*, 473 F.2d 1090 (2d Cir. 1973), *cert. denied*, 414 U.S. 1146 (1974); *Almenares* v. *Wyman*, 453 F.2d 1075 (2d Cir. 1971), *cert. denied*, 405 U.S. 944 (1972). §1337, however, has been successfully invoked in a suit involving the National School Lunch Program. See *Richmond Welfare Rights Organ.* v. *Snodgrass*, 525 F.2d 197 (9th Cir. 1975).

[172] 28 U.S.C. §1331.

Claims of right arising in grant-in-aid disputes will normally be based on federal statutes, regulations, guidelines, and agreements. The complex of rights and duties between grantors and grantees, and the express or implied rights of third parties, is created by virtue of federal law. Thus, federal question jurisdiction will be the normal basis of federal court adjudicatory power in grant-in-aid controversies.[173] Jurisdiction attaches if plaintiff states in his pleading an arguable claim of right under the laws and regulations applicable to the particular grant,[174] although patently frivolous assertions will not suffice.[175] The mere fact, however, that a grantee is federally funded does not convert its every action into a federal question. If federal standards of conduct have not been imposed on the particular grantee activity claimed to be illegal, the case does not arise under federal law.[176]

The $10,000 amount-in-controversy requirement for federal question jurisdiction has not proven to be a major barrier. Federal courts have been liberal in their economic valuation of the "right to be protected or extent of injury to be prevented."[177] It is beyond our scope to explore in any detail the valuation problems which may arise in federal grant controversies. We shall only highlight some recurring themes.

Federal grants rarely involve less than $10,000 and if the plaintiff can show that the grant is jeopardized in some way, or its full value to him is not being realized because of illegal grantor or grantee conduct, the courts will normally accept the amount of the grant as the economic value of the lawsuit.[178] Alternatively, the value of a particular component of the grant may be the relevant measuring stone. The cost of providing mandated citizen participation, for example, has been used in cases where participa-

---

[173] See, e.g., *Philadelphia Anti-poverty Action Comm. v. Rizzo*, 502 F.2d 306 (3d Cir. 1974), cert. denied, 419 U.S. 1108 (1975).

[174] See, e.g., *Norton v. Blaylock*, 285 F. Supp. 659, 662 (W.D. Ark. 1968), aff'd, 409 F.2d 772 (8th Cir. 1969) ("whether well or ill founded the complaint is based on federal grounds").

[175] See, e.g., *Stanturf v. Sipes*, 335 F.2d 224 (8th Cir. 1964), cert. denied, 379 U.S. 977 (1965).

[176] See *Hines v. Cenla Community Action Comm., Inc.*, 474 F.2d 1052 (5th Cir. 1973) (firing of employee by grantee).

[177] See *Marquez v. Hardin*, 339 F. Supp. 1364, 1370 (N.D. Calif. 1969) (dicta).

[178] See, e.g., *Silva v. East Providence Housing Auth.*, 390 F. Supp. 691 (D. R.I. 1975); *Afton Alps, Inc. v. United States*, 392 F. Supp. 543 (D. Minn. 1974); *Community Action Programs Executive Directors Ass'n v. Ash*, 365 F. Supp. 1355 (D. N.J. 1973); *Comprehensive Group Health Servs. Bd. of Directors v. Temple Univ.*, 363 F. Supp. 1069 (E.D. Pa. 1973). But cf. *Mid-America Regional Council v. Mathews*, 416 F. Supp. 896 (W.D. Mo. 1976) (doubts whether amount sought in grant proposal is proper measure).

tory standards have not been met.[179] Particularized injury to the plaintiff is also relevant; thus, a business claiming competitive injury caused by an illegal grant activity can use its economic losses as the relevant measure.[180]

In a not insignificant number of cases, however, jurisdiction has been found lacking because of an insufficient amount in controversy.[181] The problem has been ameliorated to some extent by the 1976 amendment to Section 1331 which eliminated the dollar requirement in suits brought against the United States, its agencies, and its officers.[182] By virtue of the amendment, virtually every grant-in-aid controversy brought against the Federal Government will find a jurisdictional basis in §1331.

This does not, however, solve the jurisdictional problem when the plaintiff's primary complaint is against the grantee and when the value of the suit cannot be measured economically or does not exceed $10,000. In cases of grantee conduct which violates federal standards, the problem may sometimes be avoided by simply suing only the grantor. If, for instance, the plaintiff's complaint is that a grant is about to be awarded in violation of federal standards, the plaintiff can seek injunctive relief against the federal grantor agency. The issue is more complicated if illegality is occurring during the course of the grant, and the plaintiff's goal is to achieve corrective action rather than forfeiture of the grant. It may be possible to sue the Federal Government alone on the basis that the administrator is violating its obligation to enforce compli-

---

[179] See *New York City Coalition for Community Health* v. *Lindsay*, 362 F. Supp. 434 (S.D. N.Y. 1973); *Comprehensive Group Health Servs. Bd. of Directors* v. *Temple Univ.*, 363 F. Supp. 1069 (E.D. Pa. 1973).
[180] See *Corrugated Container Corp.* v. *Community Servs. Admin.*, 429 F. Supp. 142 (W.D. Va. 1977); *Afton Alps, Inc.* v. *United States*, 392 F. Supp. 543 (D. Minn. 1974).
[181] See *City of Milwaukee* v. *Saxbe*, 546 F.2d 693 (7th Cir. 1976) (injury to city caused by lack of enforcement of civil rights requirements in outlying areas); *Lopez* v. *Luginbill*, 483 F.2d 486 (10th Cir. 1973), *cert. denied*, 415 U.S. 927 (1974) (members of grantee advisory committee sue to get information needed to discharge their functions); *Aguayo* v. *Richardson*, 473 F.2d 1090 (2d Cir. 1973), *cert. denied*, 414 U.S. 1146 (1974) (suit challenging experimental grant program); *Davis* v. *Shultz*, 453 F.2d 497 (3d Cir. 1971) (plaintiff rehired after two weeks); *Carman* v. *Richardson*, 357 F. Supp. 1148 (D. Vt. 1973) (insufficient valuation of injury to plaintiff caused by grant violating state priorities); *Mattingly* v. *Elias*, 325 F. Supp. 1374 (E.D. Pa. 1971), *rev'd on other grounds*, 482 F.2d 526 (3d Cir. 1973) (damages from uninhabitable apartment); *English* v. *Town of Huntington*, 335 F. Supp. 1369 (E.D. N.Y. 1970) (value of equal rights immeasurable). Compare *Schreiber* v. *Lugar*, 518 F.2d 1099 (7th Cir. 1975) (illegal diversion of general revenue-sharing funds; taxpayers cannot aggregate individual damage), with *Mathews* v. *Massell*, 356 F. Supp. 291 (N.D. Ga. 1973) (same; aggregation permitted).
[182] Pub. L. 94-574, Oct. 21, 1976. See *Clark* v. *Richardson*, 431 F. Supp. 105 (D. N.J. 1977).

150 / *Rights and Remedies Under Federal Grants*

ance with grant conditions. That type of suit, however, circumscribes the permissible relief. The court could only order the defendant to begin enforcement proceedings. The matter would then have to be reinstituted at the administrative level— a tortuous and disagreeable route in view of the additional delay and cost involved. It may also lead to grant forfeiture, which is likely to be against the plaintiff's interests. Thus, in many cases effective relief —an injunction against the grantee—requires the presence of the fund recipient. It is then that the plaintiff may have to find jurisdictional authority which does not require an amount in controversy.[183]

Civil Rights Jurisdiction

In the grants field, as elsewhere, federal civil rights legislation has proved a fertile basis for federal court subject matter jurisdiction for plaintiffs who cannot meet the standards of Section 1331. The jurisdictional issues are somewhat complex, and it will aid understanding if we set forth the relevant parts of the statutes most frequently utilized by plaintiffs.

Individuals acting under color of state law may suffer civil liability under 42 U.S.C. §1983 for subjecting "any citizen of the United States or any other person within the jurisdiction thereof to the deprivation of any rights, privileges, or immunities secured by the Constitution and laws . . . ." Both damage actions and suits seeking injunctions are afforded injured parties.[184] Section 1983, however, does not provide federal court subject matter jurisdiction. For this we must turn to Section 1343 of the Judicial Code. Its third paragraph grants original jurisdiction to the federal district courts for civil actions:

> "To redress the deprivation, under color of any State law, statute, ordinance, regulation, custom or usage, of any right, privilege or immunity secured by the Constitution of the United States or by any Act of Congress providing for equal rights of citizens or of all persons within the jurisdiction of the United States." [185]

---

[183] Conceivably the plaintiff could sue both grantor and grantee, show clear jurisdiction against the Federal Government, then invoke the court's pendent jurisdiction on the claim against the grantee. Cf. *Hagans* v. *Lavine*, 415 U.S. 528 (1974). But see *Aldinger* v. *Howard*, 427 U.S. 1 (1976).

[184] See generally "Developments in the Law—Section 1983 and Federalism," 90 Harv. L. Rev. 1133, 1217–50 (1977).

[185] 28 U.S.C. §1343(3).

The next paragraph contains additional civil jurisdiction as follows:

> "To recover damages or to secure equitable or other relief under any Act of Congress providing for the protection of civil rights, including the right to vote." [186]

Neither section requires a showing of a specified amount in controversy.

If the thrust of the plaintiff's complaint is that a state grantee has violated his constitutional rights in the implementation of the grant program, Section 1983 would create substantive liability and Section 1343(3) would provide district court jurisdiction without regard to the economic value of plaintiff's claim.[187] Similarly, if the plaintiff alleges a violation of nondiscrimination provisions applicable to federal grant activities, those provisions would provide for the substantive basis of liability and Section 1343(4) would afford subject matter jurisdiction.[188]

The more difficult jurisdictional cases are when the grant conditions allegedly violated do not protect civil rights, the plaintiff does not have a constitutional claim, and federal question jurisdiction is unavailable.

For some of these cases, *Hagans* v. *Lavine* [189] offers a jurisdictional solution.[190] If the plaintiff asserts constitutional claims in his pleading which are not "insubstantial, implausible, foreclosed by prior decisions of [the Supreme Court] or otherwise completely devoid of merit," [191] the court will have jurisdiction under Sections 1983 and 1343(3). It may then utilize its pendent jurisdiction to hear the statutory claim over which it otherwise would not have subject matter jurisdiction. Then, pursuing the federal courts'

---

[186] 28 U.S.C. §1343(4).

[187] See, e.g., *Advocates for the Arts* v. *Thomson*, 532 F.2d 792 (1st Cir. 1976), *cert. denied*, 429 U.S. 894 (1976) (First Amendment); *Escalera* v. *New York City Housing Auth.*, 425 F.2d 853 (2d Cir. 1970), *cert. denied*, 400 U.S. 853 (1970) (due process). Both personal and property rights may be so asserted. *Lynch* v. *Household Fin. Corp.*, 405 U.S. 538 (1972).

[188] See, e.g., *Bartels* v. *Biernat*, 427 F. Supp. 226 (E.D. Wis. 1977) (rights of the handicapped).

[189] 415 U.S. 528 (1974).

[190] See also *King* v. *Smith*, 392 U.S. 309 (1968) (by implication); *Rosado* v. *Wyman*, 397 U.S. 397, 402–405 (1970); *Edelman* v. *Jordan*, 415 U.S. 651, 653, n. 1 (1974); *Shea* v. *Vialpando*, 416 U.S. 251, 258 (1974); *Burns* v. *Alcala*, 420 U.S. 575, 577, n. 1 (1975); *Almenares* v. *Wyman*, 453 F.2d 1075 (2d Cir. 1971), *cert. denied*, 405 U.S. 944 (1972); *Aguayo* v. *Richardson*, 473 F.2d 1090 (2d Cir. 1973), *cert. denied*, 414 U.S. 1146 (1974); *Ayala* v. *District 60 School Bd.*, 327 F. Supp. 980 (D. Colo. 1971); *Davis* v. *Robinson*, 346 F. Supp. 847 (D. R.I. 1972); *Silva* v. *East Providence Housing Auth.*, 390 F. Supp. 691 (D. R.I. 1975).

[191] *Hagans* v. *Lavine*, 415 U.S. 528, 543 (1974).

152 / *Rights and Remedies Under Federal Grants*

traditional policy of avoiding constitutional decisions if the same result can be reached on narrower grounds, it may decide the case on the statutory ground without ever reaching the constitutional issues.[192]

That still leaves plaintiffs who cannot, with a straight face, assert claims of a constitutional nature.[193] Several have tried a rather circuitous route which combines Sections 1983 and 1343 with the particular federal law which has allegedly been violated in their case. There are two branches in this argument. Both proceed from the same trunk—the text of Section 1983 which provides a cause of action against persons, acting under color of state law, who deprive another of rights secured not only by the Constitution but also by the "laws" of the United States. A literal reading of §1983 leads to the conclusion that a violation of *any* federal statute is perforce a violation of §1983, whether or not such statute protects civil rights. Once this proposition is established, jurisdiction is easily found under §1343(3) because §1983 is an "Act of Congress providing for equal rights," or under §1343(4) because §1983 is an "Act of Congress providing for the protection of civil rights."

In 1968, 1970, and 1974 the Supreme Court noted but did not decide the issue.[194] Most of the lower federal courts rejected it, unconvinced by the bootstrapping nature of the argument and fearful that it would wreak havoc with federal question jurisdiction.[195] Yet two circuits took a favorable view.[196] Finally, the Supreme Court in 1979 ruled that Section 1983 "by itself does not protect anyone against anything" and is essentially "procedural." [197] Thus, the Court ruled that the primary law allegedly violated must be a "civil rights" or "equal rights" statute in order to invoke Section 1343 jurisdiction and that the Social Security Act, including its

---

[192] See, e.g., *King* v. *Smith*, 392 U.S. 309, 312, n. 3 (1968).

[193] See, e.g., *Andrews* v. *Maher*, 525 F.2d 113 (2d Cir. 1975) (constitutional claim insubstantial).

[194] See *Hagans* v. *Lavine*, 415 U.S. 528, 533–34, n. 5 (1974); *Rosado* v. *Wyman*, 397 U.S. 397, 405, n. 7 (1970); *King* v. *Smith*, 392 U.S. 309, 311–12 (1968).

[195] See, e.g., *City of Milwaukee* v. *Saxbe*, 546 F.2d 693 (7th Cir. 1976); *Andrews* v. *Maher*, 525 F.2d 113 (2d Cir. 1975); *Lopez* v. *Luginbill*, 483 F.2d 486 (10th Cir. 1973), *cert. denied*, 415 U.S. 927 (1974); *Dorak* v. *Shapp*, 403 F. Supp. 863 (M.D. Pa. 1975); *Mattingly* v. *Elias*, 325 F. Supp. 1374 (E.D. Pa. 1971), *rev'd on other grounds*, 482 F.2d 526 (3d Cir. 1973).

[196] See *Blue* v. *Craig*, 505 F.2d 830 (4th Cir. 1974); *Gomez* v. *Florida State Employment Serv.*, 417 F.2d 569 (5th Cir. 1969).

[197] *Chapman* v. *Houston Welfare Rights Organ.*, 99 S. Ct. 1905, 1916 (1979), *aff'g Gonzalez* v. *Young*, 560 F.2d 160 (3d Cir. 1977), and *rev'g Houston Welfare Rights Organ., Inc.* v. *Vowell*, 555 F.2d 1219 (5th Cir. 1977).

grant programs, did not qualify under the common understanding of those terms.

Where Section 1983 and its jurisdictional counterparts remain viable, one must keep in mind that they afford relief only against individuals who act under color of state law and, recently,[198] municipalities. Thus, this basis of jurisdiction would be unavailable in suits against private sector grantees.

Mandamus Jurisdiction

The mandamus jurisdiction of the federal courts, which can be utilized in suits against U.S. grant officials, does not require proof of an amount in controversy. The statute vesting mandamus power in the federal district courts, 28 U.S.C. §1361, provides:

> "The district courts shall have original jurisdiction of any action in the nature of mandamus to compel an officer or employee of the United States or any agency thereof to perform a duty owed to the plaintiff."

Mandamus is appropriate only when there is a failure to act by a Federal Government official in violation of a mandatory and clear statutory command.[199] The obligation to act is usually phrased in terms of a "ministerial" act,[200] one which allows no scope for discretion.[201] Plaintiff must also demonstrate a clear right to relief and that no other adequate remedy is available.[202]

Though these strict standards governing the use of mandamus circumscribe its utility in grant-in-aid controversies, such jurisdiction has been successfully invoked in several cases. Mandamus issued where federal officials did not afford statutorily required hearing opportunities prior to withholding federal grant funds due and owing.[203] Similarly, mandamus was the indicated remedy in the impoundment cases.[204] The finding of a clear statutory

---

[198] *Monell* v. *Department of Social Servs.*, 436 U.S. 658 (1978).

[199] See *City of Milwaukee* v. *Saxbe*, 546 F.2d 693, 699–701 (7th Cir. 1976).

[200] See *Clark* v. *Richardson*, 431 F. Supp. 105, 112 (D. N.J. 1977).

[201] One district court refused to apply the traditional standard in a grant-in-aid controversy, finding the "ministerial-discretionary" distinction unworkable and holding that it could issue an order of mandamus against any grantor action which was not purely discretionary. See *Michigan Head Start Directors Ass'n* v. *Butz*, 397 F. Supp. 1124, 1137–39 (W.D. Mich. 1975). Another lower court refused a similar invitation. See *Marquez* v. *Hardin*, 339 F. Supp. 1364, 1368 (N.D. Cal. 1969).

[202] See, e.g., *State Dep't of Pub. Welfare* v. *Weinberger*, 388 F. Supp. 1304 (W.D. Tex. 1975), modified sub nom., *State Dep't of Pub. Welfare* v. *Califano*, 556 F.2d 326 (5th Cir. 1977), cert. denied, 99 S. Ct. 78 (1978).

[203] *Ibid.*; *Minnesota* v. *Weinberger*, 359 F. Supp. 789 (D. Minn. 1973).

[204] See, e.g., *Community Action Programs Executive Directors Ass'n* v. *Ash*, 365 F. Supp. 1355 (D. N.J. 1973).

obligation to expend appropriated grant funds justified the issuance of mandamus against the grant officials responsible for the impoundment. The President's failure to implement a grant program by not discharging his statutory obligation to appoint the members of an advisory committee subjected him to the mandamus jurisdiction of the federal courts.[205] Statutorily directed grant procedures can also be enforced through mandamus,[206] as can the constitutional obligations of grantor officials.[207]

In cases involving grantee violations of federal standards, the availability of mandamus to achieve corrective action is unlikely. The plaintiff would have to seek an order of mandamus against the federal grantor and in the process demonstrate not only that the violation was apparent but that the federal agency had a mandatory duty to take enforcement action.[208] One court had considerable difficulty finding such a duty:

> "... it is fair to say that if the Secretary of Agriculture learns that federal funds are being applied in a manner substantially different from the congressional mandate, it is his duty in some way to remedy the situation.... If it is brought to his attention that the States are misapplying the funds, he should take steps to insure that either the funds are applied correctly or terminated. Exactly what manner ... is the area in which he has discretion, because the statute does not spell out any specific method to insure compliance. This analysis places the primary responsibility for compliance on the States because they are given the first opportunity to comply.
>
> "Since in any situation where factual determinations are involved some mistakes will inevitably be made, the Secretary would only have to take remedial measures if the state administration were to vary in a substantial way from the Congressional mandate." [209]

This analysis is consistent with our view that federal grantor agencies generally have flexibility in determining when and how to enforce federal grant conditions.[210]

---

[205] See *Minnesota Chippewa Tribe* v. *Carlucci*, 358 F. Supp. 973 (D. D.C. 1973).
[206] See *Sansom Comm.* v. *Lynn*, 366 F. Supp. 1271 (E.D. Pa. 1973).
[207] See *Thompson* v. *Washington*, 497 F.2d 626 (D.C. Cir. 1973) (procedural due process); *Ponce* v. *Housing Auth.*, 389 F. Supp. 635 (E.D. Cal. 1975) (same).
[208] If the claim is that the federal agency has completely abdicated its duty to apply statutory grant conditions, mandamus may be available. See *Corrugated Container Corp.* v. *Community Servs. Admin.*, 429 F. Supp. 142 (W.D. Va. 1977).
[209] *Marquez* v. *Hardin*, 339 F. Supp. 1364, 1369 (N.D. Cal. 1969).
[210] See Chapter 3, notes 118–120, *supra*, and accompanying text.

Expanding Bases of Judicial Intervention / 155

Another area in which mandamus has been found inappropriate is the award process for discretionary grant applications.[211] In approving grants the grantor must often exercise judgment, even in the application of standards prescribed by statute or regulation.

U.S. Court of Claims

Suits against the Federal Government seeking damages for breach of any "express or implied contract with the United States" may be brought in the Court of Claims.[212] Prior to a 1978 amendment if the damages sought exceeded $10,000 they had to be brought in that forum; for lesser amounts the Court of Claims and the U.S. district courts had concurrent jurisdiction.[213] In 1978, however, the concurrent jurisdiction of the district courts was eliminated.[213a] Federal grant-in-aid agreements are included in these jurisdictional rules.[214]

The Demise of Government Legalese

Liberalized standing concepts and expanded bases of federal court jurisdiction have been instrumental in opening the federal courts to grant-in-aid controversies. These two, however, do not exhaust the content of the "standard litany" [215] of government defenses. In this section, we shall briefly examine the fate of another: sovereign immunity.[216]

---

[211] See *Davis* v. *Shultz*, 453 F.2d 497 (3d Cir. 1971); *Clark* v. *Richardson*, 431 F. Supp. 105 (D. N.J. 1977); *Mid-America Regional Council* v. *Mathews*, 416 F. Supp. 896 (W.D. Mo. 1976); *Carman* v. *Richardson*, 357 F. Supp. 1148 (D. Vt. 1973).
[212] 28 U.S.C. §1491.
[213] 28 U.S.C. §1346(a)(2) (1976).
[213a] §14(a) Contract Disputes Act of 1978, Pub. L. 95-563, Nov. 1, 1978, amending 28 U.S.C. §1346(a)(2).
[214] See, e.g., *Minnesota* v. *Weinberger*, 359 F. Supp. 789 (D. Minn. 1973) (welfare grants); *Arizona* v. *United States*, 494 F.2d 1285 (Ct. Cl. 1974) (highway grants); *Port Auth.* v. *United States*, 432 F.2d 455 (Ct. Cl. 1970) (disaster aid).
[215] The phrase is borrowed from Judge Robinson's opinion in the impoundment case, *Pennsylvania* v. *Weinberger*, 367 F. Supp. 1378, 1379 (D. D.C. 1973). His colleague on the U.S. District Court for the District of Columbia, Judge Gesell, also expressed impatience against the "litany," "the confusing inconsequential defenses so typical of Government legalese these days." *National Council of Community Mental Health Centers, Inc.* v. *Weinberger*, 361 F. Supp. 897, 899, 900 (D. D.C. 1973). The lawyers for the United States may be getting the message. See *Train* v. *City of New York*, 420 U.S. 35, 41, n. 7 (1975) (government abandoned the sovereign immunity defense in the Supreme Court).
[216] In the impoundment cases the government defense that the claims were nonjusticiable political questions was regularly rejected, see, e.g., *State Highway Comm'n* v. *Volpe*, 479 F.2d 1099 (8th Cir. 1973), and has not surfaced since.

156 / *Rights and Remedies Under Federal Grants*

The United States, as defendant in federal grant controversies, has consistently tried to get mileage out of a 1954 decision, *Arizona v. Hobby*.[217] In that case the Secretary of Health, Education and Welfare refused to approve Arizona's state plan for federal welfare assistance because of restrictions placed on Indian participation. Arizona then sued the Secretary. The U.S. Court of Appeals for the District of Columbia refused jurisdiction on the ground of sovereign immunity. It reasoned that the suit sought to reach money in the U.S. treasury, that the Secretary had authority to disapprove state plans, that the Administrative Procedure Act did not constitute a waiver of sovereign immunity, and that the United States had not consented to the suit.[218]

Since *Hobby*, the sovereign immunity doctrine has been riddled with so many exceptions, and these exceptions have been so broadly read, that the rule has played virtually no role [219] in the hundreds of grant-in-aid controversies which have been decided by the federal courts in the past decade.

The exception which has swallowed up the rule is that sovereign immunity cannot protect a federal official who has acted beyond his statutory powers. The "scope of authority" exception does not require a showing of a complete absence of authority to act. It applies even when the defendant had authority to act, but exercised it in violation of a statutory standard.[220] The exception has also been extended to include violations by grantor officials of agency regulations and agreements.[221] Thus, immunity from suit is waived in any case in which the plaintiff claims the grantor official violated federal law of any type. The federal courts have also rejected the *Hobby* view that the Administrative Procedure Act, in authorizing judicial review of federal agency actions, did

---

[217] 221 F.2d 498 (D.C. Cir. 1954).

[218] In response to *Hobby*, Congress eventually amended the welfare statute to provide judicial review of federal agency decisions on state plans. See *County of Alameda v. Weinberger*, 520 F.2d 344, 348–49 (9th Cir. 1975).

[219] The doctrine may still prohibit suits designated as against the United States and federal departments, see *Afton Alps, Inc. v. United States*, 392 F. Supp. 543 (D. Minn. 1974), leading to the designation of individual grantor officials as defendants.

[220] See, e.g., *Michigan Head Start Directors Ass'n v. Butz*, 397 F. Supp. 1124, 1132–36 (W.D. Mich. 1975). See also *Afton Alps, Inc. v. United States*, 392 F. Supp. 543 (D. Minn. 1974); *Community Action Programs Executive Directors Ass'n v. Ash*, 365 F. Supp. 1355 (D. N.J. 1973); *Local 2816, AFGE v. Phillips*, 360 F. Supp. 1092 (N.D. Ill. 1973); *Coalition for United Community Action v. Romney*, 316 F. Supp. 742 (N.D. Ill. 1970).

[221] See, e.g., *Thompson v. Washington*, 497 F.2d 626, 631, n. 25 (D.C. Cir. 1973).

not waive the sovereign immunity defense.²²² Finally, the prohibition against suits which may have a direct impact on the federal treasury has been ruled inapplicable in grant-in-aid cases on the theory that the plaintiff was seeking to reach federal funds already authorized and appropriated by Congress.²²³ They would not, therefore, impose additional monetary obligations on the United States.

Reviewability

The subject matter jurisdiction of the federal judiciary refers to the categories of cases congressionally authorized to be heard in those courts. Standing focuses on the party seeking to invoke such jurisdiction. In suits against nonfederal defendants, an "implied" cause of action satisfies the preliminary requirement that plaintiff state a valid claim for relief. A fourth branch in the jurisdictional thicket, which we shall now discuss, is reviewability. This concept centers on the *type of decision* which the plaintiff is seeking to have overturned by a federal court. It is applicable only in suits challenging federal agency decisions. If a nonfederal defendant is sued, the court's finding of a valid cause of action includes the determination that the defendant's action can be judicially reviewed. In suits against federal agency decisions, even if a jurisdictional basis for the category of case is found, and even if the plaintiff has been determined to have standing, the particular decision sought to be overturned may be found to have been committed to the sole and exclusive jurisdiction of the executive branch. The matter is regulated by the Administrative Procedure Act which establishes the basic proposition that, unless Congress has spoken otherwise, final agency actions not committed to the discretion of the agency may be reviewed in the federal courts.²²⁴

Only *final* decisions of federal grantor agencies may be subjected to judicial review.²²⁵ A suit charging that a federal agency

---

222 See, e.g., *Grumman Ecosystems Corp.* v. *Gainesville-Alachua County Regional Elec., Water & Sewer Facilities Bd.*, 402 F. Supp. 582 (N.D. Fla. 1975); *Carman* v. *Richardson*, 357 F. Supp. 1148 (D. Vt. 1973); *School Bd.* v. *Richardson*, 332 F. Supp. 1263 (N.D. Fla. 1971).
223 See, e.g., *Grumman Ecosystems Corp.* v. *Gainesville-Alachua County Regional Elec., Water & Sewer Facilities Bd.*, 402 F. Supp. 582 (N.D. Fla. 1975); *National Council of Community Mental Health Centers, Inc.* v. *Weinberger*, 361 F. Supp. 897 (D. D.C. 1973).
224 §10 Administrative Procedure Act, 5 U.S.C. §§701–706.
225 §10(c) *id.*, 5 U.S.C. §704.

has failed to correct administrative deficiencies might be unable to overcome the problem that no decisions have been made and there is, therefore, no action to review.[226] If a clear duty to act can be found in the grant statute or regulations, mandamus might be available to force an agency decision.[227] The plaintiff could also sue the grantee and hope to show an implied cause of action which would lead to injunctive relief.[228] Finally, the plaintiff might be able to convince the court that federal agency inaction is equivalent to final action on the particular issue.[229]

In the grant-in-aid field, Congress has addressed the topic of reviewability with infrequency. One finds in the statutes establishing formula grant programs, however, a standard section which authorizes judicial review in the U.S. courts of appeal of agency disapproval of state plans. The sections are all virtually identical with respect to appellate review, so the quoted section is representative:

> "(1) If any State is dissatisfied with the Commissioner's final action with respect to the approval of a plan submitted under this Act or with his final action under subsection (e) of this section [noncompliance] such State may, within sixty days after notice of such action, file with the United States court of appeals for the circuit in which such State is located a petition for review of that action. A copy of the petition shall be forthwith transmitted by the clerk of the court to the Commissioner. The Commissioner thereupon shall file in the court the record of the proceedings on which he based his action as provided in section 2112 of Title 28.
>
> "(2) The findings of fact by the Commissioner, if supported by substantial evidence, shall be conclusive; but the court, for good cause shown, may remand the case to the Commissioner to take further evidence, and the Commissioner may thereupon make new or modified findings of fact and may modify his previous action, and shall certify to the court the record of further proceedings.
>
> "(3) The court shall have jurisdiction to affirm the action of the Commissioner or to set it aside, in whole or in part. The judgment of the court shall be subject to review by the Supreme

---

[226] See *North Phila. Community Bd. v. Temple Univ.*, 330 F. Supp. 1107 (E.D. Pa. 1971).

[227] See notes 199–211, *supra*, and accompanying text.

[228] See notes 33–35, *supra*, and accompanying text.

[229] *Poirrier v. St. James Parish Police Jury*, 372 F. Supp. 1021 (E.D. La. 1974), *aff'd per curiam*, 531 F.2d 316 (5th Cir. 1976).

Court of the United States upon certiorari or certification as provided in section 1254 of Title 28." [230]

Final administrative action must be preceded by notice and an opportunity to be heard. If a state loses at such a hearing (or forfeits its hearing right) and disapproval is finalized, the state may seek relief in its circuit court. In *Commission on Aging of the State of Alabama* v. *Finch* [231] the grantor reallocated Alabama's formula funds to other states because the plaintiff's state plan had not been approved by the end of the fiscal year. The Fifth Circuit declined jurisdiction because the plaintiff had failed to provoke a final disapproval, and because reallocation decisions do not fall within the ambit of the special review provision. Another of these sections was also read strictly in a case in which intervenors in a conformity hearing were not allowed to appeal the agency decision because these sections refer only to dissatisfied "States." [232]

Review in the courts of appeal is similarly available when state formula funds have been cut off for noncompliance with federal requirements. These review provisions began to be inserted into grant statutes by Congress in response to federal decisions [233] which held that sovereign immunity barred lawsuits challenging such federal action.[234]

The majority of formula grant statutes contain the boilerplate clause. When Congress has inserted noncompliance and nonconformity sections in grant statutes, it has provided judicial review of such final agency actions.[235] In its absence, a state would have to seek review of a noncompliance or nonconformity decision in the federal district court under the Administrative Procedure Act, because the courts of appeal have only the jurisdiction specifically conferred by Congress.[236] The presence of such special

[230] §6(f) Library Services and Construction Act of 1956, 20 U.S.C. §351d(f).
[231] 430 F.2d 667 (5th Cir. 1970).
[232] *Arizona State Dep't of Pub. Welfare* v. *Department of Health, Educ. & Welfare*, 449 F.2d 456, 463–64 (9th Cir. 1971), cert. denied, 405 U.S. 919 (1972).
[233] See, e.g., *Arizona* v. *Hobby*, 221 F.2d 498 (D.C. Cir. 1954).
[234] See *County of Alameda* v. *Weinberger*, 520 F.2d 344, 348–49 (9th Cir. 1975); *Arizona State Dep't of Pub. Welfare* v. *Department of Health, Educ. & Welfare*, 449 F.2d 456, 463 (9th Cir. 1971), cert. denied, 405 U.S. 919 (1972).
[235] See statutory sections cited in Chapter 9, note 2, and Chapter 12, note 1, *infra*, and accompanying text.
[236] See *In re School Bd.*, 475 F.2d 1117 (5th Cir. 1973) (decision voiding grant not reviewable by court of appeals in absence of statutory authorization). But see *Gardner* v. *Alabama*, 385 F.2d 804 (5th Cir. 1967), cert. denied, 389 U.S. 1046 (1968) (inadvertent congressional omission of special judicial review in one of several related programs did not preclude appeal).

statutory review procedures has not been read as precluding other forms of review by other parties.[237]

Most federal grantor decisions do not fall under such special statutory review sections. Review must be sought under the Administrative Procedure Act. The Act provides judicial oversight of all statutorily mandated grantor decisions,[238] but precludes review of actions committed to agency discretion.[239] The distinction, however, has been virtually eradicated in favor of reviewability by the 1971 Supreme Court decision, *Citizens to Preserve Overton Park* v. *Volpe*.[240] In *Overton Park,* the Court described the discretion exemption as "very narrow." [241] It applies only in those rare instances when a court would have "no law to apply." [242] The reviewability question, therefore, is not simply whether Congress has given a federal agency options on a particular matter (the Secretary "may . . .") but whether such judgment is guided by statutory standards. If so, those same standards can be interpreted and applied by courts in reviewing the correctness of the agency judgment.

Overton Park, therefore, is another significant development in the expansion of the bases for judicial intervention in the administration of grant-in-aid programs. Federal grantor decisions involving agency judgment and discretion can be judicially reviewed under the Administrative Procedure Act, except for occasional discretionary acts which are completely unguided by norms drawn from statutes and legislative history.[243]

Under the liberalized reviewability standards courts have been open to review various types of grantor decisions. These in-

---

[237] See, e.g., *Arizona State Dep't of Pub. Welfare* v. *Department of Health, Educ. & Welfare,* 449 F.2d 456, 464, n. 9 (9th Cir. 1971), *cert. denied,* 405 U.S. 919 (1972) (program beneficiary may challenge conformity of state welfare plan in federal district court); *Carman* v. *Richardson,* 357 F. Supp. 1148, 1159 (D. Vt. 1973) (party with standing may challenge approval of grant in district court).

[238] See, e.g., *Tenants & Owners in Opposition to Redev.* v. *U.S. Dep't of Housing & Urban Dev.,* 406 F. Supp. 1024 (N.D. Calif. 1970).

[239] §10(a)(2) Administrative Procedure Act, 5 U.S.C. §701(a)(2).

[240] 401 U.S. 402 (1971).

[241] *Id.* at 410.

[242] *Ibid.*

[243] Our review of grant-in-aid cases has revealed very few instances of unguided and, therefore, unreviewable discretion. See *East Oakland-Fruitvale Planning Council* v. *Rumsfeld,* 471 F.2d 524 (9th Cir. 1972) (decision of Director of Office of Economic Opportunity whether to overturn a gubernatorial veto of a community action grant); *City of Macon* v. *Marshall,* 439 F. Supp. 1209 (M.D. Ga. 1977) (whether grant applicant made "fair and equitable" arrangements to protect employee collective bargaining rights); *Boston Pub. Housing Tenants' Policy Council, Inc.* v. *Lynn,* 388 F. Supp. 493 (D. Mass. 1974) (HUD decisions whether to enforce quality standards in public housing).

clude, in general: federal approval of discretionary grant-in-aid applications [244] and also disapproval; [245] action on specific projects to be implemented under formula grants; [246] decisions on plans which are a prerequisite to funding,[247] and modifications of such plans; [248] specific decisions required in the funding process, such as site selection for facilities; [249] evaluation reports of grantee programs and projects; [250] federal enforcement of grant-in-aid conditions; [251] approvals of grant experiments and demonstrations; [252] disallowances of federal reimbursement for grantee expenditures; [253] defunding of grantees; [254] voiding of grants; [255] determinations on the size of a recipient's formula entitlement; [256] federal agency decisions to suspend grant activities for program reasons; [257] and the imposition of special conditions on grantees.[258]

---

[244] See, e.g., *Mid-America Regional Council v. Mathews*, 416 F. Supp. 896 (W.D. Mo. 1976); *Carman v. Richardson*, 357 F. Supp. 1148 (D. Vt. 1973).
[245] See, e.g., *Advocates for the Arts v. Thomson*, 532 F.2d 792 (1st Cir.), *cert. denied*, 429 U.S. 894 (1976); *Mil-Ka-Ko Research and Dev. Corp. v. Office of Economic Opportunity*, 352 F. Supp. 169 (D. D.C. 1972), *aff'd mem.*, 497 F.2d 684 (D.C. Cir. 1974) (denial of refunding).
[246] See, e.g., *Road Review League v. Boyd*, 270 F. Supp. 650 (S.D. N.Y. 1967) (highway project).
[247] See, e.g., *Western Addition Community Organ. v. Weaver*, 294 F. Supp. 433 (N.D. Cal. 1968), *vacated sub nom.*, *Western Addition Community Organ. v. Romney*, 320 F. Supp. 308 (N.D. Cal. 1969) (relocation plan).
[248] See, e.g., *Shannon v. U.S. Dep't of Housing & Urban Dev.*, 436 F.2d 809 (3d Cir. 1969) (modification of urban renewal plan); *Sansom Comm. v. Lynn*, 366 F. Supp. 1271 (E.D. Pa. 1973) (same).
[249] See, e.g., *Jones v. Tully*, 378 F. Supp. 286 (E.D. N.Y. 1974), *aff'd per curiam*, 510 F.2d 961 (2d Cir. 1975) (public housing site selection).
[250] See, e.g., *Gaines v. Martinez*, 353 F. Supp. 780 (N.D. Tex. 1972).
[251] See, e.g., *North City Area-Wide Council, Inc. v. Romney*, 428 F.2d 754 (3d Cir. 1970), *cert. denied*, 406 U.S. 963 (1972) (citizen participation standards); *Afton Alps, Inc. v. United States*, 392 F. Supp. 543 (D. Minn. 1974) (noncompetition standards).
[252] See, e.g., *Aguayo v. Richardson*, 473 F.2d 1090 (2d Cir. 1973), *cert. denied*, 414 U.S. 1146 (1974); *Crane v. Mathews*, 417 F. Supp. 532 (N.D. Ga. 1976); *California Welfare Rights Organ. v. Richardson*, 348 F. Supp. 491 (N.D. Cal. 1972).
[253] See, e.g., *County of Alameda v. Weinberger*, 520 F.2d 344 (9th Cir. 1975).
[254] See, e.g., *Economic Opportunity Comm'n v. Weinberger*, 524 F.2d 393 (2d Cir. 1975).
[255] See, e.g., *School Bd. v. Department of Health, Educ. & Welfare*, 390 F. Supp. 13 (S.D. Fla. 1974), *rev'd on other grounds*, 525 F.2d 900 (5th Cir. 1976).
[256] See, e.g., *School Bd. v. Richardson*, 332 F. Supp. 1263 (N.D. Fla. 1971).
[257] See *Pennsylvania v. Lynn*, 501 F.2d 848 (D.C. Cir. 1974).
[258] See *AFSCME, Greater Cleveland Dist. Council 78 v. City of Cleveland*, 484 F.2d 339 (6th Cir. 1973).

5

Legal and Practical Limits on the Judicial Role

Remaining Barriers

Our survey thus far of the law concerning judicial review of grantor and grantee actions may give the impression that the judicial and not the executive branch is administering the grant-in-aid system. This section is aimed at demonstrating that, while recent developments have greatly improved the accessibility of the courts for review of grant-in-aid controversies, the power of the judiciary to overturn agency decisions is still quite limited. The section has two parts. In the first, we shall analyze the doctrine of primary jurisdiction (also called "exhaustion of administrative remedies"). This doctrine, we shall see, enables federal agencies to snatch grant-in-aid controversies away from the courts, at least temporarily, by providing an adequate administrative forum for the resolution of such disputes. The second part discusses the scope of judicial review which obtains when a plaintiff has hurdled the barriers of standing, cause of action, sovereign immunity, political question, subject matter jurisdiction, reviewability, and primary jurisdiction, and finally manages to get a federal court to look at the merits of his complaint.

Primary Jurisdiction

The doctrine of primary jurisdiction is essentially a judicial invention. Through it the courts allow federal agencies a prior opportunity to resolve disputes within their domain. If an administrative agency has established procedures for the resolution of the kind of issue brought to court, the plaintiff will not be permitted to bypass the administrative forum. When a court finds the doctrine applicable, it will stay or dismiss the plaintiff's action.[1] Judicial review is thus postponed. It is also narrowed to a review of the federal agency's decision following the hearing.

Such judicial deference permits primary responsibility for the administration and supervision of grant-in-aid programs to remain in the hands of the grantor agency, where it has been placed by Congress. It recognizes the experience and expertise of the executive in managing massive and complex social programs, and confesses the judiciary's relative lack of resources and know-how. It maintains a functional balance between the executive and judicial branches, and keeps the judicial workload within tolerable limits. The doctrine also promotes uniformity in the law by allowing a specialized agency to pass initially on administrative questions which it regularly confronts. Finally, the doctrine assists the judicial function of resolving legal questions by promoting the development of full factual records at the administrative level prior to judicial review.[1a]

Because the courts themselves have created the doctrine, they have felt relatively free to determine when it may or may not be invoked. There is "no fixed formula" [2] for its use; it is a "flexible" [3] doctrine; it requires a "case by case determination of whether, in view of the purposes of the statute involved and the relevance of the administrative expertise to the issue at hand, a court ought to defer initially to the administrative agency." [4]

An essential predicate for the rule of primary jurisdiction to

---

[1] See *Feliciano* v. *Romney*, 363 F. Supp. 656, 676 (S.D. N.Y. 1973).

[1a] The reader is advised to keep in mind that the much vaunted "expertise" and "experience" underlying deference doctrines such as primary jurisdiction may cut against the objectivity and impartiality of an administrator, thus hindering his ability to achieve "in-house" justice. This has been recognized even by federal offices. See e.g., 41 Fed. Reg. 10488, 10489 (1976) ("Executive Branch Positions on Government Procurement Recommendations"). See generally Chapter 15, *infra*.

[2] *Bradford School Bus Transit, Inc.* v. *Chicago Transit Auth.*, 537 F.2d 943, 949 (7th Cir. 1976), *cert. denied*, 429 U.S. 1066 (1977).

[3] *Feliciano* v. *Romney*, 363 F. Supp. 656, 674 (S.D. N.Y. 1973).

[4] *Ibid.* (footnote omitted).

164 / *Rights and Remedies Under Federal Grants*

come into play is the existence of an administrative forum available to the plaintiff and covering the type of complaint he has filed in court. In *Rosado* v. *Wyman*[5] welfare beneficiaries brought to the federal courts a challenge to the legality of New York's welfare program. Although procedures existed for the Department of Health, Education and Welfare to raise compliance issues, they could not be initiated by welfare recipients. The defense of primary jurisdiction was, therefore, rejected.[6] The Supreme Court suggested that if a court wished the views of the federal administrator on the litigated issues, it could invite him to participate as a party or amicus, or obtain his position informally.[7] Besides being available to the plaintiff, the administrative forum must be adequate and not an "exercise in futility."[8] If the administrative process "does not establish any machinery for the review and resolution of complaints and does not indicate what action, if any, might ever result from the expressing of a complaint, . . . plaintiffs need not embark on such an uncertain course before bringing their complaint to court."[9] Mere delay in the administrative processing of complaints, however, does not by itself make the forum inadequate,[10] although failure to include the type of issue raised in the lawsuit would.[11] If the court is uncertain about the adequacy of the administrative forum, it may request the agency to present a plan for processing of plaintiff's petition.[12]

[5] 397 U.S. 397 (1970). See also *Almenares* v. *Wyman*, 453 F.2d 1075, 1087 (2d Cir. 1971), cert. denied, 405 U.S. 944 (1972); *New York City Coalition for Community Health* v. *Lindsay*, 362 F. Supp. 434, 438 (S.D. N.Y. 1973).
[6] *Rosado* v. *Wyman*, 397 U.S. 397, 405–407 (1970). See also id. at 426 (Douglas, J., concurring). Chief Justice Burger and Justice Black dissented strongly on the primary jurisdiction ground, feeling that conformity procedures between state and federal governments would be undermined by third-party lawsuits. See id. at 430–35; *Lewis* v. *Martin*, 397 U.S. 552, 560–63 (1970).
[7] *Rosado* v. *Wyman*, 397 U.S. 397, 406–407 (1970).
[8] *Comprehensive Group Health Servs. Bd. of Directors* v. *Temple Univ.*, 363 F. Supp. 1069 (E.D. Pa. 1973). The court held that it would be futile to require an administrative appeal to the grantee-defendant which had consistently taken an adverse position.
[9] Id. at 1097 (federal regulation simply encouraged grantee to hear complaints).
[10] See *Cannon* v. *University of Chicago*, 406 F. Supp. 1257 (N.D. Ill. 1976), aff'd, 559 F.2d 1063 (7th Cir. 1976), rev'd on other grounds, 99 S. Ct. 1946 (1979).
[11] See *Shannon* v. *U.S. Dep't of Housing & Urban Dev.*, 436 F.2d 809, 820 (3d Cir. 1970) (federal agency's affirmative civil rights obligations); *Comprehensive Group Health Servs. Bd. of Directors* v. *Temple Univ.*, 363 F. Supp. 1069, 1097 (E.D. Pa. 1973) (adequacy of citizen participation).
[12] See *NAACP* v. *Wilmington Medical Center, Inc.*, 426 F. Supp. 919 (D. Del. 1977).

Legal and Practical Limits on the Judicial Role / 165

Civil rights suits arising from grant programs have frequently been dismissed for plaintiff's failure to pursue the administrative relief available.[13] In this area, federal grantor agencies have developed full and detailed procedures.[14] Departmentally initiated nonconformity and noncompliance actions against grantees have also been covered, in most cases, by procedural mechanisms.[15] Yet outside of these two areas, grantor agencies have generally not taken advantage of the opportunity to preempt judicial intervention in grant administration. Third-party challenges to the legality of grantee and grantor actions are generally not covered by the administrative complaint forums that exist, nor are numerous areas of grantor-grantee controversies. The path is open to federal grantors not only to establish their own systems for the administrative ventilation and resolution of controversies [16] but also to preempt judicial action by mandating adequate complaint mechanisms at the state and substate level.[17]

Scope of Review

The plaintiff who has successfully leaped all jurisdictional and other preliminary hurdles, and gets a federal court to review on the merits his case against a federal agency decision, should not be overly optimistic. While the court has power to overturn the agency action, this authority is carefully circumscribed. The limits on federal judicial power in reviewing the decisions of the executive branch are phrased in terms of the "scope of review."

The hard cases are when the plaintiff can show no absence of

---

[13] See *Green St. Ass'n v. Daley*, 373 F.2d 1 (7th Cir. 1967); *Cannon v. University of Chicago*, 406 F. Supp. 1257 (N.D. Ill. 1976), aff'd, 559 F.2d 1063 (7th Cir. 1976), rev'd on other grounds, 99 S. Ct. 1946 (1979); *Feliciano v. Romney*, 363 F. Supp. 656 (S.D. N.Y. 1973); *North Phila. Community Bd. v. Temple Univ.*, 330 F. Supp. 1107 (E.D. Pa. 1971); *Powelton Civic Home Owners Ass'n v. Department of Housing & Urban Dev.*, 284 F. Supp. 809 (E.D. Pa. 1968). Cf. *Bradford School Bus Transit, Inc. v. Chicago Transit Auth.*, 537 F.2d 943 (7th Cir. 1976), cert. denied, 429 U.S. 1066 (1977) (UMTA third-party complaint procedures).

[14] See Chapter 14, infra, at pp. 321–24.

[15] See Chapter 9, infra; and Chapter 12, infra, at pp. 289–91.

[16] See, e.g., §184 Elementary and Secondary Education Act of 1965, 20 U.S.C. §2834, as rewritten by §101 Education Amendments of 1978, Pub. L. 95-571, Nov. 1, 1978; *Lloyd v. Regional Transp. Auth.* 548 F.2d 1277 (7th Cir. 1977).

[17] See, e.g., §§128, 168 Elementary and Secondary Education Act of 1965, 20 U.S.C. §§2738, 2815, as rewritten by §101 Education Amendments of 1978, Pub. L. 95-571, Nov. 1, 1978; *National Ass'n of Neighborhood Health Centers, Inc. v. Mathews*, 551 F.2d 321 (D.C. Cir. 1976).

agency authority or jurisdiction,[18] no prejudicial [19] procedural irregularity,[20] no violation of mandatory requirements statutorily imposed on the grantor,[21] and no failure on the part of the decision maker to consider obligatory factors.[22] When the grantor has had discretion in making the decision and the accusation is that it has exercised poor judgment, the chances of relief are remote. The Administrative Procedure Act provides that such decisions can be overturned only if found to be "arbitrary, capricious [or] an abuse of discretion." [23] While the court may orchestrate a "thorough, probing, in-depth review" of the agency decision and make a "searching and careful" inquiry into the facts, the Supreme Court has made clear that the "ultimate standard of review is a narrow one." [24] The court is not empowered to substitute its judgment for that of the agency, and may vacate the agency decision only upon a finding of a "clear error of judgment." [25]

Under these standards, the success rate of plaintiffs challenging federal grantor discretionary decisions is a poor 10 percent.[26]

---

[18] See §10(e)(2)(c) Administrative Procedure Act, 5 U.S.C. §706(2)(c) ("in excess of statutory jurisdiction, authority, or limitations, or short of statutory right").

[19] Even if plaintiff can demonstrate an agency violation of procedural or substantive standards, such error must also be prejudicial to plaintiff's interests. See, e.g., *Mid-America Regional Council* v. *Mathews*, 416 F. Supp. 896, 906 (W.D. Mo. 1976) (violation of time limits of A-95 consultation *de minimis*); cf. Federal Rules of Civil Procedure 61 (harmless error).

[20] See §10(e)(2)(D) Administrative Procedure Act, 5 U.S.C. §706(2)(D) ("without observance of procedure required by law").

[21] See §10(e)(2)(A) Administrative Procedure Act, 5 U.S.C. §706(2)(A) ("otherwise not in accordance with law").

[22] See *Citizens to Preserve Overton Park, Inc.* v. *Volpe*, 401 U.S. 402, 416 (1971); *Shannon* v. *U.S. Dep't of Housing & Urban Dev.*, 436 F.2d 809 (3d Cir. 1970) (failure to consider racial impact of project change).

[23] §10(e)(2)(A) Administrative Procedure Act, 5 U.S.C. §706(2)(A).

[24] *Citizens to Preserve Overton Park* v. *Volpe*, 401 U.S. 402, 415–16 (1971).

[25] *Id.* at 416.

[26] Agency action in the following sampling of cases was found not to have been an abuse of discretion: *Advocates for the Arts* v. *Thomson*, 532 F.2d 792 (1st Cir.), *cert. denied*, 429 U.S. 894 (1976) (denial of grant for literary publication); *School Bd.* v. *Department of Health, Educ. & Welfare*, 525 F.2d 900 (5th Cir. 1976) (termination of grant for false assurances); *Economic Opportunity Comm'n* v. *Weinberger*, 524 F.2d 393 (2d Cir. 1975) (defunding of community action grant); *Pennsylvania* v. *Lynn*, 501 F.2d 848 (D.C. Cir. 1974) (suspension of housing program); *AFSCME, Greater Cleveland Dist. Council 78* v. *City of Cleveland*, 484 F.2d 339 (6th Cir. 1973) (imposition of special grant restriction); *South Suburban Safeway Lines, Inc.* v. *City of Chicago*, 416 F.2d 535 (7th Cir. 1969) (finding that grant would not cause competitive injury); *Kletschka* v. *Driver*, 411 F.2d 436 (2d Cir. 1969) (denial of health research grant); *School City* v. *Derthick*, 273 F.2d 319 (7th Cir. 1959) (finding that plaintiff not eligible for grant); *City of Grand Rapids* v. *Richardson*, 429 F. Supp. 1087 (W.D. Mich. 1977) (determination of grantee eligibility based on unemployment rates); *City of Benton Harbor* v. *Richardson*, 429 F. Supp. 1096 (W.D. Mich. 1977) (ranking of applications for grants); *Missouri ex rel. Missouri-St. Louis Metro. Airport Auth.* v. *Coleman*, 427 F. Supp. 1252 (D. D.C.), *vacated*, 564 F.2d 600 (D.C. Cir. 1977) (adequacy of environmental impact statement; grant approval); *Township of Ridley* v.

Legal and Practical Limits on the Judicial Role / 167

The reported court decisions demonstrate the extreme difficulty of overturning federal grantor decisions, whether the suit has been brought by a grantee or a third party. While grantor decisions may be wrong, they rarely reflect the almost total lack of rationality necessary to a finding of arbitrariness. Further, court review is of the administrative record on which the agency decision was based. The court cannot create a factual basis for the administrative decision, but can only review the facts and information which the agency took into consideration in reaching the result in dispute.[27] Absent administrative hearing opportunities, the fabric of the factual background of decisions is woven by the grantor. Having authority over the input, the grantor not only directs the desired outputs but also influences the reviewability of such decisions in court. Only an extremely careless grantor would be likely to fail

---

Blanchette, 421 F. Supp. 435 (E.D. Pa. 1976) (finding that environmental assessment not needed); *Crane v. Mathews,* 417 F. Supp. 532 (N.D. Ga. 1976) (demonstration project promotes Medicaid objectives); *Mid-America Regional Council v. Mathews,* 416 F. Supp. 896 (W.D. Mo. 1976) (no abuse in awarding grant); *Grassetti v. Weinberger,* 408 F. Supp. 142 (N.D. Cal. 1976) (denial of health research grant); *Grumman Ecosystems Corp. v. Gainesville-Alachua County Regional Elec., Water & Sewer Facilities Bd.,* 402 F. Supp. 582 (N.D. Fla. 1975) (determination of responsiveness of bid); *Afton Alps, Inc. v. United States,* 392 F. Supp. 543 (D. Minn. 1974) (finding that grant would not cause competitive harm); *Board of Educ. v. U.S. Dep't of Health, Educ. & Welfare,* 384 F. Supp. 816 (S.D. N.Y. 1974) (determination that discretionary grant application was of inferior quality); *Jones v. Tully,* 378 F. Supp. 286 (E.D. N.Y. 1974), *aff'd per curiam,* 510 F.2d 961 (2d Cir. 1975) (decision on housing project); *Northeast Community Organ., Inc. v. Weinberger,* 378 F. Supp. 1287 (D. Md. 1974) (determination of grantee ineligibility); *City of North Miami v. Train,* 377 F. Supp. 1264 (S.D. Fla. 1974) (finding of adequacy of environmental assessment); *Movement Against Destruction v. Volpe,* 361 F. Supp. 1360 (D. Md. 1973), *aff'd per curiam,* 500 F.2d 29 (4th Cir. 1974) (same; planning process adequate); *Carman v. Richardson,* 357 F. Supp. 1148 (D. Vt. 1973) (finding that grant consistent with state plan); *Gaines v. Martinez,* 353 F. Supp. 780 (N.D. Tex. 1972) (no clear error in evaluation report); *Mil-Ka-Ko Research & Dev. Corp. v. Office of Economic Opportunity,* 352 F. Supp. 169 (D. D.C. 1972), *aff'd mem.,* 497 F.2d 684 (D.C. Cir. 1974) (denial of refunding based on grantee deficiencies); *California Welfare Rights Organ. v. Richardson,* 348 F. Supp. 491 (N.D. Cal. 1972) (experiment would further welfare objectives); *School Bd. v. Richardson,* 332 F. Supp. 1263 (N.D. Fla. 1971) (determination of size of formula grant); *Monmouth Legal Servs. Organ. v. Carlucci,* 330 F. Supp. 985 (D. N.J. 1971) (grantor decision to merge two programs); *Road Review League v. Boyd,* 270 F. Supp. 650 (S.D. N.Y. 1967) (approval of highway route).

In only a handful of cases have grantor discretionary decisions been found to be arbitrary. See, e.g., *Tenants & Owners in Opposition to Redev. v. U.S. Dep't of Housing & Urban Dev.,* 406 F. Supp. 1024 (N.D. Cal. 1970) (arbitrary approval of grantee's relocation plan); *Western Addition Community Organ. v. Weaver,* 294 F. Supp. 433 (N.D. Cal. 1968), *vacated sub nom., Western Addition Community Organ. v. Romney,* 320 F. Supp. 308 (N.D. Cal. 1969) (same).

27 *South Dakota v. Volpe,* 353 F. Supp. 335, 339, 342–43 (D. S.D. 1973); *Missouri ex rel. Missouri-St. Louis Metro. Airport Auth. v. Coleman,* 427 F. Supp. 1252, 1257 (D. D.C.), *vacated,* 564 F.2d 600 (D.C. Cir. 1977). The court may order the defendant federal agency to prepare the full administrative record which underlay its decision. See *Citizens to Preserve Overton Park, Inc. v. Volpe,* 401 U.S. 402, 420 (1971).

to document its decision so as, effectively, to immunize it from judicial review.

Some types of grantor decisions, while seemingly reviewable under the Administrative Procedure Act and *Overton Park,* will not in fact be subjected to judicial review. The award of competitive grants is a good example. There is "law to apply," plenty of it. The standards under which funding proposals are to be evaluated and ranked are typically published in agency regulations in considerable detail. If a court were so inclined, it could restage a particular grant competition and determine if the grantor had abused its discretion in its ranking of a disappointed plaintiff's proposal. Courts, however, have balked at that proposition. One court suggested that such decisions be nonreviewable, voicing the fear that:

> "were a substantial evidence or abuse of discretion standard held to apply, the result would be to place a tremendous burden on the courts to digest masses of technical data before it could be decided that one grant application was so superior that it was an abuse of discretion to reject it in favor of others." [28]

Besides the magnitude of the task such review would place upon a district court, the judiciary has disclaimed having "institutional competence warranting case-by-case participation in the allocation of funds." [29]

Adequacy of the Judicial Forum

Despite the limits on judicial review and the poor success rate of their predecessors, those harmed by federal grant decisions have taken advantage of the new accessibility of federal courts in ever-increasing numbers. The bulk of such suits are brought by program beneficiaries and third parties who challenge the implementation of grant programs by the federal administering agency, the grantee, or both. Yet recent years have also witnessed a substantial increase in the number of lawsuits brought by

---

[28] *Grassetti* v. *Weinberger,* 408 F. Supp. 142, 150 (N.D. Cal. 1976) (health research grants). See also *Apter* v. *Richardson,* 510 F.2d 351, 355 (7th Cir. 1975) (same); *Kletschka* v. *Driver,* 411 F.2d 436, 443 (2d Cir. 1969) (same; complex and subtle evaluations of the technical merits of projects and personnel).

[29] *Advocates for the Arts* v. *Thomson,* 532 F.2d 792, 795–96 (1st Cir.), *cert. denied,* 429 U.S. 894 (1976).

grantees and potential grantees harmed by federal agency decisions.[30] This sharp increase may be simply the result of the elimination of prior barriers to judicial relief. It may also indicate other trends. The sudden growth of lawsuits could signal increased tensions in grantor-grantee relations. It might represent a heightened awareness of "rights" and erosion of the psychological blocks which inhibit challenges to grantors. The wave of lawsuits may also signify that the administrative forum for the resolution of such disputes is inadequate, or perceived as unfair. Whatever the underlying reasons, we doubt whether judicial process is an adequate remedial device for recipients of federal grants. Nor do we believe that increased involvement of the federal judiciary in the administration and supervision of grants-in-aid serves the interests of federal agencies and, through them, the public.

The opening of the federal courts guarantees an opportunity to be heard to grantees. To that extent, it provides a path to relief from harmful and erroneous federal agency action. But it is a long, rocky, and ultimately unsatisfactory route.

If the grantor's decision has been outside its authority, procedurally irregular, or inconsistent with substantive standards, the opportunity for judicial relief is obviously valuable. In those circumstances courts are not confined in their review function, though they will defer to some extent to the agency view on substantive questions. Those, however, are the atypical cases. Federal agencies are unlikely to pursue at length a clearly illegal course of action. The more common situation is where the agency must exercise judgment in its decisional process, and the grantee claim is that such exercise was abusive or simply wrong. The grantee argument may proceed from a different perception and emphasis on the facts of the case; it may be based on a subtly different reading of the substantive standards; or it could result from a different view on the application of the facts to the legal standard. These are precisely the cases in which the courts are confined in their review function and in which the grantee has little chance for relief. With reversals limited to cases in which the court finds "arbitrary" agency action or "clear" error of judgment, the grantee is playing against a stacked deck. And even in those few cases in which a court is willing to characterize agency action as "arbitrary," the judicial relief will typically be unsatisfactory—

---

[30] See Chapter 1, notes 15a–26a, *supra,* and accompanying text.

remand to the agency for a decision following the correct procedures or standards. The agency, already predisposed, may then affirm its original decision on other grounds.[31]

Numerous other disadvantages attend the judicial route. It is costly and time-consuming. Unless the stakes are very high, grantees may simply abandon their rights in view of the high legal costs and delay characteristic of federal court litigation. Because judicial review is available only after final agency action has been taken, the grantee must, if possible, withstand the consequences of that agency decision during the course of the lawsuit. A grantee dependent on federal funding, for example, would be hard put to survive a termination decision long enough to see a judicial action to its conclusion. Another disadvantage has already been noted. If no administrative hearing has preceded federal agency action, the facts to be reviewed in court are those which the grantor agency utilized in reaching its decision. It is the administrative record which is reviewed, not the facts which the grantee may wish to advance at the judicial hearing. Control of the factual record, therefore, rests in the hands of one of the adversaries in court—a substantial litigation advantage. Also, the court proceeding often lacks flexibility. Courts usually cannot compromise on legal principles. The question is whether the agency decision was right or wrong, not a little bit of each. When lawsuits are filed, positions tend to harden, and the chance for mutual accommodation lessens.

The ultimate disadvantage is the hostility which litigation engenders. When administrative hearing procedures have been established, grantor agencies expect them to be utilized. Grantees are not begrudged the pursuit of claims in the administrative forum. The matter is still "in-house," still a normal part of the administrative process. A lawsuit, however, casts the gauntlet. Those federal grantor officials involved in the decisional process find their actions brought to public attention and scrutinized by a different branch of government. Their business agenda is disturbed by the time demands of litigation. The "cooperative" nature of the grant-in-aid has been undermined.

People who sue normally expect and pay the price of antagonisms. Most, however, do not have a continuing relationship with their opponent which requires postlitigation cordiality. Most grantees must keep doing business with the agencies they sue, and

---

[31] Cahn & Cahn, "The New Sovereign Immunity," 81 Harv. L. Rev. 929, 942 (1968).

may suffer future harm from the ill will which litigation has fostered. Defeats for their competitive grant proposals, tightened supervision of their compliance with grant standards, careful inspection of their reports and evaluations, loss of flexibility in tailoring grants to their particular needs—all of these consequences and more may be anticipated. Grantor discretion permeates all aspects of grant-in-aid administration and may quickly be turned against disfavored grantees.

From the grantor's perspective, clear advantages accrue to the resolution of grant-in-aid controversies in an administrative forum. The adversarial tone is muted, and sensible, program-related accommodations can often be reached. Both parties can move toward the common goal of serving the ultimate beneficiaries of the grant, seeking grounds of agreement, and adjusting differences so as to maximize the efficiency of the grant. Federal law must, of course, be observed, but unless grantee practices are clearly violative of established norms (in which case dispute is unlikely), standards can be shaped and practices altered to the mutual satisfaction of grantor and grantee. Equally important, the matter remains in the hands of those with experience and knowledgeability in the management of multimillion dollar social programs.

6

The Federal Grant: A Unique Legal Creation

We have, thus far, avoided any definitions of the subject of our study, perhaps unwisely in the eyes of some. For example, we have employed the terms "grant" and "grant-in-aid" interchangeably, recognizing that some prefer to use the latter term only to describe financial assistance to state and local governments.[1] Our survey of grant statutes and regulations did not reveal any such custom or usage. Although the Federal Grant and Cooperative Agreement Act of 1977 [2] uses only the word "grant," we generally feel more comfortable with the term "grant-in-aid," probably because it explicitly contains the fundamental idea of support.

We will continue to avoid thought-stifling definitions, though now that we have surveyed the core rights, responsibilities, and remedies attending a federal grant-in-aid, we may be in a position to describe the grant in broader conceptual terms. Our basic conclusion is that the federal grant occupies a unique place in American law.

Efforts have been made to demonstrate that a grant is basically a contract and, therefore, carries with it the bag of rights and obligations traditionally associated with business agreements.[3]

---

[1] See S. Rep. No. 449, 95th Cong., 1st Sess. 9 (1977).
[2] Pub. L. 95-224, Feb. 3, 1978, 41 U.S.C. §§501–509.
[3] See Wallick & Montalto, "Symbiosis or Domination: Rights and Remedies Under Grant-Type Assistance Programs," 46 Geo. Wash. L. Rev. 159, 165–68 (1978).

Similarly, respectable authority asserts that the federal grant is more akin to a trust relationship, bringing to bear equitable principles of right and duty.[4] Writers have even explored the relevance of partnership principles to the grant-in-aid.[5] And the popular conception of a grant as a gift still strongly influences thinking in the field.[6] Yet the grant-in-aid is none of the above, although it shares elements of each. The procrustean efforts of the writers are misguided. In the end it does little good to characterize the federal grant as a contract, gift, trust, or partnership. In order to be decided correctly, any question concerning the relative rights and responsibilities of the parties to the grant must ultimately be decided by reference to the set of rules emanating from the grant statute, regulations, and agreement, all interpreted in light of the constitutional bases of federal grants, the purposes of such aid, and standard grant practices. To align the federal grant with one of the traditional fields of American law is to substitute a body of principles and doctrines evolved in a foreign context for the hard work of interpreting and evolving principles in the context of governmental assistance. While such shortcuts are not unknown,[7] they ill serve the governmental institution of grants-in-aid.

The matter is more than academic. Although the U.S. Senate admits that grant law is "primitive and underdeveloped,"[8] expanded bases of judicial review[9] are bringing into the courts more and more controversies involving grants-in-aid.[10] Increasingly judicial glosses will be placed on the vague terms and expressions now found in grant statutes and regulations. The quality of this judicial law making will be seriously affected by the bench's perception of the grant. To the extent that the analogies to schoolboy doctrine are found easy and irresistible, to that same extent will the chance of error rise. Only if the analogies are resisted will the evolution of the grant institution remain consistent with the spirit and purposes of governmental aid.

More profitable than comparisons, we believe, is a straight and simple listing of the basic attributes of the federal grant. First,

[4] See Willcox, "The Function and Nature of Grants," 22 Ad. L. Rev. 125, 128–29 (1970).
[5] See Wallick & Montalto, "Symbiosis or Domination: Rights and Remedies Under Grant-Type Assistance Programs," 46 Geo. Wash. L. Rev. 159, 168–69 (1978).
[6] See R. Scurlock, *Government Contracts and Grants for Research: A Guide for Colleges and Universities* 1 (Nat'l Ass'n of College & Univ. Business Officers 1975).
[7] See Chapter 3, note 122, *supra*, and accompanying text.
[8] See S. Rep. No. 449, 95th Cong., 1st Sess. 8 (1977).
[9] See generally Chapter 4, *supra*.
[10] See Chapter 1, *supra*, at pp. 1–7.

and probably of primary importance, is that the federal grant aims at assisting other social institutions perform public services.[11] The Federal Grant and Cooperative Agreement Act of 1977 captures that idea by requiring federal agencies to use the grant vehicle when the purpose of the payment is "support or stimulation." The key section reads in full as follows:

> "Each executive agency shall use a type of grant agreement as the legal instrument reflecting a relationship between the Federal Government and a State or local government or other recipient whenever—
>
> "(1) the principal purpose of the relationship is the transfer of money, property, services or anything of value to the State or local government or other recipient in order to accomplish a public purpose of support or stimulation authorized by Federal statute, rather than acquisition, by purchase, lease, or barter, of property or services for the direct benefit or use of the Federal Government; and
>
> "(2) no substantial involvement is anticipated between the executive agency, acting for the Federal Government, and the State or local government or other recipient during performance of the contemplated activity." [12]

The concept of giving without receiving leads one readily to the idea of a gift. The spirit is, indeed, donative, but the gift analogy fails when one adds the ingredient of enforceability. Once a federal agency makes a grant award, or even in some cases once Congress appropriates funds for a grant program,[13] the recipient is "entitled" to the funds. That means, simply, that the grantee can successfully sue if the federal agency does not come up with the promised cash, or parts thereof.[14] The gift analogy is also weakened by the host of restrictions and conditions placed on the federal grant.[15] Each federal control and standard tends to support the idea that, indeed, the United States is getting something out of the deal and, thus, moves the grant toward the world of quid pro quos. It is, at bottom, impossible not to perceive benefits flowing to the U.S. government from the grants-in-aid—promotion

---

[11] See Chapter 2, *supra*, at pp. 34–36, and Chapter 8, *infra*, at pp. 241–42.

[12] §5 Federal Grant and Cooperative Agreement Act of 1977, Pub. L. 95-224, Feb. 3, 1978, 41 U.S.C. §504.

[13] In formula programs. See Chapter 7, notes 44–46, *infra*, and accompanying text.

[14] See Chapter 1, note 16, and Chapter 4, notes 212–214, *supra*, and accompanying text.

[15] R. Scurlock, *Government Contracts and Grants for Research: A Guide for Colleges and Universities* 4 (Nat'l Ass'n of College & Univ. Business Officers 1975).

of national civil rights, healthier and cleaner environment, uniformity in government employee wages and hours of work, less disparity in public service levels throughout the country, to name a few. It remains, however, reasonably intelligible to draw lines on the basis of the "who benefits most" principle, though in some cases, such as research grants, the lines will be quite fine.[16]

A second major characteristic of the grant-in-aid is the high level of generality with which the end product—public services—is described. The focus is generally on process and goals [17] rather than detailed descriptions of the end products sought. Another way of conceptualizing this is to stress the high degree of control which the grantee has over the resulting product, unlike the normal situation of buyer control.[18] Because of this level of generality in the products sought by the Federal Government, combined with the assistance concept described above, the grantee is not liable for failure to perform, an important characteristic of the grant-in-aid.[19] In fact, the Office of Management and Budget uses this as one of the important definitional characteristics of a project grant: "The funding for fixed or known periods, of specific projects or the delivery of specific services or products without liability for damages for failure to perform." [20]

Lack of liability means several things to a grantee. One is that if the grantee has violated one or more terms of the grant, it will generally not have to reimburse the Federal Government for federal funds expended during the period of noncompliance. That includes, for example, a failure to achieve programmatic goals or to follow mandated processes.[21] A likely exception, calling for reimbursement, is the diversion of funds to unauthorized purposes.[22] Another consequence of nonliability is that the grantee, unlike the grantor, can generally terminate at will,[23] simply returning whatever federal funds and property that remain. The ability to quit

[16] See S. Rep. 449, 95th Cong., 1st Sess. 26–27 (1977).
[17] See Chapter 2, notes 87–88, *supra,* and accompanying text.
[18] See Willcox, "The Function and Nature of Grants," 22 Ad. L. Rev. 125, 129 (1970).
[19] *Id.* at 129–30.
[20] Office of Management and Budget, *Catalog of Federal Domestic Assistance* xix (1978 update).
[21] See Chapter 3, notes 188–214, *supra,* and accompanying text; Skoler, Lynch, & Axilbund, "Legal and Quasi-Legal Considerations in New Federal Aid Programs," 56 Geo. L. J. 1144, 1161 (1968).
[22] See Chapter 3, *supra,* at pp. 101–102.
[23] See Chapter 3, notes 228–230, *supra,* and accompanying text.

a project means, essentially, that the remedy of specific performance is unavailable to the United States.[24]

The Supreme Court land grant cases [25] involved Acts of Congress based on the Territorial Clause.[26] They would seem to have little relevance in establishing grant principles for modern grant-in-aid statutes established under the Spending Clause.[27] For example, the doctrine of the *San Francisco* case that land grant conditions are specifically enforceable is explicitly based on the plenary congressional power under the Territorial Clause,[28] and can have little relevance outside that context. Despite the fundamental differences between modern grants-in-aid and the land grants, writers unfortunately cite these old cases for the proposition that today's grants are contracts with obligations enforceable by both sides.[29] Courts, too, are prone to the same mistake.[30]

We have demonstrated that the "voluntary quit" is a constitutionally required principle in federal grant programs established under the Spending Clause.[31] Federal standards are imposed by virtue of the consent of the grantee, not through constitutional sources of power independent of the Spending Clause. Once that consent ends, so does federal power. Many grant programs, however, stem from an independent basis of federal authority. Grants awarded by the Department of Defense, for example, do not flow from the power to promote the general welfare but, rather, from the military clauses in the Constitution.[32] In these cases, there is no constitutional need to permit a grantee to drop the project before its termination date. The question of mandating performance is one of agency choice. When, however, an agency opts to require specific performance of grantee obligations, it is necessarily undercutting the "assistance" principle.

Similar trade-offs may occur in grant programs which, by their nature, permit great detail in the description of the desired end

---

[24] See Chapter 3, notes 215–230, *supra*, and accompanying text.
[25] *Burke v. Southern Pac. R.R.*, 234 U.S. 669 (1914); *United States v. Northern Pac. R.R.*, 256 U.S. 51 (1921); *United States v. City & County of San Francisco*, 310 U.S. 16 (1940).
[26] U.S. Const. art. IV, §3, cl. 2.
[27] U.S. Const. art. I, §8, cl. 1.
[28] *United States v. City & County of San Francisco*, 310 U.S. 16, 29–30 (1940).
[29] See, e.g., R. Scurlock, *Government Contracts and Grants for Research: A Guide for Colleges and Universities* 4 (Nat'l Ass'n of College & Univ. Business Officers 1975); Wallick & Montalto, "Symbiosis or Domination: Rights and Remedies Under Grant-Type Assistance Programs," 46 Geo. Wash. L. Rev. 159, 165, n. 34 (1978).
[30] E.g., *United States v. Frazer*, 297 F. Supp. 319, 322–23 (M.D. Ala. 1968).
[31] U.S. Const. art. I, §8, cl. 1. See Chapter 3, notes 85–109, and accompanying text.
[32] See, e.g., U.S. Const. art. I, §8, cl. 1 (Common Defense Clause).

products. These would include federal support of construction activities—roads, highways, sewage plants, hospitals, schools—and also "development" projects. Because the desired products can be specified in the grant agreement with reasonable detail, leading to the possibility of measuring performance accurately at the end of the work, liability for inadequate performance is easily imposed. And to avoid half-built structures, specific performance during the term of the project is sensible. In both cases contractual principles are adopted despite the fact that funds are paid under a grant. Thus, the Environmental Protection Agency, for example, has adopted numerous typical contract rules in the administration of its construction grants.[33]

Another basic feature of the federal grant is the lack of negotiation by the grantee prior to the award.[34] The federal agency unilaterally determines, on its own or pursuant to a statutory formula, the project's cost and awards that amount. The terms accompanying the grant award are similarly nonnegotiable. They are imposed by federal statute and regulation, and usually cannot be waived by the grantor agency. Thus, rights and responsibilities under a grant-in-aid are unilaterally determined by the United States.[35] The grantee retains only the right to reject the award.

Unlike traditional contracts, or even federal procurement contracts,[36] what is stated in the grant agreement is usually of minor importance in determining grantor and grantee rights and duties. The grant statute, grantor agency regulations, and central directives are all applicable and controlling.[37] An important grant principle, which deviates from traditional contract rules, is that one party, the United States, can unilaterally modify the terms of the relationship during the term of the grant. By statute or regulation the United States can impose additional obligations under

---

[33] See 35 C.F.R. pt. 30, subpts. H–J.

[34] For a description of the grant application process, see cases cited in Chapter 7, note 72, *infra,* and accompanying text.

[35] See Chapter 3, *supra,* at pp. 53–63.

[36] Federal procurement contracts generally contain all relevant clauses and rules, unlike grant agreements which usually incorporate applicable rules by reference. A principle parallel to that discussed in this paragraph of the text exists in the procurement field. Called the "Christian Doctrine," it holds that procurement regulations have the force of law and will be read into contracts if not actually incorporated. G. L. *Christian & Assocs.* v. *United States,* 312 F.2d 418 (Ct. Cl.), *cert. denied,* 375 U.S. 954 (1963).

[37] See Chapter 3, *supra,* at pp. 53–59.

178 / *Rights and Remedies Under Federal Grants*

the agreement,[38] although constitutional restrictions on the impairment of contracts limit that power to some degree.[39]

A further feature of the federal grant-in-aid is the cost-sharing principle. Because the grant is considered as primarily for the benefit of the recipient, it is regularly considered appropriate that the grantee share in the financing of project costs.[40] On the other hand, the recipient of a federal procurement contract expects to be paid fully for its services.

The above are the major and inherent features of the federal grant-in-aid. We may also add some functional ways in which grants differ from federal contracts.[41] Unlike federal procurement law, the terms of grant awards are characterized by a high degree of vagueness and gaps. The rights and duties of grantors and grantees are, consequently, frequently unclear. Similarly, administrative dispute resolution machinery is in a primitive stage of development, and Due Process rights are not generally recognized. Unlike the procurement field which is governed by substantive codes,[42] grant regulations are promulgated agency-by-agency, program-by-program, leading to a vast network of repetitive and frequently inconsistent rules. Finally, many of the conditions imposed on federal grantees differ from those required of federal contractors.[43]

New legislation imposes the obligation on each federal agency to determine whether its financial relationships are, in each case, for the direct benefit or use of the Federal Government, for the support or stimulation of the recipient, or for the support and stimulation of the recipient with substantial federal involvement.[44] Procurement contracts, grant agreements, and cooperative agreements must be utilized in the case of each such finding, respectively, though the statute does not dictate any of the clauses in

---

[38] *Thorpe* v. *Housing Auth.*, 393 U.S. 268, 279 (1969).

[39] *Id.* at 278–79.

[40] R. Scurlock, *Government Contracts and Grants for Research: A Guide for Colleges and Universities* 5 (Nat'l Ass'n of College & Univ. Business Officers 1975).

[41] See *id.* at 21–22 for a comparison of grants and contracts on 21 points.

[42] See, e.g., 41 C.F.R. pts. 1-1-1-30 (federal procurement regulations); cf. Office of Federal Procurement Policy, "Uniform Rules of Procedure for Boards of Contract Appeals and Related Regulations," 44 Fed. Reg. 12519 (1979).

[43] Compare Chapter 2, *supra*, at pp. 45–52, with R. Scurlock. *Government Contracts and Grants: A Guide for Colleges and Universities* 28–357 (Nat'l Ass'n of College & Univ. Business Officers 1975).

[44] §§4–6 Federal Grant and Cooperative Agreement Act of 1977, Pub. L. 95-224, Feb. 3, 1978, 41 U.S.C. §§503–505.

such instruments. The primary effect of the Act will be felt in the field of research and development where the practice had arisen in several federal agencies of avoiding competitive bidding by utilizing grants instead of contracts.[45] The bulk of the federal grant-in-aid programs will be undisturbed since there can be little dispute about their essentially supportive or stimulative nature.

---

[45] See S. Rep. No. 449, 95th Cong., 1st Sess. 23–24 (1977). Correct identification of an instrument as a "contract" will also place the resolution of controversies under the Contract Disputes Act of 1978, Pub. L. 95-563, Nov. 1, 1978, 41 U.S.C. §§601–613, rather than the haphazard grants disputes system described throughout this book.

7

Due Process and Federal Grants

Basic Principles

"Due process" has become a household phrase. Its revolutionary movement in recent years out of the cabin of judicial proceedings and into the fields of administrative action has widened its impact to the extent that millions of Americans are both protected in many of their activities and sensitized to the potential protection in others.[1]

Despite its popularization, understanding the meaning of Due Process is most difficult for it is a genus which we can ultimately know only by a study of the myriad of species it subsumes. A series of variables composes each species, and in turn each of those variables demands particularized investigation of the factual context in which fair process is demanded.

Due Process claims against the United States are based on the Fifth Amendment,[2] while the claim against a state grantee which

---

[1] See generally Nowak *et al., Constitutional Law* 476–514 (1978); Tribe, *American Constitutional Law* 501–63 (1978); Friendly, "Some Kind of Hearing," 123 U. Pa. L. Rev. 1267 (1975); Mashaw, "The Supreme Court's Due Process Calculus for Administrative Adjudication in *Mathews* v. *Eldridge*: Three Factors in Search of a Theory of Value," 44 U. Chi. L. Rev. 28 (1976); Mashaw, "The Management Side of Due Process: Some Judicial and Litigation Notes on the Assurance of Accuracy, Fairness, and Timeliness in the Adjudication of Social Welfare Claims," 59 Cornell L. J. 772 (1974); Monaghan, "Of 'Liberty' and 'Property,'" 62 Cornell L. Rev. 405 (1977); Tribe, "Structural Due Process," 10 Harv. Civ. Rights-Civ. Lib. L. Rev. 269 (1975); Van Alstyne, "Cracks in the 'New Property': Adjudicative Due Process in the Administrative State," 62 Cornell L. Rev. 445 (1977); Note, "Statutory Entitlement and the Concept of Property," 86 Yale L. J. 695 (1977).
[2] U.S. Const. amend. V.

has acted against the interests of a subgrantee would be premised on the Fourteenth.[3] The constitutional standards are, for the most part, identical.[4] While the emphasis here is on *constitutional* rights, we should stress that a grievance by a grantee that it has received inadequate notice and opportunity to be heard may be founded on other legal sources. The claim may arise under *statutory* hearing requirements allegedly violated by the federal or state grantor,[5] or violations by the grantor of its own procedural *regulations*.[6]

For constitutional adjudication, the opening inquiry is whether the interests allegedly invaded by the actions of another merit attention of that stature. Process is owed when "liberty" and "property" interests are threatened.[7] Those chameleons, we are told, "gather meaning from experience" and "relate to the whole domain of social and economic fact."[8] Human aspirations and greed being what they are, we are guaranteed an endless procession of claims that the interests being invaded by government are sufficiently substantial and asserted with enough justification to be covered under one or more of those words.

We also need to find a deprivation, which requires measurement of the impact of governmental action on the claimant's interest.[9] Is it a sufficient taking of or injury to what rightfully belongs to another as to warrant judicial concern? The search into the impact on the well-being of an individual or entity becomes even more particularized when a constitutionally protected interest and sufficient deprivation are found so that the next inquiry, what process is "due," must be made. The more substantial the asserted harm, the more protection is needed.[10] In measuring that impact we are forced to enter the home and life of the Due Process claimant.[11] Because no one suffers "in general," we look to and measure the specific hurts resulting from the government's action.

---

[3] U.S. Const. amend. XIV, §1.

[4] See, e.g., *Curry v. McCanless*, 307 U.S. 357, 370 (1939); *Twining v. New Jersey*, 211 U.S. 78, 101 (1908); *French v. Barber Asphalt Paving Co.*, 181 U.S. 324, 329 (1901); *Regents of the Univ. of Cal. v. Bakke*, 438 U.S. 265, 367, n. 43 (1978) (Brennan, J., concurring and dissenting); H. Meyer, *The History and Meaning of the Fourteenth Amendment* 126 (1977).

[5] See, e.g., *Arizona State Dep't of Pub. Welfare v. Dep't of Health, Educ. & Welfare*, 449 F.2d 456, 479, n. 29 (9th Cir. 1971), *cert. denied*, 405 U.S. 919 (1972).

[6] See, e.g., *Economic Opportunity Comm'n v. Weinberger*, 524 F.2d 393 (2d Cir. 1975).

[7] U.S. Const. amend. V; U.S. Const. amend. XIV, §1.

[8] *National Mut. Ins. Co. v. Tidewater Transfer Co.*, 337 U.S. 582, 646 (1949) (Frankfurter, J., dissenting).

[9] See notes 117–124, *infra*, and accompanying text.

[10] See, e.g., *Mathews v. Eldridge*, 424 U.S. 319, 341 (1976).

[11] See, e.g., *Goldberg v. Kelly*, 397 U.S. 254, 264 (1970).

Ordinarily, some process will have been afforded before or after the deprivation, which takes us to another variable. Given the particular interest, the particular type of invasion, and the particular harms suffered, was the particular process offered what was "due?" Because the constitutional command tells nothing about either the purposes of process or the kinds of procedures that must be followed, we must delve into history, common sense, and modern procedural theory and practice to inform our judgment. We know, at least, that the processes attending the visitation of doom upon an individual must be "fair," and that fairness in the American procedural context means that (1) the procedures followed are likely to produce correct decisions, on the law and facts, in most cases,[12] and (2) the affected individual has been allowed some voice in the decisional process.[13] But both of these guideposts will vary in content as we move from one factual context to another. Given lesser interests, invasions, and injuries, we will tolerate procedures which involve greater margins of error and lesser participation of the Due Process claimant. As the magnitudes of these three variables increase, "fairness" changes to stricter tolerances and greater opportunity for the affected party to influence the outcome.

A further factor in the Due Process equation is the extent to which additional procedural safeguards mandated by the judiciary are likely to increase fairness in the decision-making process, compared to the costs of such improvements.[14] Free from the constraints of time and resources, we could theoretically devise procedural systems which reduce the chance of error in individual cases to virtually zero. Similarly, we could guarantee full participation by the affected party in every step of the proceedings, from investigation through decision. We could also impose our ideal

[12] See, e.g., *Mathews* v. *Eldridge*, 424 U.S. 319, 344 (1976) ("procedural due process rules are shaped by the risk of error inherent in the truth-finding process"). Professor Tribe characterizes this as the "instrumental" approach to procedural Due Process. See Tribe, *American Constitutional Law* 503–506 (1978). It is severely criticized for lacking human and traditional values in Mashaw, "The Supreme Court's Due Process Calculus for Administrative Adjudication in *Mathews* v. *Eldridge*: Three Factors in Search of a Theory of Value," 44 U. Chi. L. Rev. 28 (1976).

[13] Professor Tribe calls this the "intrinsic" view of Due Process and describes it as follows:

"it grants to the individuals or groups against whom government decisions operate the chance to participate in the process by which those decisions are made, an opportunity that expresses their dignity as persons."

Tribe, *American Constitutional Law* 502 (1978). The importance of party participation in adjudicative systems has been measured and verified empirically. See J. Thibaut & L. Walker, *Procedural Justice: A Psychological Analysis* (1975).

[14] See, e.g., *Mathews* v. *Eldridge*, 424 U.S. 319, 348 (1976).

system on all forms of government action which affect all forms of interests. In this world, however, time and resources are finite, often painfully so. Thus, the process which is "due" must be practical, taking all the other variables into consideration. In one case we may be willing to incur substantial expense in increasing only slightly the probabilities of correct decisions if the dangers of less accurate systems are too great. In another case the projected costs of improvements may be seen to outweigh the benefits to human rights. The cost-benefit calculation, like the measurement of the other variables, must be made within the context of the specific Due Process claim.

Finally, in the realm of administrative agency action we must consider the impact which proposed procedures would have on other governmental functions.[15] An important consideration in the implementation of procedural safeguards in the grant-in-aid field is that the financing of increased procedural fairness (to grantor and grantee alike) must necessarily come from fixed program budgets. Every dollar devoted to achieving greater procedural justice for one grantee is a dollar diverted from providing services and benefits to the ultimate program beneficiaries.[16] Unlike courts, executive offices are not primarily in the business of providing Due Process. Though the executive branch, no less than the judicial or congressional, can only act in accordance with constitutional mandates and restrictions,[17] its basic responsibility is to "take care that the laws be faithfully executed. . . ."[18] The role of agencies is directed to the achievement of conduct control, via regulatory programs, or the enhancement of the social welfare,

---

[15] In *Wolff* v. *McDonnell*, 418 U.S. 539 (1974), for example, the procedures for imposing disciplinary sanctions on prisoners did not include a right of confrontation and cross-examination of adverse witnesses because of potential prison disruption and retaliation. See *id*. at 568. In *Goss* v. *Lopez*, 419 U.S. 565 (1975), which dealt with student suspensions, notice and informal conferences were considered adequate in view of the detrimental effect more formal proceedings might have on the education mission:

"Brief disciplinary suspensions are almost countless. To impose in each case even truncated trial-type procedures might well overwhelm administrative facilities in many places and, by diverting resources, cost more than it would save in educational effectiveness. Moreover, further formalizing the suspension process and escalating its formality and adversary nature may not only make it too costly as a regular disciplinary tool but also destroy its effectiveness as part of the teaching process."
Id. at 583.

[16] See Friendly, "Some Kind of Hearing," 123 U. Pa. L. Rev. 1268, 1276 (1975); cf. *Mathews* v. *Eldridge*, 424 U.S. 319, 348 (1976) (cost of pretermination disability hearings would come out of trust fund).

[17] Tribe, *American Constitutional Law* 502 (1978).

[18] U.S. Const. art. III, §3.

via the dispensation of benefits—both, of course, pursuant to statutory directives. Inexorably, such activity involves the decision of specific cases, many of which produce harmful effects on individuals and entities. The question of procedural fairness then becomes relevant, whether as a question of constitutional obligation or of good government. But it remains subsidiary to the executive mission. With that in mind, we may logically assert that granting Due Process to individuals may adversely affect the "interests" of the government, defined as the primordial goals and functions of agencies. When we divert too much of an executive department's resources to the pursuit of Due Process, we stifle its ability to regulate or to dispense benefits. Strict procedures may also have counterproductive programmatic effects. The problem is deeper than the diversion of dollars from the program side to the administration side of grant-in-aid budgets. Judicial-type procedures require heavy investments of time and energy by the parties to the dispute. An ongoing grant program will inevitably suffer when its leadership is battling in judicial or administrative forums, particularly in the case of small grantee organizations with limited staff. In short, the question of Due Process in agency decision making must be seen within the broad scope of agency functions, an inquiry which perforce requires a particularized examination of the agency involved in the Due Process dispute.

While our conceptual framework has implied, thus far, the typical situation of judicial review of agency procedures under constitutional standards, and has emphasized the multifaceted and particularized nature of that review, the same problem has another important dimension. We cannot forget that both legislatures and executive departments are subject to constitutional commands. In legislating and regulating, both must honor the demands of Due Process. To a degree this is basically the same theme, with the variant that these branches must guess at the standards which are, or may be, imposed by judicial interpretation of the constitutional norm. Yet even if the constitutional prescriptions do not attach in a particular setting, the legislature must consider whether as a question of discretion it should provide procedural protections in each of its programs. And, in the face of legislative silence or vagueness, the agency entrusted with the administration of a program must pursue the same inquiry.

Thus, an investigation of "due process" in any governmental program, or set of programs, has to be dual to be complete. If constitutional protections apply, the primary task will be to ascertain the relevant constitutional standards and their implications for the program and parties under review. That first-level analysis will, however, do no more than determine what is minimally required. The legislature and administering agency may, of course, go beyond those threshold standards. This leads to a second level of analysis probing whether for programmatic reasons strict procedural safeguards should attend decisions involving individual cases. Many of the factors involved in the constitutional probe continue to be involved, but the analysis widens to embrace considerations of program effectiveness and the like. A third type of analysis may be required where the constitutional standards are found inapplicable. Free from externally imposed criteria, the legislative or executive question whether and what process should be offered becomes purely one of social policy and program design.

Grantee Due Process: Threshold Considerations

Given the complex, individualized nature of the Due Process probe, as well as the various postures of the analysis, one must question whether it is profitable or, indeed, possible to generalize in an area as broad as federal grant programs. Because Due Process "unlike some legal rules is not a technical conception with a fixed content unrelated to time, place, and circumstances," [19] and is "flexible and calls for such procedural protections as the particular situation demands," [20] Supreme Court decisions are simultaneously too broad and too narrow to be as instructive as one would like. The guiding principles enunciated under the Due Process Clauses of the Fifth and Fourteenth Amendments, such as the famous formulations in *Mullane*,[21] are helpful springboards for analysis, but do not carry us far because of their generality. On the other hand, the Due Process decisions of the Court, with their great attention

---

[19] *Cafeteria & Restaurant Workers Union, Local 473* v. *McElroy*, 367 U.S. 886, 895 (1961).

[20] *Morrissey* v. *Brewer*, 408 U.S. 471, 481 (1972).

[21] "Many controversies have raged about the cryptic and abstract words of the Due Process Clause but there can be no doubt that at a minimum they require that deprivation of life, liberty or property by adjudication be preceded by notice and opportunity for hearing appropriate to the nature of the case." *Mullane* v. *Central Hanover Bank & Trust Co.*, 339 U.S. 306, 313 (1950).

"An elementary and fundamental requirement of due process in any proceeding which is to be accorded finality is notice reasonably calculated, under all the circumstances, to apprise interested parties of the pendency of the action and afford them an opportunity to present their objections." *Id.* at 314.

to the details of individual circumstances, are such narrow holdings that one hesitates to use them much beyond their specific factual context.[22]

Nevertheless, as long as federal agencies dispense grants the analysis cannot be avoided. The size and structure of the grant-in-aid system are such that hundreds of individualized decisions about specific grantees and petitioners for grants must be made daily, thousands weekly, and hundreds of thousands yearly. Many of those decisions clearly or arguably prejudice grantees. While at one time it was thought that no process need be afforded recipients of governmental "privileges," the conceptual breakthrough which shifted statutorily bestowed benefits into the category of procedurally protected property[23] has deprived governmental agencies of the luxury of nonconcern. In each grant-in-aid program, first Congress, then the administering agency, must ask whether it can adversely affect grantee interests without affording some process and, if not, what type of process is demanded.

The operational reality of grant programs, therefore, forces the Due Process analysis, however difficult and imponderable. It shall be demonstrated that in various situations the Constitution most probably reaches adverse grantor action, and when it does not, good public policy calls for some notice and opportunity to be heard. This leads to the need for procedural codes to be drafted and published. It would be possible but horrendously impractical for the government to instruct its grant officials to construct on an *ad hoc* basis fair proceedings for each individual case that comes along.[24] Uniform standards can achieve evenhanded treatment of similarly situated grantees. They can ease the administrative burden by freeing grant officials from the difficult and frequent task of judging the process to be afforded in particular instances. They also provide advance security to the grantee which may wish to evaluate the effects of its conduct not only in terms of substantive legal standards but also by the procedural context in which issues will be raised and resolved.

Thus, the drafting of administrative procedural codes for use in the processing of conflicts within the federal grant-in-aid system

---

[22] See, e.g., *Mathews* v. *Eldridge*, 424 U.S. 319 (1976).

[23] See Chapter 1, notes 69–73, *supra*, and accompanying text.

[24] The fact that administrative agencies improvise hearing procedures for particular disputes does not, by itself, invalidate the process. If the procedures actually followed comport with the relevant fairness principles, they will be upheld, even if the agency has violated a statutory directive to promulgate hearing procedures. See, e.g., *Economic Opportunity Comm'n* v. *Weinberger*, 524 F.2d 393 (2d Cir. 1975).

is an imperative feature of the grant system. It is also one of its most complicated tasks. Our preceding examination of the multifaceted nature of Due Process shows that one measures the need for and appropriateness of hearing opportunities by the specifics of the individual case. This indicates, at the least, that one procedural code cannot serve for all possible federal grantor actions which adversely impact on grantees. The question then becomes whether it is possible to categorize government actions by type, utilizing the factors of a Due Process analysis as the classifying criteria. Prototypal decisions could be tested by: the type of grantee interest which is being affected; the impact on that interest; other possible impacts on grantees; the needs of the Federal Government; and the costs and benefits of procedural alternatives. Communality among types of grantor actions might be found, permitting the drafting of a few sets of procedures to cover the different categories.

One might trigger the use of such codes not by fixing the types of grantor actions covered by each but by calling upon the federal grantor to choose the process to be applied according to a Due Process analysis of the case under consideration. For example, the grantor would determine on the particular facts the kind of grantee interests being affected, the possible adverse impacts on the particular grantee, the type of grantee, the federal interests involved, and the benefits and detriments of the various procedural alternatives. While such a system would have the advantage of adaptability and flexibility in the choice of process, and would avoid the dangers of prejudgment, it has the obvious disadvantage of burdening administrators with complex, individual decisions and their concomitant uncertainties.

A combination of the two methods might be an optimum solution. Each procedural code would state the types of grantor actions it covers, but would permit grantees to present unique circumstances which justify the utilization of another code more protective of grantee interests. The burden would be on an objecting grantee to show that an alternative process is due.

One further preliminary question remains. Is it possible to cut across grant-in-aid programs and draft a set of procedural codes applicable to all? Recall that dozens of federal departments administer hundreds of different grant-in-aid programs under scores of federal statutes.[25] If each grant-in-aid program requires, as we suggest, several different hearing mechanisms, and if each federal grantor agency goes its own way in developing these codes, we may be inundated by a procedural avalanche. In fact, this is precisely what is occurring.[26]

We can perceive no serious problems arising from consolidated procedural codes which extend to certain grantor actions in all grant-in-aid programs. A grant termination, for example, would have the same effects and potential consequences whether imposed by HEW, HUD, or any of the other grant-giving federal agencies. While the substance of programmatic conditions varies, of course, from grant to grant, the processes of issue formulation, fact presentation, ascertainment of legal standards, and decision need not differ between agencies. The desirability of common processes is highlighted by the existence of numerous standard federal requirements which apply to many or all grant programs. Grantees of different agencies facing similar charges should have identical procedural rights as a matter of intergrantee equity.

Federal judicial procedure has been consolidated for four decades. The multiple advantages of such a unified procedural system would similarly accrue to the executive branch and those who deal with it.[27]

The Property Question

A central question in determining grantee Due Process rights is whether the grant-in-aid qualifies as "property" within the meaning of the Fifth Amendment so as to offer procedural safeguards. We shall approach that question by analyzing the two basic postures of the grantee—seeker and holder—but, preliminarily, we must examine the meaning of that elusive word.

Constitutionally protected property includes government funds which are being transferred to individuals under government benefit programs. In a variety of contexts the judiciary has so

---

[25] See Chapter 1, *supra,* at pp. 8–9.
[26] We have studied more than 50 different grant-in-aid procedural codes (apart from civil rights procedural regulations) during the course of our research.
[27] Cf. Office of Federal Procurement Policy, "Uniform Rules of Procedure for Boards of Contract Appeals and Related Regulations," 44 Fed. Reg. 12519 (1979). See Davis, "Informal Administrative Action: Another View," 26 Am. U. L. Rev. 836, 836–38 (1977).

ruled.[28] In *Board of Regents of State Colleges* v. *Roth*,[29] Mr. Justice Stewart generalized from these cases as follows:

> "Certain attributes of 'property' interests protected by procedural due process emerge from these decisions. To have a property interest in a benefit, a person clearly must have more than an abstract need and desire for it. He must have more than a unilateral expectation of it. He must, instead, have a legitimate claim of entitlement to it. It is a purpose of the ancient institution of property to protect those claims upon which people rely in their daily lives, reliance that must not be arbitrarily undermined. It is a purpose of the constitutional right to a hearing to provide an opportunity for a person to vindicate those claims.
>
> "Property interests, of course, are not created by the Constitution. Rather, they are created and their dimensions are defined by existing rules or understandings that stem from an independent source such as state law—rules or understandings that secure certain benefits and that support claims of entitlement to those benefits." [30]

We are directed to look, for the legitimacy of claimed entitlements, to the statutes originating the program of benefits or other interests. In the context of government grants that would be, of course, the authorizing grant-in-aid law and appropriations legislation, as well as conforming regulations. We may also, it appears, broaden our knowledge by reading such statutes in the light of customary practices and understandings. This means, presumably, the traditions of grant administering agencies will be relevant and, perhaps, other indicia outside of the statute which support or defeat grantee reliance on federal funding.

---

[28] See, e.g., *Goldberg* v. *Kelly*, 397 U.S. 254 (1970) (welfare benefits); *Mathews* v. *Eldridge*, 424 U.S. 319 (1976) (social security); *Sockwell* v. *Maloney*, 554 F.2d 1236 (2d Cir. 1977) (foster care payments); *Schneider* v. *Whaley*, 541 F.2d 916, *explained on rehearing*, 548 F.2d 394 (2d Cir. 1976) (day-care services); *Green* v. *Dumke*, 480 F.2d 624 (9th Cir. 1973) (students' federal aid); *Don* v. *Okmulgee Mem. Hosp.*, 443 F.2d 234 (10th Cir. 1971) (admission to staff of public hospital); *Escalera* v. *New York City Housing Auth.*, 425 F.2d 853 (2d Cir.), *cert. denied*, 400 U.S. 853 (1970) (public housing); *Kletschka* v. *Driver*, 411 F.2d 436 (2d Cir. 1969) (transfer of government employee as disciplinary measure); *Klein* v. *Mathews*, 430 F. Supp. 1005 (D. N.J. 1977) (nursing home services); *Hairston* v. *Drosick*, 423 F. Supp. 180 (S.D. W.Va. 1976) (public school education; admittance of handicapped); *Ponce* v. *Housing Auth.*, 389 F. Supp. 635 (E.D. Cal. 1975) (rent increase in public housing).

An individual has no constitutional right to government benefits while the determination of eligibility is being made and may be burdened with proving the qualifying factors. *Lavine* v. *Milne*, 424 U.S. 577 (1976).

[29] 408 U.S. 564 (1972).

[30] *Id.* at 577.

190 / *Rights and Remedies Under Federal Grants*

This we shall do, but we should first consider two more preliminary matters.

Our survey of the statutory scene reveals extremely erratic congressional behavior on the topic of grantee procedural rights. Some statutes provide prior hearing rights for certain kinds of adverse grantor actions, while others involving the same program format and action are silent. From field to field, we see the handiwork of different congressional committees, some extremely solicitous of grantee needs, others seemingly callous. One is tempted to reason not from property to procedure, but backwards. Simply put, if Congress did not choose to afford hearing rights in a particular statute, it could not have intended any entitlements of Due Process stature.

This type of reasoning was rejected in *Arnett* v. *Kennedy*.[31] Justice Rehnquist, who wrote the Court's opinion, pointed out that while a federal employee had a statutory right to be discharged only for cause, the very law which granted that tenure also explicitly specified that in the discharge process a trial or hearing was not required. Therefore, he argued, the employee's "right" to continued federal employment was defined and limited by the congressional procedural standard.[32] A majority of the Court, however, rejected this approach. Justice Powell saw it leading

> "directly to the conclusion that whatever the nature of an individual's statutorily created property interest, deprivation of that interest can be accomplished without notice or a hearing at any time. The view misconceives the origin of the right to procedural due process. That right is conferred not by legislative grace, but by constitutonal guarantee. While the legislature may elect not to confer a property interest in federal employment, it may not constitutionally authorize the deprivation of such an interest, once conferred, without appropriate procedural safeguards. As our cases have consistently recognized, the adequacy of statutory procedures for deprivation of a statutorily created property interest must be analyzed in constitutional terms." [33]

Justice Marshall added the thought that the Rehnquist logic "would amount to nothing less than a return, albeit in somewhat different garb, to the thoroughly discredited distinction between rights and privileges which once seemed to govern the application of procedural due process." [34]

[31] 416 U.S. 134 (1974).
[32] *Id.* at 152.
[33] *Id.* at 166–67 (Powell, J., concurring).
[34] *Id.* at 211 (Marshall, J., dissenting).

A second threshold question is whether the Due Process analysis may be affected by the nature of grantees. Eligibility for federal grants-in-aid is ordinarily restricted to states, units of local government, and nonprofit organizations. A feature which distinguishes the grant from other forms of property is that the recipient holds and administers the funds for the benefit of others.[35] Although the grant does provide jobs, offices, and perquisites to officers and employees of the grantee, that is only a necessary means for channeling benefits to another group. Because the purposes of the grant-in-aid statute are to provide benefits to this different population and not to the individuals comprising the grantee organization, one might argue that procedural Due Process attaches only to the ultimate beneficiary.

The argument carries some weight. If, for example, a grantor defunds an organization, its officials cannot complain about their individual sufferings. They have, in fact, been deprived of funds used, among other things, to pay their salaries, and that is doubtlessly a serious personal setback. Nevertheless, their employment has only been incidental to the broader purpose served by the grant program. Any grant-in-aid statute transfers funds not to help the individuals employed by the grantee but rather to capacitate them to help others.[36] The relevant injury which may lay claim to Due Process protections is, therefore, to that capacity to carry out the grant program.

The grant funds are in that sense a limited property in the hands of the grantee; they are "owned" only for the fiduciary purposes specified by the grant statute and regulations. But to conclude that this caretaker status incapacitates the grantee from asserting any Due Process rights is erroneous.

First, as organizations, grant recipients have purposes and needs which go beyond the predilictions of their individual members. Whether the grantee is a local government, state, or nonprofit association, it will have a mission, defined by local law and

---

[35] See Chapter 2, notes 29–33, *supra*, and accompanying text.

[36] A major exception is the grant program which includes as a goal the employment of members of the recipient population on the grantee organization's staff. See, e.g., statutes cited in Chapter 2, note 109, *supra*; §223 Community Services Act of 1974, 42 U.S.C. §2810:

"In the conduct of all component programs under this part, residents of the area and members of the groups served shall be provided maximum employment opportunity, including opportunity for further occupational training and career advancement. The Director shall encourage the employment of persons fifty-five and older as regular, part-time and short-term staff in component programs."

documents, which is independent of the goal of any grant-in-aid the entity may receive. The organization's capacity to implement its chartered mission can suffer harm from adverse actions of federal grantors, and that harm is distinct from the individual sufferings of the organization's agents. Further, the theory underlying federal grants is that they "aid" other institutions in our society carry out public purposes.[37] This is the essence of both "new" and "cooperative" federalism. The grantee is not a mere mechanical conduit for the transfer of funds or services from the Federal Government to individuals. Rather, it is premised to be an independent agency with the primary responsibility of carrying out social missions of its own choice, the federal grant being an aid *to that body*. The property created by a grant-in-aid is, therefore, one of capacitation—the means for carrying out the organizational goals of the grantee. If the federal statute is read as supporting a legitimate claim of entitlement to those means and if such claim is not a unilateral expectation but rather a justifiable reliance, one should readily conclude that sufficient property exists in the grantee organization to invoke constitutional protection.

Second, as a practical matter the extension of Due Process guarantees to grantees is both a logical and necessary corollary of their extension to ultimate beneficiaries. Except for the Social Security program, the Federal Government has opted to provide a great variety of social welfare benefits to individuals through intermediary grantees. In a number of programs, the ultimate recipients have been found to have a claim of entitlement to such benefits of sufficient merit to call forth constitutional process.[38] If the funds are cut off at the pass by adverse federal action against the grantee, the procedural safeguards of those waiting in town will be rendered nugatory.

The example of *Goldberg* v. *Kelly* [39] is instructive. That case held that welfare recipients cannot have their monthly benefits terminated without being afforded a quasi-judicial hearing prior to such action. The specific program involved was Aid to Families With Dependent Children,[40] a typical federal grant-in-aid activity in which the United States funds states and their units of local

[37] See §5 Federal Grant and Cooperative Agreement Act of 1977, Pub. L. 95-224, Feb. 3, 1978, 41 U.S.C. §504.
[38] See note 28, *supra*.
[39] 397 U.S. 294 (1970).
[40] Title IV-A, Social Security Act, 42 U.S.C. §§601–611.

government to help them provide financial aid to needy families. If New York State or one of its subdivisions could be arbitrarily deprived of federal assistance, each of the individual recipients is thereby deprived of federal aid without *any* administrative procedural safeguards. That would be the practical effect of denying the applicability of Due Process to grantees.

To avoid such a questionable result the grantee's procedural protections must be coextensive with those of its beneficiaries. Logically, this is easily achieved by considering the grantee as a representative of the interests and rights of those to whom it passes on funds or benefits. When the imminent federal action will adversely impact on both the grantee and its beneficiary population, the representational role of the grantee is not a fiction. While grantee and beneficiary interests are frequently antagonistic, when both find themselves in the same camp opposing the Federal Government their interests are likely to coalesce sufficiently so that realistically the grantee can be said to represent the beneficiary group, or at least is presumptively entitled to that role. Further, the grantee always has a double agency. It represents the Federal Government by virtue of the federal law brought into play by the grant. It is an agent (in a nontechnical sense) carrying out the federal will. But under state law it is also an agent to its beneficiary population and is entrusted with the responsibility of the welfare of that group.

Under the representational theory posed above, not only is the grantee able to invoke the procedural safeguards accorded its beneficiaries but can argue from the position of an ultimate beneficiary. We have noted that the degree of harm to be suffered is relevant to a determination of the kind of procedural safeguards that are due. Arguing from the posture of an organization, a grantee would appear to be limited to showing the adverse effects on its service capacities. Arguing as a surrogate of the ultimate beneficiaries, the grantee can bring to bear the degree of individual suffering that the federal action might entail.

Seekers of Formula Grants

Even before a grant is awarded, there may be a sufficiently strong claim of entitlement by eligible applicants to call forth Due Process protections. The legitimacy of this proposition is clearest with respect to the grant program involving automatic entitlements of statutorily [41] or administratively [42] determined formula amounts. In this category of grant-in-aid program, Congress has essentially removed from the administrator discretion as to the choice of grantee and the amount to be awarded. The grantee will be, in most cases, a state, and appropriated funds will be allocated among the state on the basis of a statutory formula. While there is an application process, it usually invloves no more than the submission of a state plan—a series of assurances by the state that it will comply with the various conditions set forth in the statute. The administering agency is directed to approve the state's submission if it conforms to federal requirements, and to make payments accordingly. Some statutory variations require the state to submit, additionally, annual program plans detailing the projected use of funds.[43] In this latter situation there is, similarly, no grantor discretion to reject conforming uses of the federal funds, nor to establish the amount of grants based on the federal agency's appreciation of relative needs.

For this type of grant program, the applicant's claim of entitlement appears to solidify with the congressional appropriation of funds. Once federal dollars have been made available for distribution, the functions of the administering agency are primarily ministerial.[44] The lesson of the "impoundment" decisions is that when Congress mandates the distribution of funds the

[41] See, e.g., §102 Elementary and Secondary Education Act of 1965, 20 U.S.C. §2702, as rewritten by §101 Education Amendments of 1978, Pub. L. 95-561, Nov. 1, 1978:

". . . the Commissioner shall, in accordance with the provisions of this title, make payments to State educational agencies for grants made on the basis of entitlements created under this title."

[42] Federal agencies will frequently adopt a distribution formula even though Congress has vested them with discretion to determine grantees and amounts. For example, §4(b)(1) Child Abuse Prevention and Treatment Act, 42 U.S.C. §5103(b)(1), authorizes but does not direct HEW to make grants to states for child abuse and neglect prevention and treatment programs. §4(d), id., 42 U.S.C. §5103(d), requires the agency to design criteria to promote equitable distribution of grants across the country, and orders that citizens of each state be able to receive assistance from at least one grant project "[t]o the extent possible." HEW has cleverly satisfied the latter requirement by establishing a mandated formula distribution to each state of a portion of the yearly appropriation, see 45 C.F.R. §1340.3-7, while retaining discretion over the balance of funds. See id., pt. 1340, subpart B. Since agency regulations have the force of law, see Chapter 3, note 22, supra, and accompanying text, Due Process rights attach to an entitlement of funds created by agency rules to the same extent as if the statute had created the entitlement.

[43] See, e.g., §108 Vocational Education Act of 1973, 20 U.S.C. §2308. Some required plans combine both assurances and programmatic descriptions. See, e.g., §613 Education of the Handicapped Act, 20 U.S.C. §1413.

[44] See, e.g., State Highway Comm'n v. Volpe 479 F.2d 1099, 1107, n. 8 (8th Cir. 1973).

executive branch must comply. Cut to their kernal, these cases all turned on whether Congress intended that the appropriated funds be expended. This, in turn, was determined by the statutory language ("shall" versus "may"), bolstered by any available legislative history.[45] The fact, therefore, that the funds have not yet been transferred to the states does not defeat the idea that a property interest, in the constitutional sense, exists in the presumptive grantee the moment Congress funds the program.[46]

The federal agency does have the responsibility of reviewing state submissions under these formula programs for compliance with statutory standards. Following such review it can determine against the applicant. Yet the property interest in the eligible applicant—its justifiable reliance on the provision of funds—requires that any such rejection be accompanied by constitutional Due Process safeguards.

While most of the major federal grant programs follow the formula-plan pattern, several drop the state as a central recipient. Although the amount of each state's entitlement is legislatively earmarked, eligible entities within each state apply directly to the Federal Government for funds to be awarded out of the state allot-

---

[45] See, e.g., *Train* v. *City of New York*, 420 U.S. 35 (1975) (grants for waste water treatment facilities); *Train* v. *Campaign Clean Water, Inc.*, 420 U.S. 136 (1975) (same); *Iowa ex rel. State Highway Comm'n* v. *Brinegar*, 512 F.2d 722 (8th Cir. 1975) (per curiam; highway funds); *State Highway Comm'n* v. *Volpe*, 479 F.2d 1099 (8th Cir. 1973) (highway funds); *Kennedy* v. *Mathews*, 413 F. Supp. 1240 (D. D.C. 1976) (nutrition program for elderly); *Louisiana* v. *Weinberger*, 369 F. Supp. 856 (E.D. La. 1973) (library grants); *Illinois ex rel. Bakalis* v. *Weinberger*, 368 F. Supp. 721 (N.D. Ill. 1973) (grants to strengthen instruction in academic subjects); *Pennsylvania* v. *Weinberger*, 367 F. Supp. 1378 (D. D.C. 1973) (grants to strengthen departments of education); *Community Action Programs Executive Directors Ass'n* v. *Ash*, 365 F. Supp. 1355 (D. N.J. 1973) (summer neighborhood youth corps program); *National Council of Community Mental Health Centers, Inc.* v. *Weinberger*, 361 F. Supp. 897 (D. D.C. 1973) (community mental health center grants); *Oklahoma* v. *Weinberger*, 360 F. Supp. 724 (W.D. Okla. 1973) (library services and construction grants); *Local 2677, AFGE* v. *Phillips*, 358 F. Supp. 60 (D. D.C. 1973) (community action grants); cf. *City of Los Angeles* v. *Adams*, 556 F.2d 40 (D.C. Cir. 1977) (impoundment by appropriations committees).

[46] The entitled party must assert its rights, however, before congressional authorization has lapsed. After congressional authorization for the expenditure of grant funds has expired or appropriations are exhausted, a court lacks constitutional authority to order that the grant be made even if illegal grantor action in denying the grant can be shown. *National Ass'n of Regional Councils* v. *Costle*, 564 F.2d 583, 588–90 (D.C. Cir. 1977); *Township of River Vale* v. *Harris*, 444 F. Supp. 90, 93 (D. D.C. 1978). If suit is filed before the grantor's budget authority has lapsed or appropriations are depleted, the court can protect its ability to remedy possible wrongs against the plaintiff by enjoining the expenditure of appropriations and suspending the operation of a lapse period. See *National Ass'n of Regional Councils* v. *Costle*, supra at 588–89.

ment. Sometimes Congress uses mandatory language for the funding of eligible applications; [47] sometimes discretionary.[48]

The applicability of constitutional Due Process to these grantees is less clear. While the total amounts to be expended in each state are predetermined, the size of the grant to eligible applicants is ordinarily left to the discretion of the administering agency.[49] With the loss of certainty in amount, one cannot be sure that any property rights have vested in the eligible grantees upon congressional funding of the program. The point might be made that the federal grantor agency can defeat the statutory interstate distribution of appropriations when it is deciding which proposals to fund and at what levels from entities within each state. Yet that problem would exist whether or not applicants had hearing rights, and its solution must surely be political rather than procedural. It may be that in this type of grant program we cannot avoid basing our Due Process conclusions on the choice of language employed by Congress in the authorizing statute. Some uneasiness may be felt in attaching constitutional consequences to the congressional choice of a word or two in rambling grant-in-aid statutes.[50] But this is the essence of the Due Process determination. Through the distinction between "the Secretary *may* approve" and "the Secretary *shall* approve" the extent of the grant applicant's rights is known.

A third variety of formula funding involves institutional grants. Rather than using an interstate distribution mechanism, Congress focuses on the class of organizations it wishes to aid and

---

[47] See, e.g., §413D(b)(1)(B)(i) Higher Education Act of 1965, 20 U.S.C. §1070b-3(b)(1)(B)(i) (supplemental educational opportunity grants): "From the sums apportioned (or reapportioned) to any State, the Commissioner shall allocate amounts to institutions which have submitted applications. . . ."

[48] See, e.g., §§103–105 Local Public Works Capital Development and Investment Act, 42 U.S.C. §§6702–6704 ("The Secretary is authorized to make . . ."); §221(a) Community Services Act of 1974, 42 U.S.C. §2808(a) (Community Action Program; "The Director may provide financial assistance . . ."); §511 Community Services Act of 1974, 42 U.S.C. §2928 (Head Start; "The Secretary may . . . provide financial assistance . . ."); §706(a)(1) Emergency School Aid Act, 20 U.S.C. §1605(a)(1) ("The Assistant Secretary is authorized to make a grant . . ."); §502(b)(1) Older Americans Act of 1965, 42 U.S.C. §3056(b)(1) ("The Secretary is authorized to enter into agreements . . .").

[49] See, e.g., §413D(b)(1)(B)(ii) Higher Education Act of 1965, 20 U.S.C. §1070b-3(b)(1)(B)(ii).

[50] See Mason, "Current Trends in Federal Grant Law—Fiscal Year 1976," 35 Fed. B. J. 163, 170 (1976). Compare *Pennsylvania v. Lynn*, 501 F.2d 848, 854 (D. D.C. 1974): "[D]iscerning Congress's intent to bestow or withhold discretion to suspend the programs in their entirety is not a simple matter of tallying the 'shalls' and 'mays' and finding that the 'mays' have it. Logic, and precedent . . . require more." (Footnote omitted.)

creates a formula for determining the size of grants to each. The state in which the institution is located ordinarily does not intervene. Institutional applications containing the data required to make the formula determination and required assurances are submitted directly to the Federal Government. In programs of this nature, once the size of an institution's grant is determined and the application papers are in order the federal grantor lacks discretion to refuse the payment. While the amount of each institution's grant may be reduced on a pro rata basis to fit the total amount of grants within the available appropriation,[51] each eligible institution is guaranteed a formula amount.[52]

The argument that Due Process protects this category of grant parallels the argument for formula-plan programs. The mandatory and predetermined method of grant distribution established by the authorizing legislation creates "property" in the eligible grantees, in the constitutional sense, once Congress funds the program.

An additional consideration supports this constitutional conclusion with respect to mandated formula grants. In his description of the attributes of property interests shielded by procedural Due Process, Justice Stewart in the *Roth* case stresses the concept of reliance.[53] Planning and progress would be impossible if one could not count on today's resources being available tomorrow and if the in-flow of reasonably expected resources could be arbitrarily stopped. The concept of justifiable reliance is directly relevant to the formula grant. Besides achieving rough equity in the distribution of federal dollars among the states, the formula technique serves the vital purpose of enabling states, local governments, colleges, hospitals, and other institutions to plan on the basis of reasonably accurate estimates of future receipts. Admittedly, some uncertainty always attends the final grant since in all but a few [54] formula programs Congress reserves the power to

[51] See, e.g., §770(b) Public Health Service Act, 42 U.S.C. §295f(b); §810(b) Public Health Service Act, 42 U.S.C. §296e(b).
[52] See, e.g., §770(a) Public Health Service Act, 42 U.S.C. §295f(a) (health professions capitation grants: "The Secretary shall make annual grants . . ."); §810(a) Public Health Service Act, 42 U.S.C. §296e(a) (nursing school capitation grants: "The Secretary shall make annual grants . . ."); §§202, 203 Higher Education Act of 1965, 20 U.S.C. §§1022, 1023 (college library grants: "The Commissioner shall make basic grants . . ."; "The Commissioner shall make supplemental grants . . ."); §§420(a)(1), (d)(1) Higher Education Act of 1965, 20 U.S.C. §§1070e-1(a)(1), (d)(1) (veterans' cost-of-instruction: "each institution of higher education shall be entitled . . ."; "The Commissioner shall pay . . .").
[53] See text, *supra*, at p. 189.
[54] See Chapter 2, note 52, *supra*.

determine, from year to year, whether to appropriate funds and how much to spend. Nevertheless, most formula grant programs have achieved sufficient respectability and stability that one can gauge with fair accuracy the amount that the President will budget and the Congress will appropriate. The applicant data that are slotted into the distribution formula are known or can reasonably be approximated so that an eligible grantee can predict within tolerable limits the size of next year's grant. In fact, federal offices assist grantees in their advance planning by providing program-by-program estimates of future federal dollar allotments months before funds are actually appropriated. For example, the federal regional councils have assumed the function of distributing to governors estimates of each state's entitlement under each formula program. The estimates are initially based on the appropriations recommended in the President's annual budget and are subsequently revised according to actual appropriations. If a national program is defunded or severely cut, storm signals will ordinarily have been raised far enough in advance for grantees to lay contingency plans.

Thus, the formula system of distributing federal grants permits and, more, actively encourages reliance by presumptively eligible grantees on the future receipt of reasonably certain amounts of federal assistance. The amount of actual reliance by governments and institutions on such future income should not be underestimated. For instance, a budget for a typical state government will depend on receipts from the Federal Government, mostly from formula grants, amounting to over one quarter of the total budget. Since these allocations must be matched with local funds, many on a dollar-for-dollar basis, it is not unusual for more than one third of a government's budget to be tied up in federal programs. Decisions essential to government planning such as tax rates, employment levels, and allocation of resources are based, therefore, to an important extent on the future receipt of federal funds. The same is increasingly true for city and county governments. The reliance on federal funds of school systems, hospitals, universities, and nonprofit community groups may be equally acute.

The formula grant, therefore, provides a paradigm example of actual, justifiable reliance in the *Roth* sense sufficient to invoke procedural Due Process. Undermining of this reliance by arbitrary grantor actions would have such seriously deleterious effects on the structure and functioning of American government that it rarely occurs. Yet the track record and good faith of federal grantor agencies, as well as their political sensitivity, are an insufficient bulwark against illegal deprivations. Only open and full hearing opportunities can provide applicants for formula grants with the measure of security that their reliance requires.

Before considering other kinds of grants, we should note a curious inconsistency in the typical formula program. Competing political considerations will usually produce an incredibly prolix and complicated distribution formula requiring quantities of wisdom to decipher and sophisticated data-gathering and computer technology to implement. Congress will also carefully select its phraseology to insure that the mandatory nature of the distribution is known. More often than not, as we shall see, Congress will afford notice and hearing opportunities to eligible grantees whose funding is denied in whole or in part.[55] Yet in the same statute we will often find a provision authorizing the administering agency to determine, apparently unilaterally, whether a grantee will "need" the full amount of its statutory share.[56] If the administrator's calculation of needs is less generous than the formula's, he can slice off any "excess" and reallot it among the other eligible grantees. In the event of such a determination, the reallotment provision is invariably silent on the question of grantee hearing rights; at most, the grantor is obliged to announce its intention to reallocate in the *Federal Register*.[57]

---

[55] See Chapter 12, note 1, *infra*, and accompanying text.
[56] §906(b) Older Americans Act of 1965, 42 U.S.C. §3056d(b), while prolix, is typical:
"The amount allotted for projects within any State . . . for any fiscal year which the Secretary [of Labor] determines will not be required for such year shall be reallotted, from time to time and on such dates during such year as the Secretary may fix, to projects in other States in proportion to the original allotments to projects within such States . . . for such year, but with such proportionate amount for any of such other States being reduced to the extent it exceeds the sum the Secretary estimates that projects within such State need and will be able to use for such year; and the total of such reductions shall be similarly reallotted among the States whose proportionate amounts were not so reduced. . . ."
[57] See Chapter 12, notes 21–22, *infra*, and accompanying text. Compare §502(d)(2) Older Americans Act of 1965, 42 U.S.C. §3056(d)(2), as added by §105(b)(2) Comprehensive Older Americans Act Amendments of 1978, Pub. L. 95-458, Oct. 18, 1978:
"The Secretary [of Labor] shall review on his own initiative or at the request of any public or private nonprofit agency or organization, or an agency of the State government, the distribution of programs under this title within the State including the distribution between urban and rural areas within the State. For each proposed reallocation of programs within a State, the Secretary shall give notice and opportunity for a hearing on the record by all interested individuals and make a written determination of his findings and decision."

The sense of such provisions is obvious. In its statutory formulas Congress can only roughly match the size of grants with the respective needs of the various eligible jurisdictions by preselecting relevant but approximate factors. If the program is not grossly underfunded so that no jurisdiction's needs are met, the statute will ordinarily produce a degree of imbalance in the matching of funds and needs. The reallotment provisions attempt to square away the two. As the real and current exigencies of a jurisdiction become known to the grantor agency through its review of applications and plans, it is authorized to make *ad hoc* adjustments of the formula allotments.

Such provisions are disturbingly unclear as to the amount of a jurisdiction's allotment than can be shuffled elsewhere. Their literal text would support a conclusion that the federal grantor could, theoretically, perceive no need in a particular state for the program funds and reallot the entire amount elsewhere, even if the jurisdiction had applied for the funds.

Social problems addressed by federal grant-in-aid programs are ordinarily national in scope, and, if regional, eligibility for grants will be defined in regional terms.[58] Thus, some amount of need for the funds will be found in all eligible jurisdictions, making remote the possibility of a reallotment of an applicant's total funds. Yet that possibility would appear to exist under statutory reallotment provisions and their implementing regulations.[59] More important, the reallotment procedure moves the grantor agency into a discretionary role. While these provisions seem to authorize the grantor to tinker a little in discretionary fashion with the amount of the formula grant, they do not textually set limits to prevent the grantor from tinkering a lot. Further, the basis for exercising discretion—the federal agency's perception of the degree of a particular social problem in a particular jurisdiction—is a hotly contentious item. Apart from the inherent difficulties in making that type of decision on the merits, the grantor may be tempted to use its reallotment discretion to express its discontentment (*sub silencio,* of course) with the grantee on other fronts. Nothing would be easier than to spank a grantee for its past uses of federal funds, perceived to be unwise by the grantor though not illegal, by reallotting away its future funds. If no hearing procedures need

---

[58] See, e.g., Title V, Public Works and Economic Development Act of 1965, 42 U.S.C. §§3181–3196 (regional economic development).

[59] See, e.g., 45 C.F.R. §130.42 (reallotment of library funds).

be afforded on such decisions, the shroud of secrecy surrounding such grantor action might make the temptation irresistible.

One might try to construct an argument à la Rehnquist from the statutory silence on hearing rights in this situation. The reasoning would be that Congress knows how to give hearing rights when it so desires, for in a statute containing the reallotment section there typically will be other provisions requiring notice and an opportunity to be heard prior to the grantor's rejection of a state plan or termination of the grant for noncompliance with federal standards. The omission of hearing opportunities in the reallotment provision must be read, the argument continues, as intentional, confirming and stressing the discretionary nature of the reallotment process. Thus, if the formula applicant has a property interest in the expected grant it is a property limited by the grantor's authority to divest it, at least partially, free from procedural constraints.

Fortunately, in light of the majority view in *Arnett* the argument would not be accepted. Since the formula grant statute as a whole (including an appreciation of the import of any reallotment authority) contemplates an investiture of property in eligible grantees, we turn to the Constitution for an understanding of the procedural protections that must attend any attempt to divest this interest. We must then read procedural protections into any attempt to deprive the grantor of its property interest, including reallotment. Remember, however, that the scope of such protection may vary according to the degree of detriment and the practical problems facing the bureaucracy administering the program. While process may attach, its details depend on the nature of the particular reallotment action.

Seekers of Discretionary Grants

The most humble seekers of federal grants are those applying for funds under programs which bestow upon the administering agency discretion both as to the choice of grantees and the amount of the award. These are known as "competitive," or "discretionary," or "project" grants.[60] About three quarters of all federal programs fall in this category. While most are modestly funded research,

[60] See Chapter 2, notes 66–76, *supra,* and accompanying text; Tomlinson, *supra,* Chapter 1, note 55, at 601.

training, or demonstration programs, some of the larger service projects are established on this basis.[61]

Before sketching the constitutional picture, which is not promising on the whole, we should emphasize that while applicants whose proposals for discretionary grants are rejected do not have a constitutional right to an administrative opportunity to be heard on that decision,[62] they are not totally bereft of protection. Some ability exists to obtain judicial review of the negative grantor action. The fact that the granting agency has discretion in the award process does not completely insulate the decisional process from judicial inspection when issues are raised to which "law" may be applied.[63] Thus, if the grantor agency has promulgated standards under which proposals will be tested and also procedures for such testing, the courts may inquire whether those standards and procedures have in fact been utilized in the particular case.[64] Similarly, judicial review is available to determine whether the federal agency correctly applied statutory eligibility rules,[65] and whether it properly implemented statutory allocation mandates.[66] In cases in which a formula grant to a state agency is being distributed on the state level to subgrantees, the courts are open to challenges

---

[61] It is often difficult to discern when a federal grant program has ceased to be a demonstration type and has acquired the characteristics of an established service program. See *California Welfare Rights Organ.* v. *Richardson,* 348 F. Supp. 491, 498 (N.D. Cal. 1972). A program would seem to no longer be a demonstration when its shape is federally determined (whether by statute or regulation), when it has been funded substantially over several years, when a large number of grants are made throughout the country, and when the focus is on the provision of services rather than the production of knowledge. Compare, e.g., §§101–104 Community Services Act of 1974, 42 U.S.C. §§2711–2714 (economic opportunity research, demonstrations, and pilots), and §553, *id.,* 42 U.S.C. §2929b (Follow Through demonstration), with §§551, 552, *id.,* 42 U.S.C. §§2929, 2929a (Follow Through service projects), and Title IV, *id.,* 42 U.S.C. §§2901–2906 (migrant farmworker programs).

[62] *Advocates for the Arts* v. *Thomson,* 532 F.2d 792, 797 (1st Cir.), cert. denied, 429 U.S. 894 (1976); *East Oakland-Fruitvale Planning Council* v. *Rumsfeld,* 471 F.2d 524, 535–36 (9th Cir. 1972) (by implication); *Northeast Community Organ., Inc.* v. *Weinberger,* 378 F. Supp. 1287, 1292 (D. Md. 1974).

[63] *Apter* v. *Richardson,* 510 F.2d 351 (7th Cir. 1975); *East Oakland-Fruitvale Planning Council* v. *Rumsfeld,* 471 F.2d 524 (9th Cir. 1972).

[64] E.g., *Advocates for the Arts* v. *Thomson,* 397 F. Supp. 1048 (D. N.H. 1975), aff'd, 532 F.2d 792 (1st Cir.), cert. denied, 429 U.S. 894 (1976); *City of Grand Rapids* v. *Richardson,* 429 F. Supp. 1087 (W.D. Mich. 1977); *Mid-America Regional Council* v. *Mathews,* 416 F. Supp. 896 (W.D. Mo. 1976); *Grassetti* v. *Weinberger,* 408 F. Supp. 142 (N.D. Cal. 1976); *School Bd.* v. *Richardson,* 332 F. Supp. 1263 (N.D. Fla. 1971).

[65] *Board of Educ.* v. *Dep't of Health, Educ. & Welfare,* 532 F.2d 1070 (6th Cir. 1976); *School City* v. *Derthick,* 273 F.2d 319 (7th Cir. 1959); *Michigan Head Start Directors Ass'n* v. *Butz,* 397 F. Supp. 1124 (W.D. Mich. 1975); *Northeast Community Organ., Inc.* v. *Weinberger,* 378 F. Supp. 1287 (D. Md. 1974).

[66] *Clark* v. *Richardson,* 431 F. Supp. 105 (D. N.J. 1977); *City of Benton Harbor* v. *Richardson,* 429 F. Supp. 1096 (W.D. Mich. 1977); *Lewis* v. *Richardson,* 428 F. Supp. 1164 (D. Mass. 1977).

that the state agency violated dollar distribution rules imposed by the Federal Government.[67]

Assuming, however, that the thrust of the complaint is that the agency unfairly ranked the applicant's proposal (but did not violate any statutory directive or established procedure), the courts will not intercede. Having "no particular institutional competence warranting case-by-case participation in the allocation of funds," [68] the courts will not second-guess agencies on questions such as the relative merits of numerous proposals, technical soundness of applications, the competence of applicant personnel, and the like.[69]

The reason constitutional protection under the Due Process Clause does not apply is that one would have considerable difficulty demonstrating any property interest in the applicant for such grants prior to an award. The authorizing statutes create no expectations of grants, nor do program regulations; [70] at most, eligible applicants can only hope for objective and honest consideration of their proposals. That aspiration does not reach Fifth Amendment dimensions. Applicants for competitive grants must look to Congress and grantor agencies for procedural protection in the administrative consideration of their applications. Although the Federal Government has taken positive steps to promote fair evaluation of project grant proposals, such efforts do not include hearing opportunities for rejected applications.[71]

Projects seeking the expansion of knowledge through research, the creation of capability through training, and the development of improved methodology through demonstrations require

[67] *School Comm.* v. *Anrig*, 520 F.2d 577 (1st Cir. 1975).

[68] *Advocates for the Arts* v. *Thomson*, 532 F.2d 792, 795–96 (1st Cir.), *cert. denied*, 429 U.S. 894 (1976).

[69] *Kletschka* v. *Driver*, 411 F.2d 436, 443 (2d Cir. 1969); *Grassetti* v. *Weinberger*, 408 F. Supp. 142, 150 (N.D. Cal. 1976). But see *City of Benton Harbor* v. *Richardson*, 429 F. Supp. 1096 (W.D. Mich. 1977); *Mid-America Regional Council* v. *Mathews*, 416 F. Supp. 896 (W.D. Mo. 1976).

[70] A grantor agency may decide to use a formula to distribute discretionary funds, although it is not statutorily compelled to do so. See note 42, *supra*. Compare, e.g., §§312, 313 Public Health Service Act, 42 U.S.C. §§244-1, 245a (1976), with 42 C.F.R. §§58.2–58.3 (1977) (training grants to schools of public health). If such policy is officially promulgated, it can be strongly argued that a property interest has been created in the grantee once the program has been funded by Congress. See text *supra* at pp. 193–95. Probably to guard against this occurrence, a recent allocation regulation of the Environmental Protection Agency states: "Allotments are not an absolute entitlement of funds for any State; rather, they represent the amount of a grant the State can receive if the State's work program supports that level of funding and is approved by the Regional Administrator." 40 C.F.R. §35.706, 42 Fed. Reg. 56053 (1977) (interim regulation).

[71] See Chapter 12, notes 27–48, *infra*, and accompanying text.

careful, discriminate selection of the groups and individuals to be funded.[72] One understands the need to screen applicants with a close eye on their capabilities, past performance, resource base, proposed activities, and the like. Because the number of proposals far exceeds the number of grants to be made,[73] evaluation is necessarily one of relative merits. Applicants are ranked against each other, with the basis for choice often being a narrow distinction. Also, these projects cannot be premoulded. The authorizing statute can, at best, set the broad goals to be achieved, leaving to executive agencies the yearly task of determining, in the light of current knowledge and needs, the specific thrusts to be funded. The nature of such endeavors mandates against both congressional predetermination of grantees and amounts, and applicant participation in the funding decisional process.

A number of competitive grant programs, however, are primarily service oriented.[74] Their aim is to provide a package of specific benefits to particular segments of the population. The mould for such programs is usually cast in Washington with little flexibility offered grantees. Eligibility for such benefits, the types of services to be offered, and the organizational structure for their delivery are detailed in the statute and implementing regulations. Both the development of projects and their implementation involve, for the grantee, a mostly mechanical tracking of federal guidelines. The need for such services in various jurisdictions can be measured in advance with fair accuracy, leading to the possibility of a formula distribution of funds.

It is often difficult to discern why Congress has chosen for such programs the discretionary rather than the formula grant structure. The central factor appears to be the desire for flexibility in grantee selection. Nongovernmental community groups are

[72] For detailed descriptions of the grant application review processes employed by federal agencies, see *Washington Research Project, Inc.* v. *Dep't of Health, Educ. and Welfare*, 366 F. Supp. 929 (D. D.C. 1973), rev'd in part, 504 F.2d 238 (D.C. Cir. 1974), cert. denied, 421 U.S. 963 (1975) (National Institute of Mental Health); *City of Benton Harbor* v. *Richardson*, 429 F. Supp. 1096 (W.D. Mich. 1977) (Economic Development Administration); *Grassetti* v. *Weinberger*, 408 F. Supp. 142 (N.D. Cal. 1976) (National Institutes of Health); *Board of Educ.* v. *Dep't of Health, Educ. & Welfare*, 384 F. Supp. 816 (S.D. N.Y. 1974) (Office of Education). For insights on proposal review by state agencies distributing formula funds, see *Advocates for the Arts* v. *Thomson*, 397 F. Supp. 1048 (D. N.H. 1975), aff'd, 532 F.2d 792 (1st Cir. 1976), cert. denied, 429 U.S. 894 (1976) (grants for the promotion of the arts); *School Comm.* v. *Anrig*, 520 F.2d 577 (1st Cir. 1975) (grants to schools for elementary and secondary education); *Nicholson* v. *Pittenger*, 364 F. Supp. 669 (E.D. Pa. 1973) (same).

[73] See, e.g., *Board of Educ.* v. *Dep't of Health, Educ. & Welfare*, 384 F. Supp. 816, 818, n. 4 (S.D. N.Y. 1974).

[74] See Chapter 2, notes 73–76, *supra*, and accompanying text.

made eligible to apply for such grants, either exclusively or along with governmental units.[75] And once choice between various eligible entities is made part of the grant award process, the possibility disappears that any group has a legitimate claim of entitlement prior to an award. The concept of discretion in the award of governmental benefits belies the legitimacy of reliance on the future receipt of funds—to this extent, at least, the traditional concept of governmental benefits being "privileges" has continuing validity.

Both Congress and administering agencies have generally not distinguished, for Due Process purposes, between discretionary initial awards and discretionary continuation awards for existing projects. In both cases, minimal opportunities are afforded to argue the merits of grant applications.[76] The practice seems beyond constitutional challenge. If in a particular program Congress has conceded discretion to the administering agency for both new and subsequent awards, the Due Process analysis is essentially the same for both categories of funding. In the former, there is no legitimate expectation of an initial award; in the latter, there is no right to funding beyond the project period for which the first award was made. In both cases, the amount of the award is subject to grantor discretion, and in neither instance can the applicant claim that it is the only one eligible for funding.

Nonetheless, a substantial practical difference can be shown. The disappointed applicant for new project funding has lost little beyond the time, energy, and resources invested in the preparation and submission of the grant application. One may concede that for many programs that process is costly and the frustration of rejection acute. But the possibility of failure was always live and known in advance. Nor have any individuals or organizations suffered the loss of existing benefits from the rejection. On the other hand, the refunding question is whether to continue an ongoing effort. Defunding of such a project may have serious adverse consequences both on the grantee organization and on the population being serviced by the project.

Another section will advance the argument that such differ-

---

[75] See, e.g., §456(a) Comprehensive Employment and Training Act of 1973, 29 U.S.C. §929(a):
"The Secretary [of Labor] may make agreements with Federal, State, or local agencies, . . . or private organizations for the establishment and operation of Job Corps centers. . . ."

[76] See Chapter 12, *infra*, at pp. 296–306.

entiating considerations should motivate both Congress and the executive branch to develop adequate procedural safeguards for the refunding of discretionary projects. In most cases, however, that would not be a duty of constitutional origin. Because our primary understanding of whether a property interest in continued funding exists in the grantee must come from the grant statute and regulations, their implicit or explicit denial of refunding entitlements would make short shrift of any Fifth Amendment argument. The harm that might befall a particular grantee and its service population is constitutionally relevant only after the applicability of the Due Process Clause is demonstrated.[77]

In some refunding cases a course of conduct by the grantor agency might produce a different constitutional result. Even though the grant statute and regulations bestow discretion on the government in continuation grant decisions, the grantor could conceivably deal away that otherwise absolute power of refusal. If, for example, it could be proved that a grantor explicitly guaranteed refunding to a particular recipient, both reliance and a claim of entitlement might be legitimated. According to Justice Stewart, property interests may be created not only by "existing rules" but also by "understandings."[78] A guarantee of further financial support might also be read into certain grantor actions. A combination of signals from the grantor might transform a grantee's refunding hopes from expectation to entitlement. Such might consist of a glowing grantor evaluation of the project, or budget and programmatic approvals inconsistent with a winding down of the activity, or undue delay in notifying the grantee that refunding will not be forthcoming. These actions might together or individually create considerably more than an expectation of continued financing. Because the argument is not that the grantor by its prior course of conduct is precluded from denying the grant but rather that its acts have produced such reliance and expectation that it would be fundamentally unfair to deny refunding without affording the grantee a *hearing opportunity*, the finding of a constitutional right to such would not have seriously detrimental effects on the grant system. Nor is it disturbing to have constitutional protections arise on an *ad hoc* basis. While the grantor agency would face the practical problem of determining when it must give Due Process hearings because of its course of

[77] See notes 7–8, *supra*, and accompanying text.
[78] *Board of Regents of State Colleges* v. *Roth*, 408 U.S. 564, 577 (1972).

action in a particular project, constitutional protections are latent in any situation where the government can harm another. Since a basic Due Process inquiry is whether a sufficient interest in a thing has been created by law or conduct to make a claim constitutionally recognizable, we must accept the possibility that sufficient interests might vest by federal grantor action, even when that action falls short of an award, so that deprivation by denial of refunding must be surrounded by fair procedures.

Parenthetically, this possibility might be a roadblock in another path to the goal of injecting larger doses of fairness in the process of refunding projects. Despite the absence of constitutional duty, federal grantor agencies should improve equity and even-handedness in the refunding process by providing, in advance, detailed guidelines as to the circumstances under which projects will and will not be refunded.[79] While a grantor agency might agree to the desirability of such guidelines, it justifiably would look askance at the responsibility of giving a Due Process hearing every time it denies an applicant refunding. But under our prior analysis that might be the consequence of clear refunding rules and procedures. To the extent that grantors give advance and detailed notice of the conditions under which refunding can be expected, they would open themselves to Due Process requirements. Should the latter be viewed as strongly undesirable, the grantor may take the easy course of playing its refunding cards close to the vest.

Holders of Federal Grants

The preceding section explored the applicability of Fifth Amendment procedural protections to those applying for federal grants and concluded that even prior to a grant award a property interest may be found in the applicant for some types of formula grants, but not for discretionary awards except under exceptional circumstances.

This part focuses on Fifth Amendment coverage of grant recipients during the term of the grant, normally one year.[80] The Due Process analytical framework remains the same, but the route to constitutional protection is simple and direct. Once the grant award is made, no reasonable argument can be advanced that the

---

[79] For a review of current administrative practices, see Chapter 12, notes 55–65, *infra*, and accompanying text.

[80] See Chapter 12, note 53, *infra*, and accompanying text.

property interest in the federal funds has not been transferred to the grantee. Even if the payment system is reimbursement rather than advances or letters of credit,[81] the fact that the money technically remains in the federal treasury does not alter the commitment of the grantor to finance allowable grantee costs. Nothing in federal grant statutes would lead to a different conclusion. On the contrary, once the grant is made payment provisions in federal statutes are regularly couched in mandatory terms.[82] Postaward grantee reliance on the uninterrupted flow of funds, as scheduled, is not only justifiable but essential for the success of federally financed projects. Staff must be employed, space rented, supplies acquired, commitments made to third parties, beneficiaries selected, committees constituted, and dozens of additional decisions and actions effectuated from a basis of economic security.

Thus, we can quickly conclude that a property right vests in the grantee after the award—a right to the funds in hand or the funds committed to be transferred, as the case may be.[83] Such a finding then calls into play Due Process protection.

While the practice is not universal, in most formula programs the grantor will not terminate a grant without affording the grantee notice and hearing opportunities.[84] Our conclusion that property rights accrue to an eligible applicant for a formula grant even prior to the official award makes the postaward constitutional case apparent. In those formula programs in which neither the statute nor regulations provide such rights, we can feel confident that the Fifth Amendment will rectify the omission.

The simplicity of the analysis, however, ends here, for most federal grantor agencies do not offer Due Process to recipients of discretionary grants even after an award and during the course of a project.[85]

[81] Most grant statutes contain a section or clause authorizing the grantor agency to determine whether the payment system shall be by advances or reimbursement and also the size of installments. See, e.g., §620(b) Education of the Handicapped Act, 20 U.S.C. §1420(b). Office of Management and Budget instructions provide details on the grantor selection of payment methods. See OMB Cir. A-102, *supra*, Chapter 1, note 83, at Attachment J; OMB Cir. A-110, *supra*, Chapter 1 note 83, at Attachment I.

[82] See, e.g., §620(a) Education of the Handicapped Act, 20 U.S.C. §1420(a) ("The Commissioner shall make payments"); §111(a)(1) Vocational Education Act, 20 U.S.C. §2311(a)(1) ("The Commissioner shall pay"); §1611(a) Public Health Service Act, 42 U.S.C. §300 p-1(a) ("the Secretary shall . . . make such payment").

[83] *Red School House, Inc. v. Office of Economic Opportunity*, 386 F. Supp. 1177 (D. Minn. 1977). A preliminary question may be whether a commitment of grant funds occurred. See, e.g., *Township of River Vale v. Harris*, 444 F. Supp. 90 (D. D.C. 1978).

[84] See generally Chapter 9, *infra*.

[85] See generally Chapters 10, 11, *infra*.

The Office of Management and Budget cursorily instructs grantor agencies as follows:

> "The grantor agency may terminate any grant in whole, or in part, at any time before the date of completion, whenever it is determined that the grantee has failed to comply with the conditions of the grant. The grantor agency shall promptly notify the grantee in writing of the determination and the reasons for the termination, together with the effective date." [86]

Although the instruction does not explicitly deny grantor agencies the power to concede hearing rights either before or after termination, a unilateral termination decision is its clear thrust. Grantees get, according to the text, no more than prompt notice of when and why their funding shall cease. Some federal agencies have simply copied the instruction in their own program regulations, thus affording no pretermination process or, in some cases, even no posttermination process to the recipient of a discretionary grant.[87] Others have provided the grantee with only advance notice and an opportunity to protest in writing or an informal meeting to respond to the proposed termination before it is effected.[88]

We have been unable to find language in any statute establishing a program of discretionary grants which authorizes, explicitly or implicitly, a termination by the government without affording the grantee an opportunity to be heard. The termination power has arisen, presumably, as a necessary administrative tool supported implicitly by the agency authority to approve program regulations and its mandate to administer the program. While the necessity of such power may readily be conceded, the need to exercise such power free from grantee participation is not so easily seen. Keeping in mind that the exercise of the termination power is conditioned upon a finding of grantee noncompliance, a closed door decisional process is not justified. Certainly the informational base

---

[86] OMB Cir. A-102, *supra*, Chapter 1, note 83, at Attachment L, para. 5(a). See also OMB Cir. A-110, *supra*, Chapter 1, note 83, at Attachment L, para. 4(a) (federal sponsoring agency "may reserve" termination right).

[87] See, e.g., 45 C.F.R. §74.115(a), 43 Fed. Reg. 34076 (1978) (Department of Health, Education and Welfare); 7 C.F.R. pt. 1948, exh. A, pt. B, para. 17(a), 43 Fed. Reg. 14289 (1978) (Department of Agriculture grant agreement termination clause); Chapter 10, note 72, *infra*, and accompanying text. Compare 45 C.F.R. §1050.115-5 (Community Services Administration; termination only after hearings required by grant statute).

[88] See, e.g., 40 C.F.R. §30.920-3 (Environmental Protection Agency); 45 C.F.R. §1424.8 (National Institute of Education); National Science Foundation, *Grant Policy Manual* §663, 42 Fed. Reg. 38770 (1977); Office of Human Development, *Grants Administration Manual* ch. 9, 42 Fed. Reg. 21076 (1977).

upon which such decisions are made can only be improved by affording grantees a formal opportunity to present evidence and argument. In fact, the grantee will ordinarily have the best access to relevant data since its own policies and actions are under review. To answer that grantors can acquire such information through reviews, inspections, and interviews with grantee employees and beneficiaries is not satisfactory. Unilateral power to collect evidence carries too much danger that the grantor will sift and screen at its pleasure, thus building a slanted record to prove a point. To the extent that relevant information is not sought or is ignored, the risk of incorrect findings increases. Additionally, the grantor, answerable only to itself, may abuse the termination power or use it as a threat to force grantee compliance with debatable dictates. Inadequate grantee participation in the decisional process may also lead to inappropriate remedies for noncompliance; corrective action may be feasible and desirable, yet working from scanty information the grantor may inappropriately levy the doom of termination. Finally, speed and efficiency are hardly sufficient justifications. If, in a particular situation, the grantor must move quickly to prevent the illegal expenditure of federal funds, summary suspension will be available.[89] Unilateral determinations are more efficient, but that very efficiency is what produces higher risks of error. And to close down a project by mistake is to lose the prior investment of the Federal Government entirely.

On a broader level, unchecked termination power in federal grantors is antithetical to the very nature and functioning of the grant-in-aid system. To operate effectively, both grantors and grantees must move toward common goals. The primary mission of the administering agency is to achieve programmatic goals set forth in the grant-in-aid statute. The methods by which those goals are achieved must be, of course, consistent with statutory directives, leading to the policing powers of the grantor. But that is a consideration subsidiary to the main purpose of achieving program success, whether it be research, training, demonstrations, services, construction, or education. The batting average of a grantor is not determined by the number of hands it catches in the till, but by the number of hands it launches which are successfully doing the job. The cooperative nature of a grant-in-aid venture requires close grantor-grantee relations throughout the project, even within the context of a possible violation of federal standards.

[89] See Chapter 11, *infra*, at pp. 286, 288.

Due Process and Federal Grants / 211

The maize of ambiguous federal conditions facing every grantee virtually guarantees some instance or degree of noncompliance, even for the most sophisticated and well-intentioned recipient.[90] The potential for conflict and contention is, thus, ever present. Should grantor-grantee hostility prevent the free interchange of information and opinion, the energy of both is likely to be diverted from the actualization of program goals to bickering over the compliance issues. A danger of compliance procedures which shut out grantee participation from investigation through decision is that they are quite likely to promote such hostility.

Federal agency practice is, of course, worthy of respect. Courts defer not only to written rules and standards of federal agencies but also to their uniform operating practices.[91] Still, one gets the impression that the prevalent notion that procedural rights do not extend to the holder of a discretionary grant may be a result of the failure to distinguish between the significantly different grantee interests, in both a constitutional and practical sense, before and after a grant award. While discretion attends the award of federal funds, once the grants are made, as we have demonstrated, sufficient property accrues to the grantee to call forth the protections of Due Process. Another explanation might be that these grantor customs predate the procedural Due Process revolution and simply have not been reexamined in light of *Goldberg* v. *Kelly*[92] and its kin. If that is the case, we submit that the time for reevaluation is at hand. HEW's voluntary adoption of a grant appeals system in 1975 for review of adverse actions taken against recipients of discretionary awards was a major breakthrough.[93] Unfortunately, few other federal grantor agencies have followed suit.[94]

The Liberty Question

The grantee claim to procedural Due Process naturally focuses on the deprivation of property—dollars being the currency of the grant. Yet the Fifth Amendment also protects "liberty" interests,

[90] See, e.g., Tomlinson, *supra*, Chapter 1, note 55, at 610–11.
[91] See, e.g., *Shea* v. *Vialpando*, 416 U.S. 251, 262–63, n. 11 (1974); *New York State Dep't of Social Servs.* v. *Dublino*, 413 U.S. 405, 420–21 (1973); *Carleson* v. *Remillard*, 406 U.S. 598, 601 (1972); *Dandridge* v. *Williams*, 397 U.S. 471, 481 (1970).
[92] 397 U.S. 254 (1970).
[93] See Chapter 10, *infra*, at pp. 281–83, for a description of the system.
[94] See Chapter 1, notes 96–99, *supra*, and accompanying text.

212 / *Rights and Remedies Under Federal Grants*

and there may be some value in that concept for the federal grantee facing termination or other severe sanctions.

At first blush (and at second also!), the connection between the loss of a federal grant and the loss of "liberty" does not surface. The grantee organization remains free to come and go, poorer but hopefully wiser. But liberty in the sense of freedom of movement does not exhaust the meaning of that constitutional term. The Supreme Court has not hesitated to sweep into procedural Due Process, under the liberty concept, a variety of interests not involving bodily restraint.[95]

The two which are most relevant to the recipient of a government grant are the interests in preserving one's good name and in engaging in fruitful business relationships. The Court has voiced concern about the stigmatic effects which adverse governmental action may have on an individual. Unfavorable employment decisions, for example, if accompanied by charges of misconduct might seriously harm an individual's "standing and associations in his community."[96] Such a stamp of disapproval might effectively impose on the individual "a stigma or other disability that foreclose[s] his freedom to take advantage of other employment opportunities."[97] The harm is to *future opportunities*, thus precluding reliance on the procedural protections afforded property interests by the Fifth and Fourteenth Amendments. We must conceptually distinguish reputational harm from the injury produced by the deprivation of property, even though the two are, realistically, intertwined. The former results from the findings which lead to the taking, as opposed to the prejudicial impact of the taking itself. The damage to be measured is not the debilitating present effects of the property deprivation but the loss of future opportunities caused by the badge of dishonor. Thus, even though a Due Process claimant may be found not to have an interest which qualifies as property, the reputational damage suffered may be sufficiently severe to require constitutional protection. The right to pursue

[95] See, e.g., *Meyer* v. *Nebraska*, 262 U.S. 390, 399 (1923), which included within protected "liberty":

"not merely freedom from bodily restraint but also the right of the individual to contract, to engage in any of the common occupations of life, to acquire useful knowledge, to marry, to establish a home and bring up children [and] to worship God according to the dictates of . . . conscience."

See generally Monaghan, "Of 'Liberty' and 'Property,'" 62 Cornell L. Rev. 405, 411–34 (1977).

[96] *Board of Regents of State Colleges* v. *Roth*, 408 U.S. 564, 573 (1972).

[97] *Id.* at 573.

one's goals free from the debilitating effects of unjust and unfounded governmental accusations is an aspect of liberty safeguarded by the Constitution, for when "a person's good name, reputation, honor, or integrity is at stake because of what the government is doing to him, notice and an opportunity to be heard are essential." [98]

In *Paul* v. *Davis* [99] the Court required a showing not only that government action harmed an individual's reputation but also that this, in turn, substantially affected a more tangible interest such as employment. This has been viewed as a substantial erosion of the protection previously conceded reputational interests.[100] It does not affect our analysis, however, since we stress the harm to future funding opportunities which reputational damage to grantees may cause.

While such principles have evolved mainly in the context of government accusations against individuals, the potentiality for harm and the need for procedural protection are equally acute when the government moves against organizational recipients of government grants. A decision by the Federal Government to suspend, terminate, or void a grant necessarily involves a tentative or final determination that the grantee organization has engaged in some misconduct, whether malfeasance or nonfeasance. A grant may be voided, for instance, if substantial misrepresentations are discovered to have been made in the grant application, or if receipt and administration of the grant are found to be beyond the grantee's authority.[101] Suspension and termination both require a finding that the grantee is in violation of the grant statute, regulations, or agreement. Therefore, whenever the grantor defunds, wholly or partially, within the term of the grant, the potential exists for reputational harm to the grantee.

The damage of concern is the loss of future gains caused by the findings which resulted in adverse grantor action. Grantees, whether governmental units or private nonprofit groups, are ordinarily dedicated to the provision of public services. The

---

[98] *Wisconsin* v. *Constanineau*, 400 U.S. 433, 437 (1971).
[99] 424 U.S. 693 (1976).
[100] E.g., Tribe, *American Constitutional Law* 527–32 (1978).
[101] See *In re School Bd.*, 475 F.2d 1117 (5th Cir. 1973). There is a surprising lack of reference in grant-in-aid regulations to the agency power to void a grant for material misrepresentation in the grant application or for lack of grantee authority. For two examples, see 45 C.F.R. §185.45(b), 43 Fed. Reg. 36250 (1978) (voiding emergency school grants for ineligibility arising subsequent to grant); 42 C.F.R. §64.7(c) (material misrepresentation in NIH grant applications).

relevant inquiry, therefore, is whether a finding of misconduct in the administration of a federal grant may have ripple effects which substantially hinder the achievement of that public service mission. The focus is not on damage to individuals within the organization —that is a separate subject involving different considerations—but rather on reputational harm to the organization itself. The grantee can act, of course, only through individuals and a finding of organizational misconduct is, perforce, a determinaton of individual derelictions. But the grant is awarded to the organization, the commitments are its own, and the acts of officers and employees of the grantee are attributable to it. Thus, a determination of grant mismanagement is a finding applicable to the organization, whether it be the result of the errant behavior of one member of the grantee body or of the combined action of many.

Section 1006(b)(5) of the Legal Services Corporation Act [102] dramatically illustrates this principle. To a degree unknown to grant-in-aid statutes this provision controls the conduct of employees of grantee bodies. The prohibitions and directives of grant statutes are ordinarily addressed to grantee organizations. This statute, however, speaks directly to employee activities and prohibits personnel of grant recipients from engaging in, or promoting, riots, civil disturbances, violation of court injunctions, certain political activity, public demonstrations, pickets, boycotts, strikes, and any "illegal" activity. Special mechanisms are instituted to monitor enforcement of this and other grant conditions.[103] The corporation is explicitly authorized by Section 1006(b)(5) to suspend and terminate the grant of any organization whose employee(s) is found to have violated these prescriptions.[104]

Without question, fault-based government decisions can have substantially detrimental effects on the future ability of the grantee organization to carry out its chartered mission. One primary effect will be to prejudice the grantee in its efforts to obtain future grants from the Federal Government. It is common practice in discretionary grant programs to include as a factor in funding

---

[102] 42 U.S.C. §2996(b)(5).

[103] See Chapter 3, notes 71–74, *supra,* and accompanying text.

[104] See also the hearing notice published at 42 Fed. Reg. 38018–19 (1977) which gives as the reason for an intended denial of refunding "the ineffective and improper use of Federal funds in paying the salaries of personnel whose breach of the duty of care owed to children enrolled in the program resulted in the deaths of two of them."

decisions the "past performance" of the applicant.[105] Relevant past history includes not only an evaluation of the degree of success of prior projects but also an adherence by the grantee to programmatic requirements. Regulations are ordinarily couched in terms of past compliance with the requirements of the specific program under which funds are again being solicited, but sometimes the grantee's past performance under other programs of the same agency or similar projects funded by any federal agency is considered relevant.[106] Even if a "past performance" policy is not officially announced, one may surmise that findings of an applicant's past noncompliance, if known by grantor officials reviewing the application, will always be considered a relevant, detrimental factor. Thus, whether or not there is an announced policy on the subject, and whether or not an announced policy limits the range of inquiry to past defaults under specific programs, it is likely that information of this nature in grantor hands will harm a grantee's chances for future awards.

Considering that an applicant for a discretionary federal grant is afforded no opportunity to be heard on the merits of its proposal or its capacity to administer the grant,[107] we easily see the dangers implicit in federal agency use of past performance as an award criterion. Because the argument is that future harm is relevant to Due Process rights in a federal noncompliance action, we presume that a grantee (which is now seeking new funds) was not afforded adequate administrative hearing rights before or after a noncom-

[105] See, e.g., 42 C.F.R. §50.106(d) (health services programs); *City of Lebanon* v. *Dep't of Housing & Urban Dev.*, 422 F. Supp. 803, 806 (M.D. Pa. 1976); *Grassetti* v. *Weinberger*, 408 F. Supp. 142, 146 (N.D. Cal. 1976); *Silva* v. *East Providence Housing Auth.*, 390 F. Supp. 691, 693, n. 1 (D. R.I. 1975). In *Southern Mut. Help Ass'n* v. *Califano*, 574 F.2d 518 (D.C. Cir. 1977), reputational injury provided sufficient harm for a refunding applicant to have standing to challenge a denial of continuation funds. In its analysis, the court stressed the past performance factor:

"Reputation, especially that established by past performance, is a key element in agency grant decisions, and an organization that acquires a bad reputation in the grant community based on poor performance will have a difficult burden to overcome in securing new grants. . . . While SMHA has in the past obtained grants from agencies other than HEW, most of its programs are of the type supported by appropriations channeled through HEW. It is not difficult to imagine the inhospitable reception that would be given to future applications from an organization that has been accused of violating departmental regulations, misusing grant funds, and engaging in activities that create conflicts of interest. The effect of HEW's action in this case, therefore, is to endanger SMHA's ability to obtain future grants, the very lifeblood of its existence."

Id. at 524 (footnotes omitted).

[106] See, e.g., 45 C.F.R. §187.5(a)(2) (projects for education of Indian children); 45 C.F.R. §46.121(b) (past compliance with regulation protecting human subjects).

[107] See Chapter 12, *infra*, at pp. 296–300.

pliance decision. That grantor action may have been correct, but we suspect that the unilateral nature of the decisional process has significantly augmented the chances of an erroneous determination. Thus, the spectre is raised of a grantee being condemned again and again for actions which may well have been perfectly legal and proper, without ever having the opportunity to correct the record and, indeed, without even knowing that its grant applications are being rejected for past "sins." [108]

The ambiguity of the "past performance" factor is also disturbing. Program regulations do not specify whether there must be an official finding of noncompliance in past projects in order for the factor to be relevant in the review of a grantee's new funding requests. They refer vaguely to whether the applicant adhered to or complied with program terms and conditions, the law, and the regulations.[109] It is theoretically possible for federal officials to disapprove a funding proposal on the belief that the applicant improperly operated a previous grant project, even though the question of noncompliance was never raised. One may consider that possibility remote and, in any event, an abusive use of review criteria. It is not, however, unlikely in the common situation in which the grantee/applicant heavily relies on funds under particular programs administered by the same subdivision of a regional or national federal office. Those who review proposals, and particularly those who sign off on awards, are likely to be familiar with, or informed of, an applicant's performance under other grants. Since this decisional process is shielded from outside scrutiny, one must be particularly reluctant to rely on the good faith of officials; even if it is abusive, it would be unreviewable.

In most situations of alleged noncompliance, the errors and defects perceived by the government are informally brought to the attention of the grantee. Depending on the type of violation and the individuals involved on both sides, the matter may be pursued amicably or hostilely. While most administrators recognize the self-defeating nature of a termination decision and, hence, the preferability of obtaining compliance,[110] the methods employed to achieve compliance vary greatly. If the infraction is innocent and

---

[108] Grant rejection notices tend to be quite vague concerning the reasons for disapproval. We have found only one provision in a statute or regulation requiring specification of the grounds upon which the federal rejection of a competitive grant application is based. See §710(d)(2) Emergency School Aid Act, 20 U.S.C. §1609(d)(2).

[109] See, e.g., 45 C.F.R. §187.5.

[110] See Chapter 3, notes 169–180, *supra,* and accompanying text.

obvious, a simple nudge will usually be sufficient to produce corrective action. Yet that is not the prototype context. Grantees are usually sophisticated and wise enough to avoid obvious violations of the grant. Most of the alleged illegalities will stem from unclear federal policies or a confusing backdrop of facts. In more cases than not, noncompliance allegations are likely to be highly debatable. Ideally, the parties will openly and honestly exchange information and arguments, identify areas of agreement and disagreement, discuss alternative solutions, and move toward compromises when feasible. Program modifications effectuated by the grantee as a result of such negotiations are not necessarily evidence that the grantee violated the law but, rather, a mutual accommodation of conflicting views. The question whether there was, in fact, a violation of federal law need not ever be resolved. Such accommodations are to be encouraged and, indeed, are required by some grant statutes.[111] Yet, if following successful negotiations the same or a different federal agency were to consider the matter as evidence of noncompliance in past projects and a negative factor in the review of new funding proposals from the grantee, a deterrent to the favored policy of negotiation has been created. Worse, the conclusion of poor past performance may be incorrectly premised on the sole fact that the grantee did revise its operations. Thus, to protect its reputation and, hence, its capability of attracting future funds, a grantee may well force a compliance hearing and determination even though conciliation would best serve the interests of both sides.

All too commonly the federal grantor does not seek an interchange of ideas and information with the grantee. This occurs most frequently when no compliance hearing is available to recipients, the government thus being relatively free from outside inspection. An ultimatum is presented. Both "facts" and "policies" are handed to the grantee with little chance for debate and rebuttal, and the grantor specifies the corrective action that must be taken. Failure to take such steps, it is announced, will result in a termination of the grant. Consider the grantee's dilemma. The Federal Government may be totally wrong on the facts, on the policy, or on the corrective action required. Because a formal opportunity to argue the contrary is not open, whether there is noncompliance becomes, incredibly, an irrelevant factor from the grantee's perspective. The more meaningful question is whether

[111] See Chapter 3, note 180, *supra,* and accompanying text.

it will be worthwhile to continue the grant given the nature of the conditions being imposed by the grantor. If the conditions do not violate strong policies of the grantee and if the project will still be viable and valuable, the grantee complies. But whether the project continues or is terminated, there is a "finding" of noncompliance to be potentially used by federal agencies in the review of future applications from that grantee. The inherent unfairness of that situation should be apparent.[112]

Future penalties for past offenses have generally been the handiwork of federal administering agencies. Only occasionally has Congress required that a review of a grantee's past performance be an element in the decisional process on future grants. One such example can be found in Title III-B of the Public Health Service Act which provides formula grants to states for comprehensive health planning and services. Section 314(d)(3) of the Act directs HEW to review annually the activities undertaken by each state to determine if it has honored the assurances contained in the grant agreement.[113] A finding of noncompliance can lead to a termination of the current grant until the deficiencies have been corrected; further, HEW is directed not to approve any future grant applications in the absence of sufficient assurance that the state will conform to federal requirements in the future. Significantly, such a finding must be preceded by notice and an opportunity to be heard.

Title XV of the same Act establishes a national network of federally funded health systems agencies and state health planning and development agencies.[114] Each of these entities must be designated by HEW. An annual decision is made whether to continue the designation and, hence, the organization's eligibility for Title XV funds. For both types of agencies, HEW is instructed to review annual performance, including compliance with federal requirements, prior to redesignation. While the statute is silent on hearing rights,[115] by regulation the department affords prior written notice of the reasons for not renewing the agreement and an opportunity

---

[112] One program regulation includes past compliance with grant terms and conditions as a criterion in the evaluation of proposals. It explicitly provides that if the application is rejected on this basis, the applicant must be afforded prior "notice and an opportunity to rebut the basis for the decision." 45 C.F.R. §153.12(b)(12), 42 Fed. Reg. 57292 (1977) (noncommercial educational broadcasting facilities).
[113] 42 U.S.C. §246(d)(3).
[114] §§1501–1536 Public Health Service Act, 42 U.S.C. §§300k–330n-5.
[115] See §§1515(c), 1521(b) id., 42 U.S.C. §§300"l"-4(c), 300m(b).

for a hearing before an officer or employee specially designated by the Secretary.[116]

Although the adverse impact on future federal funding possibilities is the most serious harm which reputational damage will ordinarily produce, a holding of noncompliance by the federal grantor could debilitate the ability of the grantee organization to achieve its goals in numerous other ways. The existence and degree of other harms would depend, of course, on the context of each case. While the violation of federal law must in each instance be sufficiently serious to justify termination, the degree of reputational harm may depend on both the type of violation and the amount of publicity it generates. To function successfully, a grantee organization, whether a government agency or a nonprofit group, needs the approval of its beneficiary population, other entities that provide support services, and the larger community of politicians and taxpayers. A publicized disapprobation involving grounds such as pervasive discrimination, financial mismanagement, breaches of client confidentiality, and improper fund uses might predictably weaken the support network to a point where fundamental fairness requires that the grantee be given an adequate opportunity to respond.

The Range of Deprivations

Grantees may be offended by many different types of grantor actions which affect, to some degree, the property held. Virtually any interference with a grantee's freedom, during the course of a project, may be said to impinge on its right to the grant funds, for that right includes use as well as possession. The protected interest of the grantee extends to the bundle of activities which comprises a grant project—from organization through expenditure. Although possession and use are highly conditioned, they cannot be adversely affected without a determination that such conditions have been violated. The punch line, then, is that federal grantors cannot act upon the grantee in any way during the course of a grant without affording notice and an opportunity to be heard.

---

[116] See 42 C.F.R. §122.108 (health systems agencies); 42 C.F.R. §123.108 (state health planning and development agencies). Compare 42 C.F.R. pt. 110, subpt. I, 43 Fed. Reg. 32254–56 (1978) (no hearing opportunity for Health Maintenance Organization).

That startling principle is, of course, wrong. The denouement is avoided (along with government paralysis) by the constitutional need to find not that property or liberty has been affected but that it has been "deprived." That word, along with its grandiose brethren in the Due Process Clause, may be fuzzy, but it at least informs us that governmental actions must be substantially harmful before the need for procedural safeguards arises. We also know from the Supreme Court that the concept of deprivation is of double relevance: first, it is one of the keys which opens the procedural safe; second, once the safe's door swings open the nature and degree of deprivation continues to be relevant to the determination of which procedural gems we must withdraw.[117]

This section will not attempt to elaborate a constitutional analysis for each of the grantor actions which might amount to deprivations in the constitutional sense. That task would be overwhelming, given the multiplicity of events which occur during the life of each grant and the varying factual circumstances of each. Instead, some general approaches will be suggested.

In its primary sense a deprivation is a taking, a bereaving, a removal of something from the possession of another.[118] In the federal grants context the paradigm example is an order to return federal dollars or to stop using them. Yet the varying factual contexts in which that order may issue complicate any straightforward conclusion. If the order arrives at a humming grantee office 90 days after the project has begun, we would have little difficulty talking about constitutional deprivations and procedural fairness. If it happens, however, on the second day of a project when little has been launched besides a party to celebrate the arrival of an award letter, our appreciation of loss is considerably diminished. While property may have vested in the grantee in the latter case, the absence of prejudicial reliance lessens our sympathy. Similarly, a grant may be terminated toward the end of a project when few dollars remain in the till and employees are cleaning out their desks. Absent reputational damage, such minor economic deprivation appears not to deserve the stature of a constitutional case.

Shifts in our sense of equity are produced by our responses to degree of harm. We wish not to demean the majestic concept

---

[117] See *Mathews* v. *Eldridge*, 424 U.S. 319, 334 (1976):
"[R]esolution of the issue whether the administrative procedures provided here are constitutionally sufficient requires analysis of the governmental and private interests that are affected."
[118] *Webster's New Collegiate Dictionary* 223 (1961).

of Due Process of law by invoking it in relatively trivial matters. The three cases above are technically indistinguishable if all we must find to invoke constitutional process is a government taking of an interest that qualifies as protected property or liberty. The deprivation, therefore, must be of significant dimension measured in terms of injury to the affected party. A yardstick is applied to each individual case to see if the alleged harm meets a threshold test of substantiality.[119]

An alternative is to consider that any governmental taking of constitutionally qualified property or liberty, regardless of its dimension, springs the Due Process Clause, with the magnitude of injury being relevant only to the question of the type of process which is due. The problem with that approach is that the actor often does not know what process is demanded until long after the event. In the case of minimal deprivations, minimal procedural safeguards will be required. But their precise content will depend on *post hoc* judicial evaluation of the equity of the particular case. In cases of small harms the actor may have guessed wrong as to the type of notice and hearing opportunity constitutionally required, or, as is more likely, may have assumed not unreasonably that no process was needed. Its action then becomes a constitutional violation with all the consequences: voiding of the act, reparation of harm, civil rights remedies.[120] And all of the above occurs even though the deprivation caused injury only to principle and not to people. This untoward result is avoided by requiring some basic level of substantiality of the deprivation before the constitutional requirement is found applicable; parties that meet

---

[119] We propose this test of substantiality fully recognizing that the Supreme Court has not articulated standards distinguishing *de minimis* from substantial government actions. Compare *Joint Anti-Fascist Refugee Comm.* v. *McGrath*, 341 U.S. 123, 168 (1951) (Frankfurter, J., concurring) ("grievous loss of any kind"), with *Fuentes* v. *Shevin*, 407 U.S. 67, 87 (1972) ("a significant property interest"), and *Goss* v. *Lopez*, 419 U.S. 565, 576 (1975) ("as long as a property deprivation is not *de minimis* its gravity is irrelevant"). See *Escalera* v. *New York City Housing Auth.*, 425 F.2d 853, 864 (2d Cir. 1970), *cert. denied*, 400 U.S. 853 (1970) (even small rent increases burden public housing tenants enough to call for due process). See generally *Thompson* v. *Washington*, 497 F.2d 626, 635–36 (D.C. Cir. 1973) ("what constitutes a deprivation of constitutional significance remains an abiding question"); *Human Resources Management, Inc.* v. *Weaver*, 442 F. Supp. 241, 248 (D. D.C. 1978) (eligibility for SBA minority procurement a "relatively low-order [property] interest"). The fact that the Supreme Court has permitted the award of nominal damages for violations of constitutional Due Process rights, see *Carey* v. *Piphus*, 435 U.S. 247 (1978), does not mean that trivial deprivations are litigable. Rather, some deprivations, though substantial, do not cause damage easily measured in economic terms, such as the 20-day student suspensions in *Carey*.

[120] See generally "Developments in the Law—Section 1983 and Federalism," 90 Harv. L. Rev. 1133 (1977).

this threshold test may then argue that Due Process required greater safeguards than what was afforded in view of the particular injuries caused.

We cannot, therefore, be sure that all federal grantor actions of a particular type must be attended by Due Process. Even the classic example of a taking, a grant termination, may result in such inconsequential harm that constitutional principles are not involved. Yet because in the great majority of cases a grant termination will, in fact, cause substantial harm, we can comfortably presume that terminations must ordinarily meet Due Process standards, and legislate and regulate accordingly. In the same category of presumptively substantial injury we may also include a withholding of formula funds. Because a property interest is created in eligible institutions at the moment funds are appropriated, a nonconformity withholding is effectively a taking even though federal funds have not yet been transferred. In the great majority of cases the act of withholding will result in considerable prejudice to the grantee. Formula allocations are usually substantial and heavy reliance on the uninterrupted receipt of yearly allocations can typically be demonstrated. A third class of federal grantor action which we may consider a prima facie constitutional deprivation is the recoverey for past illegal expenditures effectuated by dipping into a grantee's future allocations under the same or a different program.

At the other end of the spectrum, a wide variety of grantor actions may be taken without affording hearing opportunities. Most are exempt because they are not deprivations. Grantors discharge their obligations to assure compliance with federal terms and conditions by issuing directives, not by cleaning house themselves. The grantee is instructed to improve its reports, reform its financial management system, modify its eligibility requirements, reconstitute its citizen advisory board, and so forth. It is only when sanctions are imposed because the grantee has ignored or faultily carried out such instructions that the deprivation occurs.

In the middle we find the tough cases. Examples include: allocations of funds pursuant to the statutory formula when a recipient claims that its allotment falls below what it believes to be the correct amount; reallocation of formula funds to others based on the agency's perception of a grantee's lack of need for the full allotment; disallowance of costs as improper or insufficiently documented. In all of these cases *if the grantee is right* it has effectively been deprived of its property. Yet thousands of such decisions must be made each year by the Federal Government. If a set of hearing rights must attend each such decision, an intolerable burden would be placed on the grant-in-aid system. On the other hand, such actions may substantially injure grantees. To afford only the judicial forum for the ventilation of the grantee's position would not comport with modern standards for administrative Due Process.[121]

Our proposal for a threshold test of substantiality may aid us in reconciling these conflicting interests. We need a range of economic decisions which the government can make without having to hear or read contrary arguments from the grantee. It would simply be too burdensome to permit grantees to challenge formally each $50 cost disallowance or relatively insubstantial variations between their formula calculations and those of the grantor. The threshold test could be quantified as a percentage of the total grant. We might, for example, start requiring procedural safeguards if the government's financial action results in a loss to the grantee amounting to 5 percent of the grant,[122] recognizing, of course, that any attempt to quantify substantiality must necessarily be somewhat arbitrary. At that point, notice and an opportunity to be heard must be afforded. The details of the process due after the threshold will then depend on the seriousness of the deprivation and the types of issues involved.

A difficult situation is also presented by the grant suspension. Because a compliance decision favoring the grantee will release the federal payments, the act of suspension causes no final taking. Yet, like the case of the welfare recipient afforded only a posttermination administrative hearing,[123] a temporary suspension of payments may have destructive effects on a grantee. Those effects can only be known by a study of the individual case. At one extreme, a well-healed grantee may have sufficient reserves to withstand several weeks of suspension without appreciable effects. On the other side, even a week's suspension may tumble a fragile grantee organization. And in the middle rest hundreds of cases of differing types and degrees of harm. Because the ability of each grantee to withstand a suspension will be unique, the deprivation caused by a suspension must be measured on a case-by-case basis.

[121] See Chapter 1, notes 66–67, *supra*, and accompanying text.
[122] Cf. 45 C.F.R. §1067.2-4 (20% or greater reduction in grant gives right to show-cause hearing).
[123] See *Goldberg* v. *Kelly*, 397 U.S. 254 (1970).

It would not be unreasonably burdensome to require the grantor agency to evaluate in each case whether a suspension would have sufficiently detrimental effects on a grantee to require, in fairness, a prior notice and opportunity to be heard. The agency could also factor into its analysis the government's need to protect federal funds by stopping their use as soon as possible.[124]

---

[124] See Chapter 11, note 20, *infra*, and accompanying text.

8

The Right of States to Fair Process

We have spoken thus far as if states were like individuals in terms of Due Process protections. When we speak of "states" in this chapter, we include local units of government. The issue under review, whether constitutional Due Process extends to state and local governments, would be decided the same for either level of government under any type of analysis.[1]

Contrary to our assumption, this section will reveal that under the present status of the law a state cannot claim Fifth Amendment protection from arbitrary federal action.[2] Those readers who are still with us may justifiably complain about having been led down a dead-end street. We have cause, however, for not starting with this critical question. We will argue that the existing law is wrong, that states should be accorded constitutional Due Process, and that recent Supreme Court decisions[3] support that conclusion. To understand the arguments one needs a primer in Due Process within the framework of grants-in-aid, such as has been provided in the preceding chapters.

We have yet to examine the extent to which Congress and the executive branch have legislated procedural protections for actual or potential recipients of grants-in-aid. That survey, in the following chapters, will reveal a surprising lack of concern for applicant/grantee procedural rights. A meaningful opportunity to be heard

[1] See, e.g., *National League of Cities* v. *Usery*, 426 U.S. 833 (1976).
[2] See *South Carolina* v. *Katzenbach*, 383 U.S. 301, 323–24 (1966).
[3] See, e.g., *National League of Cities* v. *Usery*, 426 U.S. 833 (1976).

is not afforded to grantees for many types of detrimental federal agency decisions. In various "entitlement" (formula) programs Congress has required that federal actions disapproving state plans or halting the flow of federal funds for noncompliance with federal requirements be preceded by reasonable hearing opportunities for the affected states.[4] But numerous formula programs are silent on the matter.[5] To a very limited extent nongovernmental grantees of discretionary awards have rights to be heard on certain adverse financial decisions.[6] A minority of federal agencies have responded to concerns for procedural fairness by enacting, through their regulatory power, postdecision appeals.[7] The upshot of our survey of statutes and regulations is that for many types of decisions in many programs there is no legal obligation, outside of a possible constitutional duty, on federal grantors to weigh the grantee's position either before or after their final decision.

Grant recipients which are not state and local governments can combat this neglect with Fifth Amendment rights, for the obligation imposed on all branches of the Federal Government not to deprive others of liberty and property without due process of law extends to individuals [8] and corporations.[9] But what about governmental grant recipients? Can they turn to the Constitution when neither Congress nor the executive branch has extended the mantle of procedural protection? Even when some type of hearing opportunity has been extended by law, can governmental grantees challenge its adequacy under constitutional principles? Given the fact that the bulk of grant-in-aid funds is channeled to or through state and local governments,[10] the answers to these questions are of substantial public import. This section will search out answers.

To some the answer may be a quick and confident "no." There is Supreme Court "law" on the point—right on point. Yet it is extremely strange law. In the one case in which the Court directly addressed the issue, it dedicated a total of 43 words to its

---

[4] See Chapter 9, note 2, and Chapter 12, note 1, *infra*, and accompanying text.
[5] See Chapter 9, note 3, and Chapter 12, note 2, *infra*, and accompanying text.
[6] See Chapter 10, *infra*, at pp. 272–77, 281–84; Chapter 11, *infra*, at pp. 286–88; and Chapter 12, *infra*.
[7] See Chapter 1, note 99, *supra*, and accompanying text.
[8] For instances involving individuals receiving benefits and services under federal grants, see cases cited in Chapter 7, note 28, *supra*.
[9] See, e.g., *Blake v. McClung*, 172 U.S. 239, 259 (1898); *Sinking Fund Cases*, 99 U.S. 700, 718–19 (1878).
[10] See Chapter 1, note 103, *supra*, and accompanying text.

disposition, finding that the states have no right to Due Process from the Federal Government:

> "The word 'person' in the context of the Due Process Clause of the Fifth Amendment cannot, by any reasonable mode of interpretation, be expanded to encompass the States of the Union, and to our knowledge this has never been done by any Court." [11]

Perhaps as a demonstration of the audacity of the proposition, Chief Justice Warren cited as direct authority only 41 words of conclusory *dicta* in a state court footnote.[12] Lest this was not sufficiently convincing, he then offered as an analogy some conclusory *dicta* of the Fifth Circuit to the effect that the United States is not a "person" under the Fourteenth Amendment.[13] One should not draw the conclusion that the Chief Justice's law clerks had a bad day. The digests simply offered little in the way of direct precedent for the proposition. If his clerks had served up the contrary holding in *State* v. *Anderson*,[14] knowledge apparently hidden from the Chief Justice, perhaps we would have been spared the labor of leveling 10,000 words at the Chief Justice's 43! There is, admittedly, considerable law on the question whether governments are "persons" under constitutional clauses other than the Fifth Amendment.[15] But each of those clauses has its own purpose, spirit, history, and problems, and we shall not examine them.

The peculiarity of this summary treatment in *South Carolina* v. *Katzenbach* resides in the combination of two facts: (1) the question is certainly one of importance, involving a basic element of federal-state relations; and (2) the Supreme Court has never lacked for words, even on relatively trivial matters.

The brevity of the Supreme Court analysis (or, better, the lack thereof) naturally leads one to think that the conclusion is so very apparent—states are not entitled to Due Process—that there is nothing much to discuss. The Fifth Amendment's protective shield covers "any person" and a state is not a person. End matter. The lower federal courts, obliged by *stare decisis,* have since 1966 faithfully and uncritically echoed the Supreme Court pronounce-

---

[11] *South Carolina* v. *Katzenbach*, 383 U.S. 301, 323–24 (1966).
[12] *International Shoe Co.* v. *Cocreham*, 246 La. 244, 266, n. 5, 164 So.2d 314, 322, n. 5 (1964).
[13] *United States* v. *City of Jackson*, 318 F.2d 1, 8 (5th Cir. 1963).
[14] 220 Minn. 139, 146, 19 N.W.2d 70, 73 (1945).
[15] See, e.g., *Pennsylvania* v. *New Jersey*, 426 U.S. 660, 665 (1976) (Privileges and Immunity Clause and the Fourteenth Amendment Equal Protection Clause do not apply to states).

ment.[16] This, however, also cuts in the other direction. He who dares challenge the obvious does not have to confront contrary reason and logic. In that sense the task is considerably easier, assuming that strong arguments can be brought to bear on the proposition that the Constitution can and should be read as affording procedural protections to states in their grant-in-aid dealings with the United States.

Our task, therefore, is to show that the "obvious" is, in fact, doubtful. In so doing we shall reverse the typical path of lawyer's logic. We will start with a showing of the illogical results which accrue in the real world to a denial of Due Process to recipients of grants-in-aid which are states. We shall then consider some possible arguments which might be raised in support of these results. Once we have demonstrated, hopefully, that it makes little sense to deny Due Process protections to the states, at least in the grant-in-aid context, we shall search the Constitution for an appropriate source for those protections.

Assuming that the Supreme Court cannot be tempted to discard its cursory pronouncements, neither Congress nor the executive branch nor the judiciary is constitutionally obliged to afford state grantees a day-in-court. Congress may or may not extend such protection, depending on its particular mood. The executive branch, as part of its responsibility for administering grants-in-aid, could opt for grantee procedural rights when Congress has not addressed the issue, but has chosen to do so infrequently. The federal courts are presently open to grantees for judicial review of federal agency actions, but that jurisdiction is limited to post-decision review and subject to congressional modification. It is, therefore, theoretically possible for the Federal Government to cut off a state's "entitlement" funds in patent violation of substantive grant standards without having to listen to even a whisper from the grantee. We could use that draconian possibility as our

---

[16] See *Connecticut State Dep't of Pub. Welfare v. Dep't of Health, Educ. & Welfare*, 448 F.2d 209, 212 (2d Cir. 1971); *Arizona State Dep't of Pub. Welfare v. Dep't of Health, Educ. & Welfare*, 449 F.2d 456, 478 (9th Cir. 1971), cert. denied, 405 U.S. 919 (1972); *Stiner v. Califano*, 438 F. Supp. 796, 799, n. 3 (W.D. Okla. 1977); *Carroll v. Finch*, 326 F. Supp. 891, 894 (D. Alas. 1971). The Second Circuit has wondered whether *South Carolina v. Katzenbach*, 383 U.S. 301 (1966), applies to cities seeking Fifth Amendment protection. The court did not consider the issue foreclosed, but found it "difficult to see how a city can be a 'person' if its progenitor is not." *Aguayo v. Richardson*, 473 F.2d 1090, 1100 (2d Cir. 1973), cert. denied, 414 U.S. 1146 (1974). Maybe because the *Katzenbach* ruling runs contrary to common sense, some courts have missed the point completely. See, e.g., *City of Milwaukee v. Saxbe*, 546 F.2d 693, 698 (7th Cir. 1976).

starting point in the constitutional analysis, as our chief horror in the parade. We choose, however, to begin from a point closer to reality—the typical situation in which the state grantee has no right to be heard in an administrative forum but can challenge final agency action in the courts.

Many federal grant-in-aid programs offer the administering agency a choice in the type of grantee it will fund. It is quite common for state and local governments to compete with private institutions for discretionary grants. Let us assume that State X and Corporation Y have each been awarded a grant under the same program. Neither the statute authorizing the award nor the program regulations afford administrative hearing opportunities in the event that the grantor decides to terminate the grant. The federal grantor finds that both grantees have violated some federal condition (a discretionary but debatable finding) and terminates both grants without affording prior notice and opportunity to be heard to either grantee. We know from our study of Due Process that Corporation Y marches into court and quickly gets an injunction against the termination on the basis of its Fifth Amendment hearing rights. The federal agency is judicially instructed not to take any final, harmful action without first affording Y a hearing suitable to the occasion. Because the contemplated action is drastic, the occasion will likely call for the full bag of procedural safeguards—lawyers, confrontation, cross-examination, and so forth. Corporation Y also gets an opportunity to negotiate a settlement, a chance to advance its interpretation of the law, a crack at altering the agency's perception of the facts, the right to demonstrate how the purported federal policy is antithetical to the program's purposes, and a final determination by an impartial official or tribunal. State X, which has entered the same courtroom at the same time with the same program, gets crucified. We have already shown how, ultimately, judicial review of federal agency action is unsatisfactory and we shall not belabor the point here.[17] State X gets the law's delays, the problem of running a program without federal support, the financial burden of a protracted proceeding, a factual record consisting only of a reconstituted administrative record of the basis of the final agency action, and a meager chance to convince a court, already predisposed to the defendant under the deference policies, that the grantor agency has acted arbitrarily and in abuse of its discretion.

[17] See Chapter 5, *supra*, at pp. 165–71.

A variant on the above scenario is the situation in which under the relevant grant statute State X must be afforded "reasonable" hearing opportunities prior to a noncompliance finding. Not untypically, the federal agency has translated that statutory language into a procedural scheme which lacks ingredients considered essential under constitutional Due Process.[18] Because the agency has implementation power to which the courts give great deference, and because the procedural right stems from the statute and not the Constitution, a judge would be hard put to find that the agency has violated the statutory mandate. The court need not give respect to agency positions in determining what the Constitution requires, but must abide by agency views, if not patently contrary to the statutory language and purpose, as to the best way of implementing statutory dictates. Thus, once again, Corporation Y gets the better procedural deal. Because it is a federal court and not Congress which determines what process the Fifth Amendment commands, whether Congress has conceded statutory hearing rights to Corporation Y, or, if it has, the rights it has given, is immaterial. If the Congress and the executive branch have not afforded constitutionally satisfactory safeguards, the judiciary will correct the deficiency.

A third incongruence which results from the denial of constitutional protection to state grantees results from the effects which fund cutoffs have on the ultimate, individual beneficiaries of these programs. We know that an individual receiving benefits under a government program has a property interest in those benefits sufficient to qualify for Due Process protection. The principle covers entitlements distributed to the individual either by state or federal government.[19] We suspect that Due Process guarantees extend to those who are not currently receiving benefits, but who are eligible under the relevant statutes and regulations and have made application.[20] We do not know, however, whether the individual beneficiary has procedural rights under the Constitution if a federal agency indirectly cuts off his entitlements (actual or potential) by taking adverse financial action against the grantee.

[18] See Chapter 15, *infra*, at pp. 346–49.
[19] See, e.g., *Goldberg* v. *Kelly*, 397 U.S. 254 (1970) (state distribution of welfare benefits to individuals); *Mathews* v. *Eldridge*, 424 U.S. 319 (1976) (Federal Government distribution of disability benefits to individuals).
[20] See Nowak et al., *Constitutional Law* 492 (1978) (concept of "present enjoyment" undefined).

To our knowledge this issue has yet to be resolved by a court.[21]

One might take the seemingly sensible position that the ultimate effect of such federal decisions is the deprivation of property interests held by individuals and they must, therefore, be afforded some type of hearing. But that position runs squarely against congressional practice. When Congress has given hearing rights in the context of noncompliance and nonconformity decisions by federal grantors, it has vested such rights only in the states.[22] Similarly, the executive branch gives individual beneficiaries only the limited right to intervene in state hearings.[23] As intervenors, their participatory rights are sharply curtailed.[24] Significantly, the intervention right did not arise as a consequence of Due Process considerations. It was derived from a judicial finding in *National Welfare Rights Organization* v. *Finch*[25] that program beneficiaries had standing to seek judicial review of federal grantor decisions which would adversely affect them. Exclusion of such individuals from the decisional process at the agency level would prejudice their right to judicial review by limiting them to the facts and issues presented by the government parties. Hence, intervention rights stemmed from rights to seek judicial review and not from constitutional Due Process.

The unanimous view of Congress and the executive branch might, of course, be constitutionally wrong. It may be based on pre-*Goldberg*[26] practices kept in effect by inertia and inattention. Nonetheless, the judiciary must strain to uphold the constitutionality of Acts of Congress. A rather obvious defense of the practice is that Due Process aims at affording one the chance to be heard on one's claimed rights, not on the rights of others. The fact that grant funds are ultimately parceled to individuals does not alter the facts that the grant-in-aid is made to the state, that the

---

[21] The issue was posed to the District of Columbia Circuit, but was not resolved because of a disposition on other grounds. *National Welfare Rights Organ.* v. *Finch*, 429 F.2d 725, 734–35, ns. 33 & 34 (D.C. Cir. 1970). In *Schneider* v. *Whaley*, 541 F.2d 916, *explained on rehearing*, 548 F.2d 394 (2d Cir. 1976), the constitutional issue was skirted because HEW hearing regulations were found applicable.

[22] See statutes cited in Chapter 9, note 2, and Chapter 12, note 1, *infra*. If the federal action is based on the *ultimate recipient's conduct* and affects that person, the Federal Government directly owes Due Process to such recipient. See *Hathaway* v. *Mathews*, 546 F.2d 227 (7th Cir. 1976).

[23] E.g., 45 C.F.R. §16.58(a)(1).

[24] E.g., 45 C.F.R. §16.58. Compare 45 C.F.R. §213.15(b) (1977) (welfare conformity hearings; those within "zone of interests" may petition to participate as parties).

[25] 429 F.2d 725 (D.C. Cir. 1970).

[26] *Goldberg* v. *Kelly*, 397 U.S. 254 (1970).

state is the contracting party, that the state is the primary beneficiary of federal largesse, and that the network of rights and responsibilities runs primarily between grantor and grantee. *Goldberg* and its progeny offer procedural safeguards when government acts against individuals based on its perception of the facts of the individual case and the law and policy as applied to that particular instance. Hearing rights shield one from governmental misperceptions of one's individual circumstances or misapplications of the law to those precise circumstances. The hearing claimed by an individual upon the occurrence of grant-in-aid terminations would have nothing to do with that individual's circumstances. It would involve state policies, practices, and action. In these instances to afford hearing rights to individuals would be to wrest *Goldberg* out of its context and substantially depart from its thrust and purpose.

This is likely to be the correct view. But it has dramatic effects when combined with the presumed absence of constitutional Due Process rights in states. The result is to condone administrative cutoffs of important benefits to thousands of recipients *without affording prior notice and an opportunity to be heard to anyone*. A state is under no legal compulsion to cover the deficit caused by the interruption of federal funding with local resources while pursuing its remedy in the courts. The political pressure on a state to do so will depend on the popularity of the affected program and the state's fiscal circumstances. The frequent strain on state and local budgets and the traditional unpopularity of many welfare programs might combine to interdict temporary state financing. Thus, the spectre of shutting down a large social program is not imaginary. The resulting anomoly is that an adjudicative proceeding closely approximating the judicial model is constitutionally mandated before the government can deprive Mrs. Jones of her monthly $50 welfare check, while thousands of welfare and other social program beneficiaries, including Mrs. Jones, can be administratively stripped of $50 million in benefits without *constitutional* compulsion of a prior hearing.

This incongruence might tempt a court not to grant Due Process rights to the state grantee (after all, it would have to defy those 43 Supreme Court words) but to vest the hearing right in individual program beneficiaries. That leaves us somewhat more content, but puzzled. Is Mrs. Jones now the champion of New York State? Since *she* has the hearing rights, *she* must logically lead the battle. Her lawyers, assuming she chooses to be represented, frame the issues, marshal the facts, present the witnesses, research the law, write the briefs, and so forth. Would the state then be allowed to intervene to protect its right to judicial review? A curious reversal of the *Finch* situation, indeed!

It is beyond our purview to pursue further this example of the law's mysterious paths. We will rest with the observation that these and, assuredly, other strange consequences attend a denial of Due Process rights to states. Above these specific difficulties lies the disturbing broader problem of reconciling the absence of state procedural rights with the concept of "cooperative federalism" embodied in the grant-in-aid system. That mutual venture insists on some mutuality of right, and certainly procedural equity, between the Federal Government and its state and local government customers. Fair procedure oils the wheels of business, and no less the business of promoting the country's welfare in spending $106 billion a year under some 800 domestic grant programs. Federal agencies have always recognized this. Rarely will a major defunding action be carried out without lengthy negotiations.[27] Even in the absence of constitutional, statutory, or regulatory command we doubt whether a federal grantor would deny hearing rights on any issue of major importance. That is, nonetheless, a question of good will, of grace, of individual discretion. That is precisely what shifts the power balance strongly to the Federal Government in the grant-in-aid system—and that balance, we assert, must be realigned on the basis of grantee *rights*.

We presume that the first defense of the Supreme Court's pronouncement will be that our scenarios are unreal. None will eventuate because the states, as states, will exercise their clout in Congress to protect themselves from arbitrary assertions of federal power. An individual needs constitutional protection because of his helplessness in the face of governmental power. States, on the other hand, control their potential oppressors through power in Congress and do not need constitutional solicitude. That, it will be asserted, is basic in the structure of our federal system.

Before responding, we must be more precise about the nature of this argument. "State" is not used in the sense of the conglomeration of individuals, businesses, and other private entities located within certain borders. Its meaning is the formal sense—

[27] See Chapter 3, notes 171–180, *supra*, and accompanying text.

the entity which governs that conglomeration. It is the composite of state officials, both elected and appointed, deriving their authority from the state constitution and law. The distinction is critical. The argument carries no weight if one visualizes, in putting content in the federalism argument, a state resident calling up his U.S. Senator. The Bill of Rights is unnecessary under that vision. "Persons" are constitutionally protected from arbitrary federal power because it is contemplated that the Senator will not take the call. To have meaning the argument must focus on the supposed power of state officials. *They* are the ones stripped of constitutional protection in their official dealings with the United States. Thus, the proper vision must be a state governor, legislator, or department head calling upon the state's congressional delegation for support. The precise question, therefore, is whether the federal structure created by the Constitution offers sufficient political protection to these officials so that judicial protection under the Fifth Amendment is unnecessary.

We will deal with the argument on two levels, theoretical and actual. Our position is that political developments, constitutional amendments, and Supreme Court decisions have destroyed whatever theoretical validity the argument may once have had, and that as a factual matter the record shows that the states have been unable to protect themselves in either Congress or the executive branch on the matter under study.

The best statement of the theoretical argument was made by Professor Wechsler of Columbia Law School in 1954.[28] It is both fascinating and instructive to see how time has destroyed every argument he advances in support of the thesis. First, he argues that federal law is interstitial, extraordinary, an extremely small fraction of the corpus. Those who call for federal action have a heavy burden of convincing Congress that the issue is proper for national as opposed to normal, traditional state concern.[29] That view was clearly debatable then, and two and one-half decades of subsequent congressional activism have certainly placed the burden on those who oppose federal intervention. Second, he advances some mechanisms which states can utilize to control Congress. Though admitting that the Seventeenth Amendment eliminated state legislatures' control of the Senate by providing

[28] Wechsler, "The Political Safeguards of Federalism: The Role of the States in the Composition and Selection of the National Government," 54 Colum. L. Rev. 543 (1954) (hereinafter cited as "Wechsler").
[29] *Id.* at 544–46.

for popular election of Senators,[30] he points to state control of voter qualifications [31] and the power to shape electoral districts.[32] Both powers are now moribund. State ability to determine the qualification of electors has been viscerated by constitutional amendments [33] and Supreme Court activism under the Equal Protection Clause.[34] Control over the shape of congressional districts is now in the hands of the federal judiciary under the "one-man, one-vote" rule.[35] The importance of national political parties is mentioned by Professor Wechsler as a force contrary to state political power, but given no great significance.[36] The present day importance of the media and the high costs of financing media campaigns have made national party alignments and policies of paramount importance in congressional elections to the detriment of state party allegiances. Halfheartedly the mechanism of selecting presidential electors is advanced as a demonstration of how the President responds to state legislatures,[37] but we doubt that Professor Wechsler would seriously dispute the proposition that today the President responds to the people and very little to state legislators and governors.

The reality of congressional politics is that Senators and Representatives respond to their constituents and not to state officials. One writer finds it "difficult to hypothesize weighty issues for which the interests of the state, in the abstract, would in practice be of force comparable to the interests of various constituent groups—voters and lobbyists will almost always be of paramount concern to the legislator." [38] It has been shown how social welfare lobbyists are instrumental in the enactment and longevity of

---

[30] *Id.* at 546.
[31] *Id.* at 548–49.
[32] *Id.* at 549–52.
[33] U.S. Const. amend. XV (no disenfranchisement based on race or color); amend. XIX (no voter qualification based on sex); amend. XXIV (no poll tax); XXVI (no denial of franchise based on age if voter 18 or older).
[34] U.S. Const. amend. XIV, §1, cl. 4. State restrictions on voter qualifications are actively reviewed by the Supreme Court. See, e.g., *Harper* v. *Virginia Bd. of Elections,* 383 U.S. 663 (1966).
[35] See, e.g., *Baker* v. *Carr,* 369 U.S. 186 (1962); *Reynolds* v. *Sims,* 377 U.S. 533 (1964); *Kirkpatrick* v. *Preisler,* 394 U.S. 526 (1969). The districting process has been accurately described as "largely mechanical." See Tribe, "Unraveling *National League of Cities:* The New Federalism and Affirmative Rights to Essential Government Services," 90 Harv. L. Rev. 1065, 1071 (1977).
[36] Wechsler, *supra* note 28, at 546.
[37] *Id.* at 553.
[38] Note, "Municipal Bankruptcy, The Tenth Amendment, and The New Federalism," 89 Harv. L. Rev. 1871, 1885, n. 115 (1976).

federal grants-in-aid.[39] On an issue of state noncompliance these private forces, and the voters they represent, will frequently be aligned against the state. A congressman would often be hard put to offer political support to the state in view of the contrary pulls from his constituency and his duty to protect his federal program from (for all he knows) enervating state tactics.

The record shows that whatever state power that exists in Congress has been feebly exercised to protect states from arbitrary grantor actions. One notes with fascination that it took Congress *11 years* to react to a judicial decision holding that a state had no forum, not even judicial, to challenge a federal agency decision cutting off its funds under the *largest* federal grant-in-aid program.[40] Since that breakthrough, Congress has afforded states notice and hearing opportunities in most major formula programs, but far from all. State recipients of federal competitive grants get no protection. And for many types of adverse federal decisions no administrative forum is afforded states under any grant program.

It may be that Congress has considered the matter of marginal importance or has not considered the matter at all, apart from an occasional brief foray. The protective provisions that exist are, in the great majority of cases, most likely the handiwork of draftsmen borrowing the boiler plate of predecessor statutes. The important point is that constitutional protection is needed from inadvertent as well as intentional traps. Judicial blue-penciling of congressional oversights can only go so far. Without a constitutional source of authority one would imagine great judicial difficulty in supplying procedures inadvertently omitted by Congress, particularly when there is likely to be no supporting legislative history.

Courts have, indeed, liberally required fair procedures, but only after identifying authority for judicial action such as the

[39] See, e.g., Advisory Commission on Intergovernmental Relations, *The Intergovernmental Grant System: An Assessment and Proposed Policies: Summary and Concluding Observations* 68 (1978):

"Politically, the functional triads that have always formed the national basis for program enactments have multiplied in recent years. These forces (consisting of middle level administrators, subcommittee members, and interest group spokesmen) have not only a national, but frequently a state or local base as well."

[40] In 1954 the District of Columbia Circuit held that the doctrine of sovereign immunity barred judicial review of an HEW nonconformity decision. *Arizona* v. *Hobby*, 221 F.2d 498 (D.C. Cir. 1954). §1116 Social Security Act, 42 U.S. §1316, which provides states an administrative hearing and judicial review of nonconformity decisions, was added by Congress in 1965 in response to *Hobby* and "to strengthen federalism." See *County of Alameda* v. *Weinberger*, 520 F.2d 344, 348–49 (9th Cir. 1975).

Fifth Amendment [41] or reading such rights into a statute in order to avoid a finding of unconstitutionality under the Due Process Clause.[42] The premise of a majority of Justices writing in *Arnett v. Kennedy* [43]—that Congress may determine what property entitlements it will concede, but the Court will rule on the propriety of procedures attending the deprivation of those entitlements—can be seen as an exhibition of judicial muscle flexing in a domain of particular judicial competence and expertise. Professor Tribe has suggested that

> "the *Arnett* Court's allocation of responsibility between the political and judicial branches rests on a notion of the special relevance of judicial expertise, and the comparative irrelevance of legislative competence, in making process-oriented decisions. Values of accuracy, participation and predictability are matters that judges are continually required to consider and balance; conversely, legislative ability to adjust competing economic and political interests has little to do with designing fair ways to resolve factual disputes. Indeed, if the courts have any special competence at all it is to be found in the area of fair dispute resolution." [44]

The point is not to invite free-wheeling judicial imposition of procedural rules in the absence of constitutional or statutory authority but, rather, to counteract the second line of defense of those 43 words. If the fear be expressed that in extending constitutional procedural rights to the states the courts will be thrusting themselves unduly into the interplay of the state and the Federal Government, the answer then becomes that establishing rules of the game is the normal business of the courts. Questions of power allocations are not involved, just the process of exercising state and congressionally determined powers. Judicial intervention is to be invited, not repulsed, if Professor Tribe is right in suggesting that courts have a particular expertise in greasing the wheels of government.

We have tried to demonstrate, thus far, that the lack of Due Process for the states may produce some surprisingly undesirable consequences; that the cooperative nature of the grant-in-aid system can best be served by affording state grantees such protection;

---

41 See, e.g., *Powelton Civic Home Owners Ass'n v. Dep't of Housing & Urban Dev.*, 284 F. Supp. 809, 830–31 (E.D. Pa. 1968); *Barnes v. Tarrytown Urban Renewal Agency*, 338 F. Supp. 257, 260–61 (S.D. N.Y. 1971); *Cole v. Lynn*, 389 F. Supp. 99, 103–104 (D. D.C. 1975).
42 See, e.g., *Thompson v. Washington*, 497 F.2d 626 (D.C. Cir. 1973).
43 416 U.S. 134 (1974). See Chapter 7, notes 31–34, *supra*, and accompanying text.
44 Tribe, *American Constitutional Law* 536–37 (1978).

that the states can not and have not been able to protect themselves in Congress; and that judicial umpiring of the federal-state game will be beneficial and not disruptive. Now we shall search for a doctrinal basis for achieving the indicated result.

The natural starting point is the Due Process Clause of the Fifth Amendment and the *Katzenbach* pronouncement that the word "person" cannot be expanded to encompass the states "by any reasonable mode of interpretation." [45] Let us be unreasonable for a while. First, a Supreme Court decision apparently shares our irrationality. In the *Thorpe* [46] case a government housing agency challenged the imposition of additional grant requirements by HUD subsequent to the execution of the grant agreement. One argument made by the government defendant was that the new HUD regulations violated the constitutional prohibition on the impairment of contracts which applied, by way of Fifth Amendment Due Process, to the Federal Government.[47] Note that a government agency was, thus, sneaking under the protective shield afforded "persons" by the constitutional text. The Court reached the argument on the merits and held that the grant agreement was not impaired.[48] It did not deny Durham Housing Authority the right to claim such protection. One would be quite hesitant to suggest that the Supreme Court inadvertently missed a point which seemed so obvious to the Court in *Katzenbach* only three years before. While the Due Process right of governments was not discussed in the *Thorpe* opinion, it was an essential predicate to the Court's disposition on the merits.

Second, our unreasonableness stems primarily from the historical underpinning of the Fifth Amendment and not from any textual or result-measured illogic.[49] The word "person" in the

---

[45] *South Carolina* v. *Katzenbach*, 383 U.S. 301, 323 (1966).
[46] *Thorpe* v. *Housing Auth.*, 393 U.S. 268 (1969).
[47] See *Lynch* v. *United States*, 292 U.S. 571, 579 (1934).
[48] *Thorpe* v. *Housing Auth.*, 393 U.S. 268, 279 (1969). Recent congressional legislation, Pub. L. 95-291, June 12, 1978, 42 U.S.C. §1397a note, clearly impairs the obligations of the United States under grant agreements with states, but its constitutionality is not likely to be tested because the law resulted from a compromise negotiated between HEW and 19 states. See generally H.R. Rep. No. 1114, pts. I & II, 95th Cong., 2d Sess. (1978). The law deprives federal courts of jurisdiction over lawsuits claiming reimbursement for social services provided under the welfare program, limiting courts to the financial compromise struck in the law.
[49] The Supreme Court has consistently read the word "person" expansively when it fit in with the goals of the command under review. For two recent examples, see *City of Lafayette* v. *Louisiana Power & Light Co.*, 435 U.S. 389, 394–97 (1978) ("person" in federal antitrust laws covers municipalities); *Pfizer, Inc.* v. *Government of India*, 435 U.S. 910 (1978) (foreign nations are a "person" entitled to bring treble damage actions under Clayton Act).

Fifth Amendment means human beings and (with some straining) their corporate alter egos [50] because that is what the drafters of the Magna Carta, the statute of Edward III, the 1692 Massachusetts colonialists, and our Constitution had in mind.[51] Are we to be constitutionally ruled from their graves? In 1791 no one could have envisioned a federal system in which the United States bankrolls with $85 billion 25 percent of the operations of state and local governments. The basic problem at that time was precisely the opposite: how to finance a national government in view of existing state tax systems and protectionist tariffs.[52] The Sixteenth Amendment, ratified in 1913, gave rise to the tremendous imbalance in federal-state fiscal capability which, in turn, gave the United States the luxury of dealing out large numbers of federal dollars to the states. The fact that dozens of Supreme Court decisions applaud the great value of the Due Process Clause as the protector of human rights [53] should not be read as precluding its expansion, when consistent with the spirit of that constitutional norm, to afford procedural protection to the states in their business dealings with the United States. We will not enter a debate as to when the Constitution should and should not be read as a "living" document.[54] We will refer only to Professor Corwin's magnificent pun:

> "[I]t is a fact that in certain early printings of the Constitution the 'common defense and general welfare' clause appears separately paragraphed, while in others it is set off from the 'lay and collect' clause by a semicolon and not, as modern usage would require, by the less awesome comma. To be sure, the semicolon may have been due in the first instance to the splattering of a goose quill

[50] See *Santa Clara* v. *Southern Pac. R.R. Co.*, 18 F. 385, 402–404 (C.C.D. Cal. 1883), aff'd, 118 U.S. 394 (1886).
[51] See H. Meyer, *The History and Meaning of the Fourteenth Amendment* 128–29 (1977); R. Mott, *Due Process of Law* 4, n. 11, 14–16 (1926). For brief but effective warnings against overreliance on the "intent of the Framers" approach to constitutional interpretation, see Greenawalt, "The Enduring Significance of Neutral Principles," 78 Colum. L. Rev. 982, 1014–16 (1978).
[52] See Dam, "The American Fiscal Constitution," 44 U. Chi. L. Rev. 271, 274 (1977). The Federal Government was to be financed mostly by customs revenues. *Id.* at 284.
[53] See, e.g., *Shelley* v. *Kraemer*, 334 U.S. 1, 22 (1948).
[54] See Munzer & Nichol, "Does the Constitution Mean What It Always Meant?," 77 Colum. L. Rev. 1029 (1977), for a good review of the varying philosophies. The authors conclude:
"The Constitution has remained vital largely because its provisions have proved adaptable to the changing needs of a developing society. It does not mean what it always meant." *Id.* at 1029 (footnote omitted).

that needed trimming, for it is notorious that the fate of nations has often turned on just such minute *points*." [55]

For the historicists and literalists who rebel at the idea of injecting new meaning into old words, we offer an alternative constitutional route. The Tenth Amendment, which reserves to the states or to the people the powers not delegated to the United States by the Constitution, was officially escorted to its grave by Professor Corwin in 1950.[56] It had not survived the mortal blows of Supreme Court decisions under the commerce, spending, and necessary and proper clauses which found vast national powers in the Constitution.[57] Since few powers had not been delegated to the United States by the Constitution, the Tenth Amendment became a repository only for gross congressional excesses.[58] Recently the coffin bell began to jingle. Strange quiverings were noted in the *remains* (touché!) of state power as the Burger Court began to survey the federal-state scene. [59] Then, still rather surprisingly, a youngster called federalism jumped out of the coffin in 1976.[60] Not a resurrection, because we know that much of the old corpus of states rights is still dead. Rather, a rebirth—a fledgling whose ultimate shape and size can only be determined by time.

We will leave to others [61] the job of penetrating the mysteries of *National League of Cities* v. *Usery*.[62] It is beyond our scope to

[55] Corwin, "The Passing of Dual Federalism," 36 U. Va. L. Rev. 1, 6 (1950).
[56] See *id., passim.*
[57] For a review of the decisions concerning federal-state powers prior to the Burger Court, see Note, "Municipal Bankruptcy, The Tenth Amendment, and The New Federalism," 89 Harv. L. Rev. 1871, 1871–74 (1976).
[58] See, e.g., *Oregon* v. *Mitchell,* 400 U.S. 112 (1970) (congressional legislation lowering voting age to 18 in all state elections violates Constitution).
[59] The Burger Court federalism-based decisions are summarized in Tribe, "Unraveling *National League of Cities:* The New Federalism and Affirmative Rights to Essential Government Services," 90 Harv. L. Rev. 1065, 1068–69, ns. 18–20 (1977). See also Note, "Municipal Bankruptcy, The Tenth Amendment, and The New Federalism," 89 Harv. L. Rev. 1871, 1874–78 (1976).
[60] See *National League of Cities* v. *Usery,* 426 U.S. 833 (1976). The Court struck down, on federalism grounds, the 1974 amendments to the Fair Labor Standards Act which had extended federal minimum wage and maximum hour provisions to almost all state and municipal employees. *Maryland* v. *Wirtz,* 392 U.S. 183 (1968), which upheld such regulation of state hospital and school employees, was overruled. 426 U.S. at 840.
[61] See, e.g., Michelman, "States' Rights and States' Roles: Permutations of 'Sovereignty' in *National League of Cities* v. *Usery,"* 86 Yale L. J. 1165 (1977); Tribe, "Unraveling *National League of Cities:* The New Federalism and Affirmative Rights to Essential Government Services," 90 Harv. L. Rev. 1065 (1977); Note, "Municipal Bankruptcy, The Tenth Amendment and The New Federalism," 89 Harv. L. Rev. 1871 (1976). Attempts to extend the principles of *National League of Cities* to exercises of congressional power under the spending clause are discussed *supra* at Chapter 2, notes 20–27, and accompanying text.
[62] 426 U.S. 833 (1976).

fathom its implications for the future power boundaries between states and the union. Our primary theme is the procedural exercise of conceded powers. For our purposes the relevance of *National League of Cities* is its affirmation of the importance of states in our system of government. Our argument is essentially of the *a fortiori* type. If the Supreme Court was willing in that case to rediscover a domain of untouchable state power and authority, it would certainly be receptive to a considerably more modest plea, in the name of federalism, of procedural equity for the states in the face of admitted national power exercised arbitrarily.

The Tenth Amendment textually does not help us. It refers to the distribution of powers, not to processes for their implementation. But that is a "minute point" which need not detain us long. *National League of Cities* itself did not explicitly ground its decision in the Tenth Amendment.[63] It drew authority from the structure of federalism in the Constitution as a whole, a respectable mode of dealing with federalism issues.[64] We can, therefore, be forgiven for suggesting the same approach. Constitutional Due Process applies to the states not because it is mandated by the Fifth Amendment or the Tenth Amendment but because the federal-state system created by the entire Constitution demands it when viewed in the light of present day realities.[65]

Some type of argument could be constructed from a *parens*

[63] See Tribe, "Unraveling *National League of Cities:* The New Federalism and Affirmative Rights to Essential Government Services," 90 Harv. L. Rev. 1065, 1067, n. 17 (1977); Note, "Municipal Bankruptcy, The Tenth Amendment and The New Federalism," 89 Harv. L. Rev. 1871, 1879, n. 66 (1976).

[64] For example, the doctrine of intergovernmental tax immunity is derived from the federal structure of government created by the Constitution and not from any specific constitutional clauses. See Dam, "The American Fiscal Constitution," 44 U. Chi. L. Rev. 271, 290–91 (1977).

[65] In two cases which anteceded the Burger Court's federalism decisions, states sought procedural fairness by way of the Tenth Amendment, apparently conceding that *South Carolina* v. *Katzenbach*, 383 U.S. 301 (1966), precluded use of the Fifth Amendment. See *Connecticut State Dep't of Pub. Welfare* v. *Dep't of Health, Educ. & Welfare*, 448 F.2d 209, 212 (2d Cir. 1971); *Arizona State Dep't of Pub. Welfare* v. *Dep't of Health, Educ. & Welfare*, 449 F.2d 456, 478–79 (9th Cir. 1971), *cert. denied*, 405 U.S. 919 (1972). The Second Circuit did not consider the question, finding that the particular hearing given to the state was procedurally fair. *Connecticut State Dep't of Pub. Welfare, supra*, at 212. The Ninth Circuit rejected the proposition, stating:

"To go further and read the Tenth Amendment as incorporating specific guarantees of procedural fairness would exceed even an expansive reading of the Amendment's proper scope. At very most the Amendment reserves certain powers to the states . . . it assuredly does not incorporate a Bill of Procedural Rights for the states."

Arizona State Dep't of Pub. Welfare, supra, at 479. The authority of the Ninth Circuit decision has, of course, been weakened by the subsequent invigoration of constitutional federalism, and is distinguishable from our idea which derives procedural fairness from the Constitution as a whole.

patriae theory. The idea might be that in grant-in-aid programs the state is essentially the alter ego of the citizens to whom the funds are ultimately directed. The state, therefore, should be able to piggyback on their constitutional rights to fair process.[66] We refrain from further analysis, however, because we reject the basic premise that state recipients of federal grants are representing anybody else. The state itself has the proprietary interest in the federal funds and has standing to defend them in court from federal attack.[67] A natural corollary of this position is that ultimate program beneficiaries do not have Due Process rights when state grantee action is challenged by the Federal Government because of the secondary nature of their interest. Thus, there are no rights to be inherited by the states. We also note little weakening of the *Frothingham v. Mellon*[68] position that, in defending the federal interest in disputes with the states concerning federal aid programs, the United States and not the states represents the citizenry.[69] Finally, it is a tortuous path to a sensible destination better reached by our suggested route.

Two points will conclude this chapter. First, we should emphasize the modest nature of our proposal. According procedural fairness (judicially defined) to the states does not alter the fundamental relationships between the national government and its partners in governance. On the contrary, it promises to *avoid* dislocation of whatever working balance has been politically struck at any point in time.[70] Insisting that the states be given a voice in the partnership simply affirms their dignity, essentiality, and

---

[66] See *Arizona State Dep't of Pub. Welfare v. Dep't of Health, Educ. & Welfare*, 449 F.2d 456, 478–79 (9th Cir. 1971), *cert. denied*, 405 U.S. 919 (1972).

[67] See Chapter 2, notes 31–33, and Chapter 4, notes 40–44, *supra*, and accompanying text.

[68] 262 U.S. 447, 485–86 (1923).

[69] See, e.g., *Pennsylvania v. Kleppe*, 533 F.2d 668 (D.C. Cir.), *cert. denied*, 429 U.S. 977 (1976); *Arizona State Dep't of Pub. Welfare v. Dep't of Health, Educ. & Welfare*, 449 F.2d 456, 479 (9th Cir. 1971), *cert. denied*, 405 U.S. 919 (1972); *Carroll v. Finch*, 326 F. Supp. 891, 894 (D. Alaska 1971).

[70] See Note, "Municipal Bankruptcy, The Tenth Amendment and The New Federalism," 89 Harv. L. Rev. 1871, 1888 (1976) (footnote omitted):

"Theoretically, the process examination is based on the fundamental justification for tenth amendment judicial scrutiny: that it serves as a check on congressional representation of the autonomy interests of the states. Requirements that state interests be articulated and state participation in the operation of congressional measures encouraged, where feasible, represent one means by which the courts, in accordance with the purposes of their involvement, are able to ensure that the interests of the states have been fully considered. Moreover, such participation and dialogue may serve to shore up the process of political interest bargaining without displacing that process as the primary forum for resolving both policy and federalism conflicts."

The Right of States to Fair Process / 243

ability to contribute. Unilateral decisional power in the hands of the Federal Government, on the other hand, promises the contrary. Procedure does control substance in any system which gives one party to a dispute the exclusive right to determine the law, the facts, and the results of particular controversies.

Second, should the Supreme Court definitively resolve the issue against the states, we simply redirect our plea to Congress. Through the insertion of appropriate language in grant-in-aid statutes Congress can quickly remedy the deficiencies we have discussed. That, indeed, may prove to be the easier route. It is difficult to imagine any political arguments against procedural justice for the states. Remember that we are not seeking methods to enable states to play fast and loose with federal grant standards. The petition is nothing more than for an adequate forum for a state to demonstrate that, in a particular case, it has not violated its duties under the Supremacy Clause. If, as we strongly suspect, the present procedural lagunas are more a result of inadvertence than conscious decision, Congress is likely to act as the march of time lays bare the defects. The essential difference between the constitutional and congressional routes is that in the former the courts shape the process that is due, while in the latter the job falls on Congress. That, too, presents no great difficulties. What the courts have found to be essential to procedural fairness under the Fifth Amendment can readily serve as a model for congressional action in legislating, under the spending power, grant-in-aid dispute mechanisms. And even if Congress cannot be moved to act, the executive branch can remedy the situation through its rule-making power. As the administrator of this mass of social welfare programs, the executive branch, one would hope, should be intensely interested in methods of promoting cordial state relations.

9

Grantee Hearing Rights: Withholding of Entitlements

Congressional Practice

A formula program presumes repetitive annual appropriations by Congress, unlike project grants which are of limited duration. The formula grant will ordinarily provide yearly federal subsidies to ongoing state and local government activities, or sometimes to nongovernmental bodies like private universities and hospitals. In the typical situation, the administering federal agency will have no choice as to grantee.[1] The recipients will be those

---

[1] The degree to which Congress has and may create, through grant programs, new local institutions to provide services in competition with state and local government programs is beyond the purview of this work. See generally Moynihan, *Maximum Feasible Misunderstanding: Community Action in the War on Poverty* (1969), for a detailed analysis of one such congressional effort. Where government has traditionally and substantially provided services of this type supported by a grant program, Congress will not ordinarily tamper with that structure. Restraint is reflected in the eligibility section of a grant-in-aid statute in which only governmental units are made eligible for grants. Such restricted eligibility would prevent a grantor agency from considering an alternative sanction, recommended by the Administrative Conference of the United States, of transferring the grant to another body. See Recommendation 71-9, "Enforcement of Standards in Federal Grant-in-Aid Programs," 1 C.F.R. §305.71-9. Congress has, however, authorized such transfers from one public agency to another, or even from a public to a private organization, in areas where state and local governments are not the exclusive agents for the provision of services. See, e.g., Chapter 15, note 16, *infra*, and accompanying text; §304(c) Older Americans Act of 1965, 42 U.S.C. §3024(c); §102 Comprehensive Employment and Training Act of 1973, 29 U.S.C. §812:

"In any area for which no prime sponsor has been designated or where the Secretary

bodies with exclusive authority to provide the particular governmental service: state agencies, cities, counties, school systems, and the like.

Should noncompliance with formula grant conditions occur, it is theoretically possible for the United States to terminate the grant. A new entitlement will come along, however, and one must consider the applicability of the sanction to the fresh injection of funds. Because illegality has permeated only the expenditure of funds for a particular fiscal year, to deprive the recipient of the new funds would be unduly harsh, and to divert the funds to a different recipient not possible. If the noncompliance is of a continuing nature, however, it would be senseless to award the funds and then immediately terminate. And at the core of the sanction problem is the ever-present reality that the real losers are innocent program beneficiaries.

The congressional solution has been, generally, to impose the deterrent and sanction of withholding payments—payments of federal formula funds are suspended until the grantee brings the program into compliance with federal law. Withholding is, thus, unlike a termination, which ends both further funding and the grantor-grantee relationship. No finality is contemplated by the federal action. Rather, the grantee's monetary entitlements are stockpiled until the compliance dispute is resolved.

In most grant programs in which Congress has utilized the formula device for distributing funds among the states, it has explicitly provided for grantee hearing rights prior to noncompliance withholding by the administrator.[2] The practice, however,

---

has taken an action . . . which results in employment and training services not being provided in such area, the Secretary shall use funds allocated to such prime sponsor to make payments directly to public agencies or private nonprofit organizations. . . ."

[2] See, e.g., §314(g)(3) Public Health Service Act, 42 U.S.C. §246(g)(3) (comprehensive health planning and services); §§1611(b), 1612(a) Public Health Service Act, 42 U.S.C. §§300p-1(b), 300p-2(a) (health facilities); §507 Social Security Act, 42 U.S.C. §707 (crippled children services; maternal and child health services); §6(e) Library Services and Construction Act of 1956, 20 U.S.C. §351d(e); §1004(c) National Defense Education Act of 1958, 20 U.S.C. §584(c); §11(a) Act of Sept. 23, 1950, Pub. L. 81-815, 20 U.S.C. §641(a) (impact aid; construction); §186(a) Elementary and Secondary Education Act of 1965, 20 U.S.C. §2836(a), as rewritten by §101 Education Amendments of 1978, Pub. L. 95-561, Nov. 1, 1978 (education of disadvantaged children; hearing "on the record"); §108(b) Higher Education Act of 1965, 20 U.S.C. §1007(b) (university community services; lifelong learning); §415D(a) id., 20 U.S.C. §1070c-3(a) (state student incentives); §607(b) id., 20 U.S.C. §1127(b) (undergraduate instructional equipment); §708(a)(2) id., 20 U.S.C. §1132a-7(a)(2) (undergraduate academic facilities); §308(a) Adult Education Act of 1966, 20 U.S.C. §1207(a); §109(c) Vocational Education Act, 20 U.S.C. §2309(c) (state program); §§134, 135 Developmental Disabilities Services and Construction Act, 42 U.S.C. §§6064, 6065; §101(c)

Rehabilitation Act of 1973, 29 U.S.C. §721(c) (state formula grants for vocational rehabilitation); §307(d) Older Americans Act of 1965, 42 U.S.C. §3027(d) (formula grants for senior citizen services); §404 Social Security Act, 42 U.S.C. §604 (aid to families with dependent children); §1904 *id.*, 42 U.S.C. §1396c (Medicaid); §2003(e) *id.*, 42 U.S.C. §1397b(e) (social services); §312(b) Coastal Zone Management Act, 16 U.S.C. §1458(b) (state administration grants); §401(h) Federal Civil Defense Act of 1950, 50 U.S.C. app. §2253(h) (state and local support); §111 Housing and Community Development Act of 1974, 42 U.S.C. §5311 (block grants); §509 Omnibus Crime Control and Safe Streets Act, 42 U.S.C. §3757 (block grants); §309(g) *id.*, 42 U.S.C. §3739(g) (antitrust enforcement); §226 Juvenile Justice and Delinquency Prevention Act, 42 U.S.C. §5636; §18(f) Occupational Safety and Health Act, 29 U.S.C. §667(f); §507 Intergovernmental Personnel Act of 1970, 42 U.S.C. §4767; §§519(3), 604 Community Services Act of 1974, 42 U.S.C. §§2928h(3), 2944 (community action; Head Start); §105(e) Clean Air Act of 1963, as amended by Pub. L. 95-95, Aug. 7, 1977, 42 U.S.C. §7405(e).

The most comprehensive noncompliance provisions we encountered are found in §106 Comprehensive Employment and Training Act of 1973, 29 U.S.C. §816. After providing for mandatory investigation of noncompliance allegations, the section authorizes the Secretary of Labor to terminate or suspend financial assistance in whole or in part and order appropriate sanctions and corrective actions upon finding a violation of any provision in the Act or regulations. The Secretary may require repayment of misspent funds from the grantee's own funds or from future allocations. In addition, if such misspending amounts to "fraud or abuse," a prime sponsor may be required to maintain planned program levels despite the reduced amount of federal financing resulting from recovery action. The section also focuses on specific types of violations. A pattern or practice of civil rights violations *must* lead to the revocation of a prime sponsor's plan and termination of financial assistance, failing informal resolution of the matter. This sanction *may* be imposed by the Secretary, after unsuccessful negotiations, for various specific illegalities, including: failure to serve "equitably" eligible segments of the population; incurring "unreasonable" administrative costs; not giving "due consideration" to the funding of programs of "demonstrated effectiveness"; underserving areas of chronic or concentrated unemployment; material delay in spending funds; failure to provide employment and training matched to participant capabilities; and a catchall—"otherwise materially failing to carry out the purposes and provisions of this Act or the regulations promulgated pursuant to this Act." All sanctions must be preceded by notice and opportunity for a hearing.

The most confused provision we have found was added in late 1978 to the program of federal operational aid to "impacted" schools. The section reads:

"Each local educational agency which is adversely affected or aggrieved by any action of the Commissioner [of Education] under this title shall be entitled to a hearing on, and review of, such action in the same manner as if such agency were a person under the provisions of chapters 5 and 7 of title 5, United States Code."

§5(g) Act of Sept. 30, 1950, 20 U.S.C. §240(g), as added by §1008 Education Amendments of 1978, Pub. L. 95-561, Nov. 1, 1978. The congressional intent was to provide a formal Administrative Procedure Act hearing and judicial review to local educational agencies suffering losses, such as application denials and payment withholdings, at the hands of the Commissioner. See H.R. Rep. No. 95-1137, 95th Cong., 2d Sess. 114, 172–73 (1978). Careless draftsmanship, unfortunately common in grant statutes, may have caused a failure in the implementation of this intent. First, the section is redundant. The word "person" was already defined in the APA so as to include a local educational agency. See §§2(2), 10(b)(2) Administrative Procedure Act, 5 U.S.C. §§551(2), 701(b)(2) (" 'person' includes . . . [a] public or private organization"). Second, the APA only gives formal hearings when the program statute provides that the "case . . . be determined on the record after opportunity for an agency hearing." §5(a), *id.*, 5 U.S.C. §554(a). See Chapter 15, note 30, *infra*. This is what the quoted section was apparently trying to do, but technically failed because the grant statute, Act of Sept. 30, 1950, 20 U.S.C. §§236–246, does not use the magic words (apart from §5(g)) and §5(g) is itself a redundancy. Third, an abundance of case law had already established the grantees' right of judicial review under the APA when harmed by federal agency action. See Chapter 4, notes 224–258, *supra*, and accompanying text.

is far from universal, and a significant number of major formula programs contain no mention of Due Process rights.³

The reasons for such inconsistency cannot be found in the differing purposes of the various formula programs. Whatever the specific goal, all federal grant programs are conditional—i.e., conditioned upon grantee compliance with a set of requirements imposed by the statute creating the program and by implementing agency regulations. Standard grant conditions run across program lines, providing a core of uniform operating principles for this type of federal activity. Programmatic specifications are tailored to the needs of the particular grant activity. Both kinds of requirements are ordinarily mandatory.⁴ This means that breach of one or more of these conditions places federal payments automatically in jeopardy for violation of federal law and grantee assurances. All

---

³ See, e.g., Title X, Public Health Service Act, 42 U.S.C. §§300–300a-8 (family planning services); Title XVI-F, *id.*, 42 U.S.C. §300t (area health service development funds); Comprehensive Alcohol Abuse and Alcoholism Prevention, Treatment and Rehabilitation Act of 1970, 42 U.S.C. §§4541–4593; Drug Abuse Office and Treatment Act of 1972, 21 U.S.C. §§1101–1194; Title IV-B, Social Security Act, 42 U.S.C. §§620–626 (child welfare services); Child Nutrition Act of 1966, 42 U.S.C. §§1771–1787 (school breakfast; nonfood assistance; special milk program); National School Lunch Act of 1946, 42 U.S.C. §§1751–1769a; §304 Public Works and Economic Development Act of 1965, 42 U.S.C. §3153 (supplemental state grants); §308 Coastal Zone Management Act, 16 U.S.C. §1456a (energy impact grants); Land and Water Conservation Fund Act of 1965, 16 U.S.C. §§460L-4 to 460L-11 (outdoor recreation); Title IX, Social Security Act, 42 U.S.C. §§1101–1108 (state grants; unemployment insurance); Wagner-Peyser Act of 1933, 29 U.S.C. §§49–49k (state employment services); Airport and Airway Redevelopment Act of 1970, 49 U.S.C. §§1701–1743; Urban Mass Transit Act of 1964, 49 U.S.C. §§1601–1618; Federal Aid Highway Act of 1973, 23 U.S.C. §§101–407; Solid Waste Disposal Act, 42 U.S.C. §§6901–6987; Safe Drinking Water Act, 42 U.S.C. §§300f to 300j-9; Federal Water Pollution Control Act, 33 U.S.C. §§1251–1376.

A comical example of a failure to mention hearing rights occurs in §425 General Education Provisions Act, 20 U.S.C. §1231b-2. This section requires state education agencies to afford hearings on the record to local education agencies disappointed with proposed SEA funding decisions or whose grant will be terminated by the SEA for noncompliance with federal law. The LEA can appeal final SEA action to the Commissioner of Education. If the SEA fails to provide adequate hearings or does not comply with the Commissioner's decision, *all* federal assistance to the SEA "shall forthwith terminate," seemingly without any hearing.

⁴ Congress can, of course, expressly limit the reach of its grant requirements or the sanctions for noncompliance. For example, the Aid to Families With Dependent Children Program prohibits grantees from imposing certain residence requirements as a condition of eligibility. §402(b) Social Security Act, 42 U.S.C. §602(b). If in administering the program local welfare agencies violate the requirement and the state agency is aware of the practice, the Secretary can terminate payments, but only when the violation involves "a substantial number of cases." §404(a)(1) *id.*, 42 U.S.C. §604(a)(1). The same law provides another example. While each state must have a conforming child support program in order to qualify for federal AFDC payments, see §402(a)(27) *id.*, 42 U.S.C. §602(a)(27), a failure to comply could not be found, prior to January 1, 1977, if the state was making a "good faith effort" to implement the program and, after that date, noncompliance can be sanctioned only by reducing a state's AFDC reimbursement by 5 percent. See §§404(c), 404(d) *id.*, 42 U.S.C. §§604(c), 604(d).

248 / *Rights and Remedies Under Federal Grants*

federal agencies with authority to adopt regulations necessary to carry out a grant-in-aid statute have power to sanction noncompliance; while various statutes expressly authorize such action, the absence of such authorization is not fatal to the power. Since federal grantors cannot be placed in the position of condoning illegal uses of government funds, the withholding sanction must be considered inherent to the function of grant supervision and administration.[5] Thus, all grants are subject to either withholding or termination for infraction of federal requirements, and all grant programs implicitly contain potential Due Process issues.

Varying congressional practices on the question of grantee hearing rights appear to be more accidental than purposeful. The authorizing legislation for grant programs originates in different congressional committees according to the subject matter of the program.[5a] Clusters of grant programs coming out of a particular committee will contain numerous similar or identical statutory provisions borrowed from prior efforts of the same committee. For standard situations, such as noncompliance enforcement, the relevant "boiler plate" which the committee has evolved over the years will be automatically incorporated in the new grant statute. Because of this, we can see repetitive patterns in different fields. For example, nutrition programs originating in the agricultural committees do not contain any mention of enforcement of federal requirements in the authorizing statutes and, hence, do not address the Due Process question.[6] The same is true for grant-in-aid statutes in the fields of public works and economic development,[7] land use,[8] transportation,[9] and environmental protection.[10] On the

---

[5] See, e.g., *Nebraska Dep't of Rds. v. Tiemann*, 510 F.2d 446 (8th Cir. 1975); *Maryland v. Mathews*, 415 F. Supp. 1206 (D. D.C. 1976); *United States v. City of Chicago*, 411 F. Supp. 218 (N.D. Ill. 1976), *modified*, 549 F.2d 415 (7th Cir. 1977), cert. denied, 434 U.S. 875 (1978); *Gaines v. Martinez*, 353 F. Supp. 780 (N.D. Tex. 1972); *Marquez v. Hardin*, 339 F. Supp. 1364 (N.D. Cal. 1969).

[5a] See generally Subcomm. on Intergovernmental Relations, Senate Comm. on Governmental Affairs, 95th Cong., 1st Sess., *Table of Federal Programs: Presentation of Federal Programs by Budget Function, Authorizing Legislation, and Legislative Comm. Jurisdiction* (Comm. Print 1977).

[6] See Child Nutrition Act of 1966, 42 U.S.C. §§1771–1788; National School Lunch Act of 1946, 42 U.S.C. §§1751–1769a.

[7] See, e.g., Public Works and Economic Development Act of 1965, 42 U.S.C. §§3121–3246h; Local Public Works Capital Development and Investment Act of 1976, 42 U.S.C. §§6701–6710.

[8] See Land and Water Conservation Fund Act of 1965, 16 U.S.C. §§460L-4 to L-11.

[9] See Federal-Aid Highway Act of 1973, 23 U.S.C. §§101–407; Urban Mass Transit Act of 1964, 49 U.S.C. §§1601–1618; Airport and Airway Redevelopment Act of 1970, 49 U.S.C. §§1701–1730.

[10] See Clean Air Act of 1963, 42 U.S.C. §§7401–7641; Solid Waste Disposal Act, 42 U.S.C. §§6901–6987; Federal Water Pollution Control Act, 33 U.S.C. §§1251–1376.

other hand, health, education, and welfare statutes regularly contain provisions dealing with noncompliance and grantee Due Process rights. Perfect consistency is, of course, not to be found, given the idiosyncrasies of draftsmen and committees.[11] Nothing binds legislative counsel to yesterday's stock language. An adventurous draftsman will, indeed, look into other areas for adaptable clauses. But overall one can see the handiwork of specific congressional committees.

An important point is that in no grant-in-aid statute will one find an express denial of hearing rights to a grantee facing a withholding sanction. When Congress has addressed the question in specific statutes, it has invariably afforded hearing rights; thus, one may easily find a cumulative congressional judgment that, at least with respect to formula grants, deprivation of the grant without hearing opportunities would be inconsistent with Due Process. If the statute is silent on the issue of hearing rights, it will be because the topic of condition enforcement is not addressed at all, or the grantor agency is not explicitly instructed to terminate grants for noncompliance.[12] One cannot, therefore, read into such silence an intention of Congress to deny hearing rights. Lack of congressional directives delegates the Due Process question to the administrator to be decided under constitutional or administrative law principles.

In an earlier day, Congress designated itself as an appeal board if the administering agency denied a formula grant to a state.[13] Today's busy Congress cannot handle such individual adjudications, and the appeal to Congress is rarely found in grant statutes as a formal review procedure. A threatened grantee can, of course, informally try to utilize political pressure; in fact, most major compliance and conformity questions are attended by intense congressional involvement.[14]

The common practice presently employed is to direct the designated administrator to provide a grantee hearing. Section 6(e) of the Library Services and Construction Act of 1956, one of

[11] For example, explicit withholding authority exists for all state formula grants under the Social Security Act, see note 2, *supra*, except, inexplicably, for the child welfare services program. See Title IV-B Social Security Act, 42 U.S.C. §§620–626.
[12] See, e.g., §141 Federal-Aid Highway Act of 1973, 23 U.S.C. §141 (state certification of compliance with requirements).
[13] §4 Agricultural College Act of 1890, 7 U.S.C. §326; §16 Smith-Hughes Vocational Education Act, 20 U.S.C. §26.
[14] See, e.g., M. Derthick, *The Influence of Federal Grants: Public Assistance in Massachusetts* 207–208 (1970).

the earlier federal grant programs, exemplifies the standard statutory language:

> "Whenever the Commissioner [of Education], after reasonable notice and opportunity for a hearing to the State agency administering a program submitted under this Act, finds—
> "(1) that the program has been so changed that it no longer complies with the provisions of this Act, or
> "(2) that in the administration of the program there is a failure to comply substantially with any such provisions or with any assurance or other provision contained in the basic State plan,
> "then, until he is satisfied that there is no longer any such failure to comply, after appropriate notice to such State agency he shall make no further payments to the State under this Act or shall limit payments to programs or projects under, or parts of, the programs not affected by the failure, or shall require that payments by such State agency under this Act shall be limited to local or other public library agencies not affected by the failure." [15]

Under this section a finding of noncompliance must be *preceded* by notice and a hearing. This tends to insure an adequate informational base before the imposition of sanctions. One may also assume that the tremendously disruptive effect of federal fund withholding on grantee beneficiary populations has motivated Congress to minimize the chance of erroneous cutoffs.

Neither here nor in analogous sections does Congress attempt to specify the details of the required notice and hearing, preferring, instead, to let the administering agency flesh out "reasonable" procedures. A legislature will ordinarily resort to broad standards when it cannot anticipate the types of future actions which will fall under the statute's directives. To the executive branch or judicial system is delegated the responsibility of working out casuistically the implications and coverage of the legislative norms. Here, however, we are not concerned with prescription or authorization of future conduct unforeseeable in its detail, but, instead, procedural rights which can function equitably across the total range of specific noncompliance contexts. Sometimes the reliance on other bodies to provide the details is based on the presumed greater expertise of a coordinate branch on the subject matter. While agencies administering federal grants may have a greater understanding of the practical difficulties of affording grantee hearing rights and of the strains placed on agency re-

---

[15] 20 U.S.C. §351d(e).

sources, these agencies certainly have no edge over Congress on the topic of procedural fairness. Moreover, because the grantor is inevitably an adversary party in a noncompliance proceeding, the obvious danger arises that it will stack the procedural deck in its own favor. The very pressures which Due Process hearings produce may incline the grantor, in evolving the rules of the game, to smooth the functioning of grant administration by shortcutting on grantee hearing opportunities. The more procedural safeguards afforded grantees, the greater the cost in time and resources in adjudicating issues of compliance with federal standards. Recognizing that such an investment cuts into program budgets for the delivery of services, the grantor may easily be tempted to devise the least expensive and time-consuming procedures possible. When factual and legal issues are complex, as they are likely to be in contested proceedings, the quick route to resolution is usually the least secure route. Such delegation might be defensible if Congress were totally naive about the matter. But the legislators and their advisors are equally capable of understanding and effectuating the constitutional mandates of Due Process, and, in fact, have established detailed Due Process rights when so inclined.[16] We question, therefore, the wisdom of delegating to administrators the determination of what is a "reasonable" scheme of procedural protection for grantees.

A third feature of the section worthy of note is that there is no explicit obligation placed on the Commissioner to establish in advance, by regulation or otherwise, a procedural code under which noncompliance issues will be ventilated. Unless there is a specific directive to issue certain regulations, the administering agency can decide which issues it will address in its regulations.[17] Busy with its duty to flesh out the "substantive" aspects of the

[16] See, e.g., §440(b) General Education Provisions Act, 20 U.S.C. §1232i(b) (Due Process rights of local education agencies accused of civil rights violations); §615 Education of the Handicapped Act, 20 U.S.C. §1415 (procedural safeguards for handicapped; hearing rights on appropriateness of educational program); H.R. Rep. No. 95-1137, 95th Cong., 2d Sess. 143 (1978) ("due process hearing procedure" for state and local education agencies).

[17] Even if Congress directs the administering agency to issue regulations, the latter may sometimes ignore the mandate. For example, the law prohibiting sex discrimination in federally assisted education programs "authorized and directed" each federal department and agency awarding educational grants, loans, and contracts to "effectuate" the prohibition "by issuing rules, regulations, or orders of general applicability." §902 Education Amendments of 1972, Pub. L. 92-318, 20 U.S.C. §1682. Regulations, however, were not forthcoming and Congress, two years later, directed the Secretary of Health, Education and Labor to prepare and publish regulations within 30 days. §844 Education Amendments of 1974, Pub. L. 93-568, 20 U.S.C. §1681 n.

grant statute and to get the money working quickly and efficiently, the federal agency is likely to put off indefinitely the question of the type of notice and hearing it will afford if a compliance controversy should arise. This is precisely what has occurred. In the great majority of cases, no procedures have been administratively established, even for programs containing statutory language like Section 6(e).[18] We have argued elsewhere that reliance on *ad hoc* improvisations of hearing procedures is an unacceptable practice.[19]

The library program, like most formula grants, utilizes a state agency as a distribution center for federal funds. The agency acts as a conduit to other units of government or private entities which establish and conduct the actual programs and projects.[20] If the state agency is itself in the public library business, it too can sponsor projects. Thus, the basic formula grant is parceled out by the grantee, the state agency, by a series of subgrants. Elsewhere in this book we shall discuss the Due Process rights of subgrantees;[21] for now, a few brief comments will aid our understanding of this typical section.

The dissection of the formula grant into numerous subgrants multiplies considerably the number of obligations emanating from the grant award and, hence, the number of possible noncompliance situations. Each subgrantee organization is subject to all federal conditions imposed by the statute and regulations which are not, by their terms or nature, exclusively a grantee responsibility.[22] The statute and regulations will be incorporated in each subgrant, and ordinarily the grantee will require each of its clients to provide the same set of assurances submitted by the grantee to the Federal Government. Limits on the uses of federal funds, for example, follow the federal dollars. So do all standard grant requirements, such as nondiscrimination and reporting conditions.

[18] See note 65, *infra*, and accompanying text.
[19] See Chapter 7, note 24, *supra*, and accompanying text.
[20] The subgrant system is implied rather than explicit in many formula statutes. Library grants, for instance, are made pursuant to state long-range and annual programs which specify the particular activities which will be funded. §§6(a), (d) Library Services and Construction Act of 1956, 20 U.S.C. §§351d(a), (b). Most of these activities are actually carried out by subgrantees, see §3 *id*., 20 U.S.C. §351a (various definitions of providers of services), which is made explicit by program guidelines. 45 C.F.R. pt. 130, Appendix B.
[21] See Chapter 13, *infra*.
[22] See, e.g., OMB Cir. A-102, *supra*, Chapter 1, note 83, at para. 6 ("Except where they are specifically excluded, the provisions of the attachments of this circular shall be applied to subgrantees performing substantive work under grants that are passed through or awarded by the primary grantee . . ."); OMB Cir. A-110, *supra*, Chapter 1, note 83, at para. 5 (same); 7 C.F.R. §246.6, 42 Fed. Reg. 43215 (1977) (state agency agreement with subgrantees).

Also, the grantee may be held liable for each and every violation, whether committed by itself or by a subgrantee. Because the state agency is the recipient of *all* the federal funds by virtue of the formula grant, it bears responsibility for the proper expenditure of every dollar even when it has funneled them to other entities. A violation of federal conditions by the subgrantee is, therefore, perforce a violation by the grantee-subgrantor.[23] This, in turn, leads to the possibility that the violative actions of one of the utlimate recipient organizations may endanger the grants to all recipients.

This conclusion is both confirmed and ameliorated by a reading of Section 6(e). A "failure to comply" with federal conditions "in the administration of the program" includes not only grantee defaults but also failures in the carrying out of projects by subgrantees. The "program" is the totality of the activities sponsored with federal funds, including all activities of delegate entities.[24] In common grant parlance, "administration" includes all actions of all fund recipients. The amelioration is the "pinpoint" provision. Explicit authorization is conceded to the Commissioner to impose sanctions only on those subgrantees ("local or other public library agencies") violating the Act or assurances.[25] While authority is also bestowed on the Commissioner to shut off funds completely, the strong implication of the section is that this drastic remedy should be pursued only if the violation is vitiating all activities being developed with federal funds. If, for example, a state's public libraries practice *de facto* or *de jure* racial discrimination, a total stoppage of federal funds would be appropriate, while a more selective sanction should be applied if the illegal practice is uncovered in just one library. Similar authority is conferred to divide the program into components ("parts of") and impose sanctions on separable elements.[26] If, for instance, the construction phase of the program is found to violate grant conditions, it would ordinarily be irrational to deny funds for the acquisition of books and the provision of library services.

[23] See, e.g., 29 C.F.R. §97.165(a) (termination of the grant if grantee violates regulations or grant conditions or "permits a subgrantee" to do so).

[24] Cf. Note, "Administrative Cutoff of Federal Funding Under Title VI: A Proposed Interpretation of Program," 52 Ind. L. J. 651 (1977).

[25] Cf. §602 Civil Rights Act of 1964, 42 U.S.C. §2000d-1: ". . . such termination or refusal shall be limited to the particular political entity, or part thereof, or other recipient as to whom such a finding has been made. . . ."

[26] Cf. §602, *id.*, 42 U.S.C. §2000d-1: ". . . such termination or refusal . . . shall be limited in its effect to the particular program, or part thereof, in which such noncompliance has been so found. . . ."

254 / *Rights and Remedies Under Federal Grants*

Observe that notice and a hearing are offered exclusively to the state agency. As previously explained, a violation of grant terms always places the state agency in a noncompliance posture; thus, the grantee is directly affected by an adverse finding in all cases and it is logical to afford it hearing rights. But the alleged violation may be charged only to a specific subgrantee, and, indeed, we have just noted that the penalty may be imposed only on that violator. Hearing rights are commonly denied subgrantees in federal grant programs, a practice we shall explore in another chapter.[27]

The provision under study and its kin are disturbingly vague about the effects of a stop payment. No problem is presented if a finding of noncompliance is overturned on appeal;[28] presumably the grantee will be immediately restored all retained payments. But if a violation is proved and later corrected, the important question arises whether the grantee is entitled to the funds accumulated between the date withholding began and the date compliance was achieved.

One can draw no comfortable conclusions from the statutory language. "[H]e shall make no further payments . . . or shall limit payments" is the way the fiscal action is ordinarily phrased in these sections;[29] such is often described as a "withholding" and the funds are considered "withheld."[30] These words and phrases primarily stop the disbursement of federal funds from the agency to the grantee and would similarly authorize the grantor to put a hold on unobligated federal funds already in the hands of the grantee. They do not, however, offer guidance with respect to the government's disposition of the retained funds once compliance has been achieved.

---

[27] See Chapter 13, *infra*.

[28] Almost all noncompliance and nonconformity sections provide for judicial review of the federal agency's final action. See, e.g., §6(f) Library Services and Construction Act of 1956, 20 U.S.C. §351d(f). The state may file a review petition in the U.S. court of appeals for the circuit in which the state is located. Agency findings of fact supported by substantial evidence are conclusive. Further review in the U.S. Supreme Court is available by certiorari or certification. But see, e.g., §314(g)(3) Public Health Service Act, 42 U.S.C. §246(g)(3) (no judicial review).

[29] See, e.g., §6(e) Library Services and Construction Act of 1956, 20 U.S.C. §351d(e); §308(a) Adult Education Act of 1966, 20 U.S.C. §1207(a); §135 Developmental Disabilities Services and Construction Act, 42 U.S.C. §6065; §1904 Social Security Act, 42 U.S.C. §1396c. Compare §108(b) Higher Education Act, 20 U.S.C. §1007(b) ("the State will not be regarded as eligible to participate in the program until . . .").

[30] See, e.g., §434(b) General Education Provisions Act, 20 U.S.C. §1232c(b). One statutory section explicitly states that funds are withheld "pending" corrective action, §1611(b)(2) Public Health Service Act, 42 U.S.C. §300p-1(b)(2), thus making it clear that retained funds are not forfeited.

An example may serve to clarify the nature of the problem. Assume the following facts. At the begining of the fiscal year, a state is allocated $1 million as its formula share of appropriated library funds. On that same day, a compliance hearing begun in the previous year ends with a decision unfavorable to the grantee. The payment system established for the program is on a quarterly basis—the grantee estimates its needs for each trimester and draws that amount, with appropriate adjustments for miscalculations in previous periods. The federal share is 50 percent of all eligible expenditures. It takes six months for the state to achieve compliance, during which period the state has maintained the program at previous service levels by the simple expedient of spending its entire local share. Because of the noncompliance finding, the full $1 million has been retained by HEW. Is the grantee now entitled to $500,000 for each of the last two quarters?

Several factors coalesce to suggest an affirmative answer. The grantor is not authorized to disburse the state's allocation to other states because the reallotment authority is conditioned on a finding of insufficient need for the funds, not on compliance issues.[31] The money, therefore, will still be available. Second, the funds upon allotment belong to the state. Nothing appears to have occurred before or during the withholding period to strip the state of that ownership. Although noncompliance has been found, the illegality has not infected the million dollar allocation because those funds have never been utilized. The grantee commitment is to expend federal funds only according to federal standards; now that the program has been brought into compliance the grantee can expend the allocation in accordance with all applicable standards. Third, if the federal grantor were inclined to deprive the state of funds, it would have no criteria for determining how much of the allotment to retain permanently. Because none of the federal dollars has been expended, there is no way to calculate the amount of any fiscal penalty. It would be impermissible to retain half of the allocation on the ground that half a year has passed. The grant statute and regulations do not require a state to spread the use of its allocation evenly throughout the year; on the contrary, the state can ordinarily draw on its federal funds as need arises.[32]

[31]See, e.g., §5(b) Library Services and Construction Act of 1956, 20 U.S.C. §351c(b) ("[t]he amount . . . which the Commissioner deems will not be required . . .").
[32] See, e.g., 45 C.F.R. pt. 100b, subpts. E, F (methods and procedures for grant payments; Office of Education state-administered programs).

256 / *Rights and Remedies Under Federal Grants*

Finally, a fiscal penalty should not be readily implied.[33] Depriving our hypothetical state of its federal allocation will have the probable effect of closing down all library projects for the remainder of the year even though compliance has been achieved. The result of that action will be felt primarily by library users who are most likely blameless.

A technical obstacle to the release of federal funds remains. Recall that the state must provide 50 percent of the total program costs for each year. In our hypothetical example, that would appear to be no problem because the state financed the first two quarters of operations entirely with local resources. But these matching dollars must have been expended for eligible program activities. The commitment of the United States is to pay half of each dollar expended for library services which are authorized by the grant statute and regulations.[34] To the extent that expenditures from state revenues were for impermissible uses under federal standards they could not count as matching funds. Thus, federal funds from the allocation will be released only in an amount equivalent to what the grantee can demonstrate is a qualified match. The state, however, can deal with any shortfall by the expedient of adding additional local dollars in the latter part of the fiscal year.

Our conclusion that upon proving compliance a state is entitled to the withheld funds may be challenged on the ground that it removes the effectiveness of withholding as a deterrent to the violation of federal standards. The answer is that withholding itself is a sufficient deterrent. In the example, if the state had not corrected its infractions it would have been without funds for library programs for the second half of the fiscal year. Also, the state cannot delay compliance indefinitely because federal funds will revert to the U.S. treasury if not obligated by the state by a certain time, either by the end of the fiscal year for which they are allocated [35] or the following year.[36] Moreover, it is rarely wise to

---

[33] See Chapter 3, *supra*, at pp. 98–100.

[34] See §§7(b)(1), 102, 202, 302, 402 Library Services and Construction Act of 1956, 20 U.S.C. §§351e(b)(1), 353, 355b, 355e-1, 362.

[35] See, e.g., §413 General Education Provisions Act, 20 U.S.C. §1226.

[36] See, e.g., §4(b) Library Services and Construction Act of 1956, 20 U.S.C. §351b(b); §412(b) General Education Provisions Act, 20 U.S.C. §1225(b). Compare §6(b)(4) Land and Water Conservation Fund Act of 1964, 16 U.S.C. §460L-8(b)(4) (three fiscal years); §103(c) Housing and Community Development Act of 1974, 42 U.S.C. §5303(c) (appropriated sums "shall remain available until expended"). For a broad review of the judicial power to reinstate lapsed funds in light of illegal grantor actions, see *Jacksonville Port Auth.* v. *Adams,* 556 F.2d 52 (D.C. Cir. 1977).

stockpile program revenues. The state may find itself with a large amount of categorical dollars which it must expend for federally defined purposes in a short period of time. It cannot hire hundreds of additional librarians for a three-month period to avoid the loss of funds to the federal treasury, because it will have to deal with those employees and the people who have gotten used to their services once the period expires. It might be able to buy thousands of new books, but such improvisations would ordinarily be programmatically unwise.

One is struck by a paradox commonly found in provisions such as Section 6(e). Although hearing rights are initially afforded on the issue of noncompliance, no comparable procedural protection is found on the question whether the grantee has subsequently brought its program into conformity. The statute appears to vest in the Commissioner complete discretion to determine when reforms have been sufficient to make the program consistent with federal standards. That issue and its resolution are as important as the initial adverse decision. The deprivation of grant funds is initially effected by the finding of a violation, but may be continued in force by grantor action or inaction on the question of later compliance. It is imperative, and probably constitutionally required, to afford adequate hearing rights on such subsequent determinations. It is also advisable for Congress to provide some mechanism by which the grantee could reasonably compel the administrator to review and determine the question of compliance when the grantee has taken what it considers to be sufficient corrective action.[37]

Noncompliance provisions in formula programs are boringly repetitive in structure and language. We have, however, uncovered a few variations.

Section 616(a) of the Education of the Handicapped Act provides additional sanctions for violations.[38] The Commissioner of Education, after finding against the grantee, is directed to withhold payments under that Act and is permitted to stop the flow of federal funds under any other program (presumably, under his jurisdiction) providing assistance to handicapped children. Also, after receiving notice of a noncompliance hearing, state and local educational agencies must "by means of a public notice, take

[37] Cf. 45 C.F.R. §168.82, 42 Fed. Reg. 64570 (1977) (procedures to reinstate educational institutions).
[38] 20 U.S.C. §1416(a).

such measures as may be necessary to bring the pendency of [such] action to the attention of the public within the jurisdiction of such agency. . . ." [39] This requirement forces governmental grantees to expose their possibly illegal conduct to public light, thus increasing the pressure on such grantees to correct alleged deficiencies quickly and docilely. Because the termination of federal payments is likely to impact severely on the beneficiary population, and potentially on taxpayers if local revenues are utilized to cover the deficit, the idea of public notice can hardly be faulted. The condition does, however, place the grantee in a poor bargaining position, even if its case is good. The public is unlikely to unravel the complexities of compliance questions in this highly technical field, and the mere initiation of a compliance proceeding by the Federal Government will probably be taken as evidence, whatever the merits, of local government failures. Pressure to keep the dollars flowing will force accommodation to the federal position, even if the grantee would otherwise be likely to prevail on the matter.

In federal formula programs which support the construction of facilities, one sometimes finds an additional clause covering the situation where compliance is impossible.[40] Under these circumstances, the federal agency is authorized to withhold further payments, in whole or part, until the grantee has returned or arranged for the repayment of illegally expended funds. For example, if a building violates federally approved plans and specifications or other grant requirements, it may be impossible or unfeasible to remedy the deficiency. Similarly, when a federally financed facility is transferred to another party for uses inconsistent with the grant purpose and agreement, it may be impossible for the grantee to regain title and possession. The government is then authorized to sue to recoup the federal outlays from the grantee.[41]

The presence of the repayment sanction in the context of compliance impossibility helps us resolve a separate but related question. We previously concluded that federal funds withheld after a formal noncompliance finding must be returned once the

---

[39] §616(a) Education of the Handicapped Act, 20 U.S.C. §1416(a). Compare Administrative Conference of the United States, Recommendation 71-9, "Enforcement of Standards in Federal Grant-in-Aid Programs," 1 C.F.R. §305.71-9 (public disclosure by federal agency).

[40] See, e.g., §1612(b)(2) Public Health Service Act, 42 U.S.C. §300p-2(b)(2) (health facilities construction).

[41] See, e.g., §225 Community Mental Health Centers Act, 42 U.S.C. §2689m.

deficiencies have been satisfactorily corrected. The finding, however, may be not only that the program is presently violative of federal standards but also that federal funds were illegally spent for a period of time prior to the finding. The issue then arises whether a grantee can be subjected to forfeiture (via lawsuits or reductions in future payments) of the amount of such funds. Silence on the question in the typical statutory noncompliance provision tends to support a conclusion that the grantor lacks recapture power, but one could convincingly argue that the withholding sanction does not negate the existence of other grantor enforcement powers considered necessary to proper grant administration, and that the illegality of the expenditure must always give rise to an adequate federal remedy. Yet Congress can, if it desires, limit the range of sanctions for federal grant noncompliance. The existence of explicit authority to seek repayment in some federal grant statutes, under the specified circumstance of compliance impossibility, strongly suggests an intentional limitation on enforcement powers and sanctions when illegal practices have been cured and when recapture is not explicitly authorized.[42] The result is not implausible or undesirable. The fact that a recapture of federal funds is likely to produce a future reduction in program services, thus sanctioning the innocent beneficiaries of the grant, is enough reason to forego such a remedy. Further, past expenditures are likely to have been dedicated to program purposes even though the grantee was in violation of grant terms and the expenditures were technically tainted. Assume, for example, that the grantee violated citizen participation requirements because its citizen board was improperly constituted. The grantee commitment is to expend federal funds only by way of a conforming organizational structure, making the expenditure of every federal dollar during the period of nonconformity illegal. But the grantee expenditures were providing authorized services and benefits to beneficiaries. To recapture the dollars in situations like

[42] See generally Chapter 3, *supra*, at p. 103. See, e.g., §11(a) Act of Sept. 23, 1950, Pub. L., 81-815, 20 U.S.C. §641(a) (". . . no further payment will be made under this Act with respect to such agency until there is no longer any failure to comply or the diversion or default has been corrected or, if compliance or correction is impossible, until such agency repays or arranges for the repayment of Federal moneys which have been diverted or improperly expended."); §106(g) Comprehensive Employment and Training Act of 1973, 29 U.S.C. §816(g) ("The Secretary may withhold funds otherwise payable under this Act in order to recover any amounts expended in any fiscal year in violation of any provision of this Act, any regulation promulgated pursuant to this Act, or any term or condition of assistance under this Act.").

this would be inequitable. It does, therefore, make sense for Congress to "forgive and forget" once compliance is achieved.[43]

The place of the Due Process hearing has been left to the discretion of the federal administering agencies. Not surprisingly, they have usually chosen Washington, D.C., the location of their central offices.[44] Occasionally, in their discretion, they may move the hearing location to a regional office.[45] This places a tremendous burden on grantees located far from Washington and the regional office, particularly if a factual controversy will require the attendance of witnesses. This issue is addressed, to our knowledge, in only one grant statute, the revised [46] Vocational Education Act. Section 109(f) requires the Commissioner of Education to prescribe and implement regulations which assure that any noncompliance hearing will be held within the state.[47] But the tortured language of that section seems to apply only to discretionary project grants made to local governments and school districts, and does not require compliance hearings involving state formula funds to be held within the state.

We often find hearing rights attached to grantor enforcement of *specific* federal conditions. Statutory sections which extend the reach of a condition to all federal programs, or groups of federal programs, will often contain language affording notice and an opportunity to be heard prior to a finding that the particular condition has been violated.[48] Such hearing rights are not redun-

---

[43] See generally Chapter 3, *supra*, at pp. 98–103. The major exception is when a grantee has diverted funds to unauthorized purposes. In this situation, recapture of federal funds is clearly justified, but the grant statute or regulations should still explicitly establish the government's recovery power. See §104(e) Community Development Act of 1977, Pub. L. 95-128, Oct. 12, 1977, amending §104(d) Housing and Community Development Act of 1974, 42 U.S.C. §5304(d); §119(h) *id.*, 42 U.S.C. §5318(h), as added by §110(b) Community Development Act of 1977, Pub. L. 95-128, Oct. 12, 1977; §308(b)(6) Coastal Zone Management Act, 16 U.S.C. §1456a(b)(6); 15 C.F.R. §931.97.

[44] See, e.g., 45 C.F.R. §111.5. Compare 45 C.F.R. §115.66(c) (place fixed by Commissioner or his designee "with due regard to the mutual convenience of the parties"); 45 C.F.R. §168.75(b)(3), 42 Fed. Reg. 64569 (1977) (designated OE official sets date and place).

[45] See, e.g., 45 C.F.R. §1386.92; 45 C.F.R. §213.13 (1977).

[46] §202(a) Education Amendments of 1976, Pub. L. 94-482, Oct. 12, 1976, substantially revised the Vocational Education Act of 1963, 20 U.S.C. §§2301–2463.

[47] 20 U.S.C. §2309(f).

[48] See, e.g., §§601–603 Civil Rights Act of 1964, 42 U.S.C. §§2000d–2000d-1 (prohibits racial discrimination in any program receiving federal financial assistance; grantee right to hearing on the record); §§901, 902 Education Amendments of 1972, 20 U.S.C. §§1681, 1682 (prohibits sex discrimination in any educational program receiving federal aid; grantee right to hearing on the record); §438 General Education Provisions Act, 20 U.S.C. §1232g (termination of educational grants for violation of student privacy rights; hearing rights implicitly given); §407 Drug Abuse Office and

dant because even if the particular program in which the violation occurs contains a noncompliance provision, it will refer only to violations of that act and not the violation of terms imposed by other federal statutes.

Within a grant statute, Congress will sometimes provide a hearing opportunity if compliance with a particular requirement is put in question by the grantor, even though no hearing rights are afforded for alleged violations of any of the other conditions imposed by the statute. For example, Title I of Public Law 81-874 establishes a program to provide grants to maintain and operate schools impacted by federal activities.[49] The statute prohibits states from taking such assistance into account in determining their distribution of state funds to local education agencies.[50] The additional federal assistance to a school will, of course, be negated if the state lowers its allotment of funds because of the federal contribution. Federal payments under the Act can be reduced or terminated if the Commissioner finds that such substitution of

---

Treatment Act of 1972, 21 U.S.C. §1174 (discrimination against drug abusers by hospitals; hearing rights prior to suspension or revocation of federal aid); §321 Comprehensive Alcohol Abuse and Alcoholism Prevention, Treatment and Rehabilitation Act of 1970, 42 U.S.C. §4581 (discrimination against drug abusers by hospitals; hearing rights prior to suspension or revocation of federal aid); §335(e) Public Health Service Act, 42 U.S.C. §245h(e) (hospital denial of admitting privilege to member of National Health Service Corps; opportunity for hearing on the record); §1310 Public Health Service Act, 42 U.S.C. §300e-9 (state or local government failing to offer employees a health maintenance organization option subject to termination of payments under six formula health programs; prior notice and opportunity for hearing). Compare §§504, 505 Rehabilitation Act of 1973, 29 U.S.C. §§794, 794a (prohibits discrimination against the handicapped in any program receiving federal financial assistance; incorporates hearing provision of another statute). But see §704 Public Health Service Act, 42 U.S.C. §292d (prohibits schools of medicine receiving federal financial aid from engaging in sex discrimination; no explicit hearing rights); §855 Public Health Service Act, 42 U.S.C. §298b-2 (prohibits nursing schools supported with federal funds from engaging in sex discrimination; no explicit hearing rights); §408 Drug Abuse Office and Treatment Act of 1972, 21 U.S.C. §1175 (hospitals must maintain confidentiality of drug abuse patient records; no explicit grantee hearing rights); §333 Comprehensive Alcohol Abuse and Alcoholism Prevention, Treatment and Rehabilitation Act of 1970, 42 U.S.C. §4582 (hospitals must maintain confidentiality of alcohol abuse patient records; no explicit grantee hearing rights); §1521 Public Health Service Act, 42 U.S.C. §300m (failure of state to enter into designation agreement for a state health planning and development agency jeopardizes state's formula health funding; no explicit hearing rights).

Federal agencies will occasionally impose requirements applicable to all, or some, of their grant programs under their regulatory powers. Hearings rights are ordinarily not given in explicit terms. See, e.g., 45 C.F.R. pt. 46 (protection of human subjects; violation grounds for termination of any HEW grant); 45 C.F.R. pt. 70 (1977) (HEW standards for grantee personnel systems; question of noncompliance not addressed); 45 C.F.R. pt. 71 (interagency day-care requirements; noncompliance grounds for termination).

[49] Act of Sept. 30, 1950, Pub. L. 81-874, 20 U.S.C. §§236–246.
[50] §5(d) *id.*, 20 U.S.C. §240(d).

funds has occurred. Prior to action by the Commissioner, hearing rights are afforded to any state or local education agency which will be affected by a reduction or termination. Yet Title I is replete with terms governing the award and expenditure of federal funds, and the violation of any one of these conditions may lead to the termination of federal payments. If a grantee claims Due Process rights when noncompliance with any of these other conditions is charged, the natural reaction would be to assume that Congress by implication denied them.[51] Whether or not the Constitution is ultimately held to provide such rights independent of the legislative intent, the ambiguity of such statutes is undesirable.[52]

Even more confusing are the cases in which Congress grants hearing rights for any noncompliance action, then repeats such rights within other sections of the statute imposing particular program conditions. Let us look at a major grant statute as it stood prior to its 1978 revision. Title I of the Elementary and Secondary Education Act provided notice and an opportunity to be heard prior to any withholding for violation of assurances.[53] One such assurance was that participation in Title I programs would be afforded, on an equitable basis, to eligible children in private schools.[54] The section imposing this requirement had its own notice and hearing provisions. We could easily live with such redundancy if the language in the two sections were identical. But the general provision spoke of an opportunity for a "hearing," while the more specific section afforded a hearing "on the record." Thus, doubt was created as to the type of hearing which the Commissioner had to afford in the former situation.[55]

---

[51] In fact, the Office of Education appears to have taken that very position with respect to the impact aid program established under Pub. L. 81-874. See 45 C.F.R. §111.2(c) (noncompliance hearing procedures apply to impact aid under Pub. L. 81-815 but not under Pub. L. 81-874). A 1978 statutory amendment may have resolved the problem. See note 2, *supra*.

[52] See also §770(b)(2)(E) Public Health Service Act, 42 U.S.C. §295f-1(b)(2)(E) (denial of health professions capitation grant for noncompliance with specific requirement must be preceded by hearing; no hearing rights for denial or termination of grant on other grounds); §206(c)(6) Community Mental Health Centers Act, 42 U.S.C. §2689e(c)(6) (grantee given "opportunity to respond" to reduction of discretionary grant for insufficient efforts to secure payments for services; no hearing rights for denial or termination of grants).

[53] §146 Act of Sept. 30, 1950, Pub. L. 81-874, 20 U.S.C. §241j (1976).

[54] §141A *id.*, 20 U.S.C. §241e-1 (1976).

[55] The statute now provides for a *less* formal opportunity to be heard when the Commissioner finds a violation of the equitable participation rule. Compare §130 (b)(4)(A) Elementary and Secondary Education Act of 1965, 20 U.S.C. §2740(b)(4)(A), as rewritten by §101 Education Amendments of 1978, Pub. L. 95-561, Nov. 1, 1978

One must usually look to the authorizing legislation (which might be an act, or a title of an act, or a part of a title of an act, or a subpart of a part of a title of an act) for each program to determine the statutory hearing rights, if any. In 1974 Congress attempted to speak more broadly to the question of hearing rights when it added Section 434(c) to the General Education Provisions Act. This provision read at that time, in part:

> "Whenever the Commissioner, after reasonable notice and an opportunity for hearing, finds that there has been a failure, by any recipient of funds under any applicable program, to comply substantially to the terms to which such recipient has agreed in order to receive such funds, the Commissioner shall notify such recipient that further payments will not be made to such recipient under that program until he is satisfied that such recipient no longer fails to comply with such terms. Until the Commissioner is so satisfied, no further payments shall be made to such recipient." [56]

"[A]ny applicable program" is defined elsewhere [57] as the grant programs of the Office of Education and the National Institute of Education, which comprise the substantial majority of the educational initiatives of the national government. Thus, in one pronouncement Congress extended Due Process rights to grantees under more than 150 different programs, both formula and competitive.[58]

As originally proposed by the Senate, the focus of the section was quite distinct. It aimed to make the terms of a grant agreement specifically enforceable in court,[59] which, parenthetically, is some evidence that federal standards cannot be specifically enforced without congressional authorization.[60] This remedy was deleted in conference,[61] without changing the reference to com-

---

(written objections; show cause appearance before Commissioner), with §186(a) *id.*, 20 U.S.C. §2836(a) (hearing "on the record"). This amendment conforms to the practice under the Emergency School Aid Act which contains the requirement without affording a grantee hearing, see §§710(a)(12), 712(c) Emergency School Aid Act, 20 U.S.C. §§1609(a)(12), 1611(c), and the Office of Education by regulation affording only an informal conference on the issue. See 45 C.F.R. §185.42.

[56] 20 U.S.C. §1232c(c) (1976), as added by §511(a) Education Amendments of 1974, Pub. L. 93-380, Aug. 21, 1974.

[57] §§400(b), (c)(1)(A) General Education Provisions Act, 20 U.S.C. §§1221(b), (c)(1)A).

[58] As of the time of writing, the Office of Education and the National Institute of Education are together administering 163 separate grant programs, 54 of which are of the formula type.

[59] See S. Rep. No. 93-763, 93d Cong., 2d Sess. 63 (1974).

[60] See Chapter 3, notes 215-230, *supra,* and accompanying text.

[61] See S. Rep. No. 93-1026, 93d Cong., 2d Sess. (1974), in *1974 U.S. Code Cong. & Admin. News* 4248.

264 / *Rights and Remedies Under Federal Grants*

pliance with "the terms to which such recipient has agreed." This explains the variance from the usual provision which requires compliance with the statute, regulations, and assurances. Because the terms of a typical grant agreement include the requirement of complying with all applicable statutes and regulations, the different phraseology in Section 434(c) would ordinarily have been insignificant. A second thrust of the amendment as passed by the Senate was to offer administrative review to any person or agency aggrieved by the action or inaction of the Commissioner of Education. This, too, was deleted in conference. Concerning noncompliance questions, the Senate proposal included hearing rights only if all or a portion of a state's funds were withheld. This was intended as a "consolidation" of "standard provisions." The conference committee expanded this to all OE and NIE programs without explaining the reasons for increased coverage. The real impact of the section was the extension of Due Process rights to recipients of educational grants of a competitive nature. The great majority of formula programs already contained the right to notice and a hearing prior to a withholding of funds; [62] competitive grant statutes did not.[63] We are unfortunately left without insight into the congressional motivation behind the only significant change brought about in 1974 by the passage of that section.

The matter is now history because the Education Amendments of 1978 [63a] thoroughly revised the enforcement and Due Process system for recipients of OE and NIE grants. A comprehensive set of sanctions, procedures, and appeals is now established at both the federal and state levels.[63b]

While the 1974 and 1978 amendments obviated the need to write noncompliance provisions into new education grant statutes, they failed in several cases to remove comparable provisions from existing statutes. For a number of programs, therefore, two different statutory sections cover the same topic. This may lead to problems where the language is not identical.[64]

---

[62] See notes 2, 50, 52, 54, 55, *supra,* and accompanying text.
[63] See Chapter 10, *infra,* at pp. 272–79.
[63a] Pub. L. 95-561, Nov. 1, 1978.
[63b] §§425, 434, 451–456 General Education Provisions Act, 20 U.S.C. §§1231b-2, 1231c, 1234e.
[64] For example, the library program continues to have its own noncompliance section, §6(e) Library Services and Construction Act of 1956, 20 U.S.C. §351d(e). The congressional intent is to conform the education grant statutes piecemeal. See H.R. Rep. No. 95-1137, 95th Cong., 2d Sess. 143–44 (1978).

Administrative Practice

Three basic propositions emerge from our review of the regulations of federal grantor agencies. First, outside of mandated hearing procedures to consider allegations of civil rights violations by grantees, the majority of federal formula grants do not have regulations establishing the processes by which noncompliance isues will be determined.[65] Second, even if the statute establishing the program specifies that payments will not be withheld until the grantee has been given prior notice and an opportunity to be heard, the administering agency in many cases has not implemented the requirement by regulation [66] or has simply copied verbatim the statutory language in its program rules.[67] Third, if a statute establishing a formula grant program is silent on the issue of hearing rights, the grantor agency is most likely to either leave

[65] Our project surveyed more than 130 formula grants. The hearing provisions cited below cover about one fourth of these. In the remainder, program regulations are silent or refer generally to the right to be heard before noncompliance sanctions are imposed without specifying hearing procedures. See, e.g., 45 C.F.R. §1361.5 (noncompliance in the state vocational rehabilitation program). For detailed hearing procedures, see 45 C.F.R. §§115.68–115.69, 42 Fed. Reg. 15549 (1977) (compliance hearing on nonsupplantation requirement); 45 C.F.R. pt. 111 (hearings for application rejection in impact aid programs and for noncompliance under impact aid construction program); 45 C.F.R. §§168.71–168.84, 42 Fed. Reg. 64567 (1977) (institutional noncompliance hearings; student financial assistance programs); 45 C.F.R. §§1386.80–1386.112 (nonconformity-noncompliance hearings under developmental disabilities program); 45 C.F.R. pt. 213 (1977) (nonconformity-noncompliance hearings; welfare, Medicaid, social services grants); 45 C.F.R. §§99.60–99.67 (noncompliance hearings for violations of student privacy rights); 32 C.F.R. §1803 (nonconformity hearings for civil defense grants); 24 C.F.R. §570.913(c) (noncompliance hearings for community development grants); 28 C.F.R. §§18.31–18.35 (noncompliance hearings for crime control grants); 29 C.F.R. §§97.190–97.198 (noncompliance hearings for comprehensive employment and training grants); 29 C.F.R. §1950.12 (noncompliance hearings for occupational safety and health grants); 5 C.F.R. §900.204 (noncompliance hearings for intergovernmental personnel grants); 45 C.F.R. §1067.1 (noncompliance hearings for community action grants); 45 C.F.R. §1303.4 (noncompliance hearings for Head Start and Native Americans grantees); 45 C.F.R. §1206.1 (hearings for noncompliance and refunding denials for domestic volunteer grants); 45 C.F.R. pt. 1606, 43 Fed. Reg. 32769 (1978) (legal services grants; hearing procedures for noncompliance); 40 C.F.R. §30.920 (noncompliance hearings for air and water grants).

[66] See, e.g., 42 C.F.R. pt. 51, subpt. B (comprehensive public health service grant regulations); 42 C.F.R. pt. 53 (health facilities grant regulations); 42 C.F.R. pt. 51a, subpt. A (crippled children services grant regulations); 45 C.F.R. pt. 119 (strengthening education departments grant regulations); 45 C.F.R. pt. 192 (state student incentive grant regulations); 45 C.F.R. pt. 171 (undergraduate instructional equipment grant regulations); 45 C.F.R. pt. 170, subpt. B (undergraduate facility grant regulations); 45 C.F.R. pt. 166 (adult education grant regulations).

[67] See, e.g., 45 C.F.R. §116.20; 45 C.F.R. §130.41; 45 C.F.R. §141.10; 45 C.F.R. §117.2(h); 45 C.F.R. §118.20; 45 C.F.R. §173.15(b); 45 C.F.R. §104.291; 45 C.F.R. §1361.5(a); 45 C.F.R. §1321.20(a); 45 C.F.R. §1324.10(a).

the matter unregulated [68] or assume in its program regulations that it may withhold grant payments without a hearing.[69]

No general directives from the Office of Management and Budget or other coordinating federal agency have established hearing procedures which are obligatory on grantor agencies; nor, apparently, have recommended models been provided.[70] Each federal agency is free to establish whatever grantee process it believes is due under each of its grant programs. This has resulted in a bewildering array of hearing procedures for those programs in which the grantor agency has decided to issue regulations on the subject.[71] Some communality can be found in structure, in the kinds of procedural provisions included, and in the phrasing of those provisions. Draftsmen of these codes have liberally borrowed from the efforts of others. To some extent we can, therefore, speak of "typical" rules of procedure, but must keep in mind that multiple variations exist as we go from code to code.

We can best approach an analysis of the process afforded by grantor agencies by setting forth the basics of a fairly standard set of administrative rules governing noncompliance hearings under a particular program. Major variants found in other codes can then be compared.

We will select regulations of the Office of Education which provide grantee hearings if a state may be subject to a loss of operational grants for school assistance in areas impacted by federal activity.[72] Section 5 of the establishing Act prohibits states from taking such "impact" assistance into account in determining the amount of state funds to be allocated to elementary and secondary school systems.[73] Noncompliance by a state may lead to a stoppage or reduction of payments, but the statute directs that

---

[68] See, e.g., 23 C.F.R. pts. 420, 450, 520–99, 630 (program regulations for formula highway grants); 49 C.F.R. pts. 601, 613 (urban mass transportation formula grants). The Economic Development Administration, which administers several formula grants, speaks of a "cancellation or termination action" for grantee failure to adhere to requirements without offering details. See 13 C.F.R. §305.99.

[69] The Federal Aviation Administration, for example, offers only an opporunity for reconsideration if a formula airport grant is withheld. See 14 C.F.R. §152.64(d). The Food and Nutrition Service, which administers formula grants under the National School Lunch Act of 1946, 42 U.S.C. §§1751–1769a, and the Child Nutrition Act of 1966, 42 U.S.C. §§1771–1788, simply notifies the grantee in writing of the withholding, the reasons for the action, and its effective date. See 7 C.F.R. §210.19. See also 13 C.F.R. §317.75 (formula grants to local governments for public works projects).

[70] Cf. §2(c) Exec. Order No. 11764, 39 Fed. Reg. 2575 (1974), 42 U.S.C. §2000d-1 (directs Department of Justice to issue hearing procedures for discrimination cases).

[71] See Chapter 7, note 26, *supra*, and accompanying text.

[72] 45 C.F.R. §§115.68–115.69.

[73] §5(d) Act of Sept. 30, 1950, Pub. L. 81-874, 20 U.S.C. §240(d).

"[w]henever a State educational agency or local educational agency will be adversely affected by the operation of this subsection, such agency shall be afforded notice and an opportunity for a hearing prior to the reduction or termination of payments pursuant to this subsection." [74]

Under the regulations, if the Commissioner of Education makes a "determination" that Section 5 has been violated, he must provide affected state and local educational agencies with notice of this decision and their right to a hearing. Both notice and a hearing, if requested, must take place prior to any imposition of sanctions. The regulations impose an obligation on the Commissioner to state the basis for his decision "in sufficient detail for the agencies to respond." Recipients of a notice may request a hearing within 30 days. Both noncompliance and nonconformity hearings are usually triggered in this fashion. Section 5 regulations, however, contain an untypical alternate route to a hearing. A state or local educational agency may initiate a hearing prior to a determination by the Commissioner. A state which is uncertain whether existing or planned funding actions violate Section 5 can, thus, get an advance reading on the legality of its position; similarly, a local educational agency can protect itself from state action which might jeopardize its funds by precipitating a compliance hearing. Also, the Commissioner can call a hearing if he has "reason to believe" that a state is violating the requirement. If the proceedings are initiated in this way, they may produce a "determination" of noncompliance. The way the regulations are drafted, it appears that the state or local education agency could then request another compliance hearing, even though there would seem to be little purpose served by a second hearing.

The issues of fact and law to be determined are formulated by the grantee in its request for a hearing. This cuts against most hearing regulations which give the hearing officer(s) power to define the issues to be considered.[75] The intention is most likely to promote a narrowing of the questions of fact and law by enabling the grantee to challenge less than all of the contentions specified in the noncompliance notice.

Both the time and place of the hearing are fixed by the Commissioner "with due regard to the mutual convenience of the

---

[74] §5(d)(2)(A) *id.*, 20 U.S.C. §240(d)(2)(A).
[75] See, e.g., 45 C.F.R. §16.65. Compare 45 C.F.R. §81.52 (pleadings as under Federal Rules of Civil Procedure).

268 / *Rights and Remedies Under Federal Grants*

parties." The Commissioner also selects the decision maker. He may choose one or more hearing officers from within or without the Office of Education, in his discretion.

The regulation does not specify the powers of a hearing officer(s) in the conduct of the proceeding. It does, however, authorize the adjudicator to determine that the controversy does not involve factual disputes and to thereby limit the hearing opportunity to written submissions or an informal conference.

In all cases the grantee has the right to be represented by counsel. If a hearing is held to resolve factual disputes, the grantee is guaranteed additional trial rights: to present witnesses; to cross-examine witnesses orally or through written questions; and to obtain a record of the proceedings.

The panel or hearing officer is directed to render an "initial" decision based on written findings and to provide copies to all parties. This decision and findings are forwarded to the Commissioner who may certify it as the final decision without further proceedings. He may also, in his discretion, review the case, with or without further proceedings, and reverse or modify the decision. All the parties are notified of his final determination with a written statement of the grounds.

The Section 5 regulation prohibits the Office of Education from suspending or terminating grant payments if an appropriate request for a hearing is made. When the final decision is adverse to the grantee, all payments under the Act are stopped. A state may, however, resume federal payments by restoring to local school systems the state aid which was determined to have been wrongfully withheld.

The program just reviewed has a companion which provides grants for construction of school facilities in areas containing unusually large numbers of federal employees or federally connected individuals.[76] The statute establishing this program contains standard language requiring notice and an opportunity to be heard prior to a withholding of payments for violation of any of the requirements imposed by the Act and regulations.[77]

A separate regulation [78] governs noncompliance hearings under this construction program. This procedural code follows the same basic format as that just reviewed, with some additional features. Default by the grantee in failing to request a hearing

[76] Act of Sept. 23, 1950, Pub. L. 81-815, 20 U.S.C. §§631–647.
[77] §11(a) *id.*, 20 U.S.C. §641(a).
[78] 45 C.F.R. pt. 111.

Grantee Hearing Rights / 269

within a specified period following notice, or in failing to appear at the hearing, is "deemed to be a waiver of the right to a hearing . . . and consent to the Commissioner making a decision on the basis of such information as is available to him." [79] The regulation also makes clear that the setting of a hearing does not preclude the grantee from informally requesting the Commissioner to reconsider his decision, but any such request cannot be a ground for postponing the hearing.[80]

The regulation adds some detail to the hearing process. Like many such codes, it authorize the hearing officer to issue "proper" rules of procedure for the conduct of the hearing, and specifies that:

"[t]echnical rules of evidence shall not apply to hearings . . . but rules or principles designed to assure production of the most credible evidence available and to subject testimony to test by cross-examination or by other means shall be applied by the hearing officer where reasonably necessary. All documents and other evidence offered or taken for the record shall be open to examination by the parties and opportunity shall be given to refute facts and arguments advanced on either side of of the issues . . ." [81]

Unlike the scheme in the Section 5 regulation, a hearing officer can, but need not, render a decision. He is given the option of certifying the record to the Commissioner for a final decision, accompanied by recommended findings and a proposed decision.[82] Another variant is that if the record is so certified, or if the Commissioner exercises his discretion to review an initial decision, the grantee is given the opportunity to submit its contentions in writing.[83]

An important element of Due Process is the guarantee that the decision maker will consider only evidence which has been presented at the hearing in arriving at a decision. This protection is found in many of the administrative hearing codes. For example, the hearing procedures for litigating violations of grant conditions by institutions of higher education receiving student aid funds specify that "[f]indings of fact shall be based only on evidence considered at the hearing and matters of which official notice has been taken. " [84] This regulation also provides a written appeal of

[79] 45 C.F.R. §111.2(c).
[80] 45 C.F.R. §111.4.
[81] 45 C.F.R. §111.7(b).
[82] 45 C.F.R. §111.8.
[83] 45 C.F.R. §111.9.
[84] 45 C.F.R. §168.77(a), 42 Fed. Reg. 64569 (1977). See also 45 C.F.R. §213.27 (1977):

right to the Commissioner of Education,[85] an unusual practice.[86] One other unique aspect of the higher education regulation merits attention. Most noncompliance procedural rules do not specify the effects of an adverse finding in terms of the types of sanctions which may be imposed, or their duration, or how they may be lifted. This regulation, however, meticulously spells out the potential sanctions and their effects. It makes an important modification of traditional practice by specifying that a finding of noncompliance with Title IV of the Higher Education Act need not result in a termination of funding. The decision may impose special conditions on the grantee rather than stopping federal grant payments. Such conditions may limit the number of students at an institution who may receive federal aid, establish a ceiling on Title IV payments for tuition and fees, impose special bonding requirements on the institution, or establish "other conditions as may be determined to be reasonable and appropriate." [87] A termination of payments may be extended to any or all of the 11 student aid programs established under Title IV, and stops the authority of both the institution and the Commissioner to make additional student aid awards or incur any other new obligations under the terminated program.[88] The termination decision may also specify the corrective action which the violator must take to achieve compliance, including the payment to the Office of Education of any funds illegally spent. Such repayment may be achieved by offsetting the amount against any grant funds to which the institution is entitled. An unusually severe penalty is that reinstatement of eligibility cannot be obtained for 18 months from the effective date of the termination.[89] At that time, the institution may make a written

---

"Letters expressing views or urging action and other unsponsored written material regarding matters in issue in a hearing will be placed in the corresponding section of the docket of the proceeding. These data are not deemed part of the evidence or record in the hearing."

[85] 45 C.F.R. §168.77(c)(1), 42 Fed. Reg. 64569 (1977).

[86] In the great majority of hearing procedures, review by the head of the federal department or agency is discretionary. The practice follows the recommendations of the Administrative Conference of the United States. See Recommendation 68-6, "Delegation of Final Decisional Authority Subject to Discretionary Review by the Agency," 1 C.F.R. §305.68-6.

[87] 45 C.F.R. §168.79, 42 Fed. Reg. 64570 (1977).

[88] 45 C.F.R. §168.80(a), 42 Fed. Reg. 64570 (1977).

[89] 45 C.F.R. §168.82(a), 42 Fed. Reg. 64570 (1977). The regulation is ambiguous as to whether the prohibition is just against an institution's requesting reinstatement or whether it prohibits the Office of Education from reinstating eligibility within 18 months.

showing that compliance has been achieved. If the Commissioner does not reinstate eligibility, or does so only partially, the institution gets only "an opportunity to show cause" why the Commissioner is in error.

The newer hearing codes tend to be quite elaborate; as each drafting effort builds upon its successors, it adds more and more procedural detail. Some of the more important provisions now commonly found in regulations are: burden of proof placed on the administrator proposing sanctions, unless the issue is whether the recipient failed to take required action; [90] intervention of third parties which may be affected by the decision, usually at the discretion of the hearing officer; [91] *amicus curiae* participation, ordinarily limited to written submissions; [92] rules concerning judicial notice of non-record facts, with prior opportunity to rebut such facts; [93] expanded discovery provisions, sometimes adopting the practice under the Federal Rules of Civil Procedure; [94] authorization for grantees to pay, within limits, the cost of legal representation and other litigation expenses with grant funds; [95] authorization for the grantor and grantee to negotiate a settlement of the dispute before and after the hearing; [96] authority granted to the hearing officer to modify or waive any procedural rule upon determination that no party will be unduly prejudiced and the ends of justice will be served thereby; [97] detailed specification of the authority of the hearing officer, including the right to hold pretrial conferences, to decide motions, to examine witnesses, and to control the conduct of parties and attorneys; [98] control over *ex parte* written and oral communications to the hearing officer; [99] and prohibitions on interlocutory appeals from rulings of the presiding officer.[100]

---

[90] See, e.g., 45 C.F.R. §1303.4-4(d).
[91] See, e.g., 45 C.F.R. §1386.94(b).
[92] See, e.g., 45 C.F.R. §1386.94(c).
[93] See, e.g., 45 C.F.R. §1067.1-7(L).
[94] See, e.g., 45 C.F.R. §1386.103.
[95] See, e.g., 45 C.F.R. §1206.1-9. This section, like others, limits counsel fees to $100.00 per day unless the grantor authorizes a higher rate. A proposed Legal Services Corporation regulation, permitting "the reasonable and customary rate for an attorney practicing in the locality of the counsel so retained," was rejected in the final regulation in favor of one pegging the hourly rate to federal salary levels. See Chapter 15, notes 57–59, *infra*, and accompanying text.
[96] See, e.g., 45 C.F.R. §1386.81(b).
[97] See, e.g., 45 C.F.R. §16.51.
[98] See, e.g., 45 C.F.R. §1386.101.
[99] See, e.g., 45 C.F.R. §1206.1-7(b)(2).
[100] See, e.g., 45 C.F.R. §16.71.

10

Terminations of Competitive Grants

Statutory Rights

Federal agencies have traditionally assumed the power to terminate a grant without a prior hearing if the award was discretionary and if the agency was in possession of evidence indicating noncompliance.[1] No express authority for this policy can be found in federal grant-in-aid statutes, either generically [2] or in particular acts. The statutes authorizing the award of competitive grants do not, in the great majority of cases, contain any language whatsoever referring to grantee failure to comply with the terms of the award. Nor do they speak of grant termination. There is, therefore, no call to focus attention on the question of Due Process. Congressional judgment on the matter usually does not exist at all.

One of the few exceptions is found in the programs which originated in the antipoverty legislation.[3] Owing to the turbulence attending the community action programs and their high incidence of compliance controversies,[4] Congress built into these pro-

---

[1] See, e.g., *Silva v. East Providence Housing Auth.* (II), 565 F.2d 1217 (1st Cir. 1977).

[2] The only generic provision on the subject is §453(c) General Education Provisions Act, 20 U.S.C. §1234b, which affords prior notice and an opportunity for a hearing and covers both formula and discretionary grants of the Office of Education and the National Institute of Education.

[3] Economic Opportunity Act of 1964, Pub. L. 88-452.

[4] See H.R. Rep. No. 866, 90th Cong., 1st Sess., in *1967 U.S. Code Cong. & Admin. News* 2448, 2450–51, 2491. §301 Economic Opportunity Amendments of 1967, Pub. L. 90-222, Dec. 23, 1967, added a section to the Economic Opportunity

grams a full set of Due Process rights for recipients of grants.[5] Financial assistance under the Act cannot be terminated by the Community Services Administration for the recipient's failure to comply with grant terms and conditions until "reasonable notice and opportunity for a full and fair hearing" have been afforded.[6] The pattern of hearing rights under the Community Services Act does not follow the standard congressional practice of affording Due Process rights for formula grants but not for discretionary awards. Community action funds are distributed among the states by formula,[7] yet discretion rests in the grantor in the designation and funding of community action agencies.[8] Head Start funds are similarly subject to an interstate formula,[9] with grantor discretion in the selection of grantees and determination of funding levels.[10] Hearing rights are also afforded for some of the nonformula, direct, discretionary grants authorized by the Act.[11] Yet numerous other grants authorized by the Act do not carry hearing rights, even if they are not research and demonstration but rather service programs.[12]

The Legal Services Program, which originated in the Economic Opportunity Act,[13] contains comparable hearing rights;[14] it also expressly authorizes the Legal Services Corporation "to insure the compliance of recipients and their employees with the provisions of this title and the rules, regulations, and guidelines pro-

---

Act imposing stiff federal criminal penalties for theft and willful misapplication of grant and contract funds awarded under the Act and the use of duress to secure kickbacks from employees. See §626 Community Services Act of 1974, 42 U.S.C. §2971f. The number of successful prosecutions has not been inconsiderable. See, e.g., *United States v. Minyard*, 461 F.2d 931 (9th Cir. 1972); *United States v. Cogwell*, 486 F.2d 823 (7th Cir. 1973), cert. denied, 416 U.S. 959 (1974); *United States v. Hill*, 495 F.2d 1245 (5th Cir.), cert. denied, 419 U.S. 1052 (1974); *United States v. June*, 503 F.2d 442 (8th Cir. 1974); *United States v. Riddick*, 519 F.2d 645 (8th Cir. 1975), cert. denied, 425 U.S. 960 (1976).

[5] See §§519, 557, 604, 809 Community Services Act of 1974, 42 U.S.C. §§2928h, 2929c, 2944, 2991h.

[6] §§519(3), 557(c), 604(3), 809(2), 1011(2) id., 42 U.S.C. §§2928h(3), 2929c(c), 2944(3), 2991h(2), 2996j(2).

[7] See §225 id., 42 U.S.C. §2812.

[8] See §§221(a), 222(a) id., 42 U.S.C. §§2808(a), 2809(a).

[9] See §513 id., 42 U.S.C. §2928b.

[10] See §§511, 514 id., 42 U.S.C. §§2928, 2928c.

[11] See §551 id., 42 U.S.C. §2929 (Follow Through); §803 id., 42 U.S.C. §2991b(a) (Native Americans).

[12] See, e.g., Title IV, id., 42 U.S.C. §§2901–2906 (migrant farm workers); Title VII, id., 42 U.S.C. §§2981–2985g (community economic development).

[13] Economic Opportunity Act of 1964, Pub. L. 88-452.

[14] §1011 Community Services Act of 1974, 42 U.S.C. §2996j. The domestic volunteer services program, which stems from the original antipoverty legislation, also has Due Process rights. See §412 Domestic Volunteer Services Act of 1973, 42 U.S.C. §5052.

274 / *Rights and Remedies Under Federal Grants*

mulgated pursuant to this title, and to terminate, after a hearing . . . financial support to a recipient which fails to comply." [15] Although power to terminate competitive grants for grantee misconduct has always been exercised by federal agencies, the provision just quoted is one of only two instances in which Congress has not left such authority to implication or inference.

The other example is found in the legislation which establishes a modest program of grants for arts and humanities projects.[16] Amidst sections establishing grant requirements, one finds the following language:

> "Whenever the Chairperson, after reasonable notice and opportunity to be heard, finds that—
>
> "(1) a group is not complying substantially with the provisions of this section;
>
> "(2) a state agency is not complying substantially with the provisions of this section; or
>
> "(3) any funds granted to a group or state agency have been diverted from the purposes for which they were allotted or paid;
>
> "the Chairperson shall immediately notify the Secretary of the Treasury and the group or state agency with respect to which such finding was made that no further grants will be made under this section to such group or agency until there is no longer any default or failure to comply or the diversion has been corrected, or, if compliance or correction is impossible, until such group or agency repays or arranges repayment of the Federal funds which had been improperly divested or expended." [17]

The most interesting feature of this section is the borrowing of the withholding enforcement technique common to formula grants. A noncompliance finding in a competitive grant program need not lead to termination if, in its discretion, the grantor determines that correction is possible and that the merits of the project are sufficient to justify its continuation. Yet the termination sanction is available and, in fact, the agency regulations will usually indicate that this is the expected result of a noncompliance finding.[18] As in the formula programs, the quoted provision seems

---

[15] §1006(b)(1) Community Services Act of 1974, 42 U.S.C. §2996e(b)(1).
[16] Arts and Humanities Act of 1965, 20 U.S.C. §§951–968.
[17] §5(h) Arts and Humanities Act of 1965, 20 U.S.C. §954(h) (arts grants); §7(f)(7) *id.*, 20 U.S.C. §956(f)(7) (identical provision; humanities grants).
[18] See OMB Cir. A-102, *supra*, Chapter 1, note 83, at App. L., paras. 4, 5; OMB Cir. A-110, *supra*, Chapter 1, note 83, at App. L., paras. 3, 4.

to contemplate a continuation of grant payments once compliance is achieved. Choice is thereby shifted to the grantee. It may determine that the burden of compliance, including the repayment of illegally expended federal funds, is or is not too onerous to warrant continuation of the project. Placing that decision in the grantee's hands curtails the possibility of grantor abuse in the selection of sanctions. It permits the continuation of projects which have foundered on the technicalities of federal grant requirements but which are providing valuable benefits and services. On the other hand, it lessens the deterrent effect of sanctions. For example, a grantee could consciously choose to divert federal funds to purposes known to be impermissible. Since the repayment obligation appears to arise only if the grantee wishes to receive further federal payments,[19] it could respond to a noncompliance finding by closing down the project.[20] And by affording the additional alternative of correcting and continuing, the provision would seem to lessen grantee inhibitions about violating grant requirements.

A common thread connecting the programs discussed above is that the recipients of grants are likely to be community groups.[21]

[19] This follows from our premise that the federal grantor cannot pursue past illegal expenditures without express authority by statute or regulations. See Chapter 3, *supra,* at pp. 98–100.

[20] This would be true, of course, for any program in which the federal agency has no express authority to recover federal funds already spent in violation of federal standards. A grantee can normally terminate a grant project at will. See Chapter 3, *supra,* at p. 107; Office of Human Development, *Grants Administration Manual* ch. 9, sec. C, para. 2, 42 Fed. Reg. 21076 (1977):
"When the grantee wishes to terminate grant support unilaterally, the authorized grantee official shall provide written notification to the granting office, setting forth the reasons for such termination, the effective date, and in the case of partial terminations, the portion to be terminated. The responsible granting official shall provide the grantee with written acknowledgement of the notice and written instructions regarding termination or close-out procedures";
45 C.F.R. §100a.496(a)(2) (Office of Education direct grants):
"grants or contracts may be terminated in whole or in part . . . [b]y the recipient, upon written notification to the Commissioner, setting forth the reasons for the termination, the effective date and in the case of partial terminations, the portion to be terminated";
45 C.F.R. §100b.495 (Office of Education state grants):
"If a State desires at any time not to participate in a Federal program . . . the State shall refund to the Federal Government any unexpended or unobligated funds which have been paid to the State agency under such Federal program";
Rubinstein v. Mayor of Baltimore, 295 F. Supp. 108 (D. Md. 1969). But see OMB Cir. A-102, *supra,* Chapter 1, note 83, at App. L., para. 5(b) ("when both parties agree"); OMB Cir. A-110, *supra,* Chapter 1, note 83, at App. L., para. 4(b)(same).

[21] See generally S. A. Levitan, *The Great Society's Poor Law: A New Approach to Poverty* 109–31 (1969); H. W. Hallman, *Neighborhood Control of Public Programs: Case Studies of Community Corporations and Neighborhood Boards* (1970) (hereinafter cited as H. W. Hallman).

While state agencies, local governments, school systems, and other institutions which traditionally provide public services may be eligible for grants, the bulk of the funds under community action, domestic volunteers, legal services, and arts and humanities is intended for "grass-roots" organizations. The delivery of public services by nonprofit community organizations has been chiefly stimulated and nurtured by federal grants, with the above programs at the core of the effort. The express concern with compliance issues in such grant statutes, which bypass traditional institutional service providers, may reflect a distrust of the ability and willingness of community groups to abide by grant requirements.[22] This concern may be legitimate, given the "technicalities" which abound in the field of federal grants, the prevalent unfamiliarity with federal grant law, and rampant ambiguity attending federal requirements. In addition, a community group's lack of political accountability may be seen as a serious obstacle to the prevention of legal carelessness.[23] Such grants, by establishing "competing" providers of public services, also create intense friction with the executive and political branches of state and local governments.[24] To survive in the face of such formidable adversaries, these experiments in alternative mechanisms of service delivery must be structured and administered with exceptional care. Each dereliction of each community grantee weakens the political and policy foundation for such an effort.

On the other hand, the presence of these special provisions can be viewed in a quite different light.[25] The executive branch has never doubted its authority to police grantee activities and to terminate for violations of federal standards, even though no express or even implied authority appeared in the grant-in-aid statute. One might consider such provisions as superfluous, except to the extent that they concede hearing rights to grantees. That, indeed, is their practical effect. If they did not exist, administrators would enforce compliance through threats of and actual termina-

[22] See, e.g., H.R. Rep. No. 866, 90th Cong., 1st Sess., in *1967 U.S. Code Cong. & Admin. News* 2428, 2447–51.

[23] H. W. Hallman, *supra,* note 21, at 214–18.

[24] See, e.g., H.R. Rep. No. 866, 90th Cong. 1st Sess., in *1967 U.S. Code Cong. & Admin. News* 2428, 2447–51; Selover, W.C., "The View From Capitol Hill: Harassment and Survival," in *On Fighting Poverty: Perspectives From Experience* 158–86 (J.L. Sundquist ed. 1969).

[25] Sections in grant statutes establishing grantee Due Process rights are rarely discussed in congressional committee reports. They receive either no mention or are repeated verbatim in section-by-section analyses. In most cases, we are left to speculate about legislative motive and intent.

tions, but without affording grantees hearing opportunities. Because the real impact of these provisions is to guarantee Due Process rights to grantees, one may emphasize their shield rather than their sword attributes. In this light, a different set of concerns and purposes may be advanced. For instance, because community groups are particularly dependent on grantor good will (their grants are discretionary) and especially unfamiliar with the intricacies of federal grant law, they can be seen as needing exceptional protection from grantor overreaching. Because of the fragile nature of their very being, they need an adequate forum to expose tenuous accusations.

When Congress speaks of compliance questions in competitive grant statutes without mentioning grantee hearing rights, the natural tendency is to imply that Congress did not intend to concede such rights. This, for instance, is the import of Title XV of the Public Health Service Act which established a major federal initiative in the delivery of health services.[26] The thrust of the legislation is to improve the delivery of health care through the creation of a national network of health systems agencies and state health planning and development agencies. Both types of agencies are offered federal financing to improve health planning and administration. The Secretary of HEW enters into yearly agreements, and he is instructed to review the operations of each grantee not less often than once each year to determine if the agency is complying with the statute's requirements and its commitments under the agreement.[27] The Secretary may terminate agreements with state agencies prior to the end of their term upon a determination that the agencies are not complying with or effectively carrying out their provisions.[28] The only Due Process requirement is that the Secretary give notice to the state's governor. Similarly, unilateral power is seemingly vested in the Secretary on the yearly decision to renew such agreements.[29] Health systems agencies fare no better. The following actions can be taken by the Public Health Service without, apparently, any formal mechanism of protest and challenge: reject the governor's designation of a health services area; [30]

[26] National Health Planning and Resources Development Act of 1974, §§1501–1536 Public Health Service Act, 42 U.S.C. §§300k–300n-5.
[27] See §§1522(c), 1535(a) Public Health Service Act, 42 U.S.C. §§300m-1(c), 300n-4(a).
[28] §1521(b)(3)(B) *id.*, 42 U.S.C. §300m(b)(3)(B).
[29] See §1521(b)(4) *id.*, 42 U.S.C. §300m(b)(4).
[30] See §1511(b)(3)(B)(i) *id.*, 42 U.S.C. §300"1"(b)(3)(B)(i).

revoke a conditional designation of a health systems agency; [31] cancel the final designation if the grantor determines that the designee is not complying with or effectively carrying out the agreement; [32] terminate the agreement, within a project year, and substitute another entity; [33] and overturn the agency's disapproval of a federal health grant to another entity within the jurisdiction.[34]

The dearth of hearing rights is surprising. The amount of planning and administration grants under Title XV is determined by formula,[35] the intention being regularly to provide such funds to each finally designated agency; also, other grants under the Act are of a formula type.[36] Because refusal to renew a designation or a revocation of the designation within the term effectuates a cutoff of entitlement funds, one would expect hearing rights equivalent to those in most formula programs. The distinguishing feature is, perhaps, that these grantor actions do not deprive a jurisdiction of its health funds since a new entity will become the recipient.

Congress rarely disqualifies a governmental or nonprofit institution from receiving federal funds for illegal acts under grant programs. At most, the entity will lose funds under the particular program in which the violation occurs, still retaining its eligibility for grants under other programs and subsequent grants in the program involving the finding of noncompliance. An important exception is found in Title IV of the Higher Education Act of 1965,[37] which provides federal support for a variety of student aid activities. The eligibility of an institution for assistance under any of the Title IV programs can be limited, suspended, or terminated for violation of any provision of Title IV and its regulations,[38] or for "substantial misrepresentation of the nature of its educational program, financial charges, or employability of its graduates." [39] Perhaps because most of an institution's Title IV funds are nondiscretionary entitlements and students, the intended beneficiaries, will not be able to receive the support from alternate grantees if

[31] See §1515(b)(3) id., 42 U.S.C. §300"1"-4(b)(3).
[32] See §1515(c)(1) id., 42 U.S.C. §300"1"-4(c)(1).
[33] See §1515(d) id., 42 U.S.C. §300"1"-4(d).
[34] See §1513(e)(2) id., 42 U.S.C. §300"1"-2(e)(2).
[35] See §1516(b) id., 42 U.S.C. §300"1"-5(b) (health systems agency grants); 42 C.F.R. §123.204 (grants to state health planning and development agencies).
[36] See §1640 Public Health Service Act, 42 U.S.C. §300t (area health services development funds).
[37] 20 U.S.C. §§1070–1089.
[38] §497A Higher Education Act of 1965, 20 U.S.C. §1088f-1.
[39] §497A(c) id., 20 U.S.C. §1088f-1(c).

their institution loses its eligibility, the Commissioner must afford notice and an opportunity to be heard on the record prior to an adverse finding. Similarly, a hospital is entitled to a hearing on the record prior to a loss of eligibility for federal health grants because it has denied admitting privileges to a qualified member of the National Health Service Corps.[40]

Eligibility may be terminated in some programs not because of the recipient's poor or illegal performance but because the area served by the grantee no longer qualifies for funding. Public works, public employment, and economic development programs sometimes aim to inject federal funds only into areas of exceptional economic need.[41] Economic indicators, such as levels of unemployment, trigger eligibility for government aid, or extra quantities of assistance, on and off. If an area is receiving financial assistance, one would expect a prior hearing on the question of continued eligibility because of the adverse impact a program shutdown would have on area residents. Also, the entitlement may be statutorily vested upon a showing of qualifying economic indicators.[42] Yet in the major program of this nature, the Public Works and Economic Development Act of 1965,[43] no hearing rights are given by statute or regulations if the Secretary of Commerce, pursuant to his mandated annual review, withdraws his designation of an economic development district or area.[44]

Certain health education funds are targeted to areas of health manpower shortage.[45] As in the case of economic development area designations, no hearing rights are available to challenge either initial or subsequent area eligibility determinations.[46]

[40] §335(e) Public Health Service Act, 42 U.S.C. §254h(e).
[41] See, e.g., Title VI, Comprehensive Employment and Training Act of 1973, 29 U.S.C. §§961–970 (countercyclical public service employment); §903 Public Works and Economic Development Act of 1965, 42 U.S.C. §3243 (economic adjustment assistance; areas of economic deterioration); §1002 id., 42 U.S.C. §3246a (job opportunities; high unemployment areas).
[42] See, e.g., §604 Comprehensive Employment and Training Act of 1973, 29 U.S.C. §964 (". . . [funds] shall be allocated . . ."); §§304(a), (b) Public Works and Economic Development Act of 1965, 42 U.S.C. §§3153(a), (b) ("[s]uch funds shall be apportioned; [f]unds apportioned . . . shall be available"). But see, e.g., §101(a) id., 42 U.S.C. §3131(a) (Secretary of Commerce "authorized . . . to make direct grants").
[43] 42 U.S.C. §§3131–3246h.
[44] See §§402, 403(c) Public Works and Economic Development Act of 1965, 42 U.S.C. §§3162, 3171(c); 13 C.F.R. §§302.40, 303.10.
[45] See §332 Public Health Service Act, 42 U.S.C. §254e.
[46] Ibid. See also 42 C.F.R. pt. 5, 43 Fed. Reg. 1586 (1978).

280 / *Rights and Remedies Under Federal Grants*

Regulations

We have already seen that Office of Management and Budget circulars establish, for competitive grants, the operational principle that no hearing is necessary before such a grant is terminated for cause.[47] The directives are silent on the question of post-termination hearing opportunities, thus leaving the matter to each agency's discretion. One finds with monotonous regularity provisions comparable to the OMB directives in grant program regulations.[48] Grantees are warned that failure to comply with grant legislation, regulations, or terms may result in withholding of payments or termination of the grant. While notice is given before the imposition of sanctions, no hearing is provided. Grantees are sometimes also advised that the same consequences can be expected if material representations in the grant application are found to be substantially false.[49]

Despite the severity of the language in such regulations, it is unusual for federal agencies to terminate grants without affording the grantee a chance to bring correctable practices into conformity. Most grantors recognize the serious consequences of a termination and its often self-defeating nature. For example, one grant administration manual recognizes the importance of such a decision in the following announcement:

> "the decision to terminate grant support represents a serious judgment that must reflect a thorough analysis of all relevant factors. It is based on a determination that the grantee has failed to comply with one or more of the terms and conditions of the grant, and that such failure is of sufficient magnitude to warrant the termination of grant support." [50]

Though it is not obligatory, most federal agencies after discovering substantial grantee noncompliance will notify grantees of their findings, specify the steps which must be taken to achieve compliance, and offer a reasonable time for corrective action.[51] If the grantee does not respond in acceptable fashion, the grantor will probably suspend the authority of the grantee to obligate federal funds. During the period of suspension, the recipient will be given

---

[47] See Chapter 7, note 86, *supra*, and accompanying text.
[48] See, e.g., 45 C.F.R. §74.115(a), 43 Fed. Reg. 34076 (1978) (HEW).
[49] See, e.g., 45 C.F.R. §64.7(c) (NIH training grants).
[50] Office of Human Development, *Grants Administration Manual* ch. 9, sec. B, para. 1, 42 Fed. Reg. 21047, 21076 (1977).
[51] See, e.g., ch. 9, sec. B, *id.*, 42 Fed. Reg. 21047, 21076 (1977).

a further opportunity to take corrective action. Failing this, the grant will be terminated.

The Department of Health, Education and Welfare, which administers more than half of all federal competitive grants,[52] affords an appeal following termination of such a grant.[53] Although the regulation, 45 C.F.R. Part 16, refers to an "appeals process," it actually establishes a procedure for a full adjudicative hearing; it is appellate only in the sense that a termination decision has already been reached by a branch of HEW. Because that prior decision carries no presumptions of correctness and, in fact, is not reviewed for error, the "appeal" is akin to a trial *de novo*.

The regulation covers programs of the Office of Education and National Institute of Education, yet terminations of grants awarded by these agencies had to be *preceded* by a hearing opportunity under Section 434(c) of the General Education Provisions Act,[54] before its 1978 revision. Thus, the regulations of the Office of Education speak of termination "after affording the recipient reasonable notice and an opportunity to be heard," [55] and insure this result by postponing the effective date of a termination until a final decision is rendered following a Part 16 hearing.[56] The National Institute of Education employs the same technique.[57]

Unlike other grant hearing codes, Part 16 establishes a court, denominated the "Departmental Grant Appeals Board," which sits regularly to adjudicate various grant disputes within its jurisdiction. The board is not independent of the department; on the contrary it is established within the Office of the Secretary, and its members, including the chairman, are selected by the head of HEW. While members of the board may be department employees, one may not sit on a hearing panel if he has "been associated with the case to be appealed either directly or by reason of organizational affiliation." [58]

The board's jurisdiction is limited by both the type of dispute

[52] As of the time of writing, the Department of Health, Education and Welfare is administering 312 separate competitive grant programs.
[53] 45 C.F.R. pt. 16. A separate Audit Hearing Board was established by the Office of Education to hear appeals from audit disallowances of expenditures under Title I of the Elementary and Secondary Education Act. See 37 Fed. Reg. 23002 (1972); 41 Fed. Reg. 28568 (1976). This function will be assumed by the new Education Appeal Board. See §451 General Education Provisions Act, 20 U.S.C. §1234.
[54] 20 U.S.C. §1232c(c) (1976).
[55] 45 C.F.R. §100a.495(a)(3).
[56] 45 C.F.R. §100a.495(h).
[57] See 45 C.F.R. §1424.8(h).
[58] 45 C.F.R. §16.4(b).

and the type of program involved. It may adjudicate controversies which concern: termination of a grant, in whole or part, for noncompliance; determinations that expenses paid with grant funds were not allowable or insufficiently documented; disapproval of requests to incur expenditures; decisions on cost allocation plans and indirect cost rates; and voiding of grants.[59] The program within which the dispute occurs must involve "direct, discretionary, project grants."[60] This definition may cause ambiguity with respect to coverage of hybrid programs containing both formula and discretionary elements. For example, distribution of funds among the states is determined by formula in the emergency school aid program,[61] but specific grants are awarded on a competitive, project basis.[62] The Office of Education originally opted to provide prior hearings on the formula-state-plan noncompliance model.[63] Later, the Office of Education adopted a Part 16 review for controversies in this program, citing as grounds a shortage of administrative law judges and the absence of a statutory mandate for "formal adjudication."[64] If the statute calls for different procedures for the termination of a competitive grant, Part 16 is inapplicable.[65]

A hearing may be sought by a grantee which is officially notified of an adverse determination. The board chairman has power to determine whether jurisdictional prerequisites have been met. These include: a written notice of an adverse determination; application for a hearing made within the prescribed time; grantor decision of a type within the board's jurisdiction; a program covered by Part 16; and grantee exhaustion of any informal review procedures which the grantor agency has established by regulation.[66]

---

[59] 45 C.F.R. §16.5(a).
[60] 45 C.F.R. §16.2(a).
[61] §705 Emergency School Aid Act, 20 U.S.C. §1604.
[62] §706 id., 20 U.S.C. §1605.
[63] 45 C.F.R. §185.45 (1977).
[64] 45 C.F.R. §185.45, 43 Fed. Reg. 36250 (1978).
[65] For example, Follow Through grants, though competitive, can be terminated only after a "full and fair hearing," see §554(c) Community Services Act of 1974, 42 U.S.C. §2929c(c), which is provided by 45 C.F.R. §158.84.
[66] 45 C.F.R. pt. 75 provides informal procedures for resolving cost allocation plan and indirect cost rate disputes arising from HEW grants. A grantee dissatisfied with a plan or rate decision is offered the opportunity to argue informally for reversal to the program's regional director. 45 C.F.R. §§50.401–50.406 establishes procedures which must be exhausted before a grantee of the Public Health Service can invoke Part 16. An adverse decision of the type covered by Part 16 may be submitted to a PHS review committee. The committee is provided "all background materials" by the grantor and, at its option, may invite the parties

Hearing procedures substantially follow the format of noncompliance and nonconformity hearings established for formula grant programs, including full rights to present, test, and rebut testimonial and written evidence. One important difference is that the grantor agency which adversarily defends its prior determination in the board proceeding is given full authority to revoke or modify an unfavorable decision. The hearing panel's determination is "initial" and may be reviewed at the discretion of the head of the constituent agency whose grant action is under attack. The decision of this official is final. Therefore, while Part 16 requires the final decision maker to base his decision upon the evidence and argument below, and mandates a "written statement of the grounds for such modifications or reversal," [67] the finality of the decision precludes further administrative review.

The Community Services Administration, ACTION, the Office of Human Development, and the Legal Services Corporation have fleshed out detailed procedures pursuant to their statutory mandates to provide a "full and fair hearing" prior to a termination of competitive grants awarded under the Community Services Act and the Domestic Volunteer Services Act.[68] Three different but virtually identical regulations establish such hearings,[69] and a fourth borrows from and improves on the lot.[70] The grantee is entitled to detailed notice of the grounds supporting termination and an opportunity for a hearing prior to imposition of sanctions. The burden is on the federal grantor agency to prove

---

to "discuss" the matter and to submit additional information. 45 C.F.R. §204.4 (1977) provided an informal review of grant decisions of the now defunct Social and Rehabilitation Service. A grant appeals officer would "reconsider the determination appealed from considering any material submitted by the grantee and any other material necessary." Compare 45 C.F.R. §201.14 (1977) which implements the statutory requirement, §1116(d) Social Security Act, 42 U.S.C. §1316(d), that a state be given, on request, reconsideration of the disallowance of federal payments under the welfare, medical assistance, and social services programs. While an evidentiary hearing is not contemplated, the reconsideration of regional decisions is conducted by the head of the grantor agency; the state has a right to inspect the material submitted by the regional office; the state can submit additional written evidence and argument; a conference with the agency head is available, including a transcript of the meeting; and the decision must be in writing, based on the administrative record, and justified by the facts and law.

[67] 45 C.F.R. §16.10(d).
[68] See notes 5, 14, *supra*.
[69] See 45 C.F.R. §1067.1 (hearings prior to termination of community action grants); 45 C.F.R. §1303.4 (hearings prior to termination of Head Start or Native Americans grants); 45 C.F.R. §1206.1 (hearings prior to termination of domestic volunteer grants).
[70] See 45 C.F.R. pt. 1606, 43 Fed. Reg. 32769–72 (1978). The Legal Services Corporation's new hearing procedure in cases of intended grant terminations is discussed in Chapter 15, *infra*, at pp. 354–55.

284 / Rights and Remedies Under Federal Grants

the violation, unless the question involves grantee failure to take required steps under the grant commitment. The hearing examiner may be either the official authorized to make the grant or an independent hearing officer. In the latter case, an initial decision is reviewable by such grantor official on exceptions and briefs. Full opportunities are afforded to submit and rebut evidence, oral and documentary, and a hearing transcript is available. Findings of fact and conclusions of law are made on the record. A final appeal to the agency head is allowed as of right, and this official may hold further hearings, permit briefs, or review on the basis of the record and arguments below, as he deems convenient.

Project grants made by federal agencies other than the four reviewed in the preceding paragraphs may apparently be terminated without either a pre- or post-termination hearing.

The hearing procedure set up in 45 C.F.R. Part 16 by HEW is not mandated by statute; rather, it is an example of the development of Due Process rights by grantor agencies.[71] Such examples, unfortunately, are relatively uncommon.[72] More typical are provisions like the following:

> "(b) *Termination for cause.* The Department may terminate a state agency's participation in the program in whole, or in part, whenever it is determined that the State agency has failed to comply with the conditions of the program. The Department shall promptly notify the State agency in writing of the termination, together with the effective date, and shall allow the State 30 days to respond. In instances where the State does respond, the Department shall inform the State of its final determination no later than 30 days after the State responds. A State agency shall terminate a sponsor's participation in the program by written notice whenever it is determined by [the Food and Nutrition Service] or the State agency that the sponsor has failed to comply with the conditions of the program. . . ." [73]

Some agencies may provide an informal post-termination review process based on written submissions.[74]

---

[71] See also 42 C.F.R. §§122.108, 123.108 (hearing opportunity if designation agreements under Title XV of the Public Health Service Act are terminated; statute does not require such hearings); 38 C.F.R. §17.285 (Veterans Administration; Exchange of Information Grant Program).

[72] See generally Chapter 1, notes 96–99, *supra*.

[73] 7 C.F.R. §225.18(b), 43 Fed. Reg. 4632 (1978) (proposed rule: Summer Food Service Program for Children).

[74] See, e.g., National Science Foundation, *Grant Policy Manual* §665, 42 Fed. Reg. 38746, 38770–71 (1977).

11

Grant Suspensions

Because our discussion of grant "suspension" in this chapter uses that word in a particular sense, we must commence with some terminological analysis. The words "suspension" and "withholding" could be equally used to describe the situation in which the grantor has already determined grantee noncompliance (whether or not the finding is the result of a hearing) and is retaining grant funds until correction is satisfactorily achieved. In fact, Congress commonly speaks of "withholding,"[1] while the executive branch refers to "suspension."[2]

That, however, is not the only situation in which grant funds may be retained for violations of federal standards. Because in various programs grantees are afforded notice and an opportunity to be heard prior to the imposition of any sanction, the need may arise to stop federal payments before a noncompliance decision is reached. We need to be able to describe and distinguish withholding in this other situation because of its different Due Process implications. Some modern federal grant statutes refer to such predetermination action as a "suspension,"[3] and we shall follow that practice.

[1] See statutory provisions cited in Chapter 9, note 2, *supra*. But see §407(b)(1) Drug Abuse Office and Treatment Act of 1972, 21 U.S.C. §1174(b)(1) ("suspension" after finding of noncompliance); §321(b)(1) Comprehensive Alcohol Abuse and Alcoholism Prevention, Treatment and Rehabilitation Act of 1970, 42 U.S.C. §4581(b)(1) (same).

[2] See, e.g., OMB Cir. A-102, *supra*, Chapter 1, note 83, at Attachment L., para. 2(d); OMB Cir. A-110, *supra*, Chapter 1, note 83, at Attachment L., para 2(b).

[3] See, e.g., §519(2) Community Services Act of 1974, 42 U.S.C. §2928h(2); §412(1) Domestic Volunteer Services Act of 1973, 42 U.S.C. §5052(1).

286 / *Rights and Remedies Under Federal Grants*

We can quickly summarize the rules which our statutory survey has revealed. In the great majority of grant statutes, whether formula or competitive, Congress neither authorizes nor prohibits such pretermination or prewithholding suspensions. Not speaking to the matter, it has no occasion to deal with hearing opportunities prior to the imposition of a suspension. That practice holds true even in statutes which contain noncompliance provisions.[4] In the small cluster of laws in which the topic is covered, Congress has afforded grantees "reasonable notice and an opportunity to show cause why such action should not be taken";[5] the show cause opportunity, however, may be denied if the grantor considers that an "emergency situation" is presented.[6] It is interesting to note that the legislative committee which authorized the Commissioner of Education to suspend grant payments pending the outcome of a termination proceeding warned against a misuse of the power to harass school districts and other grant recipients.[7]

In the absence of contrary directives from Congress, federal agencies have traditionally assumed the power to suspend assistance upon receiving information of grantee violations of grant conditions.[8] Suspension can be effected without affording the grantee any hearing rights, formal or informal.[9] OMB circulars instruct federal administrators as follows:

> "All Federal grantor agencies shall provide procedures to be followed when a grantee has failed to comply with the grant award stipulations, standards, or conditions. When that occurs, the grantor agency may, on reasonable notice to the grantee, suspend the grant, and withhold further payments, or prohibit the grantee

[4] See, e.g., statutory sections cited in Chapter 10, notes 27–34, *supra*.

[5] See §604(2) Community Services Act of 1974, 42 U.S.C. §2944(2) (community action programs); §519(2) *id.*, 42 U.S.C. §2928(h)(2) (Head Start); §809(1) *id.*, 42 U.S.C. §2991h(1) (Native Americans); §554(b) *id.*, 42 U.S.C. §2929c(b) (Follow Through); §1011(1) *id.*, 42 U.S.C. §2996j(1) (Legal Services Program: due process hearing within 30 days of suspension); §412(1) Domestic Volunteer Service Act of 1973, 42 U.S.C. §5052(1) (emergency suspension limited to 30 days); §§434(b)(2), 453(c) General Education Provisions Act, 20 U.S.C. §§1232c(b)(2), 1234b(c) (covers all grant programs of Office of Education and National Institute of Education).

[6] The Act last cited in the preceding footnote does not contain the "emergency situation" exception. See also §106(e) Comprehensive Employment and Training Act of 1973, 29 U.S.C. §816(e).

[7] See S. Rep. No. 1026, 93d Cong., 2d Sess., in *1974 U.S. Code Cong. & Admin. News* 4248, 4249.

[8] See, e.g., OMB Cir. A-102, *supra*, Chapter 1, note 83, at Attachment L; OMB Cir. A-110, *supra*, Chapter 1, note 83, at Attachment L.

[9] See, e.g., 13 C.F.R. §317.75(a) (local public works program).

from incurring additional obligations of grant funds, pending corrective action by the grantee or a decision to terminate. . . ."[10]

During the period of suspension the grantee is unable to obligate federal funds without specific authorization, although it can make payments on costs incurred prior to the effective date of the suspension. Thus, in the absence of quickly available nonfederal financial resources, a notice of suspension will immediately stop a project. In most federal programs, this can be done on suspicion alone. There is no standard requiring grantor agencies to act only on the basis of a *prima facie* case or substantial evidence. Nor are grantees guaranteed a chance, prior to suspension, to rebut whatever evidence the grantor has at hand. Most federal agencies will, in fact, give some warning and opportunity to respond. For example, the Office of Human Development of HEW states the following:

> "When conditions are identified which may be serious enough to cause the granting office to consider termination, the grantee institution shall be advised by letter of the nature of the problem and that failure to correct the deficiency may result in suspension or termination of the grant. The grantee shall respond in writing within thirty (30) days of the date of such letter, describing the action or the plans designed to correct the deficiency.
>
> "If a satisfactory written response to the letter described above is not received within thirty (30) days of the date of such letter, the granting office may issue a notice suspending authority to obligate grant funds in whole or in part. The notice of suspension will be sent by certified mail (return receipt requested), shall set forth the effective date of the suspension, and shall identify any costs which may be incurred by the grantee during the period of suspension."[11]

If a grantor is required to give notice and a hearing before it can withhold on a formula grant or terminate a competitive grant, some protest rights will be ordinarily given to a grantee before payments are suspended. Some statutes so require;[12] in other cases the right is created by regulation.[13]

The Community Services Administration is obliged to afford

[10] OMB Cir. A-102, *supra,* Chapter 1, note 83, at Attachment L., para. 4; OMB Cir. A-110, *supra,* Chapter 1, note 83, at Attachment L., para. 3.
[11] Office of Human Development, *Grants Administration Manual* ch. 9, sec. B., paras. 2–3, 42 Fed. Reg. 21047, 21076 (April 22, 1977).
[12] See note 5, *supra.*
[13] See note 11, *supra,* and accompanying text.

recipients "reasonable notice and an opportunity to show cause why such action should not be taken" before it suspends financial assistance.[14] The agency has interpreted the show cause requirement as being satisfied by: notice of intent to suspend which offers details concerning the alleged breach or threatened breach of federal requirements; notice of the suspension's effective date; grantee opportunity to oppose the action through the submission of written materials; and the right to an informal meeting to argue against suspension.[15] There are, however, no standards governing the reviewing officer's decision. Presumably, if the grantor can make any reasonable showing of a probable violation, the suspension will go into effect.

Regulations of other agencies either follow the above pattern [16] or are even more vague, simply referring to the grantee's right to show cause at an informal meeting.[17]

Even if the agency's policy is to give an informal hearing opportunity prior to suspension of payments, it retains the authority to cut off federal payments immediately in a situation of "emergency." [18] Such situations have been variously and vaguely defined as: where the grantor believes that there has been an illegal use of program funds and that immediate action is necessary to protect the integrity of the grant program; [19] where the risk of substantial injury to or loss of project funds and property is sufficiently serious to outweigh the policy favoring a prior show cause opportunity; [20] where criminal violations may be involved; [21] or cases in which violation of any law, regulation, or guideline is so serious that immediate suspension is justified.[22]

---

[14] See §604(2) Community Services Act of 1974, 42 U.S.C. §2944(2). See also §§169(a), 186(a) Elementary and Secondary Education Act of 1965, 20 U.S.C. §§2816(a), 2836(a), as rewritten by Education Amendments of 1978, Pub. L. 95-561, Nov. 1, 1978; §434(b)(2) General Education Provisions Act, 20 U.S.C. §1232c(b)(2).

[15] 45 C.F.R. §1067.1-4.

[16] See, e.g., 45 C.F.R. §1303.4 (Head Start; Native Americans); 45 C.F.R. §1206.1-4 (domestic volunteer programs). Compare 45 C.F.R. §168.75 (suspension of institutional eligibility for grants under the Higher Education Act; despite different phraseology the procedure is basically the same). The new regulations of the Legal Services Corporation are discussed in Chapter 15, *infra,* at pp. 354–55.

[17] See, e.g., 45 C.F.R. §100a.495(f) (programs of Office of Education); 45 C.F.R. §1424.8(f) (programs of National Institute of Education).

[18] Such power is either explicitly given by statute, see notes 5–6, *supra,* or assumed under the agency's regulatory power. See, e.g., 29 C.F.R. §98.16(c) (comprehensive employment and training program).

[19] *Ibid.*

[20] See 45 C.F.R. §1206.1-4(c)(1)(i) (domestic volunteer programs).

[21] See 45 C.F.R. §1303.4(a)(2) (Head Start).

[22] See 45 C.F.R. §1206.1-4(c)(1)(iii) (domestic volunteer programs).

12

Rights of Applicants for Federal Funds

In the last three chapters our focus was on adverse grantor actions during the term of a grant based on the recipient's failure to adhere to federal requirements. This chapter takes us to a prior point in time—when the affected entity has been frustrated in its efforts to obtain federal funding. We shall review the statutory and administrative Due Process rights of applicants for government aid in three distinguishable situations: when the request is for entitlement funds provided under a formula program; when the applicant is seeking a discretionary grant; and when a grantee seeks refunding of a competitive grant project.

Formula Funding Decisions

In formula programs requiring the approval of a state plan, Congress typically requires the Federal Government to offer the state notice and opportunity to be heard prior to disapproval.[1]

[1] See, e.g., §1603(b) Public Health Service Act, 42 U.S.C. §300o-2(b) (health facilities); §237(c) Community Mental Health Centers Act, 42 U.S.C. §2689t(c); §182 Elementary and Secondary Education Act of 1965, 20 U.S.C. §2832, as rewritten by §101 Education Amendments of 1978, Pub. L. 95-561, Nov. 1, 1978 (education of disadvantaged children); §6(c)(3) Library Services and Construction Act of 1956, 20 U.S.C. §351d(c)(3); §5(g) Act of Sept. 30, 1950, Pub. L. 81-874, 20 U.S.C. §240(g), as added by §1008 Education Amendments of 1978, Pub. L. 95-561, Nov. 1, 1978; §1004(b) National Defense Education Act of 1958, 20 U.S.C. §584(b); §6(c) Act of Sept. 23, 1950, Pub. L. 81-815, 20 U.S.C. §636(c) (impact aid; construction); §108(a) Higher Education Act of 1965, 20 U.S.C. §1007(a) (university community services; lifelong learning program); §415D(a) *id.*, 20 U.S.C. §1070c-3(a) (state student incentives); §607(a) *id.*, 20 U.S.C. §1127(a) (undergraduate instruc-

There are, however, more than a few exceptions.[2] In most cases, one finds in the same statutory section prior hearing opportunities for both grantor action rejecting a state plan (nonconformity) and grantor action withholding payments (noncompliance).[3]

The format for nonconformity sections is simple and fairly standard: "The Secretary shall not finally disapprove any State plan submitted under this Act, or any modification thereof, without first affording the agency administering the plan reasonable notice and opportunity for a hearing." [4] As in hearing opportunities for noncompliance, process must precede final grantor action,

---

tional equipment); §§704(b), 708(a)(1) *id.*, 20 U.S.C. §§1132a-3(b), 1132a-7(a)(1) (undergraduate academic facilities); §1001(c) *id.*, 20 U.S.C. §1135(c) (state plans for community colleges); §306(b) Adult Education Act of 1966, 20 U.S.C. §1205(b); §613(c) Education of the Handicapped Act, 20 U.S.C. §1413(c) (state assistance); §109(b)(1) Vocational Education Act, 20 U.S.C. §2309(b)(1) (state program); §133(c) Developmental Disabilities Services and Facilities Construction Act, 42 U.S.C. §6063(c); §101(b) Rehabilitation Act of 1973, 29 U.S.C. §721(b) (state formula grants for vocational rehabilitation); §104(d) Comprehensive Employment and Training Act of 1973, 29 U.S.C. §814(d) (plan of prime sponsor); §307(c) Older Americans Act of 1965, 42 U.S.C. §3027(c) (state formula grants for social services for elderly); §105(e) Clean Air Act of 1963, as amended by Pub. L. 95-95, Aug. 7, 1977, 42 U.S.C. §7405(e); §223(d) Juvenile Justice and Delinquency Prevention Act, 42 U.S.C. §5633(d); §510 Omnibus Crime Control and Safe Streets Act of 1968, 42 U.S.C. §3758.

[2] See, e.g., §314(d)(3) Public Health Service Act, 42 U.S.C. §246(d)(3) (comprehensive health planning and services); Title X, *id.*, 42 U.S.C. §§300–300a-8 (family planning services); Title XVI, pt. F, *id.*, 42 U.S.C. §300t (area health services development funds); Title V, Social Security Act, 42 U.S.C. §§701–716 (crippled children services; maternal and child health services); Comprehensive Alcohol Abuse and Alcoholism Prevention, Treatment and Rehabilitation Act of 1972, 42 U.S.C. §§4541–4593; Drug Abuse Office and Treatment Act of 1972, 21 U.S.C. §§1101–1194; §418B Higher Education Act of 1965, 20 U.S.C. §1070d-3 (education information centers); §493C *id.*, 20 U.S.C. §1088b-3 (student financial assistance training); §619 Education of the Handicapped Act, 20 U.S.C. §1419 (state incentive grants); Title III, pt. C, Education Amendments of 1976, 20 U.S.C. §§2501–2565 (state career education planning); Title IV, pt. B, Social Security Act, 42 U.S.C. §§620–626 (child welfare services); Child Nutrition Act of 1966, 42 U.S.C. §§1771–1787 (school breakfast; nonfood assistance; special milk program); National School Lunch Act of 1946, 42 U.S.C. §§1751–1769a; §304 Public Works and Economic Development Act of 1965, 42 U.S.C. §3153 (supplemental state grants); §306 Coastal Zone Management Act, 16 U.S.C. §1455 (state administration grants); §308 *id.*, 16 U.S.C. §1456a (energy impact grants); Federal Civil Defense Act of 1950, 50 U.S.C. app. §§2251–2297 (state and local support); Housing and Community Development Act of 1974, 42 U.S.C. §§5301–5319; Land and Water Conservation Fund Act of 1965, 16 U.S.C. §§460L-4–460L-11 (outdoor recreation); Title IX, Social Security Act, 42 U.S.C. §§1101–1108 (state grants; unemployment insurance); Wagner-Peyser Act of 1933, 29 U.S.C. §49–49k (state employment services); Occupational Safety and Health Act, 29 U.S.C. §§651–678; Airport and Airway Redevelopment Act of 1970, 49 U.S.C. §§1701–1743; Urban Mass Transit Act of 1964, 49 U.S.C. §§1601–1618; Federal Aid Highway Act of 1973, 23 U.S.C. §§101–407; Intergovernmental Personnel Act of 1970, 42 U.S.C. §§4701–4772; Solid Waste Disposal Act, 42 U.S.C. §§6901–6987; Safe Drinking Water Act, 42 U.S.C. §§300f–300j-9; Federal Water Pollution Control Act, 33 U.S.C. §§1251–1376.

[3] See statutes cited in Chapter 9, note 2, and note 1, *supra.*

[4] §1004(b) National Defense Education Act of 1958, 20 U.S.C. §584(b).

and Congress leaves procedural details to the executive branch under the broad guideline of reasonableness.[5] We also find in *noncompliance* sections a reference to "changes" in state plans which make them "no longer" consistent with federal requirements.[6] This might appear to be redundant in view of the need for a "modification" to conform to the statute's requirements. It covers, however, the distinct occurrence where a state changes the operation of its program, either formally or *de facto,* without submitting the change for federal approval. In the three possible nonconformity situations—disapproval of a plan, disapproval of a modification of a plan, and a finding of a plan change effected without submission—the sanction is the withholding of federal payments until conformity has been achieved.

One finds infrequent variants on the above theme. An important exception is contained in Section 1116 of the Social Security Act which covers federal review of state plans in three major formula programs: Aid to Families With Dependent Children, Medicaid, and Social Services.[7] This section varies from the standard format in two essentials. First, it prevents undue delay by the Department of Health, Education and Welfare in the review of state submissions by imposing time limits within which the agency must act. Absent stipulations to the contrary, HEW must make a conformity determination within 90 days of receiving a state plan, hold a hearing within 60 days of a state's request for reconsideration, and make a final decision within 60 days after conclusion of the proceeding. Since a state has up to 60 days to decide whether to request reconsideration, under the statute's timetable nine months can be consumed between the date of the plan's submittal and the final conformity decision. It can be even longer if the state and the department agree to extend any of the time periods. Second, the provision makes clear that federal payments can be withheld during the period of plan review, including reconsideration, but if the plan is found consistent with federal law HEW

---

[5] We shall not review the details of conformity hearings established by agency regulations because of their similarity to noncompliance hearings. In addition to the regulations cited in Chapter 9, note 65, *supra,* see 45 C.F.R. §§104.281–104.289 (hearing procedures for challenges to vocational education plans); 15 C.F.R. pt. 925 (procedures for approval of coastal zone management programs). Several agencies provide one set of hearing procedures for both types of issues. See, e.g., 28 C.F.R. pt. 18 (crime control grants).

[6] See statutory sections cited in Chapter 9, note 2, *supra.*

[7] 42 U.S.C. §1316. The procedures for conformity hearings are set forth in 45 C.F.R. pt. 213 (1977).

must restitute "forthwith in a lump sum . . . any funds incorrectly withheld or otherwise denied."

We have seen that the statutes authorizing the withholding of formula funds for noncompliance permit the sanction to be limited to those projects or activities in which the illegality occurs.[8] That possibility might also arise in a state plan proceeding. The particular federal requirement for which the state's assurance is found to be inadequate might apply only to an identifiable portion of the federal payments. For example, federal formula grants typically require states to provide a range of specified services to program beneficiaries. If a state plan did not provide for one of such services, it might be desirable to reduce the formula grant by an amount equivalent to the omitted activity's estimate cost while approving and funding the remainder of the plan. Such partial reduction would have to be backed by a requirement of full conformity within a reasonable time; otherwise, states would simply pick and choose among the supposedly mandatory services. It might also be that the state is providing the required service, but its level or quality violates the federal standard. In this case, the reason for not totally shutting off federal payments is even more compelling, particularly if the state is making good faith efforts to comply. Yet the power of federal agencies to impose partial sanctions for nonconformity is ambiguous. The standard nonconformity provisions are seemingly couched in "all or nothing" terms. The plan, it appears, must be completely acceptable before any funds are released. And whether the power exists or not, a federal agency can always disclaim such authority as a pressure tactic in its bargaining with state agencies.

We have uncovered one instance in which a grant statute addresses the above problem. The old Title III of the Elementary and Secondary Education Act of 1965 contained the following provision:

> "The Commissioner may, if he finds that a State plan for any fiscal year ending prior to October 1, 1978, is in substantial compliance with the requirements set forth in subsection (b) of this section, approve that part of the plan which is in compliance with such requirements and make available . . . to the State that part of the State's allotment which he determines to be necessary to carry out that part of the plan so approved. The remainder of the amount which such State is eligible to receive . . . may be made

---

[8] See Chapter 9, notes 20–26, *supra*, and accompanying text.

available to such State only if the unapproved portion of that State plan has been so modified as to bring the plan into compliance with such requirements: *Provided,* That the amount made available to a State pursuant to this subsection shall not be less than 50 per centum of the maximum amount which the State is eligible to receive under this section." [9]

The state, acting through an agency designated by the governor or by a state law, usually has sole responsibility for the development and submission of the application for formula funds, even though the program calls for a pass-through of the funds to other entities within the state. Whether the plan conforms to federal requirements is obviously a matter of concern to these ultimate organizational recipients, yet the grant statutes contain no formal mechanism for their participation.[10] Instead, conformity issues are apparently considered the exclusive domain of the federal administering agency and the designated state agency. Programmatic decisions are similarly entrusted to the state, though where and how federal funds are put to use is of vital importance to project sponsors within the state. The revised Vocational Education Act departs from this mold by requiring the participation of various affected groups in the development of both the basic state vocational education plan and the programmatic plans required to be submitted annually.[11] One or more of the groups for which participation is statutorily required may appeal to the Commissioner of Education the final decision of the state vocational education board on either type of plan. After notice and opportunity for a hearing at which both the board and the objecting group appear, the Commissioner may reject a decision which is not supported by substantial evidence.

Formula grants do not always require the submission of a state plan. In some programs, although the amount of a state's total yearly entitlement is calculated by applying the formula set forth in the authorizing law, institutions within the state which are eligible for grants apply directly to the Federal Government.[12] Statutes structured in this way sometimes indicate that the eligible

[9] §305(c) Elementary and Secondary Education Act of 1965, 20 U.S.C. §844a(c) (1976).
[10] See Chapter 13, notes 4–6, *infra,* and accompanying text.
[11] §§107(a)(1), 108(a)(1) Vocational Education Act of 1963, 20 U.S.C. §§2307(a)(1), 2308(a)(1). Implementing hearing regulations are found at 45 C.F.R. §§104.281–104.289, 42 Fed. Reg. 53828 (1977).
[12] See Chapter 7, notes 47–48, *supra,* and accompanying text.

applicants have a right to a grant, even though the federal administering agency has authority to determine an appropriate amount.[13] Others are phrased in a way which vests the grantor with discretion to choose the applications it will fund out of the state's allotment.[14] Programs of this latter type leave unanswered the question whether the administrator must fund sufficient applications in a sufficient amount to exhaust the state's total entitlement. A different type of formula approach does not predetermine each state's yearly entitlement, but rather calculates by formula the entitlement of each eligible institution. Grants for college libraries [15] and "capitation" support to schools, [16] for example, follow this last format.

Once Congress departs from the state plan model, it almost invariably [17] omits applicant hearing rights if an eligible institution is not funded or receives what it considers an inadequate amount.[18] Despite this practice, we have argued that when the statute phrases the grant award process in a way which indicates that conforming applications from eligible institutions must be funded, Due Process requires an opportunity to be heard on an adverse funding decision. Unfortunately, federal agencies seem to disagree. For example, institutions of higher education which are displeased with panel recommendations concerning their yearly level of student aid funding are offered only the opportunity to request reconsideration by the regional commissioner and to submit a written case. A further review by a national panel is available, but that body considers no new evidence or argument.[19]

One additional incongruity deserves mention before we move to funding decisions in other types of grant programs. While formula grants are structured and phrased in a way which leads to the conclusion that each state has a right to its allotment, the

[13] See Chapter 7, notes 47, 49, *supra*, and accompanying text.
[14] See Chapter 7, note 48, *supra*, and accompanying text.
[15] See, e.g., §203 Higher Education Act of 1965, 20 U.S.C. §1023; 45 C.F.R. §131.23 (supplemental college library grants).
[16] See, e.g., §810(a) Public Health Service Act, 42 U.S.C. §296e(a); 42 C.F.R. pt. 52, subpt. K (capitation grants to nursing schools).
[17] The major exceptions are found in the Community Action and Head Start programs. See Chapter 10, note 6, *supra*, and accompanying text.
[18] Compare, e.g., Title IX, Older Americans Act of 1965, 42 U.S.C. §§3056-3056f (1976) (formula allocations among states for employment projects for elderly; no state plan; no hearing rights on application rejections); with §305(d) *id.*, 42 U.S.C. §3025(d) (1976) (hearing rights on state plan rejection; formula grants for social services projects).
[19] See 45 C.F.R. §144.4a (National Defense Education Act student loans); 45 C.F.R. §176.7 (supplemental educational opportunity grants); 45 C.F.R. §175.7 (work-study grants); 45 C.F.R. §144.7 (Higher Education Act loans).

authorizing statutes do not contain mechanisms by which a state can challenge a federal agency's calculation of the size of the entitlement. We have uncovered only one exception. Subsections 510(b) and 510(c) of the Omnibus Crime Control and Safe Streets Act of 1968 [20] require a formula grant applicant to be given both a hearing and a rehearing if it "has been given a grant in a lesser amount than such applicant believes appropriate." Such rights also extend to the rejection of a grant application or the discontinuance of an existing grant in whole or part. This is a rarity. In all other cases, to our knowledge, neither the grantor's initial state-by-state allotments nor its reallotment decision following a finding that one or more states do not need their full allotment is accompanied by hearing rights. At most, the federal agency publishes the respective entitlements in the *Federal Register* under statutory mandate [21] or its own grant policy.[22] Because such determinations (other than a finding of state need) appear to be achieved by the mechanical slotting of economic and demographic statistics into the statutory formula, one might not be concerned by the absence of grantee hearing rights. Indeed, Congress will occasionally try to avoid disputes about the accuracy of federal agency allocation calculations by attributing finality to the administrative decision.[23] If, however, the property is considered vested in the grantee prior to such allocation, the Due Process Clause might override the congressional intent and require notice and a hearing.[24] But the process involves much more than mechanical computer runs. First, the accuracy of the statistics used by the grantor may be hotly debatable. While formula statutes attempt to avoid

[20] 42 U.S.C. §§3758(b), (c).
[21] See, e.g., §§108(b), 123(d) Comprehensive Employment and Training Act of 1973, 29 U.S.C. §§818(b), 825(d). Under these sections: (1) allotments under statutory formulas must be published in the *Federal Register;* (2) formulas used by the Secretary of Labor to distribute discretionary funds (with some exceptions) must be similarly published in proposed form with proposed amounts and then finalized through the *Federal Register;* (3) the Secretary must give 30 days notice to the public, the governor of the state, and the grantee affected by a proposed reallotment. They may submit comments which are to be considered by the Secretary prior to publishing his final reallocation decision in the *Federal Register*. See also §2002(a)(2) Social Security Act, 42 U.S.C. §1397a(a)(2) (required promulgation of state entitlements for social services); 42 Fed. Reg. 43670 (1977) (fiscal year 1979 promulgation).
[22] See, e.g., 42 Fed. Reg. 38573 (1977) (reallocation of child care nonfood assistance funds); 5 C.F.R. §900.301(a) and 42 Fed. Reg. 46565 (1977) (allocation of intergovernmental personnel fiscal year 1978 grant funds); 42 Fed. Reg. 54126 (1977) (apportionment of urban mass transit capital and operating funds).
[23] E.g., §6(b) Land and Water Conservation Fund Act of 1964, 16 U.S.C. §460L-8(b).
[24] See Chapter 7, *supra,* at pp. 193–95.

such arguments by establishing the sources of such statistics,[25] their collection, compilation, and currency may be flawed. Errors in the process may translate into substantial losses of dollars—entitlement dollars—which lead to the constitutional Due Process requirement of an opportunity to be heard. Second, the statutory formulas allocating federal funds among the states are probably the most prolix, complicated, confusing, and incomprehensible provisions to be encountered in the statutes-at-large.[26] Their interpretation may be a source of considerable controversy, with substantial shifts in the distribution of dollars resulting from one reading or another. It would seem elementary that the parties affected by those interpretative decisions be given a voice in the process.

Discretionary Initial Grant Awards

Not surprisingly, Congress does not afford Due Process rights of any type to disappointed applicants for discretionary federal grants. This is true whether the funds sought are to start or to continue a project, although for the latter some rights are found in two grant statutes.[27]

We have encountered few instances in which Congress has given an opportunity for a full administrative hearing to seekers of a grant which is fully discretional with the administering agency. One exceptional provision is found in the Omnibus Crime Control and Safe Streets Act of 1968.[28] It concedes both hearing

[25] See, e.g., §102(b) Housing and Community Development Act of 1974, 42 U.S.C. §5302(b) (data and reports of Bureau of the Census and Office of Management and Budget). Compare §123(d)(1) Comprehensive Employment and Training Act of 1973, 29 U.S.C. §825(d)(1) (allotments based "on the latest available data and estimates satisfactory to the Secretary").

[26] See, e.g., §106 Housing and Community Development Act of 1974, 42 U.S.C. §5306.

[27] See statutes cited in notes 50–52, *infra*.

[28] §510 Omnibus Crime Control and Safe Streets Act of 1968, 42 U.S.C. §3758. Hearing procedures are found in 28 C.F.R. pt. 18. See also §510(g) Housing Act of 1949, 42 U.S.C. §1480(g), as added by §503 Housing and Community Development Amendments of 1978, Pub. L. 95-557, Oct. 31, 1978:

"[T]he Secretary shall have the power to—

. . .

"(g) issue rules and regulations which assure that applicants denied assistance under this title or persons or organizations whose assistance under this title is being substantially reduced or terminated are given written notice of the reasons for denial, reduction or termination and are provided at least an opportunity to appeal an adverse decision and to present additional information relevant to that decision to a person, other than the person making the original determination, who has authority to reverse the decision."

A unique provision was recently enacted as part of a new program for elderly

Rights of Applicants for Federal Funds / 297

and rehearing rights to disappointed applicants for formula and also discretionary crime control grants, even if a grant has been awarded in an amount below the applicant's expectations. Another statute provides a second opportunity to a rejected application. The Emergency School Aid Act instructs HEW not to disapprove finally in whole or part an application for funds submitted by a local educational agency without first notifying the applicant of the "specific reasons" for the disapproval and giving it an opportunity to modify the application.[29] While this second chance is more than is afforded other solicitors of competitive grants, HEW still retains full power to remain unimpressed with the proposed project, and need not hear argument from the applicant.[30]

If enough frustrations are suffered by applicants for discretionary grants, they can, of course, request Congress to convert the grant program into one of mandated formula grants. An interesting occurrence of this nature involved the distribution of discretionary funds by the Department of Commerce under the Local Public Works Capital Development and Investment Act, which is aimed at stimulating the economy through the funding of small public works projects throughout the country.[31] The extreme administrative burden caused by the rapid creation and funding of the program and by the congressional intent to get the money into the field as soon as possible led to a considerable breakdown in the grant application review process.[32] In response, Con-

---

Indians. Perhaps because of the special legal, social, and historical status of Indian tribes, a hearing right is given for denial of these applications in the following terms:

"Whenever the Commissioner [of Education] determines not to approve an application . . . he shall—

"(1) state his objections in writing to the tribal organization within 60 days after such decision;

"(2) provide to the extent practicable technical assistance to the tribal organization to overcome his stated objections; and

"(3) provide the tribal organization with a hearing, under such rules and regulations as he may prescribe."

§604(e) Older Americans Act of 1965, 42 U.S.C. §3057c(e), as added by §106 Comprehensive Older Americans Act Amendments of 1978, Pub. L. 95-478, Oct. 18, 1978. Another explanation for the hearing right is that the grant is phrased in terms of an entitlement, see §604(c) *id.*, 42 U.S.C. §3057c(c) (the Commissioner "shall" approve any complying application), although the Commissioner of Education has discretion to determine the amount of the grant.

[29] §710(d)(2) Education Amendments of 1972, 20 U.S.C. §1609(d)(2).

[30] See 45 C.F.R. §185.14(c)(3).

[31] Local Public Works Capital Development and Investment Act, 42 U.S.C. §§6701–6710.

[32] See H.R. Rep. No. 20, 95th Cong., 1st Sess., in *1977 U.S. Code Cong. & Admin. News Pamphlet No. 5* 716, 721.

298 / *Rights and Remedies Under Federal Grants*

gress set aside 70 million dollars in the second round of funding to be expended "only for grants for any public works project the application for a grant for which . . . was not received, was not considered, or was rejected solely because of an error by an officer or employee of the United States." [33] Congress also withdrew the authority of the department to determine the interstate distribution of funds and wrote a mandatory allocation formula into the statute.[34]

Federal agencies have not utilized their administrative powers to act where Congress has not. Our survey of grant-in-aid regulations reveals few instances in which an applicant for an initial competitive grant is given an opportunity to argue its case, either before or after rejection of the submission. The most an applicant can expect is a statement of reasons for the rejection and an opportunity to resubmit the proposal.[35] Reconsideration of the adverse decision can usually be requested,[36] but is unlikely to be fruitful. Agencies could, of course, provide greater applicant input if they so desired. In a recent program regulation, for instance, disappointed applicants for project grants are offered an opportunity to rebut, in writing or in an informal meeting, the basis for the adverse decision.[37] However, that is, and will continue to be, the rare exception.[38] The great volume of grant applications, the close choices that must necessarily be made on the relative merits of

[33] §108(a)(2) Local Public Works Capital Development and Investment Act, 42 U.S.C. §6707(a)(2), as amended by §105 Pub. L. 95-28, May 13, 1977.

[34] §108(a)(3) Local Public Works Capital Development and Investment Act, 42 U.S.C. §6707(a)(3), as amended by §105 Pub. L. 95-28, May 13, 1977.

[35] See, e.g., 45 C.F.R. §100a.27 (Office of Education project grants); 45 C.F.R. §1403.11 (National Institute of Education project grants). But see 7 C.F.R. pt. 1900, subpt. B, 43 Fed. Reg. 52461 (1978) (Farmers Home Administration; full hearing rights for disappointed grant applicants).

[36] See, e.g., 45 C.F.R. §121f.30 (education of the handicapped personnel training grants): "If an applicant wishes to request reconsideration of a decision concerning action taken on its application for assistance, a letter making such request must be sent to the Commissioner within 30 days of the receipt of the letter of notification of such action"; 29 C.F.R. §97.292 (petition for reconsideration of denial of migrant farmworkers' grant; review by official not involved in original decision).

[37] 45 C.F.R. §187.5(b).

[38] Even though a program vests discretion in the application process to the grantor agency, it may contemplate the award of at least one grant in each eligible area to an entity which has been specially qualified or designated. Such grants are more akin to negotiated contracts than competitive grants and usually call for greater grantor-applicant cooperation in the development of proposals. See, e.g., 15 C.F.R. §920.46(b) (negotiation of coastal zone management grants); 42 C.F.R. §110.605 ("fair hearings" for applicants for qualification as health maintenance organizations).

proposals, and the difficult judgments on applicant capabilities militate against a more open process.

Because no administrative processes are available to test the validity and objectiveness of grantor decisions on funding proposals, the agency power of rejection approaches the absolute. Though the executive branch remains accountable to Congress for its action, the volume of business precludes more than passing oversight. The Administrative Conference of the United States has characterized grantor authority in the award process as "unchannelled discretion." [39] The Conference has approached the problem of potential abuse of such discretion by exhorting federal grantors to develop and publicize clear and detailed standards governing the grant award process. Agencies are urged to: provide timely and public notice of the availability of grant funds; [40] offer detailed descriptions of the objectives of the particular grant program and the specific criteria which will be utilized in evaluating proposals; [41] set forth the requirements which will be imposed on recipients; [42] describe the procedures utilized by the agency to review grant applications; [43] and afford detailed reasons for the rejection of proposals.[44]

The Department of Health, Education and Welfare, the agency with the lion's share of competitive grant programs, has faithfully adhered to the recommendations of the Conference. For almost every currently authorized and funded grant program of the department one can find a regulation implementing that particular activity. Such regulations, besides setting forth grant conditions, describe the application process and the criteria under which proposals will be judged. Such criteria are reasonably precise and are often translated into point values making possible a

[39] Administrative Conference of the United States, Recommendation 74-2, "Procedures for Discretionary Distribution of Federal Assistance," 1 C.F.R. §305.74-2(a).
[40] Administrative Conference of the United States, Recommendation 71-4, "Minimum Procedures for Agencies Administering Discretionary Grant Programs," 1 C.F.R. §305.71-4(1).
[41] Administrative Conference of the United States, Recommendation 74-2, "Procedures for Discretionary Distribution of Federal Assistance," 1 C.F.R. §305.74-2(B).
[42] Id. at §305.74-2(B)(3).
[43] Administrative Conference of the United States, Recommendation 71-4, "Minimum Procedures for Agencies Administering Discretionary Grant Programs," 1 C.F.R. §305.71-4(2).
[44] Id. at §305.71-4(4).

300 / *Rights and Remedies Under Federal Grants*

ranking by score of each proposal.[45] As priorities and goals shift from year to year, changes are announced in the *Federal Register,* as are application deadlines.[46]

Outside HEW, practice is varied. Some agencies offer considerable advance notice of the availability of project grants and sufficient detail on the process of application submission and review,[47] while others seemingly prefer to maintain a shroud of secrecy over their grant activity.[48]

Refunding Proposals

Because an ongoing activity may be involved, refunding of a discretionary grant project involves factors considerably different from the appraisal of a proposal to start up a project.[49] In general, Congress has not taken note of the difference. An exception is found in the Community Services Act of 1974 which specifically addresses the refunding process and affords grant recipients notice and an opportunity to "show cause" why the federal agency should not deny continuation funding.[50] One also finds this procedural right in the Domestic Volunteer Services Act.[51] In just three cases

---

[45] See, e.g., 45 C.F.R. §§194.8, 194.30, 42 Fed. Reg. 40207 (1977) (criteria for evaluating public service education grant proposals); 45 C.F.R. §§172.20–172.137, 42 Fed. Reg. 47235–36 (1977) (requirements for Teacher Corps grant applications).

[46] See 42 Fed. Reg. 37254 (1977) for a typical HEW grant announcement.

[47] See, e.g., 42 Fed. Reg. 37075 (1977) (Employment and Training Administration; notice of intent to fund HEP and CAMP projects); 42 Fed. Reg. 33240, 37208 (1977) (Community Services Administration; information, application, procedures, and grant requirements for special crisis intervention program; allocation formula and allotments); 42 Fed. Reg. 38397 (1977) (guidelines for various National Endowment for the Arts grants); 42 Fed. Reg. 44025 (1977) (National Science Foundation; physically handicapped in science program); 42 Fed. Reg. 60976 (1977) (National Science Foundation; guidelines for resource center for science and engineering grants); 42 Fed. Reg. 54310 (1977) (Forest Service; regulations for Youth Conservation Corps grants); 42 Fed. Reg. 54314 (1977) (Department of the Interior; regulations for Youth Conservation Corps grants); 42 Fed. Reg. 54586 (1977) (Civil Service Commission; request for proposals for national training grants); 42 Fed. Reg. 58984 (1977) (HUD; innovative community development grants); 42 Fed. Reg. 63798 (1977) (Department of Agriculture; research grants announcement); 43 Fed. Reg. 5440 (1978) (LEAA; operating principles and funding guidelines for criminal intelligence systems grants).

[48] See, e.g., 42 Fed. Reg. 37580 (1977) (Agricultural Marketing Service; vague guidelines on marketing grants).

[49] See Chapter 7, *supra*, at pp. 205–207.

[50] See §554(b) Community Services Act of 1974, 42 U.S.C. §2929c(b) (Follow Through); §604(2) *id.*, 42 U.S.C. §2944(2) (community action; migrant grants).

[51] See §412(1) Domestic Volunteer Services Act of 1973, 42 U.S.C. §5052(1).

are the recipients of a discretionary grant afforded a full hearing prior to an adverse refunding decision.[52]

Standard federal agency practice is to limit project periods to one year, even though the funded activity may be of a type which has no natural termination point.[53] Research and demonstrations can be programmed for finite periods, with minor adjustments for miscalculations in the time needed to achieve project goals. If the goal is, however, to offer needed services to discrete beneficiary groups, the only logical stopping point is when the need ends, usually an unpredictable event. Grantor agencies have generally not distinguished in the award process between these two types of projects.[54] When the time comes to seek refunding for an additional year (usually referred to as a "continuation grant"), the grantee has no greater claim to competitive federal funds than when it originally sought them. The grantor retains discretion to deny the continuation grant without affording hearing opportunities. To insure that there is no misunderstanding about the matter, one agency regularly includes in its program regulations the following warning to recipients of discretionary grants:

> "Neither the approval of any application nor any grant award shall commit or obligate the United States in any way to make any additional, supplemental, continuation or other award with respect to any approved application or portion thereof. For continuation support, grantees must submit separate applications annually, at such times and in such form and manner as the Secretary may direct." [55]

Some agencies have recognized, however, that one-year funding with renewed competition for further grants is often programmatically undesirable. Service oriented projects can achieve little in 12 months; by the time the activity becomes fully functional, the first year is usually at an end. Even the most carefully designed

[52] See §519(3) Community Services Act of 1974, 42 U.S.C. §2928h(3) (Head Start); §809(2) id., 42 U.S.C. §2991h(2) (Native Americans); §1011(2) id., 42 U.S.C. §2996j(2) (legal services).

[53] See, e.g., 45 C.F.R. §160e.5(a) (consumers' education program): "While grant applications may be filed proposing multi-year projects, it is expected that a substantial proportion of projects funded by the Commissioner in any fiscal year will have a project duration of only one year." But see, e.g., 45 C.F.R. §1340.1-11 (child abuse prevention and treatment grants): "programs and projects may be approved for a period not to exceed five years. Program and project budgets must be submitted and will be reviewed and approved annually."

[54] Dozens of program regulations contain no separate criteria for the review of continuation grant proposals. See, e.g., 28 C.F.R. pt. 18 (LEAA grants); 29 C.F.R. pts. 94, 97, 98 (special employment and training grants).

[55] The agency is the Public Health Service. See, e.g., 42 C.F.R. §52c-5(d).

programs need constant modifications to improve their functioning to a point where their true value can be seen; thus, if the federal grant aims at launching activities with the expectation that local funds will be found for continuation, forcing a first-year decision to assume the costs or not would be unwise. Similarly, few demonstrations can produce valid data and information in the short span of 12 months.

Desirous of maximizing the opportunity for project stability and of promoting long-range planning, some agencies have established a multiyear funding system.[56] Tied to the appropriations process, federal grantors cannot guarantee funding beyond one year. They can, however, commit themselves to project periods extending beyond one year subject only to the conditions of compliance with grant terms and of subsequent congressional funding. They have not, however, gone quite this far.

An opportunity is provided in the initial grant application to request multiyear support.[57] The applicant must justify the need for continuation grants and provide budget estimates for future years. If the application is approved, besides determining the amount of the first-year award the federal agency can indicate its intent to provide support beyond the initial project period. That commitment, however, is highly conditional. Although grantees seeking continuation support will compete with each other for new funds and not with first time applicants, the grantor retains discretion to allocate new appropriations between the two groups. While grant statutes frequently determine the percentage of the total appropriation which the federal agency must dedicate to the different categories of authorized assistance, they do not ordinarily mandate a division of appropriations between new competitive fundings and refundings. In addition, applications for continuation grants are reviewed to determine not only whether the grantee has satisfied its legal obligations [58] but also whether the project has demonstrated its "effectiveness" [59] and "continues to offer promise for success." [60] Even if these can be shown, performance during the first year will be reviewed to ascertain whether the grantee has made satisfactory progress in achieving the project's

---

[56] See, e.g., 45 C.F.R. §121.5.
[57] See, e.g., 45 C.F.R. §123.04(b).
[58] See, e.g., 45 C.F.R. §160e.5(d)(2)(i): "If the grantee has complied with the grant terms and conditions, the Act, and applicable regulations."
[59] See, e.g., 45 C.F.R. §160e.5(d)(2)(ii).
[60] See, e.g., 45 C.F.R. §159.7(b)(3).

goals and objectives as set forth in its work plan.[61] While site visits, progress reports, and other data might verify effectiveness and continued promise, that may not be enough because performance is to be measured by what the grantee promised to achieve in its initial grant application. Another criterion for review is whether the grantee has cooperated by instituting modifications "recommended" by the grantor; this is usually phrased as the degree to which the recipient has made "the constructive changes proposed as a result of the ongoing evaluation."[62] This condition demonstrates how the refunding power overtly acts as a tremendous lever to obtain grantee acquiescence in federal agency programmatic views. Even if all of the above criteria are satisfied, the grantee is still not assured continued aid. Its project must continue to fall within federal agency priorities.[63] Considerable discretion is vested in the administering agency to determine the specific types of projects it will fund in carrying out the grant-in-aid statute's broad policies and goals. As the agency gathers experience and information, its grant focus will shift. The fact that a project fits within the agency's priorities in one year does not preclude a denial of continuation support when in a subsequent year the agency decides to move in new directions. Finally, program regulations ordinarily hammer home the grantor discretion retained in the refunding process by including a vague criterion such as "the extent to which continuation of federal financial assistance is in the best interests of the Government."[64]

As a practical matter applicants for refunding stand a considerably better chance of getting a federal grant than original applicants, particularly if an intention to provide multiyear support has been expressed. Because delay may be seriously detrimental to grantee personnel, they also get more rapid consideration of their refunding proposals.[65] A working relationship has been established with a federal office which, if interactions have been cordial, will normally lead to favorable reviews. The grantor is likely to perceive increasing returns on its investment in the second, third, and fourth years of a project when the bugs have been worked out and efficiency is at its highest. While the multi-

[61] See, e.g., 45 C.F.R. §159.7(b)(2).
[62] See, e.g., 45 C.F.R. §187.6(d)(2).
[63] See, e.g., 45 C.F.R. §160e.5(d)(2)(iii).
[64] See, e.g., 45 C.F.R. §160e.5(d)(2)(iv).
[65] See, e.g., 40 C.F.R. §30.335 (refunding of Environmental Protection Agency grants; review conducted "expeditiously" and generally no extramural review required).

year commitment turns out, on examination, to be moral and not legal, it still has force. The universal bureaucratic disinclination to shut down an ongoing activity is also at work. Negative funding decisions which displace people and services are naturally harder to reach than denials of first-time funding where the loss is only the time and resources expended in the development of a proposal.

Yet, at bottom, the applicant for refunding has no greater rights, either substantive or procedural, than applicants for initial competitive grants. No "right" to refunding emerges from the grant-in-aid statutes or the administrative regulations.[66] Nor is the applicant provided procedural mechanisms for testing whether the grantor agency has dealt with its continuation proposal according to the review standards it has announced. Absent special statutory directives, no formal opportunities for hearings or argument are provided applicants for continuation grants.

Though not established on a formula grant basis, some programs [67] are intended to provide continuing federal support for services whose need is not expected to dwindle or disappear. For political or financial reasons, the recipient is not expected or required to assume an increasing percentage of project costs; rather, the federal share of expenses remains constant. Though this type of program vests discretion on initial and continuation funding in the administrator, it is similar to formula programs in the expectation of continuing congressional appropriations and the implicit presumption that grantees which abide by federal requirements will be regularly refunded. They approach but do not quite reach a mandated grant. The difficulty of predetermining by formula a reasonable grant amount for each recipient appears to be the main reason why a formula system is not used in many service programs.[68] A second reason is that various organizations, both governmental and private, may be able to accomplish the project goals, and

---

[66] In *Southern Mut. Help Ass'n v. Califano*, 574 F.2d 518 (D.C. Cir. 1977), a rather unique case, HEW failed to specify clearly in the grant instruments that the project was funded for one year, with only the possibility of multiyear support over five years. Thus, the court held that the project period was five years, that the denial of "refunding" was really a termination, and that, accordingly, the grantee was entitled to a termination hearing under 45 C.F.R. pt. 16.

[67] Programs of this nature include: Public Works and Economic Development Act of 1965, 42 U.S.C. §§3121–3246h; §329 Public Health Service Act, 42 U.S.C. §254b (migrant health services); Title VII, Elementary and Secondary Education Act of 1965, 20 U.S.C. §§3221–3261, as rewritten by §101 Education Amendments of 1978, Pub. L. 95–561, Nov. 1, 1978 (bilingual education).

[68] See generally *Categorical Grants*, Chapter 1, note 6, *supra*, at 39, 109–11, 197–211.

competition among service providers is considered beneficial.[69] Some programs, it appears, could easily be converted to a formula fund distribution system.[70] Whatever the reason, in this type of program, one may find a statutory right to notice and an opportunity to be heard prior to a denial of refunding.

The Legal Services Corporation Act, for example, requires the corporation (LSC) to "prescribe procedures to insure that . . . an application for refunding shall not be denied . . . unless the grantee, contractor, person or entity receiving financial assistance under this title has been afforded reasonable notice and an opportunity for a timely, full and fair hearing." [71] In addition, the Act directs LSC to afford grantees which have filed a timely refunding application interim funding sufficient to maintain their level of activities until the refunding decision has been made.[72] This latter requirement assures that meritorious projects will not be delayed to death.

LSC has liberally interpreted "denial" to include not only absolute terminations but also any funding decision which selectively reduces a grantee's annual rate of financial support or which imposes restrictions which would force the grantee to reduce its level of legal services to eligible clients.[73] Hearing rights are comparable to those afforded states in nonconformity and noncompliance actions. Applications for refunding are to be submitted at least four months before the current grant expires, and LSC "shall" act upon them "as soon as practicable." If LSC preliminarily determines that refunding will be denied, it so notifies applicants, specifying in detail the supporting reasons and facts and accompanying the notice with copies of all relevant documents. Within 15 days a grantee may request review of this preliminary decision. The president of the corporation designates an LSC official as a hearing officer, but such individual cannot have been "directly" involved in the preliminary determination. If the matter cannot

[69] See, e.g., §101 Public Works and Economic Development Act of 1965, 42 U.S.C. §3131.
[70] See, e.g., Title VII, Elementary and Secondary Education Act of 1965, 20 U.S.C. §§3221–3261, as rewritten by §101 Education Amendments of 1978, Pub. L. 95-561, Nov. 1, 1978 (bilingual education).
[71] §1011(2) Community Services Act of 1974, 42 U.S.C. §2996j(2).
[72] §1007(a)(9) *id.*, 42 U.S.C. §2996f(a)(9).
[73] See 45 C.F.R. §1606.2(b), 43 Fed. Reg. 32770 (1978). The corporation amended Part 1606, making the same procedures applicable to both grant terminations and refunding denials and substantially improving the hearing rights of grantees. See 43 Fed. Reg. 32769–72 (1978). These amendments are discussed in Chapter 15, *infra*, at pp. 354–55.

306 / *Rights and Remedies Under Federal Grants*

be informally resolved at a required prehearing conference, the parties quickly proceed to a hearing. In addition to the standard guarantees of full participation, the LSC regulation provides procedural rights not found in other programs. Both the informal conference and the hearing are held whenever possible "at a place convenient to the applicant and the community affected," thus relieving the applicant of the usual burden of litigation in the District of Columbia. Although the LSC regulation does not adopt the federal discovery rules, the applicant can call and examine LSC officials involved in the preliminary determination upon a showing of good cause.

Despite its overall concern for grantee Due Process, the regulation apparently places the burden of proof on the refunding applicant. The review is aimed at affording

> "a full and fair opportunity for the applicant to demonstrate that its application for refunding should not be denied or that the preliminary determination was based on erroneous information or was arbitrary or capricious." [74]

It also follows the standard practice of placing the ultimate decisional power in the agency head.[75]

While the community action program has the same attribute of implied permanency as legal services, Congress opted for a "show cause" [76] opportunity rather than a "full and fair hearing." This has been administratively interpreted as requiring only that the grantee tentatively denied refunding be given a chance to state its case through written submissions and/or an informal meeting with the grantor official authorized to make the grant or his designee.[77]

---

[74] 45 C.F.R. §1606.8, 43 Fed. Reg. 32770–71 (1978).

[75] See 45 C.F.R. §1606.15, 43 Fed. Reg. 32772 (1978). The Head Start and Native Americans programs, administered by HEW, contain similar requirements of providing a "full and fair hearing" to applicants for refunding. See note 52, *supra*, and accompanying text. Head Start procedural regulations comparable to those of the Legal Services Corporation are found in 45 C.F.R. pt. 1303, subpt. C, and the Native Americans regulations incorporate these procedures by reference. 45 C.F.R. §1336.59, 42 Fed. Reg. 3789 (1977).

[76] See §604 Community Services Act of 1974, 42 U.S.C. §2944. See also §412 Domestic Volunteer Service Act of 1973, 42 U.S.C. §5052 (refunding of domestic volunteer grants must not be denied without affording "reasonable notice and opportunity to show cause why such action should not be taken"); §554(b) Community Services Act of 1974, 42 U.S.C. §2929c(b) (same; Follow Through grants).

[77] See 45 C.F.R. §1067.2-4(b). See also 45 C.F.R. §1206.2-4(c) (same for denials of refunding by ACTION). The Follow Through regulation simply copies the statutory requirement without offering details. See 45 C.F.R. §158.84(d).

13

Subgrantees

Most formula grant programs involve a pass-through of funds. The basic allotment is made to a state agency which, in turn, grants the funds to eligible institutions throughout the state. We refer to these ultimate recipients as "subgrantees," while recognizing that in some programs the state agency does not actually award the funds but rather approves the grant application and forwards it to the Federal Government for final approval.

Our review of the adverse decisions which the federal grantors may take against the primary recipient of formula funds has shown that in the majority of programs Congress explicitly concedes notice and hearing rights prior to nonconformity and noncompliance decisions. In this chapter we shall consider the procedural rights of subgrantees. The inquiry is dual. Subgrantees may be harmed by federal sanctions taken against the grantee which stop federal payments to the state agency and, consequently, interrupt the flow of funds to subgrantees.[1] They may also be adversely

---

[1] If the Federal Government takes action directly against the subgrantee based on its noncompliance or ineligibility, the Federal Government must give the subgrantee a Due Process hearing. *Hathaway* v. *Mathews,* 546 F.2d 227 (7th Cir. 1976). In this case HEW tried to argue that it had no privity relationship with the subgrantee and that the plaintiff should deal with the state grantee and not HEW. The court blasted that argument:

"To accept this argument would be to exalt legal formalism over reality. Simply because HEW makes payments to the states, rather than directly to the provider, does not mean that there is not an important relationship between the provider and the federal government. . . . [T]o deny Hathaway the right to bring an action against the federal government simply because federal funds come to her through the conduit of the State is to deny that it is the federal government, and not the State, which threatens to cause her injury. We will not subscribe to such a palpable fiction." *Id.* at 229.

308 / Rights and Remedies Under Federal Grants

affected by state agency actions. Their applications to the state for a share of the federal formula funds may be rejected or approved at disappointing funding levels. The state agency could also impose sanctions on the subgrantee for noncompliance with grant requirements, including termination of the subgrant.

In the great majority of grant programs, the power of grantees to impose sanctions on those receiving pass-through funds is not explicitly given by statute or regulation.[2] Indeed, this chapter is so short precisely because of the lack of federal norms governing the relationship between grantees and subgrantees. It is a shadowy world of inferences and, presumably, custom. Despite the absence of explicit norms we must presume that grantees have power over subgrantees; otherwise, the main recipient could not give assurances of compliance to the Federal Government. It has been our experience that grantees, left to their own devices, typically pass on down to those below all the standards to which they have been subjected by the Federal Government. Whether *additional* requirements can be imposed on subgrantees is a matter which eventually will have to be dealt with.[3]

Despite the effects which federal fund cutoffs have on subgrantees, the operating principle which emerges from grant-in-aid statutes is that the Federal Government need deal only with its primary recipient, the state agency, on compliance and conformity questions. When granted, hearing rights belong exclusively to the state.[4] This principle holds true even if a noncompliance issue arises from the activities of a subgrantee,[5] or if the Federal Government rejects a state-approved grant application submitted by a subgrantee.[6] Title II of the Education of the Handicapped Act

---

[2] But see Chapter 3, notes 93–117, *supra,* and accompanying text; 45 C.F.R. §118.27(c): "The State educational agency shall establish procedures for termination, during the project period, of programs and projects which are not operating in compliance with (1) any provisions of this Act and regulations of this part, or (2) any requirement set forth in the approved State plan or in the approved project application . . ."; 7 C.F.R. §246.17(c), 42 Fed. Reg. 43221 (1977): "A State agency shall terminate a local agency's participation under the program whenever it is determined by [the Food and Nutrition Service] or the State agency that the local agency has failed to comply with the requirements of the program"; 45 C.F.R. §121a.194, 42 Fed. Reg. 42485 (1977) (education of handicapped grants; withholding of LEA funds by SEA).

[3] See 47 U.S.L.W. 2160 (Sept. 12, 1978) (OMB memorandum encouraging state grantees to develop standardized reporting forms for subgrantees).

[4] See statutory sections cited in Chapter 9, note 2, and Chapter 12, note 1, *supra.*

[5] See, e.g., §223 Community Mental Health Centers Act, 42 U.S.C. §2689k.

[6] See, e.g., §1604(d) Public Health Service Act, 42 U.S.C. §300o-3(d) (medical facilities projects).

contains a rare exception. Both the administering state agency and any "affected" subgrantee receive notice and an opportunity to be heard before the Commissioner invokes the withholding sanction for noncompliance with federal law.[7] We should also mention that occasionally a federal agency will provide by regulation for participation of right by subgrantees if the noncompliance hearing was provoked by the subgrantee's actions.[8]

Subgrantee procedural rights are more commonly found with respect to adverse state agency actions. In most formula programs in which a state qualifies for a grant by submitting a state plan, the state agency must give assurances that it will give a fair hearing opportunity to entities which apply to the agency for a share of the federal funds.[9] Program regulations usually leave the structuring of adequate hearing procedures completely up to the state. One such regulation reads: "[T]he State agency shall establish such rules and regulations as will provide an opportunity for an appeal to and a fair hearing before the State agency to every applicant for a construction project who is dissatisfied with any action of the State agency regarding its application." [10] Such regulations leave the subgrantee only with a compliance complaint that the state agency has set up an inadequate review process. It cannot appeal to the Federal Government on the merits of grantee actions in the specific case.[11]

One provision of law deals comprehensively with the issue of procedural equity for subgrantees. It is Section 425 of the General Education Provisions Act [12] which extended, upon its

[7] §616(a) Education of the Handicapped Act, 20 U.S.C. §1416(a).
[8] See, e.g., 45 C.F.R. §1303.4 (Head Start); 45 C.F.R. §1050.115 (Community Action).
[9] See, e.g., §1603(a)(8) Public Health Service Act, 42 U.S.C. §3000-2(a)(8) (medical facilities projects); §§303(a)(8), (10) Omnibus Crime Control and Safe Streets Act of 1968, 42 U.S.C. §§3733(a)(8), (10); §307(a)(5) Older Americans Act of 1965, 42 U.S.C. §3027(a)(5).
[10] 42 C.F.R. §53.124. But see 45 C.F.R. §104.182 (vocational educational grants): "The State Board, in its five-year State plan shall . . . (b) describe the procedures for affording eligible recipients reasonable notice of an opportunity for a hearing, for providing a written record of hearing, and for informing the recipient in writing of the decisions and reasons therefore"; 15 C.F.R. §§931.112(m), 931.114(d) (elaborate procedures for intrastate distribution of energy impact grant funds).
[11] See, e.g., 28 C.F.R. §18.32. If the program involves discretionary grant applications submitted through a central state body, disapproval by such agency is usually reviewable by the grantor. See e.g., §425 General Education Provisions Act, 20 U.S.C. §1231b-2. If the basic state grant is discretionary, it is unusual to find hearing rights conceded to disappointed applicants for subgrants. There are, however, precedents for granting hearing rights in this situation. See 7 C.F.R. §246.25, 42 Fed. Reg. 43223 (1977) (special supplemental food program for women, infants, and children).
[12] 20 U.S.C. §1231b-2.

310 / *Rights and Remedies Under Federal Grants*

enactment in 1974, hearing opportunities to all subgrantees receiving or requesting federal education funds from state educational agencies. The provision is notable for its comprehensiveness and detail. Its first paragraph reads as follows:

> "In the case of any applicable program under which financial assistance is provided to (or through) a State educational agency to be expended in accordance with a State plan approved by the Commissioner, and in the case of a program provided for in Title I of the Elementary and Secondary Education Act of 1965, any applicant or recipient aggrieved by the final action of the State educational agency, and alleging a violation of State or Federal law, rules, regulations, or guidelines governing the applicable program, in (1) disapproving or failing to approve its application or program in whole or part, (2) failing to provide funds in amounts in accord with the requirements of laws and regulations, (3) ordering, in accordance with a final State audit resolution determination, the repayment of misspent or misapplied Federal funds, or (4) terminating further assistance for an approved program, may within thirty days request a hearing. Within thirty days after it receives such a request, the State educational agency shall hold a hearing on the record and shall review such final action. No later than ten days after the hearing the State educational agency shall issue its written ruling, including reasons therefor. If it determines such final action was contrary to Federal or State law, or the rules, regulations, and guidelines, governing such applicable program it shall rescind such final action."

If the state does not rescind its action, an appeal is provided to the Commissioner of Education who may overturn or modify erroneous state decisions. The Commissioner, however, must accept the state educational agency findings of fact which are supported by substantial evidence. Review is also limited to alleged SEA violations of federal law, regulations, or guidelines. A decision of the SEA based on state law which is consistent with federal requirements is nonreviewable.

Section 425 also contains a discovery rule which we have found to be unique. The third paragraph of the provision requires each state educational agency to

> "make available at reasonable times and places to each applicant or recipient under a program to which this section applies all records of such agency pertaining to any review or appeal such applicant or recipient is conducting under this section, including records of other applicants."

It is interesting to note that no comparable right is afforded, at least by statute,[13] to a grantee challenging federal agency action.

In enacting Section 425 Congress intended to provide two new rights to local educational agencies: the right to a hearing before the state educational agency and the right to an appeal to the Federal Government.[14] The latter did, indeed, work a substantial change since educational grant statutes did not theretofore provide federal review of SEA decisions on applications or compliance issues involving subgrantees. The right to a hearing before the SEA, however, was already established in almost all of the programs covered by the new section. The statement in the committee report that "[u]nder present practice, when a State agency's plan has been approved by the Commissioner of Education for operation of a program, the State agency issues regulations and makes decisions regarding the distribution of funds without affording the local educational agencies an opportunity to contest either" [15] was demonstrably untrue.[16] Because Congress did not repeal these duplicative sections, some confusion may result as to the hearing requirements. For example, some of the sections which supposedly did not exist require that the SEA afford a local educational agency notice and an opportunity to be heard *before* finally disapproving a grant application.[17] Section 425 requires a hearing *after* final action of the SEA. Thus, a literal reading of these sections leads one to conclude that an LEA can insist on two hearings before the SEA and then appeal to the Commissioner of Education.[18] We can, however, effect a reconciliation if we take into

[13] Some regulations covering hearing procedures permit parties to utilize the liberal discovery provisions of the Federal Rules of Civil Procedure. See Chapter 9, note 94, *supra*.

[14] See H.R. Rep. No. 93-805, 93d Cong., 2d Sess., *1974 U.S. Code Cong. & Admin. News* 4093, 4153.

[15] *Ibid.*

[16] See, e.g., §141(c) Act of Sept. 30, 1950, Pub. L. 81-874, 20 U.S.C. §241e(c) (1976); §§303(a)(3), 313 (b) National Defense Education Act of 1958, 20 U.S.C. §§443(a)(3), 453(b); §305(b)(12) Elementary and Secondary Education Act of 1965, 20 U.S.C. §844a(b)(12) (1976); §603(4) Higher Education Act of 1965, 20 U.S.C. §1123(4); §704(a)(5) *id.*, 20 U.S.C. §1132a-3(a)(5).

[17] See, e.g., §305(b)(12) Elementary and Secondary Education Act of 1965, 20 U.S.C. §844a(b)(12) (1976).

[18] Provisions such as §425 of the General Education Provisions Act, 20 U.S.C. §1231b-2, obviate the need to write comparable provisions into new grant statutes since they cover all programs, both existing and future, of a particular federal agency. Sometimes, however, draftsmen might overlook such general provisions in writing subsequent legislation. The 1975 revision of the Education of the Handicapped Act, 20 U.S.C. §§1401–1461, for example, requires SEAs to "provide procedures to assure that final action with respect to any application submitted by a local education agency or an intermediate educational unit shall not be taken

account the fact that Section 425 hearings are limited to claims that the SEA action violated state or federal law. If the LEA claim is simply that the SEA erroneously exercised admitted discretion, Section 425 is inapplicable, but the broader hearing provisions found in the particular grant statute can be invoked.

In covering only educational programs involving state plans, Section 425 essentially distinguishes between formula and discretionary grants. The principle of entitlement [19] is, therefore, carried on down one level to the subgrantees. Due Process is afforded because the statute creates a right to the subgrant in eligible local educational agencies and other entities which qualify for pass-through funds, assuming, of course, that formally correct applications are submitted. If the federal grantor has discretion in the award, we do not find comparable hearing rights when the application needs approval by a state agency before submission to the Federal Government.[20]

While we have found the greatest concern for subgrantee rights in the education field, the programs emanating from the "war on poverty" contain a similar set of rights. The Community Action and Head Start programs are operated through primary grant recipients in each state which, in turn, screen grant applications from local groups which wish to carry out projects within the geographical area covered by the Community Action or Head Start agency.[21] For both programs, a "timely and expeditious appeal" to the administering federal agency is provided to agencies and organizations whose applications to serve as "delegate agencies" have

---

without first affording . . . reasonable notice and an opportunity for a hearing." §613(a)(8) *id.*, 20 U.S.C. §1413(a)(8). This apparent inadvertence leads to the same double hearing possibility noted in the text. See also §106(a)(4) Vocational Education Act, 20 U.S.C. §2306(a)(4) (same). This legislation is unusual in providing judicial review of state agency action on grant applications. See §109(e) *id.*, 20 U.S.C. §2309(e). The provision was borrowed from the old Title III of the Elementary and Secondary Education Act. See §305(f) Elementary and Secondary Education Act, 20 U.S.C. §844a(f) (1976).

[19] See Chapter 7, *supra*, at pp. 193–95.

[20] See, e.g., §532(c)(2) Higher Education Act, 20 U.S.C. §1119a(c)(2). LEA applications for discretionary teacher training grants require SEA approval. If such approval is withheld, the applicant only has the right to "request further consideration" by the SEA. Implementing regulations authorize dissatisfied local educational agencies or institutions of higher education to petition the Commissioner of Education; however, the petition is not to review the state agency decision but rather to direct the state agency to give further consideration to the grant application. 45 C.F.R. §197.12, 43 Fed. Reg. 1762, 1767–68 (1978).

[21] §§210(a)(1), 211(e), 212(a), 515 Community Services Act of 1974, 42 U.S.C. §§2790(a)(1), 2191(e), 2795(a), 2928d.

Subgrantees / 313

been rejected or not acted upon within a reasonable period of time.[22]

A final example of subgrantee hearing rights is drawn from Title XV of the Public Health Service Act. This legislation authorizes health systems agencies and state health planning and development agencies to review and comment on all applications for federal health grants made by other organizations which provide health services within their region.[23] This review is aimed at promoting the rational use of federal health funds within a jurisdiction by avoiding duplication and overlap and by aiming dollars at the greatest needs. While the Public Health Service can override an adverse clearinghouse review, it is anticipated that the Federal Government will exercise such power sparingly. Any applicant for federal funds subject to such review is accorded the right to adequate notice, an opportunity to submit information to the reviewing agency, written findings which state the basis for decision, and a public hearing if adversely affected by such review.[24]

The subgrantee rights to notice and an opportunity to be heard in education, Community Action, and Head Start may give the impression that it is standard for Congress to afford Due Process to local groups which must apply to or through a state's central grant recipient. In numerous other programs, however, no comparable statutory rights are granted even though the grants are distributed by statutory formula and eligible subgrantees are entitled to pass-through funding.[25]

---

[22] §§519(1), 604(1) Community Services Act of 1974, 42 U.S.C. §§2928h(1), 2944(1). See 45 C.F.R. pt. 1303, subpt. B (Head Start), and 45 C.F.R. §1050.115 (Community Action) for implementing regulations. The "appeal" is effectuated through informal meetings and the submission of written materials.
[23] §1513(e) Public Health Service Act, 42 U.S.C. §300"1"-2(e).
[24] §1532 Public Health Service Act, 42 U.S.C. §300n-1.
[25] See, e.g., §1604(d) Public Health Service Act, 42 U.S.C. §300o-3(d) (medical facilities); §237(c) Community Mental Health Centers Act, 42 U.S.C. §2689t(c); §133(c) Developmental Disabilities Services and Facilities Construction Act, 42 U.S.C. §6063(c).

14

Two Special Cases

In this chapter we shall briefly examine two areas in which a considerable degree of uniqueness characterizes administrative enforcement procedures. The two special cases are polar extremes. In one—nondiscrimination requirements in grant programs—Congress and the executive branch have comprehensively regulated the manner and method by which federal agencies may police the substantive civil rights standards. We shall observe an elaborate system of enforcement, including meticulous attention to the Due Process rights of grantees charged with civil rights violations. The area is singular in that this one type of federal condition has been culled from the others and given substantial attention. The other case—termination of fellowships and training grants—presents a quite contrary picture. Fellowships and traineeships awarded to individuals may be cut off on the grounds of violation of the conditions of the award without a glimmer of fair process. Because it is our opinion that such deprivations constitute a paradigm example of when constitutional fair process is due, we have chosen to review with care the enforcement scheme in this area.

Nondiscrimination

In the most sweeping terms possible Congress has declared that federal grant dollars shall be free from discrimination based on considerations of race, color, national origin, handicap, sex, and age. Title VI of the Civil Rights Act of 1964 [1] has provided the model: "No person in the United States shall, on the ground of race, color, or national origin, be excluded from participation in, be denied the benefits of, or be subjected to discrimination under any program receiving Federal financial assistance." [2]

Besides providing the model substantive prohibition, Title VI has also been copied in its accompanying enforcement details by later statutes and regulations which expanded the ban to discrimination based on handicap,[3] sex,[4] and age.[5] We shall, therefore, focus on the Title VI format and then note any material variances

[1] §§601–605 Civil Rights Act of 1964, 42 U.S.C. §§2000d–2000d-4.
[2] §601 id., 42 U.S.C. §2000d.
[3] §504 Rehabilitation Act of 1973, 29 U.S.C. §794:
"No otherwise qualified handicapped individual in the United States . . . shall, solely by reason of his handicap, be excluded from the participation in, be denied the benefits of, or be subjected to discrimination under any program or activity receiving Federal financial assistance."
The Rehabilitation Act defines "handicapped individual," for purposes of §504, as:
"any person who (i) has a physical or mental impairment which substantially limits one or more of such person's major life activities, (ii) has a record of such an impairment, or (iii) is regarded as having such an impairment. For purposes of sections 503 and 504 as such sections relate to employment, such term does not include any individual who is an alcoholic or drug abuser whose current use of alcohol or drugs prevents such individual from performing the duties of the job in question or whose employment, by reason of such current alcohol or drug abuse, would constitute a direct threat to property or the safety of others."
§7(7) id., 29 U.S.C. §706(7). For details concerning implementation of §504 by the executive branch, see notes 74–83, infra, and accompanying text.
Special types of handicap have occasionally been covered by specific civil rights provisions. §904 Education Amendments of 1972, 20 U.S.C. §1684, prohibits the denial of admission to a federally supported educational program or activity on the ground of blindness or severely impaired vision. §407 Drug Abuse Office and Treatment Act of 1972, 21 U.S.C. §1174, requires federally supported hospitals to refrain from discriminating against drug abusers and addicts in admission or treatment solely because of that condition. §321 Comprehensive Alcohol Abuse and Alcoholism Prevention, Treatment, and Rehabilitation Act of 1970, 42 U.S.C. §4581, provides identical protection to alcohol abusers and alcoholics.
[4] §§901–907 Education Amendments of 1972, 20 U.S.C. §§1681–1686. §901 id., 20 U.S.C. §1681, contains the substantive standard:
"No person in the United States shall, on the basis of sex, be excluded from participation in, be denied the benefits of, or be subjected to discrimination under any education program or activity receiving Federal financial assistance, except . . ."
For details concerning implementation of §901 by the executive branch, see notes 84–100, infra, and accompanying text.
[5] Age Discrimination Act of 1975, 42 U.S.C. §§6101–6107. §303 id., 42 U.S.C. §6102, contains the substantive standard:
"Pursuant to regulations prescribed under section 304 of this Act . . . no person in the United States shall, on the basis of age, be excluded from participation in, be denied the benefits of, or be subjected to discrimination under any program or activity receiving Federal financial assistance."
For details concerning implementation of §303 by the executive branch, see notes 101–109, infra, and accompanying text. Regulations, and hence the §303 prohibition, cannot be put in force prior to July 1, 1979. See §304(a)(5) id., 42 U.S.C. §42 U.S.C. §6103(a)(5).

316 / *Rights and Remedies Under Federal Grants*

encountered in the other civil rights provisions. Title VI standards and procedures are contained in various documents which we shall examine *seriatim:* the statute; a presidential directive; regulations of the coordinating federal agency; and substantive and procedural regulations of federal grantor agencies.

Racial Discrimination

Title VI sweeps within its prohibition on racial discrimination all federal assistance programs providing grants, loans, or contracts,[6] and excepts only federal insurance and loan guarantees.[7] Primary enforcement responsibility is placed in the federal departments and agencies which administer covered programs. These are ordered to implement Title VI by means of rules and regulations consistent with the objectives of the nondiscrimination standard and the particular assistance programs to which it is applied.[8] Such regulations are to be approved by the President,[9] who subsequently delegated this responsibility to the Attorney General.[10] Although agencies are broadly permitted to enforce the civil rights standard by "any . . . means authorized by law," [11] the basic remedial tool is fiscal: Grantor agencies may terminate financial aid, may refuse to award such assistance, and may shut off grant funds in programs involving continuous financing.[12] Several limitations, however, control the sanction power.[13] First, no sanctions are to be imposed until the grantee has been notified of its failure to comply and given an opportunity to achieve compliance by voluntary means. Second, aid may not be refused or curtailed absent an express finding on the record, based on an administrative hearing, of grantee noncompliance. Third, the fiscal sanction shall be limited to the particular political entity or recipient found in violation.

[6] §604 Civil Rights Act of 1964, 42 U.S.C. §2000d-3, exempts "employment practices" of employers, employment agencies, and labor organizations. However, Exec. Order 11246, 30 Fed. Reg. 12319 (1965), provides nondiscrimination standards and procedures parallel to those in Title VI for construction activities financed by federal grants, contracts, loans, insurance, or guarantees. Numerous agencies have promulgated procedural rules applicable specifically to proceedings under Exec. Order 11246. See, e.g., 45 C.F.R. pt. 82.
[7] §602 Civil Rights Act of 1964, 42 U.S.C. §2000d-1.
[8] *Ibid.*
[9] *Ibid.*
[10] See Exec. Order 11247, 30 Fed. Reg. 12327 (1965); Exec. Order 11764, 39 Fed. Reg. 2575 (1974).
[11] §602 Civil Rights Act of 1964, 42 U.S.C. §2000d-1.
[12] *Ibid.*
[13] *Ibid.*

Thus, if a grant has been parceled out to subgrantees, the grantee cannot be punished for any violations of its customers. Similarly, the sanction must be tailored to "the particular program, or part thereof" in which noncompliance is proved. Fifth, fiscal action is not effective until 30 days after the grantor has filed with the House and Senate committees having jurisdiction over the involved program a written report of its decision and grounds. Finally, judicial review of the administrator's action is explicitly provided.[14]

By Executive Order the presidential power to approve agency regulations has been delegated to the Attorney General [15] who, in turn, delegated responsibility to the Assistant Attorney General for Civil Rights.[16] The order not only vests approval power but also authorizes the Attorney General to coordinate agency enforcement of Title VI by prescribing mandatory standards and procedures.[17]

The Department of Justice initially promulgated a set of broad advisory guidelines.[18] The thrust of these guidelines is the offering of advice on how to achieve compliance with the nondiscrimination standard without unduly jeopardizing the flow of benefits and services to the ultimate grant-in-aid beneficiaries. The statutory requirement of initial efforts to secure voluntary compliance is emphasized:

> "Title VI requires that a concerted effort be made to persuade any noncomplying applicant or recipient voluntarily to comply with Title VI. Efforts to secure voluntary compliance should be undertaken at the outset in every noncompliance situation and should be pursued through each stage of enforcement action. Similarly, where an applicant fails to file an adequate assurance or apparently breaches its terms, notice should be promptly given of the nature of the noncompliance problem and of the possible consequences thereof, and immediate effort made to secure voluntary compliance." [19]

In addition, the guidelines suggest various alternatives to what they describe as the "ultimate" [20] sanction of terminating aid or

---

[14] §603 Civil Rights Act of 1964, 42 U.S.C. §2000d-2.
[15] See note 10, *supra*, and accompanying text.
[16] See 28 C.F.R. pt. 42, subpt. F *passim*.
[17] §1 Exec. Order 11764, 39 Fed. Reg. 2575 (1974).
[18] 28 C.F.R. §50.3.
[19] *Id.* at para. I-C.
[20] *Id.* at para I-A.

318 / *Rights and Remedies Under Federal Grants*

refusing to fund a proposal. In cases involving applications for noncontinuing assistance or initial applications for programs of continuing assistance, agencies are authorized to defer "temporarily" action on such applications pending initiation and completion of Title VI procedures, including voluntary compliance attempts.[21] In cases of deferral, proceedings should be "conducted without delay and completed as soon as possible." [22] For ongoing grant programs, however, deferral of funding decisions is considered inappropriate presumably because of the severe impact on program operations. Federal funds must be paid out according to grantor commitments until a noncompliance decision has been formally rendered, although the grantor may limit the payout of funds to short periods.[23] The guidelines also suggest alternatives not involving the fiscal sanction. They suggest suits to obtain specific performance of Title VI assurances, as well as lawsuits to compel compliance with constitutional or other statutory provisions requiring nondiscrimination.[24] Two interesting recommended alternatives involve "by-passing a recalcitrant central agency applicant in order to obtain assurances from, or to grant assistance to complying local agencies," [25] or "by-passing all recalcitrant non-Federal agencies and providing assistance directly to the complying ultimate beneficiaries." [26]

In programs involving the distribution of federal funds to subgrantees through a central state recipient, the guideline instructs grantor agencies to impose enforcement responsibilities on the main grantee.[27]

Ten years after the promulgation of the guidelines described

---

21 *Id.* at para. II-A.
22 *Id.* at para. I-A.
23 *Id.* at para. II-B.
24 *Id.* at para. I-B-1. We have previously discussed the unclear state of the law concerning the ability of federal agencies to obtain specific performance of grant conditions. See Chapter 3, notes 215–230, *supra,* and accompanying text. Title VI does not specifically authorize such relief, and the Department of Justice guidelines speak only in terms of the "possibilities" of suits to obtain specific performance. HEW, however, specifically mandates that all HEW financial assistance programs require Title VI assurances which "include provisions which give the United States a right to seek its judicial enforcement." 45 C.F.R. §80.4(a)(1). HEW Form 441, "Assurance of Compliance With the Department of Health, Education and Welfare Regulation Under Title VI of the Civil Rights Act of 1964," which accompanies all HEW applications, provides, *inter alia:* "The Applicant recognizes and agrees that such Federal financial assistance will be extended in reliance on the representations and agreements made in this assurance, and that the United States shall have the right to seek judicial enforcement of this assurance."
25 28 C.F.R. §50.3, para. I-B-2(3).
26 *Id.* at para. I-B-2(4).
27 *Id.* at para. III.

above, the Department of Justice, undoubtedly unhappy with federal agency Title VI performance, put in force a regulation aimed at promoting active implementation of the Title VI nondiscrimination standard and at standardizing Title VI procedures.[28] The Attorney General ordered federal agencies administering programs subject to Title VI to approve, with prior clearance of the Department of Justice, implementing regulations and guidelines.[29] The agency Title VI guidelines must contain descriptions, for each covered grant-in-aid program, of: the nature of Title VI coverage; methods of enforcement; examples of prohibited practices in the context of particular programs; required or suggested remedial action; and requirements concerning data collection, complaints, and public information.[30]

The new regulation goes considerably beyond the statute itself in its control of agency enforcement of Title VI. Agencies and their grantees are required to disseminate to the public information concerning the Title VI program, including the nondiscrimination requirements, the rights of individuals under the Act and regulations, and the procedures for asserting those rights.[31] Agencies must collect data and information from grantees sufficient to permit effective enforcement of Title VI.[32] Each grantor is required to have a civil rights office at both the national and regional levels with responsibility for making or reviewing Title VI determinations.[33] The regulation identifies three major areas of compliance activity. One is the review of grant applications for the purpose of determining compliance prior to the approval of federal financial assistance.[34] The assurances required by the grantor agency and accompanying data are checked for completeness and responsiveness. A second area is postapproval compliance review.[35] Each federal grantor agency must establish and maintain an "effective program" of this nature. This requires not only periodic submission of compliance reports by grantees but also field investigations of a representative number of major recipients. The third compliance area involves the receipt and processing of

[28] 28 C.F.R. pt. 42, subpt. F, 41 Fed. Reg. 52669 (1976).
[29] Id. at §42.403.
[30] Id. at §42.404.
[31] Id. at §42.405.
[32] Id. at §42.406.
[33] Id. at §42.407(a).
[34] Id. at §42.407(b).
[35] Id. at §42.407(c).

complaints of discrimination by program beneficiaries and others.[36] Each federal agency must establish procedures for the prompt processing and disposition of such complaints. All complaints having "apparent merit" must be investigated, and both the complainant and the accused applicant/recipient of federal aid must be notified of the results. The regulation authorizes the federal agency to shift the initial responsibility of processing Title VI complaints to its grantees, but the grantor must verify the adequacy of the grantee's complaint procedures, must get a report of each complaint and investigation, and must retain the power to review grantee decisions. For programs involving formula grants to state agencies which then enter into subgrants, the state recipient is obliged to establish a Title VI program containing at least the same standards imposed on federal agencies by the regulations.[37]

The Department of Justice regulation requires each federal grantor to assign sufficient personnel to its Title VI program so as to "ensure effective enforcement."[38] The agencies are also instructed to develop a written enforcement plan.[39] The plan must set out priorities and procedures for enforcement and address, at a minimum:

> "the method for selecting recipients for compliance reviews, the establishment of timetables and controls for such reviews, the procedure for handling complaints, the allocation of its staff to different compliance functions, the development of guidelines, the determination as to when guidelines are not appropriate, and the provision of civil rights training for its staff."[40]

It is beyond our scope to review the Title VI regulations issued by grantor agencies in compliance with the Department of Justice guidelines.[41] We will, however, take a quick look at the

---

36 *Id.* at §42.408.
37 *Id.* at §42.410.
38 *Id.* at §42.414.
39 *Id.* at §42.415.
40 *Ibid.* See 43 Fed. Reg. 7048 (1978) for the fiscal year 1978 annual operating plan of HEW's Office for Civil Rights. The plan covers enforcement of all of HEW's civil rights obligations. OCR has 1,102 professional staff conducting its activities, and is allocating 55% of its investigative staff to the investigation of complaints and the balance to compliance reviews. *Id.* at 7050. It is estimated that 6,431 complaints will be handled, see *ibid.*, and compliance reviews will cover 30 different areas. See *id.* at 7055.
41 See, e.g., 7 C.F.R. pt. 15 (Department of Agriculture); 10 C.F.R. pt. 4 (Atomic Energy Commission); 32 C.F.R. pt. 1811 (Defense Civil Preparedness Agency); 33 C.F.R. pt. 24 (Coast Guard); 15 C.F.R. pt. 8 (Department of Commerce); 32 C.F.R. pt. 300 (Department of Defense); 45 C.F.R. pt. 1010 (Community Services

manner in which the Department of Health, Education and Welfare has implemented Title VI, the Executive Order, and the Attorney General's guidelines and directives.

HEW has enacted a procedural code governing the conduct of Title VI compliance hearings which closely resembles the judicial model.[42] The proceedings are triggered by a notice to the applicant/recipient ("respondent") which details the fiscal action HEW proposes to take, the legal basis for such action, and the matters of fact or law asserted as the basis for the fiscal sanction.[43] The notice either sets a time or place for a hearing, or authorizes the recipient of the notice to request a hearing by a specified date.[44] This notice is normally sent by the division of HEW which administers the particular program, although the department's general counsel represents HEW at the proceeding.[45] Issues for the hearing are formulated by the notice, the respondent's answer, and the subsequent amendments to both.[46] The hearing is conducted by a hearing examiner appointed pursuant to the Administrative Procedure Act.[47] In a written designation the examiner is either authorized to make a final decision or to certify the hearing record with his proposed findings of fact and law to a reviewing authority designated by the Secretary of HEW.[48] At the hearing respondents may appear by counsel or *pro se*.[49] Testimony is to be given orally under oath or affirmation at the hearing, with both parties having the right to introduce evidence and to cross-examine adverse witnesses.[50] The examiner has broad authority to make

---

Administration); 45 C.F.R. pt. 8 (Environmental Protection Agency); 7 C.F.R. pt. 1890 (Farmers Home Administration); 24 C.F.R. pt. 200 (Federal Housing Administration); 50 C.F.R. pt. 3 (Fish and Wildlife Service); 41 C.F.R. pt. 101-6 (General Services Administration); 24 C.F.R. pt. 1 (Department of Housing and Urban Development); 43 C.F.R. pts. 17, 17a (Department of the Interior); 22 C.F.R. pt. 209 (Agency for International Development); 29 C.F.R. pt. 31 (Department of Labor); 30 C.F.R. pt. 41 (Mining Enforcement and Safety Administration); 14 C.F.R. pt. 1250 (National Aeronautics and Space Administration); 45 C.F.R. pt. 611 (National Science Foundation); 13 C.F.R. pt. 113 (Small Business Administration); 22 C.F.R. pt. 141 (Department of State); 18 C.F.R. pt. 302 (Tennessee Valley Authority); 49 C.F.R. pt. 21 (Department of Transportation); 38 C.F.R. pt. 18 (Veterans Administration); 5 C.F.R. pt. 900, subpt. E (1976) (Civil Service Commission); 28 C.F.R. pt. 42, subpt. C (Department of Justice).

[42] 45 C.F.R. §§80.6–80.10, pt. 81.
[43] 45 C.F.R. §§80.9(a), 81.51.
[44] 45 C.F.R. §80.9(a).
[45] See 45 C.F.R. §81.21(b).
[46] 45 C.F.R. §§81.51–81.53.
[47] 45 C.F.R. §§80.9(b), 81.61.
[48] 45 C.F.R. §§80.10(a), 81.62.
[49] 45 C.F.R. §§80.9(c), 81.11.
[50] 45 C.F.R. §§80.9(d), 81.72–81.73.

rulings necessary to the conduct of a fair hearing, to avoid delay, and to maintain order, including prehearing conferences, rulings on procedural motions, requiring prehearing statements and trial briefs, excluding or receiving evidence, and otherwise regulating the course of the hearing.[51] The exclusive record for decision is the transcript of the evidence, the exhibits, and all papers and requests filed in the proceeding.[52]

If the hearing examiner issues a final decision, either party may request discretionary review by the Secretary of HEW.[53] The Secretary may also decide on his own to review the decision.[54] If the case is to be reviewed by the Secretary, the parties have the right to submit written arguments.[55] If the hearing examiner is authorized only to certify the record and recommend a decision, the final decision rests in the reviewing authority.[56] This procedure is appellate. The Secretary's designee decides on the basis of the certified record, the examiner's recommendations, the parties' briefs, and oral argument if permitted.[57] The reviewing authority's final decision may then be appealed to the courts, or the losing party may first seek discretionary Secretarial review.[58]

If the respondent is found to have violated Title VI, HEW's regulation authorizes the issuance of an order providing for the suspension, termination, refusal to grant, or refusal to continue federal assistance.[59] In addition, the order may contain "such terms, conditions, and other provisions as are consistent with and will effectuate the purposes of [Title VI] and this regulation. . . ." These additional sanction powers include that of denying future aid under any HEW assistance program "unless and until [the respondent] corrects its noncompliance and satisfies the responsible Department official that it will fully comply with the regulation." An applicant/recipient which is subject to an order finding continuing noncompliance with Title VI and denying eligibility for HEW assistance may "at any time" request reinstatement of eligibility.[60] The request must be supported with infor-

[51] 45 C.F.R. §81.63.
[52] 45 C.F.R. §§80.9(d)(2), 81.92.
[53] 45 C.F.R. §§80.10(e), 81.106.
[54] Ibid.
[55] 45 C.F.R. §81.106.
[56] 45 C.F.R. §§80.10(a), 81.104(b).
[57] 45 C.F.R. §§81.104(b), 81.105.
[58] 45 C.F.R. §§80.10(e), 81.106.
[59] 45 C.F.R. §80.10(f).
[60] 45 C.F.R. §80.10(g)(2).

mation demonstrating that compliance with Title VI has been achieved or that the terms of the order have been satisfied.[61] If HEW denies the request, the petitioner is entitled to an "expedited" Part 81 hearing.[62]

While many of the elements of judicial civil procedure have been incorporated into the HEW Title VI adjudication process, significant variances can be noted. One major distinction is that HEW as an institution plays the role of both prosecutor and judge. Whether or not an individual has initiated the proceedings by way of a complaint of discrimination, the controversy is litigated between HEW, represented by its general counsel, and the grantee. If an independent hearing examiner is given decisional power and if the Secretary, in his discretion, chooses not to intervene, an impartial tribunal has been provided. But the Secretary may opt to have a department official act as the decisional authority and may himself ultimately decide any case. Another important distinction is that the penalties which may be imposed for Title VI violations are not clearly defined. While the fiscal sanctions are reasonably precise, the HEW regulation provides additional remedial power without specifying its content. For example, whether the grantee can be subjected to an order requiring repayment of illegally expended funds is unclear. Similarly, it is ambiguous whether a grantee can be subjected to a claim of damages by the individual suffering discrimination [63] and, more generally, the extent to which the order can attempt to remedy the effects of past discrimination.[64]

Several variances from traditional judicial procedure typify the administrative adjudicatory hearing. The rules of evidence, for example, do not apply, although the officer conducting the hearing is advised to apply "principles designed to assure the production of the most credible evidence available and to subject testimony to test by cross-examination. . . ." [65] Additionally, the hearing officer has considerable discretion to permit the introduction of depositions and affidavits as direct evidence even though a party to the proceeding may not have the opportunity to cross-examine the affiant/deponent.[66] The officer may also modify or

---

[61] 45 C.F.R. §§80.10(g), 81.121(a).
[62] 45 C.F.R. §§80.10(g)(3), 81.121.
[63] See Chapter 4, *supra*, at pp. 137–42.
[64] See *Regents of the Univ. of Cal.* v. *Bakke*, 438 U.S. 265 (1978).
[65] 45 C.F.R. §80.9(d)(2).
[66] 45 C.F.R. §§81.73, 81.75, 81.76.

324 / *Rights and Remedies Under Federal Grants*

waive any procedural rule "upon determination that no party will be unduly prejudiced and the ends of justice will be thereby served." [67] Finally, neither party to the proceeding is entitled to prehearing discovery.

In addition to providing a procedural code for adjudicatory hearings, the HEW Title VI regulations comply with Department of Justice directives by: detailing the programs to which the Title VI prohibitions apply; [68] specifying the types of discriminatory acts which are prohibited, with illustrative examples; [69] explaining the content and reach of Title VI assurances which applicants for and recipients of HEW assistance must provide; [70] outlining the Department's procedures for receiving, investigating and resolving complaints of racial discrimination; [71] and establishing the basic requirements for the compliance reports submitted to the operational divisions of HEW.[72] Of particular interest is the requirement that the civil rights assurance forms drafted by the component agencies of HEW must contain a provision giving the grantor the right to seek judicial enforcement of its terms.[73]

Discrimination Based on Handicap

The structure created around the prohibition against handicap discrimination in federally supported activities is almost identical to the Title VI enforcement scheme.[74] Unlike Title VI, which speaks rather extensively to implementation norms, Section 504 of the Rehabilitation Act of 1973 as originally passed simply stated the rule, with no exceptions [75] and no guidance concerning implementation.[76] Identity between handicap and racial civil rights enforcement was initially achieved, however, through implement-

[67] 45 C.F.R. §81.4.
[68] 45 C.F.R. pt. 80, app. A.
[69] 45 C.F.R. §§80.3, 80.5.
[70] 45 C.F.R. §80.4.
[71] 45 C.F.R. §80.7.
[72] 45 C.F.R. §80.6.
[73] 45 C.F.R. §80.4(a)(1). See note 24, *supra,* and accompanying text.
[74] The only major difference we have noted is that federal agencies must require recipients of financial aid to conduct a self-evaluation of their compliance with §504 Rehabilitation Act of 1973, 29 U.S.C. §794, and implementing regulations. See 45 C.F.R. §85.5(b)(2). HEW's own requirements for grantee self-evaluations are set forth at 45 C.F.R. §84.6(c).
[75] Unlike Title VI which exempts employment practices, see note 6, *supra,* §504 applies to grantee hiring of staff. See 45 C.F.R. §§85.52–85.55. But see *Trageser v. Libbie Rehab. Center, Inc.,* 590 F.2d 87 (4B Cir. 1978).
[76] See note 3, *supra.*

ing regulations, and in 1978 Congress amended the title to incorporate within it "[t]he remedies, procedures, and rights set forth in Title VI of the Civil Rights Act of 1964." [77]

In 1976 President Ford issued Executive Order 11914 [78] to implement the Section 504 standard which had, theretofore, been largely ignored by federal grantor agencies. The order designated the Secretary of Health, Education and Welfare as the coordinator of the implementation program and instructed him to establish standards for determining who is handicapped and guidelines for determining what are discriminatory practices. Each federal agency providing federal aid was ordered to issue implementing regulations consistent with the directives of the Secretary of HEW.[79] The Title VI focus on voluntary compliance is adopted in the Executive Order, as well as the expedient of fiscal sanctions following a posthearing finding of noncompliance. Like Title VI, the order limits fiscal sanctions to "the particular program or activity or part thereof with respect to which there has been such a finding of noncompliance."

HEW guidelines and coordinating directives became effective on January 13, 1978.[80] Rather than creating an independent enforcement system, the HEW regulation instructs federal agencies to adopt the same enforcement and hearing procedures utilized for Title VI.[81] The regulation also defines both "recipient" [82] and "federal financial assistance" [83] in a way which makes program coverage identical with the Title VI program.

Sex Discrimination

Congressional extension of the civil right to be free from discrimination based solely on sex has been more cautious than

[77] §505(2) Rehabilitation Act of 1973, 29 U.S.C. §794a(2), as added by §120 Rehabilitation, Comprehensive Services, and Developmental Disabilities Amendments of 1978, Pub. L. 95–602, Nov. 6, 1978.
[78] 41 Fed. Reg. 17871 (1976).
[79] HEW ordered federal agencies to publish proposed rules no later than April 13, 1978, and final regulations no later than 135 days after the close of the comment period. 45 C.F.R. §85.4(b).
[80] 45 C.F.R. pt. 85, 43 Fed. Reg. 2132 (1978).
[81] 45 C.F.R. §85.5(a).
[82] The definition of "recipient" includes all subgrantees. See 45 C.F.R. §85.3(d). Compare 28 C.F.R. §50.3, para. III.
[83] Neither the Rehabilitation Act of 1973, 29 U.S.C. §§701–796i, nor Exec. Order 11914 defines "Federal financial assistance," despite the multitudinous forms of federal aid. HEW has excluded, like Title VI, procurement contracts and federal insurance and guarantees. Compare §602 Civil Rights Act of 1964, 42 U.S.C. §2000d-1, and 45 C.F.R. §80.13(f) with 45 C.F.R. §85.3(e).

the ban on race and handicap prejudice. The major prohibition against sexual discrimination is found in Title IX of the Education Amendments of 1972.[84] Unlike its counterparts in Title VI and the Rehabilitation Act, the ban on sexual discrimination is not extended to all federal assistance programs; rather Title IX is limited to "any education program" receiving federal financial aid.[85] This has led to the need, in noneducational federal grant activities, to extend the ban on a program-by-program basis.[86]

Title IX was closely patterned after Title VI not only in the prohibitory language [87] but also in the enforcement structure. Each federal agency administering an assistance [88] program covered by Title IX is directed to issue implementing regulations [89] approved by the President.[90] Fiscal sanctions, such as the denial or termination of grants, can be utilized to enforce the civil rights standard, but no penalties can be imposed until efforts to secure voluntary compliance have been unsuccessful and a finding of noncompliance has been made after notice and opportunity for a hearing on the record. Fiscal sanctions must be limited to the particular entity found in violation and to the particular programs in which sexual discrimination has occurred. By regulation the nondiscrimination prohibition is made applicable to subrecipients of federal assistance,[91] and the statute clearly contemplates that

---

[84] 20 U.S.C. §§1681–1686. Title IX was preceded by two sections of the Public Health Service Act which prohibited sex discrimination in admissions to federally supported (including loan guarantees) graduate schools of medicine and health and nurse training schools. See §704 Public Health Service Act, 42 U.S.C. §292d, as added by §207 Pub. L. 91-519, Nov. 2, 1970, and renumbered by §201(c) Pub. L. 94-484, Oct. 12, 1976; §855 Public Health Service Act, 42 U.S.C. §298b-2, as added by §11 Pub. L. 92-158, Nov. 18, 1971, and renumbered by §941(k)(1) Pub. L. 94-63, July 29, 1975. Both sections continue in force and are implemented by a separate HEW regulation. See 45 C.F.R. pt. 83.

[85] §901(a) Education Amendments of 1972, 20 U.S.C. §1681(a).

[86] See, e.g., §132 Comprehensive Employment and Training Act of 1973, 29 U.S.C. §834; §109 Housing and Community Development Act of 1974, 42 U.S.C. §5309; §110 Local Public Works Capital Development and Investment Act of 1976, 42 U.S.C. §6709.

[87] See note 4, *supra*.

[88] Only procurement contracts, loan guarantees, and insurance are excluded. See §902 Education Amendments of 1972, 20 U.S.C. §1682; 45 C.F.R. §86.2(g).

[89] The command was ignored by federal grantor agencies. In §844 Pub. L. 93-380, Aug. 21, 1974, 20 U.S.C. §1681 note, Congress ordered the Secretary of HEW to publish implementing regulations. Final regulations were issued by HEW on June 4, 1975. 40 Fed. Reg. 24128 (1975). Although various federal agencies other than HEW offer financial support to education programs, they apparently continue to ignore the directive to issue regulations.

[90] §902 Education Amendments of 1972, 20 U.S.C. §1682. Unlike race and handicap discrimination, no presidential order has issued concerning sex discrimination.

[91] 45 C.F.R. §86.2(h).

only the entity actually violating Title IX will suffer fiscal sanctions.[92] Nevertheless, HEW's form of assurance contains the following stipulation:

> "The Applicant hereby agrees that it will . . . [a]ssure itself that all contractors, subcontractors, subgrantees or others with whom it arranges to provide services or benefits to its students or employees in connection with its education program or activity are not discriminating on the basis of sex against these students or employees." [93]

The accompanying explanation makes clear that the recipient has a continuing obligation to ensure that its subrecipients are not discriminating and must monitor their activities. This opens the possibility that HEW can sanction both the grantee and the subgrantee—the grantee for violation of its monitoring obligation and the subgrantee for its violation of Title IX—despite the "pinpointing" clause in Section 902.[94] Final actions must be postponed for 30 days pending congressional review of "a full written report of the circumstances and the grounds for such action." Like Title VI, judicial review of final agency action is explicitly provided.[95]

In its implementing regulation HEW has followed the normal enforcement pattern. The hearing rules and mechanisms of Title VI are adopted *in toto*.[96] The nondiscrimination obligation is extended to recipients by way of assurances which accompany grant applications.[97] Recipients must disseminate widely their Title IX responsibilities [98] and must establish procedures to process grievances.[99] Also, recipients are obliged to perform self-evaluations of their degree of compliance with Title IX.[100]

Age Discrimination

Although the law prohibiting unreasonable discrimination based on age in federal assistance programs was enacted in Novem-

---

[92] Compare Chapter 9, *supra*, at pp. 252–53.
[93] HEW Form 639 A (3/77), "Assurance of Compliance With Title IX of the Education Amendments of 1972 and the Regulation Issued by the Department of Health, Education and Welfare in Implementation Thereof," at E12.
[94] §902 Education Amendments of 1972, 20 U.S.C. §1682.
[95] §903 *id.*, 20 U.S.C. §1683.
[96] 45 C.F.R. §86.71.
[97] 45 C.F.R. §86.4.
[98] 45 C.F.R. §86.9.
[99] 45 C.F.R. §86.8(b).
[100] 45 C.F.R. §86.3(c).

328 / *Rights and Remedies Under Federal Grants*

ber 1975,[101] the prohibition is effective only "pursuant to regulations" [102] and these cannot take effect prior to July 1, 1979.[103] Thus, as of the time of writing, this civil rights program has yet to be launched.[104]

When established, the enforcement techniques will parallel those of the other civil rights since the Age Discrimination Act of 1975 borrows heavily from its predecessors. Voluntary compliance efforts, fiscal sanctions, and prior hearing opportunities are basic features of the enforcement program.[105] The statute varies from its brethren in one important aspect. As originally enacted, Section 305(e) of the Act [106] made federal agency enforcement the "exclusive remedy" for age discriminations. The law, thus, dealt explicitly with the question, which has troubled the courts,[107] whether a private cause of action may be implied under a grant condition. This negative position was mollified in the 1978 amendments to the Act. The statute now authorizes "any interested person" to bring a suit to enjoin violations of the age discrimination standards established in the Act and regulations.[108] A prevailing plaintiff is also entitled to be paid costs and reasonable attorney's fees by the other side. The conference committee on this legislation, however, conditioned the bringing of private injunctive actions on the exhaustion of available administrative remedies.[109] The statute also precludes private injunctive suits if "at the time the action is brought the same alleged violation by the same defendant is the subject of a pending action in any court of the United States."

---

[101] Age Discrimination Act of 1975, Title III, Pub. L. 94-135, Nov. 28, 1975, 42 U.S.C. §§6101–6107.

[102] §303 *id.*, 42 U.S.C. §6102.

[103] §304(a)(5) *id.*, 42 U.S.C. §6103(a)(5).

[104] HEW is given the role of coordinator. See §304(a)(1) *id.*, 42 U.S.C. §6103(a)(1); 43 Fed. Reg. 8756 (1978) (notice of intent to issue proposed regulations); 43 Fed. Reg. 56428 (1978) (proposed rules).

[105] §305 Age Discrimination Act of 1975, 42 U.S.C. §6104. §306 *id.*, 42 U.S.C. §6105, provides judicial review of federal agency action.

[106] 42 U.S.C. §6104(e) (1976).

[107] See Chapter 4, notes 9, 33–39, 141–151, *supra*, and accompanying text.

[108] §§305(e), (f) Age Discrimination Act of 1975, 42 U.S.C. §§6104(e), (f), as amended by §401(c) Comprehensive Older Americans Act Amendments of 1978, Pub. L. 95-478, Oct. 18, 1978. The statute does not explicitly preclude a claim for damages within the suit for injunctive relief, but the legislative history makes clear that this was the congressional intent. See H.R. Rep. No. 95-1150, 95th Cong., 2d Sess. 40 (1978).

[109] See H.R. Conf. Rep. No. 95-1618, 95th Cong., 2d Sess. 87 (1978).

Fellowships

Although this book has focused on federal assistance to institutions, we shall briefly discuss the Due Process rights of individuals who hold fellowships and traineeships from the United States. Our research has uncovered serious constitutional deficiencies in the treatment of such individuals—a neglect sufficiently egregious to merit exposure and analysis.

Those holding federal training and study awards are subject, like institutional grantees, to a series of conditions placed on the grant. One will be a performance standard, typically phrased in extremely vague terms. We find in the agency regulations the power to cut off the federal stipend to a fellow or trainee for "material fail[ure] to comply with the terms and conditions" [110] of the award, for failure to "carry out the purpose for which made," [111] for being "unfit or unable to carry out the purposes of the traineeship," [112] for "unsatisfactory" performance," [113] for not making "satisfactory progress," [114] and for not being "in the best interests of the United States." [115] An individual suffering cancellation of federal assistance of this type is entitled, by statute [116] and regulation,[117] to *no* administrative Due Process. Only when the revocation is based on grounds of disloyalty or immorality is there an entitlement to prior notice and opportunity to be heard.[118] Similarly recipients of federal student aid get Due Process rights if their aid is cut off for convictions of crime or violations of institutional rules, but not if the reason is "other misconduct" or unsatisfactory progress.[119]

---

110 See, e.g., 42 C.F.R. §66.109(a) (PHS National Research Service Award).
111 *Ibid.*
112 See, e.g., 42 C.F.R. §61.17 (Public Health Service fellowships); 42 C.F.R. §86.39(b) (OSHA traineeships); 42 C.F.R. §63.6 (NIH traineeship).
113 *Ibid.*
114 See, e.g., 42 C.F.R. §123.43(d) (bilingual education fellowships).
115 §1001(g) National Defense Education Act, 20 U.S.C. §581(g).
116 See, e.g., Title IV, Public Health Service Act, 42 U.S.C. §§281–289"1"-8; §1001(g) National Defense Education Act, 20 U.S.C. §581(g): "Nothing contained in this Act shall prohibit the Commissioner from refusing or revoking a fellowship award under sections 461–465 of this Act, in whole or in part, if the Commissioner is of the opinion that such award is not in the best interests of the United States."
117 See, e.g., 42 C.F.R. §61.17; 45 C.F.R. §123.43(d); 45 C.F.R. §187.79 (opportunity to rebut in writing or in informal meeting); 42 C.F.R. §63.6; 42 C.F.R. §66.109; 42 C.F.R. §86.39 (written rebuttal unless Secretary determines oral presentation is desirable).
118 See 42 C.F.R. §61.15; 45 C.F.R. pt. 147. Hearings are conducted pursuant to the procedures set forth at 45 C.F.R. pt. 10.
119 §497 Higher Education Act of 1965, 20 U.S.C. §1088f.

330 / *Rights and Remedies Under Federal Grants*

The above system was created at a time when the prevailing norm was that recipients of governmental benefits do not hold constitutionally protected property.[120] Although *Goldberg* v. *Kelly* [121] and subsequent cases [122] cast a rather clear shadow over these regulations, neglect has likely kept them in force.

It is most difficult to construct an argument supporting the validity of these regulations. Once awarded, the fellowship becomes a valuable property justifiably held by the recipient. The conditions under which the recipient may be deprived of that property call for the finding of facts and their application to legal standards, both being adjudicative processes. Cancellation of a fellowship will typically cause substantial hardships to the recipient, perhaps of sufficient degree that a prior hearing is constitutionally mandated and, certainly, of sufficient magnitude that at least a subsequent administrative hearing is called for.[123] The hearing, at either time, could not be satisfied by opportunities to make written submissions or have an informal meeting. Given the critical importance of individual facts in these fund cutoffs, only an evidentiary hearing following the judicial model would be sufficient.

Our conclusions are reinforced by an appreciation of the "liberty" interests affected by the termination of a fellowship.[124] In most cases the termination will be based on a finding of individual fault—the performance standards being phrased in terms of fitness, ability, and performance. Those who hold such fellowships are likely to be severely prejudiced in their future career opportunities by the fault-based black spot of a fellowship cancellation. Thus, not only does the fellow or trainee lose a present opportunity for training and education but his future is undoubtedly bleaker because of the opprobrium attaching to the cancellation.

---

[120] See Chapter 1, notes 69–73, *supra,* and accompanying text.
[121] 397 U.S. 254 (1970).
[122] See cases cited in Chapter 7, note 28, *supra.*
[123] See Chapter 7, *supra,* at pp. 181–84.
[124] See Chapter 7, *supra,* at pp. 211–19.

15

Guideposts for Reform

"I submit that larger legislative management is necessary and desirable, that, indeed, there is no other way to prevent the anarchical proliferation. . . . [I]t is only by unhurried canvassing of all the issues in a field, the systematic rooting out of inconsistencies, the time-consuming search for information that can shape and inform policy, that the entire corpus of a field of law can be evaluated and reframed." [1]

"The history of American freedom is, in no small measure, the history of procedure." [2]

My original plan was to stop here. The task of surveying the scene, working through some basic concepts, and testing the metes and bounds of Due Process in the context of federal grants has been arduous. It would suffice, I thought, to lay the groundwork for whatever reform this work would suggest. The next step, the formidable task of fleshing out the details of change, could be left to others. A decision not to attempt the "development" phase of my ideas would also spare me the anguish of seeing my reform proposals sink in the quicksand of government lethargy.

The temptation to at least sketch out a new system, however, has been irresistible. It also tidies up what might otherwise seem cowardly incomplete. While most of this chapter is but a synthesis of ideas previously posited, our concept of a Grant Disputes Board

[1] H. Wechsler, "Comment on American Legal Institution," in *Legal Institutions Today and Tomorrow* 303, 307 (M. Paulsen ed. 1959).
[2] *Malinski v. New York*, 324 U.S. 401, 414 (1945) (Frankfurter, J., concurring).

332 / *Rights and Remedies Under Federal Grants*

might lend focus to what otherwise might seem to be scattered complaints.

A Grantee Bill of Procedural Rights

The Office of Management and Budget is presently conducting, pursuant to congressional directives, a study to determine the feasibility of creating a "comprehensive system of guidance for federal assistance programs."[3] That fancy language translates into a set of basic rules governing, among other forms of federal aid, grants. A type of legal code is envisioned, a consolidation of the operational legal principles now spread through dozens of statutes, hundreds of regulations, and thousands of pages of handbooks.[4] It is instructive to note that OMB has not been ordered to prepare such a code; rather, it is to determine whether such a set of common principles *can* be created to the advantage of the grant-in-aid system. Such is the complexity of the field. "Can the beast be tamed?" is the question posed, a sorry commentary on the state of public law in the United States.

In any event, we are happy to report that consolidation is both possible and desirable, at least in that part of the law of federal grants which deals with enforcement of federal conditions and the resolution of grantor-grantee disputes. We recommend a simple statute which could be called the Bill of Procedural Rights for Grantees. It would contain a set of Due Process principles which guarantees to the clients of federal grant-giving agencies a fair forum for the ventilation of controversies. Such a Bill of Procedural Rights need not await the development of a comprehensive code of grant-in-aid rules. Its justification is relevant regardless of the precise content of the norms of conduct imposed on grantees and the obligations of grantors.

This work demonstrates the high degree of repetition among federal grant statutes and regulations. The same rule is established in the same language in scores of statutes and regulations. The few differences have little to do with the particular grant program being regulated but rather are products of the preferences and idio-

[3] §8 Federal Grant and Cooperative Agreement Act of 1977, Pub. L. 95-224, Feb. 3, 1978, 41 U.S.C. §507.
[4] See 43 Fed. Reg. 27504, 27504–27505 (1978) (proposed study guide): "... a government-wide set of assistance guidance or regulations ... a centrally developed set of regulations for direct use without substitutes or duplication by agencies. ..."

syncrasies of the particular legislative draftsman. We can, therefore, enact a Due Process law and system for all grant programs and repeal the particular provisions found in particular grant statutes. Congressional action is the best implementation alternative, because only Congress can consolidate and repeal in a comprehensive fashion. A second advantage of congressional action is that grant-giving agencies are more likely to comply than if an OMB directive, for example, or even a presidential order tried to accomplish the same result. Agencies could refer to their obligations to implement the congressional intent expressed in the grant statutes under their jurisdiction.[5] But if Congress cannot be moved to act, it would be within the domain of OMB to establish a set of standard principles as an aspect of grant management. As long as such principles embodied greater procedural rights for grantees than required under grant statutes, there would be no conflict with positive law.

Notice and Opportunity To Be Heard

In the materials that follow we shall highlight the main features of the proposed Bill of Procedural Rights and then discuss implementing structures and procedures. We will not, for the most part, recapitulate what we believe is constitutionally mandated and what is simply a matter of good government. Due Process deals with the specific instance, and here we are generalizing. This particular proposed system is not of constitutional obligation, although most of the federal agency action listed below invokes some type of process as a Fifth Amendment necessity.

Our Bill of Procedural Rights will guarantee grantees notice and an opportunity to be heard if any federal agency action adversely affects them. All federal grant administrators would be covered, and the definition of grant and grantee would track the definitional efforts under the Federal Grant and Cooperative Agreement Act.[6] We would, however, fully include subgrantees in

[5] See Advisory Commission on Intergovernmental Relations, *The Intergovernmental Grant System: An Assessment and Proposed Policies: Summary and Concluding Observations* 6 (1978):

"The attempts to improve coordination among programs have demonstrated that federal agencies have few incentives to standardize, simplify or 'target' their activities. Their primary concern (shared by most Congressional committees which oversee them, as well as most interest groups) is to be able to account for and make effective use of each specific grant program they administer. This naturally leads to differences in requirements and procedures."

[6] Pub. L. 95-224, Feb. 3, 1978, 41 U.S.C. §§501–509.

334 / *Rights and Remedies Under Federal Grants*

all cases in which the actions of the federal grantor adversely affect them, whether directly, as when the federal agency moves against the subgrantee, or indirectly, as when action against the principal recipient ripples downward.

We would specifically include within the guarantees of notice and hearing rights the following types of federal agency decisions:

- Rejection of state plans (or any comparable document) and of modifications of such plans;
- Withholding of entitlement funds;
- Allocation of formula funds;
- Actions stripping a jurisdiction of all or part of its formula funds under the grantor's reallocation authority;
- Termination of grants, including fellowships and traineeships, within their term;
- Voiding of grants for misrepresentations in the grant application;
- Adverse redeterminations of area eligibility for grants;
- In programs in which the grant is to a designated provider of services, such as a health systems agency, action stripping the grantee of such designation, whether during or at the end of the grant term;
- Suspension of a grant;
- Denial of a continuation award in service-oriented programs where a denial of refunding will substantially affect individual program beneficiaries;
- Denial of federal reimbursement for grantee costs, refusal to permit certain expenditures, or cost disallowances;
- Decisions on indirect cost rates;
- Decisions on grantee requests to modify the approved budget;
- Action on requests for a finding that a noncomplying program, project, or plan has been corrected and that deferrals or sanctions should be lifted.

We have discussed each of these types of actions in preceding chapters and have shown how they prejudice grantees and individual beneficiaries of grantee efforts, regardless of the particular grant activity. Across the spectrum of federal grant programs service activities will ordinarily be closed wholly or partially because of any of the above actions. Their inherent capability of harm, a constitutionally recognized deprivation of "property" in most cases, is what springs the need for procedural protection.

Later we shall recommend variances in procedure to deal with varying degrees of substantiality in the harm. That recommendation concerns cases which carry the right to a hearing, and it attempts to vary the formality of the proceeding according to the seriousness of the federal action. At this point we must repeat an idea previously set forth [7] that some federal actions, even those involving economic loss to grantees, are not takings of sufficient magnitude to constitute "deprivations" in a constitutional sense. We posited the idea that the Constitution does not mandate Due Process in every case in which government action affects someone's liberty or property. Admitting the arbitrariness of the dividing line, we suggested a threshold level of substantiality in the harm.[8] Below this level constitutional requirements do not apply.

The fact that the constitutional standard of Due Process is inapplicable, however, does not mean that we must similarly limit our proposal. We may recommend and the government may adopt procedures which offer protections greater in coverage and more solicitous in content than are mandated by the Constitution. The Fifth Amendment sets minimum not maximum standards. Thus, we may and should consider whether access to procedural rights should be limited by some degree of harm. We previously suggested a *constitutional* minimum of 5 percent of the total grant as a rough guess at substantiality.[9] Now we must decide whether to afford greater access to hearing rights as a question of good government rather than constitutional principle.

Our first tendency is to adopt the constitutional minimum as a method of keeping our procedural systems from being clogged by trivial matters. Further reflection reveals the unsoundness of that impulse when considered in light of our later recommendation for an informal adjudicative system through which small controversies can be rapidly processed. We have no basis for presuming that grantees would pursue small or frivolous claims just because an adjudicative system exists to process them. Grantees as well as grantors incur costs in such pursuits. In most cases involving small cost disallowances, budget modification disallowals, required corrective actions, and other daily administrative decisions, it would

---

[7] See Chapter 7, *supra*, at pp. 219–22.
[8] See Chapter 7, note 122, *supra*, and accompanying text.
[9] *Ibid.*

be irrational for a grantee to do anything other than accept the federal judgment. We can guess that many of these matters would not be resolved differently, or substantially differently, after an adjudicative hearing, and that grantees are smart enough to know this. Thus, the presumption closer to common sense is that only seriously debatable matters would be brought into the adjudicative system, and not even all of these. Grantees would likely accept a number of questionable federal decisions because a fight simply is not worth the trouble. We would not, therefore, anticipate a burdensome rash of trivial and one-sided matters. Further, nothing would preclude the later establishment of jurisdictional minima if our hunch is wrong.

On the other hand, without strong evidence of overuse we have difficulty justifying exclusionary rules based on the type of grantor action or the dollar value. Both factors require the adoption of rules which would necessarily deprive grantees of an administrative hearing on the basis of considerations which might not hold in the particular case. If we tried to establish a flexible system in which unique circumstances could be counted in determining jurisdiction to adjudicate, we would invite probably as much trouble as if we let in *ab initio* all claims of adverse federal action.

Thus, we recommend that, in addition to the listed federal grantor actions, grantees be allowed to challenge through adjudicative process any federal administrator actions claimed to be adverse to grantee interests.

The "Timing" Issue

The "timing" of our notice and hearing—whether they shall be granted before or after agency action becomes final—will also be influenced by the degree of harm. The Due Process rule is that if a deprivation will cause substantial, immediate hardship it must be *preceded* by the hearing opportunity, absent powerful needs for quicker government action.[10] Let us analyze two of the listed adverse actions to see workings of the "timing" rule.

Federal agency decisions concerning the allocation of formula grants are of major importance to entitlement grantees. Because so many dollars are involved in the formula programs—infrequently less than $100 million—agency decisions concerning both

[10] See, e.g., *Goldberg v. Kelly*, 397 U.S. 254 (1970).

the workings of frequently indecipherable statutory formulas and the data to be utilized will shift large amounts from one jurisdiction to another. Those decisions, therefore, produce significant effects on the ability of grantees to perform the services contemplated by the grant program. Some of these actions are policy decisions beyond the reach of adjudicative process. Some, however, relate to the specific demographic and other data of the entitlement jurisdictions and would be suitable for fact adjudication. An entitled grantee could argue, therefore, that it should be given notice and a hearing before the allotment of formula funds is finalized. Nonetheless, a prior opportunity to be heard must be denied because it would produce an intolerable burden on the grant system. The start-up and refunding dates of federal programs would be delayed for indeterminate periods while each recipient is given its hearing opportunity, most of which, we guess, would confirm the federal decision. In almost all programs such delay would be unacceptably prejudicial to the interests of those served by the government activity. The public interest in having appropriated funds put to their intended use as quickly as possible would outweigh the particular harm which a grantee might suffer from errors in the allocation process.[11] The grantee's need for process before the allocation is completed is also tested by the adequacy of post-decision review.[12] Assuming that a portion of the appropriated funds is held by the federal agency for subsequent installment payments, as is typical practice, funds would be available to compensate a short-changed grantee. Thus, after the allocations are announced and initial payments made, accelerated hearings may be held and errors remedied while unobligated funds are still in the federal bank.

In comparison, the balance swings to the other side on reallotment decisions. Grant statutes authorize the administrator to switch to other jurisdictions the portion of any allocation which is not needed by a recipient.[13] In this situation a prior hearing would protect the recipient from undue harm—damage to its fiscal capacity and, thus, the loss of services for its beneficiaries, both based on presumably erroneous federal action—with only minor disadvantages to the grant program. Also, a hearing following a

[11] See *Clark* v. *Richardson*, 431 F. Supp. 105 (D. N.J. 1977); *City of Grand Rapids* v. *Richardson*, 429 F. Supp. 1087 (W.D. Mich. 1977); *Lewis* v. *Richardson*, 428 F. Supp. 1164 (D. Mass. 1977).
[12] See, e.g., *Mathews* v. *Eldridge*, 424 U.S. 319 (1976).
[13] See Chapter 7, notes 56-59, *supra*, and accompanying text.

reallotment might produce a dollarless victory for the prejudiced grantee. If the reallotted funds have been obligated to another, it might prove impossible to recall them because of prejudice to the third party. Reallotments frequently occur late in a fiscal year when grantee spending rates are better known, and the appropriations for the particular fiscal year may be exhausted by the time the reallotment decision is reversed. The grantee would, thus, be left only with an appeal to Congress for an additional appropriation to remedy the mistake.[14]

Most of the other adverse actions specifically listed above would necessitate a prior hearing. Congress has usually judged that withholding of formula funds for noncompliance and rejection of state plans for nonconformity are sufficiently detrimental to require a hearing before decisions are finalized.[15] Terminations, voiding, area eligibility redetermination, grantee redesignation, and certain denials of refunding are akin. All involve complete cessation of federal funding, the worst available federal sanction. The remaining instances, on the other hand, would ordinarily involve less than the full grant. The degree of possible harm to the grantee would then depend on the percentage of the grant affected by the federal action. The common situation of cost disallowances provides the best example. One would not want to burden the grant system with prior hearing rights on $5000 disallowances in multimillion dollar programs. Still, cost disallowances may involve substantial sums and severely harm grantees. A possible solution is to require prior notice and adjudication when federal decisions would affect a significant percentage of the grant, like 20 percent. If a federal decision involves a lesser portion of the grant, the affected party could normally withstand the temporary financial loss pending corrective action. A stay of federal action could be authorized for the exceptional case in which the reviewing authority is convinced that significant prejudice to the grantee would result even though the bulk of the grant was untouched.

Similar flexibility is needed in the case of suspensions. The Federal Government needs the ability to prevent, without undue delay, the diversion of federal funds to illegal or impermissible purposes. Funds could be squandered, with little chance of re-

[14] Courts cannot order Congress to appropriate money. See Chapter 7, note 46, *supra*.
[15] See statutes cited in Chapter 9, note 2, and Chapter 12, note 1, *supra*.

covery, during the period of sending notice and setting and holding a hearing on the question of suspension. On the other hand, a suspension of federal payments (or authorization to spend federal funds) can stop a project cold and, if it drags on, can be as effective as a termination in its destructive effects. Thus, any suspension which has been imposed without a prior hearing must be of limited duration; some type of quick and informal hearing opportunity must be given in all cases to the grantee to show that suspension would be inappropriate, either because federal funds are not endangered, the grantee is in a precarious situation, or the individual beneficiaries will unduly suffer; and in those cases in which even a temporary suspension will work a severe hardship on the grantee and the federal need for immediate action is minimal, a full hearing must precede suspension.

Sanctions

A Grantee Bill of Procedural Rights must address several problems we have encountered in our study of the remedial powers of federal grantor agencies. The first is rampant ambiguity in the sanctions attending violations of federal rules. Statutes and regulations generally do not specify the types of sanctions which may be imposed for grantee noncompliance with federal standards, nor are details offered concerning the sanctions that are mentioned. It would seem an elemental aspect of fair procedure to warn grantees of the consequences which their mistaken actions might produce. The second basic problem is that of proportionality—sanctions must parallel derelictions in kind and degree. The concept found in most grant programs that the violation of any grant condition can lead to termination of the entire grant, though rarely if ever invoked, is a frightfully unfair premise on which to base a system of cooperative efforts. A third difficulty is, perhaps, irremediable. Because of constitutional considerations, grantees must be allowed to opt out of grant programs, at least at the end of project terms. Therefore, grantees cannot be forced to comply with federal standards beyond an agency's threatening and causing the loss of federal financial participation. The only effectiveness in the fiscal sanction is in the threat; any time the sanction is actually levied there is a total remediation failure. There is no violation of federal program standards because there is no longer a federal program. Still, the United States could openly and honestly accept this constitutional limit on remedial power. Although the principle of voluntariness is firmly established by Supreme Court decisions, there is no clear-cut admission at the level of executive regulations. It might also be possible, once the remedial problem was tagged and accepted, to devise alternatives to the self-defeating fiscal sanction.

Let us now address in greater detail each of these problems, starting with the last.

The stress on "voluntary" compliance found in the enforcement sections of nondiscrimination rules must be universally invoked in grant programs. Fiscal sanctions *always* frustrate the goals of grants-in-aid, of whatever type; hence, it is universally preferable to achieve compliance with federal standards than to impose financial penalties. Each federal agency must be instructed to limit such penalties to those cases in which sincere negotiations have been fruitless. If future compliance is assured, past deviations must be forgiven, except, perhaps, when there has been a diversion of federal funds to clearly impermissible uses. Because recovery of past illegal expenditures would necessarily come out of program funds, whether federal or local, the current beneficiaries of the grant project would suffer the penalty. That unseemly and unfair consequence should be avoided whenever possible.

In cases in which a grantee refuses, after a hearing and negotiations, to abide by federal standards, alternatives to total withholding or termination should be created. One possibility might be the imposition of fiscal penalties for the duration of the noncompliance. Penalties could be large enough to act as a prod to future compliance, while not so heavy as to curtail program operations significantly. The lowering of service levels caused by the fiscal penalty might generate sufficient political pressure at home to cause a change of grantee policy. The United States cannot tolerate, however, the violation of some federal standards, like nondiscrimination. When grant conditions reach this stature a penalty for their violation would be an unacceptable remedy. Certain standards must be met or federal aid totally withdrawn. An alternative for such cases might be the transference of federal financing to another service provider. If the grant eligibility section of the particular statute broadly includes various types of public and nonpublic entities, the federal agency can seek out a substitute grantee, strip the recalcitrant recipient of federal funds, and transfer them to the new client. This would avoid penalizing innocent program beneficiaries in order to enforce standards. In many programs, however, the eligibility sections are not so flexible,[16] and special statutory authority would be needed to accomplish the transfer.[17] If state law does permit an alternative in the provision of public services, such as the state doing the job normally discharged by local governments or nonprofit private groups providing government-type services, agencies should have authority to transfer grants in cases of noncompliance findings and lack of remediation.

On the question of proportionality there is a strong need to tailor a better fit between crime and punishment. The guiding premise must be that no federal standard contained in a grant-in-aid program is more important than the program itself. If the principles underlying such standards are sufficiently important and if constitutional power exists, Congress can impose them independent of grant assistance. When they are imposed as a condition on the receipt of federal funds, however, it is either because such standards are thought to improve the product resulting from the grant or because federal funds cannot be tainted by or promote practices contrary to national policies. It would be a perversion of the grant system to whip grantees and ultimate program beneficiaries for the sake of national purposes only indirectly related to the grant system. Unless there is considerable deceit underlying the system, one must accept the premise that the purpose of a grant-in-aid is to provide social services, or build hospitals, or improve highway safety and not to end racial or sexual discrimination, or to improve state and local personnel practices, or to save

[16] See Chapter 9, note 1, *supra*. For example, in two thirds of the formula grant programs only states are eligible for grants. *Categorical Grants*, Chapter 1, note 6, *supra*, at 98. This problem is dealt with in a recent amendment to the Age Discrimination Act by linking expanded grant eligibility directly to the fiscal sanction. The following is the specific language added:

"Whenever the head of any Federal department or agency . . . withholds funds pursuant to subsection (a), he may, in accordance with regulations he shall prescribe, disburse the funds so withheld directly to any public or non-profit private organization or agency, or State or political subdivision thereof, which demonstrates the ability to achieve the goals of the Federal statute authorizing the program or activity while complying with [nondiscrimination rules]."

§305(b) Age Discrimination Act of 1975, 42 U.S.C. §6104(b), as added by §401(d) Comprehensive Older Americans Act Amendments of 1978, Pub. L. 95-478, Oct. 18, 1978.

[17] We cannot imagine where the First Circuit got the idea that without statutory authority a grantor can convert an assistance program into a direct federal development program through the takeover of unsuccessful projects. See *Silva* v. *East Providence Housing Auth.* (II), 565 F.2d 1217, 1224 (1st Cir. 1977).

the environment by means of conditions on grants aimed at other goals.

This premise leads to certain desirable limits on the sanction power. One is "pinpointing," isolating the particular agent and activity responsible for violation of federal law and restricting sanctions to that party and program, or part thereof. Grantees should not be held responsible for violations by subgrantees unless the culpability is a blatant failure to monitor and enforce program rules, a violation distinct from that of the subgrantee; one subgrantee should never suffer because of the violations of another; activities should be separated when the violation has occurred in one element of a program; and violations of the main recipient should not prejudice, to the extent possible, subgrantees. It would also appear advisable to refrain from spreading the fiscal sanction to other grants untainted by the illegal practice. Recent legislation permits a federal agency to enforce compliance with program standards by halting federal funds not only for the grant program in which the violation occurs but also for other separate and untroubled grants.[18] That extraordinary sanction power would need explicit congressional authorization. We are, therefore, counseling Congress to tie such sanction power only to exceptionally important federal standards or to conditions which have produced unusually serious enforcement problems.

We would not object to the practice of the Department of Labor under which a grantee suffering a fiscal penalty is expected to maintain program levels as previously promised.[19] Holding the grantee to commitments based on the prior anticipated level of federal financing effectively imposes a double penalty on the grantee —loss of federal funds and additional matching required by the shortfall. Nonetheless, the sanction is directly related to the party and program in which the violation occurred and does not elevate any particular standard to a pinnacle of importance greater than the program itself. Indeed, insisting on the original commitment protects the program beneficiaries from reductions in service levels caused by grantee illegalities. If the double sanction is unambiguously part of the program rules, no grantee could complain of being trapped. And while the degree of the sanction might seem harsh, an administrator could not be faulted for employing it as a method of enforcing standards without prejudicing project levels.

[18] See §616(a) Education of the Handicapped Act, 20 U.S.C. §1416(a).
[19] See Chapter 3, note 196, *supra,* and accompanying text.

Finally, the Grantee Bill of Procedural Rights should specify the sanctions available to a grantor agency, avoiding buck-passing clauses such as "any other means authorized by law." For instance, the issue whether grant conditions will be specifically enforceable and, if so, under what circumstances should not be left to judicial resolution. That question is too important to the grant system to be left to conjecture, as it still is. The conditions under which suspension of federal payments is permissible should be specifically fixed, with careful avoidance of such broad authorizations that suspension can be invoked on a grantor whim. The present grant system has also been particularly vague about the circumstances under which grantors can seek recovery of federal funds illegally spent, either by deductions from future grants or by debt suits. Hopefully such recoveries would be limited to the use of federal funds for unauthorized activities, but at a minimum the important step of specifying sanction parameters, whatever they be, would lead toward greater grantee equity. Similar detail should be offered on the sanctions of withholding, termination, and voiding of grants.

If established by Congress, a Grantee Bill of Procedural Rights might also be a convenient place to resolve the question whether private parties may sue grantees under federal grant standards and what type of judicial relief will be available. We will not repeat our lengthy analysis of the confusing and complex current situation.[20] The Supreme Court failed, in the 1978–1979 term,[21] to clarify the ambiguities of *Lau* v. *Nichols*[22] and *Bakke*.[23] The opinion of Mr. Justice Stevens in *Cannon* v. *University of Chicago*,[23a] recently decided, adds welcome detail to our understanding of the process by which courts may imply private remedies under federal statutes. His reliance, for instance, on statutory language "which expressly identifies the class Congress intended to benefit"[23b] as opposed to more general congressional interdictions may overly presume a care for and precision in language which we know to be absent in the massive grant-in-aid statutes. It does, none-

---

[20] See Chapter 4, notes 8–9, 30–39, 67, 141–150, *supra*, and accompanying text.

[21] Because it ruled against plaintiff on the merits, the Court was able to skirt the implication question in *Southeastern Community College* v. *Davis*, 99 S. Ct. 2361, 2366, n. 5 (1979), which involved alleged discrimination against the handicapped under §504 Rehabilitation Act of 1973, 29 U.S.C. §794.

[22] 414 U.S. 563 (1974).

[23] *Regents of the Univ. of Cal.* v. *Bakke*, 438 U.S. 265 (1978).

[23a] 99 S. Ct. 1946 (1979).

[23b] *Id.* at 1954.

theless, express a workable rule of thumb for Congress, the courts, grantors, and grantees. One finds strength in Mr. Justice Powell's dissenting opinion in *Cannon* that the implication doctrine unwisely places basic policy decisions in the hands of "relatively uninformed federal judges who are isolated from the political process," [23c] and that the doctrine, also unwisely, allows Congress to avoid the "hard political choices" involved in the issue of private versus public enforcement of federal standards.[23d] But the judicial groping for a fictitious congressional intent has yet to be averted. In our proposed bill Congress could at least signal its general feeling about private enforcement of federal grant standards, leaving room for contrary positions in specific grant-in-aid statutes.

Denials of Grant Applications

We have explored the difficulties involved in providing a forum for disappointed applicants for federal grants.[24] While grantor agencies could be required to give more detailed reasons why a proposal was not funded, it would be virtually impossible to provide a hearing opportunity, even informal. First, most timely grant applications are rejected on a basis of comparative merits. The agency will have announced a prior intention to fund a certain number of proposals within a particular dollar range. The question, therefore, is not whether the losing application was satisfactory but whether it was more promising than others. To reexamine this question, the entire evaluation process would have to be restaged. That would place an intolerable burden on the grant system, particularly if the distribution of funds were stayed pending the rerun. Second, even if we were willing to sponsor a second evaluation process, there would be no standards under which it could be said that the second round results were more satisfactory than the first. Assuming that the first round was procedurally regular, it would be an extremely rare case in which the results could be said to be clearly wrong. The evaluators would have exercised judgment on subjective questions such as the proposal's promise, staff competency, innovative techniques, and so forth. The second set of results would be no more "valid" than the first, just different. Third, in this area of grants we have a problem

[23c] *Id.* at 1975.
[23d] *Id.* at 1981.
[24] See Chapter 7, notes 70–73, *supra,* and accompanying text.

of volume. For each winning competitive grant proposal we typically find dozens of losers.²⁵ In opening the door to hearing opportunities, we must be prepared to have thousands step in. Given the subjective nature of the original evaluative decisions, we are reasonably certain that hearing opportunities are not worth the cost and trouble.

Still, we are troubled by any system in which large amounts of public funds are distributed free from inspection, control, and review. To remedy the problem of such "unchannelled discretion," the Administrative Conference of the United States has focused on improvements in the methodology employed by grantor agencies in the distribution of competitive grants.²⁶ That leaves, however, the problem of superficially clean processes producing sullied results because of irregularities in individual cases. Because an agency has announced certain evaluation procedures and standards does not guarantee that those rules have, in fact, been applied. One might also guess that to the extent such system is shielded from inspection, the probability of distortion increases.

That is, indeed, why a losing applicant for federal funds may get judicial review of the agency decision, even in discretionary grant programs. Such review is limited to questions of procedural regularity and law.²⁷ Did the agency violate the grant statute, its own regulations, or some other law? Did it follow its announced procedures in evaluating plaintiff's proposal?

The Grantee Bill of Procedural Rights should maintain this limited review of agency decisions on grant proposals, though we will later recommend that review be shifted to an administrative court. Only in the case of a refunding proposal rejection which leads to substantial prejudice to individual beneficiaries should the merits of the agency decision be probed.

The Grant Disputes Board

We could rest here. If our proposed set of rights met with favor in Congress or in OMB and were enacted, the existing grant dispute machinery would be obliged to incorporate and apply the fairness tenets previously set forth. That would be a rather large

---

[25] A dramatic example is provided by the local public works program. Local Public Works Capital Development and Investment Act of 1976, 42 U.S.C. §§6701–6736. Some 20,000 grant applications were rejected in the funding competition for the first year. See Commission on Federal Paperwork, *Public Works* 11 (1977).

[26] See Chapter 12, notes 39–44, *supra,* and accompanying text.

[27] See Chapter 5, notes 18–22, *supra,* and accompanying text.

step forward, an overdue and substantial improvement in the grant-in-aid system.

We would be shielding our eyes, however, to a fundamental flaw in the existing administrative structure for the resolution of controversies in grant programs. While we are unhappy with the sprawling network of boards and procedural codes, we could live with the resulting confusion, waste, and inefficiency. The grantee institution that deals with multiple federal agencies might get frustrated at times, such duplicative machinery might cost too much, and the system might produce lack of uniformity and even-handedness among grantees; nonetheless, this all could be seen as a tolerable consequence of the rich diversity of statutes and agencies. We cannot, however, accept any public adjudicative system, authorized to strip an entity of its property and give it to another, in which the government plays the triple role of adversary, judge, and arbiter of the procedural rules.[28]

Cut to the core, that is, indeed, what our study of administrative systems for the adjudication of grant disputes has revealed. Such is not surprising for agencies have followed the pattern of the Administrative Procedure Act,[29] though not legally bound to do so.[30] That structure contemplates some degree of independence

[28] The problem of massive numbers of controversies, each of relatively small public importance, must usually be considered in appraising procedural fairness in the administrative state. See, e.g., Gardner, "The Informal Actions of the Federal Government," 26 Amer. U. L. Rev. 799 (1977); Mashaw, "The Management Side of Due Process: Some Theoretical and Litigation Notes on the Assurance of Accuracy, Fairness, and Timeliness in the Adjudication of Social Welfare Claims," 59 Cornell L. Rev. 772 (1974). That problem assuredly underlay the Supreme Court's impatient brushing aside of the argument that the multiple role of the Social Security hearing examiner violated Due Process. See *Richardson v. Perales*, 402 U.S. 389, 410 (1971). Grant controversies, however, are characterized by neither unwieldy volume nor relative unimportance, and we need not concern ourselves with the administrative problems involved in processing millions of small claims.

[29] §§5–8 Administrative Procedure Act, 5 U.S.C. §§554–557. See Chapter 9, notes 72–100, *supra*, and accompanying text.

[30] APA adjudication procedures apply when a case of adjudication is "required by statute to be determined on the record after opportunity for an agency hearing . . . ." §5(a) Administrative Procedure Act, 5 U.S.C. §554(a). This requirement is to be strictly interpreted. J. O. Freedman, *Crisis and Legitimacy: The Administrative Process and American Government* 151–52 (1978). Some grant statutes specifically require a hearing "on the record" prior to certain grantor decisions, see, e.g., §502(d)(2) Older Americans Act of 1965, 42 U.S.C. §3056(d)(2), as added by §105(b)(2) Comprehensive Older Americans Act Amendments of 1978, Pub. L. 95–458, Oct. 18, 1978; §509 Omnibus Crime Control and Safe Streets of 1968, 42 U.S.C. §3757, as amended by §122(a) Crime Control Act of 1976, Pub. L. 94-503, Oct. 5, 1976; §186(a) Elementary and Secondary Education Act of 1965, 20 U.S.C. §2836(a), as rewritten by §101 Education Amendments of 1978, Pub. L. 95–561, Nov. 1, 1978, but the great majority either have no hearing requirement, see statutory sections cited in Chapter 9, note 3, and Chapter 12, note 2, *supra*, or provide for prior notice and a "reasonable" hearing opportunity without specifying that it must be on the record. See statutory sections cited in Chapter 9, note 2, and Chapter 12, note 1, *supra*.

in the decision maker, at least at the beginning. An employee of the government agency involved in the dispute, or panel of such, will be appointed by the agency head to adjudicate the controversy.[31] One party to the dispute, therefore, gets to pick the judge, something our judicial system would not tolerate.[32] Certain efforts are made to secure a degree of impartiality. The decision maker cannot have played a role in the agency decision which led to the hearing.[33] If the adjudicator comes from the agency's corps of administrative law judges, his job and salary are protected from agency retaliatory acts.[34] Efforts are also made to shield the hearing examiner from agency pressure on the issue, such as by prohibiting *ex parte* communications.[35] Nonetheless, the simple fact remains that employees of the same government agency are acting as prosecutor and judge, and, hence, the agency itself plays that antithetically dual role. It may be that in the great majority of cases the system in fact works fairly and objectively. Nevertheless, in all cases the *perception of fairness* must necessarily be lacking.[36] From the perspective of those grantees harmed by decisions emanating from the system, it can only seem that HEW, for example, has both accused and judged the recipient. To point out that the HEW Grant Appeals Board is located in a separate building and responds by way of a separate chain to the Secretary is no satis-

[31] See, e.g., 32 C.F.R. §1803.6(a); 28 C.F.R. §18.52(a); 29 C.F.R. §98.47(f); 5 C.F.R. §900.204(d)(2). But see 24 C.F.R. §570.913(d) (administrative law judge in all community development program noncompliance procedures).

[32] And eventually, perhaps, the administrative system too. The Legal Services Corporation Act was recently amended to provide for independent hearing examiners for matters involving grant terminations, suspensions, and denials of refunding. §16 Legal Services Corporation Act Amendments of 1977, Pub. L. 95-222, Dec. 28, 1977, amending §1011(2) Community Services Act, 42 U.S.C. §2996j(2). The corporation has provided for the independence of the examiner in the following terms:

"The presiding officer shall be appointed by the President, and shall be a person who is familiar with legal services and supportive of the purposes of the Act, who is independent, and who is not an employee of the Corporation."

45 C.F.R. §1606.8, 43 Fed. Reg. 32770 (1978). The grantee may challenge the credentials and impartiality of the examiner, but the President has the last word. See 45 C.F.R. §1606.8(b)–(d), 43 Fed. Reg. 32770–71 (1978). While an improvement, the Legal Services Corporation system still permits one adversary to choose the judge.

[33] §5(d) Administrative Procedure Act, 5 U.S.C. §554(d). This principle is not explicitly stated in the agency hearing regulations.

[34] §11 Administrative Procedure Act, U.S.C. §§5362, 7521.

[35] §5(d) Administrative Procedure Act, 5 U.S.C. §554(d). See, e.g., 45 C.F.R. §1206.1-7(b)(2).

[36] See, e.g., *Offut v. United States*, 348 U.S. 11, 14 (1954) (Frankfurter, J.) ("[j]ustice must satisfy the appearance of justice"). See generally Mashaw, "The Supreme Court's Due Process Calculus for Administrative Adjudication in *Mathews v. Eldridge*: Three Factors in Search of a Theory of Value," 44 U. Chi. L. Rev. 28, 52–54 (1976).

348 / *Rights and Remedies Under Federal Grants*

factory answer. Political and bureaucratic pressures on employees ebb and flow within the Byzantine structures of that behemoth. To adjudicate in favor of a grantee is necessarily to rule against one or more colleagues, some usually of considerably greater rank. One should not burden human nature with such hard decisions.

The lack of real independence of the initial decision maker, however, is not the greatest evil. For after considerable precautions are taken to insure a trial-type hearing, including many of the procedural protections offered defendants in civil and criminal trials,[37] the matter then gets turned over to the agency for final decision. Whether the hearing body is asked to make a recommended decision or is asked to make a "final" determination, the agency head (or his delegate) has the last word, the real decisional power. Power to review and overturn the decision or recommendation of hearing examiners is uniformly vested by agency regulation in the agency head.[38] While that power is to be exercised on the basis of the record of the proceedings,[39] judicial review can only correct arbitrary and capricious action. Thus, a decision in favor of a grantee which the agency head dislikes can be overturned whenever some degree of reason would support a contrary result.

The grant "appeals" system of HEW is even more suspicious. Cases are prosecuted against grantees by "constituent agenc[ies]" (operating divisions) of HEW. After a panel of the HEW Grant Appeals Board renders its decision following an adjudicative hearing, whether "initial" or "final," power is then vested in the constituent agency to modify or reverse the panel decision.[40] Here there is not even a pretense of separating functions.

This is not to suggest that grantee rights are regularly and systematically despoiled by such procedures. No evidence exists, one way or the other. To our knowledge the disputes system has never been empirically studied. In practice it may be that the heads of federal agencies and their appointees may be able to resist organizational pressure and to render fair and objective decisions. At bottom, however, that would be a matter of grace and not law.

[37] See Chapter 9, notes 72–100, *supra*, and accompanying text.
[38] §8(b) Administrative Procedure Act, 5 U.S.C. §557(b). See, e.g., 32 C.F.R. §1803.6(a); 24 C.F.R. §570.913(j)-(m); 28 C.F.R. §18.57; 29 C.F.R. §98.48; 5 C.F.R. §900.204(g); 45 C.F.R. §1050.
[39] §8(c) Administrative Procedure Act, 5 U.S.C. §557(c). See, e.g., 24 C.F.R. §570.913(m); 29 C.F.R. §98.48; 5 C.F.R. §900.204(g).
[40] See 45 C.F.R. §16.10(c).

If just one grantee is unjustly treated by an administrative system which could have been structured more fairly with no adverse costs, we would be dissatisfied. Also, if we are correct in our evaluation that the grant system is "heating up"—that an ever-increasing flow of grantor-grantee disputes can be expected—it would be wise not to wait for systematic flaws to reveal themselves in the form of manhandled grantees.

The fact that the outlines of existing administrative dispute systems are sanctioned by the Administrative Procedure Act does not discourage us. That system was devised in 1946 to handle the multitude of regulatory matters of the Federal Government.[41] At that time, grant outlays amounted to a small percentage of the federal budget and involved only a few programs.[42] It is essentially a structure evolved to handle high-volume, low-impact agency decisions. The procedures were also adopted at a time when government grants and benefits were not considered entitlements.[43] If there is real substance to the current Supreme Court doctrine of statutory entitlements, and there is no reason to believe otherwise, procedures must be evolved which treat the new property, to the extent feasible, with the same dignity as the judicial system treats the old.

Before we reach our proposal for an alternative system, we should ventilate one more complaint, a small one. Agencies are presently free to devise their own dispute procedures. When Congress has spoken to the matter of grantor-grantee controversies, it has generally left the matter of devising "reasonable" procedures to grantor agencies.[44] We have argued that agencies are too involved to devise fair systems. That matter should be governed by statute, at least in terms of the essential elements of fair process. We suggest, therefore, that a Bill of Grantee Procedural Rights include procedural specifications, perhaps along the lines we suggest below.

[41] The adjudicatory principles of the Administrative Procedure Act were "aimed at the statutory hearings held by the big agencies which wield drastic powers of control, for example the Federal Communications Commission . . . the Civil Aeronautics Board . . . the Federal Trade Commission . . . or the Securities and Exchange Commission." B. Schwartz & H.W.R. Wade, *Legal Control of Government: Administrative Law in Britain and the United States* 109 (1972).
[42] See *Special Analysis H,* Chapter 1, note 43, *supra,* at 184, Table H-5.
[43] See Chapter 1, notes 69–73, *supra,* and accompanying text.
[44] See Chapter 9, *supra,* at pp. 250–52.

350 / *Rights and Remedies Under Federal Grants*

Jurisdiction and Structure

We favor the creation of an administrative court [44a] charged with the duty of adjudicating all disputes arising from federal grant programs. We call it the Grant Disputes Board, though Grant Administrative Board would have a more appealing acronym.

Nothing terribly new is pretended. Judge Friendly suggested a few years ago that the problem of mass justice in the administrative state could probably be best dealt with by informal proceedings conducted by truly independent administrative bodies.[45] The loss of protection through procedural formality would be covered by greater confidence in the impartiality of the adjudicatory body. We shall utilize this concept in suggesting a branch of the Grants Dispute Board which will handle high-volume types of matters without oral hearings. Nor is the idea of an administrative court novel, such having existed for many years in Europe.[46] We have borrowed from both places in concept, though blame for the details is ours alone.

[44a] In the procurement field considerable support existed for consolidation of adjudicative boards into just one or two boards to hear all procurement disputes. Such consolidation was a "hotly debated" issue. Testimony of O. S. Hiestand, General Counsel to the Commission on Government Procurement, *The Contract Disputes Act of 1978: Hearings on H.R. 664, H.R. 3745, H.R. 4713, H.R. 4739, H.R. 9975 and H.R. 11002 Before the Subcomm. on Administrative Law and Governmental Relations of the House Comm. on the Judiciary*, 95th Cong., 1st Sess. 188 (1977). Administrators in high positions supported major consolidation. See *id.* at 70–71 (testimony of Lester A. Fettig, Administrator, Office of Federal Procurement Policy); 41 Fed. Reg. 10488, 10489 (1976) (Hugh E. Witt, Administrator for Federal Procurement Policy); *The Contract Disputes Act of 1978: Joint Hearings on S. 2292, S. 2787 and S. 3178 Before the Subcomm. on Federal Spending Practices and Open Government of the Comm. on Governmental Affairs and the Subcomm. on Citizens and Shareholders Rights and Remedies of the Comm. on the Judiciary*, 95th Cong., 2d Sess. 87 (1978) (Irving Jaffee, Deputy Assistant Attorney General). While Congress opted not to create a single board, some consolidation is expected by virtue of the requirement that a workload study justify the creation of individual agency boards. §8(a)(1) Contract Disputes Act of 1978, Pub. L. 95-563, Nov. 1, 1978, 41 U.S.C. §607(a)(1); Commission on Government Procurement, *Report of the Commission on Government Procurement*, vol. IV, at 21 (1972). Lacking sufficient volume, smaller agencies will have to utilize the board of another agency. §8(c) Contract Disputes Act of 1978, Pub. L. 95-563, Nov. 1, 1978, 41 U.S.C. §607(c).

[45] Friendly, "Some Kind of Hearing," 123 U. Pa. L. Rev. 1267, 1289 (1975).

[46] See generally L. Neville Brown & J. F. Garner, *French Administrative Law* 17–75 (1967); von Mehren & Gordley, *The Civil Law System: An Introduction to the Comparative Study of Law* 108–20 (2d ed. 1977); I. Zamir, "The Control of Administrative Acts by the Ordinary Courts," in I. Englard, ed., *Israeli Reports to the Ninth International Congress of Comparative Law* (Jerusalem, 1974). While two distinguished professors of administrative law have rejected the idea of incorporating the European model in British and American administrative systems, their frame of reference consisted exclusively of regulatory and individual benefit proceedings and did not consider grant-in-aid disputes. B. Schwartz & H.W.R. Wade, *Legal Control of Government: Administrative Law in Britain and the United States* 314–24 (1972). Similarly, federal regulatory agencies have been the focus of the proposals for ad-

The Board would have original and exclusive jurisdiction of all disputes between grantors and grantees and would sit in each of the 10 federal regions (with power to circulate within regions) so that justice would be conveniently accessible to grantees across the country. While the Board would be part of the executive branch, it would be insulated to the highest degree possible from presidential and congressional political pressure.

The principle of comprehensive and exclusive jurisdiction would bestow the Board with a multitude of relatively minor matters such as reimbursement arguments, indirect cost rate decisions, and budget controversies. Quasi-judicial hearing mechanisms would clearly be unsuitable, both for grantors and grantees, to resolve these matters. On the other hand, these disputes might be of substantial importance; after all, it was a series of reimbursement issues that Congress recently settled for $543,000,000.[47] We need, therefore, a dual system within the Board—one for the quick and efficient resolution of lesser matters and another permitting more thorough consideration of disputes of considerable impact.

For our dividing line we can borrow the classic technique in determining judicial jurisdiction—the amount in controversy. Matters heard within the "formal" system must involve, say, $20,000 or more. That access rule could not, however, be inflexible. The requirements of Due Process are not always measured in monetary terms alone. For example, a fellowship might not reach that jurisdictional amount. We would still want to give the holder of such a grant a full, formal hearing if threatened with its loss because of the potentially severe personal repercussions. Therefore, all terminations, suspensions, and voiding of fellowships, traineeships, and other individual grants (not benefits) would be entitled to formal process. In more general terms, it would probably be wise to permit any matter to be moved from the "informal" to the "formal" branch of the Board on a showing that, under the particular circumstances, a substantial deprivation may occur even though the financial impact is under $20,000. The inability of a small grantee institution to withstand a lesser financial loss or suspension might justify a transfer, as might a showing

---

ministrative courts which have emanated from the various government reform commissions which Presidents are wont to establish. See J. O. Freedman, *Crisis and Legitimacy: The Administrative Process and American Government* 8 (1978).

[47] See Pub. L. 95-291, June 12, 1978, 42 U.S.C. §1397a note.

352 / *Rights and Remedies Under Federal Grants*

that the controversy is likely to harm the reputation of the grantee and, hence, its future fund-raising opportunities. Conversely, the parties to the dispute should be able to opt for the informal branch even though the case would qualify for a trial-type hearing. The jurisdictional amount would not apply to the denial of original or continuation competitive grants. For these cases, review would be limited as previously suggested and would be placed in the informal branch. An exception would be made, as explained, for denials of refunding which would substantially affect individual beneficiaries. These cases would be entitled to formal adjudication.

We would be inclined to preclude judicial review of Board decisions, even on a capricious and arbitrary standard. If the Grant Disputes Board is an independent, quality operation, no reason readily appears to clog the system with appeals to "superior" courts, other than discretionary review by the Supreme Court of constitutional issues and questions of great public importance. The constitutionally required opportunity to be heard does not encompass a right to be heard more than once when a meaningful hearing has been originally given.[48] Nor does the Constitution mandate access to the lower federal courts, at least in these cases.[49] The federal bench has no special competence in the analysis and interpretation of grant statutes, and, in fact, might welcome the relief from docket congestion which exclusive administrative jurisdiction would provide.[50] We would also bring within the Board's exclusive jurisdiction all grant disputes arising under federal law. While controversies between grantees and subgrantees stemming from questions of state law would be inappropriate for Board jurisdiction, those involving the grant statute, regulation, agreement, and other federal requirements should be of Board cognizance, at least on appeal from state board decisions.

Whether third-party claims of right under federal grant statutes should be folded into the system is a difficult question in view of the present lack of guidance from the Supreme Court on the propriety of implying private claims for relief under grant standards and conditions.[51] If injunctive and declaratory relief

---

[48] See, e.g., *Ross v. Moffitt*, 417 U.S. 600, 606, 610–11 (1973) (state not constitutionally obliged to provide appeal to criminal defendant).
[49] Jurisdiction of the lower federal courts is determined by Congress. U.S. Const. art. III, §1.
[50] See, e.g., *Economic Opportunity Comm'n v. Weinberger*, 524 F.2d 393, 404–408 (2d Cir. 1975) (Friendly, J., concurring).
[51] See Chapter 4, note 67, *supra*.

continues to be widely available, it would make good sense to at least place primary jurisdiction in the Grant Disputes Board. We would also see little difficulty in making that jurisdiction exclusive. It would be inadvisable to create concurrent decisional systems in view of the desirability of evolving uniform grant principles under which the same rules would apply to parties subject to the same federal standards. On the other hand, if damages may be claimed under implied claims for relief, those traditional actions would be better tried within the federal judicial system.

Procedures

Here we shall highlight the essential procedural details for both branches of the Board, without pretending to be devising a complete procedural code.

The formal branch should be structured so as to comply in all cases with Due Process. The basic elements of fair procedure outlined in *Goldberg* v. *Kelly* [52] should be met. That includes: reasonably detailed notice of the reasons for agency action that is final or proposed (it could be either depending on the "timing" requirement) and of the opportunity for a Board hearing; [53] an impartial decision maker which, of course, is satisfied through the independence of the Board and its members; an opportunity to appear personally or to be represented at the proceeding by counsel or another; the chance to present evidence and to challenge, through cross-examination, the adversary's proof; and a written decision based only on the record evidence and applicable legal standards.

In many cases justice would be denied if the grantee or losing applicant for funds were not given some opportunity to probe the agency files. While agency action may have been based on erroneous information or illegal practices, the agency may, when challenged, change its grounds.[54] Although the latter might have been adequate to uphold the agency action if it were the original basis of decision, it should be rejected as a *post hoc* rationalization. For

[52] 397 U.S. 254 (1970). See generally Levinson, "Elements of the Administrative Process: Formal, Semi-Formal, and Free Form Models," 26 Amer. U. L. Rev. 872 (1977).
[53] See *Memphis Light, Gas & Water Div.* v. *Craft*, 436 U.S. 1, 13–15 (1978) (utility customers facing cutoff entitled to notice of availability of dispute procedures).
[54] See Cahn & Cahn, "The New Sovereign Immunity," 81 Harv. L. Rev. 929, 935–36 (1968).

354 / *Rights and Remedies Under Federal Grants*

example, an agency might reject a grant proposal on the basis of a policy which conflicts with its own regulations or the grant statute, yet defend its action at a Board hearing on the ground that the proposal lacked sufficient merit. On the other hand, one would hesitate to introduce into the grant system the cost, delay, and complication produced by liberal discovery rules. The Legal Services Corporation has devised what might be a workable compromise:

> "The presiding officer may, at the pre-hearing conference or at any subsequent appropriate time prior to completion of the hearing, require the Corporation or the recipient, on sufficient notice, to produce a relevant document in its possession, to make a report not unduly burdensome to prepare, or to produce a person in its employ to testify, if any might offer a relevant and substantial addition to the accuracy or completeness of the record. . . ." [55]

It would also appear reasonable and not an undue burden on the grant system to permit the exchange of a reasonable number of interrogatories to be answered by the parties under oath and utilizing information possessed by the agency or institution.

The new disputes regulation of the Legal Services Corporation has other progressive features which deserve mention. It explicitly places the burden on the corporation to prove, by a preponderance of the evidence, "any disputed fact relied upon as justification for termination or denial of refunding; . . . ." [56] The burden question is all too often ignored or missed in agency procedural rules. The regulation also authorizes grantees to pay for attorney fees out of grant funds,[57] something essential for the adequate representation of nongovernmental grantees. Unfortunately, the corporation backed up from its original rule which permitted compensation of grantee lawyers "at the reasonable and customary rate for an attorney practicing in the locality of the counsel so retained." [58] The new rule binds grantees to the compensation rate of government lawyers, lacking special permission from the corporation.[59] It is doubtful whether competent counsel could be secured at that rate and, even if they could, it is not fair to permit one party to a formal adjudication to have the power to

---

[55] 45 C.F.R. §1606.9(c), 43 Fed. Reg. 32771 (1978).
[56] 45 C.F.R. §1606.11(a), 43 Fed. Reg. 32771 (1978).
[57] 45 C.F.R. §1606.16, 43 Fed. Reg. 32772 (1978).
[58] 45 C.F.R. §1606.17, 41 Fed. Reg. 18083 (1976) (superceded).
[59] 45 C.F.R. §1606.16, 43 Fed. Reg. 32772 (1978).

determine the competency of its adversary's counsel through control of the purse strings. A third notable feature of the regulation is that if a grantee wins it is entitled to reimbursement by the corporation for reasonable and actual litigation expenses.[60] Because grant funds finance the proceeding, even if the grantee wins its beneficiaries will lose to the extent that legal services funds are so diverted. Reimbursement, therefore, returns the grantee to its pre-proceeding financial posture, the status quo prior to corporation error.

We are, in essence, suggesting the maintenance of considerable formality in the processing of the substantial grant disputes appearing on the "formal" side of the Board's jurisdiction. That formality will, of course, have its costs. We anticipate and expect the delay and expense of quasi-judicial process, though we hopefully shed some of the less indicated judicial baggage. We would not, however, anticipate an overload on the "formal" side. Despite the great number of grant programs and transactions, the serious disputes to which this process applies will be relatively small in number. The grantor agencies will continue to be obliged to push and prod grantees toward settlement, thus ending many a controversy before it reaches the Board. The very formality of the procedure will discourage grantees from pursuing idle claims. Many a matter will not involve serious factual dispute. These can be quickly processed through summary procedures which would be authorized to the Board as they are to agencies at the present time.[61]

In the "informal" branch we are willing to sacrifice accuracy in decision making at the altar of speed and cost. Cases would be submitted primarily on the basis of documents, with oral hearings only at the Board's initiative. After providing written notice with reasons to the grantee of the final adverse action, the grantor simply implements its decision unless an appeal is taken and the Board stays the action. Unless the "timing" question requires a prior hearing, most of these decisions will be accepted and no controversy develops at all; even if a prior hearing opportunity must be offered, it will frequently be declined because the federal action is clearly right. The grantee may "appeal" the decision or proposed decision to a member or panel of the Board. The grantor then justifies its decision by submitting a written file to the Board,

[60] 45 C.F.R. §1606.17, 43 Fed. Reg. 32772 (1978).
[61] See, e.g., 45 C.F.R. §16.60(c).

356 / *Rights and Remedies Under Federal Grants*

containing its analysis and documentation with a copy to the grantee. The grantee, in turn, submits its written case in rebuttal. At the discretion of the presiding officer or panel, witnesses may be called to resolve fact disputes or clarify ambiguities. The member or panel then renders a final written decision based on the submissions. No appeals would be allowed, although motions for reconsideration by a larger panel of the Board might be advisable to cure egregious misconception of the law or facts revealed in the written opinion.

Justifications

We end where we started—with the thought that realistic opportunities to be heard must be given to states, local governments, and private institutions that join with the Federal Government in governance through the grant-in-aid. The system of shared power will function more smoothly if the right to be heard is recognized and honored, and the increased inputs of grantees will add to the creativeness and rationality of the multitudinous decisions arising in this massive American enterprise. Those are, indeed, unverifiable expectations. Even if new structures were created with those goals in mind, it would be difficult to prove with any assurance that the purposes had actually been realized. But because what we are proposing stems from notions thought fundamental to American justice for centuries, we need not be too disturbed by the lack of hard data.

Many paths are open to those goals, including dozens of better structured hearing boards—one for each grant-giving department, administration, board, foundation, commission, office, corporation, and agency. We feel, however, that consolidation and simplification can produce additional advantages. Not to be overlooked are the benefits derived from eliminating hundreds upon hundreds of rules from statutes and regulations. The man-hours spent printing, distributing, searching out, reading, comparing, and applying these redundancies should not be denigrated. Though a new governmental structure would arise, we would not bemoan this modest addition to the vast bureaucracy because we would expect considerable savings through the elimination of grant dispute machinery in each of the agencies. We would obviously be inviting grantees to use the system, which would lead to an overall increase in the volume of litigated controversies. That, however, is an acceptable price of extending Due Process to new areas and agencies, particularly in view of the likelihood that such procedural rights would have eventually been accorded. Consolidation might also lead to efficiencies in case processing resulting from expertise and systematization.

Beyond cost considerations lie the questions of equity. Our Grant Disputes Board would obviously deal with the "perception of fairness" problem created by the present prosecutor-judge structure. It would also promote consistency of decision through the making and use of precedents. That would promote intergrantee equity by cutting across program lines and ensuring that identical grant standards are interpreted and applied equally. We thus envision a body of clear, comprehensible, and consistent grant doctrine emerging from the Board. With its exclusive and limited jurisdiction the Board members would quickly develop expertise on grant matters. This would lead, presumably, to a more rational filling of the many interstices in the grant statutes and regulations than the present scattering of cases to district courts throughout the country. It would, finally, skirt the judicial pitfalls of excessive cost, susceptibility to delay, and rigidity in procedure.[62]

Encouraging movement in the direction of our recommended Grants Disputes Board can be noted. Recent legislation mandates the creation of an "Education Appeal Board" within the Office of Education.[63] Several features of this legislation are to be applauded. First is the explicit legislative recognition that "due process" standards apply to grantees.[64] It should be noted that the Education Appeal Board will be hearing mostly appeals from state and local education agencies, the recipients of the formula grants to which the new system exclusively applies. This is tacit congressional recognition of the need to interpose constitutional procedural norms between the Federal Government and state and local government grantees. Second, the aim is to consolidate the many scattered provisions relating to enforcement and judicial review into one statute. The new Part E of the General Education Provisions Act [65]

---

[62] See *Memphis Light, Gas & Water Div.* v. *Craft*, 436 U.S. 1, 19–21 (1978).

[63] §451 General Education Provisions Act, 20 U.S.C. §1234, as added by §1231 Education Amendments of 1978, Pub. L. 95-561, Nov. 1, 1978.

[64] See H.R. Rep. No. 95-1137, 95th Cong., 2d Sess. 141 (1978) ("due process hearing procedure"); *id*. at 179 (same).

[65] §§451–456 General Education Provisions Act, 20 U.S.C. §§1234–1234e, as added by §1231 Education Amendments of 1978, Pub. L. 95-561, Nov. 1, 1978.

358 / Rights and Remedies Under Federal Grants

aims at superceding each of the comparable provisions found in particular grant-in-aid statutes, though repeals of duplicative sections will take place piecemeal.[66] A third commendable facet of the legislation is the composition of the board. The Secretary of HEW appoints the board members, in consultation with the Assistant Secretary for Education and the Commissioner of Education; yet no more than one third of the members can be officers or employees of HEW and each hearing panel, including the entire board when it sits as a panel, must have a majority composed of individuals who are not full-time employees of the Federal Government. Thus, the legislation opts for true independence in the decision maker. The fourth promising feature in the design of this board is that its decisions are administratively final. The Commissioner of Education or Secretary of HEW does not appear to have final decisional power; [67] rather, a losing grantee may immediately seek judicial review of the board's decision.[68] Finally, while the Commissioner of Education is authorized to establish the board's procedures for the processing of cases, he must conform to the procedural protections offered by the Administrative Procedure Act.[69]

---

[66] See H.R. Rep. No. 95-1137, 95th Cong., 2d Sess. 141–42 (1978). Compare 45 C.F.R. pts. 200, 228a, 300, 430, 43 Fed. Reg. 38318 (1978) (proposed; same model followed in hearing regulations for four major grant programs).

[67] The new provisions on their face vest finality in board decisions, but some doubt is injected by the following language from the House Conference Report:

"The managers stress that the Secretary and the Commissioner may not delegate the making of decisions under their legal authority for enforcement to the Appeal Board, which includes a majority of persons who are not Federal employees. The Secretary and the Commissioner can utilize the reviews and advice of an appeals board in reaching their enforcement decisions, but cannot totally delegate their authority to persons or groups of persons who are not Federal officials."

H.R. Conf. Rep. No. 95-1573, 95th Cong., 2d Sess. 320 (1978). This language should not be read as undercutting the finality given to board decisions by Congress in the statute. Rather, it should be read as a curb on the statutory power of the commissioner to delegate "other proceedings" to the board. See §451(a)(4) General Education Provisions Act, 20 U.S.C. §1234(a)(4), as added by §1231 Education Amendments of 1978, Pub. L. 95-561, Nov. 1, 1978.

[68] See §455 *id.*, 20 U.S.C. §1234d. As is typical, the board's findings of fact are conclusive when supported by "substantial evidence."

[69] The procedural norms of §§5, 7, 8 Administrative Procedure Act, 5 U.S.C. §§554, 556, 557, are incorporated by reference. See §451(e) General Education Provisions Act, 20 U.S.C. §1234(e), as added by §1231 Education Amendments of 1978, Pub. L. 95-561, Nov. 1, 1978.

16

No Man's Land

"According to this [cooperative] conception, the National Government and the States are mutually complementary parts of a *single* governmental mechanism all of whose powers are intended to realize the current purposes of government according to their applicability to the problem at hand. It is thus closely intertwined with the multiple-purpose conception of national power and with recent enlarged theories of the function of government generally."

"[I]n this area of overriding significance, the traditional checks to human fallibility are strangely absent.... We are confronted then with a vast no man's land at the heart of our legal system—territory off limits to the courts and beyond the ken of the traditional legal process. This is more than anomaly—such a no man's land is the antithesis of democracy itself."

Hand-in-hand or hand-at-throat? The first statement was by Professor Corwin in a seminal article on the new federal-state-local structure that had emerged, by 1950, as a result of expanded judicial readings of the national power and "inducements primarily of a pecuniary kind" resulting from the United States' "greater financial strength."[1] At that time the eminent constitutionalist was surveying a quite modest system of federal grants. Only 5.3 percent of the national budget was devoted to grants-in-aid, mostly matching payments for state welfare programs.[2] The

[1] Corwin, "The Passing of Dual Federalism," 36 U. Va. L. Rev. 1, 20–21 (1950).
[2] See *Special Analysis H*, Chapter 1, note 43, *supra*, at 184, Table H-5.

360 / Rights and Remedies Under Federal Grants

Cahns, authors of the second quote, wrote their scathing indictment of the grant system almost two decades later—a time when most of the modern grants were in place.[3] The Great Society legislation peaked in an incredible outpour of domestic assistance legislation in 1965,[4] three years before the Professors Cahn wrote about the mistreatment of grantees. Differing time perspectives quite possibly explain the dichotomous visions. In Corwin's time the Federal Government was working peacefully with state administrators in a few service areas.[5] The grant was a "gift" and the mystique of federal expertise had not yet been dissipated by the social program bunglings which were to come. In 1968, on the other hand, infant domestic assistance programs sprawled all over the landscape. The Eighty-Ninth Congress alone at least tripled the content of Title 42 of the *United States Code*. In the quick-step march toward social justice during those years neither Congress nor the executive branch paused to consider elements of fairness in the multiple facets of the grantor-grantee relationship. Corwin's "cooperative" imagery still held sway, and, magically it seemed, under hundreds of programs billions of dollars would pass from hand to hand without dispute.

At the time of this writing 10 more years have passed. While dozens of programs have come, gone, and been consolidated, most of the Great Society's output remains, as do the older programs of the 1940s and 1950s. Six Congresses have worked on the legislative products of the Eighty-Ninth and have added their own domestic initiatives. Over the same time span the Supreme Court brought Due Process to the administrative state.[6]

One would expect a better blend today than we have encountered. Ten years of experience and oversight have resulted in surprisingly few "checks to human fallibility" in the federal grants field. We have documented some change and progress. But for the most part the "no man's land" is still out there, a feudal world of grantor kings and grantee serfs.

---

[3] Cahn & Cahn, "The New Sovereign Immunity," 81 Harv. L. Rev. 929, 930, 971 (1968).
[4] See, e.g., Cappalli, "Federal Financing in the Commonwealth of Puerto Rico," 38 U.P.R. L. Rev. 1, 16–19 (1970).
[5] Primarily, public assistance (50.8% of all grant funds to state and local governments), maternal and child health (5.6%), highways (19.4%), and vocational education (3.7%). See *Categorical Grants,* Chapter 1, note 6, *supra,* at 22, Table I-5.
[6] See Mashaw, "The Supreme Court's Due Process Calculus for Administrative Adjudication in *Mathews* v. *Eldridge:* Three Factors in Search of a Theory of Value," 44 U. Chi. L. Rev. 28, 28, n.1 (1976) (Supreme Court administrative Due Process decisions from 1969 to 1975).

The absence of procedural fairness is, we think, an important problem deserving attention. It is, however, merely symptomatic of an even broader problem—the exclusion of the federal grant-in-aid from the realm of the law.

We averted to the pervasive lack of legal craftsmanship in the opening pages of this book. The federal grant is a legal creature in only the crudest sense—that of a sovereign command. The grant stems from a statute which must be obeyed. Similarly, each of the lower order commands generates enforceable rights and obligations. The remaining senses of "law," however, are absent to a large degree. Careful attention to language is lacking, as are the definitional penumbras brought to other statutory fields by the common law. One reads grant statutes nakedly, stripped of the understandings brought to legal language by history, precedent, custom, and scholarship. On the point of ambiguity the words of one appellate court,[7] struggling with a difficult civil rights issue, are particularly meaningful:

> "HEW's failure to adopt guidelines applicable to higher education . . . completely undermines the effectiveness of any effort towards Title VI compliance, either through negotiation or through administrative hearings. Neither party, nor the administrative law judge, has any working knowledge of what constitutes 'compliance,' thereby reducing the entire process to a meaningless exchange of theory rather than a determination of fact."

Anyone who has spent time trying to understand the meaning of grant statutes and regulations is not surprised that the National Institute of Education concluded, after a foray into the world of grant compliance, that "the law and regulations are not written clearly enough to be understood by those who implement the program."[8] What is less readily understood is that this lack of precision and comprehensibility effectively transfers governmental power away from federal, state, and local officials and into the hands of federal and federally supervised auditors. Fear of audit exceptions leading to costly disallowances, in combination with the legal insecurity bred by poorly written rules, leads inevitably to grantees developing the *most legally acceptable* programs and

---

[7] *Mayor of Baltimore* v. *Mathews*, 562 F.2d 914, 922 (4th Cir. 1977), *vacated then aff'd*, 571 F.2d 1273, *cert. denied*, 99 S. Ct. 184 (1978).

[8] See H.R. Rep. No. 95-1137, 95th Cong., 2d Sess. 49 (1978).

projects and not the soundest activities from the perspective of the program's goals.[9]

Systemization is also absent—the internal ordering of principles and their replication in comparable areas which characterize mature legal systems. Vast unfilled chasms weave through grant statutes, leaving major areas of the grant without direction. Agency regulations fill and shore but little, leaving much to practice and *ad hoc* invention. At the same time, incredible redundancy marks the field. While the unique programmatic elements of each grant program must, of course, be separately regulated, a considerable body of operational principles is common to all or many grants—disputes procedures being but one. Where a single well-expressed principle or rule could efficiently cover all federal grants, hundreds are used, with idiosyncratic twists, turns, and traps unnecessarily offering varying treatments of the same matter. The law's hearty desire for similar dispositions of similar cases is notably missing. Each grantee gets its own statute, regulation, manual, and individualistic grantor interpretation, whether or not the same issue is constantly being faced throughout the Federal Government. To be sure, some standardization has occurred and we have duly noted it. Nevertheless, the field of federal grants remains in large part a dangerous no man's land for both the weathered and the fledgling grantee.

What is there about the federal grant field which has caused the legal profession to look the other way? Lawyers, after all, can create order as well as chaos, clarity as well as confusion. Is there some flaw in the free market system which is keeping lawyers from gravitating toward that yearly $106,000,000,000 pot. That *is* about $265,000 worth of business per lawyer in America, with the pot growing mammothly every year.

Despite the large dollar figures, grants-in-aid would never amount to more than a small niche within American law. Grant agreements number probably less than one for every other lawyer, the large dollar totals resulting from a relatively small number of spectacularly large grants to states and local governments. The average lawyer would continue to be better off worrying about criminals, corporations, consumers, and contracts. Nevertheless, the federal grant may become an important specialty, particularly

[9] See *id*. at 26: "Several other findings . . . have led the Committee to believe that districts are simply not aware of the flexibility afforded them to design and operate Title I programs under the present legal framework, or else may be avoiding unfamiliar alternatives for fear of audit exceptions."

in light of the recent expansion of the federal grant partnership. One observer emphasizes that

> "[t]he participants now include all those of the Johnson era—the federal government, all the states, some special districts, some urban cities and counties, some school districts and some nonprofit units—as well as a whole range of new ones: all local general governments, almost all school districts, some additional special districts and authorities, and over 1800 substate regional units. Put differently, the eligibility and entitlement provisions of general revenue sharing, the Comprehensive Employment and Training Act, and the Community Development Block Grant—to mention only the more obvious—have greatly expanded the "partnership," and Carter's recent urban policy draft report promises to extend that partnership still further." [10]

One can anticipate a considerable increase in the pressure on Congress and the executive branch to improve equity and rationality as more players, including lawyers, enter the grant system. That, indeed, may explain the emergence in the Ninety-Fifth Congress of cornerstone grant legislation, the Federal Grant and Cooperative Agreement Act.[11] That legislation orders federal agencies to structure their assistance agreements according to basic aims (support or stimulation of the grantee versus primary benefit to the Federal Government) and arrangements (little versus large federal involvement). Although we may question Congress's architectural technique—building from the top down—we welcome the opening step toward rationalization. At a minimum the Grant Act will commence a widespread dialogue which will likely include many of the issues of grantee equity I have struggled with in this work. My hope is to have contributed constructively to the coming debate.

---

[10] Walker, "A New Intergovernmental System in 1977," 8 Publius 101, 102 (1978).
[11] Pub. L. 95-224, Feb. 3, 1978, 41 U.S.C. §§501-509.

Table of Books, Articles, Reports, and Other Secondary Sources

Advisory Commission on Intergovernmental Relations
—*Fiscal Balance in the American Federal System* (1967)   10, 34, 36, 42
—*The Intergovernmental Grant System: An Assessment and Proposed Policies: Categorical Grants: Their Role and Design* (1978)   3, 38
—*The Intergovernmental Grant System: An Assessment and Proposed Policies: Improving Federal Grants Management* (1977)   72
—*The Intergovernmental Grant System: An Assessment and Proposed Policies: Summary and Concluding Observations* (1978)   65, 81, 138, 236, 333
Albert
—"Standing to Challenge Administrative Action: An Inadequate Surrogate for Claim for Relief," 83 Yale L.J. 425 (1974)   114
Altshuler
—*Community Control: The Black Demand for Participation in Large American Cities* (1970)   49
Berney et al.
—*Legal Problems of the Poor: Cases and Materials* (1975)   1
Brown & Garner
—*French Administrative Law* (1967)   350
Bruff & Gelhorn
—"Congressional Control of Administrative Regulation: A Study of Legislative Vetoes," 90 Harv. L. Rev. 1369 (1977)   57
Burke
—"The Threat to Citizen Participation in Model Cities," 56 Cornell L. Rev. 751 (1971)   49
Cahn & Cahn
—"The New Sovereign Immunity," 81 Harv. L. Rev. 929 (1968)   14, 21, 22, 59, 85, 170, 353, 360
Cahn & Passett, eds.
—*Citizen Participation: Effecting Community Change* (1971)   49
Cappalli
—*Federal Aid to Puerto Rico* (1970)   39
—"Federal Financing in the Commonwealth of Puerto Rico," 38 U.P.R.L. Rev. 1 (1970)   13, 360

366 / Rights and Remedies Under Federal Grants

Comment
—"Congressional Oversight of Administrative Discretion: Defining the Proper Role of the Legislative Veto," 26 Am. U. L. Rev. 1018 (1977)   57
—"Federal Constitutional Spending Power: A Search for Limits," 70 Nw. U. L. Rev. 293 (1975)   33
—"Toward New Safeguards on Conditional Spending: Implications of *National League of Cities v. Usery*," 26 Am. U. L. Rev. 726 (1977)   32

Commission on Federal Paperwork
—*Education* (1977)   9
—*Employment and Training Programs* (1977)   74
—*Public Works* (1977)   345

Commission on Government Procurement
—*Report of the Commission on Government Procurement,* vol. IV   350

Corwin
—"National-State Cooperation—Its Present Possibilities," 8 Am. Law School Rev. 687 (1937)   11
—"The Passing of Dual Federalism," 36 U. Va. L. Rev. 1 (1950)   240, 359

Dam
—"The American Fiscal Constitution," 44 U. Chi. L. Rev. 271 (1977)   239, 241

Davis
—*Administrative Law Text* (1972, 3d ed.)   17
—"Informal Administrative Action: Another View," 26 Am. U. L. Rev. 836 (1977)   188

Department of the Treasury
—*Federal Aid to States: Fiscal Year 1977* (undated)   25

Derthick
—*The Influence of Federal Grants: Public Assistance in Massachusetts* (1970)   12

Englard, ed.
—*Israeli Reports to the Ninth International Congress of Comparative Law* (Jerusalem, 1974)   350

Freedman
—*Crisis and Legitimacy: The Administrative Process and American Government* (1978)   346, 351

Friendly
—"Some Kind of Hearing," 123 U. Pa. L. Rev. 1267 (1975)   180, 183, 350

Gardner
—"The Informal Actions of the Federal Government," 26 Am. U. L. Rev. 799 (1977)   346

George
—"Development of the Legal Services Corporation," 61 Cornell L. Rev. 681 (1976)   69

Greenawalt
—"The Enduring Significance of Neutral Principles," 78 Colum. L. Rev. 982 (1978)   239

Grodzins
—*The American System* (1966)   10, 12, 25, 81

Table of Books, Articles, Reports / 367

Hallman
—*Neighborhood Control of Public Programs: Case Studies of Community Corporations and Neighborhood Boards* (1970)   217, 276

Harbert
—*Federal Grants-in-Aid: Maximizing Benefits to the States* (1976)   12, 34

Heller
—*New Dimensions of Political Economy* (1966)   13

Jones
—"The Rule of Law and the Welfare State," 58 Colum. L. Rev. 143 (1958)   18

Kirp
—"Community Control, Public Policy, and the Limits of the Law," 68 Mich. L. Rev. 1355 (1970)   49

Kramer
—*Participation of the Poor: Comparative Community Case Studies in the War on Poverty* (1969)   49

Leach
—*American Federalism* (1970)   10, 12, 14, 24, 81

Levinson
—"Elements of the Administrative Process: Formal, Semi-Formal, and Free Form Models," 26 Amer. U. L. Rev. 872 (1977)   353

Levitan
—*The Great Society's Poor Law: A New Approach to Poverty* (1969)   275

Mashaw
—"The Management Side of Due Process: Some Theoretical and Litigation Notes on the Assurance of Accuracy, Fairness, and Timeliness in the Adjudication of Social Welfare Claims," 59 Cornell L.J. 772 (1974)   180, 346
—"The Supreme Court's Due Process Calculus for Administrative Adjudication in *Mathews v. Eldridge*: Three Factors in Search of a Theory of Value," 44 U. of Chi. L. Rev. 28 (1976)   180, 182, 347, 360

Mason
—"Current Trends in Federal Grant Law—Fiscal Year 1976," 35 Fed. B.J. 163 (1976)   15, 22, 53, 107, 196

Meyer
—*The History and Meaning of the Fourteenth Amendment* (1977)   181, 239

Michelman
—"States' Rights and States' Roles: Permutations of Sovereignty in *National League of Cities v. Usery*," 86 Yale L.J. 1165 (1977)   240

Monaghan
—"Of 'Liberty' and 'Property,' " 62 Cornell L. Rev. 405 (1977)   180, 212

Mott
—*Due Process of Law* (1926)   239

Moynihan
—*Maximum Feasible Misunderstanding: Community Action in the War on Poverty* (1969)   49, 244

Munzer & Nichol
—"Does the Constitution Mean What It Always Meant?" 77 Colum. L. Rev. 1029 (1977)   239

Mushkin & Cotton
—*Sharing Federal Funds for State and Local Needs: Grants-in-Aid and PPB Systems* (1969)   34, 142

Note
—"Administrative Cutoff of Federal Funding Under Title VI: A Proposed Interpretation of Program," 52 Ind. L.J. 651 (1977)   253
—"Depoliticizing Legal Aid: A Constitutional Analysis of the Legal Services Corporation Act," 61 Cornell L. Rev. 734 (1976)   69
—"Developments in the Law—Section 1983 and Federalism," 90 Harv. L. Rev. 1133 (1977)   150, 221
—"Emerging Concepts of Federalism: Limitations on the Spending Power and National Health Planning," 34 Wash. & Lee L. Rev. 1133 (1977)   33
—"Municipal Bankruptcy, the Tenth Amendment, and the New Federalism," 89 Harv. L. Rev. 1871 (1976)   32, 235, 240, 241, 242
—"Participation of the Poor: Section 202 (a) (3) Organizations Under the Economic Opportunity Act of 1964," 75 Yale L.J. 599 (1966)   49
—"Statutory Entitlement and the Concept of Property," 86 Yale L.J. 695 (1977)   180

Nowak *et al.*
—*Constitutional Law* (1978)   108, 131, 180, 230

Office of Federal Procurement Policy
—"Uniform Rules of Procedure for Boards of Contract Appeals and Related Regulations"   188

Office of Management and Budget
—*A-95: What It Is. How It Works.* (1976)   133
—*Catalog of Federal Domestic Assistance* (1978)   9, 37, 175
—"Special Analysis H, Federal Aid to State and Local Governments," in *Special Analysis, Budget of the United States Government* (1978)   10

Reagan
—*The New Federalism* (1972)   13, 25, 33, 34, 81

Reich
—"Individual Rights and Social Welfare: The Emerging Legal Issues," 74 Yale L.J. 1245 (1965)   18
—"The New Property," 73 Yale L.J. 733 (1964)   18
—"Social Welfare in the Public-Private State," 114 U. Pa. L. Rev. 487 (1966)   18

Rein & Miller
—"Citizen Participation and Poverty," 1 Conn. L. Rev. 221 (1968)   49

Schwartz & Wade
—*Legal Control of Government: Administrative Law in Britain and the United States* (1972)   349

Scurlock
—*Government Contracts and Grants for Research: A Guide for Colleges and Universities* (1975)   56, 173, 174, 176, 178

Selover
—"The View From Capitol Hill: Harassment and Survival," in *On Fighting Poverty: Perspectives From Experience* (1969)   276

Skoler, Lynch, & Axilbund
—"Legal and Quasi-Legal Considerations in New Federal Aid Programs," 56 Geo. L.J. 1144 (1968)   175

Subcommittee on Intergovernmental Relations, Senate Committee on **Governmental Affairs**
—*Table of Federal Programs: Presentation of Federal Programs by Budget Function, Authorizing Legislation, and Legislative Committee Jurisdiction* (Comm. Print 1977)   248

Thibaut & Walker
—*Procedural Justice: A Psychological Analysis* (1975)   182

Thomas & Luken
—"Balancing Incentives and Conditions in the Evolution of a Federal Program: A Perspective on Construction Grants for Waste Water Treatment Plants," 4 Publius 43 (1974)   42

Tomlinson & Mashaw
—"The Enforcement of Federal Standards in Grant-in-Aid Programs: Suggestions for Beneficiary Involvement," 58 U. Va. L. Rev. 600 (1972)   13, 14, 46, 47, 98, 201, 211

Tribe
—*American Constitutional Law* (1978)   108, 180, 182, 188, 213, 237
—"Structural Due Process," 10 Harv. Civ. Rights-Civ. Lib. L. Rev. 269 (1975)   180
—"Unraveling *National League of Cities:* The New Federalism and Affirmative Rights to Essential Government Services," 90 Harv. L. Rev. 1065 (1977)   235, 240, 241

Van Alstyne
—"Cracks in the 'New Property': Adjudicative Due Process in the Administrative State," 62 Cornell L. Rev. 445 (1977)   180
—"The Demise of the Right-Privilege Distinction in Constitutional Law," 81 Harv. L. Rev. 1439 (1968)   18

Verkuil
—"The Emerging Concept of Administrative Procedure," 78 Colum. L. Rev. 258 (1978)   22

von Mehren & Gordley
—*The Civil Law System: An Introduction to the Comparative Study of Law* (1977)   350

Walker
—"A New Intergovernmental System in 1977," 8 Publius 101 (1978)   363

Wallick & Montalto
—"Symbiosis or Domination: Rights and Remedies Under Grant-Type Assistance Programs," 46 Geo. Wash. L. Rev. 159 (1978)   14, 172, 173, 176

Watson
—"Congress Steps Out: A Look at Congressional Control of the Executive," 63 Calif. L. Rev. 983 (1975)   57

Webster
—*Webster's New Collegiate Dictionary* (1961)   220

Wechsler
—"Comment on American Legal Institutions," in *Legal Institutions Today and Tomorrow* 303 (M. Paulsen ed. 1959)   331
—"The Political Safeguards of Federalism: The Role of the States in the Composition and Selection of the National Government," 54 Colum. L. Rev. 543 (1954)   234, 235

Willcox
—"The Function and Nature of Grants," 22 Ad. L. Rev. 125 (1970)   23, 107, 173, 175, 234

Woodward
—"Reality and Social Reform: The Transition From Laissez-Faire to the Welfare State," 72 Yale L.J. 286 (1962)   34

Zamir
—"The Control of Administrative Acts by the Ordinary Courts," in I. Englard, ed., *Israeli Reports to the Ninth International Congress of Comparative Law* (Jerusalem, 1974)   350

Table of Statutes Cited

Act of July 2, 1862

§§1-8, 7 U.S.C. §§301-308, 45

Act of September 23, 1950

§§1-17, 20 U.S.C. §§631-647, 38, 268

§6(c), 20 U.S.C. §636 (c), 289
§11(a), 20 U.S.C. §641 (a), 245, 259, 268

Act of September 30, 1950

§§1-842, 20 U.S.C. §§236-246, 38, 261

§5(d), 20 U.S.C. §240(d), 261, 266
§5(d)(2)(A), 20 U.S.C. §240(d)(2)(A), 267
§5(g), 20 U.S.C. §240(g), 246, 289
§141(c), 20 U.S.C. §241e(c) (1976), 311
§141A, 20 U.S.C. §241e-1 (1976), 262
§146, 20 U.S.C. §241j (1976), 262

Administrative Procedure Act

§§1-12, 5 U.S.C. §§551-706, 1305, 3105, 3344, 5362, 7521

§2(2), 5 U.S.C. §551(2), 246
§3(a)(1), 5 U.S.C. §552(a)(1), 21
§4(a)(2), 5 U.S.C. §553(a)(2), 63
§5, 5 U.S.C. §554, 346, 358
§5(a), 5 U.S.C. §554(a), 246, 346
§5(d), 5 U.S.C. §554(d), 346, 347
§6, 5 U.S.C. §555, 346
§7, 5 U.S.C. §556, 346, 358
§8, 5 U.S.C. §557, 346, 358
§8(b), 5 U.S.C. §557(b), 346, 348
§8(c), 5 U.S.C. §557(c), 346, 348

§10, 5 U.S.C. §§701-706, 147, 157
§10(a), 5 U.S.C. §702, 111, 113
§10(a)(2), 5 U.S.C. §702(a)(2), 160
§10(b)(2), 5 U.S.C. §701(b)(2), 246
§10(c), 5 U.S.C. §704, 157
§10(e)(2)(A), 5 U.S.C. §706(2)(A), 166
§10(e)(2)(c), 5 U.S.C. §706(2)(c), 166
§10(e)(2)(D), 5 U.S.C. §706(2)(D), 166
§11, 5 U.S.C. §5362, 347
§11, 5 U.S.C. §7521, 347

Adult Education Act of 1966

§§302-315, 20 U.S.C. §§1201-1211b

§306(c), 20 U.S.C. §1205(c), 290
§308(a), 20 U.S.C. §1207(a), 245, 254

Age Discrimination Act of 1975

Title III, Older Americans Amendments of 1975, 42 U.S.C. §§6101-6107, 51, 315, 328

§303, 42 U.S.C. §6102, 315, 328
§304(a)(1), 42 U.S.C. §6103(a)(1), 328
§304(a)(5), 42 U.S.C. §6103(a)(5), 315, 328
§305, 42 U.S.C. §6104, 328
§305(b), 42 U.S.C. §6104(b), 341
§305(e), 42 U.S.C. §6104(e) (1976), 328
§305(e), 42 U.S.C. §6104(e), 328
§305(f), 42 U.S.C. §6104(f), 328
§306, 42 U.S.C. §6105, 328

Agricultural College Act of 1890

§§1-6, 7 U.S.C. §§321-329

§4, 7 U.S.C. §326, 249

372 / Rights and Remedies Under Federal Grants

Airport and Airway Development Act of 1970

§§2-208(a)-(f), 49 U.S.C. §§1701-1742, 39, 247, 248, 290

Appalachian Regional Development Act of 1965

§§1-405, 40 U.S.C. app. §§1-405, 37

Arts and Humanities Act of 1965

§§2-210, 20 U.S.C. §§951-968

§5(h), 20 U.S.C. §954(h), 274
§7(f)(7), 20 U.S.C. §956(f)(7), 274

Child Abuse Prevention and Treatment Act

§§2-7, 42 U.S.C. §§5101-5106

§4(b)(1), 42 U.S.C. §5103(b)(1), 194
§4(d), 42 U.S.C. §5103(d), 194

Child Nutrition Act of 1966

§§2-19, 42 U.S.C. §§1771-1788, 247, 266, 290

§17, 42 U.S.C. §1786, 45

Civil Rights Act of 1964

§§101-1106, 42 U.S.C. §§2000a-2000h-6

Title VI, 42 U.S.C. §§2000d-2000d-4, 20, 51, 137, 315
§601, 42 U.S.C. §2000d, 260, 315
§602, 42 U.S.C. §2000d-1, 95, 253, 260, 316, 325
§603, 42 U.S.C. §2000d-2, 260, 317
§604, 42 U.S.C. §2000d-3, 316

Clean Air Act Amendments of 1977

Pub. L. 95-95, Aug. 7, 1977

§105(e), 42 U.S.C. §7405(e), 246

Clean Air Act of 1963

§§101-403, 42 U.S.C. §§7401-7642, 248

§105(e), 42 U.S.C. §7405(e), 290

Coastal Zone Management Act

§§302-318, 16 U.S.C. §§1451-1464

§306, 16 U.S.C. §1455, 290
§308, 16 U.S.C. §1456(a), 247
§308(b)(6), 16 U.S.C. §1456a(b)(6), 100, 260
§312(b), 16 U.S.C. §1458(b), 246

Community Development Act of 1977

Pub. L. 95-128, Oct. 12, 1977, 102

§104(e), 42 U.S.C. §5304(d), 260
§110(b), 42 U.S.C. §5318, 260

Community Mental Health Centers Act

§§201-244, 42 U.S.C. §§2689-2689aa

§206(c)(6), 42 U.S.C. §2689e(c)(6), 262
§223, 42 U.S.C. §2689k, 308
§225, 42 U.S.C. §2689m, 103, 106, 258
§237(c), 42 U.S.C. §2689t, 289, 313

Community Services Act of 1974

§§2-1013, 42 U.S.C. §§2701-2996l

§101, 42 U.S.C. §2711, 202
§102, 42 U.S.C. §2712, 202
§103, 42 U.S.C. §2713, 202
§104, 42 U.S.C. §2714, 202
§210(a)(1), 42 U.S.C. §2790(a)(1), 312
§211, 42 U.S.C. §2791, 45, 50
§211(e), 42 U.S.C. §2791(e), 312
§212, 42 U.S.C. §2795, 45
§212(a), 42 U.S.C. §2795(a), 312
§213, 42 U.S.C. §2796, 45
§221(a), 42 U.S.C. §2808(a), 196, 273
§222(a), 42 U.S.C. §2809(a), 273
§223, 42 U.S.C. §2810, 191
§225, 42 U.S.C. §2812, 273
§242, 42 U.S.C. §2834, 133
Title IV, 42 U.S.C. §§2901-2906, 202, 273
§511, 42 U.S.C. §2928, 196, 273
§513, 42 U.S.C. §2928b, 273
§514, 42 U.S.C. §2928c, 273
§515, 42 U.S.C. §2928d, 312
§519(1), 42 U.S.C. §2928h(1), 313
§519(2), 42 U.S.C. §2928h(2), 285, 286
§519(3), 42 U.S.C. §2928h(3), 246, 273, 301

Table of Statutes Cited / 373

§551, 42 U.S.C. §2929, 202, 273
§552, 42 U.S.C. §2929a, 202
§553, 42 U.S.C. §2929b, 202
§557, 42 U.S.C. §2929c, 273
§557(b), 42 U.S.C. §2929c(b), 286, 300, 306
§557(c), 42 U.S.C. §2929c(c), 282
§602, 42 U.S.C. §2942, 57
§604, 42 U.S.C. §2944, 24, 246, 306
§604(1), 42 U.S.C. §2944(1), 313
§604(2), 42 U.S.C. §2944(2), 286, 300
§604(3), 42 U.S.C. §2944(3), 273
§626, 42 U.S.C. §2971f, 273
Title VII, 42 U.S.C. §§2981-2988g, 273
§723(a)(4), 42 U.S.C. §2983b(a)(4), 52
§803, 42 U.S.C. §2991b(a), 273
§809, 42 U.S.C. §2991h, 273
§809(1), 42 U.S.C. §2991h(1), 286
§809(2), 42 U.S.C. §2991h(2), 273, 301
§1004(f), 42 U.S.C. §2996c(f), 68
§1006(b)(1), 42 U.S.C. §2996e(b)(1), 24, 274
§1006(b)(2), 42 U.S.C. §2996e(b)(2), 24
§1006(b)(5), 42 U.S.C. §2996e(b)(5), 69
§1007(a)(9), 42 U.S.C. §2996f(a)(9), 305
§1007(d), 42 U.S.C. §2996f(d), 68
§1007(f), 42 U.S.C. §2966f(f), 131
§1011, 42 U.S.C. §2996j, 24
§1011(1), 42 U.S.C. §2996j(1), 286
§1011(2), 42 U.S.C. §2996j(2), 273, 301, 305, 347

Comprehensive Alcohol Abuse and Alcoholism Prevention, Treatment and Rehabilitation Act of 1970

§§2-603, 42 U.S.C. §§4541-4593, 290

§302(a), 42 U.S.C. §4572(a), 40
§321, 42 U.S.C. §4581, 51, 261, 315
§321(b)(1), 42 U.S.C. §4581(b)(1), 285
§333, 42 U.S.C. §4582, 261

Comprehensive Employment and Training Act Amendments of 1978

Pub. L. 95-524, Oct. 27, 1978, 67, 74

Comprehensive Employment and Training Act of 1973

§§2-809, 29 U.S.C. §§801-999, 10, 74

§102, 29 U.S.C. §812, 244
§104, 29 U.S.C. §814, 24
§104(d), 29 U.S.C. §814(d), 290
§106, 29 U.S.C. §816, 24, 68, 246
§106(a), 29 U.S.C. §816(a), 68, 69, 74
§106(b), 29 U.S.C. §816(b), 68
§106(d)(1), 29 U.S.C. §816(d)(1), 74
§106(e), 29 U.S.C. §816(e), 286
§106(g), 29 U.S.C. §816(g), 103, 104, 259
§106(i), 29 U.S.C. §816(i), 95
§106(l), 29 U.S.C. §816(l), 141
§108(b), 29 U.S.C. §818(b), 295
§108(b)(2), 29 U.S.C. §818(b)(2) (1976), 67
§122(c)(1), 29 U.S.C. §824(c)(1), 52
§123(d), 29 U.S.C. §825(d), 295
§123(d)(1), 29 U.S.C. §825(d)(1), 296
§123(g), 29 U.S.C. §825(g), 103
§125, 29 U.S.C. §827, 52
§131, 29 U.S.C. §833, 51
§132, 29 U.S.C. §834, 51, 326
Title II, pts. A-C, 29 U.S.C. §§841-852, 38
Title II-D, 29 U.S.C. §§853-859, 38
Title III, 29 U.S.C. §§871-886, 38
Title IV, 29 U.S.C. §§891-945, 38
§456(a), 29 U.S.C. §929(a), 205
Title VI, 29 U.S.C. §§961-970, 38, 279
§604, 29 U.S.C. §964, 279
Title VIII, 29 U.S.C. §§991-999, 38

Comprehensive Older Americans Act Amendments of 1978

Pub. L. 95-478, Oct. 18, 1978, 199, 297, 328, 341, 346

Contract Disputes Act of 1978

Pub. L. 95-563, Nov. 1, 1978, 53, 155, 350

§§2-15, 41 U.S.C. §§601-613, 37, 53, 179

§8(a)(1), 41 U.S.C. §607(a)(1), 350
§8(c), 41 U.S.C. §607(c), 350

Crime Control Act of 1976

Pub. L. 94-503, Oct. 5, 1976

§122(a), 42 U.S.C. §3757, 346

374 / Rights and Remedies Under Federal Grants

Declaratory Judgment Act

28 U.S.C. §2201, 147

Developmental Disabilities Services and Construction Act

§§102-145, 42 U.S.C. §§6001-6081

§133(c), 42 U.S.C. §6063(c), 290, 313
§134, 42 U.S.C. §6064, 245
§135, 42 U.S.C. §6065, 245, 254

Domestic Volunteer Services Act of 1973

§§101-505, 42 U.S.C. §§4591-5085

§412, 42 U.S.C. §5052, 24, 273, 306
§412(1), 42 U.S.C. §5052(1), 285, 286, 300

Drug Abuse Office and Treatment Act of 1972

§§101-504, 21 U.S.C. §§1101-1194, 247, 290

§407, 21 U.S.C. §1174, 51, 260, 315
§407(b)(1), 21 U.S.C. §1174(b)(1), 285
§408, 21 U.S.C. §1175, 261

Economic Opportunity Act of 1964

Pub. L. 88-452, Aug. 20, 1964, 272, 273

Economic Opportunity Amendments of 1967

Pub. L. 90-222, Dec. 23, 1967, 272

Education Amendments of 1972

Pub. L. 92-318, June 23, 1972

Title IX, 20 U.S.C. §§1681-1686, 51, 351
§901, 20 U.S.C. §1681, 260, 315
§901(a), 20 U.S.C. §1681(a), 326
§902, 20 U.S.C. §1682, 251, 260, 326, 327
§903, 20 U.S.C. §1683, 327
§904, 20 U.S.C. §1684, 315

Education Amendments of 1974

Pub. L. 93-380, Aug. 21, 1974

§844, 20 U.S.C. §1681n, 251

Education Amendments of 1976

Pub. L. 94-482, Oct. 12, 1976, 260

Title III-C, §§331-336, 20 U.S.C. §§2501-2506, 290

Education Amendments of 1978

Pub. L. 95-561, Nov. 1, 1978, 45, 47, 58, 74, 75, 76, 77, 78, 87, 88, 95, 102, 104, 194, 245, 246, 262, 264, 288, 289, 304, 305, 357

Education of the Handicapped Act

Title VI, Elementary and Secondary Education Amendments of 1969, 20 U.S.C. §§1401-1461, 311

§602(1), 20 U.S.C. §1401(1), 50
§612(2)(B), 20 U.S.C. §1412(2)(B), 50
§612(2)(C), 20 U.S.C. §1412(2)(C), 50
§613, 20 U.S.C. §1413, 194
§613(a)(11), 20 U.S.C. §1413(a)(11), 50
§613(c), 20 U.S.C. §1413(c), 41, 290
§615, 20 U.S.C. §1415, 51, 251
§616(a), 20 U.S.C. §1416(a), 97, 257, 258, 309, 342
§619, 20 U.S.C. §1419, 38, 290
§620, 20 U.S.C. §1420, 41
§620(a), 20 U.S.C. §1420(a), 208
§620(b), 20 U.S.C. §1420(b), 208

Elementary and Secondary Education Act of 1965

§§101-1006, 20 U.S.C. §§2701-3386, 38

§102, 20 U.S.C. §2702, 194
§111(a)(2), 20 U.S.C. §2711(a)(2), 49
§128, 20 U.S.C. §2738, 75, 165
§130(b)(4)(A), 20 U.S.C. §2740(b)(4)(A), 262
§162(b), 20 U.S.C. §2802(b), 77
§164, 20 U.S.C. §2811, 47, 75
§164(c), 20 U.S.C. §2811(c), 75
§167, 20 U.S.C. §2814, 47
§168, 20 U.S.C. §2815, 75, 165
§169, 20 U.S.C. §2816, 76

Table of Statutes Cited / 375

§169(a), 20 U.S.C. §2816(a), 287
§169(b), 20 U.S.C. §2816(b), 77
§169(c), 20 U.S.C. §2816(c), 77, 95
§169(d), 20 U.S.C. §2816(d), 76
§170, 20 U.S.C. §2817, 74
§170(a), 20 U.S.C. §2817(a), 102
§170(b), 20 U.S.C. §2817(b), 75, 76
§170(c), 20 U.S.C. §2817(c), 76, 87, 102
§170(d), 20 U.S.C. §2817(d), 75
§170(e), 20 U.S.C. §2817(e), 76, 88
§171(a), 20 U.S.C. §2821(a), 78
§182, 20 U.S.C. §2832, 298
§182(b), 20 U.S.C. §2832(b), 77
§184, 20 U.S.C. §2834, 75, 165
§185, 20 U.S.C. §2835, 78
§185(a), 20 U.S.C. §2835(a), 102
§185(b), 20 U.S.C. §2835(b), 87, 102
§186, 20 U.S.C. §2836, 78
§186(a), 20 U.S.C. §2836(a), 245, 263, 346
§186(c), 20 U.S.C. §2836(c), 95
§305(b)(12), 20 U.S.C. §844a(b)(12) (1976), 311
§305(c), 20 U.S.C. §844a(c) (1976), 293
§305(f), 20 U.S.C. §844a(f) (1976), 312
Title VII, 20 U.S.C. §§3221-3261, 304
§731, 20 U.S.C. §3241, 58

Emergency School Aid Act*

Title VII, Education Amendments of 1972, 20 U.S.C. §§1601-1619

§705, 20 U.S.C. §1604, 282
§706, 20 U.S.C. §1605, 282
§706(a)(1), 20 U.S.C. §1605(a)(1), 196
§710(a)(12), 20 U.S.C. §1609(a)(12), 263
§710(d)(2), 20 U.S.C. §1609(d)(2), 216, 297
§712(b), 20 U.S.C. §1611(b), 263
§712(c), 20 U.S.C. §1612(c), 263

Federal-Aid Highway Act of 1973

23 U.S.C. §§101-407, 38, 247, 290

23 U.S.C. §128, 49
23 U.S.C. §141, 249

* Repealed effective Sept. 30, 1979, by §601(b)(2) Education Amendments of 1978, Pub. L. 95-561, Nov. 1, 1978.

Federal Civil Defense Act of 1950

§§2-307, 50 U.S.C. app. §§2251-2297, 290

§401(h), 50 U.S.C. app. §2253(h), 24, 246

Federal Grant and Cooperative Agreement Act of 1977

§§2-10, 41 U.S.C. §§501-509, 20, 37, 172, 333

§4, 41 U.S.C. §503, 178
§5, 41 U.S.C. §504, 174, 178, 192
§6, 41 U.S.C. §505, 64, 178
§8, 41 U.S.C. §507, 332
§10(b), 41 U.S.C. §509(b), 64

Federal Water Pollution Control Act

§§101-517, 33 U.S.C. §§1251-1376, 39, 247, 248, 290

General Education Provisions Act

Title IV, Education Amendments of 1972, 20 U.S.C. §§1221-1234e, 22

§400(b), 20 U.S.C. §1221(b), 263
§400(c)(1)(A), 20 U.S.C. §1221(c)(1)(A), 263
§412(b), 20 U.S.C. §1225(b), 256
§413, 20 U.S.C. §1226, 256
§425, 20 U.S.C. §1231b-2, 247, 264, 309
§425(a), 20 U.S.C. §1231b-2(a), 76
§431, 20 U.S.C. §1232, 57
§434, 20 U.S.C. §1232c, 78, 264
§434(b), 20 U.S.C. §1232(b), 254
§434(b)(2), 20 U.S.C. §1232(b)(2), 286, 288
§434(c), 20 U.S.C. §1232c(c) (1976), 263
§435(b)(1), 20 U.S.C. §1232d(b)(1), 72, 77, 78
§438, 20 U.S.C. §1232g, 70, 260
§440(b), 20 U.S.C. §1232i(b), 251
§451, 20 U.S.C. §1234, 264, 357
§451(a)(4), 20 U.S.C. §1234(a)(4), 264, 358
§451(e), 20 U.S.C. §1234(e), 264
§452, 20 U.S.C. §1234a, 87, 264
§452(e), 20 U.S.C. §1234a(e), 88, 264

376 / *Rights and Remedies Under Federal Grants*

General Education Provisions Act— *Cont'd*

§453, 20 U.S.C. §1234b, 105, 264, 272
§453(c), 20 U.S.C. §1234b(c), 264, 286
§454, 20 U.S.C. §1234c, 87, 104, 264
§454(e)(2), 20 U.S.C. §1234c(e)(2), 105
§455, 20 U.S.C. §1234d, 264, 358
§456, 20 U.S.C. §1234e, 88, 264, 358

Health Professions Educational Assistance Act of 1976

Pub. L. 94-484, Oct. 12, 1976, 326

§201(c), 42 U.S.C. §292d, 326

Health Training Improvement Act of 1970

Pub. L. 91-519, Nov. 2, 1970, 326

§207, 42 U.S.C. §292d, 326

Higher Education Act of 1965

§§101-1208, 20 U.S.C. §§1001-1145c

§108(a), 20 U.S.C. §1007(a), 289
§108(b), 20 U.S.C. §1007(b), 245, 254
§202, 20 U.S.C. §1022, 197
§203, 20 U.S.C. §1023, 197, 294
Title IV, 20 U.S.C. §§1070-1089, 278
§413D(b)(1)(B)(i), 20 U.S.C. §1070b-3(b)(1)(B)(i), 196
§413D(b)(1)(B)(ii), 20 U.S.C. §1070b-3(b)(1)(B)(ii), 196
§415D(a), 20 U.S.C. §1070c-3(a), 289, 245
§418B, 20 U.S.C. §1070d-3, 290
§420(a)(1), 20 U.S.C. §1070e-1(a)(1), 197
§420(d)(1), 20 U.S.C. §1070e-1(d)(1), 197
§493(c), 20 U.S.C. §1088b-3, 290
§497, 20 U.S.C. §1088f, 329
§497A, 20 U.S.C. §1088f-1, 278
§497A(c), 20 U.S.C. §1088f-1(c), 278
§532(c)(2), 20 U.S.C. §1119a(c)(2), 312
§603(4), 20 U.S.C. §1123(4), 311
§607(a), 20 U.S.C. §1127(a), 289
§607(b), 20 U.S.C. §1127(b), 245
§704(a)(5), 20 U.S.C. §1132a-3(a)(5), 311
§704(b), 20 U.S.C. §1132a-3(b), 290
§708(a)(1), 20 U.S.C. §1132a-7(a)(1), 290

§708(a)(2), 20 U.S.C. §1132a-7(a)(2), 245
§1001(c), 20 U.S.C. §1135(c), 290
§1202, 20 U.S.C. §1142(a), 50

Housing Act of 1937

§§2-12, 42 U.S.C. §§1437-1437j

§8, 42 U.S.C. §1437(f), 130

Housing Act of 1949

§§2-527, 42 U.S.C. §§1441-1490g

§510(g), 42 U.S.C. §1480(g), 296

Housing and Community Development Act of 1974

§§101-120, 42 U.S.C. §§5301-5319, 10, 38, 290

§102(b), 42 U.S.C. §5302(b), 296
§103(c), 42 U.S.C. §5303(c), 296
§104(d), 42 U.S.C. §5304(d), 102, 260
§106, 42 U.S.C. §5306, 296
§109, 42 U.S.C. §5309, 128, 326
§111, 42 U.S.C. §5311, 24, 246
§119(h), 42 U.S.C. §5318(h), 102, 260

Housing and Community Development Amendments of 1978

Pub. L. 95-557, Oct. 31, 1978, 296

Inspector General Act of 1978

Pub. L. 95-452, Oct. 12, 1978, 70

Intergovernmental Cooperation Act of 1968

§§101-604, 42 U.S.C. §§4201-4244, 20

§401(b), 42 U.S.C. §4231(b), 133

Intergovernmental Personnel Act of 1970

§§2-513, 42 U.S.C. §§4701-4772, 290

§507, 42 U.S.C. §4767, 246

Joint Funding Simplification Act of 1974

§§1-12, 42 U.S.C. §§4251-4261, 20

Judicial Code

§1331, 28 U.S.C. §1331, 147
§1337, 28 U.S.C. §1337, 147
§1343(3), 28 U.S.C. §1343(3), 150
§1343(4), 28 U.S.C. §1343(4), 151
§1346(a)(2), 28 U.S.C. §1346(a)(2), 155
§1491, 28 U.S.C. §1491, 155

Juvenile Justice and Delinquency Prevention Act

§§101-341, 42 U.S.C. §§5601-5751, 38

§223(a)(19), 42 U.S.C. §5633(a)(19), 41
§223(d), 42 U.S.C. §5633(d), 290
§226, 42 U.S.C. §5636, 246

Land and Water Conservation Fund Act of 1965

§§1(b)-201, 16 U.S.C. §§460L-4 to 460L-11, 22, 39, 247, 248, 290

§6(b), 16 U.S.C. §4606L-8(b), 295
§6(b)(4), 16 U.S.C. §460L-8(b)(4), 256

Legal Services Corporation Act

Title X, Community Services Act of 1974, 42 U.S.C. §§2996-2996k, 68

§1006(b)(5), 42 U.S.C. §2996(b)(5), 214
§1011, 42 U.S.C. §2996(j)(2), 301

Legal Services Corporation Act Amendments of 1977

Pub. L. 95-222, Dec. 28, 1977

§16, 42 U.S.C. §2996j(2), 347

Library Services and Construction Act of 1956

§§2-404, 20 U.S.C. §§351-364, 38

§3, 20 U.S.C. §351(a), 252
§4(b), 20 U.S.C. §351b(b), 256
§5(b), 20 U.S.C. §351c(b), 255
§6(a), 20 U.S.C. §351d(a), 252
§6(c)(3), 20 U.S.C. §351d(c)(3), 289
§6(d), 20 U.S.C. §351d(d), 252
§6(e), 20 U.S.C. §351d(e), 245, 250, 254, 264
§6(f), 20 U.S.C. §351d(f), 159, 254
§7(b)(1), 20 U.S.C. §351e(b)(1), 256
§102, 20 U.S.C. §353, 256
§202, 20 U.S.C. §355b, 256
§302, 20 U.S.C. §355e-1, 256
§402, 20 U.S.C. §362, 256

Local Public Works Capital Development and Investment Act of 1976

§§101-111, 42 U.S.C. §§6701-6710, 10, 248, 345

§103, 42 U.S.C. §6702, 196
§104, 42 U.S.C. §6703, 196
§105, 42 U.S.C. §6704, 196
§106(f)(2), 42 U.S.C. §6705(f)(2), 52
§108(a)(2), 42 U.S.C. §6707(a)(2), 298
§108(a)(3), 42 U.S.C. §6707(a)(3), 45, 298
§110, 42 U.S.C. §6709, 51, 326

National Defense Education Act of 1958

§§101-1112, 20 U.S.C. §§401-602

§303(a)(3), 20 U.S.C. §443(a)(3), 311
§313(b), 20 U.S.C. §453(b), 311
§1001(9), 20 U.S.C. §581(g), 329
§1004(b), 20 U.S.C. §584(b), 289, 290
§1004(c), 20 U.S.C. §584(c), 245

National Environmental Policy Act of 1969

§§101-209, 42 U.S.C. §§4321-4347, 20

National School Lunch Act of 1946

§§2-21, 42 U.S.C. §§1751-1769a, 38, 247, 248, 266, 290

Nurse Training Act of 1971

Pub. L. 92-158, Nov. 18, 1971, 326

§11, 42 U.S.C. §298b-2, 326

Occupational Safety and Health Act of 1971

§§2-33, 29 U.S.C. §§651-678, 290

§18(f), 29 U.S.C. §667(f), 66, 246

Older Americans Act of 1965

§§101-608, 42 U.S.C. §§3001-3057g

§304(c), 42 U.S.C. §3024(c), 244
§304(d)(1)(A), 42 U.S.C. §3024(d)(1)(A), 41
§304(d)(1)(B), 42 U.S.C. §3024(d)(1)(B), 41
§305(d), 42 U.S.C. §3025(d) (1976), 294
§306(a)(6)(G), 42 U.S.C. §3026(a)(6)(G), 50
§307(a)(5), 42 U.S.C. §3027(a)(5), 309
§307(a)(11), 42 U.S.C. §3027(a)(11), 50
§307(c), 42 U.S.C. §3027(c), 290
§307(d), 42 U.S.C. §3027(d), 246
Title V, 42 U.S.C. §§3056-3056f, 39
§502(b)(1), 42 U.S.C. §3056(b)(1), 196
§502(d)(2), 42 U.S.C. §3056(d)(2), 199, 346
§506(a), 42 U.S.C. §3056d(a), 40
§506(a)(1), 42 U.S.C. §3056d(a)(1), 40
§506(b), 42 U.S.C. §3056d(b), 199
§604(c), 42 U.S.C. §3057c(c), 297
§604(e), 42 U.S.C. §3057c(e), 297
Title IX, 42 U.S.C. §§3056-3056f (1976), 45, 294

Omnibus Crime Control and Safe Streets Act of 1968

§§100-704, 42 U.S.C. §§3701-3796c, 10, 38

§100, 42 U.S.C. §3701, 35
§303(a)(8), 42 U.S.C. §3733(a)(8), 309
§303(a)(10), 42 U.S.C. §3733(a)(10), 309
§309(g), 42 U.S.C. §3739(g), 246
§509, 42 U.S.C. §3757, 24, 246, 346
§510, 42 U.S.C. §3758, 290, 296
§510(b), 42 U.S.C. §3758(b), 295
§510(c), 42 U.S.C. §3758(c), 295

Pub. L. 94-505, Oct. 15, 1976

Title II, 42 U.S.C. §§3521-3527, 70

Pub. L. 94-574, Oct. 21, 1976

§2, 28 U.S.C. §1331, 149

Pub. L. 95-291, June 12, 1978

§§1-6, 42 U.S.C. §1397a note, 6, 351

Public Health Service Act

§§2-1706, 42 U.S.C. §§201-300u-5

Title III-B, 42 U.S.C. §§243-247c, 38
§312, 42 U.S.C. §244-1 (1976), 203
§313, 42 U.S.C. §245a (1976), 203
§314(d)(3), 42 U.S.C. §246(d)(3), 66, 218, 290
§314(g)(3), 42 U.S.C. §246(g)(3), 79, 245, 254
§329, 42 U.S.C. §254b, 304
§332, 42 U.S.C. §254(e), 279
§335(e), 42 U.S.C. §254h(e), 261, 279
Title IV, 42 U.S.C. §§281-289"1"-8, 329
§704, 42 U.S.C. §292d, 51, 261, 326
§770(a), 42 U.S.C. §295f(a), 197
§770(b), 42 U.S.C. §295f(b), 197
§770(b)(2)(E), 42 U.S.C. §295f-1(b)(2)(E), 262
§810(a), 42 U.S.C. §296e(a), 197, 294
§810(b), 42 U.S.C. §296e(b), 197
§855, 42 U.S.C. §298b-2, 51, 261, 326
Title X, 42 U.S.C. §§300 to 300a-8, 38, 247, 290
§1310, 42 U.S.C. §300e-9, 261
§§1501-1536, 42 U.S.C. §§300k-300n-5, 33, 218, 277
§1511(b)(3)(B)(i), 42 U.S.C. §300"1"(b)(3)(B)(i), 277
§1512, 42 U.S.C. §300"1"-1, 45
§1513, 42 U.S.C. §300"1"-2, 45
§1513(e), 42 U.S.C. §300"1"-2(e), 313
§1513(e)(2), 42 U.S.C. §300"1"-2(e)(2), 278
§1515(b)(3), 42 U.S.C. §300"1"-4(b)(3), 278
§1515(c), 42 U.S.C. §300"1"-4(c), 218
§1515(c)(1), 42 U.S.C. §300"1"-4(c)(1), 278
§1515(d), 42 U.S.C. §300"1"-4(d), 278
§1516(b), 42 U.S.C. §300"1"-5(b), 278
§1521, 42 U.S.C. §300m, 261
§1521(b), 42 U.S.C. §300m(b), 218
§1521(b)(3)(B), 42 U.S.C. §300m(b)(3)(B), 277
§1521(b)(4), 42 U.S.C. §300m(b)(4), 277
§1522(c), 42 U.S.C. §300m-1(c), 277
§1532, 42 U.S.C. §300n-1, 313
§1535(a), 42 U.S.C. §300n-4(a), 277
Title XVI, 42 U.S.C. §§300o-300t, 38, 290
§1602(b), 42 U.S.C. §300o-1(6), 70

Table of Statutes Cited / 379

§1603(a)(8), 42 U.S.C. §300o-2(a)(8), 309
§1603(b), 42 U.S.C. §300o-2(b), 289
§1604(b)(1)(J), 42 U.S.C. §300o-3(b)(1)(J), 126
§1604(d), 42 U.S.C. §300o-3d, 308, 313
§1611(a), 42 U.S.C. §300p-1(a), 208
§1611(b), 42 U.S.C. §300p-1(b), 79, 245
§1611(b)(2), 42 U.S.C. §300p-1(b)(2), 254
§1612(a), 42 U.S.C. §300p-2(a), 245
§1612(b), 42 U.S.C. §300p-2(b), 102
§1612(b)(2), 42 U.S.C. §300p-2(b)(2), 258
§1612(c), 42 U.S.C. §300p-2(c), 69, 106
Title XVI-F, 42 U.S.C. §300t, 247
§1640, 42 U.S.C. §300t, 278

Public Works and Economic Development Act of 1965

§§1-1008, 42 U.S.C. §§3121-3246h, 248, 304

§101, 42 U.S.C. §3131, 305
§304, 42 U.S.C. §3153, 247, 290
§304(a), 42 U.S.C. §3153(a), 279
§304(b), 42 U.S.C. §3153(b), 279
§402, 42 U.S.C. §3162, 279
§403(c), 42 U.S.C. §3171(c), 279
Title V, 42 U.S.C. §§3181-3196, 34, 200
§702, 42 U.S.C. §3212, 52
§903, 42 U.S.C. §3243, 279
§1002, 42 U.S.C. §3246a, 279

Public Works Employment Act of 1976

Pub. L. 94-369, July 22, 1976

Title II, 42 U.S.C. §§6721-6736, 10
§212, 42 U.S.C. §6732, 24

Public Works Employment Act of 1977

Pub. L. 95-28, May 13, 1977

§105, 42 U.S.C. §6707(a)(2), 298
§105, 42 U.S.C. §6707(a)(3), 298

Rehabilitation Act of 1973

§§2-733, 29 U.S.C. §§701-796i, 38, 325

§7(7), 29 U.S.C. §706(7), 315
§101(b), 29 U.S.C. §721(b), 290
§101(c), 29 U.S.C. §721(c), 246
§103, 29 U.S.C. §723, 51
§504, 29 U.S.C. §794, 51, 261, 315, 324, 343
§505, 29 U.S.C. §794a, 261
§505(2), 29 U.S.C. §794a(2), 325

Rehabilitation, Comprehensive Services, and Developmental Disabilities Amendments of 1978

Pub. L. 95-602, Nov. 6, 1978, 325

Safe Drinking Water Act

Title XIV, Public Health Service Act, 42 U.S.C. §§300f to 300j-10, 247, 290

Smith-Hughes Vocational Education Act

§§1-18, 20 U.S.C. §§11-28

§16, 20 U.S.C. §26, 249

Social Security Act

§§1-2007, 42 U.S.C. §§301-1397f

Title IV-A, 42 U.S.C. §§601-611, 192
§401, 42 U.S.C. §601, 39
§402(a), 42 U.S.C. §602(a), 43, 51
§402(a)(1), 42 U.S.C. §602(a)(1), 50
§402(a)(3), 42 U.S.C. §602(a)(3), 50
§402(a)(4), 42 U.S.C. §602(a)(4), 51
§402(a)(10), 42 U.S.C. §602(a)(10), 51
§402(a)(27), 42 U.S.C. §602(a)(27), 247
§402(b), 42 U.S.C. §602(b), 247
§403, 42 U.S.C. §603, 39
§404, 42 U.S.C. §604, 246
§404(a)(1), 42 U.S.C. §604(a)(1), 247
§404(c), 42 U.S.C. §604(c), 247
§404(d), 42 U.S.C. §604(d), 247
Title IV-B, 42 U.S.C. §§620-626, 38, 247, 248, 290
§423, 42 U.S.C. §623, 41
Title V, 42 U.S.C. §§701-716, 290
§507, 42 U.S.C. §707, 245
Title IX, 42 U.S.C. §§1101-1108, 247, 290

380 / Rights and Remedies Under Federal Grants

Social Security Act—Cont'd

§1102, 42 U.S.C. §1302, 57
§1106, 42 U.S.C. §1306, 52
§1115, 42 U.S.C. §1315, 55
§1116, 42 U.S.C. §1316, 236, 283, 291
§1116(d), 42 U.S.C. §1316(d), 283
Title XIX, 42 U.S.C. §§1396-1396k, 38
§1902(a), 42 U.S.C. §1396a(a), 43
§1904, 42 U.S.C. §1396c, 254
Title XX-A, 42 U.S.C. §§1397-1397f, 38
§2002(a)(1), 42 U.S.C. §1397a(a)(1), 6, 48
§2002(a)(2)(A), 42 U.S.C. §1397a(a)(2)(A), 295
§2003(b), 42 U.S.C. §1397b(b), 48
§2003(c)(1), 42 U.S.C. §1397b(c)(1), 49
§2003(e), 42 U.S.C. §1397b(e), 246

Social Security Amendments of 1977

Pub. L. 95-216, Dec. 20, 1977

§402, 42 U.S.C. §603(j), 47

Solid Waste Disposal Act

§§1002-8007, 42 U.S.C. §§6901-6987, 247, 248, 290

§8001(a), 42 U.S.C. §6981(a), 43
§8004(c), 42 U.S.C. §6984(c), 44
§8006(b)(2), 42 U.S.C. §6986(b)(2), 44

Special Health Revenue Sharing Act of 1975

Pub. L. 94-63, July 29, 1975

§941(k)(1), 42 U.S.C. §298b-2, 326

Special Projects Act*

§§1-4, §§402(b)-409, 20 U.S.C. §§1851-1853, §§1861-1867

§405(h), 20 U.S.C. §1864(h), 44

State and Local Fiscal Assistance Act of 1972

* Repealed effective Sept. 30, 1979, by §301(b) Education Amendments of 1978, Pub. L. 95-561, Nov. 1, 1978.

§§101-145, 31 U.S.C. §§1221-1265, 9

§121, 31 U.S.C. §1241, 46
§122, 31 U.S.C. §1242, 46
§123, 31 U.S.C. §1243, 46
§123(b), 31 U.S.C. §1243(b), 24

Uniform Relocation Assistance and Real Property Acquisitions Policies Act of 1970

§§101-305, 42 U.S.C. §§4601-4655, 20, 52

United States Constitution

Article I, §8, cl. 1, 29, 176
Article III, §1, 352
Article III, §3, 183
Article IV, §3, cl. 2, 176
Article VI, cl. 2, 54

Amendment V, 180
Amendment XI, 140
Amendment XIV, §1, 181
Amendment XIV, §1, cl. 4, 235
Amendment XV, 235
Amendment XIX, 235
Amendment XXIV, 180, 235
Amendment XXVI, 235

Urban Mass Transit Act of 1964

§§2-22, 49 U.S.C. §§1601-1618, 247, 248, 290

Vocational Education Act of 1963

§§101-195, 20 U.S.C. §§2301-2461, 38, 66, 260

§106(a)(4), 20 U.S.C. §2306(a)(4), 312
§107(a)(1), 20 U.S.C. §2307(a)(1), 293
§108, 20 U.S.C. §2308, 194
§108(a)(1), 20 U.S.C. §2308(a)(1), 293
§109(a)(1), 20 U.S.C. §2309(a)(1), 66
§109(b)(1), 20 U.S.C. §2309(b)(1), 290
§109(c), 20 U.S.C. §2309(c), 245, 312
§109(e), 20 U.S.C. §2309(e), 312
§109(f), 20 U.S.C. §2309(f), 260
§111(a)(1), 20 U.S.C. §2311(a)(1), 208

Wagner-Peyser Act of 1933

§§1-12, 29 U.S.C. §§49-49k, 247, 290

Table of Citations to the Code of Federal Regulations

1 C.F.R. §305.68-6, 270
1 C.F.R. §305.71-4(1), 299
1 C.F.R. §305.71-4(2), 299
1 C.F.R. §305.71-4(4), 299
1 C.F.R. §305.71-9, 69, 93, 244, 258
1 C.F.R. §305.74-2(a), 299
1 C.F.R. §305.74-2(B), 299
1 C.F.R. §305.74-2(B)(3), 299
5 C.F.R. pt. 900, subpt. E, 321
5 C.F.R. pt. 900, subpt. F, 52
5 C.F.R. §900.204, 24, 265
5 C.F.R. §900.204(d)(2), 347
5 C.F.R. §900.204(g), 348
5 C.F.R. §900.301(a), 295
7 C.F.R. pt. 15, 320
7 C.F.R. §210.19, 266
7 C.F.R. §225.18(b), 284
7 C.F.R. §246.6, 252
7 C.F.R. §246.24, 51
7 C.F.R. §246.25, 309
7 C.F.R. pt. 1890, 321
7 C.F.R. pt. 1900, subpt. B, 298
7 C.F.R. pt. 1948, 209
10 C.F.R. pt. 4, 320
13 C.F.R. pt. 113, 321
13 C.F.R. §302.40, 279
13 C.F.R. §303.10, 279
13 C.F.R. §305.99, 266
13 C.F.R. §317.75, 266
13 C.F.R. §317.75(a), 286
14 C.F.R. §152.64(d), 266
14 C.F.R. pt. 1250, 321
15 C.F.R. pt. 8, 320
15 C.F.R. §920.46(b), 298
15 C.F.R. pt. 925, 291
15 C.F.R. §931.97, 106, 107, 260
15 C.F.R. §931.112(m), 309

15 C.F.R. §931.114(d), 309
18 C.F.R. pt. 302, 321
22 C.F.R. pt. 141, 321
22 C.F.R. pt. 209, 321
23 C.F.R. pt. 420, 266
23 C.F.R. pt. 450, 266
23 C.F.R. pts. 520-599, 266
23 C.F.R. pt. 630, 266
24 C.F.R. pt. 1, 321
24 C.F.R. pt. 24, 24
24 C.F.R. pt. 200, 321
24 C.F.R. §570.4, 60
24 C.F.R. §570.913, 4
24 C.F.R. §570.913(c), 265
24 C.F.R. §570.913(d), 347
24 C.F.R. §570.913(j)-(m), 348
24 C.F.R. §570.913(m), 348
28 C.F.R. pt. 18, 24, 301
28 C.F.R. §§18.31-.35, 265
28 C.F.R. §18.32, 309
28 C.F.R. §18.52(a), 347
28 C.F.R. §18.57, 348
28 C.F.R. pt. 42, 319
28 C.F.R. pt. 42, subpt. C, 321
28 C.F.R. pt. 42, subpt. F, 317, 319
28 C.F.R. §42.403, 319
28 C.F.R. §42.404, 319
28 C.F.R. §42.405, 319
28 C.F.R. §42.406, 319
28 C.F.R. 42.407(a), 319
28 C.F.R. §42.407(b), 319
28 C.F.R. §42.407(c), 319
28 C.F.R. §42.408, 320
28 C.F.R. §42.410, 320
28 C.F.R. §42.414, 320
28 C.F.R. §42.415, 320
28 C.F.R. §50.3, 317, 318

382 / Rights and Remedies Under Federal Grants

29 C.F.R. pt. 31, 321
29 C.F.R. pt. 94, 301
29 C.F.R. pt. 97, 301
29 C.F.R. §97.165(a), 72, 96, 253
29 C.F.R. §§97.190-.198, 265
29 C.F.R. §97.292, 298
29 C.F.R. pt. 98, 301
29 C.F.R. §98.15(b), 100
29 C.F.R. §98.16, 24
29 C.F.R. §98.16(c), 288
29 C.F.R. §§98.40-.46, 67
29 C.F.R. §98.46, 67
29 C.F.R. §98.47(f), 347
29 C.F.R. §98.48, 348
29 C.F.R. §1950.12, 265
30 C.F.R. pt. 41, 321
31 C.F.R. §§51.200-.225, 24
31 C.F.R. §52.90, 24
32 C.F.R. pt. 300, 320
32 C.F.R. pt. 1803, 24, 265
32 C.F.R. §1803, 265
32 C.F.R. §1803.6(a), 347, 348
32 C.F.R. pt. 1811, 320
33 C.F.R. pt. 24, 320
35 C.F.R. pt. 30, subpts. H-J, 177
38 C.F.R. §17.285, 284
38 C.F.R. pt. 18, 321
40 C.F.R. pt. 30, 24
40 C.F.R. §30.335, 303
40 C.F.R. §30.920, 265
40 C.F.R. §§30.920-3, 209
40 C.F.R. §35.706, 203
40 C.F.R. §35.744, 50
41 C.F.R. pts. 1-1 to 1-30, 178
41 C.F.R. pt. 101-6, 321
42 C.F.R. pt. 5, 279
42 C.F.R. §50.106(d), 215
42 C.F.R. pt. 51, subpt. B, 265
42 C.F.R. pt. 51a, 265
42 C.F.R. pt. 52, subpt. K, 294
42 C.F.R. §52c-5(d), 301
42 C.F.R. pt. 53, 265
42 C.F.R. §53.124, 309
42 C.F.R. §54a.102, 40
42 C.F.R. §57.13, 61
42 C.F.R. §§58.2-.3 (1977), 203
42 C.F.R. §61.15, 329
42 C.F.R. §61.17, 329
42 C.F.R. §63.6, 329
42 C.F.R. §64.7(c), 213
42 C.F.R. §66.109, 329
42 C.F.R. §66.109(a), 329
42 C.F.R. §86.39, 329
42 C.F.R. §86.39(b), 329
42 C.F.R. pt. 110, subpt. I, 219

42 C.F.R. §110.605, 298
42 C.F.R. §122.108, 219
42 C.F.R. §123.108, 219, 284
42 C.F.R. §123.204, 278
43 C.F.R. pt. 17, 321
43 C.F.R. pt. 17a, 321
45 C.F.R. pt. 8, 321
45 C.F.R. pt. 10, 321
45 C.F.R. pt. 16, 21, 24, 281, 304
45 C.F.R. §16.2(a), 282
45 C.F.R. §16.4(b), 281
45 C.F.R. §16.5(a), 282
45 C.F.R. §16.10(c), 348
45 C.F.R. §16.10(d), 287
45 C.F.R. §16.51, 271
45 C.F.R. §16.58, 231
45 C.F.R. §16.58(a)(1), 231
45 C.F.R. §16.60(c), 355
45 C.F.R. §16.65, 267
45 C.F.R. §16.71, 271
45 C.F.R. pt. 46, 261
45 C.F.R. §46.121(b), 215
45 C.F.R. §§50.401-.406, 282
45 C.F.R. §64.7(c), 280
45 C.F.R. pt. 70 (1977), 261
45 C.F.R. pt. 71, 261
45 C.F.R. pt. 74, 20
45 C.F.R. §74.115(a), 209, 280
45 C.F.R. pt. 75, 282
45 C.F.R. pt. 80, 324
45 C.F.R. §80.3, 324
45 C.F.R. §80.4, 324
45 C.F.R. §80.4(a)(1), 318, 324
45 C.F.R. §80.5, 324
45 C.F.R. §80.6, 324
45 C.F.R. §§80.6-.10, 321
45 C.F.R. §80.7, 324
45 C.F.R. §80.9(a), 321
45 C.F.R. §80.9(b), 321
45 C.F.R. §80.9(c), 321
45 C.F.R. §80.9(d), 321, 322
45 C.F.R. §80.9(d)(2), 321, 322, 323
45 C.F.R. §80.10(a), 321, 322
45 C.F.R. §80.10(e), 322
45 C.F.R. §80.10(f), 322
45 C.F.R. §80.10(g), 323
45 C.F.R. §80.10(g)(2), 322
45 C.F.R. §§81.51-.53, 321
45 C.F.R. §80.13(f), 325
45 C.F.R. §81.4, 324
45 C.F.R. §81.11, 321
45 C.F.R. §81.21(b), 321
45 C.F.R. §81.51, 321
45 C.F.R. §§81.51-53, 321
45 C.F.R. §81.52, 267

Table of Citations to the Code of Federal Regulations / 383

45 C.F.R. §81.61, 321
45 C.F.R. §81.62, 321
45 C.F.R. §81.63, 322
45 C.F.R. §§81.72-.73, 321
45 C.F.R. §81.73, 324
45 C.F.R. §81.75, 324
45 C.F.R. §81.76, 324
45 C.F.R. §81.92, 321, 322
45 C.F.R. §81.104(b), 322
45 C.F.R. §81.105, 322
45 C.F.R. §81.106, 322
45 C.F.R. §81.121, 323
45 C.F.R. §81.121(a), 323
45 C.F.R. pt. 82, 316
45 C.F.R. pt. 83, 326
45 C.F.R. §84.6(c), 324
45 C.F.R. pt. 85, 325
45 C.F.R. §85.3(d), 325
45 C.F.R. §85.3(e), 325
45 C.F.R. §85.4(b), 325
45 C.F.R. §85.5(a), 325
45 C.F.R. §85.5(b)(2), 324
45 C.F.R. §§85.52-.55, 324
45 C.F.R. §86.2(g), 326
45 C.F.R. §86.2(h), 326
45 C.F.R. §86.3(c), 327
45 C.F.R. §86.4, 327
45 C.F.R. §86.8(b), 327
45 C.F.R. §86.9, 327
45 C.F.R. §86.71, 327
45 C.F.R. §§99.60-.67, 70, 265
45 C.F.R. pt. 100a, 20
45 C.F.R. §100a.27, 298
45 C.F.R. §100a.53(b), 99
45 C.F.R. §100a.483, 60
45 C.F.R. §100a.495(a)(3), 281
45 C.F.R. §100a.495(f), 288
45 C.F.R. §100a.495(h), 281
45 C.F.R. §100a.496(a)(2), 107, 275
45 C.F.R. pt. 100b, 20, 255
45 C.F.R. pt. 100b, subpt. E, 255
45 C.F.R. pt. 100b, subpt. F, 255
45 C.F.R. §100b.495, 275
45 C.F.R. §104.182, 309
45 C.F.R. §§104.281-.289, 293
45 C.F.R. §104.291, 265
45 C.F.R. pt. 111, 265, 268
45 C.F.R. §111.2(c), 262, 269
45 C.F.R. §111.4, 269
45 C.F.R. §111.5, 260
45 C.F.R. §111.7(b), 269
45 C.F.R. §111.8, 269
45 C.F.R. §111.9, 269
45 CFR. §115.66(c), 260
45 C.F.R. §§115.68-.69, 69, 265, 266

45 C.F.R. §116.6, 69
45 C.F.R. §116.20, 265
45 C.F.R. §117.2(h), 265
45 C.F.R. §118.19, 69
45 C.F.R. §118.20, 265
45 C.F.R. pt. 119, 265
45 C.F.R. §121.5, 302
45 C.F.R. §§121a.110-.151, 60
45 C.F.R. §121a.194, 308
45 C.F.R. §121a.236, 59
45 C.F.R. §121a.602, 69
45 C.F.R. §121f.30, 298
45 C.F.R. §123.04(b), 302
45 C.F.R. §123.43(d), 329
45 C.F.R. pt. 130, 252
45 C.F.R. §130.41, 265
45 C.F.R. §130.42, 200
45 C.F.R. §131.23, 294
45 C.F.R. §134.102, 69
45 C.F.R. §141.10, 265
45 C.F.R. §144.4a, 294
45 C.F.R. §144.7, 294
45 C.F.R. pt. 147, 329
45 C.F.R. §153.12(b)(12), 218
45 C.F.R. §158, 282
45 C.F.R. §158.84(d), 306
45 C.F.R. §159.7(b)(2), 303
45 C.F.R. §159.7(b)(3), 302
45 C.F.R. §160e.5(a), 301
45 C.F.R. §160e.5(d)(2)(i), 302
45 C.F.R. §160e.5(d)(2)(ii), 302
45 C.F.R. §160e.5(d)(2)(iii), 303
45 C.F.R. §160e.5(d)(2)(iv), 303
45 C.F.R. pt. 166, 265
45 C.F.R. §§168.71-.84, 265
45 C.F.R. §168.75, 288
45 C.F.R. §168.75(b)(3), 260
45 C.F.R. §168.77(a), 269
45 C.F.R. §168.77(c)(1), 270
45 C.F.R. §168.79, 270
45 C.F.R. §168.80(a), 270
45 C.F.R. §168.82, 257
45 C.F.R. §168.82(a), 280
45 C.F.R. pt. 170, subpt. B, 265
45 C.F.R. pt. 171, 265
45 C.F.R. §§172.20-.137, 300
45 C.F.R. §173.15(b), 265
45 C.F.R. §175.7, 294
45 C.F.R. §176.7, 294
45 C.F.R. §185.14(c)(3), 297
45 C.F.R. §185.42, 263
45 C.F.R. §185.45 (1977), 282
45 C.F.R. §185.45, 282
45 C.F.R. §185.45(b), 213
45 C.F.R. §187.5, 216

45 C.F.R. §187.5(a)(2), 215
45 C.F.R. §187.5(b), 298
45 C.F.R. §187.6(d)(2), 303
45 C.F.R. §187.79, 329
45 C.F.R. pt. 192, 265
45 C.F.R. §194.8, 300
45 C.F.R. §194.30, 300
45 C.F.R. §197.12, 312
45 C.F.R. pt. 200, 358
45 C.F.R. §201.6(c), 94
45 C.F.R. §§201.10-.13, 66
45 C.F.R. §201.13(b), 94
45 C.F.R. §201.14, 283
45 C.F.R. §204.4, 283
45 C.F.R. pt. 213, 265, 291
45 C.F.R. §213.13, 260
45 C.F.R. §213.15, 231
45 C.F.R. §213.27, 269
45 C.F.R. pt. 228a, 358
45 C.F.R. §246.17(c), 358
45 C.F.R. pt. 300, 358
45 C.F.R. pt. 430, 358
45 C.F.R. pt. 611, 321
45 C.F.R. pt. 1010, 320
45 C.F.R. §1050, 348
45 C.F.R. §§1050.80-1 to .80-3, 50, 65
45 C.F.R. §1050.115, 313
45 C.F.R. §§1050.115-1 to .121, 24
45 C.F.R. §1050.115-5, 209
45 C.F.R. §1067.1, 265, 283
45 C.F.R. §1067.1-4, 288
45 C.F.R. §1067.1-7(L), 271
45 C.F.R. §1067.2-4, 223
45 C.F.R. §1067.2-4(b), 306
45 C.F.R. §1068.25-1 to .25-2, 60
45 C.F.R. pt. 1206, 24
45 C.F.R. §1206.1, 265, 283
45 C.F.R. §1206.1-4, 288
45 C.F.R. §1206.1-4(c)(1)(i), 288
45 C.F.R. §1206.1-4(c)(1)(iii), 288
45 C.F.R. §1206.1-7(b)(2), 271, 347
45 C.F.R. §1206.1-9, 271
45 C.F.R. §1206.2-4(c), 306

45 C.F.R. §1302.3-1, 61
45 C.F.R. pt. 1303, subpt. B, 313
45 C.F.R. pt. 1303, subpt. C, 306
45 C.F.R. §1303.4, 265, 283, 288, 309
45 C.F.R. §1303.4(a)(2), 288
45 C.F.R. §1303.4-4(d), 271
45 C.F.R. §1321.20(a), 265
45 C.F.R. §1324.10(a), 265
45 C.F.R. §1336.59, 306
45 C.F.R. pt. 1340, subpt. B, 194
45 C.F.R. §§1340.1-.11, 301
45 C.F.R. §1340.3-7, 194
45 C.F.R. §1361.5, 265
45 C.F.R. §1361.5(a), 265
45 C.F.R. §§1386.80-.112, 265
45 C.F.R. §1386.81(b), 271
45 C.F.R. §1386.92, 260
45 C.F.R. §1386.94(b), 271
45 C.F.R. §1386.94(c), 271
45 C.F.R. §1386.101, 271
45 C.F.R. §1386.103, 271
45 C.F.R. §1403.11, 298
45 C.F.R. §1424.8, 209
45 C.F.R. §1424.8(f), 288
45 C.F.R. §1424.8(h), 281
45 C.F.R. §1424.10(a)(2), 107
45 C.F.R. §§1603.5-.6, 69
45 C.F.R. pt. 1606, 24, 265, 283
45 C.F.R. §1606.2(b), 305
45 C.F.R. §1606.8, 306, 347
45 C.F.R. §1606.8(b)-(d), 347
45 C.F.R. §1606.9(c), 354
45 C.F.R. §1606.11(a), 354
45 C.F.R. §1606.15, 306
45 C.F.R. §1606.16, 354
45 C.F.R. §1606.17, 354
45 C.F.R. pt. 1618, 24
45 C.F.R. §1618.5(a), 94
45 C.F.R. pt. 1623, 24
49 C.F.R. pt. 21, 321
49 C.F.R. pt. 601, 266
49 C.F.R. pt. 613, 266
50 C.F.R. pt. 3, 321

Table of Cases

A

Aasum v. Good Samaritan Hosp. 64
Adams v. Richardson 80
Advocates for the Arts v. Thomson 5, 151, 161, 166, 168, 202, 203, 204
Afton Alps, Inc. v. United States 63, 130, 148, 149, 156, 161, 167
Aguayo v. Richardson 55, 109, 143, 147, 149, 151, 161, 228
Alabama Power Co. v. Ickes 129
Aldinger v. Howard 150
Allied-City Wide, Inc. v. Cole 2
Almenares v. Wyman 147, 151, 164
Amalgamated Transit Union, Local 519 v. LaCrosse Municipal Transit Util. 34, 109, 115
American Ass'n of Councils of Medical Staffs of Private Hosps., Inc. v. Mathews 63
American Federation of Government Employees (AFGE)
—Local 2677 v. Phillips 19, 113, 124, 126, 195
—Local 2816 v. Phillips 119, 124, 126, 156
American Federation of State, County, and Municipal Employees (AFSCME), Greater Cleveland Dist. Council 78 v. City of Cleveland 60, 161, 166
Andrews v. Maher 152
Apter v. Richardson 5, 123, 168, 202
Arizona
—v. Hobby 4, 156, 235
—v. United States 5, 155
Arizona State Dep't of Pub. Welfare v. Department of Health, Educ. & Welfare 6, 31, 49, 85, 94, 159, 160, 181, 228, 241, 242
Arnett v. Kennedy 191, 237
Arthur C. Logan Mem. Hosp. v. Toia 80, 85
Ascherman v. Presbyterian Hosp. of Pac. Medical Center, Inc. 64
Association of Data Processing Serv. Organs. v. Camp 112, 130
Ayala v. District 60 School Bd. 151

B

Baker v. Carr 109, 235
Barlow v. Collins 112
Barnes v. Tarrytown Urban Renewal Agency 125, 137, 237
Barnhart v. Brinegar 54
Barrera v. Wheeler 83
Bartels v. Biernat 91, 151
Batterton v. Francis 12, 31, 42, 58
Beal v. Doe 19
Benson v. City of Minneapolis 49
Berry v. Housing & Home Fin. Agency 2, 110, 111, 129
Black v. Beame 137, 139
Blake v. McClung 225
Blue v. Craig 152
Board of Educ. v. U.S. Dep't of Health, Educ. & Welfare 5, 167, 202, 204
Board of Pub. Instruction v. Finch 6
Board of Regents v. Roth 189, 206, 212
Bossier Parish School Bd. v. Lemon 106, 116, 137
Boston Pub. Housing Tenants' Policy Council, Inc. v. Lynn 116, 160
Bradford School Bus Transit, Inc. v. Chicago Transit Auth. 114, 130, 163, 165

Bromley-Heath Modernization Comm. v. Boston Housing Auth. 63
Brown v. Housing Auth. 63
Buckley v. Valeo 30
Burke v. Southern Pac. R.R. 176
Burns v. Alcala 151

C

Cafeteria & Restaurant Workers Union, Local 473 v. McElroy 185
Califano v. Sanders 147
California By and Through the Dep't of Transp. v. United States 5, 80
California ex rel. Dep't of Transp.
—v. United States 5, 21
—v. United States (II) 5
California Welfare Rights Organ. v. Richardson 42, 55, 65, 161, 167, 202
Cannon v. University of Chicago 64, 115, 136, 137, 139, 164
Carey v. Piphus 221
Carleson v. Remillard 54, 83, 211
Carman v. Richardson 124, 149, 155, 157, 160, 161, 167, 343
Carroll v. Finch 228, 242
Center for Auto Safety v. Tiemann 63, 124, 137
Chacon v. Hodgson 49
Chapman v. Houston Welfare Rights Organ., Inc. 152
Christian, G. L., & Assocs. v. United States 177
Citizens to Preserve Overton Park, Inc. v. Volpe 160, 166, 167
City of Beaver Falls v. Economic Dev. Admin. 5, 35, 121
City of Benton Harbor v. Richardson 5, 121, 122, 166, 202, 203, 204
City of Grand Rapids v. Richardson 5, 35, 123, 166, 202, 337
City of Hartford
—v. Hills 55, 144
—Towns of Glastonbury 22, 55, 143, 144, 145
City of Hialeah v. U.S. Housing Auth. 19
City of Lafayette v. Louisiana Power & Light Co. 238
City of Lebanon v. U.S. Dep't of Housing & Urban Dev. 215
City of Los Angeles v. Adams 5, 19, 195
City of Macon v. Marshall 5, 34, 160, 182

City of Milwaukee v. Saxbe 113, 149, 152, 153, 228
City of New York
—v. Diamond 6, 63
—v. Richardson 22
City of N. Miami v. Train 167
Clark v. Richardson 5, 35, 122, 149, 153, 155, 202, 337
Clement Martin, Inc. v. Dick Corp. 3, 70, 128, 131
Clinton Community Hosp. Corp. v. Southern Md. Medical Center 130
Coalition for United Community Action v. Romney 49, 55, 136, 156
Cole v. Lynn 14
Commission on Aging v. Finch 6, 159
Community Action Programs Executive Directors Ass'n v. Ash 4, 119, 122, 124, 148, 153, 156, 195
Community Progress, Inc. v. Martinez 5, 49, 90
Comprehensive Group Health Servs. Bd. of Directors v. Temple Univ. 49, 109, 136, 148, 164
Connecticut State Dep't of Pub. Welfare v. Department of Health, Educ. & Welfare 6, 32, 228, 241
Cook v. Oshner Foundation Hosp. 70, 116, 126
Cornell Univ. v. Fiske 46
Corrugated Container Corp. v. Community Servs. Admin. 130, 149, 154
Cort v. Ash 115
Corum v. Beth Israel Medical Center 54, 70, 109, 116, 126
County of Alameda v. Weinberger 5, 14, 54, 156, 159, 161, 236
County of Los Angeles
—v. Adams 6, 33, 85
—v. Coleman 32
Crane v. Mathews 59, 161, 167, 181
Crockin, M. M., Co. v. Portsmouth Redev. & Housing Auth. 115
Curry v. McCanless 181
Cuyahoga Metro. Housing Auth. v. Harmody 86

D

Dandridge v. Williams 12, 211
Davis
—v. Robinson 151
—v. Shultz 49, 149, 155
—v. Southeastern Community College 343

Don v. Okmulgee Mem. Hosp. 64, 189
Dorak v. Shapp 152
Duke Power Co.
—v. Carolina Environmental Study Group, Inc. 146
—v. Greenwood 129

E

East Oakland-Fruitvale Planning Council v. Rumsfeld 6, 160, 202
Economic Opportunity Comm'n v. Weinberger 5, 119, 161, 166, 168, 186, 352
Edelman v. Jordan 140, 151
English v. Town of Huntington 54, 125, 149
Escalera v. New York City Housing Auth. 16, 159, 189, 221
Euresti v. Stenner 106, 126
Evans v. Lynn 113, 143

F

Feliciano
—v. Romney (I) 49, 163, 165
—v. Romney (II) 163
Flast v. Cohen 108, 130
Fletcher
—v. Housing Auth. 14
—v. Romney 110
Florida
—v. Mathews (I) 6, 82
—v. Mathews (II) 5
—v. Weinberger 6
French v. Barber Asphalt Paving Co. 181
Frothingham v. Mellon 3, 30, 108, 130, 131
Fuentes v. Shevin 221

G

Gaines v. Martinez 89, 135, 161, 167, 248
Gardner v. Alabama 6, 94, 100, 159
Gart v. Cole 2, 125
Gibson & Perin Co. v. City of Cincinnati 109, 126
Goldberg v. Kelly 16, 18, 51, 181, 189, 192, 223, 230, 231, 330, 336, 352
Gomez v. Florida State Employment Serv. 115, 139, 152
Gonzales v. Young 152

Goss v. Lopez 183, 221
Graham v. Richardson 18, 55
Grassetti v. Weinberger 5, 167, 168, 202, 203, 204, 215
Green v. Dumke 189
Green St. Ass'n v. Daley 111, 165
Grumman Ecosystems Corp. v. Gainesville-Alachua County Regional Elec., Water & Sewer Facilities Bd. 14, 59, 129, 157, 167
Guran, M. B., Co. v. City of Akron 115, 116, 128

H

Hagans v. Lavine 150, 151, 152
Hairston v. Drosick 189
Hardin v. Kentucky Utils. Co. 130
Hardy v. Leonard 113
Harper v. Virginia Bd. of Elections 235
Harrison-Halstead Community Group, Inc. v. Housing & Home Fin. Agency 2, 111
Hathaway v. Mathews 229, 307
Helvering v. Davis 29, 30
Hergenreter v. Hayden 85
Hills v. Gautreaux 82
Hines v. Cenla Community Action Comm., Inc. 64, 127, 148
Hood River County v. United States By and Through the Dep't of Labor 119, 120, 135
Hospital Ass'n of New York State, Inc. v. Toia 5
Housing Auth. v. U.S. Housing Auth. 63
Houston Welfare Rights Organ., Inc. v. Vowell 152
Human Resources Management, Inc. v. Weaver 14, 21, 221
Hunt v. Washington State Apple Advertising Comm'n 112

I

Illinois ex rel. Bakalis v. Weinberger 4, 195
Indiana ex rel. Indiana State Bd. of Pub. Welfare v. Ewing 4
International Shoe Co. v. Cocreham 227
Iowa ex rel. State Highway Comm'n v. Brinegar 195
Ivanhoe Irrigation Dist. v. McCracken 29, 32

388 / *Rights and Remedies Under Federal Grants*

J

Jacksonville Port Auth. v. Adams 5, 121, 256
James v. Valtierra 82
Johnson
—v. Morton 109, 127
—v. Redevelopment Agency 54, 111
Joint Anti-Fascist Refugee Comm. v. McGrath 221
Jones v. Tully 113, 125, 137, 161, 167
Justice v. Board of Educ. 59, 83

K

Kennedy v. Mathews 41, 195
King v. Smith 1, 11, 12, 32, 55, 94, 151, 152
Kirkpatrick v. Preisler 235
Klein v. Mathews 189
Kletschka v. Driver 6, 166, 168, 189, 203
Knoxville Progressive Christian Coalition v. Testerman 110, 113, 131

L

Lau v. Nichols 31, 32, 116, 123, 137, 343
Lavine v. Milne 189
Lee v. Macon County Bd. of Educ. 6
Lewis
—v. Martin 164
—v. Richardson 5, 123, 124, 202, 337
Lloyd v. Regional Transp. Auth. 104, 115, 116, 137, 165
Lopez v. Luginbill 49, 85, 115, 136, 149, 152
Louisiana v. Weinberger 4, 195
Lower East Side Neighborhood Health Council-South, Inc. v. Richardson 49, 136
Lower Kensington Civic Ass'n v. Watson 49
Lynch
—v. Household Fin. Corp. 151
—v. United States 238

M

Malinski v. New York 331
Mando v. Beame 115, 124
Marable v. Alabama Mental Health Bd. 6
Marquez v. Hardin 148, 153, 154, 248

Martinez v. Mathews 49
Maryland
—v. Mathews 5, 14, 50, 54, 248
—v. Wirtz 240
Maryland Nat'l Capital Park & Planning Comm'n v. Lynn 6, 54
Mathews
—v. Eldridge 15, 181, 182, 185, 186, 189, 220, 230, 337
—v. Massell 109, 132, 149
Mattingly v. Elias 116, 149, 152
Mayor of Baltimore v. Mathews 5, 361
Memphis Light, Gas & Water Div. v. Craft 16, 353, 357
Meyer v. Nebraska 212
Michigan Head Start Directors Ass'n v. Butz 5, 122, 153, 156, 202
Mid-America Regional Council v. Mathews 5, 121, 148, 155, 161, 166, 167, 202, 203
Mil-Ka-Ko Research & Dev. Corp. v. Office of Economic Opportunity 6, 161, 167
Minnesota v. Weinberger 153, 155
Minnesota Chippewa Tribe v. Carlucci 122, 154
Miree v. DeKalb County 116, 137, 139, 140
Missouri ex rel. The Missouri-St. Louis Metro. Airport Auth. v. Coleman 121, 166, 167
Monell v. Department of Social Servs. 153
Monmouth Legal Servs. Organ. v. Carlucci 6, 14, 167
Morrissey v. Brewer 185
Mourning v. Family Publications Service, Inc. 57
Movement Against Destruction v. Volpe 167
Mullane v. Central Hanover Bank & Trust Co. 185

N

NAACP v. Wilmington Medical Center, Inc. 164
NAACP-Santa Rosa-Sonoma City Branch v. Hills 49, 113, 124
Named Individual Members of the San Antonio Conservation Soc'y v. Texas Highway Dep't 86
National Ass'n of Neighborhood Health Centers, Inc. v. Mathews 54, 112, 122, 165

National Ass'n of Regional Councils v. Costle 6, 39, 195
National Consumer Info. Center v. Gallegos 5
National Council of Community Mental Health Centers, Inc. v. Weinberger 4, 42, 119, 155, 157, 195
National League of Cities v. Usery 32, 225, 240
National Mutual Ins. Co. v. Tidewater Transfer Co. 181
National Welfare Rights Organ. v. Finch 41, 229, 231
Natonabah v. Board of Educ. 73
Natural Resources Defense Council, Inc. v. Costle 34, 98
Nebraska Dep't of Rds. v. Tiemann 5, 32, 248
New York City Coalition for Community Health v. Lindsay 49, 60, 109, 115, 136, 149, 164
New York State Dep't of Social Servs. v. Dublino 12, 13, 211
Nicholson v. Pittenger 204
North Carolina ex rel. Morrow v. Califano 6, 33
North City Area-Wide Council, Inc. v. Romney 49, 59, 92, 136, 161
Northeast Community Organ., Inc. v. Weinberger 5, 167, 202
North Phila. Community Bd. v. Temple Univ. 49, 158, 165
Norton v. Blaylock 127, 148
Norwalk CORE v. Norwalk Redev. Agency 125

O

Offut v. United States 347
Ohio v. U.S. Civil Serv. Comm'n 3, 32
Oklahoma
—v. U.S. Civil Serv. Comm'n 3, 31, 83, 116
—v. Weinberger 5, 195
Oregon v. Mitchell 240
Organized Migrants in Community Action, Inc. v. James Archer Smith Hosp. 115, 126
Owens v. School Comm. 49

P

Paducah Junior College v. Secretary of Health, Educ. & Welfare 4, 111

Paul v. Davis 213
Pennsylvania
—v. Kleppe 242
—v. Lynn 161, 166, 196
—v. New Jersey 227
—v. Weinberger 4, 155, 195
People's Housing Dev. Corp. v. City of Poughkeepsie 115, 128
Pfizer, Inc. v. Government of India 238
Philadelphia Anti-Poverty Action Comm. (PAAC) v. Rizzo 85, 86, 147
Pittsburgh Hotels Ass'n v. Urban Redev. Auth. 2, 111, 129
Poirrier v. St. James Parish Police Jury 80, 100, 106, 115, 124, 158
Ponce v. Housing Auth. 154, 189
Port Auth. v. United States 6, 155
Powelton Civic Home Owners Ass'n v. Department of Housing & Urban Dev. 125, 165, 237
Pullman, Inc. v. Volpe 109, 128

Q

Quern v. Mandley 31, 81

R

Red School House, Inc. v. Office of Economic Opportunity 5, 14, 208
Regents of the Univ. of Cal. v. Bakke 115, 121, 123, 181, 323, 343
Rental Housing Ass'n v. Hills 112, 130
Reynolds v. Sims 235
Rhodes v. City of Chicago 81
Richardson
—v. Belcher 18
—v. Perales 346
Richmond Welfare Rights Organ. v. Snodgrass 82, 84, 85, 147
Road Review League v. Boyd 125, 161, 167
Rocky Ford Housing Auth. v. U.S. Dep't of Agriculture 122, 124
Romeo Community Schools v. U.S. Dep't of Health, Educ. & Welfare 6
Rosado v. Wyman 2, 29, 31, 54, 58, 83, 84, 86, 94, 123, 151, 152, 164
Ross v. Moffitt 352
Rubinstein v. Mayor of Baltimore 6, 107, 127, 275

S

Saine v. Hospital Auth. 70, 115, 126, 137, 139
Sansom Comm. v. Lynn 137, 154
Santa Clara v. Southern Pac. R.R. Co. 239
Schlesinger v. Reservists Comm. to Stop the War 109
Schneider v. Whaley 189, 229
School Bd.
—v. Department of Health, Educ. & Welfare 14, 99, 100, 161, 166
—v. Richardson 6, 18, 31, 161, 167, 202
School Board, In re 6, 100, 159, 213
School City v. Derthick 4, 166, 202
School Comm. v. Anrig 5, 49, 203, 204
School Crossing Guards Ass'n v. Beame 109
Schreiber v. Lugar 115, 132, 149
Shannon v. U.S. Dep't of Housing & Urban Dev. 125, 161, 164, 166
Shapiro v. Thompson 18, 46, 143
Shaw v. Governing Bd. 85
Shaw-Henderson, Inc. v. Schneider 110, 128
Shea v. Vialpando 151, 211
Shelley v. Kraemer 239
Shepheard v. Godwin 49, 85, 131, 132
Sierra Club v. Morton 112
Silva
—v. East Providence Housing Auth. 124, 148, 151, 215, 272
—v. East Providence Housing Auth. (II) 124, 341
Simkins v. Moses H. Cone Mem. Hosp. 70
Simon v. Eastern Ky. Welfare Rights Organ. 113, 120, 145
Sinking Fund Cases 226
Smith v. Board of Comm'rs 17
Sockwell v. Maloney 189
South Carolina v. Katzenbach 225, 227, 228, 238, 241
South Dakota v. Volpe 6, 167
Southeastern Community College v. Davis 343
Southern Mut. Help Ass'n. v. Califano 1, 5, 35, 215, 304
South Suburban Safeway Lines, Inc. v. City of Chicago 109, 114, 130, 131, 166
Spokane County Legal Servs., Inc. v. Legal Servs. Corp. 5
Stanback v. Harris 92
Stanturf v. Sipes 64, 70, 148
State v. Anderson 227
State Dep't of Pub. Welfare v. Weinberger 5, 14, 153
State Highway Comm'n v. Volpe 4, 155, 194, 195
Steward Mach. Co. v. Davis 29, 30, 31
Stiner v. Califano 34, 228

T

Talbot v. Romney 125
Tenants & Owners in Opposition to Redev. (TOOR) v. U.S. Dep't of Housing & Urban Dev. 160, 167
Tennessee Elec. Power Co. v. Tennessee Valley Auth. 112, 129
Texas
—v. United States 5, 18, 54, 119
—v. United States By and Through the Community Servs. Admin. 91
Texas Acorn v. Texas Area 5 Health Systems Agency, Inc. 49
Thompson v. Washington 124, 154, 156, 221, 237
Thorpe v. Housing Auth. 62, 116, 178, 238
Torres v. Butz 59, 85
Townsend v. Swank 55, 82
Township of Benton v. County of Berrien 5
Township of Ridley v. Blanchette 113, 125, 137, 167
Township of River Vale v. Harris 5, 195, 208
Trageser v. Libbie Rehab. Center, Inc. 324
Train
—v. Campaign Clean Water, Inc. 195
—v. City of New York 4, 155, 195
Troutman v. Shriver 130, 131, 134
Twining v. New Jersey 181

U

Ulster County Community Action Comm., Inc. v. Koenig 49
United States
—v. Bossier Parish School Bd. 4, 106
—v. Brady 57, 100
—v. Butler 29, 31, 33

—v. City and County of San Francisco 176
—v. City of Chicago 92, 248
—v. City of Jackson 227
—v. Cogwell 273
—v. County School Bd. 4, 80, 106
—v. Frazer 80, 176
—v. Hill 273
—v. Independent School Dist. No. 1 4, 80, 100
—v. Jefferson County Bd. of Educ. 21, 62
—v. June 273
—v. Madison County Bd. of Educ. 4, 106
—v. Minyard 273
—v. Northern Pac. R.R. 176
—v. Orleans 12, 64
—v. Riddick 273
—v. Students Challenging Regulatory Agency Procedures (SCRAP) 112, 113
—v. Sumter County School Dist. No. 2 4, 80, 106
—v. Virginia 5

V

Vermont v. Brinegar 5, 32
Village of Arlington Heights v. Metropolitan Housing Dev. Corp. 124

W

Warth v. Seldin 113, 145
Washington Research Project, Inc. v. Department of Health, Educ. & Welfare 204
West Coast Constr. Co. v. Oceano Sanitary Dist. 63, 109, 128
Western Addition Community Organ. v. Weaver 92, 125, 161, 167
Wheeler v. Barrera 12, 31, 83, 86
Window Sys., Inc. v. Manchester Mem. Hosp. 109, 128
Wisconsin v. Constantineau 213
Wolff v. McDonnell 183
Wu v. National Endowment for Humanities 6
Wyman v. James 81
Wyoming ex rel. Wyoming Agricultural College v. Irvine 121

Index

A

Administrative Conference of the United States 69, 299, 345
Administrative Procedure Act 63, 321
   Citizens to Preserve Overton Park v. *Volpe* 160, 168
   dispute resolution procedures 346, 349, 358
   judicial review of federal grantor agency as remedy 109, 111, 113–114, 156–157, 159–160, 166, 168
Advisory Commission on Intergovernmental Relations 34
Age discrimination, finding of (*See* Notice and hearing rights)
Age Discrimination Act of 1975 328
Aid to Families With Dependent Children Program 1, 94, 192, 291
Antirecession grants 10
Applicants, rights of (*See* Due Process; Notice and hearing rights; Standing to sue)
Arts and Humanities Act of 1965 274–275
Associational standing (*See* Standing to sue)

B

Beneficiaries, rights of (*See* Due Process; Notice and hearing rights; Standing to sue)
Block grants 10, 12
Buckley Amendment 70

C

Catalog of Federal Domestic Assistance, classification scheme of 9

Categorical grants (*See* Grants-in-aid, federal)
CETA (*See* Comprehensive Employment and Training Act)
Civil Rights Act of 1964, Title VI 20, 137, 315–316
Coastal Zone Management Act 100–101
Commerce, Department of
   discretionary grants, conversion to formula grants 297–298
   funds recovery, methods for 101
Community Action Program
   beneficiaries' standing to sue 123
   subgrantee hearing rights 312–313
Community Development Block Grant Program 60
Community Services Act of 1974 283
   grant monitoring system 68
   notice and hearing provisions
      grant termination 273
      refunding proposals 300
Community Services Administration, notice and hearing provisions of 273, 283–284, 287–288
Competitive grants (*See* Project grants)
Compliance (*See* Enforcement and monitoring of grant conditions)
Comprehensive Employment and Training Act (CETA)
   grant monitoring procedures 67–68
   purpose 119
   recovery of illegal expenditures, authorization for 102–104
   remedies under 141–142
Continuation grants, hearing rights of applicants for (*See* Notice and hearing rights)
Contract law, nature of 53–54
Cooperative federalism (*See* Grants-in-aid, federal)

394 / *Rights and Remedies Under Federal Grants*

Courts, jurisdiction of 146–147
  appeals to, disadvantages of 168–171
  civil rights 150–153
  Court of Claims, U.S. 155
  Due Process, states' right to 236–237
  federal grantor agencies
    preemption by 162–165
    review of 109, 111, 113–114, 156–161, 166, 168, 228
  federal question 147–150
  Hagans v. *Lavine* 151
  limitations on 165–168
  mandamus jurisdiction 153–155
  private cause of action 109, 137–142, 343–344
  reform proposals 344–345

D

Defense, Department of 176
Deferral of grant funds (*See* Enforcement and monitoring of grant conditions)
Department of (*See* specific department names)
Discretionary grants (*See* Project grants)
Discrimination, finding of (*See* Notice and hearing rights)
Discrimination, hearing right for finding of (*See* Notice and hearing rights)
Disputes resolution (*See* Due Process)
Domestic Volunteer Services Act 283, 300
Due Process (*See also* Notice and hearing rights)
  administrative procedural codes, proposed 185–188
  Arnett v. *Kennedy* 190, 203, 237
  beneficiaries' right to 192–193, 230, 242
  Board of Regents of State Colleges v. *Roth* 189, 197, 198
  constitutional criteria 181–182
  definition 180–181
  deprivation, need to determine extent of 181–182, 219–224, 335
  disputes resolution
    inequity of 346–349, 359–363
    reform proposals 350–358
  economic factors 182–184
  federal agency obligation to provide 15–16
  Goldberg v. *Kelly* 192, 211, 231, 232, 330, 352

  grantor agency functioning, effect on 183–184
  justifiable reliance as requirement 189
    formula grants 197–199
    project grants 206–207
  liberty, protection of 181, 211–212
    future business opportunities 214–219
    good reputation 212–214, 330
    Paul v. *Davis* 213
  methods for providing, hierarchy of 184–185
  Mullane v. *Central Hanover Bank & Trust Co.* 185
  property
    applicants' claims to 193–197, 203–205
    expectation of refunding as 205–207
    federal funds as 188–189
    fellowships as 330
    reallotment process effect on 199–201
    recipients' claims to 207–208
    service capacity as 191–193
  states' right to
    court granting of 236–237
    declining power of states as reason for 234–235
    denial of 225–233
    federalism concept as grounds for 240–243
    National League of Cities v. *Usery* 32–33, 240–241
    South Carolina v. *Katzenbach* 227, 238
    state, definition of 233–234
    State v. *Anderson* 227
    state v. person issue 227, 238–240
    statutory provision for 236, 243
Durham Housing Authority 238

E

Economic Opportunity, Office of 134
Economic Opportunity Act of 1964 69, 119, 127
  notice and hearing provisions 272–274
Education, Office of (*See* Education grant programs)
Education Amendments of 1972 326–327

Education Amendments of 1978 78, 87, 104–105, 264
Education and Labor Committee, House of Representatives 73, 76, 79, 87–88
Education Appeal Board 104–105, 357–358
Education grant programs
  disputes resolution system 357–358
  enforcement procedures 87, 104–105, 264
  health education programs 279
  monitoring procedures 66, 69, 73–79
  noncompliance sanctions 257–258, 270–271, 292–293
  notice and hearing rights 261–264, 278–279, 281–282, 297
    location of hearings 260
    regulations for 266–269
    subgrantee rights 308–309
Education of the Handicapped Act
  noncompliance, sanctions for 257–258
  subgrantee hearing rights 308–309
Elementary and Secondary Education Act of 1965
  partial sanctions for nonconformity 292–293
  Title I program 83
    monitoring procedures 73–79
    notice and hearing provisions 262
    recovery of illegal expenditures, authorization for 87
Emergency Employment Act 124
Emergency School Aid Act 297
Enforcement and monitoring of grant conditions
  compliance, monitoring of 63–79
    central offices for 70–71
    complaints, investigation of 66–69
    compliance, absence of standards to determine 257
    grantee special reports 70
    on-site inspections 66
    standard practices 65–66
    subgrantee, supervision of 71–79
  condition enforcement, problem of 90–92
  federal grantor payment obligation 97
  fiscal sanctions 84–85, 95–96
    County of Alameda v. *Weinberger* 56
    Gardner v. *Alabama* 100
    program-by-program application 97–98

  self-defeating aspect of 86, 93–94, 245
  hierarchical authority of 61–62
  informal enforcement 79–80, 94–95, 216–217
  legal basis
    agency regulations 58–59
    "crosscutting" national policies 59
    federal authorizing statutes 54–58
    grantee assurances 59–60
    individualized agreements 60–61
    supplemental directives 62–63
  limitations on 82–90
    examples 85–86
    states' rights 82–85, 103–104
  noncompliance hearing, public notice of 257–258
  offense and sanction, need for proportionality between 90–92
  permissible sanctions, need to define 92–93
  recovery of illegal expenditures 87–88, 98–103, 258–260
  reform proposals 339–344
  specific performance as remedy 104–107, 176–177
  state educational agencies, responsibilities of 73–79
  subgrantee compliance 71–79
    federal and agency conditions, applicability of 71–72
    supervision of 72–73
  suspension of funds 285
  Wheeler v. *Barrera* 83
  withholding of entitlements 245
    disposition of retained funds 254–257
Entitlement grants (*See* Formula grants)
Environmental Protection Agency 177
Executive Order 11914 325

F

Fair process (*See* Due Process)
Farmers, federal payments to 30
Federal Grant and Cooperative Agreement Act of 1977 20, 172, 174, 333, 363
Federal Security Administration 4
Federalism, cooperative (*See* Grants-in-aid, federal)
Fellowships, termination of 329–330
Fifth Amendment (*See* Due Process)
Fiscal sanctions (*See* Enforcement and monitoring of grant conditions)

396 / *Rights and Remedies Under Federal Grants*

Formula grants
  definition 9
  matching ratio 41–42, 48
  standard characteristics 39–42, 244–245
  state and local services
    equalization of 36–37
    stimulation of 36
    support of 34–36
  types 38–39
Fourteenth Amendment (*See* Due Process)

G

General Education Provisions Act 357–358
  grant monitoring procedures 78–79
  notice and hearing provisions
    grant terminations 263–264, 281
    subgrantees' rights 309–312
General Welfare Clause (*See* Sovereignty, federal intervention in state and local)
Grantees
  as "caretaker" or channel of federal funds 36, 191–192
  nonliability of 175–176
  redress opportunities, factors affecting 15–16
  reluctance to file suit against grantors, reasons for 17–19, 23–24
  types and numbers, table of 8
  "voluntary quit" right 175–176
Grantors
  control over grantees, extent of 13–15
  decisions, final authority for 165–168
  primary jurisdiction in disputes 162–165
Grants Administration Manual, OHD 61–62, 95
Grants-in-aid, federal
  A-95 consultation system 133–134
  administrative departments and agencies, number of 9
  annual agreements concerning, number of 17
  conditional nature 17, 247–248
  contracts and grants, differences between 178–179
  "cooperative federalism" as means of implementing 11–13, 25–26, 192, 240–243
    King v. *Smith* 1, 11
    Cornell University v. *Fiske* 46
  expenditures, annual 10–11, 239
  federal grant law
    components of 19–21
    confusion regarding 22–23, 173
    courts' attitudes toward 22
  HEW percentage of 281
  litigation regarding, expansion of 1–10
    plaintiffs involved in 2–4
    reasons for 7–10
  misconceptions concerning 172–173
  negotiation concerning, lack of 177–178
  programs, number of 9
  purposes and types 9–10, 34–45
    research and demonstration 37, 42–44
    service 204–205
    state and local services, support of 34–42, 174–175, 244–245
  requirements 45–52
    administrative conditions 47–48
    constitutional bases 28–34
    eligibility, determination of 50–51
    focus on "input," reasons for 47, 175
    maintenance-of-effort condition 48–49
    matching ratio 41–42, 44, 48, 178
    National League of Cities v. *Usery* 32–33, 240–241
    national policies, conformity to 51–52
    Oklahoma v. *United States Civil Service Commission* 31
    programmatic conditions 48–50
    Tenth Amendment 29, 31–34
    Thorpe v. *Housing Authority* 62–63, 238
  rights v. privileges issue 17–18, 174–175, 186
  state and local revenues, percentage of 11, 131, 198, 239
  state sovereignty, intrusion into 28
    constitutional basis 29–30, 35, 80
    limitations 84
    state acceptance, voluntary aspect of 30–34, 46, 55, 81, 82, 106
  voluntary withdrawal from, grantee 82–84, 104–105, 107

H

Handicap-based discrimination
  hearing right for finding of 324–325
  victims, standing to sue 136

Head Start Program 273, 312–313
Health, Education and Welfare, Department of (HEW) 358
  appeal system 23, 164, 211, 281–284, 347–348
  conformity decisions, time period for 291–292
  grant monitoring procedures 70–72, 218–219
  grant statute, obligation to enforce 56
  health services, annual review of 277–278
  nondiscrimination by grantees, enforcement of 8, 325, 327
  nonrecovery of federal welfare payments 100
  program regulations, specificity of 299–300
  project grants, number of 281
  recovery of illegal expenditures, methods for 102
  sovereign immunity 156
  states, settlement of lawsuits with 6
  Title VI compliance hearings 321–324
Health care services (*See* Public Health Service Act)
Hearing rights (*See* Notice and hearing rights)
HEW (*See* Health, Education and Welfare, Department of)
Higher Education Act of 1965 270, 278–279
Hill-Burton Act 3, 124, 126, 138
Housing Act of 1937 129, 130
Housing and Community Development Act 101, 128
Housing and Urban Development, Department of (HUD)
  grant control authority 14–15
  regulations in circulars, binding nature of 62–63
  suits against 144
HUD (*See* Housing and Urban Development, Department of)
Human Development, Office of (OHD) 61, 95
  grant suspension, instructions for 287
  grant termination, hearing rights for 283–284
Human Resources Committee, Senate 67

I

Illegal expenditures, recovery of (*See* Enforcement and monitoring of grant conditions)
Immunity, sovereign 156–157
Implied cause of action (*See* Private cause of action)
Intergovernmental Cooperation Act of 1968 20, 133

J

Joint Funding Simplification Act of 1974 20
Judicial review (*See* Courts, jurisdiction of)
Jurisdiction of courts (*See* Courts, jurisdiction of)
Justice, Department of
  desegregation, implementation by grant requirements 4
  nondiscrimination, guidelines and regulations for 317–320

L

Labor, Department of
  grant monitoring procedures 67–68
  recovery of illegal expenditures, methods for 103
  sanctions, effectiveness of 342
Land grants
  cases regarding 176
  requirements of 45–46
LEA (Local Educational Agency) (*See* Education grant programs)
Legal Services Corporation
  disputes resolution system 354–355
  grant enforcement regulations 95
  grant monitoring procedures 68–69
  notice and hearing provisions 273–274, 283–284
Legal Services Corporation Act
  employees of grantee organizations, control of behavior of 69, 214
  refunding process, notice and hearing rights under 305–306
Legal Services Program 1, 273
Liberty, protection of (*See* Due Process)
Library grants 252
Library Services and Construction Act of 1956 249–253, 257

398 / *Rights and Remedies Under Federal Grants*

Local Educational Agency (LEA) (*See* Education grant programs)
Local Public Works Capital Development and Investment Act 297–298

M

Management and Budget, Office of (OMB) 11, 20, 64, 72, 107, 175, 266, 332
   A-95 consultation system 133–134
   grant suspensions or terminations, instructions for 209, 280, 286–287
   grants, definition of 9
   recovery of illegal expenditures, authorization for 99
Medicaid Program 291
Medical Facilities Construction Program 102
Monitoring procedures (*See* Enforcement and monitoring of grant conditions)

N

National Environmental Policy Act of 1969 20, 137
National Institute of Education (NIE) 73, 263–264, 281, 361
National Planning and Resources Development Act 33
NIE (*See* National Institute of Education)
Noncompliance, remedies for (*See* Enforcement and monitoring of grant conditions)
Noncompliance and nonconformity findings, hearing rights for (*See* Notice and hearing rights)
Nondiscrimination standards, hearing rights for noncompliance with (*See* Notice and hearing rights)
Notice and hearing rights (*See also* Due Process)
   applicants' rights
      formula grants 289–293
      grant size, disputes concerning 294–296
      institutions as applicants 293–294
      project grants 202–203, 296–300
      refunding proposals 300–306
   beneficiaries' rights 293
   Congress as appeal board 249
   discrimination findings 314–316
      age discrimination 327–328
      handicap-based discrimination 324–325
      HEW compliance hearings 321–324
      racial discrimination 316–320
      sex discrimination 325–327
   extension of 263–264
   fellowships, termination of 329
   hearings, location of 260
   recipients' rights 208–211
   reform proposals 333–339
   specific federal conditions, hearing rights for 260–262
   statutory provision
      inconsistency of 190, 225–226
      repetition within same statute 262
   subgrantees' rights 252–254, 307–313
   suspension of funds
      agency regulations 286–288
      as distinct from "withholding" 285
      statutory provision 286
   termination, project grants
      absence of rights 272, 277–278
      agency regulations 280–284
      statutory provision 272–279
   withholding of formula funds
      agency regulations 265–271
      definite procedures, lack of 250–252
      disposition of retained funds 254–257
      statutory provision 245–250
      subgrantees' rights 252–254
      subsequent compliance determination 257

O

Office of (*See* specific office name)
OHD (*See* Human Development, Office of)
OMB (*See* Management and Budget, Office of)
Omnibus Crime Control and Safe Streets Act of 1968 295–297

P

Primary jurisdiction 163–165
   Rosado v. *Wyman* 164
Private cause of action
   Administrative Procedure Act 109
   Cannon v. *University of Chicago* 343–344

civil rights 136–137
congressional creation 141–142
Grantee Bill of Procedural Rights 343
implications 138–139
Lau v. *Nichols* 137, 343
Miree v. *DeKalb County* 139–140
precedents 139–140
Regents of the Univ. of Cal. v. *Bakke* 343
solution 140–141
Supreme Court 343
Project grants
definition 9
eligibility for 43–44, 278–279
HEW percentage of 281
matching ratio 44, 48
purposes 37, 42, 204
standard characteristics 43
Property interests, protection of (*See* Due Process)
Public Health Service 61, 277–278, 313
Public Health Service Act
grant directives 218
notice and hearing provisions
absence of 277–279
subgrantee rights 313
Public Law 81-874 261–262
Public Works and Enconomic Development Act of 1965 279

R

Racial discrimination
hearing rights for finding of 316–324
victims, standing to sue 137
Reallotment process 199–201
Commission on Aging of the State of Alabama v. *Finch* 159
Recipients, rights of (*See* Due Process; Notice and hearing rights; Standing to sue)
Recovery of illegal expenditures (*See* Enforcement and monitoring of grant conditions)
Refunding, hearing rights of applicants for (*See* Notice and hearing rights)
Rehabilitation Act of 1973 136, 324–325
Remedies, grantee withdrawal from grant program 82–84, 104–105, 107
Remedies, grantor (*See* Enforcement and monitoring of grant conditions)
Remedies, private 109, 137–142, 343–344
Revenue sharing 9, 46

S

Sanctions, fiscal (*See* Enforcement and monitoring of grant conditions)
SEA (State Educational Agency) (*See* Education grant programs)
Sex discrimination
hearing rights for finding of 325–327
victims, standing to sue 136
Sixteenth Amendment (*See* Due Process)
Social and Rehabilitation Service 94
Social Security Act 152–153
conformity decisions, time period for 291–292
Social Services Program 291
Sovereign immunity 156–157
Arizona v. *Hobby* 156
Sovereignty, federal intervention in state and local 28
constitutional basis 29–30, 35, 80
limitations 84
state acceptance, voluntary aspect of 30–34, 46, 55, 81, 82, 106
Steward Machine Company v. *Davis* 30–31
withdrawal from grant program as remedy 82–84, 104–105, 107
Spending Clause 176
Butler; United States v. 29–30
Steward Machine Company v. *Davis* 30–31
Standing to sue 108–109
Apter v. *Richardson* 123
associational standing, requirements for 112
Association of Data Processing Serv. Organs. v. *Camp* 130
City of Hartford v. *Towns of Glastonbury* 143–146
Clark v. *Richardson* 122
damage suits
problems of 137–139
state power regarding 140
statutory provision for 141–142
extended application of 112, 117–118
Flast v. *Cohen* 108, 130–131
Frothingham v. *Mellon* 30, 130, 131, 242
grantees, right to challenge federal actions
grant applicants, unsuccessful 119–123
state and local grantees 118–119, 126–127, 242
Hines v. *Cenla Community Action Committee, Inc.* 127

400 / *Rights and Remedies Under Federal Grants*

Standing to sue—*Cont'd*
  Hood River County v. *United States By & Through the Dep't of Labor* 119
  Johnson v. *Morton* 127
  reform proposals 343–344
  Sansom Committee v. *Lynn* 125
  Simon v. *Eastern Kentucky Welfare Rights Organization* 113, 120–121, 145
sovereign immunity issue 156–157
special interest groups, rights of 132–133
  agencies entitled to A-95 notification 134–135
  citizens excluded from required participation 135–136
  victims of discrimination 136–137
"spillover" issue 142–146
third parties, rights of 111–113
  beneficiaries 123–126, 231
  bidders, unsuccessful 128–129
  businesses, private 127–130
  denial of 110–111
  determination of 114–117
  employees of grantee organizations 126–127
  judicial review of federal agencies 109, 111, 113–114
  landlords, private 130
  National Welfare Rights Organization v. *Finch* 231
  officials, special 127
  taxpayers, federal and local 130–132
  Troutman v. *Shriver* 134–135
  uncertainty regarding 109–110
  Warth v. *Seldin* 145
State Educational Agency (SEA) (*See* Education grant programs)
State Medical Facilities Construction Program 70
States' right to Due Process (*See* Due Process)

Subgrantees (*See* Enforcement and monitoring of grant conditions; Notice and hearing rights)
Supremacy Clause (*See* Sovereignty, federal intervention in state and local)
Suspension of grant funds (*See* Enforcement and monitoring of grant conditions)

T

Tenth Amendment (*See* Due Process)
Termination of grant funds (*See* Enforcement and monitoring of grant conditions)
Territorial Clause 176
  City & County of San Francisco; United States v. 176
Traineeships, termination of 329–330

U

Uniform Relocation Assistance and Real Property Acquisitions Policy Act of 1970 20

V

Vocational Education Act
  beneficiaries, participation in state plan development 293
  grant monitoring procedures 66
  hearings location, determination of 260

W

Withholding of funds, hearing rights for (*See* Notice and hearing rights)

TEXAS A&M UNIVERSITY-TEXARKANA